ROUTLEDGE HANDBOOK OF MODERN ECONOMIC HISTORY

The *Routledge Handbook of Modern Economic History* aims to introduce readers to important approaches and findings of economic historians who study the modern world. Its short chapters reflect the most up-to-date research and are written by well-known economic historians who are authorities on their subjects.

Modern economic history blends two approaches – cliometrics (which focuses on measuring economic variables and explicitly testing theories about the historical performance and development of the economy) and the New Institutional Economics (which focuses on how social, cultural, legal, and organizational norms and rules shape economic outcomes and their evolution). Part I of the *Handbook* introduces these approaches and other important methodological issues for economic history.

The most fundamental shift in the economic history of the world began about two and a half centuries ago when eons of slow economic change and faltering economic growth gave way to sustained, rapid economic expansion. Part II examines this theme and the primary forces economic historians have linked to economic growth, stagnation, and fluctuations – including technological change, entrepreneurship, competition, the biological environment, war, financial panics, and business cycles.

Part III examines the evolution of broad sectors that typify a modern economy including agriculture, banking, transportation, healthcare, and entertainment. It begins by examining an equally important "sector" of the economy that scholars have increasingly analyzed using economic tools – religion. Part IV focuses on the work force and human outcomes – including inequality, labor markets, unions, education, immigration, slavery, urbanization, and the evolving economic roles of women and African-Americans.

The text will be of great value to those taking economic history courses as well as a reference book useful to professional practitioners, policy makers and the public.

Robert Whaples is Professor of Economics at Wake Forest University, USA.

Randall E. Parker is Professor of Economics at East Carolina University, USA.

ROUTLEDGE HANDBOOK OF MODERN ECONOMIC HISTORY

Edited by
Robert Whaples and Randall E. Parker

LONDON AND NEW YORK

First published 2013 by Routledge

2 Park Square, Milton Park, Abingdong, Oxfordshire OX14 4RN
52 Vanderbilt Avenue, New York, NY 10017

Routledge is an imprint of the Taylor & Francis Group, an informa business

First issued in paperback 2019

British Library Cataloguing in Publication Data
A catalogue record for this book is available from the British Library

Library of Congress Cataloging in Publication Data
Routledge handbook of modern economic history / edited by Robert Whaples and Randall E. Parker.
    p. cm.
Includes bibliographical references and index.
1. Economic history–1918- 2. Economic history–1750-1918. 3. Economics. I. Whaples, Robert. II. Parker, Randall E., 1960- III. Title: Handbook of modern economic history.
HC51.R68 2012
330.9–dc23

                2012025168

ISBN: 978-0-415-67704-2 (hbk)
ISBN: 978-0-367-86621-1 (pbk)

Typeset in Bembo
by Taylor & Francis Books

CONTENTS

Contents

LIST OF FIGURES

LIST OF TABLES

NOTES ON CONTRIBUTORS

Dan Bogart is Associate Professor of Economics at the University of California – Irvine. His research on the economic history of transportation has been published in the *American Economic Journal: Economic Policy*, *Explorations in Economic History*, *Economic History Review*, *Journal of Economic History*, and *Journal of Urban Economics*.

Jenny Bourne is Professor of Economics at Carleton College. She is the author of *The Bondsman's Burden: An Economic Analysis of the Common Law of Southern Slavery* (Cambridge University Press, 1998). Her research has been published in the *Journal of Economic History*, *National Tax Journal*, and *Social Science Quarterly*.

Joyce Burnette is Professor of Economics at Wabash College. Her book *Gender, Work, and Wages in Industrial Revolution Britain* (Cambridge University Press, 2008) won the Economic History Society's First Monograph Prize. Her research has been published in the *Agricultural History Review*, *Economic History Review*, *Explorations in Economic History*, and *Journal of Economic History*.

Louis P. Cain is Professor of Economics at Loyola University Chicago and Adjunct Professor at Northwestern University. He is the author (with the late Jonathan Hughes) of *American Economic History* (Prentice Hall, 8th edition, 2011) and (with Donald Patterson) *The Children of Eve: Population and Well-Being in History* (Wiley-Blackwell, 2012).

Scott Alan Carson is Professor of Economics at the University of Texas – Permian Basin. His research on anthropometric history has been published in numerous journals including *Economics and Human Biology*, *Explorations in Economic History*, *Journal of Economic History*, *Journal of Economic Issues*, *Journal of Interdisciplinary History*, *Journal of Population Economics*, and *Social Science History*.

Nathaniel Cline is an Assistant Professor of Economics at the University of Redlands (California). He completed his dissertation, "Growth and Stagnation in the nineteenth-century United States: Three Essays in Applied International Economics" at the University of Utah in 2012.

Philip R.P. Coelho is Professor of Economics at Ball State University. He is the author (with Robert McGuire) of *Parasites, Pathogens, and Progress: Diseases and Economic Development* (MIT

Press, 2011) and has published his research in the *American Economic Review, Economic Inquiry, Journal of Economic Behavior and Organization, Journal of Economic History*, and other scholarly journals.

Raymond L. Cohn is Emeritus Professor of Economics at Illinois State University. He is the author of *Mass Migration under Sail: European Immigration to the Antebellum United States* (Cambridge University Press, 2009) and articles on immigration in *Explorations in Economic History, Journal of Economic History*, and *Social Science History*.

Lee A. Craig is Alumni Distinguished Professor of Economics at North Carolina State University and served as Executive Director of the Cliometric Society (2000–8). He is the author of five monographs and has published in *Agricultural History, Cliometrica, Explorations in Economic History, Journal of Economic History, Journal of Law, Economics, and Organization*, and *Journal of Macroeconomics*.

Jari Eloranta is Associate Professor of Comparative Economic and Business History at Appalachian State University. He is the author of numerous studies on the economic history of war and defense in journals including *Cliometrica, Economic History Review*, and *European Review of Economic History*.

Giovanni Federico is Senior Research Fellow at the European University Institute and Director of the European Research Council's project on Market Integration and the Welfare of Europeans. He is the author of *Feeding the World: An Economic History of Agriculture, 1800–2000* (Princeton University Press, 2005).

Gerald Friedman is Professor of Economics at the University of Massachusetts. He has served as Associate Editor of the journal *Labor History* since 2003 and is the author of *Reigniting the Labor Movement* (Routledge, 2007) and *State-Making and Labor Movements: The United States and France, 1876–1914* (Cornell University Press, 1998).

Richard S. Grossman is Professor of Economics at Wesleyan University. His work on financial history has been published in the *American Economic Review, Journal of Economic History*, and *Journal of Money, Credit, and Banking*. He is the author of *Unsettled Account: The Evolution of Banking in the Industrialized World since 1800* (Princeton University Press, 2010).

Christopher Hanes is Professor of Economics at Binghamton University (SUNY). His research on business cycles has been published in numerous journals including the *American Economic Review, Quarterly Journal of Economics, Journal of Economic History*, and *Journal of Money, Credit and Banking*.

Michael Haupert is Professor of Economics at the University of Wisconsin – La Crosse. He has served as Director of the Cliometric Society since 2008, is the author of *The Entertainment Industry* (Greenwood, 2006) and scholarly articles in journals including the *American Economist, Journal of Economic History*, and *Journal of Money, Credit and Banking*.

Michael Huberman is Professor of History at the University of Montreal. He is the author of numerous studies on the history of labor markets including *Escape from the Market: Negotiating Work in Lancashire* (Cambridge University Press, 1996) and articles in the *Business History Review, Economic History Review, European Review of Economic History, Explorations in Economic History*, and *Journal of Economic History*.

Andrew Jalil is Assistant Professor of Economics at Occidental College. He completed his dissertation, "A new history of banking panics in the United States, 1825–1929: construction and implications," at University of California – Berkeley in 2010.

B. Zorina Khan is Professor of Economics at Bowdoin College. Her book *The Democratization of Invention: Patents and Copyrights in American Economic Development, 1790–1920* (Cambridge University Press, 2005) was awarded the Alice Hanson Jones Biennial Prize for an outstanding work in North American economic history.

Thomas N. Maloney is Professor of Economics and Director of the Barbara L. and Norman C. Tanner Center for Nonviolent Human Rights Advocacy at the University of Utah. His research on historical economic inequality has been published in the *Journal of Economic History*, *Economic Inquiry*, *Economics and Human Biology*, and *Explorations in Economic History*.

Robert A. Margo is Professor of Economics at Boston University. He is the author or co-author of four books, has served as editor of *Explorations in Economic History* (2003–8) and has published over 80 scholarly articles and book chapters in the *American Economic Review*, *Journal of Economic History*, *Journal of Economic Perspectives*, *Quarterly Journal of Economics*, *Review of Economics and Statistics*, *Southern Economic Journal*, and numerous other journals.

David Mitch is Professor of Economics at the University of Maryland – Baltimore County. He is the co-editor of *The Origins of the Modern Career* (Ashgate, 2004), author of *The Rise of Popular Literacy in Victorian England* (University of Pennsylvania Press, 1992) and author of articles in the *Economic History Review*, *Education Economics*, and *Journal of Economic History*.

John E. Murray is J.R. Hyde III Professor of Political Economy at Rhodes College. He is the author of *The Charleston Orphan House, Children's Lives in the First Public Orphanage in America* (University of Chicago Press, 2013), and articles in *Demography*, *Explorations in Economic History*, *Journal of Economic History*, *Population Studies*, and many other scholarly journals.

Tomas Nonnenmacher is Professor and Chair of the Economics Department at Allegheny College. His research on historical political economy and industrial organization has been published in *Explorations in Economic History*, *Journal of Economic History*, *Journal of European Economic History*, and *Research in Economic History*.

Randall E. Parker is Professor of Economics at East Carolina University. He is the author of *Reflections on the Great Depression* (Edward Elgar, 2003) and *The Economics of the Great Depression: A Twenty-First Century Look Back at the Economics of the Interwar Era* (Edward Elgar, 2007), and has published research in journals such as *Economic Inquiry*, *Journal of Macroeconomics*, and *Journal of Money, Credit, and Banking*.

Fred Smith is Associate Professor at Davidson College. His research on the economic history of urban areas has been published in *Applied Economics Letters*, *Explorations in Economic History*, *Journal of Economic History*, and *Research in Economic History*.

William A. Sundstrom is Professor of Economics at Santa Clara University. His research on the history of labor markets has been published in the *American Economic Review*, *Journal of*

Economic History, Explorations in Economic History, Industrial and Labor Relations Review, Journal of Economic Behavior and Organization, Industrial Relations, and *Research in Economic History.*

Melissa Thomasson is Associate Professor of Economics at Miami University (Ohio). Her research on the history of healthcare has been published in the *American Economic Review, Explorations in Economic History, Journal of Economic History, Social Science History,* and *Southern Economic Journal.*

Werner Troesken is Professor of Economics at the University of Pittsburgh. He is the author of *Why Regulate Utilities? The New Institutional Economics and the Chicago Gas Industry, 1849–1924* (University of Michigan Press, 1996), *The Great Lead Water Pipe Disaster* (MIT Press, 2006), and research published in the *Journal of Economic History, Journal of Human Resources, Journal of Industrial Economics, Journal of Law, Economics, and Organization,* and *Explorations in Economic History.*

Robert Whaples is Professor and Chair of Economics at Wake Forest University. He served as Director of EH.Net (2003–8) and editor of the *EH.Net Encyclopedia of Economic and Business History.* His research in economic history, consensus among economists, and coinage has been published in the *Eastern Economic Journal, Economic Inquiry, Economists' Voice, Journal of Economic History,* and *Social Science History.*

PREFACE

The *Routledge Handbook of Modern Economic History* aims to introduce readers to important approaches and findings of economic historians who study the modern world. We hope that it will serve as supplementary reading for college economic history courses as well as a reference book useful to professional practitioners, policy makers, and the public. Its short chapters reflect the most up-to-date research and are written by well-known economic historians who are authorities on their subjects.

Modern economic history blends two approaches – cliometrics (which focuses on measuring economic variables and explicitly testing theories about the historical performance and development of the economy, as exemplified by the approach of Robert Fogel) and the New Institutional Economics (which focuses on how social, cultural, legal, and organizational norms and rules shape economic outcomes and their evolution, as exemplified by the approach of Douglass North). Part I of the *Handbook* introduces these approaches and other important methodological issues for economic history.

The most fundamental shift in the economic history of the world began about two and a half centuries ago when eons of slow economic change and faltering economic growth gave way to sustained, rapid economic expansion. Part II examines this theme and the primary forces economic historians have linked to economic growth, stagnation, and fluctuations – including technological change, entrepreneurship, competition, the biological environment, war, financial panics, and business cycles.

Part III examines the evolution of broad sectors that typify a modern economy including agriculture, banking, transportation, healthcare, and entertainment. It begins by examining an equally important "sector" of the economy that scholars have increasingly analyzed using economic tools – religion.

Part IV focuses on the work force and human outcomes – including inequality, labor markets, unions, education, immigration, slavery, urbanization, and the evolving economic roles of women and African-Americans.

The editors are grateful to over two dozen scholars for volunteering to write these informative chapters. We hope that users will learn as much as we did in reading these carefully written chapters, each of which aims to provide the consensus view on its subject. Readers may be disappointed that additional topics – such as aging, energy markets, trade, natural resources, property rights, central banking, housing markets, and demographic changes – do not receive chapter-length coverage. Unfortunately, we were not able to convince well-known scholars working in these areas to contribute chapters. The dissemination of knowledge has a high opportunity cost for academics, whose professional incentives are to publish more specialized, technical work in refereed journals.

PART I

The methods of modern economic history

1

ECONOMIC HISTORY AND CLIOMETRICS

Louis P. Cain and Robert Whaples

As this *Handbook* demonstrates, economic history is an active field that investigates a wide range of topics. The dominant method used by economic historians over the past half-century is cliometrics. The name "cliometrics" comes from joining "Clio" (the Greek Muse of history) with "metrics" (measurement), but cliometrics goes an important step beyond merely measuring historical events. It structures its measurements with economic theory, especially (but by no means exclusively) the neoclassical theory that has dominated economics for several generations. It often develops explicit models of how economic agents (such as households and firms), as well as entire economies, have behaved and interacted historically. Thus, in addition to measuring economic outcomes, cliometrics seeks to understand their causes. This chapter outlines the development of cliometrics and helps put the other chapters in this *Handbook* into context by examining how cliometrics is practiced.

The cliometric revolution

In the first half of the twentieth century, economic historians rarely appealed to explicit economic theory, but relied more on an accumulation of facts and anecdotes in describing and attempting to explain the past. Economists, on the other hand, were often accused of relying too much on theory and not enough on facts. Testing economic theories using historical facts was difficult because data were scarce. Important economic statistics, including series on prices and wages, production, and employment (thus unemployment), were few and far between, partly because the costs of retrieving them were prohibitive in that pre-computer age.

To begin bridging this gap, the National Bureau of Economic Research (NBER) was founded in 1920 to produce research firmly based on economic facts – quantitative if possible, scientific and impartial, and neutral with respect to ideology and policy. Edwin Gay (who later became the first president of the Economic History Association) argued that collecting these data would allow a "relatively dependable causeway" to be "thrown over the morasses of earlier economic history" (Gay 1930: 2–3). Gay's confidence was warranted, because during the interwar period the NBER added substantially to the statistical infrastructure for examining American economic development. Among the most important steps forward was a series of studies on income, savings, and expenditures in the United States by Simon Kuznets. Kuznets, one of three economic historians to win the Nobel Prize in Economics (Robert Fogel and

Douglass North are the others), had a great influence in developing the preliminary version of U.S. national income and product accounts, and in producing, or encouraging others to produce, long runs of historical national accounting data for the United States and elsewhere.

After the Second World War, economists increasingly focused their research on economic growth and development in hopes of preventing a return to Depression-era conditions in developed countries and of improving the lot of less developed countries. Because understanding growth requires understanding history, a new generation of scholars trained in economics departments turned their attention to economic history. When they began to read the works of older economic historians, many complained that important economic issues had been misinterpreted because of a failure to conjoin economic theory and historical data, and they pushed their colleagues to employ economic theory along with measurement.

The value of the new approach was convincingly displayed in "The economics of slavery in the ante-bellum South", one of the most influential and seminal works of cliometrics, which was then called "the new economic history." Rather than examine the mindset and motives of slaveholders, authors Alfred H. Conrad and John R. Meyer (1958) approached the subject as an investment problem. Was slavery profitable? This question had been debated without resolution for over a century. Conrad and Meyer modeled slave owners as investors with a capital asset subject to depreciation and maintenance costs. They examined historical data on cotton yields, slaves' average life spans, and prices of inputs and outputs – and calculated that owning slaves was more profitable than many other potential investments. Their finding (and extensions of it) helped create a new, lasting consensus concerning the profitability of slavery.

Only six years later, Douglass North noted:

> A revolution is taking place in economic history in the United States. It is being initiated by a new generation of economic historians who are both skeptical of traditional interpretations of U.S. economic history and convinced that a new economic history must be firmly grounded in sound statistical data. Even a cursory examination of accepted "truths" of U.S. economic history suggests that many of them are inconsistent with elementary economic analysis and have never been subjected to – and would not survive – testing with statistical data. (North 1963: 128–9)

North could point to Conrad and Meyer's work on the profitability of slavery, Robert Fogel's (1964) work finding that railroads were not indispensable to nineteenth-century American economic growth, research on the unimportance of the Civil War for accelerating U.S. industrialization (Gallman 1960), and several other projects to support the existence of a revolution.

In those years, the cliometric approach quickly resolved several ongoing debates in American economic history. For example, using a simple trade model, estimates of demand and supply elasticities, and colonial prices, the per capita burden of Britain's Navigation Acts as a per cent of colonial income was estimated to be much smaller than many supposed. Hence it was an unlikely spark for the American Revolution (Thomas 1965; McClelland 1969). Likewise, Peter Temin's (1968) analysis of sources of changes in the money supply demonstrated that the inflation and financial crisis of the 1830s had their origin in international events largely beyond President Andrew Jackson's control. Those crises would have taken place whether or not he had acted as he did regarding the Second Bank of the United States – thus fundamentally reinterpreting another important episode in American economic history.

The cliometric approach aimed to replace imprecise qualitative statements – such as "It is difficult to exaggerate the importance of this" – with precise and accurate estimates of economic magnitudes and economic relationships. As cliometricians harnessed computers, which allowed them to quickly calculate totals and averages, they also tried to estimate underlying economic relationships and marginal effects using voluminous (but previously silent and unusable) bodies of archival data. As some debates were settled, however, the new approach opened even more research questions to analysis and scrutiny.

One way to gauge the progress of cliometrics is to examine the pages of the leading economic history journal. In the early 1950s, less than 2 per cent of the pages in the *Journal of Economic History* were in cliometric articles – those which used measurement (seen in a growing number of tables) and explicit economic theory. This figure subsequently climbed to 10 per cent in the late 1950s, 18 per cent in the early 1960s, 44 per cent in the late 1960s, and 78 per cent in the early 1970s (Whaples 1991). In the late 1950s, cliometrics was seen by some as a passing fad, but by the 1970s it was the standard operating procedure for American economic historians. In the following decades, cliometrics was increasingly adopted by scholars from outside the U.S. as well. Many of the achievements of this first generation of cliometric research were surveyed in Fogel and Engerman (1971), McCloskey (1976), Lee and Passell (1979), and more recently (and retrospectively) Lyons *et al.* (2008) – all of which (sometimes breathlessly) emphasized both the novelty and important breakthroughs from the approach as it gained dominance within the United States.

Criticisms of cliometrics

The cliometric approach has had a natural appeal to historically minded researchers trained in departments of economics. In one sense, it is simply the application of standard economic tools – initially developed to understand the present – to the past. However, cliometrics has been more controversial among scholars trained in history departments.

One of the strongest early criticisms of the new method came from Fritz Redlich. In published work he expanded on a point he made most succinctly in responding to a question at an academic conference. The young questioner asked the old professor, "What is your model?" Redlich responded, "Model? I deal with the truth." One of Redlich's most telling arguments was that cliometricians focused too much on purely economic considerations and ignored the impact of institutions. He was even more strident in his attack on the use of explicit counterfactuals, which played a prominent role in the early history of cliometrics, especially in the case of Robert Fogel's influential analysis of the impact of railroads. To fully assess this impact, Fogel modeled a counterfactual world in which railroads never existed. Among other things, this required him to project the expansion of navigable waterways that would have been built had there been no railroads, and to project the consequences of that expansion, such as shifts in population. Redlich attacked such counterfactuals by calling them "figments." "Hypotheses are based on assumptions which are held to have a counterpart in reality, while figments are assumptions having no such counterparts or at least known to be irrealistic" (Redlich 1965: 484). Due to their basis in reality, hypotheses can be verified or falsified; figments can only be justified. Figments lead to economic models, and "a model is never a piece of history" (Redlich 1965: 490).

Proponents of the cliometric approach rebutted this criticism by arguing that *every* historian has a model. Without mental models to simplify the bewildering array of sensory facts, a person wouldn't be able to make it through the day. Without models to simplify the bewildering array of historical facts, no scholar could make sense of the past. Cliometricians, such as Lance Davis (1966), argued that their breakthrough was to make explicit the models that had once been implicit. For example, those who argue for the indispensability of railroads in nineteenth-century American economic growth implicitly have a model that suggests the demand for transportation was massive, that railroads offered immense advantages over other modes of transportation, and that no suitable substitute for railroads was likely to have performed as well. Fogel (1964) subjected this model to empirical tests and found it wanting. He then formalized an alternative set of assumptions about transportation demand and the shift in supply brought about by the railroads. Cliometricians celebrated this conceptual breakthrough, but debated whether or not the theoretical assumptions in Fogel's model accurately reflected the structure of the economy and whether the numbers used in it were accurate. The conclusion of the profession – especially those trained in economics – was that Fogel's modeling and measurement were convincing. In a 1995 survey, Whaples (1995: 143) found that 89 per cent of economic historians in economics departments rejected the idea that "without the building of the railroads, the American economy would have grown very little during the nineteenth century." Economic historians housed in history departments (a dwindling breed) were less convinced: 66 per cent of them rejected the idea.

Redlich was not alone in his criticism. Cliometricians were mostly economists, and their papers had to conform to economists' standards. Their method and style, and assertions of the virtues of cliometrics, alienated older economic historians in particular, and historians in general. American Historical Association President Carl Bridenbaugh lamented that some colleagues had succumbed "to the dehumanizing methods of social sciences," and warned against worshipping "at the shrine of that Bitch-goddess, QUANTIFICATION" (Bridenbaugh 1963: 326). To many contemporary American economic historians, these arguments are a quaint episode. Cliometrics is their orthodoxy; as they see it, cliometricians "won the West," imposing a "Pax Cliometrica" (McCloskey 1987: 77).

A more lasting criticism has been that the default model of cliometrics is an artifact of modern, Western thinking. Boldizzoni (2011) argues that cliometrics hasn't improved our understanding of the past but has distorted it, because its default assumption is that there are essentially universal laws of human behavior that have held at all times and in all places. Economists, he argues, have projected their belief that people are "rational maximizers" from the modern West – where the assumption may fit fairly well – to other times and places when and where it doesn't fit. The chief villain in his critique is Douglass North, a pioneer of cliometrics, who has also been an insistent critic. North has complained that cliometrics needs to focus more on institutions and their evolution. In a series of works designed to get to the fundamental forces behind long-term economic trends – including both pre-modern economic stagnation and modern growth – North and his co-authors (North 1981, 1990, 2005; North *et al.* 2009) pushed their analysis further and further back, but they never abandoned their key assumption that individuals acted out of self-interest and were constantly cognizant of costs versus benefits in making decisions.

At heart, Boldizzoni attacks cliometrics for relying on ill-considered deductions rather than wading deeply into the details of historical life and using induction to understand the logic of earlier societies and their economies. Cliometricians would rebut this by arguing that their method relies on *both* deduction and induction. Accordingly, the next section of this chapter looks at the practice of modern cliometrics and the debates among cliometricians about how to make conclusions regarding historical cause and effect.

Cliometrics in practice: multivariate regression

Perhaps the most common practice in cliometrics is to use multivariate regression analysis, which produces an estimate of the marginal impact of a variable of historical interest while holding other important factors constant. A typical example is Buffum and Whaples (1995) who seek to test the magnitude of employee-based discrimination in the labor market of the late 1800s using data on furniture workers collected by the Michigan Bureau of Labor Statistics. Their study begins with a simple economic model that assumes this market was competitive so that wages reflected workers' productivity, but that workers were also compensated for any negative workplace conditions. Using wages as the dependent variable and holding constant measurable worker characteristics (such as occupation, education, and experience) likely to influence productivity (and therefore wages), this study examines the marginal impact of variation in the ethnicity of co-workers. It finds that a one percentage point increase in the share of the work force who were not from a worker's own ethnic group increased his wage about 0.1 per cent. This is interpreted as evidence that employers had to pay their employees more when they were in close contact with co-workers they liked less (or disliked more) than members of their own group. The study also finds that workers from Protestant ethnic groups were generally paid more when working with Catholics, but concludes that the additional labor costs generated by this employee-based discrimination were probably offset by several benefits that rendered complete segregation unnecessary.

This study is typical of cliometric work that applies a widely used economic model to historical data. The regression coefficients allow the economic historian to go an important step beyond contemporary and historical accounts that agreed workers in these groups often didn't get along and disliked each other. Regression coefficients quantify how much workers disliked each other by estimating how much more they had to be paid to work with one another – or how much pay they were willing to sacrifice to work with members of their own group. The study reaches the cliometric goal by illuminating the past and also breaking ground in testing a theoretical implication – that if employees discriminate against each other they must be paid more to work with each other – that can't be tested well using modern data but can be tested with a rich historical data set.

Panel data

A more difficult task is to examine a historical change, an episode or a public policy, and convincingly determine its causes or consequences. Data sets on workers' wages often include thousands of observations, and it is clear that some explanatory variables are exogenous (that is, caused by factors outside the system). Wage regressions can be fairly straightforward to interpret because it is clear that some variables cannot influence others, making conclusions about causation more convincing. When wages are higher for middle-aged workers than for younger workers, it's fairly clear that age is driving wage and not the other way around – that getting older pushes up one's wage since earning more can't cause one to become older. However, examining the causes and consequences of events and policies is harder because it's more difficult to find plausibly exogenous determinants, and because events can be so complex that an unmeasured, omitted variable might be at work.

Panel data can help solve this problem. A panel generally consists of two dimensions – a spatial dimension that consists of cross-sectional observations (e.g. nations, states, cities, industries, firms, groups of people, or individuals) and a temporal dimension that consists of time-series observations (periodic measures of characteristics of what is being observed).

Consider this question: Did the riots in American cities in the 1960s *cause* long-term economic harm to those cities? Conventional economic theory suggests this is plausible, because a property's value is believed to reflect the discounted value of the expected net flow of utility associated with its ownership – including not only the physical quality of the structure, but also such things as security, proximity to work, family, friends and shopping, the quality of municipal services, and the taxes needed to support such services. In theory, if a riot causes a sustained decline in the perceived amenities in one location relative to others, it would register as a *relative* decline in property values. In line with this theory, examining data shows that – holding constant other factors like region, population, crime rate, segregation, and the trend in property values – property values fell more in cities hit by more severe riots (Collins and Margo 2007).

But what if the riots themselves were more severe in cities that were economically weaker, and this economic weakness accounts for *both* the lagging property values and the riots? In cases like this, economic historians look for "natural experiments" – changes or differences that plausibly arise outside the economic system, which allow one to compare situations or places that received one "treatment" with those that received another "treatment." Collins and Margo report contemporary observations that rainy weather made rioting less severe, and then estimate the impact of city-specific weather in the period following Martin Luther King's assassination – showing that (holding other factors constant) more rain in April 1968 led to less rioting. In this case, rain is used as an "instrumental variable," an exogenous variable that does not itself belong in the explanatory equation but which is correlated with the endogenous explanatory variables. Putting these pieces together (using a two-stage regression estimation framework), Collins and Margo convincingly confirm that more severe rioting had an independent, large, negative impact on urban property values. They estimate that riots decreased black-owned home values in these cities by about 10 per cent.

Among the panel data sets that are widely used in economic history are the Panel Study of Income Dynamics (PSID), the National Longitudinal Survey of Youth (NLSY), and the Union Army data of the Center for Population Economics. The PSID is a panel of U.S. families that began in 1968 and continues today. Economic, social, and health factors have been measured over individuals' lives and across generations. The NLSY is one of several panels collected by the Bureau of Labor Statistics. The most widely used of these is the National Longitudinal Survey of Youth 1979, which surveys young men and women born in the years 1957–64. The Union Army Data Set (and the U.S. Colored Troops Data Set) consists of white (and black) males mustered into the Union Army during the Civil War. Military, socio-economic, and medical information from several sources throughout their lifetimes have been collected and are part of ongoing research efforts.

Many economic historians have constructed their own panels. An important example is the panel of city-, county- and state-level New Deal spending, economic activity, and demographic data constructed by Price Fishback and his co-authors. For example, Fishback *et al.* (2007) examine the impact of New Deal spending on infant mortality, non-infant mortality, and general fertility rates in major U.S. cities between 1929 and 1940. They include controls for city characteristics, city and year fixed effects, and make use of instrumental variables (voting patterns in years prior to the Great Depression, and Congressional committee assignments, for example) that helped determine the allocation of New Deal spending. They conclude that about $2 million (measured in year 2000 dollars) in additional relief spending was associated with a reduction of one infant death, half a homicide, one suicide, 2.4 deaths from infectious disease, and one death from diarrhea in each large urban area.

Finding a convincing instrumental variable can be very challenging. The researcher needs to find a factor that helped drive the economic events but did not arise simultaneously from within the economic system. When it comes to policy analysis, this can be almost impossible because political decisions are so intricately intertwined with economic forces.

Time series

Because of the focus on economic growth, many problems in economic history involve statistical work with time-series data. Into the 1970s, statistical research on time series was largely limited to isolating trends from cycles. The procedures developed by Clive Granger, D.A. Dickey and W.A. Fuller, and others changed that. The appearance of new techniques in time-series econometrics afforded tests for characteristics in data such as Granger causality, non-stationarity in levels, structural change (unit root tests), and cointegration. These techniques quickly found their way into the research of economic historians. Even the old question of cycles or trends received a statistical update.

The typical regression only says something about correlation, but Granger won the Nobel Prize in Economics for arguing that, under certain conditions, the regression can also say something about causation. In brief, a time series of one variable is said to Granger-cause a time series of another variable if it can be shown that the first variable's values provide statistically significant information about the future values of the second variable – thus, if one time series can be used to forecast another, then one can argue that it helps cause it to vary, at least in a statistical sense. The first mention of such a test in the economic history literature appears in Michael Edelstein's (1980) discussion of a paper by Michael Bordo and Anna Schwartz at the annual Economic History Association meetings. Edelstein suggests the use of the test, but in the published paper Bordo and Schwartz (1981) argue that, while the Granger test could be used to test causality between money and the price level, or the price level and the terms of trade, they believe there is an omitted common influence affecting both the terms of trade and the price level, and this means the test is inappropriate. However, these tests are a main focus of Schwartz (1981) and her contribution toward revisiting the Great Depression contained in Brunner (1981). Her long-run results strongly suggest money Granger-caused income and not the reverse: the supply of money was not endogenously driven by the business cycle.

Stationarity is an attribute of a time series in which the mean and standard deviation are constant over time. It is important since standard econometric tools assume finite variances for the variables of the estimated model. Stationarity provides this finite variance. Thus, the first step in analyzing time-series data is to test if one's data are stationary or not. Its first appearance among economic historians is David Pope's (1984) analysis of Kondratieff cycles in Australia. The most common way to test for (non-)stationarity is to apply a Dickey-Fuller test that checks whether a unit root is present in an autoregressive model. In his examination of open market operations in the 1920s, Mark Toma (1989: 116) used this test to argue that, in a regression of the level of Federal Reserve security holdings against its lagged value and a constant, "standard test procedures reject the non-stationarity hypothesis that the lagged coefficient equals one." Within two years, such tests were common in the economic history journals.

Two (or more) time series are said to be cointegrated if they move together, if they statistically share a common stochastic drift. Alternatively, two time series are cointegrated if they are non-stationary but a linear combination of the two series is stationary. Gary Libecap (1989) examines interstate cartel production coordination in the petroleum market. If residual production by Texas was for the purpose of maintaining nominal crude oil prices, there would have to be a long-term relationship between output in Texas and market demand in the U.S. – that is, the two time series would be cointegrated. Libecap finds no statistically significant evidence that this was true.

One of the major issues confronted by time-series analysis has been to identify the timing and potential causes of the British Industrial Revolution. Many scholars have contributed to this literature, and among the major contributors are David Greasley and Les Oxley (2010). Extending the "best guess" estimates of British Industrial Production generated by Nick Crafts and Knick Harley (1992) and using an augmented Dickey-Fuller test, Greasley and Oxley (2010) divide almost 300 years of British history into five epochs: 1700–80; 1781–1851; 1852–1913; 1922–73 and 1974–92. Their times-series tests characterize the period between 1700 and

1913 as alternating between trend stationary, difference stationary, and trend stationary, so they make a case for dating the British Industrial Revolution to the second epoch, 1781–1851. As to the causes of British industrialization, their tests indicate that cotton and iron were the leading industries, and coal was a follower. Cotton had wider linkages than iron, "statistically causing paper and shipbuilding production," but they do not regard it as more important in the 1815–60 period "as bidirectional causality between iron goods and cotton output lies at the heart of the cotton, mining and metals sector" (Greasley and Oxley 2010: 1009–10). (This paper also contains an extensive overview of time-series methods used by economic historians.)

It can be argued that many of these techniques help us to understand the statistical process that generated the data, but that the *statistical* process is not necessarily the *economic* process and Granger-causality is not *economic* causality. Macroeconomists have generated competing models of the same economic process: there is no single "correct" understanding. It is safe to say that there is much work still to be done to understand and dynamically model the economy.

These examples are only a small sample of the empirical inquiries to which time-series econometrics has been employed by economic historians. Given the importance of time series to economic history and the time-series data economic historians have produced, it seems inevitable that new statistical techniques for analyzing time series, as they become available, will be adopted quickly.

Computable general equilibrium models

As historical questions have become more complicated, the models used to answer them have become more complex in accounting for feedback mechanisms and impacts that spread throughout the economy over time. For example, the economic effects of immigration ripple throughout an economy, so a comprehensive model that can capture this complexity is needed. A naïve, theory-free approach may suggest that one can isolate the impact of historical immigration on wages by simply comparing wages in cities and states where immigrants have settled with those in places they haven't. Unfortunately, this conveys virtually nothing for two reasons. First, immigrants don't usually choose their destinations randomly; given their mobility, they often select areas that have the best job-market opportunities. They are attracted to the highest-wage cities and states, so finding that wages are higher in places with a lot of immigrants could confuse cause and effect. Second, suppose that immigrants flood into a city – increasing its labor supply relative to its labor demand – pushing wages in the city down. The native-born population is not likely to react passively to this, but will begin to leave this market, entering other markets and pushing down wages in places where immigrants haven't gone. If these native-born workers are mobile enough, just enough of them will leave to make the wages in all cities approximately equal for similar jobs. The impact of immigration will be diffused across the entire economy, so looking for its impact by comparing where immigrants are and aren't located can be erroneous.

To capture the impact of immigration and other broad economic changes like trade and technological change, economic historians have turned to models of the economy that can capture the feedbacks. One influential immigration study is Hatton and Williamson (1998), which includes a computable general equilibrium model (developed in O'Rourke *et al.* 1994) of the interactions between the U.S. and UK economies during the late 1800s and early 1900s. In the U.S. model, output and factor prices are endogenously determined – that is, they arise within the system. Consumers are constrained by endowments and maximize a utility function; their income and expenditures are endogenous. There are four production activities that obey standard production functions – food, agricultural intermediates, manufacturing, and services; three primary factors of production – land, labor (divided into agricultural and non-agricultural), and capital; two imported goods; and foreign exchange. The model assumes that firms minimize costs (to maximize profits); competition is perfect; capital is perfectly mobile across sectors; non-agricultural labor is perfectly mobile between manufacturing and services; and rural–urban migration is determined endogenously by wage gaps. The model also includes an explicit consumer utility function. Equilibrium occurs when for every sector price equals costs; for every commodity, demand equals supply; and the consumers' incomes equal the rents on all endowments. The thirteen prices are endogenously determined, as are the nine activity levels. The UK model is similar but somewhat simpler. The model allows its users to examine the impact that labor flows from Britain to the U.S. had *throughout* the economy – on wages and other factor price levels, on prices of goods, on the allocation of resources, and more.

While a model such as Hatton and Williamson's can be an advance over a simpler partial-equilibrium model, it is open to many criticisms. Rosenbloom (1998) finds Hatton and Williamson's conclusion that trans-Atlantic migration (along with trade) was an important factor in explaining the narrowing of international wage gaps during this period is plausible; yet he cautions that it is difficult to adequately assess these conclusions in part because of the very complexity of the general equilibrium models on which they rest. Are the key assumptions of the model – the elasticities, interactions, and functional forms embedded in it, the calibrations of key parameters – a good reflection of reality? The very complexity of the economy necessitates the use of such complicated models, but also undermines their usefulness – and these complex models are simplifications that leave out much that may be important (e.g. immigration's impact on technological progress, culture, and institutions). Some important events in economic history – like immigration – have such complex and far-reaching impacts that even the most advanced cliometric techniques can't adequately assess them. But the bottom line is that models by their very design and nature are abstractions from the complexity of life. The job of the economic historian is to push refutable hypotheses as far as the theory and data will allow, and to confirm or reject these hypotheses based on the credible evidence that can be marshaled. Perhaps there will never be the tools to adequately address the most important and complex historical economic questions. Researchers probably will not innovate enough to create adequate methods to completely address these important questions. But it is essential to press the available technology as hard and as fully as we are able.

Conclusions

Cliometrics aspires to enhance the study of the economic past by applying the rigor of economic theory and quantitative analysis, while simultaneously using the historical record to evaluate and stimulate economic theory and to improve comprehension of long-run economic processes (Greif 1997). It is the dominant paradigm of modern economic history. At its best, this method has deepened our understanding of American and world economic history in many important ways. It is especially useful when data from the past are abundant and when scholars can agree on how the economy has functioned – and therefore how to model it. However, like any other scientific investigative technique, cliometrics cannot answer every question. Understanding the economic past is crucial to understanding the present, but it is hindered by lack of information on what occurred, individuals' motivations, and the sheer complexity of their interactions.

References

Boldizzoni, F. (2011) *The Poverty of Clio: Resurrecting Economic History*, Princeton, NJ: Princeton University Press.

Bordo, M.D. and Schwartz, A.J. (1981) 'Money and prices in the nineteenth century: was Thomas Tooke right?' *Explorations in Economic History*, 18: 97–127.

Bridenbaugh, C. (1963) 'The great mutation', *American Historical Review*, 68: 315–31.

Brunner, K. (ed.) (1981) *The Great Depression Revisited*, Boston, MA: Martinus Nijhoff Publishing.

Buffum, D. and Whaples, R. (1995) 'Fear and lathing in the Michigan furniture industry: employee-based discrimination a century ago', *Economic Inquiry*, 33: 234–52.

Collins, W.J. and Margo, R.A. (2007) 'The economic aftermath of the 1960s riots in American cities: evidence from property values', *Journal of Economic History*, 67: 849–83.

Conrad, A. and Meyer, J.R. (1958) 'The economics of slavery in the ante-bellum South', *Journal of Political Economy*, 66: 95–130.

Crafts, N.F.R. and Harley, C.K. (1992) 'Output growth and the British industrial revolution: a restatement of the Crafts–Harley view', *Economic History Review*, 45: 703–30.

Davis, L.E. (1966) 'The new economic history. II. Professor Fogel and the new economic history', *Economic History Review*, 19: 657–63.

Edelstein, M. (1980) 'Discussion of Howson and Bordo and Schwartz papers', *Journal of Economic History*, 40: 68–9.

Fishback, P.V., Haines, M.R. and Kantor, S. (2007) 'Births, deaths, and New Deal relief during the Great Depression', *Review of Economics and Statistics*, 89: 1–14.

Fogel, R. (1964) *Railroads and American Economic Growth: Essays in Econometric History*, Baltimore, Md: Johns Hopkins University Press.

Fogel, R. and Engerman, S.L. (eds) (1971) *The Reinterpretation of American History*, New York: Harper and Row.

Gallman, R.E. (1960) 'Commodity Output, 1839–1899', in National Bureau of Economic Research *Trends in the American Economic Economy in the Nineteenth Century*, Princeton, NJ: Princeton University Press.

Gay, E.F. (1930) 'Historical records', *American Economic Review*, 20: 2–3.

Greasley, D. and Oxley, L. (2010) 'Cliometrics and time series econometrics: some theory and applications', *Journal of Economic Surveys*, 24: 970–1042.

Greif, A. (1997) 'Cliometrics after 40 years', *American Economic Review*, 87: 400–3.

Hatton, T.J. and Williamson, J.G. (1998) *The Age of Mass Migration: Causes and Economic Impact*, New York: Oxford University Press.

Lee, S.P. and Passell, P. (1979) *A New Economic View of American History*, New York: Norton.

Libecap, G.D. (1989) 'The political economy of crude oil cartelization in the United States, 1933–72', *Journal of Economic History*, 49: 833–55.

Lyons, J.S., Cain, L.P. and Williamson, S.H. (2008) *Reflections on the Cliometric Revolution: Conversations with Economic Historians*, New York: Routledge.

McClelland, P. (1969) 'The cost to America of British imperial policy', *American Economic Review*, 59: 370–81.

McCloskey, D.N. (1987) *Econometric History*, Basingstoke: Macmillan.

North, D.C. (1963) 'Quantitative research in American economic history', *American Economic Review*, 53: 128–30.

——(1981) *Structure and Change in Economic History*, New York: Norton.

——(1990) *Institutions, Institutional Change and Economic Performance*, New York: Cambridge University Press.

——(2005) *Understanding the Process of Economic Change*, Princeton, NJ: Princeton University Press.

North D.C., Wallis, J.J. and Weingast, B.R. (2009) *Violence and Social Orders: A Conceptual Framework for Interpreting Recorded Human History*, New York: Cambridge University Press.

O'Rourke, K., Hatton, T.J. and Williamson, J.G. (1994) 'Mass migration, commodity market integration and real wage convergence: the late nineteenth century Atlantic economy', in T.J. Hatton and J.G. Williamson (eds) *Migration and the International Labor Market, 1850–1939*, London: Routledge.

Pope, D. (1984) 'Rostow's Kondratieff cycle in Australia', *Journal of Economic History*, 44: 729–53.

Redlich, F. (1965) '"New" and traditional approaches to economic history and their interdependence', *Journal of Economic History*, 25: 480–95.

——(1968) 'Potentialities and pitfalls in economic history', *Explorations in Entrepreneurial History*, 6: 93–108.

Rosenbloom, J.L. (1998) 'Review of *The Age of Mass Migration: Causes and Economic Impact*', EH.net, http://eh.net/book_reviews/age-mass-migration-causes-and-economic-impact.

Schwartz, A. (1981) 'Understanding 1929–33', in K. Brunner (ed.) *The Great Depression Revisited*, Boston, MA: Martinus Nijhoff Publishing.

Temin, P. (1968) 'The economic consequences of the bank war', *Journal of Political Economy*, 76: 257–74.

Thomas, R. (1965) 'A quantitative approach to the study of the effects of British imperial policy on colonial welfare: some preliminary findings', *Journal of Economic History*, 25: 615–38.

Toma, M. (1989) 'The policy effectiveness of open market operations in the 1920s', *Explorations in Economic History*, 26: 99–116.

Whaples, R. (1991) 'A quantitative history of the *Journal of Economic History* and the cliometric revolution', *Journal of Economic History*, 51: 289–301.

——(1995) 'Where is there consensus among American economic historians? The results of a survey on forty propositions', *Journal of Economic History*, 55: 139–54.

2

THE NEW INSTITUTIONAL ECONOMICS AND ECONOMIC HISTORY

Tomas Nonnenmacher

Two claims that are central to the research agenda of the New Institutional Economics (NIE) are that institutions affect economic performance and that both the causes and effects of institutions can be analyzed using economic concepts (North 1990). According to North (1990: 3), "institutions are the rules of the game in a society or, more formally, the humanly devised constraints that shape human interaction." Ostrom (2005: 3) describes institutions as "the prescriptions that humans use to organize all forms of repetitive and structured interactions, including those within families, neighborhoods, markets, firms, sports leagues, churches, private associations, and governments at all scales." Formal rules, which "say what individuals must, must not, may, can, and cannot do," and that are enforced by an "authoritative agency" are institutions (Commons [1924] 1995: 138). But so are informal norms based on custom and tradition, which can also shape economic behavior. This chapter provides an overview of several levels of institutional analysis, ranging from informal norms to specific rules, discusses the concepts of institutional efficiency and change, and concludes with some questions for future research.

The NIE draws on several research traditions in economics, including Neoclassical Economics (Eggertsson 1990), Old Institutional Economics (Rutherford 1994), and Austrian Economics (Langlois 1986). Economic historians have played a central role in generating both the theory and the empirical work of the NIE. (See Alston *et al.* (1996) for a theoretical overview and examples of these contributions.) While the NIE is in part the application of neoclassical theory to the study of institutions, it expands on neoclassical theory by introducing new conceptual tools, such as transaction costs and property rights. The scope of the NIE's analysis is very broad, and it draws from and influences other disciplines, such as political science, history, psychology, sociology, and anthropology. The NIE uses many methods to understand institutions, including mathematical and literary theory (De Alessi 1990), econometric analysis (Klein 2008), and case studies (Alston 2008a).

The NIE draws a distinction between institutions and organizations. Institutions are the "rules of the game," and organizations consist of individuals who interact repeatedly in linked situations. Organizations operate within an institutional environment and have their own institutions that govern their members' behavior. The United Nations, a central government, a stock exchange, a local pizza shop, and a college club are all organizations, and they are all objects of analysis of the NIE. According to North *et al.* (2009: 15), "Organizations consist of specific groups of individuals pursuing a mix of common and individual goals through partially coordinated behavior." Ostrom (2005: 57, 32) models organizations as being "composed of one or more (usually more) action situations," which occur when "two or more individuals are faced with a set of potential actions that jointly produce outcomes."

Williamson (2000) provides a four-level framework for categorizing social phenomena, which is used to organize the material in the rest of this chapter. He admits that additional levels could be added, suggesting a fifth level, Level 0: "Mechanisms of the mind", which captures the process by which our minds evolve. Evolutionary psychologists believe that psychological adaptions evolved in a similar way to physiological adaptations "because they solved problems related to survival and reproduction" (Confer *et al.* 2010). Level 1: "Embeddedness" includes the informal norms, customs, and traditions that are part of the cultural heritage of a society and take hundreds or even thousands of years to change. Level 2: The "institutional environment" includes basic human rights, constitutions, and rules concerning the allocation and enforcement of property rights. The rules at this level reflect the Level 1 institutions, but change more quickly. Level 3: The "governance" of contractual relations determines the choice and structure of the organization within which interactions take place. Level 3 rules are influenced by Level 2 rules, and can change within 1 to 10 years. Level 4: "Resource allocation and employment" decisions made continuously by market participants are made at the margin and determine the proper input and output levels. Since Level 4 decisions are the key unit of analysis in Neoclassical Economics, this chapter does not address them explicitly. In practice, when studying a particular institution or organization, a partial analysis must be done with other institutional arrangements held constant. The NIE has focused mainly on Level 2 and Level 3 analysis, and the bulk of this chapter is devoted to those two levels.

Other authors offer alternative frameworks for understanding institutions. Similar to Williamson, Ostrom (2005) describes four levels of analysis and outcomes: metaconstitutional situations; constitutional situations; collective-choice situations; and operational situations. Alston (2008b) maps how formal and informal institutions jointly determine property rights, which in turn affect transaction costs, production costs, and, ultimately, economic performance. Eggertsson (1990) uses three levels of analysis to organize the study of institutions: the structure of property rights, the organization of exchange, and the social and political rules. In Williamson's (2000) framework, norms affect formal rules, which affect governance structures, which affect resource allocation decisions, but there are feedback loops between all of these levels that lead to significant endogeneity. While the first two levels, the mechanisms of the mind and embeddedness, are generally spontaneous in nature, organizations are central to the analysis of the institutional environment, governance, and resource allocation and employment.

Mechanisms of the mind

A basic model of behavior in Neoclassical Economics assumes that individuals' mechanisms of the mind are those of rational egoists. They possess complete information, have "complete and consistent" valuations of outcomes that are monotonic transformations of external payoffs, and choose actions that "maximize material net benefits" given the actions of others (Ostrom 2005: 101). Modeling humans as rational egoists makes sense when examining markets that are close to being perfectly competitive; however, it is not appropriate to model humans as rational egoists in all settings (Arrow 1986; North 2005; Ostrom 2005). For instance, in situations where information costs are high, models based on bounded rationality, in which actors are assumed to be "intendedly rational but limitedly so," are more appropriate (Simon 1957: xxiv). A long tradition in Old Institutional and Austrian Economics posits that decision makers use habits and routines to compensate for their difficulties in processing information (Clark 1918; Hayek 1960), and the NIE draws from these traditions. Another assumption of human behavior is that some humans do not solely maximize material net benefits, but value "trust, reciprocity, and equity very highly" (Ostrom 2005: 131). These "conditional cooperators" can be modeled as receiving non-material benefits from cooperating that are not functions of external payoffs. Achieving a cooperative outcome, however, requires that other players also value cooperation and that the institutional environment encourages cooperation. Without the proper institutions in place, even those actors with a preference for cooperation will act egotistically (Ostrom 2005).

Embeddedness

The embedded culture of a society affects how people learn and process information as well as what kinds of formal institutions and organizations are feasible. North (2005: 71) argues that "Humans start out with genetic features which provide the initial architecture of the mind; the mind interacts with the cultural heritage and the experiences of individuals to shape learning." Greif (1994: 915) defines cultural beliefs as "the ideas and thoughts common to several individuals that govern interaction ... and differ from knowledge in that they are not empirically discovered or analytically proved." Ostrom (2005: 106) states, "When we indicate that people share a culture, it is a shorthand way of indicating that the wide diversity of mental models that individuals have invented has been reduced to a smaller set within those sharing the culture." The interpretation of culture as limiting the menu of available mental models is developed in Denzau and North (1994) and North (2005).

If culture limits the set of mental models with which people interpret their world, then culture will affect the range of possible legal and contractual outcomes. This is the argument made by Greif (1994, 2006) in his comparison of the eleventh-century Maghribi and Genoese traders. Because of their collectivist cultural beliefs, the Maghribi adopted "horizontal economic interactions" and group sanctions and enforcement, while the individualist culture of Genoa led to a "vertical social structure" with legal and political sanctions and enforcement (Greif 1994: 942). Alston *et al.* (2009) argue that shared cultural norms between hacendados and workers in Yucatán, Mexico, led to unique contractual practices that cannot be understood outside of the specific political and cultural context. On a broader scale, statistical cross-country analyses of culture often rely on measures such as the World Values Survey. Guiso *et al.* (2003) show that religion affects economic attitudes such as trust, thriftiness, and preferences for redistribution, and Knack and Keefer (1997) show that differences in the culture of trust across countries affect economic performance.

The institutional environment

The institutional environment defines the formal rules of society, such as constitutions, statutory law, and common law. While neoclassical theory traditionally ignores legal rules or assumes that they are structured in a way that allows costless transacting, laws and their enforcement are important because they create incentives for organizing economic activity (North 1990). Coase (1960) provides the NIE with the concepts needed to understand the conditions under which the legal rule affects economic efficiency. Using what has become a universal example in law and economics classes, he asks whether it matters if the state assigns property rights to farmers who are planting crops, or to neighboring ranchers whose cattle tend to wander and trample those crops. He argues that, in a frictionless market, farmers and ranchers would "agree themselves around" the property rights rule to achieve an efficient and invariant outcome. For instance, if farmers have the legal right to be free from wandering cattle, but total wealth is highest if farmers build a fence to exclude cattle, then a "Coasian" bargain would be struck in which ranchers pay farmers to build a fence. From an efficiency perspective, it would not matter how property rights were defined, as long as all of the assumptions required for achieving a frictionless market were met. The most important reason why markets are not frictionless is because of transaction costs, the costs of searching for trading partners, bargaining to an agreement, and policing and enforcing that bargain. Coase's insight has been labeled "the Coase Theorem," and, due to the ubiquity of transaction costs, the Coase Theorem has an important corollary: in the presence of transaction costs, institutional and organizational choices affect economic outcomes.

The insights of the Coase Theorem have been used to understand the formation and importance of property rights (Demsetz 1967; Barzel 1989; Libecap 1989). Property rights are the rights to use, derive income, exclude others, and transfer property. Rules concerning property are central to the institutional environment, and the state or some other organization must define, interpret, and enforce these rules. Since frictionless markets and well-defined property rights lead to the efficient allocation of society's resources, a policy prescription drawn from Coase's work is that the state should reduce transaction costs and have clear rules regarding the assignment of property rights in order to increase social wealth.

Examples of the importance of property rights abound in the economic history literature. In their seminal article on England's Glorious Revolution of 1688, North and Weingast (1989) argue that the balance of power between parliament and the monarchy enhanced property rights and generated subsequent economic growth. In their study of property rights in the Brazilian Amazon, Alston *et al.* (1999) find that having clearly defined property rights induces farmers to make greater investments in land, and that having better access to markets induces farmers to seek clearly defined rights. They also find that unclear property rights combined with poorly designed government policies increase the amount of squatting and the use of violence to settle competing claims to property. Libecap (1989) and Higgs (1982) provide examples of how poorly designed regulations allocate property rights to oil fields and salmon fisheries in a way that leads to inefficient modes of production. Property rights need not be defined and enforced by the state. As shown by Umbeck (1977) for the early years of the California gold rush and Ellickson (1989) for the whaling industry in the eighteenth and nineteenth centuries, property rights can arise out of informal norms and in the absence of formal enforcement mechanisms.

The institutions of governance

The institutions of governance operate at a level below the institutional environment and are the specific rules governing how economic activity is organized. The central question that Coase (1937: 388) asks is, "if production is regulated by price movements ... why is there any organization?" As noted earlier, Coase's answer is that search, bargaining, and enforcement costs introduce friction into the price mechanism. Entrepreneurs will choose the organizational form that minimizes the sum of production and transacting costs. While economic activity can be categorized as taking place either within the hierarchy of a firm or within a pure market setting, in practice, most activity takes place within a hybrid setting that incorporates elements of both.

The NIE replaces the assumptions that humans can process unlimited amounts of information and that the distribution of possible future outcomes is knowable with Simon's (1957) assumption that humans are boundedly rational and Knight's (1921) assumption that we live in a world of uncertainty. In this framework, the future is murky and complex contracts are "invariably incomplete" (Williamson 1985: 178). Klein *et al.* (1978) and Williamson (1971, 1985) build on

Coase's work to develop a theory of the firm that focuses on the enforcement costs of contracting and is founded on the concepts of bounded rationality, uncertainty, ex post opportunism, and specific assets. This theory analyzes the conditions under which stages of production are internalized versus outsourced: the classic "make or buy" decision. Williamson (1985) posits that interactions between market participants vary in their frequency and in the specificity of assets involved in the transaction. While a large number of market participants may interact during the initial stages of contracting, a "fundamental transformation" occurs after a significant amount has been invested in specific assets, causing the relationship between market participants to become bilateral. Once this transformation in the relationship takes place, a party that has devoted significant resources investing in assets specific to the relationship is vulnerable to opportunistic behavior. The greater the investment in a specific asset, the greater the opportunity to appropriate quasi rents, and the greater the cost of pure market transactions. Market transacting will occur when asset specificity is low, but, as asset specificity rises, alternative governance structures are needed, such as bilateral, trilateral, and unified contracting. Joskow (1987) tests the importance of relationship-specific investments in the U.S. coal market, using access to transportation and differences in regional variation in coal quality as measures of specificity. He finds that parties are more likely to rely on long-term contracting when investments are more specific, thereby reducing their exposure to opportunism and hold up.

While theories of transaction costs associated with asset specificity provide important insights into organizational choice, the institutions of governance are shaped by many other transaction costs. (See Garrouste and Saussier [2008] and Ménard [2008] for overviews and comparisons of alternative theories of the firm.) Alston and Higgs (1982) show that transaction costs associated with monitoring assets and worker effort explain the choice of a wage, sharecropping, or tenant contract on cotton plantations in the post-bellum South. Staten and Umbeck (1982) show that changes in the rules governing medical treatment encouraged higher levels of shirking among air traffic controllers in the 1970s. Olmstead and Rhode (2004) describe how asymmetric information in the early twentieth-century cattle market led some firms to organize trade in a way that accelerated the spread of bovine tuberculosis. They argue that this market failure could only be resolved through regulation of cattle markets at the national level. These three examples show the endogeneity of rules, incentives, and transaction costs. While Alston and Higgs (1982) show that the institutions of governance minimize the sum of production and transaction costs, Staten and Umbeck (1982) show that changes in rules can increase transaction costs and incentivize workers to shirk. Finally, Olmstead and Rhode (2004) show that transaction costs can be so high that restructuring the institutional environment is necessary.

Institutional efficiency and change

The phrases "inefficient institutions" and "efficient institutions" are often used in the NIE in the attempt to prescribe how to move from the former to the latter. One commonly used definition of efficiency is Pareto optimality. An allocation of resources is said to be Pareto optimal if there is no way to make one person better off without making someone else worse off. Pareto-improving trades happen constantly in the marketplace, but Pareto-improving institutional change is harder to achieve because institutional change creates winners and losers. In the presence of transaction costs, the winners may have a difficult time paying off the losers. A more general definition of efficient institutions is that they maximize economic growth and aggregate welfare. North and Thomas (1973), Alchian and Demsetz (1973), and Posner (1977) view institutions as either being efficient or on a path towards efficiency, but this view has been critiqued by Field (1981: 184) as being too functionalist in its assumption that market forces will cause the optimal set of rules to be chosen from a "book of organization blueprints." The introduction of transaction costs makes evaluating the efficiency of any institutional arrangement very difficult. Commenting on property rights research, Ostrom (1990: 216) argues that it is common for institutions to be "rejected as inefficient, without examining how these institutions may help them acquire information, reduce monitoring costs, and equitably allocate appropriation rights and provision duties."

North (2005) abandons his earlier views on the progression of institutional change towards efficient institutions and instead argues that the institutional structure of society is largely non-ergodic: it shifts over time in unpredictable ways in response to human action. David (1985) and Arthur (1988) develop a theory of path dependency that initially was applied to technological change, the most famous example of which is the persistence of the QWERTY keyboard layout. (See Liebowitz and Margolis (1995) for a critique of David's QWERTY story and an alternative framework for categorizing path dependence.) David (1985: 332) defines a sequence of events as being path dependent when "influences upon the eventual outcome can be exerted by temporally remote events, including happenings dominated by chance elements rather than systematic forces." North (1990) combines the path-dependence literature with a Coasian transaction cost analysis to argue that institutional lock-in can occur on many paths, including those that lead to "consistently poor performance." As an example of this type of analysis, Engerman and Sokoloff (2000) argue that path dependence and lock-in can explain differences in the performance of economies across the Americas. In their framework, initial factor endowments during the colonial period influenced the distribution of political and economic power, differences in power affected whether rules, such as those governing land policy and voting rights, were designed to maintain the power of the elite or encourage growth, and lock-in caused these remote differences to persist and affect economic outcomes to the present day.

Alston (2008b) provides a framework for analyzing change and persistence in the formal legal rules of society, distinguishing between the demand for and the supply of legal institutions. The demand for rules comes from the citizenry in general and from special interests. Formal rules are supplied by the government. A wide array of rules governs political organizations and therefore affects the path of institutional change. The structure of the organizations and the preferences of the individuals demanding and supplying change determines what types of rules will be passed and how they will be applied and enforced. Voters have little incentive to become aware of most issues facing government because the effects of their votes are small, as are the impacts of policies on individual voters (Downs 1957; Tullock 1967). Instead, special interests are more likely to influence the political process (Olson 1965). Many variables influence the supply side of government and the types of institutional change that occurs. These variables include whether the government is presidential or parliamentary (Carey 2008), federalist or unitary (Weingast 2008), and bicameral or unicameral (Cutrone and McCarty 2006); what rules govern the bureaucracy (McCubbins *et al.* 1987), the committee structure of the legislature (Shepsle and Weingast 1987), and the membership of the legislature (Alston *et al.* 2006); and how political parties are organized (Cox and McCubbins 1993). In times of crisis, the supply and demand for formal institutional change can increase, leading to an increase in the scale and scope of government. While the size of government generally falls after the crisis has passed, it does not fall back to its pre-crisis growth path, leading to what Higgs (1987) describes as a ratchet effect.

Recent work in the NIE continues to examine the causes and consequences of changes to the institutional environment, particularly the transition to democracy. North *et al.* (2009) provide a framework for understanding the move from a natural state to an open access order. Natural states limit access to valuable resources and activities to a select group of elite members, both to enrich that elite and to control violence. An open access order controls violence through a consolidated military and allows organizations to be formed impersonally, without any direct link to an elite coalition. The key question posed by North *et al.* is how natural states evolve into open access orders. Their answer involves satisfying three "doorstep conditions." First, elites must develop a rule of law among themselves that shares rights equally among elites. Second, public and private organizations must exist that persist beyond the life span of individual elites. Finally, the political system must control the military and the use of violence. Acemoglu and Robinson (2006) offer a formal model of the transition from authoritarian rule to democracy in which two groups, the elite and citizens, contend for political and economic power. The elite desire to extract resources from citizens, but fear that the continuation of elite rule may lead to violent revolution. In order to placate citizens, the elite grant them additional concessions and commit to continuing those concessions by switching to a democratic institutional environment. One question concerning this model is under what conditions the transition to democracy creates institutional lock-in and whether elites can regain *de facto* political and economic power in the future even after a transition to democracy.

Concluding remarks

While the idea that "institutions matter" has been accepted by many economists, there are still unanswered questions and much unexplored territory at all levels of Williamson's social analysis. The study of the causes and effects of informal institutions such as culture, norms, and beliefs is still in its early phase. The demand and supply of the formal institutional environment have been studied by economists and political scientists, but the process by which political institutions change and persist still requires much research. While the NIE includes many theories concerning the institutions of governance, these are often partial explanations and require additional integration. Finally, the NIE must refine its assumptions of human behavior and study the conditions under which those assumptions are most appropriate. These questions are only a few of the ones that will continue to make the NIE an exciting and important field of research in the future.

References

Acemoglu, D. and Robinson, J.A. (2006) *Economic Origins of Dictatorship and Democracy*, Cambridge: Cambridge University Press.

Alchian, A. and Demsetz, H. (1973) 'The property rights paradigm', *Journal of Economic History*, 33: 16–27.

Alston, L.J. (2008a) 'The "case" for case studies in *New Institutional Economics*', in É. Brousseau and J.M. Glachant (eds) *New Institutional Economics: A Guidebook*, Cambridge: Cambridge University Press.

——(2008b) 'New Institutional Economics', in S.N. Durlauf and L.E. Blume (eds) *The New Palgrave Dictionary of Economics*, 2nd edition, New York: Palgrave Macmillan.

Alston, L.J. and Higgs, R. (1982) 'Contractual mix in southern agriculture since the Civil War: facts, hypotheses, and tests', *Journal of Economic History*, 42: 327–52.

Alston, L.J., Eggertsson, T. and North D.C. (1996) *Empirical Studies in Institutional Change*, Cambridge: Cambridge University Press.

Alston, L.J., Jenkins, J.A. and Nonnenmacher, T. (2006) 'Who should govern Congress? Access to power and the salary grab of 1873', *Journal of Economic History*, 66: 674–706.

Alston, L.J., Libecap, G.D. and Mueller, B. (1999) *Titles, Conflict and Land Use: The Development of Property Rights and Land Reform on the Brazilian Frontier*, Ann Arbor, MI: University of Michigan Press.

Alston, L.J., Mattiace, S. and Nonnenmacher, T. (2009) 'Coercion, culture, and contracts: labor and debt on henequen haciendas in Yucatán, Mexico, 1870–1915', *Journal of Economic History*, 69: 104–37.

Arrow, K.J. (1986) 'Rationality of self and others in an economic system', *Journal of Business*, 59: 385–99.

Arthur, W.B. (1988) 'Self-reinforcing mechanisms in economics', in P. Anderson, K. Arrow and D. Pines (eds) *Studies in the Sciences of Complexity*, Reading, MA: Addison-Wesley.

Barzel, Y. (1989) *Economic Analysis of Property Rights*, Cambridge: Cambridge University Press.

Buss, D.M. (2001) 'Human nature and culture: an evolutionary psychological perspective', *Journal of Personality*, 69: 955–78.

Carey, J.M. (2008) 'Presidential versus parliamentary government', in C. Ménard and M.M. Shirley (eds) *Handbook of New Institutionalism*, Berlin: Springer.

Clark, J.M. (1918) 'Economics and modern psychology I', *Journal of Political Economy*, 26: 1–30.

Coase, R.H. (1937) 'The nature of the firm', *Economica*, 4: 386–405.

——(1960) 'The problem of social cost', *Journal of Law and Economics*, 3: 1–44.

Commons, J.R. (1924 [1995]) *Legal Foundations of Capitalism*, New Brunswick, NJ: Transaction Publishers.

Confer, J.C., Easton, J.A., Fleischman, D.S., Goetz, C.D., Lewis, D.M., Perilloux, C. and Buss, D.M. (2010) 'Evolutionary psychology: controversies, questions, prospects, and limitations', *American Psychologist*, 65: 110–26.

Cox, G.W. and McCubbins, M.D. (1993) *Legislative Leviathan: Party Government in the House*, Berkeley: University of California Press.

Cutrone, M. and McCarty, N. (2006) 'Does bicameralism matter?' in B.R. Weingast and D.A. Wittman (eds) *The Oxford Handbook of Political Economy*, Oxford: Oxford University Press.

David, P.A. (1985) 'Clio and the economics of QWERTY', *American Economic Review*, 75: 332–7.

De Alessi, L. (1990) 'Form, substance, and welfare comparisons in the analysis of institutions', *Journal of Institutional and Theoretical Economics*, 146: 5–23.

Demsetz, J. (1967) 'Toward a theory of property rights', *American Economic Review*, 57: 347–59.

Denzau, A.T. and North, D.C. (1994) 'Shared mental models: ideologies and institutions', *Kyklos*, 47: 3–31.

Downs, A. (1957) *An Economic Analysis of Democracy*, New York: Harper and Row.

Eggertsson, T. (1990) *Economic Behavior and Institutions*, Cambridge: Cambridge University Press.

Ellickson, R.C. (1989) 'A hypothesis of wealth-maximizing norms: evidence from the whaling industry', *Journal of Law, Economics, and Organization*, 5: 83–97.

Engerman, S.L. and Sokoloff, K.L. (2000) 'Institutions, factor endowments, and paths of development in the New World', *Journal of Economic Perspectives*, 14: 217–32.

Field, Alexander (1981) 'The problem with neoclassical institutional economics: a critique with special reference to the North/Thomas model of pre-1500 Europe,' *Explorations in Economic History*, 18: 174–98.

Garrouste, P. and Saussier, S. (2008) 'The theories of the firm', in É. Brousseau and J.M. Glachant (eds) *New Institutional Economics: A Guidebook*, Cambridge: Cambridge University Press.

Greif, A. (1994) 'Cultural beliefs and the organization of society: a historical and theoretical reflection on collectivist and individualist societies', *Journal of Political Economy*, 102: 912–50.

——(2006) *Institutions and the Path to the Modern Economy*, Cambridge: Cambridge University Press.

Guiso, L., Sapienza, P. and Zingales, L. (2003) 'People's opium? Religion and economic attitudes', *Journal of Monetary Economics*, 50: 525–56.

Hayek, F.A. (1960) *The Constitution of Liberty*, Chicago, IL: University of Chicago Press.

Higgs, R. (1982) 'Legally induced technical regress in the Washington salmon fishery', *Research in Economic History*, 7: 55–86.

Higgs, R. (1987) *Crisis and Leviathan: Critical Episodes in the Growth of American Government*, Oxford: Oxford University Press.

Joskow, P.L. (1987) 'Contract duration and relationship-specific investments: empirical evidence from coal markets', *American Economic Review*, 77: 168–85.

Klein, B., Crawford, R.A. and Alchian, A.A. (1978) 'Vertical integration, appropriable rents, and the competitive contracting process', *Journal of Law and Economics*, 21: 297–326.

Klein, P. (2008) 'The make-or-buy decision: lessons from empirical economics', in C. Ménard and M.M. Shirley (eds) *Handbook of New Institutionalism*, Berlin: Springer.

Knack, S. and Keefer, P. (1997) 'Does social capital have an economic payoff? A cross-country investigation', *Quarterly Journal of Economics*, 112: 1251–88.

Knight, F. (1921) *Risk, Uncertainty, and Profit*, New York: Houghton Mifflin.

Langlois, R. (1986) 'The New Institutional Economics: an introductory essay', in R. Langlois (ed.) *Economics as a Process: Essays in the New Institutional Economics*, Cambridge: Cambridge University Press.

Libecap, G.D. (1989) *Contracting for Property Rights*, Cambridge: Cambridge University Press.

Liebowitz, S.J. and Margolis, S.E. (1995) 'Path dependence, lock-in, and history', *Journal of Law, Economics, and Organization*, 11: 205–26.

McCubbins, M.D., Noll, R.G. and Weingast, B.R. (1987) 'Administrative procedures as instruments of control', *Journal of Law, Economics, and Organization*, 3: 243–77.

Ménard, C. (2008) 'A new institutional approach to organization', in C. Ménard and M.M. Shirley (eds) *Handbook of New Institutionalism*, Berlin: Springer.

North, D.C. (1990) *Institutions, Institutional Change, and Economic Performance*, Cambridge: Cambridge University Press.

——(2005) *Understanding the Process of Institutional Change*, Princeton, NJ: Princeton University Press.

North, D.C. and Thomas, R. (1973) *The Rise of the Western World: A New Economic History*, Cambridge: Cambridge University Press.

North, D.C. and Weingast, B.R. (1989) 'Constitutions and commitment: the evolution of institutional governing public choice in seventeenth-century England', *Journal of Economic History*, 49: 803–32.

North, D.C., Wallis, J.J. and Weingast, B.R. (2009) *Violence and Social Orders: A Conceptual Framework for Interpreting Recorded Human History*, Cambridge: Cambridge University Press.

Olmstead, A.L. and Rhode, P.W. (2004) 'The "tuberculous cattle trust": disease contagion in an era of regulatory uncertainty', *Journal of Economic History*, 64: 929–63.

Olson, M. (1965) *The Logic of Collective Action*, Cambridge, MA: Harvard University Press.

Ostrom, E. (1990) *Governing the Commons: The Evolution of Institutions for Collective Action*, Cambridge: Cambridge University Press.

——(2005) *Understanding Institutional Diversity*, Princeton, NJ: Princeton University Press.

Posner, R.A. (1977) *Economic Analysis of the Law*, 2nd edition, Boston, MA: Little, Brown.

Rutherford, M. (1994) *Institutions in Economics: The Old and New Institutionalism*, Cambridge: Cambridge University Press.

Shepsle, K.A. and Weingast, B.R. (1987) 'The institutional foundations of committee power', *American Political Science Review*, 81: 85–104.

Simon, H.A. (1957) *Models of Man*, New York: John Wiley & Sons.

Staten, M.E. and Umbeck, J. (1982) 'Information costs and incentives to shirk: disability compensation of air traffic controllers', *American Economic Review*, 72: 1023–37.

Tullock, G. (1967) *Towards a Mathematics of Politics*, Ann Arbor, MI: University of Michigan Press.

Umbeck, J. (1977) 'A theory of contract choice and the California gold rush', *Journal of Law and Economics*, 20: 421–37.

Weingast, B.R. (2008) 'The performance and stability of federalism: an institutional perspective', in C. Ménard and M.M. Shirley (eds) *Handbook of New Institutionalism*, Berlin: Springer.

Williamson, O.E. (1971) 'The vertical integration of production: market failure considerations', *American Economic Review*, 61: 112–23.

——(1985) *The Economic Institutions of Capitalism: Firms, Markets, Relational Contracting*, New York: The Free Press.

——(2000) 'The New Institutional Economics: taking stock, looking ahead', *Journal of Economic Literature*, 38: 595–613.

3

MEASURING ECONOMIC GROWTH AND THE STANDARD OF LIVING

Lee A. Craig

Defining the "standard of living"

Gross domestic product (GDP), the value of final goods and services produced within a country during a period of time, is the measure economists typically use to gauge aggregate economic activity in a modern nation state. It is essentially the sum of the product of prices and (final) quantities of goods and services destined for exchange in the market. The prices in this measure can be influenced by inflation (or deflation) – that is, a general increase (or decrease) in the price level unrelated to "real" economic activity. To control for these effects, economists hold prices constant for some "base year."[1] This adjustment yields real GDP, which is purged of any inflationary (or deflationary) effect. Real GDP, then, is a key economic indicator, and its growth represents "economic growth."

However, since real GDP captures aggregate economic activity, large countries will tend to have relatively large GDPs; conversely, small countries will have relatively small GDPs. For example, measured in U.S. dollars, in 2010 the real GDP of Indonesia is nearly four times larger than that of Norway (ADFAT 2011). However, per capita real GDP – that is, real GDP divided by population – is much higher in Norway than it is in Indonesia: $52,239 versus $4,380, again in 2010 U.S. dollars. Therefore, real GDP per capita, rather than GDP, is the standard economic indicator of "the living standard" within a modern nation state, and the growth of this measure is typically labeled an improvement in the standard of living.

Three intellectual milestones mark the history of measuring GDP, economic growth, and the standard of living. The first of these is the identification of the political or geographical unit that is to be measured. Exactly what constitutes an "economy"? More specifically, what are its political or geographical boundaries? The second addresses the conceptual issue of what represents economic activity within that unit, and how is that activity related to the standard of living. In other words, what economic activity or indicators are to be measured? Finally, there remains the practical question of how that economic activity is measured, and how its growth is characterized. What economic variables represent aggregate economic activity? Which of these measures the standard of living? And what does a higher standard of living mean? Since even the simplest notions of the economy, economic activity, and the standard of living involve many factors and variables, they necessarily have to be constrained in the actual measurement process for the concept of growth to be meaningful.

A history of measuring the standard of living

Adam Smith's *An Inquiry into the Nature and Causes of the Wealth of Nations* is arguably the pivotal contribution to the measurement of economic growth. In his uniquely verbose way, Smith grappled with exactly the three issues posed earlier. What was the geographical or political unit to be measured? What constitutes the "wealth" of that unit? And how would one go about measuring it?

With respect to the unit to be measured, Smith's era saw the advance and proliferation of the nation state, which was emerging from the medieval fiefs and divine-right monarchies of earlier ages. Consequently, in Smith's view, and that of subsequent generations of economists, the nation state was the political *and* geographical unit of interest. Henceforth, we would speak of the English or the French or the American economy.

As for the conceptual issue of what to measure, although Smith chose the word "wealth" (an indicator of accumulated riches, what economists refer to as *stock* measure) to denote the concept for which he was grasping, his crucial insight was that the *flow* of goods and services consumed by a nation's citizens indicated the nation's wealth. He wrote, "Consumption is the sole end and purpose of all production ..." (Smith 1976, Vol. 2: 179). Even before the ink dried on the first edition of *Wealth of Nations*, economic writers were already leaning towards national "income" as a more propitious indicator than wealth of aggregate economic activity.[2] It followed that an economy that could generate a lot of goods and services for its citizens to consume was a wealthy economy. From personal observation, Smith supposed England was wealthy; Scotland was not; and France was somewhere in between – though he conjectured that Scotland was growing faster than France. However, he had no systematic way of confirming such suppositions. Thus, it was the third issue, the actual measurement of aggregate economic wealth (or income), that Smith struggled with, and he never generated anything like a formal system of national income accounting.

Smith's quest to understand and measure the wealth of a nation would clearly be classified by later generations of economists as "macroeconomic" in nature. Indeed, the issue practically defined the field of macroeconomics. One can also find in Smith's work topics that later generations would label as distinctly "microeconomic." One of his key insights was that the efficiency of a nation's individual producers (including his famous description of the division of labor in a pin factory) was the pillar upon which its aggregate wealth rested; that is to say, he recognized what economists today refer to as the "microfoundations" of macroeconomics. However, it was the actual counting and summing of economic activity that defeated him. When it came to the measurement of aggregate production, consumption, and wealth, Smith only offered anecdotal evidence, primarily examples and case studies from microeconomics, and that was where he left the subject.

The economists who came after Smith and took up his quest to understand the aggregate wealth of a nation largely proceeded along two paths, which, while not divergent by nature, did not in practice converge until well into the twentieth century. One of these paths was largely theoretical. Among the topics on which these so-called "classical economists" focused was "national" income. However, their emphasis was not so much on measuring it as understanding its source. Here they wandered into the minefield of the theory of value, the key juxtaposition of which, according to Smith, was what he called "value in use" versus the "value in exchange" (Smith 1976, Vol. 1: 32), the latter of which economists would eventually come to interpret as the market price. Smith hypothesized that the exchange value of a good was equal to the value of the labor used in the good's production. Subsequent economic theorists – including Thomas Robert Malthus, David Ricardo, and Karl Marx – wrestled with this so-called "labor theory of value." The issue was important, because mathematically the sum of the value of economic transactions over some period of time would offer an estimate of aggregate or national income.[3]

When it came to using the value of a transaction as the building block for aggregate income, the questions were: When such a transaction takes place, from whence did income come, and where did it go? And how was the value of the product distributed among the factors that produced it? This was what the classical economists referred to as the "distribution of the product."[4] Here then was the question around which modern national income accounting was constructed. Despite their focus on the labor theory of value, the classical economists recognized that labor was only one factor of production; its wage only one form of payment. Land, capital, and credit were others; and their payments were labeled rent, profit, and interest (Smith 1976, Vol. 1: 58–9). Smith had noted that private consumption was the primary objective of productive activity, but expenditures were made on more than just consumption, and to fully form the consumption side of the ledger economists eventually added investment activities, government purchases, and, reflecting the geographic boundaries of national income accounting, net exports. So the value of every final transaction represented a buyer's consumption or investment, but it also generated a wage or profit for the producers.

While the classical economists struggled with the theoretical issues behind the source and distribution of national income, another less prominent group focused on the *measurement* of economic activity.[5] Space prohibits a full accounting of the individuals who contributed to the evolutionary progress that led from Adam Smith to the modern national income and product accounts.[6] However, a look at the work of four of the more prominent of these early academic "counters" gives one a feel for the evolution of the measurement of aggregate economic activity and hence economic growth. Two were Englishmen, Arthur Young and Thomas Tooke, and two were Americans, Henry Carey and David Wells. All offered seminal methodological and conceptual contributions to empirical economics.

Although he was 17 years Smith's junior, Young, a successful writer and a less successful gentleman farmer, began accumulating and processing economic data even before the publication of *Wealth of Nations*. Because of the size of the agricultural sector in pre-industrial economies, it was common at the time to identify agricultural success with national economic success. And so, over a roughly 40-year period, Young collected microlevel data on farms in England, Ireland, and France. Importantly, he made the intellectual leap from the performance of an English farm to the performance of the English economy, writing that, "From the average [performance] of a great number [of farms] we may certainly be able to calculate with much truth the general state of the whole kingdom ..." (Young 1771: 367, as quoted in Allen and Ó Gráda 1988: 94). Antedating the work of the classical economists on the distribution of output, Young divided the sources of income between landowners, laborers, and capital, and he often wrote in conceptual terms that also antedated the wide use of real per capita GDP as the key standard-of-living indicator.[7]

Tooke, a financier, was born two years before the publication of *Wealth of Nations*, and, although he engaged in the debates with the classical economists on the distribution of the product and made original contributions to monetary theory, his most lasting contribution was his insistence on bringing data to bear on his arguments. He focused on the movements in agricultural prices, and his monumental *History of Prices and the State of the Circulation*, which ran to six volumes, established a model, not much followed at the time, for the scientific investigation of economic relationships.[8] Tooke cast his net widely, studying, among other topics, money, banking, and distribution theory (Smith 2007), but it was his collection and use of data, including prices, the volume of credit and trade, and railway activity, that perpetuated his name.

Even more so than Tooke, Carey, born after Smith's death, rejected the abstract theorizing of the classical economists and "emphasized history and empirical observation" (Landreth and Colander 2002: 410–11), which, with a perspective of time not available to those earlier economists, revealed the unprecedented long-run economic growth generated by the Industrial Revolution. He argued, and attempted to demonstrate, that economic growth was driven by labor productivity – that is, output per worker – which was in turn driven by technological changes, which were happening all around. By tying the productivity of workers on the shop floor to aggregate living standards, Carey empirically established the link between micro-foundations and macrogrowth. Though his arguments were much ridiculed at the time,[9] his empirical approach was subsequently much imitated.

Despite the contributions of these early counters, which were not fully appreciated at the time but which, in terms of measuring the wealth of a nation, were more important than those of their more famous classical colleagues, neither Young, nor Tooke, nor Carey articulated a set of national income accounts. However, Wells (born 1828) did. Like Young, Wells was a pro-lific writer on a diverse set of topics. Trained as an engineer, which perhaps helped discipline his mind to the rigors of constructing a set of accounts that would generate estimates of national income, Wells constructed what were arguably the first reliable estimates of national income. Indeed, in private correspondence, Simon Kuznets, the father of modern national income account-ing, told Joseph Schumpeter that "Wells' estimates of [nineteenth-century national income] are deserving of confidence" (Schumpeter 1954: 524).

Despite Wells's breakthrough in national income accounting, in the late nineteenth century, the mainstream of Anglo-American economics revolved around price theory. John Stuart Mill's contributions on the theory of value and the subsequent work of Alfred Marshall dominated the scene.[10] However, the work of Marshall's most prominent student, John Maynard Keynes, and the onset of the Great Depression revived interest in empirical macroeconomics. After *Wealth of Nations* and Marx's *Das Kapital*, arguably the most influential volume in the history of economic thought was Keynes's *General Theory of Employment, Interest and Money*, the first edition of which was completed in 1935. In it, Keynes referred to aggregate output as "output as a whole" (1935: *passim*), but he did not define this whole, even as competing theories that were emerging to explain the Depression cried out for such a measurement.

The creation of the national income and product accounts

Arguably, the person to whom the most credit is due for ultimately supplying that measurement is Simon Kuznets, the "patron saint" of national income accounting, according to Martin Feldstein (Feldstein 1990: 10).[11] Kuznets, born in Pinsk in 1901, in what was then Czarist Russia, migrated to the United States during his college years. After concluding his graduate studies, Kuznets began working with Wesley Mitchell at the National Bureau of Economic Research (NBER). Mitchell's work focused on identifying business cycles using various economic indi-cators, such as bank clearings and railroad traffic (an approach that had its antecedents in Tooke's *History*). Kuznets contributed to the effort by refining the measurement of output and capital formation, and in 1930 his early efforts yielded his first major work, *Secular Movements in Pro-duction and Prices*. Here Kuznets moved towards systematically doing for the whole economy what Arthur Young had unsystematically done for English agriculture; that is, he created a set of prices and quantities that when multiplied and summed could yield a single number that measured aggregate economic activity, an indicator of Adam Smith's wealth of a nation.

With the onset of the Great Depression, policy makers in Washington took a serious look at the work of academic economists, such as Kuznets, and in consultation with him, in 1934, the

United States Department of Commerce produced *National Income, 1929–32*, which became the standard reference volume for the construction of national income accounts. Kuznets immediately set about expanding the study, pushing it backward (to 1919) and forward (to 1935) in time (Kuznets 1937). However, in the process of that effort, he raised some terminological and methodological questions. The primary mechanism through which those questions would be addressed was the NBER's Conference on Research in Income and Wealth, which was created through Kuznets's efforts.[12]

Formed in 1936, the Conference first convened early in 1937 and met annually for several years. From those meetings came a series of volumes containing scholarly papers on, among other things, the measurement and growth of aggregate output. Through the Conference Kuznets refined his methods and in 1941 produced his masterpiece, *National Income and Its Composition, 1919–1938*, which explains in a thousand detailed pages the methodology for aggregating transactions across the whole economy into national income.[13]

With the creation of a systematic and comprehensive methodology, the way was set to go forward with the annual production of the national income and product accounts, an activity formally managed by the Bureau of Economic Analysis within the U.S. Commerce Department. Other countries and international organizations followed suit. But neither Kuznets nor the policy makers who funded and oversaw the Commerce Department were interested in national income accounting as merely an intellectual exercise. They wanted to analyze the sources of long-run economic growth, as well as the deviations from long-run trends, which drove the business cycle. For that purpose, simply moving forward one year at a time for several decades until enough data were collected to say something intelligent about the process was unacceptable. Thus Kuznets pushed his estimates backwards in time.

Casting backwards to generate real gross national product (GNP) figures for the nineteenth century, Kuznets eventually came up with estimates that went back to 1889 (Kuznets 1961). These were subsequently revised by many scholars using different methodologies and data. Figure 3.1 shows Kuznets's original series and four subsequent revisions. Although, at first glance, the series look similar, by the end of the period, a substantial difference emerges among them. Indeed, the highest and lowest figures for 1913 differ by 14 per cent, and the differences between the rates of growth between the fastest- and slowest-growing series is greater than one half of a percentage point per annum (4.04 per cent for Kendrick's estimates versus 4.61 per cent for Romer's). Although that might seem like a small difference, consider that in two lifetimes a difference of that magnitude would generate estimates of real GDP that differed by more than a factor of two!

Space constraints prohibit a detailed explanation of the different data and assumptions that went into generating the estimates in Figure 3.1; however, Kuznets's original methodology served as the base for all of them (Balke and Gordon 1989; Johnston and Williamson 2008; Kendrick 1961; and Romer 1989).[14] A primary difference between the estimates is in the timing and magnitude of fluctuations in the business cycle. (Figure 3.2 shows the annual percentage changes in each series.) The average annual growth rate of the U.S. population between 1889 and 1913 was 1.90 per cent; thus the per capita growth rates of the series in Figure 3.1 range from 2.14 per cent to 2.71 per cent. Kuznets called this "modern economic growth," by which he meant aggregate growth rates that exceeded population growth rates by enough and for long enough that periodic downturns would not disrupt the long-run increase in the standard of living, as it was measured by per capita GDP (Kuznets 1966). Figure 3.2 reflects this phenomenon. Using, as an example, the Johnston and Williamson series, which has the median growth rate of the five series, and which goes back to 1870, we see that 13 of the 43 years show a decrease in real GDP, what might reasonably be called "recession" years, and

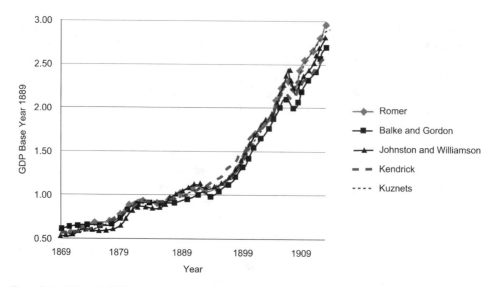

Figure 3.1 U.S. real GDP estimates, 1869–1913 (1889 = 1.00)
Sources: Balke and Gordon (1989), Johnston and Williamson (2008), Kendrick (1961), Kuznets (1961), and Romer (1989).

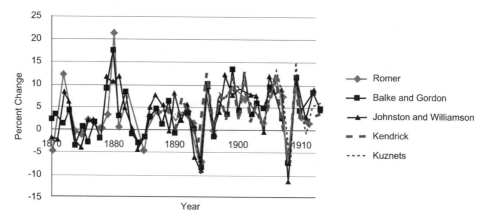

Figure 3.2 Annual per cent change in U.S. real GDP, 1870–1913
Sources: Balke and Gordon (1989), Johnston and Williamson (2008), Kendrick (1961), Kuznets (1961), and Romer (1989).

that the average decrease in real GDP during those years was 3.4 per cent. The other 30 years were growth years, with a mean increase of 7.0 per cent. In short, the standard of living roughly doubled over this period because there were more good years than bad years, and on average the good years were better than the bad years were bad. This is Kuznets's modern economic growth at work, and it is a fairly recent phenomenon in human history. In fact, Gregory Clark argues that, for the 3000 years before 1800, the average annual per capita growth rate of income was zero (Clark 2007).

Kuznets's GDP per capita provided an indicator of the living standard, but it is not without flaws. Broadly speaking, scholars have grouped these into three categories: 1) failure to reflect the distribution of income, 2) omissions or flaws in the measurement of some types of economic activity, and 3) the under-appreciation of quality-of-life issues.[15]

With respect to the distribution of income, in essence, GDP per capita gives us the output *available* for an *average* person's consumption (and investment, government expenditures, and so forth). It tells us nothing about what a *typical* person would consume. An economy could grow substantially; GDP per capita could indicate a rising standard of living; but, if all of the growth is enjoyed by, say, the top 20 per cent of the income distribution, the standard of living of the typical person or family would remain unchanged. Thus countries that appear to have a high standard of living, as measured by GDP per capita, could in fact be populated by masses of miserably poor families. In practice this is not the case. Among a large sample of countries from around the world, there is strong positive correlation between the growth of GDP per capita and the average income of the poorest 20 per cent of the population (Dollar and Kraay 2002).

As for its omissions, GDP per capita omits non-market activity, illegal activity, and the value of time spent at leisure. If you clean your house, then that economic activity does not show up in GDP; if you pay someone else to do it, it does. If your doctor writes a prescription for you and you purchase medicine from a pharmacy, then that economic activity shows up in GDP; if you purchase a controlled substance from a kid down the street, it does not. You might place a high value on fishing with your daughter, but the activity will not show up in GDP per capita. In short, GDP per capita probably understates the "true" standard of living. Furthermore, since average annual hours worked have declined by roughly 40 per cent over the past century or so in the world's richest countries (Huberman and Minns 2007), GDP per capita understates the growth in the standard of living over that time period.

Finally, one of Kuznets's students, Richard Easterlin, has argued that GDP suffers from its inability to reflect the quality of life, variously defined. In particular, he argues that there is no correlation between people's happiness and GDP per capita in the countries in which they live. This is the so-called Easterlin Paradox (Easterlin 1974). Kuznets recognized these short-comings.[16] In 1971, he received the Nobel Prize for his contributions to national income accounting, and in his Nobel address, subsequently published in the *American Economic Review*, he cautioned economists and policy makers against relying too much on real GDP or real GDP per capita as an economic indicator. He emphasized the "problem aspects of modern economic growth," which, in his view, included unexpected and "negative results" on the quality of life in industrializing countries (Kuznets 1973: 257). He hypothesized that the result might be a positive relationship between growth and the standard of living on the one hand (both conventionally measured by GDP per capita) and an increase in the inequality of the distribution of income on the other. This relationship came to be known as the "Kuznets curve."

Biological measures of the standard of living

Another student of Kuznets, Robert Fogel, himself a future Nobel Prize winner, recognized that the deterioration of the quality of life and an increase in inequality could show up in "biological indicators" of the standard of living (Fogel 2004). Among the indicators Fogel and his students focused on was human physical stature, the study of which is called "anthropometrics." The anthropometricians argued that stature serves as a good indicator of the biological well-being of a population, arguably better than per capita GDP. The consumption of nutrients – net of those exhausted during work or from fighting disease – determines whether *homo sapiens* achieve their genetic height potential. Thus stature differs from GDP per capita in that it reflects the consumption of nutrients and the biological costs associated with the production of goods and services; thus it reflects the distribution of economic output as manifest in consumption. The intensity of effort and number of hours worked, as well as working and living conditions, determine the body's demand for nutrients. When humans work harder for longer periods, or when they fight off disease, they are left with fewer nutrients for growth.

Net nutritional status, the key to human growth, is the difference between nutritional inputs and the demands of work, body maintenance, and disease. Before adulthood, a positive net nutritional status stimulates growth, while a negative net nutritional status will retard growth, *ceteris paribus*, of course.[17] Thus adult stature can be viewed as a "cumulative indicator of net nutritional status over the growth years" (Cuff 2005: 10). Changes in nutrition, working conditions, and disease environment can all influence net nutritional status, and the disease environment itself reflects public health measures (or the lack thereof), urbanization, and economic growth. Hence, stature can reveal information about the distribution of income or wealth that might be hidden in real GDP or even real GDP per capita. An economy experiencing modern economic growth and hence sustained increases in real GDP per capita, which we typically think of as indicating an increasing living standard, might be experiencing an increasingly unequal distribution of income (the Kuznets curve), such that the welfare effects of growth are not widely spread and in fact result in a worsening of the biological standard of living.

The early anthropometric work confirmed Kuznets's and Fogel's suspicions. Figure 3.3 shows the growth in real per capita GDP in 2000 dollars and the mean adult stature of white males for the United States from 1800 through 1920. As the earlier discussion notes, the GDP figures reflect the modern economic growth that sprung from the Industrial Revolution. However, the stature data reveal a troubling decline throughout the earlier decades of the nineteenth century. This so-called "antebellum paradox" has been much studied by economic historians in recent decades (see Chapter 4 in this volume), and their research suggests that, as Kuznets hypothesized, the disamenities of urbanization and industrialization initially overwhelmed their positive effects on the standard of living. Thus, although aggregate economic activity expanded more rapidly than population, generating modern economic growth, that growth did not necessarily generate an improvement in the standard of living, at least as measured by biological indicators.

If nothing else, the history of measuring economic growth teaches us that it is often unhelpful to become too dogmatic about a particular set of output estimates. As Kendrick, one of the most important contributors to the measurement of economic activity and growth noted, "there is no unique definitive set of national product estimates. The selection depends on the theoretical predilections of the estimator, the analytical purpose of the user, and the availability

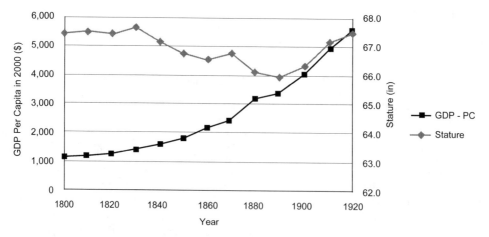

Figure 3.3 U.S. real GDP per capita and (white) adult male stature, 1800–1920
Sources: Johnston and Williamson (2008), Chanda *et al.* (2008).

of data" (1961: 21–2). In short, the successful measurement of aggregate economic activity, the standard of living, and economic growth answered many important questions in economics. It also raised many new ones. Both are important contributions to human progress.

Notes

1 Or by "chaining" them to recent time periods (Cage *et al.* 2003).
2 In modern corporate accounting, the notions of flows and stocks, income and wealth are reflected in the income statement and the balance sheet, respectively.
3 The question was originally addressed by William Petty, who antedated Adam Smith by more than a century. See Ekelund and Hébert (1983: 91).
4 In his "Plan of Work," Smith labeled the explanation of "how produce is naturally distributed" the primary objective of the first volume of *Wealth of Nations* (Smith 1976, vol. 1: 2).
5 Schumpeter collectively referred to their efforts as "factual work" (1954: 519–26).
6 For a concise discussion of many other important contributors, see Schumpeter's appropriately entitled chapter "Review of the troops" (1954: 463–526).
7 See, for example, Mingay (1975: 184–7).
8 The final two volumes were co-authored with a protégé, William Newmarch, who himself made original contributions to the collection and processing of economic data (Schumpeter 1954: 520).
9 Referring to one of Carey's volumes, John Stuart Mill said it was the "worst book on political economy I ever toiled through" (Schumpeter 1954: 516).
10 This is not to say that there were no important contributions to macroeconomics during this period. Indeed W.S. Jevons's work on index numbers, to give but one example, which was motivated by Tooke's earlier work on prices, was crucial to the subsequent construction of "real" GDP (Ekelund and Hébert 1983: 321–2).
11 In the UK, the task was initiated by two future Nobel laureates, James Meade and Richard Stone.
12 Carson (1990) offers a concise history of the Conference.
13 Kuznets subsequently refined his national income estimates to yield "gross national expenditure," which eventually became GNP, the value of final goods and services produced by the labor and property supplied by a nation's households, even if located in a foreign country. In the United States this measure was subsequently replaced by GDP in 1991. See United States Department of Commerce (2011).
14 Although Johnston and Williamson do not cite Kuznets directly, they do cite Kendrick, whose debt to Kuznets is explicit (Kendrick 1961).
15 There is a large literature on the flaws and omissions in national income accounting. For a reasonably concise summary, see Stiglitz *et al.* (2010). For an even more concise summary of why GDP per capita is nonetheless a good measure of the standard of living, see Hubbard and O'Brien (2010: 147–51).
16 It should be noted that recent research rejects the Easterlin Paradox. See, for example, Stevenson and Wolfers (2008).
17 Of course, there is a biological maximum to stature. Further consumption beyond that point merely leads to obesity (Komlos *et al.* 2008).

References

Allen, R.C. and Ó Gráda, C. (1988) 'On the road again with Arthur Young: English, Irish, and French agriculture during the industrial revolution', *Journal of Economic History*, 48: 93–125.
Australian Department of Foreign Affairs and Trade (ADFAT) (2011) 'Fact sheets', http://www.dfat.gov.au/geo/fs/nway.pdf
Balke, N.S. and Gordon, R.J. (1989) 'The estimation of prewar gross national product: methodology and new evidence', *Journal of Political Economy*, 97: 38–92.
Cage, R., Greenlees, J. and Jackman, P. (2003) 'Introducing the chained consumer price index', paper presented at International Working Group on Price Indices, Paris, May 2003.
Carson, C.S. (1990) 'The conference on research in income and wealth', in E.R. Berndt and J.E. Triplett (eds) *Fifty Years of Economic Measurement: The Jubilee of the Conference on Research in Income and Wealth*, Chicago, IL: University of Chicago Press.

Chanda, A., Craig, L.A. and J. Treme (2008) 'Convergence (and divergence) in the biological standard of living in the USA, 1820–1900', *Cliometrica*, 2: 19–48.

Clark, G. (2007) *A Farewell to Alms: A Brief Economic History of the World*, Princeton, NJ: Princeton University Press.

Cuff, T. (2005) *The Hidden Cost of Economic Development: The Biological Standard of Living in Antebellum Pennsylvania*, Aldershot: Ashgate.

Dollar, D. and Kraay, A. (2002) 'Growth is good for the poor', *Journal of Economic Growth*, 7: 195–225.

Easterlin, R. (1974) 'Does economic growth improve the human lot?' in P. David and M. Reder (eds) *Nations and Households in Economic Growth: Essays in Honor of Moses Abramowitz*, New York: Academic Press.

Ekelund, R.B. and Hébert, R.F. (1983) *A History of Economic Theory and Method*, 2nd edition, New York: McGraw Hill.

Feldstein, M. (1990) 'Luncheon in honor of individuals and institutions participating in the first income and wealth conference', in E.R. Berndt and J.E. Triplett (eds) *Fifty Years of Economic Measurement: The Jubilee of the Conference on Research in Income and Wealth*, Chicago, IL: University of Chicago Press.

Fogel, R.W. (2004) *The Escape from Hunger and Premature Death, 1700–2100: Europe, America, and the Third World*, New York: Cambridge University Press.

Hubbard, R.G. and O'Brien, A.P. (2010) *Macroeconomics*, 3rd edition, Boston, MA: Prentice Hall.

Hubbard, G., O'Brien, A. and Rafferty, M. (2012) *Macroeconomics*, Boston, MA: Prentice Hall.

Huberman, M. and Minns, C. (2007) 'The times they are not changin': days and hours of work in old and new worlds, 1870–2000', *Explorations in Economic History*, 44: 538–67.

Johnston, L.D. and Williamson, S.H. (2008) 'What was the U.S. GDP then?' MeasuringWorth, http://www.measuringworth.org/usgdp/

Kendrick, J. (1961) 'Productivity trends in the United States', National Bureau of Economic Research, http://www.nber.org/books/kend61–1

Keynes, J.M. (1935) *The General Theory of Employment, Interest and Money*, New York: Harcourt Brace Jovanovich.

Komlos, J., Breitfelder, A. and Sunder, M. (2008) 'The transition to post-industrial BMI values among U.S. children', National Bureau of Economic Research Working Papers, No. 13898.

Kuznets, S. (1930) *Secular Movements in Production and Prices*, Boston, MA: Houghton Mifflin.

——(1937) *National Income and Capital Formation, 1919–1935*, New York: National Bureau of Economic Research.

——(1941) *National Income and Its Composition, 1919–1938*, New York: National Bureau of Economic Research.

——(1961) *Capital in the American Economy: Its Formation and Financing*, Princeton, NJ: Princeton University Press.

——(1966) *Modern Economic Growth: Rate, Structure and Growth*, New Haven, CT: Yale University Press.

——(1973) 'Modern economic growth: findings and reflections', *American Economic Review*, 63: 247–58.

Landreth, H. and Colander, D.C. (2002) *History of Economic Thought*, 4th edition, Boston, MA: Houghton Mifflin.

Mingay, G.A. (ed.) (1975) *Arthur Young and His Times*, London: Macmillan Press.

Romer, C. (1989) 'The prewar business cycle reconsidered: new estimates of gross national product, 1869–1908', *Journal of Political Economy*, 97: 1–37.

Schumpeter, J.A. (1954) *History of Economic Analysis*, New York: Oxford University Press.

Smith, A. (1976) *An Inquiry into the Nature and Causes of the Wealth of Nations*, Chicago, IL: University of Chicago Press.

Smith, M. (2007) 'A survey of Thomas Tooke's contributions to political economy', *History of Economics Review*, 46: 106–35.

Stevenson, B. and Wolfers, J. (2008) 'Economic growth and subjective well-being: reassessing the Easterlin paradox', *Brookings Papers on Economic Activity*, 39: 1–102.

Stiglitz, J., Sen, A. and Fitoussi, J-P. (2010) *Mismeasuring Our Lives: Why GDP Doesn't Add Up*, New York: New Press.

United States Department of Commerce (1934) *National Income, 1929–32*, Washington, DC: Government Printing Office.

United States Department of Commerce, Bureau of Economic Analysis (2011) 'Concepts and methods of the U.S. national income and product accounts', http://www.bea.gov/national/pdf/NIPAhandbookch1–4.pdf

Young, A. (1771) *The Farmer's Tour Through the East of England*, vol. 4, London: W. Strahan.

4

ANTHROPOMETRIC HISTORY: HEIGHTS, WEIGHTS, AND ECONOMIC CONDITIONS

Scott Alan Carson

Measuring and accounting for economic growth is among the economic historian's leading objectives. To better understand living conditions during economic development, anthropometrics is the application of economic theory and statistics to changes in the dimensions of the human body.

Stature and the body mass index (BMI) are the primary measures of the biological standard of living. Stature measures the net cumulative balance between nutrition, work effort, and the disease environment before adulthood, and, because more historical height data survive, physical stature has received more attention in historical anthropometric studies. BMI measures the net current balance between nutrition, work effort, and the disease environment, and is receiving increased attention in historical studies. Therefore, to better understand historical living standards during economic development, this chapter reviews the vast amount of stature and BMI studies and considers new areas where biological measurements have become standard measurements.

Historical anthropometrics of physical stature

The use of height data to measure living standards is now a well-established method in economics and economic history (Fogel 1994: 138; Steckel 1995, 2009; Deaton 2008; Case and Paxson 2008). A population's average stature reflects the cumulative interaction between nutrition, disease exposure, work, and the physical environment (Steckel 1979: 365–7; Tanner 1962: 1–27). Genes are important determinants of individuals' heights, but genetic differences approximately cancel in comparisons of averages across most large groups and nations, so in these situations average heights accurately reflect net nutrition. When diets, health, and physical environments improve, average stature increases, and it decreases when diets become less nutritious, disease environments deteriorate, or the physical environment places more stress on the body. Therefore, when traditional economic, income, and wealth measures are unavailable, stature provides considerable insights into understanding economic and social processes – and it provides an important complement to traditional economic measures when they are available. For example, Steckel (1995: 1912) demonstrates that adult male and female heights have correlations of 0.88 and 0.82 with log per capita income.

Nineteenth-century white heights

Despite the modern correlation between stature and economic development, and the demonstration by Steckel (1983: 5) and Komlos (1987: 903) that nineteenth-century individuals' statures were positively related with income, evidence from numerous studies shows that as average incomes increased during much of the 1800s white statures paradoxically declined. Figure 4.1 shows this pattern, which is known in the U.S. as the "antebellum paradox" (Fogel *et al.* 1982; Fogel *et al.* 1983; Komlos 1987; Margo and Steckel 1983; Costa 1993). A similar pattern holds for industrializing countries in Europe, a pattern known as the "early modern growth puzzle" (Fogel *et al.* 1982: 33; Nicholas and Steckel 1991: 948; Komlos 1998).

Attempts to explain the antebellum paradox and early modern growth puzzle have focused on nutrition, access to food, inequality, disease, population density, nativity, and socioeconomic conditions. Fogel *et al.* (1983: 473–6) recognized that nutrition was a primary source for stature variation, and Fogel *et al.* (1983) and Komlos (1987: 908–19) were the first to illustrate that height varied considerably with nutritional deficiencies. Physical stature responds to access to proteins and amino acids, and Haines *et al.* (2003, Table 7) demonstrate that nineteenth-century Union Army recruits were taller in counties that had greater access to proteins and calories. Baten and Murray (2000: 359–63) and Carson (2008a: 362–6) demonstrate that taller heights were related with greater access to dairy products (Bogin 2005). Therefore, among the most established relationships in anthropometric history is a positive relationship between height and nutrition, especially calcium and animal proteins.

Because the last dollar spent on health by a wealthy individual has a smaller impact than the last dollar spent on health by a poorer individual, modern statures are inversely related with income inequality (Wilkinson and Pickett 2006: 1775; Subramanian and Kawachi 2004).

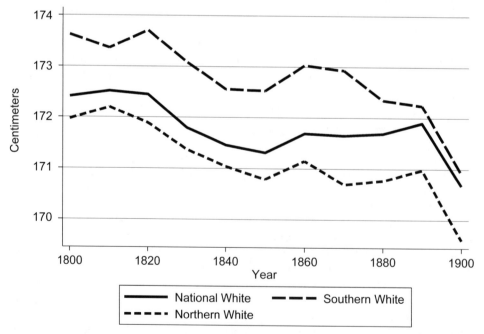

Figure 4.1 Nineteenth-century U.S. white male statures by birth year
Source: Carson (2009b).

Steckel (1983) demonstrates that historical heights were inversely related with income inequality as well. However, the relationship between stature and wealth are mixed. Wealth is a net cumulative measure for material welfare, and stature is a net cumulative measure for biological welfare. Haines *et al.* (2003: 46) find that county-level wealth was not associated with the height of Union Army recruits, while Carson (2009a: 51) finds that individual statures increased with state-level average wealth. Carson (2009a, 2010a) also demonstrates that heights were inversely related with state-level wealth inequality, and the height and wealth relationship was stable across the stature distribution. After accounting for both relative wealth inequality and absolute wealth, stature was more responsive to changes in absolute wealth than relative wealth inequality.

Inequality measures beyond income and wealth Gini coefficients have been developed to isolate the relationship between physical stature and inequality. Baten and Murray (2000) use Bavarian height coefficients of variation and find that inequality increased in the early nineteenth century. Income and wealth are also related to stages of the business cycle, and Woitek (2003: 250–5) finds that Hapsburg soldier heights were positively related with cyclical fluctuations, especially through the grain price channel. Therefore, heights were positively related with income and wealth changes and inversely related with inequality.

White statures varied regionally, and after controlling for insolation Southern whites reached taller statures than other early Americans (Carson 2009b: 155–6; Zehetmayer 2011). Part of the Southern height advantage was related to agriculture. The nineteenth-century opening of the New South to agriculture increased agricultural productivity, which was greater than elsewhere in the U.S. (Higgs 1977: 24; Margo and Steckel 1982: 519; Komlos and Coclanis 1997: 443). Before the Civil War, the South was self-sufficient in food production, and relatively high white wages and income may have also been associated with taller Southern white statures (Fogel 1994: 89, 132–3; Easterlin 1971: 41; Margo 2000). After the Civil War, the South was no longer self-sufficient in food production, and wages in the West South Central were generally lower than Midwest wages and comparable to those in the middle Atlantic region (Easterlin 1971: 41); Southern wages were in general lower than Northern wages. However, West South Central laborers' wages were comparable to those in the middle Atlantic region, and after emancipation wages in Louisiana, Mississippi, and Texas were higher than elsewhere, which may have increased Southern material and biological well-being (Rosenbloom 2002: 53, 124–5; Margo 2000; Higgs 1977: 26, 63, 102). Whites from the Great Lakes were taller than those from the Northeast and Plains. Another height pattern that has received considerable support is that migrants were taller than persisters, and the direction of the effect on height is consistent with broader geographic patterns. Internal migrants who located to the South were taller than those who immigrated to the North, and migrants to the North were shorter than migrants to the South (Carson 2009b: 155–6).

Disease and death rates have long been suspected of adversely influencing stature, and Fogel *et al.* (1983) suggest that part of the antebellum paradox and early industrial growth puzzle may be attributable to increased disease burdens and higher death rates. However, where the relationship between height and nutrition is widely agreed upon, the relationship between height and disease is less settled. Komlos (1992: 329) suggests that, since both urban black males and females were likely exposed to the same disease environments but female heights decreased at least a decade prior to male heights, disease is an unlikely source to explain the antebellum stature decline. Voth and Leunig (1996) indicate that, because individuals who survived British smallpox epidemics were shorter than those not exposed, smallpox may have been associated with shorter statures; moreover, near eradication of smallpox in the 1820s substantially improved heights. However, Heintel and Baten (1998) dismiss the significance and magnitude that smallpox had on British stature, suggesting that the Voth and Leunig findings were due to changes in military minimum stature requirements, obfuscating the measured relationship between height and smallpox. Attempting to explain declining antebellum American statures, Coelho and McGuire (2000) propose that disease environments stunted slave childhood statures. Steckel (2000) defends his earlier position that poor nutrition led to stunting and notes that poor nutrition also makes individuals more prone to disease. Haines *et al.* (2003: 406) demonstrate that height is inversely related with the crude death rate, while Carson (2010b) suggests that, because of catch-up growth, long-term institutional change is more likely than short-run disease insults to influence agricultural productivity and physical stature variation. As a result, isolating the relationship between height and disease is an area that warrants greater attention in historical stature studies.

Population density has been proposed as a variable associated with historical stature variation (Goodman and Martin 2002: 35). Height may be short when population density is low because low population density is related with limited labor specialization, failure for markets to extend, and lower increases in agricultural productivity. However, height may have decreased with population density because high population density is related with depleted resources per capita and increased disease networks that propagate disease and diminish human health (Steckel et al. 2002: 80). Carson (2009a: 47–52, 2010a: 474–6) demonstrates that physical statures both increased and decreased with population density. Statures increased with population density in states with fewer than 42 persons per square mile; maximum stature was reached in states with 42 persons per square mile, which was approximately the mid-nineteenth-century population density of Illinois. Nonetheless, stature was shorter in states with more than 42 persons per square mile.

Proximity to rivers and lakes represents access to trade routes, and whites living in close proximity to waterways may have been taller because close proximity to trade routes decreased transportation costs and increased access to nutrition during industrialization. On the other hand, proximity to waterways may have reduced stature because it facilitated the export of food and the spread of disease. Haines *et al.* (2003: 407) demonstrate that close proximity to trade routes was associated with shorter statures but do not distinguish between geographic and industrialized regions. Carson (2008b: 364, 2011c) demonstrates that whites in close proximity to Northeastern waterways were taller than whites living in counties with no access to waterways, and Northeastern industrializing centers decreased the price of acquiring nutrition. Alternatively, Southern agricultural communities that exported nutrition increased the relative price of food, which was exported to Northeastern industrial centers, and Southern whites with close proximity to the Mississippi River were shorter than individuals who were not in close proximity to waterways. Similar results are found for proximity to roads and turnpikes (Peracchi 2008).

Still other studies rely more heavily on biological explanations, specifically solar radiation. Carson (2008c, 2009b) shows a positive relationship between stature and vitamin D production. Calcium and vitamin D are required throughout life for healthy bone and teeth formation; however, their abundance for healthy skeletal development is most critical at younger ages (Wardlaw *et al.* 2004: 394–6; Tortolani *et al.* 2002: 60; Loomis 1967). In order of importance, the three most important sources of vitamin D production are the amount of time exposed to sunlight, skin pigmentation, and nativity (Holick *et al.* 1981: 590; Carson 2008c). Calcium generally comes from dairy products, and vitamin D is produced by the synthesis of cholesterol and sunlight in the epidermis's stratum basale, granulosum, and spinosum (Loomis 1967: 501; Norman 1998: 1108; Holick 2007).[1] Greater direct sunlight (insolation) produces more vitamin D, and vitamin D is related to adult terminal stature (Xiong *et al.* 2005: 228, 230–1; Liu *et al.* 2003; Ginsburg *et al.* 1998;

Uitterlinden *et al.* 2004). However, vitamin D production also depends on melanin in the stratum corneum (Norman 1998: 1108). Greater melanin (skin pigmentation) interferes with cholesterol's synthesis into vitamin D in the stratum granulosum, and darker pigmentation filters between 50 and 95 per cent of the sunlight that reaches the stratum granulosum (Loomis 1967: 502; Weisberg *et al.* 2004: 1703S; Holick, 2007: 270). Therefore, darker skin is considerably less efficient than lighter skin at producing vitamin D, and darker skin is more common in Southern latitudes where more hours of direct sunlight offset inefficient vitamin D production (Norman 1998: 1109–10). In the U.S., Southern states are closer to the equator and receive more insolation, while Northern states are farther from the equator and receive less direct sunlight. Before the mandated addition of vitamin D to the U.S. milk supply in the 1930s, statures were taller in states that received more sunlight per day.

During the nineteenth century, white statures varied by socioeconomic status, and among the most established patterns is that farmers were consistently taller than workers in other occupations (Margo and Steckel 1982: 525; Steckel 1979: 373). Farmers traditionally had greater access to superior diets and nutrition and were removed from urban environments, where disease is more easily propagated. Workers in occupations with greater exposure to direct sunlight may have also grown taller because they were exposed to greater insolation as children and produced more vitamin D, which contributed to healthy bone formation (Tortolani *et al.* 2002). Islam *et al.* (2007) demonstrate that children exposed to more direct sunlight produce more vitamin D, and, if there was little movement away from parental occupation, nineteenth-century occupations may also be a good indicator for the occupational environment in which individuals came to maturity (Margo and Steckel 1992: 520; Wannamethee *et al.* 1996: 1256–62; Nyström-Peck and Lundberg 1995: 734–7). Historical heights were taller in states that received more insolation and farmers and unskilled workers, who spent more time outdoors during adolescent ages, were taller than workers in other occupations.

Nineteenth-century black heights

Three important early studies in African-Americans' heights were Fogel and Engerman (1974), Fogel (1989), and Steckel (1986). Fogel finds that nineteenth-century adult U.S. black statures were comparable with various white samples, indicating that adult slaves received sufficient calories for work effort and to fend off disease (Komlos 1992: 327). However, using the heights of coastal slave children, Steckel (1986) demonstrates that slave children were chronically stunted compared with their white counterparts and concludes that, while adult slaves received sufficient calories to reach tall terminal statures, slave children received inadequate dietary provisions until they entered the adult slave labor force. Therefore, slave and free-black heights have received considerable attention and provide valuable insight into nineteenth-century black living standards.

Various factors led to differences between nineteenth-century black and white statures and an unexpected finding is that African-American male heights increased during the antebellum period, while white statures declined (Figure 4.2; Fogel *et al.* 1978: 465; Steckel 1986; Komlos 1992: 309; Komlos and Coclanis 1997: 445). If, however, Southern planters and overseers rationally allocated slave nutrition and medical allotments to maximize their own wealth, slave heights would have increased with antebellum slave prices and probably decreased – at least temporarily – with slavery's elimination (Rees *et al.* 2003: 22; Steckel 1995; Fogel *et al.* 1983: 464–6; Margo and Steckel 1982: 520; Komlos and Coclanis 1997: 438–42; Komlos 1998: 787; Carson 2008c, 2009b, 2010a, 2010b). In the postbellum period, black statures temporarily declined but increased in the early twentieth century (Carson 2009c). In contrast, the statures of

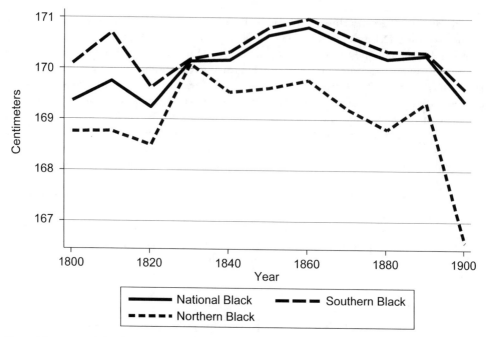

Figure 4.2 Nineteenth-century U.S. African-American male statures by year of birth
Source: Carson (2009b).

free blacks declined with industrialization and mirrored those of market-dependent nineteenth-century whites (Komlos 1992, 1998; Bodenhorn 1999: 984).

A considerable body of evidence demonstrates that nineteenth-century mulattos were taller than darker-complexioned blacks, and to explain the difference Steckel and Bodenhorn point to social practices (Steckel 1979: 375; Margo and Steckel 1982; Bodenhorn 1999: 384). An additional explanation for taller mulatto statures may be biological. Lighter-complexioned blacks were taller than darker-complexioned blacks because less melanin in the stratum corneum allowed more sunlight to penetrate the stratum granulosum, producing more vitamin D. Furthermore, the black diaspora from Africa to North American latitudes placed blacks into geographic regions where they received less direct sunlight and produced less vitamin D; therefore, Northern blacks may also have been shorter than Southern blacks because they produced less vitamin D (Xiong *et al.* 2005: 228–31; Ginsburg *et al.* 1998: 320).

Isolating the relationship between nineteenth-century black stature, income, and wealth is more elusive than for whites because slaves held no wealth before, and little wealth after, emancipation. Slave biological and material conditions probably improved during the late antebellum period, and blacks in the postbellum period devoted a higher share of their incomes to food acquisition (Higgs 1977: 102–5). Carson (2008c, 2010b) demonstrates that black statures increased during the antebellum period and declined temporarily with emancipation. Therefore, blacks fared poorly under slavery but their biological standard of living improved during the late antebellum period of prosperity, declined temporarily when slavery was eliminated, then increased as they acclimated to life beyond the slave system.

Black farmers were also taller than non-farmers, and average black unskilled workers and field hands were taller than household servants and skilled slaves (Metzer 1975: 134; Margo and Steckel 1982: 525). That unskilled black workers were also tall suggests that most unskilled workers were agricultural workers, who received sufficient nutrition allocations and worked outdoors.

Black statures also varied regionally, and Southwestern blacks reached the tallest statures (Komlos 1992: 314; Bodenhorn 1999: 384; Carson 2009b: 155). During the antebellum period, slaves were shielded from income and price variation, and, although Southwestern slavery was arduous and demanded many calories for work, Southwestern slaves lived in more recently settled and productive farmlands. After emancipation, Southwestern blacks were exposed to greater income variation and were unprepared for life beyond the slave system, either in terms of experience or human capital. The relative price of dairy and calcium were lowest in dairy-producing regions, such as the Great Lakes states, but nineteenth-century blacks were overwhelmingly native to the South, which was low in dairy production (Bodenhorn 1999: 988–93). North-eastern blacks, especially youth, encountered adverse biological environments, and contemporary reports of rickets – a result of childhood vitamin D deficiency – may have contributed to shorter Northeastern black statures (Kiple and Kiple 1977: 293–4; Tortolani *et al.* 2002: 62).

Nineteenth-century female and other minority statures

Because of data limitations, there continues to be a paucity of historical stature studies that consider the biological conditions of women. Scholars studying nineteenth-century females in England have produced considerable research, and, like males, females experienced the early modern growth puzzle. English female statures declined throughout the nineteenth century (Johnson and Nicholas 1995; Nicholas and Oxley 1996; Oxley 2004). Sunder (2011) finds that mid-nineteenth-century elite white U.S. female heights increased, and Komlos (1992) finds that black females' statures deteriorated during the early nineteenth century, at least a decade earlier than male stature decline began. Moreover, urban black women were shorter than rural black females. Using nineteenth-century state prison records, Carson (2011a) contrasts the heights of comparable U.S. African-American and white females during a period of relatively rapid economic development. White females were consistently taller than black females, and whites from the Great Lakes and Plains states and black Southwestern females were the tallest. U.S. females were tall compared with their European counterparts. The height of females began to decline in the antebellum period, possibly before that of males. The recovery of physical stature was also earlier among women than among men.

Other populations have received attention. During the nineteenth century, Mexico experienced substantial political instability, yet, because nineteenth-century Mexican populations remained near biological subsistence, Mexican biological living standards did not change appreciably. Like other populations experiencing rapid economic growth, heights in nineteenth-century Northern Mexico tended to stagnate or decline slightly during the earliest period of economic development. Agricultural output also influenced Mexican biological living conditions, and Mexican corn output probably doubled during the first half of the nineteenth century (McCaa 2000: 288). If greater corn output had been diverted into livestock feed, animal proteins may have become more abundant and improved Mexican diets. Mexican disease environments were also altered during the nineteenth century. With Mexican independence came greater strides toward improving public health. In 1804, a smallpox vaccine was introduced to the Mexican population and, later, measles and other diseases were reduced (McCaa 2000: 289). However, early forms of Mexican economic development and modernization were not accompanied by urbanization.

The statures of Chinese who emigrated from Southern China to the U.S. compared favorably with other Chinese. Between 1830 and 1870, Chinese male youth stature declined by over two centimeters and deteriorated throughout the nineteenth century, precisely when China's population growth was high, agriculture nearly collapsed, and political events created economic upheaval associated with biological privation. Chinese statures did not vary with socioeconomic status or residence. Consequently, the biological conditions facing nineteenth-century people fleeing China were deteriorating and occurred across the socioeconomic strata.

In one of the more novel applications of anthropometrics, Steckel and Prince (2001) and Prince and Steckel (2003) consider the heights of mid-nineteenth-century American Indians and find that Plains nomadic groups were tallest among a broad comparison of mid-nineteenth-century North American indigenous populations due to low population densities, close access to a high-protein food source, warmer winter clothing, barter between tribes, and more equitable living arrangements. Komlos (2003) also demonstrates that rural Georgia American Indians were quite tall.

Other areas related to historical height studies are receiving increased attention. Barker (1992) postulates that several adult health conditions are related to in-utero conditions. For example, adult hypertension and ischemic stroke have been linked to in-utero conditions, and neurological demyelination diseases have been linked to insufficient material access to iodine during the second trimester. Recent efforts also couple adult height and intelligence (Case and Paxson 2008; Deaton 2008; Mankiw and Weinzierl 2007; Maurer 2010). In one of the more original applications to historical height studies, Steckel and Prince use both Old and New World skeletal remains to study linear enamel hypoplasias, porotic hyperostosis, anemia, height, and infectious disease (Steckel *et al.* 2002).

Historical anthropometrics of the BMI

A population's average BMI (weight [kg]/height [m^2]) reflects the net current balance between nutrition, disease climate, and the work environment, and heavier nineteenth-century BMIs are evidence of more robust health (Fogel 1994: 375; Strauss and Thomas 1998). When BMI values are low, net current biological living conditions are substandard, and weight-to-height ratios may be wasted. BMIs have also been linked to modern health outcomes (Waaler 1984; Stevens *et al.* 1998: 1–7; Calle *et al.* 1999: 1097–104; Kenchaiah *et al.* 2002: 305–13; Calle *et al.* 2003: 1625–38; Pi-Sunyer 1991: 1595s–600s; Jee *et al.* 2006; Costa 1993); however, the strength of this association across sub-populations remains debatable (Henderson 2005: 340; Flegal *et al.* 2009: 240). Historical BMI studies provide important insight into the evolution of health during economic development. For BMIs of less than 20, Waaler (1984) and Koch (2011) find an inverse relationship between BMI and mortality risk. Costa (1993) and Murray (1997) apply Waaler's results to historical populations and find the modern height and weight relationship is consistent with the relationship in the past, and Jee *et al.* (2006: 780, 784–5) find the relationship is stable across racial groups. Costa (2004: 8–10) demonstrates that there were considerable differences between nineteenth-century black and white BMIs, and that blacks had greater BMI values than whites (Flegal *et al.* 2010). The health risks associated with heavier BMIs may also have been greater for whites than for blacks (Flegal *et al.* 2009: 507; Stevens *et al.* 1998; Abell *et al.* 2007; Sanchez *et al.* 2000; Stevens *et al.* 1992; Wienpahl *et al.* 1990). Costa finds that BMI values increased between 1860 and 1950, while Cutler *et al.* (2003) find that U.S. BMIs have increased since the beginning of the twentieth century; however, the majority of increased BMI values have occurred since 1980 because people consume more calories, not because they are physically less active.

An increasing number of studies consider nineteenth-century white BMI variation. Cuff (1993) finds that mid-nineteenth-century West Point cadet BMIs were low compared with modern BMI values, and placed a large proportion of young nineteenth-century Northern males into a high relative mortality risk category. Coclanis and Komlos (1995: 102–3) also find that BMI values of late nineteenth-century students at the Citadel military academy were comparable with those of West Point cadets. Carson (2009d) finds that, in contrast to modern distributions, most Southern BMI values were in normal weight ranges. There was also little change in BMI values between 1876 and 1920. Farmers were consistently heavier than non-farmers, and Southwestern men were taller and had lower BMI values than their counterparts from other regions within the U.S.

The shape of the BMI distribution tells us about a population's current biological conditions, and there are differing views about how nineteenth-century BMIs were distributed. On the one hand, BMIs may have been low because diets were meager relative to work expenditures. On the other, output growth created larger quantities of food and more nutritious diets as U.S. agricultural settlement produced greater output and more nutritious diets relative to calories consumed for work and to fend off disease. The overwhelming proportion of nineteenth-century black and white BMIs were symmetrically distributed, fell within the normal BMI category, and neither underweight nor obesity was the historical dilemma facing nineteenth-century U.S. populations. Carson (2012) finds that 17 per cent of adult white males in the 1800s were overweight or obese, as were 33 per cent of adult black males. In addition, 17 per cent of white male youths were overweight or obese, as were 17 per cent of black male youths. These historical BMIs are compared with modern U.S. values, where approximately 36 per cent of adult American men are overweight and 23 per cent are obese (Finkelstein *et al.* 2003; Sturm and Wells 2001: 231; Calle *et al.* 1999: 1103; Flegal *et al.* 2010). BMIs of less than 19 mark a threshold corresponding with increased mortality risk, and 40 per cent of West Point cadets between the ages of 20 and 21 had BMIs of less than 19 (Cuff 1993: 178). However, BMIs of black and white 20- and 21-year-olds in nineteenth-century U.S. prisons were considerably greater than the threshold of 19, and only 2.05 and 1.49 per cent of whites and blacks had BMIs of less than 19.

Morbid obesity is defined as a BMI greater than 40, and there is an alarming modern trend toward overweight and obesity (Finkelstein *et al.* 2003; Flegal *et al.* 2010; Flegal *et al.* 2009). There are numerous plausible explanations to account for this increase: behavioral, genetic, lifestyle changes, and changes in the relative price of food (Freedman 2011). Morbid obesity is also linked to type II diabetes, stroke, and cardiovascular disease (Finkelstein *et al.* 2003; Pi-Sunyer 1991: 1599s; Kenchaiah *et al.* 2002: 306–12; Calle *et al.* 2003: 1628–30). Cases of nineteenth-century black and white morbid obesity among the working class were nearly non-existent. Only 0.016 per cent of historical U.S. blacks and 0.014 per cent of whites were morbidly obese (Carson 2009d, 2012). This contrasts with 2.9 per cent in modern samples and indicates that modern Americans are more likely to be obese.

Like white heights, white BMI values (see Figure 4.3) declined throughout the nineteenth and early twentieth centuries (Carson 2008b, 2009d, 2012). Farmers had greater BMI values than workers in other occupations and were less likely to be underweight. Part of farmers' higher BMIs was probably related to physical activity, and BMIs represent an individual's composition between muscle and fat, which are related to physical activity and occupation. Occupations requiring greater physical activity are known to decrease fat and increase muscle. Modern agricultural workers use between 2.5 and 6.8 energy multiples of basal metabolic rate (Food and Agricultural Organization of the United Nations *et al.* 1985), indicating that, because they are close to nutritious diets and more physically active, farmers have sufficient calories to maintain weight. Black and white BMIs in the Northeast and Upper South were consistently lower than the Deep South and Far West (Carson 2012). BMIs were also related to industrialization and urbanization, and individuals from Philadelphia had lower BMIs and were less

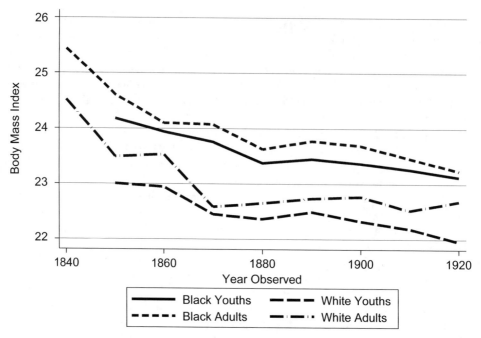

Figure 4.3 Nineteenth-century U.S. African-American and white male BMIs
Source: Carson (2012).

likely to be overweight or obese but also less likely to be underweight, suggesting that urban BMIs were more likely to be in normal weight ranges.

Much has also been written about the nineteenth-century mulatto stature advantage, and U.S. mulattos were taller than their darker-complexioned counterparts (Steckel 1979; Bodenhorn 1999: 984; Carson 2008c, 2009b). However, the relationship between BMI and skin pigmentation is more complicated than height, because blacks have greater per cent muscle mass, and muscle is heavier than fat (Flegal *et al.* 2010: 240; Flegal *et al.* 2009: 507; Fernandez *et al.* 2003; Aloia *et al.* 1999: 116; Evans *et al.* 2006). Darker-complexioned blacks were also shorter than mulattos, and shorter statures are associated with greater BMI values (Herbert *et al.* 1993: 1438; Carson 2009d: 125). Blacks were shorter, which may also reflect their basal metabolic rate and early life conditions, because shifts in relative well-being over the life cycle complicate BMI interpretation. However, modern black BMIs are greater than whites, suggesting poor early life conditions are less likely to explain greater BMI values than greater per cent muscle mass. After controlling for height, darker-complexioned blacks had greater BMI values than mulattos, indicating that the cumulative advantage of taller white statures was dominated by blacks' greater per cent muscle mass.

Conclusion and future directions

Measuring and accounting for health during economic development is augmented by the development of anthropometric measures, and a few patterns are increasingly clear. Nineteenth-century white heights experienced the antebellum paradox, where statures declined while income and wealth increased. They were positively related with income and wealth and inversely related to inequality. White heights may also have been related to stages of the business cycle;

however, because of catch-up growth, height variation may be less sensitive to the business cycle than it is to structural differences and institutional change. Nineteenth-century white height was also related to socioeconomic status, and rural farmers were taller than workers in other occupations. Heights were related to urbanization and region within the U.S., and rural Southerners were taller than other regions within the U.S. Migrants were taller than persisters, and heights were related with proximity to waterways. Northeastern whites were taller near waterways, and Southern whites were shorter near the Mississippi River. There was an inverted U-shape between height and state population density, and white heights were shorter in both sparsely and densely populated states and tallest in moderately populated states.

Nineteenth-century black heights over time differed markedly from white height variation, and enslaved black statures increased when Southern agricultural conditions in the late antebellum period improved and decreased with slavery's removal. However, like U.S. whites, free market-dependent black statures declined throughout the nineteenth century. Moreover, there was a distinct height advantage for mulattos compared with darker-complexioned blacks. Nineteenth-century socioeconomic status was also related with black height, and rural farmers were taller than workers in other occupations. Black Southerners were taller than blacks in other regions within the U.S., and black migrants were taller than persisters. Therefore, nineteenth-century black height variation was the result of complex interactions with nutrition, income, inequality, and the physical environment, and, while numerous black height patterns were comparable with those of whites, there were distinctive differences that reflected the economic, social, and physical environments in which each group came to maturity.

There are also several areas where the relationship between height and economic variables is less clear. We are in the early stages of establishing the relationships between health and in-utero conditions related with height and intelligence, and pushing the research frontier further back into the past to include underrepresented groups and paleo-peoples. Among the most promising areas of research is the relationship between height, disease, and death rates.

Diets in developed economies have undergone a nutritional transition, and nineteenth-century diets abundant in proteins, fiber, and complex carbohydrates have been replaced with simple sugars and saturated fats (Popkin 1993: 145–8). Black and white BMIs have simultaneously increased from normal to overweight and obese categories. BMIs were historically related with several economic variables, and nineteenth-century farmers consistently had higher BMI values than workers in other occupations. Heavier farmer BMI values also reflect the physical labor workers performed, and more rigorous occupational demands likely contributed to heavier farmer BMIs. Black and white BMIs were heavier in the nineteenth-century American South and lower in the industrializing North.

While these nineteenth-century stature and BMI patterns for African-Americans and whites shed light on historical health and socioeconomic patterns, the record is not complete. Researchers exploring stature patterns will continue to unearth new data sets, especially for periods following extreme poverty, such as after wars or widespread and prolonged famine. Efforts are underway that consider novel areas in stature, such as the relationships between in-utero conditions and later life conditions, and between height and intelligence. Historical BMI studies are not as advanced, and future studies will develop new data sets across the socio-economic strata. Similarly, little is known about the relationship between stature, BMI, and historical labor force participation, which is an important link between labor and health economics. Therefore, stature and BMI studies provide a vital glimpse into health during economic development and are indispensible tools in understanding economic history and historical health economics.

43

Notes

1 There are few dietary sources for vitamin D.

References

Abell, J.E., Egan, B.M., Wilson, P.W., Lipsitz, S., Woolson, R.F. and Lacklund, D.T. (2007) 'Age and race impact the association between BMI and CVD mortality in woman', *Public Health*, 122: 507–12.

Aloia, J.F., Vaswani, A., Ma, R. and Flaster, E. (1999) 'Comparison of body composition in black and white premenopausal women', *Journal Laboratory Clinical Medicine*, 129: 294–9.

Barker, D.J. (1992) 'The fetal origins of adult hypertension', *Journal of Hypertension*, 10, S39–44.

Barker, D.J.P. (1994) *Mothers, Babies, and Health in Later Life*, London: BMJ Publishing Group.

Barker, D.J.P. and Osmond, C. (1986) 'Infant mortality, childhood nutrition, and ischaemic heart disease in England and Wales', *Lancet*, 1: 1077–81.

Barker, D.J.P., Winter, P.D., Osmond, C., Margetts, B. and Simmonds, S.J. (1989) 'Weight in infancy and death from ischaemic heart disease', *Lancet*, 2: 577–80.

Baten, J. and Murray, J. (2000) 'Heights of men and women in 19th century Bavaria: economic, nutritional, and disease influences', *Exploration in Economic History*, 37: 351–69.

Bodenhorn, H. (1999) 'A troublesome caste: height and nutrition of antebellum Virginia's rural free blacks', *Journal of Economic History*, 59: 972–96.

——(2002) 'Mulatto advantage: the biological consequences of complexion in rural antebellum Virginia', *Journal of Interdisciplinary History*, 33: 21–46.

Bogin, B. (2005) 'Does milk make children grow? Relationships between milk and consumption and height in NHANES 1999–2002', *American Journal of Human Biology*, 17: 425–41.

Calle, E., Carmen R., Walker-Thurmond, K. and Thun, M. (2003) 'Overweight, obesity and mortality from cancer in a prospectively studied cohort of U.S. adults', *New England Journal of Medicine*, 348: 1625–38.

Calle, E., Thun, M., Petrelli, J., Rodriguez, C. and Meath, C. (1999) 'Body-mass index and mortality in a prospective cohort of U.S. adults', *New England Journal of Medicine*, 341: 1097–104.

Carson, S.A. (2008a) 'Health during industrialization: evidence from the nineteenth century Pennsylvania state prison system', *Social Science History*, 32: 347–72.

——(2008b) 'Health during industrialization: additional evidence from the nineteenth century Missouri state prison system', *Journal of BioSocial Science*, 40: 587–605.

——(2008c) 'The effect of geography and vitamin D on African-American stature in the 19th century: evidence from prison records', *Journal of Economic History*, 68: 812–30.

——(2009a) 'Health, wealth, and inequality: a contribution to the debate about the relationship between inequality and health', *Historical Methods*, 42: 43–54.

——(2009b) 'Geography, insolation, and vitamin D in nineteenth century U.S. African-American and white statures', *Explorations in Economic History*, 46: 149–59.

——(2009c) 'African-American and white inequality in the nineteenth century American south: a biological comparison', *Journal of Population Economics*, 22: 757–72.

——(2009d) 'Racial differences in body mass indices of men imprisoned in nineteenth century Texas', *Economics and Human Biology*, 7: 121–7.

——(2010a) 'Wealth, inequality, and insolation effects across the nineteenth century U.S. white stature distribution', *HOMO – Journal of Comparative Human Biology*, 61: 467–78.

——(2010b) 'Institutional change, geography and insolation in nineteenth century African-American and white statures in southern states', *Journal of Economic Issues*, 43: 737–56.

——(2011a) 'Height of female Americans in the 19th century and the antebellum puzzle', *Economics and Human Biology*, 92: 157–64.

——(2011b) 'Southeastern institutional change and biological variation: evidence from the nineteenth century Tennessee state prison', *Journal of Institutional Economics*, 7: 455–71.

——(2011c) 'Institutional change, stature, and northeast industrialization: evidence from the nineteenth century Philadelphia County prison', *Journal of Institutional and Theoretical Economics*, 167: 630–46.

——(2012) 'Nineteenth century race, body mass, and industrialization: evidence from American prisons', *Journal of Interdisciplinary History*, 42: 371–91.

Case, A. and Paxson, C. (2008) 'Height, health, and cognitive function at older ages', *American Economic Review*, 98: 463–7.

Coclanis, P. and Komlos, J. (1995) 'Nutrition and economic development in post-reconstruction South Carolina: an anthropometric approach', *Social Science History*, 19: 91–116.

Coelho, P. and McGuire, R. (2000) 'Diets versus disease: the anthropometrics of slave children', *Journal of Economic History*, 60: 232–46.

Cole, H., Mailath, G. and Postlewaite, A. (1992) 'Social norms, savings behavior and growth', *Journal of Political Economy*, 100: 1092–125.

Costa, D. (1993) 'Height, wealth, and disease among Native-born in the rural, antebellum north', *Social Science History*, 17: 355–83.

——(2004) 'The measure of man and older age mortality: evidence from the Gould sample', *Journal of Economic History*, 64: 1–23.

Cuff, T. (1993) 'The body mass index values of nineteenth century West Point cadets: a theoretical application of Waaler's curves to a historical population', *Historical Methods*, 26: 171–83.

Cutler, D.M., Glaeser, E.L. and Shapiro, J. (2003) 'Why have Americans become more obese?', *Journal of Economic Perspectives*, 17: 93–118.

Deaton, A. (2008) 'Height, health, and inequality: the distribution of adult heights in India', *American Economic Review*, 98: 468–74.

Dupont, H. (2003) 'Diarrheal diseases (acute)', in K.F. Kiple (ed.) *The Cambridge Historical Dictionary of Disease*, Cambridge: Cambridge University Press.

Easterlin, R. (1971) 'Regional income trends, 1840–1950', in R. Fogel and S. Engerman (eds) *The Reinterpretation of American Economic History*, New York: Harper & Row.

Evans, E.M., Rowe, D.A., Racette S.C., Ross K.M. and Mcauley E. (2006) 'Is the current BMI obesity classification appropriate for black and white post-menopausal women?', *International Journal of Obesity*, 30: 837–43.

Fernandez, J., Heo, M., Heymsfield, S., Pierson, R., Pi-Sunyer, X., Wang, Z., Wang, J., Hayes, M., Allison, D. and Gallagher, D. (2003) 'Body composition and dual energy X-ray absorptiometry in black compared to white women', *American Journal of Clinical Nutrition*, 10: 114–9.

Finkelstein, E., Fiebelkorn, I. and Wang, G. (2003) 'National medical spending attributable to overweight and obesity: how much, and who's paying?' *Health Affairs*, 30: 219–26.

Flegal, K., Carroll, M. and Ogden, C. (2010) 'Prevalence and trends in obesity among U.S. adults, 1999–2008', *Journal of the American Medical Society*, 303: 235–41.

Flegal, K., Shepherd, J., Looker, A., Graubard, B., Borrud, L., Ogden, C., Harris, T., Evenhart, J. and Schenker, N. (2009) 'Comparisons of percentage body fat, body mass index, waist circumference, and waist-stature in adults', *American Journal of Clinical Nutrition*, 89: 500–8.

Fogel, R.W. (1989) *Without Consent or Contract: The Rise and Fall of American Slavery*, New York: W.W. Norton.

——(1994) 'Economic growth, population theory and physiology: the bearing of long-term processes on the making of economic policy', *American Economic Review*, 84: 369–95.

Fogel, R.W. and Engerman, S.E. (1974) *Time on the Cross: The Economics of American Slavery*, New York: W.W. Norton.

Fogel, R.W, Engerman, S., Trussell, J., Floud, R., Pope, C. and Wimmer, L. (1978) 'Economics of mortality in North America, 1650–1910: a description of a research project', *Historical Methods*, 11: 75–108.

Fogel, R.W., Engerman, S.L., Floud, R., Steckel, R.H., Trussell, J., Wachter, K.W., Sokoloff, K., Villaflor, G., Margo, R. and Friedman, G. (1982) 'Changes in American and British stature since the mid-eighteenth century: a preliminary report on the usefulness of data on height for the analysis of secular trends in nutrition labor productivity, and labor welfare', NBER Working Paper No. 890.

Fogel, R.W., Engerman, S.L., Floud, R., Friedman, G., Margo, R.A., Sokoloff, K., Steckel, R.H., Trussell, T.J., Villaflor, G. and Wachter, K.W. (1983) 'Secular changes in American and British stature and nutrition', *Journal of Interdisciplinary History*, 18: 445–81.

Food and Agricultural Organization of the United Nations (FAO), World Health Organization (WHO) and United Nations University (UNU) (1985) *Energy and Protein Requirements FAO/WHO/UNU Expert Consultation*, Technical Report Series, No. 724, Geneva: World Health Organization.

Freedman, D.H. (2011) 'How to fix the obesity crisis', *Scientific American*, 304: 40–7.

Ginsburg, E., Livshits, G., Kobyliansky, K. and Major E. (1998) 'Gene control of human body height, weight and BMI in five ethnically different populations', *Annals of Human Genetics*, 62: 307–22.

Goodman, A.H. and Martin, D. (2002) 'Reconstructing health profiles from skeletal remains', in R.H. Steckel and J.C. Rose (eds) *The Backbone of History: Health and Nutrition in the Western Hemisphere*, Cambridge: Cambridge University Press.

Grantham-McGregor, S. (1989) 'Stunting, severe malnutrition, and mental development in young children', *European Journal of Clinical Nutrition*, 43: 403–9.

——(1995) 'A review of the studies of the effect of severe malnutrition on mental development', *Journal of Nutrition*, 125: 2233S–38S.

Haines, M., Craig, L. and Weiss, T. (2003) 'The short and the dead: nutrition, mortality and the antebellum puzzle in the United States', *Journal of Economic History*, 63: 382–413.

Heintel, M. and Baten, J. (1998) 'Smallpox and nutritional status in England, 1770–1873: on the difficulties of estimating historical heights', *Economic History Review*, 51: 360–71.

Henderson, R.M. (2005) 'The bigger the healthier: are the limits of BMI risk changing over time?', *Economics and Human Biology*, 3: 339–66.

Herbert, P., Richards-Edwards, J., Manson, J.A., Ridker, P., Cook, N., O'Conner, G., Buring, J. and Hennekens, C. (1993) 'Height and incidence of cardiovascular disease in male physicians', *Circulation*, 88: 1437–43.

Higgs, R. (1977) *Competition and Coercion: Blacks in American History, 1865–1914*, Chicago, IL: University of Chicago Press.

Holick, M.F. (1995) 'Environmental factors that influence the coetaneous production of vitamin D', *American Journal of Clinical Nutrition*, 61: 638S–645S.

——(2001) 'A perspective on the beneficial effects of moderate exposure to sunlight: bone health, cancer prevention, mental health and well being', in P. Giacomoni (ed.) *Sun Protection in Man*, Amsterdam: Elsevier.

——(2004a) 'Vitamin D: importance in the prevention of cancers, type 1 diabetes, heart disease and osteoporosis', *American Journal of Clinical Nutrition*, 79: 362–71.

——(2004b) 'Sunlight and vitamin D for bone health and prevention of autoimmune diseases, cancers, and cardiovascular diseases', *American Journal of Clinical Nutrition*, 80, supplement: 1678S–88S.

——(2007) 'Vitamin D deficiency', *New England Journal of Medicine*, 357: 266–81.

Holick, M.F., MacLaughlin, A. and Doppelt, S.H. (1981) 'Regulation of coetaneous previtamin D3 photosynthesis in men: skin pigment is not an essential regulator', *Science*, 211: 590–3.

Islam, T., Gauderman, W.J., Cozen, W. and Mack, T. (2007) 'Childhood sun exposure influences risk of multiple sclerosis in monozygotic twins', *Neurology*, 69: 381–8.

Jee, H.J., Sull, J.W., Park, J., Lee, S.Y., Ohrr, H., Guallar E. and Samet, J. (2006) 'Body-mass index and mortality in Korean men and women', *New England Journal of Medicine*, 355: 779–87.

Johnson, P. and Nicholas, S. (1995) 'Male and female living standards in England and Wales, 1812–1867', *Economic History Review*, 48: 470–81.

Kenchaiah, S., Evans, J., Levy, D., Wilson, P., Benjamin, E., Larson, M., Kannel W. and Vasan, R. (2002) 'Obesity and the risk of heart failure', *New England Journal of Medicine*, 347: 305–13.

Kiple, K. and Kiple, V. (1977) 'Slave child mortality: some nutritional answers to a perennial puzzle', *Journal of Social History*, 10: 284–309.

Koch, D. (2011) 'Waaler revisited: the anthropometrics of mortality', *Economics and Human Biology*, 9: 106–17.

Komlos, J. (1985) 'Stature and nutrition in the Hapsburg Monarchy: the standard of living and economic development in the eighteenth century', *American Historical Review*, 90: 1149–61.

——(1987) 'The height and weight of West Point cadets: dietary change in antebellum America', *Journal of Economic History*, 47: 897–927.

——(1992) 'Toward an anthropometric history of African-Americans: the case of the free blacks in antebellum Maryland', in C. Goldin and H. Rockoff (eds) *Strategic Factors in Nineteenth Century American Economic History: A Volume to Honor Robert W. Fogel*, Chicago, IL: University of Chicago Press.

——(1998) 'Shrinking in a growing economy? The mystery of physical stature during the Industrial Revolution', *Journal of Economic History*, 58: 779–802.

——(2003) 'Access to food and the biological standard of living: perspectives on the nutritional status of Native Americans', *American Economic Review*, 93: 252–5.

Komlos, J. and Alecke, B. (1996) 'The economics of antebellum slave heights reconsidered', *Journal of Interdisciplinary History*, 26: 437–57.

Komlos, J. and Brabec. M. (2011) 'The trend of mean BMI values of U.S. adults, birth cohorts 1882–1986 indicates that the obesity epidemic began earlier than hitherto thought', *American Journal of Human Biology*, 22: 631–8.

Komlos, J. and Coclanis, P. (1997) 'On the puzzling cycle in the biological standard of living: the case of antebellum Georgia', *Explorations in Economic History*, 34: 433–59.

Liu, Y.Z., Shen, F.H., Deng, H., Liu, Y.J., Zhao, L.J., Dvornyk, V., Conway, T., Li, J.L., Huang, Q.Y., Davies, K.M., Recker, R.R. and Deng, H.W. (2003) 'Confirmation linkage study in support of the X chromosome harbouring a ATL underlying human height variation', *Journal of Medical Genetics*, 40: 825–31.

Loomis, W.F. (1967) 'Skin-pigment regulation of vitamin-D biosynthesis in man: variation in solar ultra-violet at different latitudes may have caused racial differentiation in man', *Science*, 157: 501–6.

Mankiw, N.G and Weinzierl, M. (2007) 'The optimal taxation of height: a case study of utilitarian income redistribution', Harvard University Working Paper, 9–139.

Margo, R. (2000) *Wages and Labor Markets in the United States, 1820–1860*, Chicago, IL: University of Chicago Press.

——(2007) 'Government and the America dilemma', in P. Fishback (ed.) *Government and the American Economy*, Chicago, IL: University of Chicago Press.

Margo, R. and Steckel, R. (1982) 'Heights of American slaves: new evidence on nutrition and health', *Social Science History*, 6: 516–38.

——(1983) 'Heights of native born northern whites during the antebellum era', *Journal of Economic History*, 43: 167–74.

——(1992) 'The nutrition and health of slaves and antebellum southern whites', in R.W. Fogel and S. Engerman (eds) *Without Consent or Contract: Conditions of Slave Life and the Transition to Freedom*, New York: W.W. Norton.

Maurer, J. (2010) 'Height, education, and later life cognition in Latin America and the Caribbean', *Economics and Human Biology*, 8: 168–76.

McCaa, R. (2000) 'The peopling of Mexico from origins to revolutions', in M.R. Haines and R.H. Steckel (eds) *A Population History of North America*, Cambridge: Cambridge University Press.

Metzer, J.M. (1975) 'Rational management, modern business practices and economies of scale in ante-bellum southern plantations', *Explorations in Economic History*, 12: 123–50.

Murray, J.E. (1997) 'Standards of the present for people of the past: height, weight, and mortality among men of Amherst College, 1834–1949', *Journal of Economic History*, 57: 585–606.

Newman, J. (2003) 'Protein-energy malnutrition', in K. Kiple (ed.) *The Cambridge Historical Dictionary of Disease*, Cambridge: Cambridge University Press.

Nicholas, S. and Oxley, D. (1996) 'Living Standards of women in England and Wales, 1785–1815: new evidence from Newgate Prison records', *Economic History Review*, 49: 591–9.

Nicholas, S. and Steckel, R. (1991) 'Heights and living standards of English workers during the early years of industrialization', *Journal of Economic History*, 51: 937–57.

Norman, A. (1998) 'Sunlight, season, skin pigmentation, vitamin D and 25-hydroxyvatamin D: integral components of the vitamin D endocrine system', *American Journal of Clinical Nutrition*, 67: 1108–10.

Nyström-Peck, M. and Lundberg, O. (1995) 'Short stature as an effect and social conditions in childhood', *Social Science and Medicine*, 41: 733–8.

Oxley, D. (2004) 'Living standards of women in prefamine Ireland', *Social Science History*, 2: 271–95.

Peracchi, F. (2008) 'Height and economic development in Italy, 1730–1980', *American Economic Review Papers and Proceedings*, 98: 475–81.

Pi-Sunyer, F.X. (1991) 'Health implications of obesity', *American Journal of Clinical Nutrition*, 53: 1595s–1603s.

Popkin, B.M. (1993) 'Nutritional patterns and transitions', *Population Development Review*, 19: 138–57.

Prince, J.M. and Steckel, R.H. (2003) 'Nutritional success on the Great Plains: nineteenth century equestrian nomads', *Journal of Interdisciplinary History*, 33: 353–84.

Rees, R., Komlos, J., Long N. and Woitek, U. (2003) 'Optimal food allocation in a slave economy', *Journal of Population Economics*, 16: 21–36.

Riley, J.C. (1994) 'Height, nutrition, and mortality risk reconsidered', *Journal of Interdisciplinary History*, 24: 465–92.

Rosenbloom, J. (2002) *Looking for Work, Searching for Workers: American Labor Markets during Industrialization*, Cambridge: Cambridge University Press.

Sanchez, A.M., Reed, D.R. and Price, R.A. (2000) 'Reduced mortality associated with body mass index (BMI) in African Americans versus Caucasians', *Ethnicity and Disease*, 10: 24–30.

Steckel, R.H. (1979) 'Slave height profiles from coastwise manifests', *Explorations in Economic History*, 16: 363–80.

——(1983) 'Height and per capita income', *Historical Methods*, 16: 1–7.

——(1986) 'A peculiar population: the nutrition, health and mortality of American slaves from childhood through mortality', *Journal of Economic History*, 46: 721–41.

——(1994) 'Health and nutrition in the American Midwest: evidence from the height of Ohio National Guardsman', in J. Komlos (ed.) *Stature, Living Standards and Economic Development: Essays in Anthropometric History*, Chicago, IL: University of Chicago Press.

——(1995) 'Stature and the standard of living', *Journal of Economic Literature*, 33: 1903–40.

——(1996) 'Percentiles of modern height: standards for use in historical standards', *Historical* Methods, 29: 157–66.

——(2000) 'Diets versus diseases in the anthropometrics of slave children: a reply', *Journal of Economic History*, 60: 247–59.

——(2009) 'Heights of human welfare: recent developments and new directions', *Explorations in Economic History*, 46: 1–23.

Steckel, R.H. and Floud, R. (1997) *Health and Welfare during Industrialization*, Chicago, IL: University of Chicago Press.

Steckel, R.H. and Prince, J.M. (2001) 'Tallest in the world: Native Americans of the Great Plains in the nineteenth century', *American Economic Review*, 91: 287–94.

Steckel, R.H., Sciulli, P.W. and Rose, J.C. (2002) 'A health index from skeletal remains', in R.H. Steckel and J.C. Rose (eds) *The Backbone of History: Health and Nutrition in the Western Hemisphere*, Cambridge: Cambridge University Press.

Stevens, J., Cai, J., Pamuk, E., Williamson, D., Thun, M. and Woods, J. (1998) 'The effects of age on the association between body-mass index and mortality', *New England Journal of Medicine*, 338: 1–7.

Stevens, J., Keil, J.E., Rust, P.F., Tyroler, H.A., Davis, C.E. and Gazes, P.C. (1992) 'Body mass index and body girths as predictors of mortality in black and white women', *American Journal of Epidemiology*, 152: 1257–62.

Strauss, J. and Thomas, D. (1998) 'Health, nutrition, and economic development', *Journal of Economic Literature*, 37: 766–817.

Sturm, R. and Wells, K.B. (2001) 'Does obesity contribute as much to morbidity as poverty or smoking?' *Public Health*, 115: 229–36.

Subramanian, S.V. and Kawachi, I. (2004) 'Income inequality and health: what have we learned so far?' *Epidemiological Reviews*, 26: 78–91.

Sunder, M. (2011) 'Height of female Americans in the 19th century and the antebellum puzzle', *Economics and Human Biology*, 92: 165–71.

Tanner, J.M. (1962) *Growth at Adolescence*, Springfield, IL: Charles C. Thomas.

Tortolani, J., McCarthy, E. and Sponseller, P. (2002) 'Bone mineral density deficiency in children', *Journal of the American Academy of Orthopedic Surgeons*, 10, 1, 57–66.

Uitterlinden, A., Fang, Y., van Meurs, J.B., Pols, H.A. and van Leeuwen, J.P. (2004) 'Genetic and biology of vitamin D receptor polymorphisms', *Gene*, 338: 143–56.

Voth, H-J. and Leunig, T. (1996) 'Did smallpox reduce height? Stature and the standard of living in London, 1770–1873', *Economic History Review*, 49: 541–60.

Waaler, H.T. (1984) 'Height, weight, and mortality: the Norwegian experience', *Acta Medica Scandinavica*, supplement, 215: 1–56.

Wannamethee, S.G., Whincup, P., Shaper G. and Walker, M. (1996) 'Influence of father's social class on cardiovascular disease in middle-aged men', *Lancet*, 348: 1259–63.

Wardlaw, G.M., Hampl, J.S. and Disilvestro, R.A. (2004) *Perspectives in Nutrition*, 6th edition, New York: McGraw-Hill.

Weisberg, P., Scanlon, K., Li, R. and Cogswell, M.E. (2004) 'Nutritional rickets among children in the United States: review of cases reported between 1986 and 2003', *American Journal of Clinical Nutrition*, 80, supplement: 1697S–1705S.

Wienpahl, J., Ragland, D.R. and Sidney, S. (1990) 'Body mass index and 15-year mortality in a cohort of black men and women', *Journal of Clinical Epidemiology*, 43: 949–60.

Wilkinson, R.G. (1996) *Unhealthy Societies: The Effects of Inequality*, New York: Routledge.

Wilkinson, R.G. and Pickett, K.E. (2006) 'Income inequality and population health: a review and explanation of the evidence', *Social Science and Medicine*, 62: 1768–84.

Woitek, U. (2003) 'Height cycles in the 18th and 19th centuries', *Economics and Human Biology*, 1: 243–57.

Xiong, E.H., Xu, F.H., Liu, P.Y., Shen, H., Long, J.R., Elze, L., Recker, R.R. and Deng, H.W. (2005) 'Vitamin D receptor gene polymorphisms are linked to and associated with adult height', *Journal of Medical Genetics*, 42: 228–34.

Zehetmayer, M. (2011) 'The continuation of the antebellum puzzle: stature in the US, 1847–94', *European Review of Economic History*, 15, 2: 313–27.

PART II

Influences on economic growth and stagnation

5

THE CAUSES OF ECONOMIC GROWTH

Robert A. Margo

Per capita income, the ratio of gross national product to population is a widely used statistic of economic performance. One of the central features of the modern world is enormous dispersion in per capita income across countries. The study of economic growth is the study of the factors that have produced such enormous disparities over time. This chapter covers some of the essential features of modern economic growth and its causes.

Proximate causes of growth

A useful starting point is growth accounting. Growth accounting specifies an aggregate production function in which total output, Y, is a function of a set of inputs. A common aggregate production function is $Y = F(L, K, T)$.

L is the labor input, K is capital, and T is "land" and other natural resources.[1] A Cobb-Douglas or log-linear function is a convenient specification for F:

$$ln\ Y = ln\ A + \alpha_L ln\ L + \alpha_K ln\ K + \alpha_T ln\ T$$

The αs are output elasticities – for example, if $\alpha_L = 0.7$, a 10 per cent increase in L would yield a 7 per cent increase in Y, holding A, K and T constant.

Growth accountants assume that $\Sigma\ \alpha_i = 1$, which is equivalent to constant returns to scale – a simultaneous doubling of L, K and T would double Y (holding A constant). It is also convenient to assume that markets for inputs are competitive in which case the αs are equal to their respective shares of national income (for example, $\alpha_L = wL/Y$, the share of aggregate output paid to labor, or "labor's share").

Imposing the constant returns to scale assumption, and keeping in mind that the $ln\ (Y/P) = ln\ Y - ln\ P$, where P is population, we can write:

$$ln\ Y/P = ln\ A + \alpha_K ln\ K/L + \alpha_T ln\ T/L + ln\ L/P$$

Taking the derivative with respect to time and assuming the αs are fixed:

$$d\ (ln\ Y/P)/dt = d(ln\ A)/dt + \alpha_K d\ (ln\ K/L)/dt + \alpha_T d\ (ln\ T/L)/dt + d\ (ln\ L/P)/dt$$

The growth rate of per capita income is the sum of three components: the growth rate of A; a weighted average of the growth rates of capital and natural resources per worker; and the growth rate of labor force participation (L/P).

Growth in per capita income can result from increases in the level of capital per worker (K/L), natural resources per worker (T/L), or the labor force participation rate (L/P). Increases in factors complementary to labor (for example, K/L) affect output in proportion to their size moderated by the value of the output elasticity, whereas increases in labor force participation translate one-for-one into increases in per capita income.

In the nineteenth-century United States, for example, the rate of domestic savings was very high as were capital imports, resulting in substantial increases in K/L over time. As the country expanded westward, more land was brought into production, resulting in increases in T/L. Immigrants came to the country and immigrants, on average, had higher labor force participation, resulting in increases in L/P as the foreign-born share of the population increased. All three phenomena played quantitatively significant roles in raising the level of per capita income in the United States over the course of the nineteenth century (Kuznets 1971; Gallman 1986).

The term A is called "total factor productivity." A is a scaling parameter that moves Y up or down, holding factor inputs and factor shares fixed. The higher the value of A, the more efficient is the economy at turning inputs into output. The value of A is influenced by numerous forces, most importantly the state of technology, the effectiveness of factor markets in channeling productive inputs to their highest value use, and the quality and scope of economic (and other) institutions. Note that increases in A, holding K, L, T, and P fixed, generate increases in Y/P on a one-for-one basis – a 10 per cent rise in A produces a 10 per cent increase in per capita income.

The classic modern application of growth accounting is Solow (1957; see also Denison 1974). Using data for the United States in the twentieth century, Solow demonstrated that the majority of the growth in per capita income could not be explained by increases in capital per worker or land per worker, or rising labor force participation.[2] Rather, growth is explained by increases in A, total factor productivity.

The finding that increases in total factor productivity accounted for most of the rise in Y/P in the twentieth-century United States paralleled Solow's equally famous theoretical model of growth. In the Solow (1956) growth model, a representative individual maximizes the utility of lifetime consumption, subject to the aggregate production function and growth rate of factor inputs, K and L. The growth rate of L is assumed to be exogenous, but the growth rate of K depends on how much of current income is devoted to savings. In the absence of any increase in A, diminishing returns sets in and output per worker eventually falls. Given a growing population, it is necessary for A to increase if the economy is to sustain economic growth in the long run, according to the Solow growth model.

The moral of the Solow model is that, as long as population is increasing, capital accumulation cannot be a recipe for long-run growth – long-run growth requires that the level of total factor productivity increase. However, in the short run, a country might find itself temporarily with too little capital or too much. If capital per worker is below its "steady-state" or long-run level, the rate of return to capital will be high, providing an inducement to save and accumulate capital. In the short run, the higher than normal rate of capital accumulation will result in a more rapid rate of growth of output per worker – a phenomenon known as "convergence."

In evaluating the relative importance of changes in total factor productivity versus factor inputs in accounting for long-run growth, it is critical to recognize that A is measured as a "residual" rather than directly – that is, economists attempt to measure output, factor inputs, and factor shares and then infer the time path of total factor productivity after accounting for changes in factor inputs. This means that any errors in the measurement of the growth rates of output or inputs will likely cause errors in the measurement of the growth rate of total factor productivity.

Over time there have been numerous refinements in the quality of both historical and contemporary economic data and thus improvements in the accuracy of growth accounting. However, some problems of measurement are inherent in the process of economic growth itself.

In particular, it is easier to measure outputs that are tangible goods – bushels of wheat or steel ingots – than it is to measure outputs that are services. As a share of total output, services produced by the private sectors – for example, the legal profession – have increased over time relative to sectors producing tangible goods (agriculture, manufacturing, and mining). Government, too, is a much larger share of the economy today than a century ago. The output of service industries including government is often measured by the value of inputs rather than independently, which is problematic from a growth accounting perspective.

Workers are also healthier and better educated and as a result more productive. Just as new technology is frequently embodied in new capital goods, new knowledge is reflected in rising levels of educational attainment. One view (Griliches and Jorgensen 1967), albeit extreme, is that all increases in Y reflect increases in productive factors, properly measured. Most economists, however, believe that genuine increases in total factor productivity are the key factor behind long-run increases in per capita incomes.

The Solow growth model refers to a single (aggregate) economy. In the real world, economies differ in the level of A as well as factor endowments at any point in time. A country with a low value of total factor productivity due to inadequate technology benefits from technology transfer, because it does not have to re-invent the wheel (Gerschenkron 1962). Such transfer may occur privately, if individuals or businesses transport knowledge (and associated capital goods) across borders or it may be encouraged by governments (there are many historical examples) or by international organizations (for example, the World Bank). International factor markets also encourage convergence by transferring resources from low- to high-value uses. For example, if wages are low in one country relative to another – Ireland versus the United States in the 1850s – migration will encourage a narrowing of wage gaps, and this will also lead to convergence in per capita incomes. Under certain conditions, international product markets also encourage convergence through factor price equalization (Samuelson 1948). Williamson (1986) argues that "globalization" – the development and integration of international factor and product markets – has been a major force for income convergence during the past two centuries. Falling costs of international transport and communication, as well as reductions in trade barriers (for example, tariffs) facilitate such globalization and hence convergence.

The convergence debate

In understanding current differences in per capita income across countries, a central question is whether these differences are of comparatively recent origin, or else emerged sometime in the distant past. This question cannot be answered by focusing solely on the economic history of countries that are well off today. For example, Japan's per capita income in 1870 is estimated to have been $622, measured in U.S. dollars of 1985, slightly more than one-third of the estimated per capita income of today's OECD countries in the same year ($1,757).[3] That is, in 1870, Japan was a poor country by the standards of the other OECD countries in 1870. Since 1870 Japan has grown much more rapidly than the average of these other countries, and in the process has become rich itself. This type of convergence, however, is tautological (DeLong 1988). If we seek to determine the genuine role of convergence historically, we must include in the analysis the full range of experience across the world, not just rich countries today.

This important observation imposes a serious data constraint, however. Due largely to the work of Maddison (2007), economic historians have made great progress in measuring economic change in the past; however, despite progress, reliable data on per capita incomes for a large sample of countries do not extend very far back in time.[4] For example, we have plausible estimates of per capita income for the United States in 1860 but only the haziest quantitative notion of what per capita income in 1860 was in the part of Africa known today as Uganda.

An important paper by Pritchett (1997) suggests a solution to the data dilemma. Consider the ratio of per capita income in United States to per capita income in Chad, *c*. 1990, approximately 45:1. Imagine projecting the ratio back in time at the known growth rate for the United States – in effect, assuming that there was no income convergence between Chad and the United States. In fairly short order, the estimated per capita income in Chad in the past implied by this projection will fall below the level needed to sustain life.[5] That is, there must be a physiological lower bound on per capita income – otherwise the population would starve and there would be no per capita. But if there is such a lower bound, differences in per capita income between really poor countries today like Chad and rich countries today like the United States must have diverged at some point in the past – as early as 1870, according to Pritchett.

When did the "Great Divergence" actually begin? A long-standing belief is that divergence was a consequence of the "Industrial Revolution." Economic historians generally agree that industrialization began first in England, subsequently spreading to select countries in continental Europe and the United States (Mokyr 2009).

Scholars intensely debate the causes, timing, and even the basic statistics of the British case. Despite the passage of more than two centuries of scholarly investigation, many key questions remain less than fully explored or unanswered. The conventional wisdom dates the British Industrial Revolution from the first half of the eighteenth century through the first half of the nineteenth. Although initial research suggested a rather dramatic effect of industrialization on growth, more recent work by economic historians such as Crafts and Harley (1992) implies only a modest acceleration in the growth rate of per capita income. Why the impact was small is disputed. Some scholars attribute slow growth to the "crowding-out" effects that British wars had at the same time on capital formation, whereas other scholars argue that only a small portion of the British economy, in fact, was affected by industrialization (Williamson 1985; Crafts and Harley 1992). Fertility rates in England also climbed after 1800 and this put a damper on per capita income growth.

Countries that industrialized after England benefited to some extent from British mistakes as well as technological innovations, such as steam power, that developed first in England and later spread to the rest of the world. The United States, Belgium, and the Netherlands industrialized somewhat later than England but the process in these countries was well underway by the middle of the nineteenth century. Germany and Japan industrialized later, as did France. Countries in Southern and Eastern Europe, and the Mediterranean generally did not experience industrialization until the twentieth century.

Although industrialization certainly played a role in propelling the Great Divergence, recent work by Robert Allen (2001) suggests there were deeper historical roots. Allen's data on real wages for European cities date back to the middle of the fourteenth century. These data show that real wages were already rising in England and the Netherlands relative to other countries by the early seventeenth century – that is, long before the actual onset of the Industrial Revolution. In sum, Allen's data suggest that modern disparities in per capita income are not of comparatively recent origin but rather are long-standing.

Although modern disparities appear to be long-standing, they are not immutable, nor should one conclude that convergence is always necessarily weak. China and India are obvious contemporary examples. Per capita incomes in China and India were far lower than in the United States or Western Europe around 1990 but rapid growth during the past two decades has dramatically closed the gap – convergence – and the prospects for additional convergence in both countries over the next several decades are excellent. Barro and Sala-i-Martin (1992) show that per capita income differences across U.S. states converged from 1880 to 1980, although the pace of convergence is slower than implied by the Solow model. The Barro and Sala-i-Martin results are useful because they occurred within a country without internal barriers to trade or factor mobility, and with a largely common institutional framework.

Endogenous growth

Growth accounting identifies the proximate causes of economic growth and the Solow growth model identifies shifts in the rate of technological progress as the fundamental determinant of shifts in long-run "steady-state" growth. But growth accounting does not get at the fundamental causes of economic growth, unless one believes, quite erroneously, that technical innovation and factor accumulation occur exogenously. To understand long-run growth, therefore, one must understand the incentives that individuals have to innovate, the processes by which innovations diffuse, and the incentives individuals have to accumulate factors of production that are complementary to new techniques of production. Broadly speaking, "endogenous growth theory" attempts to ferret out the underlying causes of technical change and capital accumulation by focusing on such incentives.

An early, highly influential version of endogenous growth theory is Romer (1986; see also Frankel 1962). In the Romer model, aggregate production is not subject to diminishing returns (the so-called "Y = AK" model). The central idea in the AK model is that capital accumulation need not display diminishing returns because a broader notion of capital includes human capital, and greater levels of human capital lead to new knowledge and innovation and thus a higher rate of technical progress.[6] More recent versions of endogenous growth theory treat "intellectual capital" – accumulated and new knowledge – separately from human and physical capital accumulation (Aghion and Howitt 1998).

Another approach to understanding the fundamental causes of long-run growth is by concentrating on the role of institutions. In particular, well-specified, secure, and transferable property rights – "rule of law" – is an institutional feature often tied to growth. Well-specified property rights mean that ownership of a factor of production – say, a plot of land – is well defined such that clear title exists. If property rights are well specified, the use of the land for productive purposes will be the decision (primarily) of the owner. "Security" means that the owner can presume that, if, say, the land is clear or otherwise invested in, the state or another entity (person) will not claim title. "Transferable" means that the rights can be assigned, possibly through a competitive market process. The notion that property rights and related institutions are the fundamental building blocks of modern economic growth has a long history in economics but the modern version of the argument is generally attributed to Douglass North.[7]

It is easy to demonstrate empirically that countries with well-specified, secure, and transferable property rights have higher per capita incomes than countries with poorly specified, insecure property rights (if property rights are poorly specified and insecure, transferability is secondary). However, there is a chicken-and-egg problem. Are the rights a cause of per capita income, or is it that rich countries can afford to have good institutions?

A potentially useful source of evidence on the role of institutions in long-run growth is the experience of former colonies. Colonial powers established institutions of various types in the places that were colonized. It is possible that some variation in these institutions might be exogenous to other factors determining long-run growth and therefore useful in identifying the causal impact of institutions on development.

This idea is the core of a set of influential papers by Daron Acemoglu, Simon Johnson, and James Robinson (2001, 2002). They point out that current day differences in per capita income are positively correlated with measures of rule of law and the security of private property rights. In countries where the rule of law is strong and individuals are not at risk of having property expropriated, per capita income is high; the reverse is true where the rule of law is weak and property rights insecure. But are these institutions causes or consequences of growth?

To investigate this issue, Acemoglu *et al.* focus on countries that were once colonies of European powers. At or around the time of colonization, institutions were established by the mother country in the colony. In places that were densely populated (with natives) and resource-rich, Europeans established initial institutions that were "extractive" – that is, successful in generating riches at the time (slavery is the prime example). In places that were sparsely populated and resource-poor, the colonies were initially poor but early institutions had the features emphasized by North and others that were conducive to long-run growth. In the long run, therefore, there was a "reversal of fortune" (Acemoglu *et al.* 2002).

Acemoglu *et al.* show that "settler mortality" – the level of mortality experienced by the colonizers early in colonization – is a good predictor of whether initial institutions were good or bad – that is, conducive or not to long-run growth. However, much variation in settler mortality is arguably exogenous, due to differences in disease immunity.[8] Acemoglu *et al.* reason that, in places where settler mortality was high, colonizers had incentives to reap profit quickly and this often led to initial institutions that were exploitative in the short run, such as slavery. Unfortunately, bad institutions have a way of persisting. Because modern differences in per capita income developed over a long period of time, the persistence of bad institutions has terrible consequences.

Acemoglu *et al.* use settler mortality as an "instrumental variable" for an index of the current quality of economic institutions. In an ordinary least squares (OLS) regression of per capita income today on this index, the correlation is positive – but, as discussed earlier, correlation is not the same as causation. The instrumental variable estimate, however, is also positive, statistically significant, and larger in magnitude than the OLS estimate. Importantly, the positive effects of institutions on per capita income remain even with extensive controls for geography and other factors. Acemoglu *et al.* conclude, therefore, that good institutions are critical for long-run growth, and not the other way around (reverse causality).

Related work by Engerman and Sokoloff (2000) also stresses the role of institutions but features a different causal mechanism than Acemoglu *et al.* Engerman and Sokoloff focus on variation in economic performance in North and South America, stressing the role of initial factor endowments, particularly soil, climate, and geography. Some combinations of these endowments favored crops that could be grown very efficiently with slave labor. In such settings, the initial ownership of land became highly unequal. Engerman and Sokoloff show that initial land inequality is highly correlated with low rates of literacy and voting rights, even long after slavery was abolished. Endowments are also at the core of Pomeranz's (2000) highly influential analysis of why China did not industrialize at the same time as Western Europe. According to Pomeranz, European industrialization benefited from ready access to coal, unlike China. Wright (1990) also stresses the role of natural resources in explaining why United States manufacturing overtook Great Britain in the late nineteenth century.

Acemoglu *et al.*'s specific analysis has received its fair share of criticism. In particular, Albouy (forthcoming) argues that the estimates of settler mortality used in the instrumental variable regressions suffer from measurement error, and that the causal results are not robust to the countries included in the analysis. Nonetheless, the idea that poor-quality institutions established in the past for essentially arbitrary reasons might have important ramifications for present-day differences in per capita income has been highly influential in recent work on long-run growth (Diamond and Robinson 2010).

Notes

1 Sometimes Y is measured as "value added," meaning that the value of raw materials is subtracted from the value of final output.
2 The work of Solow and others on growth accounting in the twentieth century prompted similar research on the nineteenth century, as described in the text. This research concluded that growth in total factor productivity was more important as an explanatory factor in the twentieth century than in the nineteenth (Gallman 1986). The rate of technical progress, in other words, was not constant.
3 Figures are from Pritchett (1997: 5).
4 Because of the difficulties of measuring per capita income very far back in time, economic historians have also collected data on other indicators of the standard of living, such as real wages or height by age (Steckel 1995). Although extremely valuable, such additional data are not a substitute for per capita income and, in addition, carry their own set of problems. For example, there are well-known examples of countries that experienced decreases in height by age at the same time as rising per capita income (the antebellum United States is such an example). Data on real wages pertain to the portion of the labor force that worked for wages, typically a small share of the labor force historically. For the period after 1950 the situation is brighter, because of the availability of the Penn World Tables (Heston *et al.* 2011).The Penn World Tables provide consistent data on incomes and prices for a large panel of countries and are widely used in cross-country research on economic growth after the Second World War. The current version of the Penn World Tables can be downloaded from http://pwt.econ.upenn. edu/php_site/pwt_index.php
5 Data from the Penn World Tables indicate that per capita income in Chad declined after 1960, whereas in the United States it increased. If one projects actual per capita income in Chad backwards from the level in 1960 (instead of 1990), Pritchett's lower bound ($250 in 1990 U.S. dollars) is reached around the turn of the twentieth century.
6 Easterlin (1981; see also Goldin and Katz 2008) stresses formal education as a key factor in modern economic growth because of the presumed complementary relationship between educated labor and capital embodied in new technology. Economic growth is also accompanied by a shift of labor out of agriculture and a concomitant rise in urbanization. Economic historians have long argued that a higher rate of urbanization leads to more technical progress because ideas develop and diffuse more rapidly if the population is agglomerated rather than dispersed; see Jacobs (1969).
7 A useful introduction to North's views on institutions is North (1990). Critical to North's view is that economies of scale and division of labor are crucial for raising labor productivity, and that market expansion promotes both forces; hence institutions that facilitate and promote exchange are crucial to long-run development. On the role of such institutions, see also Grief (1993).
8 Because the variations in settler mortality are essentially random (exogenous), they can be used in a statistical sense to identify the effects of institutions on development. The mortality experience of settler economies is thus a type of "natural experiment" (as opposed to a laboratory experiment). The study of historical natural experiments is now a major area of research in development economics; see Nunn (2009).

References

Acemoglu, D., Johnson, S. and Robinson, J.A. (2001) 'The colonial origins of comparative development: an empirical investigation', *American Economic Review*, 91: 1369–401.
——(2002) 'Reversal of fortune: geography and institutions in the making of the modern world income distribution', *Quarterly Journal of Economics*, 117: 1231–94.

Aghion, P. and Howitt, P. (1998) *Endogenous Growth Theory*, Cambridge, MA: MIT Press.

Albouy, D. (forthcoming) 'The colonial origins of comparative development: an empirical investigation: comment', *American Economic Review*.

Allen, R. (2001) 'The great divergence in European prices from the middle ages to the First World War', *Explorations in Economic History*, 38: 411–47.

Barro, R. and Sala-i-Martin, X. (1992) 'Convergence', *Journal of Political Economy*, 100: 223–51.

Crafts, N.F.R. and Harley, C.K. (1992) 'Output growth and the British industrial revolution: a re-statement of the Crafts-Harley view', *Economic History Review*, 45: 703–30.

DeLong, J.B. (1988) 'Productivity growth, convergence, and welfare: comment', *American Economic Review*, 78: 1138–54.

Denison, E.F. (1974) *Accounting for United States Economic Growth, 1929–1969*, Washington, DC: Brookings Institution.

Diamond, J. and Robinson, J.A. (2010) *Natural Experiments of History*, Cambridge, MA: Harvard University Press.

Easterlin, R. (1981) 'Why isn't the whole world developed?', *Journal of Economic History*, 41: 1–19.

Engerman, S. and Sokoloff, K. (2000) 'History lessons: factor endowments and paths of development in the new world', *Journal of Economic Perspectives*, 14: 217–32.

Frankel, M. (1962) 'The production function in allocation and growth: a synthesis', *American Economic Review*, 52: 995–1022.

Gallman, R. (1986) 'The United States capital stock in the nineteenth century', in S. Engerman and R. Gallman (eds) *Long Term Factors in American Economic Growth*, Chicago, IL: University of Chicago Press.

Gerschenkron, A. (1962) *Economic Backwardness in Historical Perspective: A Book of Essays*, Cambridge, MA: Harvard University Press.

Goldin, C. and Katz L. (2008) *The Race Between Education and Technology*, Cambridge, MA: Harvard University Press.

Grief, A. (1993) 'Contract enforcement and economic institutions in early trade: the Maghribi traders' coalition', *American Economic Review*, 83: 525–48.

Griliches, Z. and Jorgensen, D.W. (1967) 'The explanation of productivity change', *Review of Economic Studies*, 34: 249–83.

Heston, A., Summers, R. and Aten B. (2011) *Penn World Table Version 7.0*, Center for International Comparisons of Production, Income and Prices, Philadelphia, PA: University of Pennsylvania.

Jacobs, J. (1969) *The Economy of Cities*, New York: Random House.

Kuznets, S. (1971) 'Notes on the pattern of U.S. economic growth', in R. Fogel and S. Engerman (eds) *The Reinterpretation of American Economic History*, New York: Harper and Row.

Maddison, A. (2007) *Contours of the World Economy, 1–2030 AD: Essays in Macro-Economic History*, New York: Oxford University Press.

Mokyr, J. (2009) *The Enlightened Economy: An Economic History of Britain, 1700–1850*, New Haven: Yale University Press.

North, D. (1990) *Institutions, Institutional Change, and Economic Performance*, New York: Cambridge University Press.

Nunn, N. (2009) 'The importance of history for economic development', in K. Arrow and T. Bresnahan (eds) *Annual Review of Economics*, Palo Alto, CA: Annual Reviews.

Pomeranz, K. (2000) *The Great Divergence: China, Europe, and the Making of the Modern World Economy*, Princeton, NJ: Princeton University Press.

Pritchett, L. (1997) 'Divergence, big time', *Journal of Economic Perspectives*, 11: 3–17.

Romer, P. (1986) 'Increasing returns and long-run growth', *Journal of Political Economy*, 94: 1002–37.

Samuelson, P.A. (1948) 'International trade and the equalization of factor prices', *Economic Journal*, 58: 163–84.

Solow, R. (1956) 'A contribution to the theory of economic growth', *Quarterly Journal of Economics*, 70: 65–94.

——(1957) 'Technical change and the aggregate production function', *Review of Economics and Statistics*, 39: 312–20.

Steckel, R. (1995) 'Stature and the standard of living', *Journal of Economic Literature*, 33: 1903–40.

Williamson, J. (1985) *Did British Capitalism Breed Inequality?* London: Allen and Unwin.

——(1986) 'Globalization, convergence, and history', *Journal of Economic History*, 56: 277–306.

Wright, G. (1990) 'The origins of American industrial success, 1879–1940', *American Economic Review*, 80: 651–68.

6

ECONOMIC HISTORY OF TECHNOLOGICAL CHANGE

B. Zorina Khan

Introduction

Consumers gain insights into the social value of technological innovations every time a computer crashes or the power goes off. Economists likewise agree that technological change promotes productivity gains and overall economic growth. Theoretical models variously treat inventive activity and innovation as exogenous, evolutionary, induced by economic or scientific factors, or path dependent. Economic analysis is predominantly static, whereas technological change is inherently dynamic, so it is not surprising that economic theory can illuminate, but fail to explain, the sources of advances in technology. Economic historians possess a comparative advantage in the realm of empirical analyses of changes over time, which allows them to make valuable contributions to understanding the role of technology in economic development. Accordingly, the interaction between "standard" economics and history has become more frequent and apparent in recent research.

The first modern industrial societies appeared in Western Europe and North America in the eighteenth and nineteenth centuries. The central research question is simple to pose: Why that time and those places? The answer is complex, but inextricably linked to the economic history of technological change. In the tradition of Montesquieu, an increasing number of investigators maintain that the present distribution of technical advances and global income was determined by endowments and events in the distant past. Location, climate, and the disease environment of some 13,000 years ago triggered a recursive system that altered the course of civilization, leading to economic prosperity in the West, and stagnation or decline elsewhere (Diamond 1997). According to this perspective, institutions are endogenous, for history and geography influence their choice, and the consequences of initial conditions tend to persist over the very long run.

Engerman and Sokoloff (2011) show that factor endowments shaped institutions, technology, and socioeconomic outcomes in the New World. The local climate, soils, and natural resources predisposed colonies in Latin America and the Caribbean to extractive political and socio-economic systems that perpetuated the rent-seeking of entrenched and unproductive elites. Markets were narrow, human capital investments limited to a select few, and the potential for innovation and economic growth quickly exhausted. By way of contrast, the endowments of the colonies in North America favored open-access institutions and greater equality, which encouraged market expansion, flexibility, education for the masses, and inventive activity. As such, the cumulative effect of past meta-economic endowments may well explain global inequality in the allocation of technology and income today. However, the question of whether geography has a direct or indirect effect on institutions that promote technology is still open, especially given "the reversal of fortunes" experienced in many jurisdictions (Acemoglu and Robinson 2012).

The first Industrial Revolution

The analysis of specific events, and the British Industrial Revolution in particular, provides another approach to the central issue of explaining technological change and growth paths. The term "industrial revolution" reflects earlier claims that Britain experienced a discrete structural transformation from an agrarian society to a modern economy marked by pervasive technical advances, and rapid rates of productivity and growth. Estimates of British total factor productivity during the early industrial period have since been revised downward, suggesting a less dramatic scenario, in which Britain may have been merely "precocious" rather than pre-eminent compared with such competitors as France and Holland (Crafts and Harley 1992). The industrial r/evolution itself clearly owed to the transformation of technologies in certain sectors, primarily textiles, iron and steel, and energy. Early British economic growth was unbalanced, with technological and productivity advances largely restricted to these highly capital-intensive industries, but little consensus exists about the explanation for such technical progress. The answers range from broad general factors such as politics, religion, and culture through to exquisitely precise estimates of wages and prices in firms and industries. Given the popular emphasis on mechanization and manufacturing, it is worth emphasizing that productivity gains and technical developments in agriculture provided the prerequisites for shifts into industry (Federico 2008).

On the eve of the British Industrial Revolution, China and Japan were more similar to than different from Western Europe, in terms of such important demographic, economic, and institutional factors as life expectancy, efficient goods and labor markets, effective legal systems, and respect for property rights (Pomeranz 2000). East Asian historians point out that early Chinese technologies were sophisticated and frequently far in advance of pre-industrial European achievements (Bray 1994). Thus, the "Great Divergence" that ultimately produced stagnation in Asia and industrial progress in Europe likely owed not to systematic, but to somewhat serendipitous, factors. Europeans (and Britain in particular) were able to benefit from accessible and relatively cheap energy supplies and from the resource endowments in their colonies in the New World. Allen (2009) concurs that ready access to coal facilitated the adoption of technologies that were developed to save on the relatively high costs of British labor inputs. The price of labor was also high in other locations such as Holland, but they lacked the deposits of coal that were necessary to power the industrial process.

Cultural features, broadly defined, have often been cited to explain the timing and location of the Industrial Revolution. These include religion and the role of nonconformists in technological innovation, rationalist–scientific approaches to nature, an educational approach that fosters skills among the general population, and the degree of political stability. The link between war and technology has a long scholarly tradition, and the economic concept of "creative destruction" originated with Werner Sombart's (1913) classic thesis that wars have a positive impact on industrialization and technological change. In this tradition, Rosenthal and Wong (2011) speculate that international political economy in Western Europe was more conducive to inventiveness and industrialization. In particular, the tendency for warfare and political fragmentation in Europe produced an unintended benefit: it created greater incentives for urbanization, invention, and industrial progress, compared with the centralization and political stability of imperial China. Warfare influenced the concentration of manufacturing within cities, which changed relative prices and biased European technical change toward capital-intensive technologies.

Some attribute industrialization and advances in technology to such norms as thrift, honesty, and the capacity to work hard (Landes 1999; Clark 2008). Similarly, according to Mokyr (1990, 2002, 2010), technological change and industrialization cannot be explained by standard economic variables. England benefited from the ideas and ideals of the rational scientific revolution dating from the seventeenth century that culminated in an age of "Industrial Enlightenment" (see also Jacob 1997). In the eighteenth century, exogenous discoveries about nature, changes in artisanal knowledge, and the rationalization of information combined to generate new inventions and productivity advances. Technical elites had access to scientific principles, and there was widespread diffusion of information about natural phenomena that could be manipulated to enhance economic welfare. Social agendas, appropriate institutions, and relative prices could to some extent influence incremental extensions in the set of useful knowledge, but technological ascendance owed primarily to the *dea ex machina*. Crafts (1995) contends that major technological change in Britain was idiosyncratic or random.

These theories imply that economic progress is a function of knowledge inputs whose supply is inelastic or unresponsive to economic incentives. Walt Rostow (1960) and Nathan Rosenberg (1974) contended that science and specialized knowledge comprise preconditions for economic and social progress. However, biographical information and patent records for "great inventors" credited with significantly expanding the frontiers of technology do not support the view that familiarity with formal science and engineering education played a significant role in the creation of technological innovations during early British industrialization (Khan 2010). Scientists and trained engineers were not well represented among the great British inventors until very late in the nineteenth century. Scientific endeavors of the day owed to skittish dons or aristocratic amateurs, whose efforts were directed to impractical pursuits and general principles in astronomy, magnetism, mathematics, botany, and chemistry, rather than to useful knowledge. Those great inventors who did have scientific training tended to produce innovations that were broadly distributed across sectors, rather than contributing to the key industries that were associated with productivity gains in the Industrial Revolution. England's economic advantage did not depend on advances in science or formal investments in specialized human capital. Instead, the economically valuable innovations of the eighteenth and early nineteenth centuries were largely produced by workers who benefited from apprenticeships and on-the-job learning. As such, industrialization may have owed more to a pre-industrial institution, the craft guild, which had long facilitated the acquisition of skills and technical diffusion (Epstein 1998).

North and Thomas (1973) emphasized the role of institutions in the British Industrial Revolution, and they attributed a large part of the credit to the patent system. Early studies of the British patent system concluded that, although its operation was somewhat flawed, patentees nevertheless made significant contributions to the Industrial Revolution (Dutton 1984; Sullivan 1989). Others are less sanguine, and point to the use of patents for speculation and advertising, to the inefficient rules and standards that led to a bias toward elites in the roster of patentees independently of their productivity, and to inventive activity outside the patent system (MacLeod 1988; Khan and Sokoloff 1998; Moser 2005; Khan 2011a). Dutton had highlighted the operation of markets in patented invention, but examination of the data reveals that trade in British patents was actually quite limited (Khan and Sokoloff 2004). This finding is unsurprising since British rules and standards established significant barriers to entrepreneurship and invention in the form of prohibitively high monetary and transactions costs, uncertain property rights, and

restrictions on ownership in patent property. Such features caused nationwide lobbies of manufacturers and patentees to continually express their dissatisfaction with the patent system (Khan
2005).

The high costs of patent fees and other deficiencies of the British patent system likely
encouraged some inventors to appropriate returns through alternative means, such as keeping
their discoveries secret. Several groups followed the opposite strategy of sharing technical
knowledge with competitors. Allen (1983) finds that British iron producers participated in
"collective invention," mutually exchanging information about designs and incremental innovations that lowered costs or improved performance. Similarly, Cornish steam engineers colla-
borated by circulating their findings about best practice and improvements in pumps to drain
mines, both informally and in publications (Nuvolari 2004). Cartels of cotton spinning firms in
Japan reported information on their production costs to the Ministry of Commerce during the
1880s, and the association later published in its journal reports on wages and work schedules,
machinery, and new innovations. Firms also contacted each other directly in order to find out
about improvements being implemented and this culture of cooperation led to uniformly low
costs and high productivity in the industry (Saxonhouse 1974).

In Europe, an extensive array of prizes was conferred on "deserving" inventors. Systematic
studies of prizes include an assessment of devices on display at the Crystal Palace Exhibition of
1851, the majority of which were unpatented (Moser 2005). Brunt *et al.* (2008) conclude that
prizes offered by the Royal Agricultural Society of England were effective in inducing technological innovation, although the awards seemed to be more valuable as tools of advertising
and commercialization. The grants of prizes to British great inventors were primarily connected
to status rather than to factors that might have enhanced productivity (Khan 2011a). The most
significant variable affecting the possession of a prize was an elite or Oxbridge education, which
substantially increased the odds of getting an award, despite the traditional hostility of such
institutions to pragmatic or scientific pursuits. However, specialized education in science and
engineering, patentee status, and employment in science or technology, had little or no impact
on the probability of getting a prize. In short, in Britain both patent and prize-giving institutions exhibited a bias toward recipients from privileged backgrounds. By way of contrast,
among the American great inventors, and among general inventors at annual state industrial
fairs, prizes were determined by the nature of the technology rather than the identity of their
recipients, although the conferral of prizes was idiosyncratic and not as market oriented as
patents (Khan 2011a, 2012b). American technologies at the cutting edge tended to be patented,
and few eminent inventors were associated with competitions for prizes. As such, exhibitions
offered limited opportunities for the diffusion of novel inventive information, and primarily
functioned as a forum for commercialization (Khan 2012b).

Technological innovation in the United States

Britain's early technological lead was soon eroded by other nations, and studies debate whether
that erosion owed to indigenous efforts or to international transfers and spillovers. The British
tried to prohibit the emigration of skilled artisans, machines, and technology, but were unable to
prevent such transfers. As a follower country, the United States initially benefited from the
importation of technology inputs and the diffusion of information from overseas (Jeremy 1981,
1991). For instance, Éleuthère Irénée du Pont, a student of the French chemist Lavoisier,
immigrated to the United States. He obtained funding, technical assistance, and machinery from
France, and this helped to launch the DuPont powder mill and the U.S. explosives industry early
in the nineteenth century. However, the benefits from wholesale adoption tend to be limited

because factor endowments and market conditions vary across countries, and spillovers decline sharply with distance (Keller 2002). In Britain, the textile industry employed the skill-intensive mule technology, whereas American endowments favored ring-spinning technology that economized on skilled inputs (Saxonhouse and Wright 1984). It is worth noting that the textile sector was hardly typical, and in many industries the prevalent technologies were readily apparent to anyone who was skilled in the art, with inventions that merely involved pragmatic incremental manipulations to suit local conditions (Burt 1991). In any event, indigenous U.S. technological capabilities soon proved superior to European efforts in many industries, and numerous examples indicate net flows in the opposite direction, from the United States to Europe. For instance, Charles Goodyear's patents in the 1840s for the vulcanization of rubber were not only copied in England, but also British inventors re-patented his discoveries in their own name. Similarly, Samuel Colt, Hiram Maxim, and other gun manufacturers and inventors transformed the technology of European warfare (Khan 2005). Wilkins (1970, 1974) highlighted the role of American multinational business enterprises, founded to exploit patents in sewing machines, elevators, shoemaking machinery, and electrical equipment, in spreading technological innovations to Europe.

Patents provide important insights into the sources of U.S. technological progress in the nineteenth century (Khan 2005). The United States created the world's first modern patent system. The primary features of the American patent institution gradually diffused across the globe as international patent laws became more harmonized (Penrose 1951). The U.S. patent system was deliberately designed to ensure widespread access, and featured low fees and an examination system where trained employees of the patent office certified that the patent granted comprised an original advance in the state of the art. The basic parameters of the system were transparent and predictable, in itself an aid to those who wished to obtain patent rights. In addition, American legislators were concerned with ensuring that information about the stock of patented knowledge was readily available and diffused rapidly. Numerous reported decisions before the early courts declared that, rather than unwarranted monopolies, patent rights were "sacred" and to be regarded as the just recompense to inventive ingenuity. The courts explicitly attempted to implement decisions that promoted economic growth and social welfare.

The nineteenth century proved to be an age of inventions patented by Americans. The growth in U.S. patents was especially dramatic from the 1840s through the 1870s, a period in which the per capita rate of patenting increased 15 times (Khan and Sokoloff 2001; Khan 2005). Extensive technology markets developed as early as the 1840s, when trade in patents boomed, attaining a volume of three to six times the number of patents issued (Khan 1995). There is ample evidence that such inventive activity was induced by factors that affected the appropriability of returns, over time and across place. The time series of patent grants was pro-cyclical, varying with the business cycle (Sokoloff 1988). The early take-off in per capita patenting occurred when improvements in waterways led to an expansion in market demand. Although urban and metropolitan areas excelled in inventive activity, the most significant increases were associated with formerly isolated locales that were newly exposed to larger markets. Improvements in market access led to a greater proportionate response among rural residents who were new to invention. Further evidence on the identities of nineteenth-century patentees suggests that the specific design of the patent system played a substantial role in inducing relatively ordinary individuals to reorient their efforts toward exploiting market opportunities (Sokoloff and Khan 1990). These patterns characterized both incremental and significant inventions, because great inventors in the United States were even more entrepreneurial in their efforts to use the patent system to extract returns from their technological creativity (Khan and Sokoloff 2006; Khan 2005). By way of contrast, such factors as learning-by-doing and localized knowledge spillovers did not significantly influence the course of technological development (Lamoreaux and Sokoloff 2000; Sutthiphisal 2006).

The experience of women inventors offers another perspective on the role of incentives, property rights, and legal institutions in influencing technological change. Economic historians who address the relationship between women and technology have limited their attention to the impact of technical changes on women in the household or labor market (Jellison 1993; Goldin and Katz 2002). Few systematic studies examine women's contributions to inventive activity, and some authors even deny that they made worthwhile discoveries. Cardwell's history of technology devoted no more than two paragraphs to women inventors out of a total of over 500 pages, on the grounds that "female technologists of any distinction are hard to find" (1994: 506). At the other end of the spectrum are exhaustive lists of inventions that possibly might have been attributed to women (Stanley 1993).

Patent records are incomplete indices of invention, but do permit a more objective assessment of women's contributions to technological change than the plethora of case studies featured in historical accounts (Khan 2000). Although in other regards women may have been excluded from the benefits of a democratic society, the U.S. patent system offered them equal opportunities to excel. Women were motivated by potential profits, and responded to changes in the legal system that expanded their property rights and offered greater access to potential income from their investments in inventive activity (Khan 1996). Unlike their male counterparts, women inventors disproportionately resided in rural towns and frontier areas; women in these locales, without the benefit of readily available help, likely had a greater incentive to devise inventions to help in their household tasks. The study of women inventors reminds us that technological change is far broader than the realm of machines, and encompasses improvements in diet and techniques of food preparation, more efficient processes of child-rearing, and new designs in furnishing. Female patentees were applying their creative insights to the sphere in which they had the greatest experience. In the process, as the extensive archives of assignment contracts show, many became adept participants in the flourishing market in domestic inventions. Their experience suggests that the spheres of household and market were closely linked for both men and women and, like the economy at large, the household economy was the locus of both invention and innovation (Khan 2000).

The Civil War was a turning point for women inventors, and illustrates the extent to which all categories of inventors responded to market incentives (Khan 2009). During the war, per capita patenting by women increased significantly, including such inventions as war vessels and hospital equipment. Hartcup (1988) considered the First World War to be the first technological war in history, but one doubts that he took much account of the American Civil War. Both ordinary and "great inventors" dramatically changed the rate and direction of their activities toward military technologies, and toward other areas where markets were expanding, such as prosthetics for amputees and substitutes for cotton textiles. New entrants into invention tended to be rather ordinary individuals without much technical training or wealth, who responded to perceived need by filing job-related patents for improvements. Moreover, engineering or technical expertise did not yield greater numbers of military inventions. During the war, inventors with little wealth benefited from markets in invention, which allowed them to assign or sell their rights to investors, and their material circumstances after the war improved to the extent that they caught up with their peers. Thus, the market for inventions that flourished in the middle of a devastating conflict served to allocate inventive resources toward the war effort. The war proved to be a temporary setback for both technological and economic progress, and postbellum patenting soon soared to a greater and sustained level.

Effective patent and legal institutions encouraged the securitization of property rights in invention, leading to an extensive market in technology. The potential to sell off their ideas especially benefited those technologically creative inventors without the capital to go into business and directly exploit the fruits of their ingenuity (Khan and Sokoloff 2004). The accelerated increase in the extent of the market during the 1870s promoted a Smithian process of specialization and the division of labor between invention and commercialization. Patent agencies and patent attorneys throughout the country served as intermediaries who minimized transactions costs in the market exchange of patented inventions. At the same time, patentees with a comparative advantage in technological creativity increasingly specialized in inventive activity, especially after the nature of technical inputs into inventions became more complex (Lamoreaux and Sokoloff 1996, 2001). The nineteenth century primarily remained an era of independent inventors, even among professional inventors who exhibited considerable "contractual mobility;" it was not until the twentieth century that productive patentees entered into long-term arrangements with firms, often as principals rather than as employees (Lamoreaux and Sokoloff 2005).

Conventional accounts of technological change in both manufacturing and agriculture have tended to focus on the creation and diffusion of capital-intensive machinery, and on labor-saving productivity advances. Even in the antebellum period, American agriculture was certainly more mechanized than in Britain, and this was reflected in the patent records, for fewer than 5 per cent of British patents covered inventions in this sector, relative to almost one-quarter of total patents filed in the United States (Khan 2005). Standard research has focused on the introduction and diffusion of hybrid seed corn, the substitution of the tractor for horse power, and mechanical reapers for harvesting wheat and corn. More recent contributions to the economic history of agricultural technology venture beyond the plethora of machinery and tools to highlight institutional factors, and non-machine innovations embodied in crops and livestock. For instance, although continuous-processing sugar-production technologies were associated with economies of scale, a wide range of efficient mill capacities still persisted, owing in part to adjustment costs and local institutional conditions (Dye 1998). A reexamination of the diffusion of reapers credits their adoption to changes in institutions, including the growth of local markets and cooperative sharing of reaper services by small farmers (Olmstead and Rhode 1995).

Olmstead and Rhode (2008) point out that biological innovations were pervasive in American agriculture, long before the scientific discoveries of the twentieth century. Crops were adapted to other regions, and to different soil types. New hybrid plant varieties were created, livestock selectively bred, and defenses continually devised to protect against insects, microorganisms, and animal diseases that had the potential to decimate crops and livestock. These innovations enhanced and extended the availability of arable land, while maintaining farm yields. As a result, non-mechanized technologies dramatically increased the productivity of land and labor on farms, allowing agricultural production to outpace population growth. An important part of the story relates to how institutional changes combined with and facilitated such agricultural innovations. The "dust bowl" was created because of externalities which led to an underinvestment in techniques to control the erosion of soil, a problem that was resolved by institutions for collective action that internalized the external effects (Hansen and Libecap 2004). Moreover, U.S. government agencies played a larger role in the spread of technological innovations in agriculture, introducing institutions that lowered risk and increased the return to investments in new farm technologies (Farrell and Runge 1983).

Technological achievements in the nineteenth century propelled the United States on the trajectory of productivity and economic progress that would establish it as the foremost industrial nation. However, the nature of technical progress itself was transforming toward the end of the nineteenth century. In the general population, both technology and educational inputs grew rapidly. New technologies increased the demand for skilled labor and the rates of return on human capital acquisition, and the educational system at the secondary and tertiary levels met and satisfied those needs (Goldin and Katz 2008). Specialized knowledge and science became increasingly necessary for inventive activity at the frontier. Individuals with science and engineering degrees began to dominate among the later birth cohorts of great inventors in both Britain and America (Khan 2005, 2011a). At the same time, inventive activity required larger sources of financial capital, and at times necessitated research collaborations with co-inventors trained in other disciplines. Technologically creative inventors were increasingly likely to work within corporate enterprises, which could exploit their discoveries in-house. Perhaps as a result of such factors, in the first few decades of the twentieth century there was a decline in the roster of multiple patentees and independent inventors (Lamoreaux and Sokoloff 2005). The rates of patenting that U.S. residents achieved during the second industrial revolution would not be attained again (recent increases owe to foreigners patenting in the U.S.).

Throughout American history, policy makers were aware of the trade-offs between the promotion of technological progress and the potential for monopolization (Khan 2011b). Changes in the organization of technology included the greater prominence of corporations in the creation and diffusion of inventions and innovations. The well-known industrial concentration that followed the merger movement at the turn of the century created firms with a great deal of market power. Economies of scale and scope may have engendered corporations that entrenched their positions through anticompetitive practices, but such factors also promoted technological progress through creative destruction along the lines that Schumpeter (1950) had suggested (Nicholas 2003). Although British firms have been criticized for lagging in this area, they too performed creditably by making significant investments in research and development (Edgerton and Horrocks 1994). High-technology companies such as DuPont, Eastman Kodak, and General Electric established large research laboratories that employed eminent applied scientists (Mowery 1983). Corporate research and development further benefited from spillovers in academic institutions in terms of both training and research, and the growth of pharmaceutical laboratories was associated with links to researchers in nearby universities (Furman and MacGarvie 2007). The service sector is often overlooked, but technological and organizational changes in the shift from "counting house to office" dramatically increased productivity, perhaps to a greater extent than in manufacturing, and may have accounted for U.S. competitive advantage (Broadberry and Ghosal 2002).

Conclusion

For many, it is tempting to propose that technological changes in the twenty-first century have created a new era, and that today's information technologies herald a "new economy." But convincing arguments can be made to support the claim that the truly transformative eras lie in the past. Gordon (2000) asks whether the innovations of the current information age surpass the great inventions of the second industrial revolution, and concludes that computers and the Internet do not match up to the discoveries of the late nineteenth century, which had a ratchet effect on social welfare. According to Field (2011), the 1930s comprised the most productively progressive decade of the twentieth century, because organizational and other technological advances in electrification, transportation, communications, and distribution generated high rates of total factor productivity growth and "a great leap forward." Although these perspectives are certainly valid, it is worth remembering that, since the first days of settlement, Americans have employed and enjoyed incremental improvements that satisfied the purpose of generating and diffusing information, from newspapers, through the telegraph, telephone, computers, to the Internet (Chandler and Cortada 2003). This conclusion is equally valid in other dimensions, for what stands out in any assessment of the economic history of technological change are the continuities between the past and the present.

References

Abramovitz, M. (1993) 'The search for the sources of growth: areas of ignorance, old and new', *Journal of Economic History*, 52: 217–43.

Acemoglu, D. and Robinson, J. (2012) *Why Nations Fail: The Origins of Power, Prosperity, and Poverty*, New York: Crown.

Allen, R.C. (1983) 'Collective invention', *Journal of Economic Behavior and Organization*, 4: 1–24.

——(2009) *The British Industrial Revolution in Global Perspective*, Cambridge: Cambridge University Press.

Arthur, W.B. (1989) 'Competing technologies, increasing returns, and lock-in by historical events', *Economic Journal*, 99: 116–31.

Baker, E.F. (1964) *Technology and Woman's Work*, New York: Columbia University Press.

Bray, F. (1994) *The Rice Economies: Technology and Development in Asian Societies*, Berkeley: University of California Press.

Bresnahan, T. and Trajtenberg, M (1995) 'General purpose technologies: engines of growth?' *Journal of Econometrics*, 65: 83–108.

Broadberry, S. and Ghosal, S. (2002) 'From the counting house to the modern office: explaining Anglo-American productivity differences in services, 1870–1990', *Journal of Economic History*, 62: 967–98.

Brunt, L., Lerner, J. and Nicholas, T. (2008) 'Inducement prizes and innovation', London: Centre for Economic Policy Research Discussion Paper Series, 6917.

Burt, R. (1991) 'The international diffusion of technology in the early modern period: the case of the British non-ferrous mining industry', *Economic History Review*, 44: 249–71.

Cardwell, D. (1994) *History of Technology*, London: Fontana.

Chandler, A.D. and Cortada, J.W. (2003) *A Nation Transformed by Information: How Information Has Shaped the United States from Colonial Times to the Present*, Oxford: Oxford University Press.

Clark, G. (2008) *A Farewell to Alms: A Brief Economic History of the World*, Princeton, NJ: Princeton University Press.

Crafts, N.F.R. (1995) 'Macroinventions, economic growth, and "Industrial Revolution" in Britain and France', *Economic History Review*, 48: 591–8.

Crafts, N.R. and Harley, C.K. (1992) 'Output growth and the industrial revolution: a restatement of the Crafts-Harley view', *Economic History Review*, 45: 703–30.

David, P.A. (1985) 'Clio and the economics of QWERTY', *American Economic Review*, 75: 332–7.

Diamond, J. (1997) *Guns, Germs and Steel: The Fates of Human Societies*, New York: W.W. Norton.

Dutton, H.I. (1984) *The Patent System and Inventive Activity during the Industrial Revolution, 1750–1852*, Manchester: Manchester University Press.

Dye, A. (1998) *Cuban Sugar in the Age of Mass Production: Technology and the Economics of the Sugar Central, 1899–1929*, Stanford, CA: Stanford University Press.

Edgerton, D.E.H. and Horrocks, S.M. (1994) 'British industrial research and development before 1945', *Economic History Review*, 47: 213–38.

Engerman, S.L. and Sokoloff, K.L. (2011) *Economic Development in the Americas since 1500: Endowments and Institutions*, New York: Cambridge University Press.

Epstein, S.R. (1998) 'Craft guilds, apprenticeship, and technological change in preindustrial Europe', *Journal of Economic History*, 58: 684–713.

Farrell, K.R. and Runge, C.F. (1983) 'Institutional innovation and technical change in American agriculture: the role of the New Deal', *American Journal of Agricultural Economics*, 65: 1168–73.

Federico, G. (2005) *Feeding the World: An Economic History of Agriculture, 1800–2000*, Princeton, NJ: Princeton University Press.

Field, A.J. (2011) *A Great Leap Forward: 1930s Depression and U.S. Economic Growth*, New Haven, CT: Yale University Press.

Fogel, Robert W. (1964) *Railroads and American Economic Growth: Essays in Econometric History*, Baltimore, Md: Johns Hopkins University Press.

Furman, J.L. and MacGarvie, M. (2007) 'Academic science and the birth of industrial research laboratories in the U.S. pharmaceutical industry', *Journal of Economic Behavior and Organization*, 63: 756–76.

Giovanni, F. (2008) *Feeding the World: An Economic History of Agriculture, 1800–2000*, Princeton, NJ: Princeton University Press.

Goldin, C. and Katz, L.F. (2002) 'The power of the pill: oral contraceptives and women's career and marriage decisions', *Journal of Political Economy*, 110: 730–70.

——(2008) *The Race between Education and Technology*, Cambridge, MA: Belknap Press.

Gordon, R.J. (2000) 'Does the "new economy" measure up to the great inventions of the past?' *Journal of Economic Perspectives*, 14: 49–74.

Griliches, Z. (1990) 'Patent statistics as economic indicators: a survey', *Journal of Economic Literature*, 28: 1661–707.

Hansen, Z.K. and Libecap, G.D. (2004) 'Small farms, externalities, and the dust bowl of the 1930s', *Journal of Political Economy*, 112: 665–94.

Hartcup, G. (1988) *The Wars of Invention: Scientific Developments, 1914–1918*, London: Brassey's Defence Publishers.

Hounshell, D.A. and Smith, J.K. (1988) *Science and Corporate Strategy: DuPont R&d, 1902–1980*, New York: Cambridge University Press.

Jacob, M.C. (1997) *Scientific Culture and the Making of the Industrial West*, Oxford: Oxford University Press.

Jellison, K. (1993) *Entitled to Power: Farm Women and Technology, 1913–1963*, Chapel Hill, NC: University of North Carolina Press.

Jeremy, D.J. (1981) *Transatlantic Industrial Revolution: The Diffusion of Textile Technologies between Britain and America, 1790–1830s*, Cambridge, MA: MIT Press.

——(ed.) (1991) *International Technology Transfer: Europe, Japan, and the USA, 1700–1914*, Aldershot, UK: Edward Elgar.

Keller, W. (2002) 'Geographic localization of international technology diffusion', *American Economic Review*, 92: 120–42.

Khan, B.Z. (1995) 'Property rights and patent litigation in early nineteenth-century America', *Journal of Economic History*, 55: 58–97.

——(1996) 'Married women's property laws and female commercial activity: evidence from United States patent records, 1790–1895', *Journal of Economic History*, 56: 356–88.

——(2000) '"Not for ornament": patenting activity by women inventors', *Journal of Interdisciplinary History*, 33: 159–95.

——(2005) *The Democratization of Invention: Patents and Copyrights in American Economic Development*, New York: Cambridge University Press.

——(2009) 'War and the returns to entrepreneurial innovation among U.S. patentees, 1790–1870', *Brussels Economic Review*, 52: 239–74.

——(2010) 'The evolution of useful knowledge: great inventors, science and technology in British economic development, 1750–1930', Bowdoin College Working Paper.

——(2011a) 'Premium inventions: patents and prizes as incentive mechanisms in Britain and the United States, 1750–1930', in D.L. Costa and N.R. Lamoreaux (eds) *Understanding Long-Run Economic Growth: Geography, Institutions, and the Knowledge Economy*, Chicago, IL: University of Chicago Press.

——(2011b) 'Antitrust and innovation before the Sherman Act', *Antitrust Law Journal*, 77: 757–86.

——(2012a) 'Of time and space: a spatial analysis of knowledge spillovers among patented and unpatented innovations', Bowdoin College Working Paper.

——(2012b) 'Going for gold: industrial fairs and innovation in the nineteenth-century United States', *Révue Economique* (forthcoming).

Khan, B.Z. and Sokoloff, K.L. (1998) 'Patent institutions, industrial organization and early technological change: Britain and the United States, 1790–1850', in M. Berg and K. Bruland (eds) *Technological Revolutions in Europe, 1760–1860*, London: Edward Elgar.

——(2001) 'The early development of intellectual property institutions in the United States', *Journal of Economic Perspectives*, 15: 233–46.

——(2004) 'Institutions and democratic invention in 19th-century America: evidence from "great inventors," 1790–1930', *American Economic Review*, 94: 395–401.

——(2006) 'Institutions and technological innovation during early economic growth: evidence from the great inventors of the United States, 1790–1930', in T. Eicher and C. Garcia-Penalosa (eds) *Institutions and Economic Growth*, Cambridge, MA: MIT Press: 123–58.

Lamoreaux, N.R. and Sokoloff, K.L. (1996) 'Long-term change in the organization of inventive activity', *Proceedings of the National Academy of Sciences*, 93: 12686–92.

Lamoreaux, N.R. and Sokoloff, K.L. (2000) 'The geography of invention in the American glass industry, 1870–1925', *Journal of Economic History*, 60: 700–29.

——(2001) 'Market trade in patents and the rise of a class of specialized inventors in the nineteenth-century United States', *American Economic Review*, 91: 39–44.

——(2005) 'The decline of the independent inventor: a Schumpeterian story?' NBER Working Paper, No. 11654.

Landes, D.S. (1999) *The Wealth and Poverty of Nations: Why Some Are So Rich and Some So Poor*, New York: W.W. Norton.

Liebowitz, S.J. and Margolis, S.E. (1995) 'Path dependence, lock-in, and history', *Journal of Law, Economics, and Organization*, 11: 204–26.

MacLeod, C. (1988) *Inventing the Industrial Revolution*, Cambridge: Cambridge University Press.

Mokyr, J. (1990) *The Lever of Riches: Technological Creativity and Economic Progress*, Oxford: Oxford University Press.

——(2002) *The Gifts of Athena: Historical Origins of the Knowledge Economy*, Princeton, NJ: Princeton University Press.

——(2010) *The Enlightened Economy: An Economic History of Britain, 1700–1850*, New Haven, CT: Yale University Press.

Moser, P. (2005) 'How do patent laws influence innovation? Evidence from nineteenth century world fairs', *American Economic Review*, 95: 1213–36.

Mowery, D.C. (1983) 'Industrial research and firm size, survival, and growth in American manufacturing, 1921–46: an assessment', *Journal of Economic History*, 43: 953–80.

Musson, A.E. and Robinson, E. (1969) *Science and Technology in the Industrial Revolution*, Toronto: University of Toronto Press.

Nicholas, T. (2003) 'Why Schumpeter was right: innovation, market power, and creative destruction in 1920s America', *Journal of Economic History*, 63: 1023–58.

North, D.C. and Thomas, R.P. (1973) *The Rise of the Western World*, Cambridge: Cambridge University Press.

Nuvolari, A. (2004) 'Collective invention during the British industrial revolution: the case of the Cornish pumping engine', *Cambridge Journal of Economics*, 28: 347–63.

Olmstead, A.L. and Rhode, P.W. (1995) 'Beyond the threshold: an analysis of the characteristics and behavior of early reaper adopters', *Journal of Economic History*, 55: 27–57.

——(2008) *Creating Abundance: Biological Innovation and American Agricultural Development*, New York: Cambridge University Press.

Penrose, E. (1951) *The Economics of the International Patent System*, Baltimore, Md: Johns Hopkins University Press.

Pomeranz, K. (2000) *The Great Divergence: China, Europe, and the Making of the Modern World Economy*, Princeton, NJ: Princeton University Press.

Puffert, Douglas J. (2002) 'Path dependence in spatial networks: the standardization of railway track gauge', *Explorations in Economic History*, 39: 282–314.

Rosenberg, N. (1974) 'Science, invention and economic growth', *Economic Journal*, 84: 90–108.

Rosenberg, N. and Trajtenberg, M. (2004) 'A general-purpose technology at work: the Corliss steam engine in the late-nineteenth-century United States', *Journal of Economic History*, 64: 61–99.

Rosenthal, J.L. and Wong, R.B. (2011) *Before and Beyond Divergence: The Politics of Economic Change in China and Europe*, Cambridge, MA: Harvard University Press.

Rostow, W.W. (1960) *The Stages of Economic Growth: A Non-Communist Manifesto*, Cambridge: Cambridge University Press.

Saxonhouse, G. (1974) 'A tale of Japanese technological diffusion in the Meiji period', *Journal of Economic History*, 34: 149–65.

Saxonhouse, G. and Wright, G. (1984) 'New evidence on the stubborn mule and the cotton industry, 1878–1920', *Economic History Review*, 37: 507–19.

Schumpeter, J.A. (1950) *Capitalism, Socialism and Democracy*, New York: Harper and Row.

Sokoloff, K.L. (1988) 'Inventive activity in early industrial America: evidence from patent records, 1790–1846', *Journal of Economic History*, 48: 813–50.

——(1992) 'Invention, innovation, and manufacturing productivity growth in the antebellum Northeast', in R.E. Gallman and J.J. Wallis (eds) *American Economic Growth and Standards of Living before the Civil War*, Chicago, IL: University of Chicago Press.

Sokoloff, K.L. and Khan, B.Z. (1990) 'The democratization of invention during early industrialization: evidence from the United States', *Journal of Economic History*, 50: 363–78.

Sombart, W. (1913) *Krieg und Kapitalismus*, Munich: Duncker and Humblot.

Stanley, A. (1993) *Mothers and Daughters of Invention: Notes for a Revised History of Technology*, Metuchen, NJ: Scarecrow Press.

Sullivan, R. (1989) 'England's "age of invention": the acceleration of patents and patentable invention during the industrial revolution', *Explorations in Economic History*, 26: 424–52.

Sutthiphisal, D. (2006) 'Learning-by-producing and the geographic links between invention and production: experience from the second industrial revolution', *Journal of Economic History*, 66: 992–1025.

Wilkins, M. (1970) *The Emergence of Multinational Enterprise: American Business Abroad from the Colonial Era to 1914*, Cambridge, MA: Harvard University Press.

——(1974) 'The role of private business in the international diffusion of technology', *Journal of Economic History*, 34: 166–88.

Wong, B. (1998) *China Transformed: Historical Change and the Limits of European Experience*, Ithaca, NY: Cornell University Press.

7

ECONOMIC HISTORY AND ENTREPRENEURSHIP

Robert Whaples

Entrepreneurs have played a profound role in shaping and reshaping the economy and society – both historically and in the present. When *USA Today* celebrated its twenty-fifth anniversary in 2007 by compiling a list of the 25 most influential people of the past quarter century, at the top of the list was an entrepreneur (Microsoft's Bill Gates) and not far behind were six more well-known entrepreneurs (Oprah Winfrey, Google's Sergey Brin and Larry Page, Starbucks' Howard Schultz, Wal-Mart's Sam Walton, and hip-hop impresario Russell Simmons). Likewise, since 1990, *Time* magazine has selected five entrepreneurs as Person of the Year – media magnate Ted Turner, Intel's Andy Grove, Amazon.com's Jeff Bezos, Bill Gates, and Facebook's Mark Zuckerberg. Despite this public acclaim, however, entrepreneurs are virtually absent from textbooks written by both economists and economic historians.

This chapter begins by defining entrepreneurship, examining the roles entrepreneurs play in the economy, and discussing why entrepreneurship is difficult to analyze using the standard approach of economics. It closes by examining recent research on the historical roles and impact of entrepreneurship and the actions of individual entrepreneurs.

What is entrepreneurship?

What is an entrepreneur? Unfortunately, there is much less consensus among economists about how to define this term than for other inputs to production, such as labor, capital, and natural resources. While the French roots of the term *"entreprendre"* clearly denote someone who "undertakes" a business project,[1] Hébert and Link (2009: 100–1) summarize over two centuries of economic thought by identifying 12 roles attributed to entrepreneurs: the entrepreneur is (1) a person who assumes the risk associated with uncertainty, (2) a person who supplies financial capital, (3) an innovator, (4) a decision maker, (5) an industrial leader, (6) a manager or superintendent, (7) an organizer and coordinator of economic resources, (8) the owner of an enterprise, (9) an employer of factors of production, (10) a contractor, (11) an arbitrageur, and/or (12) an allocator of resources among alternative uses. Concisely combining these roles, Sobel (2008) defines an entrepreneur as someone who "organizes, manages and assumes the risks of a business or other enterprise."

Almost all modern theories of entrepreneurship take their origin from Joseph Schumpeter (Hébert and Link 2009), who placed the innovative entrepreneur at the center of his theory of economic development.[2] In Schumpeter's view, someone "is an entrepreneur only when he actually 'carries out new combinations'" and "he loses this function when he has built up his business, when he settles down to running it as other people run their businesses." "The carrying out of new combinations we call 'enterprise'; the individuals whose function it is to carry them out we call 'entrepreneurs'" (Schumpeter 1934: 78, 74). Schumpeter identified five important types of innovations that these entrepreneurial "Carusos" introduce into the economy. These new combinations include the following:

> 1) The introduction of a new good – that is one with which consumers are not yet familiar – or of a new quality of a good. 2) The introduction of a new method of production, that is, one not yet tested by experience ... which need by no means be founded upon a discovery scientifically new, and can also exist in a new way of handling a commodity commercially. 3) The opening of a new market ... 4) The conquest of a new source of supply of raw materials or half-manufactured goods, again irrespective of whether this source already exists or whether it has first to be created. 5) The carrying out of the new organization of any industry, like the creation of a monopoly position ... or the breaking up a monopoly position. (Schumpeter 1934: 66)

Many businessmen or women do one or more of these activities occasionally, but entrepreneurs specialize in them.

Although, from Schumpeter's point of view, innovation is the key to understanding entrepreneurship's impact, it must be realized that entrepreneurs also copy the successful ideas of their competitors and it is often hard to separate innovation from replication. So, despite Schumpeter's emphasis, in common parlance the term "entrepreneur" has been applied not just to innovators but also to virtually anyone who owns and runs a business. Marshall (1920: 597) distinguished between "active" entrepreneurs – "those who open out new and improved methods of business" – and passive entrepreneurs, who "follow beaten tracks." In this view, history is full of entrepreneurs along a sliding scale from those active entrepreneurs who concentrate on innovation to the mostly passive entrepreneurs who mainly copy what others are doing but occasionally show a wisp of novelty amid their other insights.

Why studying entrepreneurship is so difficult

Despite considerable attention from Schumpeter, Marshall, Walras and other leading economists, modern economists have tended to avoid the topic of entrepreneurs and entrepreneurship because of difficulties they have dealing with entrepreneurship on both an empirical and a theoretical level. On the empirical side, it is virtually impossible to measure entrepreneurship in a meaningful way in order to quantitatively assess differences in entrepreneurship across time and space and to econometrically estimate the impact that it has had on economic structure, performance, and growth. As Hébert and Link (2009: xix) point out, "some views" of economists on the roles of entrepreneurs "are competing; some are complementary. The entrepreneur ... is a difficult person to pin down; entrepreneurship ... is a difficult activity or mindset to pin down." A growing empirical literature equates entrepreneurship with self-employment, but this can be unhelpful in at least two important ways. First, self-employed workers in many fields – landscapers, plumbers, truck drivers, accountants, day-care operators, and hair stylists, for example – rarely make economically meaningful innovations. More importantly, the most economically important entrepreneurs aren't self-employed, but rather build and manage corporations with thousands of employees.

On the theoretical side, economics arrives at fundamentally important insights by wrestling with abstract forces like "supply," "demand," and "general equilibrium," but hiding behind the shifts and movements in the black box of this system are the actions of entrepreneurs. Economists generally take markets as a given and analyze how impersonal forces like "entry" almost automatically play out. Entrepreneurs are often these entrants, but they also *create* new markets – and the sources of these creative insights and actions, which are the heart and soul of entrepreneurship, is something economic theory has a hard time handling (Casson 2010). Economics tends to focus on systems moving toward equilibrium but entrepreneurs dis-equilibrate the economy. Economics is about maximizing given a set of constraints, but entrepreneurship is also about changing the constraints that are faced – changing them in unpredictable ways that cannot easily be modeled. Neoclassic economic models often assume costless information and perfect markets. This first assumption trivializes entrepreneurial decision making and the second makes the entrepreneur superfluous – since markets anonymously coordinate everything. In standard microeconomic theory, the person (or people) running a firm:

> becomes a passive calculator that reacts mechanically to changes imposed ... by fortuitous external developments over which it does not attempt to exert any influence. One encounters no clever ruses, ingenious schemes, brilliant innovations, charisma, or any of the other stuff of which outstanding entrepreneurship is made (Baumol 2010: 14)

and that's the problem.

A well-known joke about the mind-set of economists captures this point. Two economists are walking down the street. One spots a $100 bill lying on the sidewalk and remarks, "Wow! There's a $100 bill." The other assures him, "That can't be a $100 bill. If it was, somebody would have already picked it up." The point is that economists tend to assume that profit opportunities will be obvious to everyone and, therefore, quickly seized and eliminated. Entrepreneurs, in contrast, are constantly on the lookout for opportunities, so they are the ones who recognize that something that looks like a piece of trash to everyone else may actually be a $100 bill. They search for $100 bills in places others wouldn't look – down in the storm drain, rather than on the sidewalk – and then try to figure out ways to pick up the hard-to-get bills. They don't simply *find* hundred dollar bills, they painstakingly, insightfully *make* them – and get others to collaborate with them in making them. And they often fail in these attempts, "wasting" resources when others beat them in the race to get the $100 bill or when it turns out that what others thought was a piece of trash was indeed rubbish.

An economy moves up along the supply of entrepreneurship curve when the expected payoff to entrepreneurship rises, but research suggests that deeper forces are the key to differences in the supply over time and across space. The forces that shift the supply curve are largely "non-economic," but rather are tied to social psychology, social arrangements, and cultural developments that encourage or discourage individuals from taking on entrepreneurial roles. The richest source of professional baseball players today is San Pedro de Macoris in the Dominican Republic. There is no indication that natives of San Pedro are naturally better athletes than the rest of the world's population. The key appears to be a cultural system in which success at baseball is nurtured literally from the cradle (Ruck 1991). As with baseball, so with entrepreneurship. Some societies actively encourage and foster entrepreneurship – and these are the ones in which entrepreneurship flourishes, whose supply is the greatest for a given rate of return.

Traits of successful entrepreneurs

Successful entrepreneurship involves honing a set of scarce talents and aspirations. It requires some combination of vision, good judgment, creativity, ingenuity, problem-solving abilities, hard work, persistence, leadership skills, networking abilities, courage – a willingness to take risks – and almost always the ability to *enjoy* putting these talents together in running an enterprise. These are hard to model, especially the sheer *drive* – the desire to do battle in the marketplace – that animates them all. Some have argued that entrepreneurial success is a bit like winning the lottery – it takes a lot of luck to be in the right place at the right time and head up the right path, and potentially brilliant entrepreneurial strategies may fail due to unforeseen changes in the economy and the competitive playing field (Nye 1991).

What makes entrepreneurs entrepreneurial? After interviewing 30 entrepreneurs who founded companies with market values exceeding $200 million and asking them to work their way through a 17-page problem relating to starting a new enterprise, Sarasvathy (2004) concludes that entrepreneurs are generally good causal reasoners – capable of figuring out the optimal solution to a pre-determined goal when faced with a given set of means – but that they must also be good effectual reasoners. Effectual reasoning begins with a set of means and allows the goals to emerge. Effectual reasoners begin with 1) who they are – their traits, tastes, and abilities, 2) what they know through their education and experience, and 3) who they know – then jump into action in uncharted territory knowing that plans must be made and remade as surprises emerge. The ability to deal with risks that can't be calculated (Knightian risk) is key. Predictable markets go to smart people with deep pockets who take over from entrepreneurs after the market becomes more predictable.

The history of entrepreneurship: the pre-modern era

As Baumol and Strom (2010) argue, far more than other topics in economics, the study of entrepreneurship must turn to *nonstatistical* history for the bulk of its evidence. *The Invention of Enterprise: Entrepreneurship from Ancient Mesopotamia to Modern Times* (Landes *et al.* 2010) adeptly surveys much research by economic historians on the history of entrepreneurship. In the opening chapter, Hudson argues that the typical attitude in low-surplus communities living near subsistence levels throughout much of history is that self-seeking tends to achieve gains at the expense of others. Traditional social values therefore impose sanctions against the accumulation of personal wealth and "archaic political correctness dictated" that surpluses "should be consumed, typically by public display and gift exchange, provisioning feasts at major rites of passage ... or burial of the dead. Status under such conditions is gained by giving away one's wealth" and not by entrepreneurially reinvesting it. "Profit-seeking 'economic' exchange was so great a leap that initially it seems to have been conducted mainly in association with public institutions, at least nominally. The first documented 'households' to be economically managed were those of Mesopotamia's temples" (Hudson 2010: 10–11). Thus, early entrepreneurs were faced with far different constraints than modern ones. The modern distinction between the public and private sectors was not applicable and these entrepreneurs saw no conflict of interest between their position in the temple or palace bureaucracy and the family business – but the individual payoff from entrepreneurship could be very low since gains were expected to be shared.

In contrast to this nascent positive-sum entrepreneurship of ancient Mesopotamia, Hudson argues that greatest fortunes in ancient times went to predatory entrepreneurs and were made by conquering or administering foreign lands and collecting taxes from defeated populations.

Likewise, Baumol (1990: 897) points out that if "entrepreneurs are defined, simply, to be persons who are ingenious and creative in finding ways that add to their own wealth, power, and prestige," then entrepreneurship can be productive, but also *unproductive* and *destructive*. Entrepreneurship is likely to be unproductive – a zero-sum game – when the economy gives incentives to rent-seeking. Entrepreneurship turns to destructive activities when big payoffs come from conquest, enslavement, and the extraction of tribute – and Baumol holds up ancient Rome, Medieval China, and the early Middle Ages as eras with rampant destructive entrepreneurship.[3] Thus, in pre-modern times those with entrepreneurial talents haven't been drawn toward the business world: the "dirty work of running an innovative enterprise has seemed mean and unglamorous by comparison" with heroic military action, status-enhancing friendship and rent-seeking with the rulers (Baumol and Strom 2010: 532).

One explanation of the achievement of modern economic growth is that societies finally began channeling the talents of entrepreneurs away from negative- and zero-sum activities that benefited themselves at the expense of others toward economic activities that benefited society at large. North *et al.* (2009) compare "closed access" societies – the norm throughout most of history – to modern, democratic "open access" societies, which clear away the barriers to productive entrepreneurship. They argue that, because powerful individuals always have the option of competing for resources or status through violence, these "violence specialists" stop fighting only when they perceive that it is in others' interests not to fight, an expectation that specialists must share about each other. Thus, throughout most of history, elites agree to respect each other's privileges only when they know that violence will reduce their own wealth and power. Prospering from these privileges, in turn, requires help from nonmilitary specialists in other activities. Nonmilitary elites are cemented into the ruling coalition through privileged access to vital state-supported functions like religion, justice, production, or trade. The incentives embedded in these organizations produce a "double balance" – a correspondence between the distribution of military and political power on the one hand and the distribution of economic power on the other. In "closed access" societies, access to political power, economic power, and entrepreneurship is limited because rents will be dissipated if the elite coalition gets too big. Thus the activities of many budding entrepreneurs are thwarted because they may weaken the political and economic power of the entrenched elites. In societies like this, economic growth and positive-sum entrepreneurship are stymied by the insecurity of property rights, confiscation of property, and the inability to enforce contracts because courts are not independent and many in the elite remain above the law.

The history of entrepreneurship: the modern era

As the legal infrastructure supporting entrepreneurship was built up in the modern era, other impediments remained, however. Commercial codes and laws allowing general incorporation allowed entrepreneurs to reduce risk and tap into wider financial networks, but cultural norms often diverted entrepreneurial talent. Hau, for example, argues that among the barriers to the diffusion of entrepreneurship in France in the 1800s were the attraction of gentry status and high public office for the elite, and the disdain and radical protests of intellectual and artistic elites who often despised businessmen. "A part of the entrepreneurial elite conceived enterprise as a way to gain a fortune, to buy land, and to enter into the gentry," as in the case of Auguste-Thomas Pouyer-Quertier who developed a large cotton-spinning factory, but was then elected deputy to the French parliament and eventually Minister of Finance. He began to neglect his firm, which declined – and married his daughters to noblemen (Hau 2010: 307). Factors like these, along with traditional religious beliefs, often held back the supply of entrepreneurship – which may explain why individuals from outsider groups and minority sects appear to have been disproportionately overrepresented among the ranks of entrepreneurs in many places.

Mokyr argues that one impetus to Britain's Industrial Revolution was the coupling of individuals with technical skill and entrepreneurs with commercial acumen – exemplified by the case of inventor James Watt and entrepreneur Matthew Bolton:

> The complementarity was symmetric: those with technical ability ... needed people who could run a business, understood markets, knew about the recruitment and management of workers and foremen, had access to credit and other technical consultants, and above all, were ready to accept the uncertainties of innovation. (Mokyr 2010: 187)

Mokyr identifies a culture of "gentlemen-entrepreneur" that developed in Britain, where access to credit, suppliers, partners, and opportunities was tied to a Christian code of conduct that emphasized consistency, integrity, and the fulfillment of obligations to signal that a person was a trustworthy business contact. "It was, above all, important not to come across as greedy and rapacious" (Mokyr 2010: 189). These networks allowed for risk-reducing diversification.

Casson and Godley (2010) argue that the British economy in the 1800s and early 1900s was marked by a project-based entrepreneurship in the form of thousands of free-standing companies created to invest in and develop a specific activity – often international in scope such as tin mining in Malaya, hardwood cultivation in Burma, or electric power plants in Latin America. These risky projects took considerable time to develop, their outcomes were uncertain, resources had to be irreversibly committed to them, and they often had to be undertaken on a large scale, thus requiring teams of entrepreneurs to work together.

Countering the idea of the entrepreneur as individualist, historically much entrepreneurship has occurred within family businesses. Chan's research on China suggests that many successful entrepreneurial firms started with teams of two brothers who complemented each other in talent and personalities: "one brother excelled in vision, innovation and risk-taking, while the other provided organization, systemized the books and other operations, and nurtured the staff and networked with a wide circle of associates" (Chan 2010: 482). This pattern is not unique to Asia; indeed many of the most successful entrepreneurs in American history had lesser-known brothers playing key roles in their businesses. Organizer Roy Disney complemented innovator Walt. Andrew Carnegie's brother Tom took care of many day-to-day concerns. Andrew Mellon took over and grew his successful father's business and his virtually unfailing business judgments were complemented by those of his brother, Dick. The Mellon brothers – who built up a sprawling financial and industrial empire that included Alcoa and Gulf Oil – unfailingly worked as a team (Cannadine 2008). On the other hand, when Cornelius Vanderbilt was disappointed by the business abilities of his sons, he turned to his sons-in-law to supply the complementary day-to-day organizational and management abilities to help implement his entrepreneurial innovations (Stiles 2009).

Entrepreneurship in the United States

Because it is difficult to measure entrepreneurship, it is hard to precisely pinpoint periods and places in which it has flourished and in which it has atrophied. Despite these difficulties, virtually all contemporary observers and historians have characterized the American economy as uniquely entrepreneurial. The general consensus is that the period from the end of the Civil War up to about 1920 was a "golden age" for the entrepreneur (Lamoreaux 2010, quoting Schumpeter 1942 and Hughes 1989) in which:

Americans knew the names and avidly followed the exploits of the period's 'captains of industry,' ... devoured the rags-to-riches novels of Horatio Alger, poured over P.T. Barnum's *The Art of Making Money* and other success manuals ... There was no higher goal for a young American male to pursue during this period than to become a 'self-made man' – to make a great deal of money through dint of his own hard work and 'pluck' (Lamoureaux 2010: 368–9).

McCormick and Folsom (2003) surveyed business historians to construct a list of the 25 greatest entrepreneurs in U.S. history. Seven of the 25 were born between 1835 and 1847 and, therefore, were active in business during the golden age in the decades after the Civil War.[4]

However, the rise of big business during this golden age of entrepreneurship eventually succeeded in choking off the demand for entrepreneurship, as the need for increasing amounts of capital in the railroad, petroleum, and other industries eventually left less room for the individual entrepreneur or group of partners who built, managed, and controlled their own business. Thus an entrepreneurial age matured and gave way to an era of big business, merger, and consolidation, as "organization men" began to displace entrepreneurs in driving the economy – and public attitudes began to sour toward business, especially with the onset of the Great Depression, the rise of labor unions, and regulations that hemmed in traditional entrepreneurial prerogatives and strategies. After the shared sacrifice of the Second World War, individual power and wealth – as exemplified by successful entrepreneurs – became suspect to many. However, in the last decades of the twentieth century, the tables were turned; encouragement and celebration of entrepreneurship rose again with entrepreneurial success in newer industries, especially in computers, biotech, and information technology. New technologies reduced the efficiency advantages of the largest firms and provided space for entrepreneurs to flourish (Graham 2010). Deregulation allowed the entry of new firms. The employment share of the nation's 500 largest firms fell from 20 per cent in 1970 to 8.5 per cent in 1996 – and the decline in self-employment bottomed out and began to rise (Carree and Thurik 2003). The reemergence of venture capitalists – private banks and wealthy individuals who provided investment money for start-up ventures – spurred this transition. Reestablishing a pattern of entrepreneurial firms spinning off from established firms, Silicon Valley replicated the early auto industry (Klepper 2007).

Lessons from the lives of individual entrepreneurs

Textbook economic models are a useful starting place but the complexity and dynamics of real-world economies can be grasped more clearly by examining the lives and careers of individual entrepreneurs in light of these economic models. Fortunately, there is growing stock of insightful biographies on American entrepreneurs to draw upon, including Klein (1986) on Jay Gould; Chernow (1998) on John Rockefeller; Bundles (2001) on Madam C.J. Walker, African-American beauty care products pioneer; Weightman (2003) on Frederic Tudor; Watts (2005) on Henry Ford; Nasaw (2006) on Andrew Carnegie; Stiles (2009) on Cornelius Vanderbilt; Martello (2010) on Paul Revere; Dalzell (2010) on Frank Sprague, developer of the first successful electric street car system; and Isaacson (2011) on Steve Jobs. Tedlow (2001) insightfully analyzes the careers of Andrew Carnegie, George Eastman, Henry Ford, Thomas J. Watson, Sr., Charles Revson, Sam Walton, and Robert Noyce. In addition, Klein draws a collective portrait of 26 American entrepreneurs.[5] He emphasizes their creativity and concludes that, because entrepreneurs occupy a "place on a broad spectrum of creativity that includes artists, scientists, political figures, and mathematicians, among others ... riches alone seldom if ever fulfill the inner need that drives them" (Klein 2003: xii–xiii).

A little-known entrepreneur, Frederic Tudor, exemplifies and embodies many of the themes of this chapter. Tudor ultimately introduced a new good, brought it to new markets, developed new methods of production and conquered new sources of supply – innovating in almost all of the classic Schumpeterian manners. Tudor's brilliant idea was to bring ice from the frozen ponds of New England to people sweltering in hot climates. He closely guarded his initial plans, but needn't have bothered because no one else seemed to think this was a $100 bill waiting to be picked up.

> The idea was considered so utterly absurd by the sober minded merchants as to be the vagary of a disordered brain, and few men would have been willing to stand the scoffs and sneers from those whose assistance it was necessary to obtain and aid [Tudor] in his enterprise … Merchants were not willing to charter their vessels to carry ice. The offices declined to insure and sailors were afraid to trust themselves with such a cargo. (Weightman 2003: 27)

Tudor was forced to buy his own ship to transport the ice but, as predicted, lost money on his first venture (in 1806) – not because the ice damaged the ship but because he had no effective way to market the ice in the Caribbean. Initially he knew virtually nothing about the demand for his product, how to market it, how to cut, transport and distribute it efficiently, and how to run a business. He battled predatory government officials, disease, bad weather, Jefferson's trade embargo, and disruptions due to war. He persisted as his family's wealth dwindled and he systematically discovered more efficient ways to harvest, transport, and store ice. In 1813 he was thrown into a debtors' prison but recalled:

> I smiled to think that any one should believe I was beaten, or in the slightest degree daunted in the steady purpose I had formed of accomplishing the payment of every dollar of debt and lifting myself to lord it or, if I chose, my humble creditors and his instrument. I never doubted I should accomplish what I have accomplished. (Weightman 2003: 56)

Ultimately, he built a profitable business that sold ice in the U.S. South, the Caribbean, and India. Inevitably, his success bred competition, but his understanding of the industry earned him above-normal profits and, when he fell into debt due to ill-advised speculation in the coffee market, his creditors elected not to seize his business but to allow him to run it as a surer way to assure that the debts were repaid.

Examining John Rockefeller's path from bookkeeper to Titan of the oil industry demonstrates the impact that an individual entrepreneur can have on the economy. Rockefeller's track record as a trustworthy, competent businessman made him a magnet for investors seeking to profit from the discovery of oil in Western Pennsylvania. Unlike other investors, he was in it for the long haul and so worked relentlessly and systematically to reduce refining costs, to pour his profits back into the industry, and to organize his competitors to stabilize the market. As his firm grew larger, it was in a position to negotiate rebates from railroads and build its own pipelines, magnifying its cost advantages and allowing it to purchase and merge with rivals as Standard Oil became a feared monopoly. Once this position was achieved, he and his colleagues pioneered industrial warfare techniques – including predatory price cutting, legislatively created barriers to entry, and cost-cutting innovations – to block potential entrants. Rockefeller took great personal risks, trusting that God's providence and his own intelligent business decisions would make him successful. In 1885 a vast new oil field was discovered near Lima, Ohio, but the oil's sulfur content was so high that it wasn't economically useful. Rockefeller concluded, "It seemed … impossible that this great product had come to the surface to be wasted and thrown away," and he "imported a distinguished, German-born chemist named Herman Frasch and gave him simple marching orders: Banish the odor from Lima crude and turn it into a marketable commodity." His strategy was to buy up vast quantities of this oil at rock-bottom prices and assume that Frasch would be successful. The majority of Standard's board objected, whereupon Rockefeller stunned them by pledging to fund the project with his own money. "[I]f it is a success the company can reimburse me. If it is a failure, I will take the loss" (Chernow 1998: 285). This convinced the rest of his partners to fund the project, which reaped immense profits and strengthened Standard's monopoly position. Yet, no one has a monopoly on entrepreneurial abilities, and eventually entrants found ways to crack the petroleum market, even before the Supreme Court broke up Standard Oil in 1911.

Entrepreneurs and economic growth

Historical comparisons strongly suggest that nations with more entrepreneurial cultures and stronger encouragement for entrepreneurs have higher rates of economic growth, but showing causation rather than only correlation is nearly impossible, as is quantifying the magnitude of the relationship. This correlation has been demonstrated by Acs and Szerb (2009), who find the strongest correlation between per capita income and measures of cultural support for entrepreneurship, lack of fear of the consequences of businesses failure, and networking. The countries ranking highest on Acs and Szerb's index of entrepreneurship (Denmark, Sweden, New Zealand, the U.S., Australia, and Canada) are economic leaders, while those at the bottom (Uganda, Ecuador, Bolivia, Iran, the Philippines, and Venezuela) are much less developed. Acs *et al.* (2005) attempt to explain the recent "European paradox" – European economic growth rates have lagged behind the U.S. despite high levels of investment in human capital and research. They argue that entrepreneurship is the key, that countries with stronger entrepreneurship turn these investments in knowledge into higher rates of growth. Their empirical estimates, using data on 18 countries from 1981 to 1998, suggest a positive and statistically significant impact of entrepreneurship on economic growth. Unfortunately, however, they are compelled to measure entrepreneurship via self-employment rates.

Acs *et al.* (2007) argue that a unique feature of American capitalism is that successful American entrepreneurs often become philanthropists who create foundations that, in turn, contribute to economic prosperity through knowledge creation. One prominent example is Andrew Carnegie, who argued in his essay *The Gospel of Wealth* (1889) that "the man who dies rich dies disgraced," because the wealthy man should "consider all surplus revenues which come to him simply as trust funds, which he is called upon to administer." Excess wealth should be distributed by the man who created it, because of his superior wisdom, experience, and ability to administer, according to Carnegie. With these talents, he could do more to elevate the populace than they or the state could ever do. Carnegie emphasized that wealth should not be given to "charity," but that it should go to libraries, schools, museums and other projects that helped those who would help themselves. By the time of his death in 1919, he had overseen the distribution of nearly $350 million (about $4.5 billion in 2011 dollars). John Rockefeller followed a similar path, focusing on education and medical research in his philanthropic giving. Among his foundation's achievements was a project that virtually eliminated hookworm around the world – thereby increasing the productivity of millions of poor people. The largest foundations in the U.S. were founded by some of the most successful entrepreneurs of the twentieth century including Bill Gates, Henry Ford, J. Paul Getty, Robert Wood Johnson's family

(Johnson & Johnson), W.K. Kellogg, William Hewlett, David Packard, John D. MacArthur, Gordon Moore, and the Lilly family.

Despite this additional channel of economic growth, it's hard to argue with Baumol's (2010) conclusion that the biggest gains from entrepreneurship come from the huge positive spillovers brought about by the innovations they unleash, or John Rockefeller's conclusion that his most important service wasn't through his philanthropies but passing along cost savings to the millions of customers who bought his company's products.

Notes

1 Originally the term referred to battlefield commanders and only gradually was the meaning transferred to the business world.
2 See McCraw's (2007) fascinating, Pulitzer-Prize-winning biography of Schumpeter.
3 This characterization of ancient Rome has been criticized by Temin and others.
4 Here are the ranking and birth years of these entrepreneurs: 1) Henry Ford (1863), 2) Bill Gates (1955), 3) John Rockefeller (1839), 4) Andrew Carnegie (1835), 5) Thomas Edison (1847), 6) Sam Walton (1918), 7) J.P. Morgan (1837), 8) Alfred Sloan (1875), 9) Walt Disney (1901), 10) Ray Kroc (1902), 11) Thomas Watson, Sr. (1874), 12) Alexander Graham Bell (1847), 13) Eli Whitney (1765), 14) James J. Hill (1838), 15) Jack Welch (1935), 16) Cyrus McCormick (1809), 17–18) David Packard (1912) and William Hewlett (1913), 19) Cornelius Vanderbilt (1794), 20) George Westinghouse (1846), 21) Pierre DuPont (1870), 22) Steve Jobs (1955), 23) Michael Dell (1965), 24) Thomas Watson, Jr. (1914), and 25) John Jacob Astor (1763).
5 Klein's entrepreneurs are Warren Buffett, Andrew Carnegie, Pierre DuPont, James B. Duke, William Durant, George Eastman, Thomas Edison, Henry Ford, Bill Gates, Jay Gould, Edward H. Harriman, Samuel Insull, Ray Kroc, Edwin Land, Cyrus McCormick, Robert Noyce, John Patterson, J.C. Penney, John Rockefeller, Theodore Vail, Cornelius Vanderbilt, Sam Walton, John Wanamaker, Thomas Watson, George Westinghouse, and Frank Woolworth.

References

Acs, Z. and Szerb, L. (2009) 'The global entrepreneurship index (GEINDEX)', *Foundations and Trends in Entrepreneurship*, 5: 341–435.
Acs, Z., Audretsch, D., Braunerhjelm, P. and Carlsson, B. (2005) 'Growth and entrepreneurship: an empirical assessment', CEPR Discussion Paper No. 5409.
Acs, Z., Audretsch, D., Phillips, R.J. and Desai, S. (2007) 'The entrepreneurship–philanthropy nexus: nonmarket source of American entrepreneurial capitalism', Jena Economic Research Papers.
Baumol, W.J. (1990) 'Entrepreneurship: productive, unproductive, and destructive', *Journal of Political Economy*, 98: 893–921.
Baumol, W.J. (2010) *The Microtheory of Innovative Entrepreneurship*, Princeton, NJ: Princeton University Press.
Baumol, W.J. and Strom, R.J. (2010) '"Useful knowledge" of entrepreneurship: some implications of the history', in D.S. Landes, J. Mokyr and W.J. Baumol (eds) *The Invention of Enterprise: Entrepreneurship from Ancient Mesopotamia to Modern Times*, Princeton, NJ: Princeton University Press.
Bundles, A. (2001) *On Her Own Ground: The Life and Times of Madam C.J. Walker*, New York: Washington Square Press.
Cannadine, D. (2008) *Mellon: An American Life*. New York: Vintage.
Carnegie, A. (1889) *The Gospel of Wealth*, London: F.C. Hagen.
Carree, M.A. and Thurik, A.R. (2003) 'The impact of entrepreneurship on economic growth', in Z.J. Acs and D.B. Audretsch (eds) *Handbook of Entrepreneurship Research: An Interdisciplinary Survey and Introduction*, Boston, MA: Kluwer.
Casson, M. (2010) *Entrepreneurship: Theory, Networks, History*, Cheltenham: Edward Elgar.
Casson, M. and Godley, A. (2010) 'Entrepreneurship in Britain, 1830–1900', in D.S. Landes, J. Mokyr and W.J. Baumol (eds) *The Invention of Enterprise: Entrepreneurship from Ancient Mesopotamia to Modern Times*, Princeton, NJ: Princeton University Press.
Chan, W.K.K. (2010) 'Chinese entrepreneurship since its late imperial period,' in D.S. Landes, J. Mokyr and W.J. Baumol (eds) *The Invention of Enterprise: Entrepreneurship from Ancient Mesopotamia to Modern Times*, Princeton, NJ: Princeton University Press.

Chernow, R. (1998) *Titan: The Life of John D. Rockefeller, Jr.*, New York: Random House.

Dalzell, F. (2010) *Engineering Innovation: Frank J. Sprague and the U.S. Electrical Industry*, Cambridge, MA: MIT Press.

Graham, M.B.W. (2010) 'Entrepreneurship in the United States, 1920–2000', in D.S. Landes, J. Mokyr and W.J. Baumol (eds) *The Invention of Enterprise: Entrepreneurship from Ancient Mesopotamia to Modern Times*, Princeton, NJ: Princeton University Press.

Hau, M. (2010) 'Entrepreneurship in France', in D.S. Landes, J. Mokyr and W.J. Baumol (eds) *The Invention of Enterprise: Entrepreneurship from Ancient Mesopotamia to Modern Times*, Princeton, NJ: Princeton University Press.

Hébert, R.F. and Link, A.N. (2009) *The History of Entrepreneurship*, New York: Routledge.

Hudson, M. (2010) 'Entrepreneurs: from the near eastern takeoff to the Roman collapse', in D.S. Landes, J. Mokyr and W.J. Baumol (eds) *The Invention of Enterprise: Entrepreneurship from Ancient Mesopotamia to Modern Times*, Princeton, NJ: Princeton University Press.

Isaacson, W. (2011) *Steve Jobs*, New York: Simon and Schuster.

Klein, M. (1986) *The Life and Legend of Jay Gould*, Baltimore, Md: Johns Hopkins University Press.

——(2003) *The Change Makers: From Carnegie to Gates, and How Great Entrepreneurs Transformed Ideas into Industries*, New York: Henry Holt.

Klepper, S. (2007) 'Silicon Valley: a chip off the old Detroit block', in D.B. Audretsch and R. Strom (eds) *Entrepreneurship, Growth and Public Policy*, New York: Cambridge University Press.

Lamoreaux, N. (2010) 'Entrepreneurship in the United States, 1865–1920', in D.S. Landes, J. Mokyr and W.J. Baumol (eds) *The Invention of Enterprise: Entrepreneurship from Ancient Mesopotamia to Modern Times*, Princeton, NJ: Princeton University Press.

Landes, D., Mokyr, J. and Baumol, W.J. (2010) *The Invention of Enterprise: Entrepreneurship from Ancient Mesopotamia to Modern Times*, Princeton, NJ: Princeton University Press.

Marshall, A. (1920) *Principles of Economics*, 8th edition, London: Macmillan.

Martello, R. (2010) *Midnight Ride, Industrial Dawn: Paul Revere and the Growth of American Enterprise*, Baltimore, Md: Johns Hopkins University Press.

McCormick, B. and Folsom, B.W. (2003) 'A survey of business historians on America's greatest entrepreneurs', *Business History Review*, 77: 703–16.

McCraw, T.K. (2007) *Prophet of Innovation: Joseph Schumpeter and Creative Destruction*, Cambridge, MA: Harvard University Press.

Mokyr, J. (2010) 'Entrepreneurship and the industrial revolution in Britain', in D.S. Landes, J. Mokyr and W.J. Baumol (eds) *The Invention of Enterprise: Entrepreneurship from Ancient Mesopotamia to Modern Times*, Princeton, NJ: Princeton University Press.

Nasaw, D. (2006) *Andrew Carnegie*, New York: Penguin.

North, D.C., Wallis, J.J. and Weingast, B.R. (2009) *Violence and Social Orders: A Conceptual Framework for Interpreting Recorded Human History*, New York: Cambridge University Press.

Nye, J.V. (1991) 'Lucky fools and cautious businessmen: on entrepreneurship and the measurement of entrepreneurial failure', in J. Mokyr (ed.) *The Vital One: Essays in Honor of Jonathan R.T. Hughes*, supplement to *Research in Economic History*, 6: 131–52.

Ruck, R. (1991) *The Tropic of Baseball: Baseball in the Dominican Republic*, Westport, CT: Meckler.

Sarasvathy, S.D. (2004) 'What makes entrepreneurs entrepreneurial?' Batten Briefings, Charlottesville, VA: Batten Institute, Darden Graduate School of Business Administration, University of Virginia, http://ssrn. com/abstract=909038

Schumpeter, J. (1934 [originally published 1912]) *The Theory of Economic Development*, Cambridge, MA: Harvard University Press.

Sobel, R. (2008) 'Entrepreneurship', *Concise Encyclopedia of Economics*, http://www.econlib.org/library/ Enc/Entrepreneurship.html

Stiles, T.J. (2009) *The First Tycoon: The Epic Life of Cornelius Vanderbilt*, New York: Knopf.

Tedlow, R.S. (2001) *Giants of Enterprise: Seven Business Innovators and the Empires They Built*, New York: Harper.

Watts, S. (2005) *The People's Tycoon: Henry Ford and the American Century*, New York: Knopf.

Weightman, G. (2003) *The Frozen-Water Trade: A True Story*, New York: Hyperion.

8

ECONOMIC HISTORY AND COMPETITION POLICY

Werner Troesken

This chapter considers the economic history of competition policy in the United States. The discussion is organized around five historical moments: the pre-1880 period; the creation of the Interstate Commerce Commission (ICC) in 1887; the passage of the Sherman Antitrust Act in 1890; the rise of municipally owned utilities and state utility commissions during the nineteenth and early twentieth centuries; and the privatization and deregulation movement of the 1970s and 1980s.

Antecedents of modern competition policy

The American marketplace before 1880 is sometimes characterized as "cowboy capitalism," a time and place where trade and economic activity was free and unfettered. This is correct only to the extent that one equates regulation with federal activity. Before 1880, most regulation occurred at the state and local level. Municipal governments, for example, regulated everything from the location of marketplaces to interest rates and prices. Laws regulating the location of trade sometimes had a public health rationale or were intended to prevent offensive trades, such as the slaughter of raw meat and the processing of offal, from adversely affecting nearby property owners. At the state level, governments passed bankruptcy laws, mortgage moratoria (usually declared unconstitutional), and other measures protecting farmers and debtors. Later, state laws regulated railroads and corporations (Hughes 1991; Novak 1996).

These state and local measures are sometimes interpreted as ineffectual and irrelevant, and there is some evidence to support such interpretations. For example, state-level antitrust enforcement appears to have been ineffective, though many large industrial enterprises were initially quite fearful of it, with stock prices plummeting on the announcement of prosecution (Troesken 1995). Yet in an era of (relatively) localized markets, a regulatory structure that devolved power to state and local governments might well have made economic sense. In addition, the development of state incorporation laws during this period facilitated the expansion of business and financial markets, and undermined the political corruption associated with the granting of special corporate charters (Bodenhorn 2006; Wallis 2005, 2006). There is also evidence that state regulatory regimes facilitated the development of the early telegraph industry (Nonnenmacher 2001).

The creation of the interstate commerce commission and the rise of the modern regulatory state

A convenient place to start the history of modern competition policy is with the passage of the Interstate Commerce Act (ICA) in 1887. Creating the ICC, the ICA sought to control the rates and competitive practices of interstate railroads. For a long time, traditional histories of the ICA and the ICC portrayed federal regulation of the railroads as a benevolent and rational measure that benefited farmers and other shippers. That story was based largely on four observations. First, state governments could not effectively control the rates charged by interstate railways because they were barred by the federal Constitution from interfering with economic activities that crossed state lines (Hovenkamp 1988). This constitutional obstacle was highlighted in *Wabash v. Illinois* (118 U.S. 557 1886).

Second, during the rapid inflation that accompanied the First World War, the ICC did not allow railroad rates to keep pace with the rising price level, and many private railroads were ruined (Martin 1971). One might interpret this as evidence that shippers had the upper hand at the ICC. Third, prior to federal regulation, there was greater competition on long-haul routes than on short-haul routes, giving rise to the paradoxical result that it could cost farmers more to ship short distances than long ones. Fourth, relative to agricultural commodity prices, railway rates were rising over the late nineteenth century and shipping costs could represent as much as 50 per cent of the final price of agricultural commodities (Higgs 1970). Given all this, it is easy to see why farmers might have pushed for more aggressive federal regulation.

But, starting in the 1960s, historians began questioning the traditional narrative that federal railroad regulation was all about protecting the well-being of farmers. Kolko (1965), for example, presented evidence that the railroads themselves wanted federal regulation partly as a means of helping forestall more hostile laws at the state level and of helping long-haul railroads collude. During the 1980s and 1990s, economic studies emerged to support this hypothesis. Based on event study methods, these analyses showed that the stock prices of railroads responded positively to the passage of the ICA and to subsequent court decisions affirming its regulatory powers (Binder 1985; Prager 1989). Presumably, if the ICC was designed to protect the interests of shippers, and not the railroads, stock prices would have fallen with passage of the measure. Evidence on how the ICC affected consumer welfare is mixed; depending on how one specifies the demand function, one can find either positive or negative effects on consumer welfare (Zerbe 1980; Winston 1981).

The origins and effects of federal antitrust enforcement

Modern antitrust enforcement began with passage of the Sherman Antitrust Act in 1890, the nation's first federal antitrust statute. Scholars typically appeal to one of three interpretations to explain why the Sherman Act was passed. First, the public-interest interpretation portrays the Sherman Act as a response to broad societal dissatisfaction with the trust movement. As evidence, Thorelli (1955: 133–43) points to the large number of books and articles by contemporary writers criticizing the trust movement. Further evidence for the public-interest interpretation comes from Bork (1966). Bork argues that Congressional debates over the Sherman Act reveal a clear legislative desire to promote consumer interests. In addition, scholars advancing the public-interest interpretation often emphasize the importance of populist farmers and agrarian agitation. As evidence, they cite the many petitions Congress received from farm groups requesting an antitrust law (Letwin 1965: 66–9; Thorelli 1955: 143–5).

These sources of evidence are problematic. The surveys of public opinion cited by Thorelli have been challenged by Galambos (1975), a more recent and systematic study. Surveying a broad cross section of publications from 1880 through 1940, Galambos identifies changes in the public opinion of big business. He finds that during the late 1880s and early 1890s, when Congress passed the Sherman Act, "public antagonism toward the large firm was not at a fever pitch," though it was slightly higher than it had been during the early 1880s (Galambos 1975: 64–76). Scholars have also challenged Bork's interpretation of Congressional debates. For example, Grandy (1993) reads the same debates and concludes that the primary goal of Congress was to protect the interests of small businesses, not consumers.

Also, the small business interpretation portrays the Sherman Act as an anticompetitive measure. According to this view, the Act was designed to "hamper the growth of large enterprises whose greater efficiency threatened the small business sector in many industries" (Stigler 1985). Direct evidence of the lobbying efforts of small businesses can be found in the letters of Senator John Sherman, after whom the Sherman Antitrust Act is named. Sherman received numerous letters from small oil refiners asking him to take action against Standard Oil. In response, Sherman introduced a measure amending the Interstate Commerce Act of 1887. If passed, the amendment would have prohibited the railroads from granting Standard Oil special rebates. Small oil companies, who typically did not receive such rebates, claimed the rebates gave Standard an unfair advantage. Besides introducing this amendment, Sherman also tried to appease the demands of the small oil companies by making several speeches denouncing Standard, by introducing antitrust legislation on three separate occasions, and by encouraging Ohio's attorney general to file an antitrust suit against Standard Oil (Troesken 2002).

Although this evidence clearly shows that small businesses lobbied for antitrust, it does not prove they were the dominant interest group in the political battle over antitrust; it only tells what small businesses wanted out of the battle. Moreover, there are at least two reasons to think the trusts, and not small businesses, were the dominant interest group. First, the same free-rider problems that lead economists to argue that small businesses were more powerful than consumers and farmers should also lead economists to argue that the trusts were at least as powerful as small businesses. Second, business and political historians maintain the trusts possessed significant political power in 1890 (e.g. Josephson 1934; Sklar 1988; Stephenson 1930). Given this power, it seems unlikely that the trusts would have allowed any legislation they found seriously threatening to become law.

Lastly, appeasement interpretations characterize the Sherman Act as "something of a fraud," because "it did nothing and solved nothing, except to still the cry for action against the trusts" (Friedman 1985: 464). To support this characterization, scholars frequently cite Senator Orville Platt of Connecticut. During the debate over the Sherman Act, Platt argued that his fellow senators were not interested in passing genuine antitrust legislation: they merely wanted something to appease their constituents (Josephson 1938: 460). While Platt implied that legislators passed a weak and ineffective law out of haste and indifference, many subsequent observers imply that legislators did so deliberately. The 51st Congress, they say, would never have passed a genuine antitrust law because "it was dominated at the time by many of the very industrial magnates most vulnerable to real antitrust legislation" (Fainsod and Gordon 1948: 450; Seager and Gulick 1929: 367–70). An event study confirms the appeasement hypothesis: the stock prices of major trust companies did not fall when the Act was passed, and might have even risen. This pattern suggests that investors believed the Sherman Act would not reduce the profitability of the trusts (Troesken 2000).

Evidence on the effects of antitrust enforcement after the Sherman Act run the gamut. If one examines landmark decisions dissolving large industrial enterprises such as Standard Oil and

American Tobacco, stock prices were not greatly affected by the dissolutions, in large part because the affected firms were able to contract around the court rulings at low cost (Binder 1988; Burns 1977; Prager 1992). Case studies of individual trusts suggest that market forces worked faster than antitrust regulators in disciplining monopolistic enterprises (Troesken 1998). In a series of papers, George Bittlingmayer presents evidence that antitrust enforcement is not only ineffective but rather counterproductive. Bittlingmayer (1985) argues that early antitrust enforcement gave rise to the great merger wave of the 1890s and early 1900s. Elsewhere, he shows that the threat of antitrust enforcement gave rise to financial panics during the early twentieth century (Bittlingmayer 1993, 1996). In a study of the antitrust suit against Microsoft, Bittlingmayer and Hazlett (2000) present stock-market evidence that firms in Microsoft's production and distribution chain experienced reductions in market value, suggesting that investors anticipated a breakup would not enhance efficiency but rather reduce it.

One of the few studies to find that antitrust has beneficial effects on consumer welfare is also one of the most creative and convincing. Ashenfelter and Hosken (2008) look at the impact of U.S. merger guidelines. The central difficulty any researcher faces in identifying the effect of these guidelines is building the relevant counterfactual: all mergers above a certain threshold for market power are disallowed, and as a result it is impossible to identify the effect on prices should those mergers have been allowed. Ashenfelter and Hosken, however, look at mergers that were just below the threshold and ask what happened to prices in those cases. They consider five mergers, and in four of the five they find evidence of a modest price increase. It is reasonable to assume that in the case of mergers well above the threshold the price increases would have been even larger.

Another important study suggesting antitrust regulation is effective is Mullin *et al.* (1995). Using an event study, they explore how the stock prices of rival firms and purchasers responded to the antitrust suit launched against U.S. Steel in 1911 and decided (adversely) in 1920. Their analysis, which is a model of how to perform a convincing event study, suggests that the dissolution of U.S. Steel, had it gone through, would have lowered steel prices and increased output.

State regulations of public utilities

Throughout the nineteenth century, only Massachusetts regulated utilities such as gas, electricity, water and sewer, and local transit, and even there the commission had only limited authority. At the same time, state constitutions often forbade local governments from directly regulating rates. It was not until the second decade of the twentieth century that alternative forms of municipal control gave way to state regulation. Between 1907 and 1924, nearly 30 states created state-wide regulatory commissions to govern the behavior of private utility companies (Stigler and Friedland 1962). In the review that follows, three explanations for the rise of public utility commissions are considered, and the effects of those commissions on rates and performance are reviewed.

Public utilities were (and are) natural monopolies; a single firm could service a market at lower cost than multiple firms. For example, two competing gas companies would have installed two sets of mains when only one set was required. Many economists claim that, in this context, unfettered markets did not work very well. In the short run, competition led to wasteful duplication of capital and brief price wars. In the long run, competing firms merged, consumer prices rose, and the excess capital remained. According to the traditional public-interest interpretation of utility regulation, lawmakers created state utility commissions to solve the natural monopoly problem. State commissions prevented wasteful duplication by restricting market entry. They protected consumers against producers' monopoly power by regulating rates (e.g. Gessell 1914; Stotz and Jamison 1938).

85

The natural monopoly explanation for state regulation does a good job helping historians understand some of the economic aspects of pre-regulation utility markets, particularly the high levels of market concentration. Throughout the late nineteenth and early twentieth centuries, a single firm dominated gas markets in most towns. Of the 714 towns the 1890 Census of Manufacturers identifies as having gas service, only 16 had two or more gas companies; of the 827 towns the 1900 Census identifies, only 29 had two or more gas companies (Troesken 1996: 5–6). Furthermore, for those cities in which competition emerged, it typically lasted no more than a few months' time; it did not take competing firms long to realize that merging was a much more profitable course of action. Although there are a handful of antitrust cases involving public utilities, most government officials quickly gave up on the idea that antitrust enforcement could be effectively used to combat market power in utility industries (Troesken 1996: 35–42).

Natural monopoly explanations, however, do a much poorer job accounting for the unique regulatory experience of utilities, the timing of regulatory change, or the politics behind regulation. First, declining average costs (natural monopoly) did not always induce regulation (James 1983). Second, lawmakers created nearly all state utility commissions during the 15 years following 1907. As George Priest (1993: 296) writes, "it is very hard to believe that the average cost curves of gas and electric utilities only began to slope downward after 1907." Finally, the standard natural monopoly/public-interest view assumes that lawmakers created utility commissions in response to the demands of consumers. The assumption runs counter to established historical fact. Utilities, not consumers, lobbied for state utility regulation (Blackford 1970; Troesken 1996: 79–82).

The Chicago School interpretation turns the natural monopoly story on its head. As the Chicago story goes, the problem was not that the market failed. The market worked all too well and utilities lobbied for state regulation because they believed it would undermine the market and promote monopoly (Demsetz 1968; Jarrell 1978). This interpretation suggests that the state acted as an agent for producers: the state brought producers substantial market power when the market failed. The Chicago School interpretation constitutes a powerful critique of economic regulation in general. Economists have long believed utilities provided the quintessential example of market failure: natural monopoly. If regulation failed to improve things in markets that were natural monopolies, it would surely fail in situations where claims of market failure were more tenuous.

The strongest evidence for the Chicago School explanation comes from Jarrell (1978), who isolates the political demand for state utility regulation. Suppose consumers demanded regulation to protect them against monopoly rates. If so, one would expect states where utilities charged the highest rates and earned the most profits to have been the first to create state commissions. Alternatively, suppose utilities demanded regulation to protect themselves against the low rates set by municipal regulators. In that case, one would expect states where utilities charged the lowest rates and earned the lowest profits to have been the first to create regulatory commissions. Jarrell divides states into two groups. Early regulators adopted commissions between 1912 and 1917; later regulators adopted commissions after 1917. After adjusting for cross-state variations in demand and cost conditions, Jarrell finds that electric utilities in early-regulated states charged lower rates and earned lower profits than utilities in later-regulated states.

Given this pattern, Jarrell concludes that municipal authorities set competitive rates that allowed producers a reasonable return while state regulators set rates close to monopoly levels. He rejects the idea that municipal authorities promoted unreasonably low rates after calculating the ratio of average revenue to average cost for each state. For both early-regulated states and later-regulated states, the mean ratio exceeds one. This suggests that on average electric utilities covered their costs.

In emphasizing the lobbying activities of public utility companies, the Chicago School interpretation captures a critical piece of the politics behind utility regulation. On the other hand, at least two general questions remain unanswered. First, if it were merely the lobbying of efforts of producers that gave rise to state utility regulation, why were utilities so much more successful than producers in other industries in securing regulation? Surely producers in other industries wanted monopoly profits just as much as utilities. Second, if state regulation granted utilities a sure road to monopoly profits, why did utilities wait over half a century to lobby for it? Surely utilities in 1860 desired monopoly profits as much as utilities in 1910.

In addition, although Jarrell's central finding is unassailable – it is clear utilities lobbied for state regulation – other aspects of his analysis are problematic. First, his evidence on the rates charged by municipal authorities is not evidence of municipal behavior but of the rates the courts allowed; municipal authorities often tried (but were blocked by the courts) to set much lower rates. Second, in calculating his revenue-to-cost ratios, Jarrell combines states that allowed municipal rate regulation with states that prohibited municipal rate regulation. This is inappropriate. Some state constitutions prohibited local governments from regulating utility rates without special enabling legislation, while in other states municipal governments possessed regulatory powers. Third, Jarrell's revenue-to-cost ratios are averages, and only speak to the performance of the mean firm. This is unfortunate because firms below the mean were the firms most affected by municipal regulation. It is likely that these below-the-mean firms were the ones that pushed the hardest for state regulation as a means of supplanting municipal control. If so, this would run counter to Jarrell's claim that municipal regulation was efficient and non-confiscatory (Troesken 1996: 87–9). Beyond all this, a more recent econometric analysis of the adoption of state regulatory commissions cuts against Jarrell's earlier analysis (Neufeld 2008).

Over the last 30 years, a third explanation for the creation of state utility commissions has emerged. This explanation sees state regulation as a solution to a fundamental long-term contracting problem (Goldberg 1976; Williamson 1985). The following example highlights the underlying logic. To sell gas, a gas company had to invest substantial resources in a system of mains. The investment was irrevocable. Once the mains were in the ground, the gas company could not move or sell them. Strictly speaking, the mains represented an asset-specific or non-redeployable investment. If, after the company installed its mains, the city imposed onerous price regulations or taxes, the company was stuck. It could not move or resell its mains. As a result, before installing its mains, the gas company required assurances that the city would not impose onerous regulations or taxes *ex post*. Alternatively, municipal authorities had to grant the gas company the right to use public roads to lay mains. For the city, this right represented an irrevocable investment. Once the gas company exercised its right to use public property and install its mains, the city could not meaningfully revoke that right. If the company's rates or service failed to satisfy the city, the city was stuck. As a result, before granting this property right, the city demanded a commitment that the utility would not charge excessive rates or provide poor service *ex post* (Jacobson 1989; Troesken 1996: 5–7).

According to the relational contracting interpretation, utility industries were never organized as markets, for the same reason that firms are not organized as markets: positive transaction costs. Non-redeployable investments forced utilities and municipalities to create long-term, binding contracts. Before state utility regulation, state charters and municipal franchises embodied these contracts and supplanted the market. The charter and franchise governed the behavior of both the municipality and the utility. The state charter set strict limits on the city's regulatory authority. The municipal franchise dictated the price and quality of the company's gas. State utility commissions functioned similarly. Like state charters, they prevented the city from imposing onerous regulations. Like municipal franchises, they prevented the gas company from charging high rates. Hence, the arrival of state regulation represented a change in the way cities and utilities contracted, not a move from pure and unfettered competition to widespread state intervention (Troesken 1996: 5–7).

Several pieces of evidence support the relational contracting interpretation. First, there is strong evidence of opportunistic behavior on the part of municipal authorities in the years prior to state regulation. Local politicians frequently used the promise of lower utility rates to garner votes, and, while legal protections such as substantive due process limited the ability of local governments to enforce such rates, securing legal protection through the courts was neither cheap nor timely (Troesken 1996: 76–7). Second, state regulation was associated with increased private investment in utility industries, which is consistent with the hypothesis that state regulation was functioning as a commitment mechanism (Troesken 1997; Hausman and Neufeld 2002). Case studies of specific utility industries provide clear evidence that municipal franchises and state charters were working just as the relational contracting interpretation would suggest (Priest 1993; Wilcox 1910). Moreover, it is easy to reconcile much of the corruption associated with the granting of municipal franchises to public utility companies with a relational contracting view (Troesken 2006).

As to the effects of public utility commissions on rates, the evidence is mixed and much less supportive of the Chicago School view than is often thought. In a seminal paper, Stigler and Friedland (1962) set up a natural experiment. They analyze the prices and profits of electricity utilities during the early twentieth century. During that period, regulatory regimes varied across states. Some states had utility commissions while others did not. Stigler and Friedland find that rates and profits were not significantly lower in states with utility commissions. From this, they conclude that state regulation failed to reduce rates from monopoly levels. In drawing this conclusion, Stigler and Friedland assume that, in states without regulatory commissions, utilities operated without any regulatory constraints and were, therefore, able to charge monopoly rates. This is a problematic assumption. Even in states without regulatory commissions, municipal regulations put limits on the behavior of utility companies. Sometimes local authorities directly regulated rates, but most of the time local governments used franchise contracts to put limits on utility rates (Troesken 1996: 55–78).

Moore (1970) and Meyer and Leland (1980) estimate demand and cost equations to isolate the effects of regulation. Moore uses a cross section of electric utilities operating in 1962. He finds that state regulation lowered rates from monopoly levels by only 3 per cent. Meyer and Leland pool data from 48 states over the period 1969 to 1974. These data, and the estimating procedure, allow for the possibility that the effectiveness of regulation varies over time and across space. Allowing for this possibility distinguishes Meyer and Leland's study from earlier work. They find "pervasive irregularity" in the impact of state utility commissions across states and "widespread and substantial benefits being conferred by rate of return regulation" (Meyer and Leland 1980: 562). A study of the effects of state regulation on gas rates in Chicago finds that it was effective in reducing rates below monopoly levels (Troesken 1996: 83–6).

The rise of public ownership in utility industries

Between 1880 and the 1930s, thousands of cities and towns in the United States municipalized their utility systems. While the electric, gas, and water industries all experienced sharp growth in the number and proportion of municipally owned companies during this period, growth was especially pronounced in the water industry. The number of municipally owned water companies increased by a factor of 26, from 293 in 1880 to 7,832 in 1932; and the proportion of municipally owned companies increased from 43 per cent in 1890 to 68 per cent in 1920.

Growth in the proportion of municipally owned companies did not stem solely from the fact that municipalities installed water systems at a faster rate than private enterprises. During the early twentieth century, roughly one-third of all municipally owned water companies had been privately owned at one time (Troesken 1997; Troesken and Geddes 2003).

The existing literature suggests three classes of possible explanations for the widespread municipalization of private utility companies during this period. The first class of explanations appeals to the standard arguments about market failure in the presence of declining costs, externalities, or capital market imperfections (e.g. Carey 1900; Zueblin 1918; Thompson 1925). Of the traditional market failure explanations, those appealing to natural monopoly have the least explanatory power. Natural monopoly cannot explain why there was a sudden wave of public acquisition around the turn of the century; as noted earlier, it seems unlikely that utilities only began to exhibit scale economies around 1900. Natural monopoly also cannot explain why municipal ownership was chosen in lieu of regulation to solve the problem of declining costs. Finally, natural monopoly cannot explain why municipal ownership was so much more common in the water industry than in the gas and electric industries, which also exhibited substantial scale economies.

On their face, market failure arguments based on externalities have greater explanatory power, at least in the case of water. It seems plausible that distributing pure water generated large positive externalities by reducing the risk of epidemic diseases such as typhoid fever, and by reducing the risk of conflagrations like the Great Chicago Fire. The distribution of gas and electricity exhibited no such community-wide benefits. If externalities were substantial, and private companies found it harder to internalize them than public enterprises, this could account for the inter-industry variation of public ownership. When Progressive-Era reformers champ-ioned the cause of municipal ownership, they often picked up on this line of thought, arguing that municipal ownership was particularly common in the water industry because there were serious public health concerns associated with distributing pure water. According to Progressive-Era reformers, municipal water companies were more likely than private companies to make socially beneficial, but presumably unprofitable, investments in water-purification systems because they were guided by political rather than economic motives (Troesken 1999).

The externality argument is problematic in four ways, however. First, it is not clear why public enterprises would have been able to better internalize the positive spillovers associated with distributing pure water than were private enterprises. Although it is possible that sub-sidizing private companies was politically unpopular and therefore unlikely, this line of thought suggests a contractual or political failure, not a market failure. Second, historically, all water companies, regardless of ownership regime, were legally liable to pay damages if the water they distributed caused typhoid epidemics. And there were several cases at the turn of the twentieth century in which companies were held liable for distributing tainted water. That companies had to pay damages for typhoid epidemics suggests that at least some of the externalities associated with distributing impure water would have been internalized by the firm. Third, a recent study suggests that public water companies did no better at reducing typhoid rates than did private companies. The same study also reports evidence that, as of 1900, private water companies were 2.5 times more likely than municipal companies to have invested in water-filtration systems (Troesken 1999). Finally, one could argue that fire risks were falling during the period of municipalization due to new building technologies and materials – undercutting the idea that municipal companies were necessary to better protect cities against fire.

Cutler and Miller (2006) suggest a third market failure explanation for municipal ownership, arguing that financial market imperfections make it difficult for private companies to raise the necessary capital. Municipalities, they claim, have an easier time raising the money necessary to fund an adequate water system. As evidence for this position, one might point to the fact that municipal ownership in the water industry was positively correlated with city size: water companies in large cities were more likely to have been municipally owned than were companies in small cities. There is also evidence that during the late nineteenth and early twentieth centuries private water companies were reluctant to extend water mains outside of the most densely populated areas of cities and towns, so that the people located on the periphery of cities and towns, which were less densely populated, often went without service (Troesken 2001; Troesken and Geddes 2003).

Nonetheless, the difficulties with this line of thought are twofold. First, in utility industries other than water, the correlation between city size and municipal ownership is negative, not positive. It is not clear why capital market imperfections should have impinged any more on water companies than on gas companies. Second, the assumption that cities would have had an easier time raising capital than private utility companies seems inconsistent with legal history: like private corporations during the nineteenth century, municipalities were incorporated by state governments and were typically subjected to state-imposed debt limits. The only way cities could borrow in excess of these limits was to petition state legislatures for special exemptions (Friedman 1985: 528–9).

Another class of explanations for the rise of municipally owned water companies builds on Pashigian (1976), who considers the wave of municipal takeovers that struck the urban transit industry during the mid-twentieth century. Pashigian finds that public acquisition was driven by over-zealous regulation on the part of local authorities that were captured by the riders of transit systems. These regulations undermined the profitability of local transit markets, and drove private providers into bankruptcy, necessitating municipal takeover and subsidy. Along the same lines, Peltzman (1971) reports evidence that publicly owned electric companies charged slightly lower rates than private companies largely because private companies faced a heavier tax burden. The same processes may have driven the municipal acquisition of other private utilities.

Two pieces of evidence speak in favor of a regulation-based explanation. First, broadly speaking, local governments did become more aggressive in their regulation of local utilities around the turn of the twentieth century, and this coincided with at least part of the municipal ownership movement (Troesken 1996: 55–78). Furthermore, previous research shows that increased zealousness on the part of municipal regulators discouraged private gas companies from entering specific markets and ultimately forced many local governments to construct municipally owned gas works. Second, the municipal acquisition of private waterworks was often preceded by draconian policies on the part of local politicians (Troesken 1997). For example, in Kansas City, Kansas, local authorities simply tried to seize the National Waterworks Company (a private enterprise) without paying any compensation, while elsewhere local authorities enacted confiscatory rate ordinances.

A concern with any regulation-based explanation of public acquisition is that it seems to assume irrationality or imperfect foresight. Given the high levels of idiosyncratic investments in the water industry, private investors would have likely demanded credible assurances from local authorities that unduly burdensome regulations would not be enacted *ex post*. Indeed, there is clear evidence from the gas industry that private gas companies demanded such assurances before they entered local markets (Troesken 1997). Additionally, it is not clear how a regulation-based explanation of public ownership could account for the inter-industry variation in public ownership.

A third explanation of municipal ownership builds on the relational-contracting literature already discussed in reference to state utility commissions. In particular, one might think of municipal ownership as a form of vertical integration. To see this, consider two recent studies.

Comparing the ownership of telephone systems across several countries, Levy and Spiller (1995) find that publicly owned telephone systems are most common in those nations that cannot commit to stable and reasonable regulatory policies. Comparing the ownership of urban gas systems across U.S. cities and towns in 1911, Troesken (1997) finds the same pattern: municipally owned gas companies were most common in those towns that could not credibly commit to stable and reasonable regulatory policies. According to these studies, there is a clear parallel between the city that buys its own gas company because it cannot commit to treating a private gas company fairly *ex post* and the manufacturer that acquires a potential supplier because it cannot commit to treating that supplier fairly. Although the relational-contracting literature implies that municipal ownership was probably efficient in that it reduced transactions costs, such strong efficiency implications are not a necessary part of such interpretations. Municipal ownership might well have been a second- or third-best option.

The privatization and deregulation movements of the 1970s and 1980s

The history of regulation has an odd circular quality in that many of the regulatory mechanisms created during the nineteenth and early twentieth centuries were dismantled a half-century later. For example, after creating state public utility commissions between 1900 and 1930, state governments during the 1970s and 1980s abandoned or curtailed their use of these commissions on a wide scale. The available evidence suggests that, with some important exceptions, deregulating utilities had beneficial effects (Joskow 1997; Peltzman 1989; Winston 1981). Similarly, by the turn of the twenty-first century, the same governments that had municipalized water (and other utility) systems a century earlier were now privatizing those systems and returning them to the institutional environment that had governed private water companies for much of the nineteenth century. Again this appears to have been done with positive results (Galiani *et al.* 2005; Vitale 2001).

What explains the circularity of public utility regulation and governance? At least three possibilities suggest themselves. The first possibility is that technological changes altered the viability of alternative governance regimes over time. The second possibility is that ideological changes altered the preferences of voters and policy makers. During the early twentieth century, these ideological changes led policy makers to favor state-oriented solutions; by the late twentieth century, these changes led policy makers to favor market-oriented solutions. The third possibility appeals to the work of Mancur Olson (1982), who argues that over time institutions tend to ossify and slow economic growth as entrenched interest groups work to secure a greater share of society's resources. Olson's work suggests that transitions in regulatory and governance regimes – whether from market-oriented to statist, or vice versa – can dramatically improve the operation markets.

The available evidence suggests that the circularity of public utility regulation has not been driven by ideological mistakes or technological changes, but instead by the desirability and necessity of occasional regime changes in public utility markets. More precisely, corruption was endemic to public utility markets; it existed, in some form, across all regulatory and ownership regimes. In addition, for any type of governance regime (e.g. state regulation or municipal ownership) corruption grew increasingly severe over time, and eventually became politically untenable. When corruption reached this point, politicians intervened and replaced the existing and utterly corrupt governance regime with a new regime. The institutional change broke the fully matured and corrupt relationships of the old regime, and replaced them with new corrupt relationships that also eventually matured and flourished, but this maturation took much time, and, at least initially, the new governance regime was associated with much less corruption than the old regime (Troesken 2006).

References

Ashenfelter, O. and Hosken, D. (2008) 'The effect of mergers on consumer prices: evidence from five selected case studies', NBER Working Paper No. 13859.

Binder, J.J. (1985) 'Measuring the effects of regulation with stock price data', *Rand Journal of Economics*, 16: 167–83.

——(1988) 'The Sherman Antitrust Act and the railroad cartels', *Journal of Law and Economics*, 31: 443–68.

Bittlingmayer, G. (1985) 'Did antitrust policy cause the Great Merger Wave?' *Journal of Law and Economics*, 28: 77–118.

——(1993) 'The stock market and early antitrust enforcement', *Journal of Law and Economics*, 36: 1–32.

——(1996) 'Antitrust and business activity: the first quarter century', *Business History Review*, 70: 363–401.

Bittlingmayer, G. and Hazlett, T.W. (2000) 'DOS kapital: has antitrust against Microsoft created value in the computer industry?' *Journal of Financial Economics*, 55: 329–59.

Blackford, M.G. (1970) 'Businessmen and the regulation of railroads and public utilities in California during the Progressive Era', *Business History Review*, 44: 7–19.

Bodenhorn, H. (2006) 'Bank chartering and political corruption in antebellum New York: free banking as reform', in E. Glaeser and C. Goldin (eds) *Corruption and Reform: Lessons from America's Economic History*, Chicago, IL: University of Chicago Press.

Bork, R.H. (1966) 'Legislative intent and the policy of the Sherman Act', *Journal of Law and Economics*, 9: 7–56.

Burns, M.R. (1977) 'The competitive effects of trust-busting: a portfolio analysis', *Journal of Political Economy*, 85: 717–39.

Carey, F.K. (1900) *Municipal Ownership of Natural Monopolies*, Baltimore, Md: John Murphy Company.

Cutler, D. and Miller, G. (2006) 'Water, water everywhere: municipal finance and water supply in American cities', in E. Glaeser and C. Goldin (eds) *Corruption and Reform: Lessons from America's Economic History*, Chicago, IL: University of Chicago Press.

Demsetz, H. (1968) 'Why regulate utilities?' *Journal of Law and Economics*, 11: 55–65.

Fainsod, M. and Gordon, L. (1948) *Government and the American Economy*, New York: W.W. Norton.

Friedman, L.M. (1985) *A History of American Law*, New York: Touchstone Books and Simon and Schuster.

Galambos, L. (1975) *The Public Image of Big Business in America, 1880–1940: A Quantitative Study in Social Change*, Baltimore, Md: Johns Hopkins University Press.

Galiani, S., Gertler, P. and Schargrodsky, E. (2005) 'Water for life: the impact of the privatization of water services on child mortality', *Journal of Political Economy*, 113: 83–120.

Gessell, G.A. (1914) 'Minnesota public utility rates: gas-electric-water', *Bulletin of the University of Minnesota*, 3: 1–15.

Goldberg, V. (1976) 'Regulation and administered contracts,' *Bell Journal of Economics*, 7: 426–52.

Grandy, C. (1993) 'Original intent and the Sherman Antitrust Act: a re-examination of the consumer-welfare hypothesis', *Journal of Economic History*, 53: 359–76.

Hausman, W.J. and Neufeld, J.L. (2002) 'The market for capital and the origins of state regulation of electric utilities in the United States', *Journal of Economic History*, 62: 1050–73.

Higgs, R. (1970) 'Railroad rates and the populist uprising', *Agricultural History*, 44: 291–8.

Hovenkamp, H. (1988) 'Regulatory conflict in the gilded age: federalism and the railroad problem', *Yale Law Journal*, 97: 1017–72.

Hughes, J.R.T. (1991) *The Governmental Habit Redux: Economic Controls from Colonial Times to the Present*, Princeton, NJ: Princeton University Press.

Jacobson, C. (1989) 'Same game, different players: problems in urban public utility regulation, 1850–1987', *Urban Studies*, 26: 13–31.

James, J.A. (1983) 'Structural change in American manufacturing, 1850–1890', *Journal of Economic History*, 43: 443–59.

Jarrell, G. (1978) 'The demand for state regulation of the electric utility industry', *Journal of Law and Economics*, 21: 269–96.

Josephson, M. (1934) *The Robber Barons: The Great American Capitalists, 1861–1901*, New York: Harcourt, Brace and Company.

Josephson, M. (1938) *The Politicos, 1865–1896*, New York: Harcourt, Brace, and World Company.

Joskow, P.L. (1997) 'Restructuring, competition, and regulatory reform in the U.S. electricity sector', *Journal of Economic Perspectives*, 11: 119–38.

Kolko, G. (1965) *Railroads and Regulation, 1877–1916*, Greenwood, CT: Greenwood Press.

Letwin, W. (1965) *Law and Economic Policy in America: The Evolution of the Sherman Antitrust Law*, Chicago, IL: University of Chicago Press.

Levy, B. and Spiller, P.T. (1995) 'The institutional foundations of regulatory commitment: a comparative analysis of telecommunications regulation', *Journal of Law, Economics, and Organization*, 10: 201–46.

Martin, A. (1971) *Enterprise Denied: Origins of the Decline of American Railroads, 1897–1917*, New York: Columbia University Press.

Meyer, R.A. and Leland, H.E. (1980) 'The effectiveness of price regulation', *Review of Economics and Statistics*, 62: 555–71.

Moore, T.G. (1970) 'The effectiveness of regulation of electric utility prices', *Southern Economic Journal*, 36: 365–81.

Mullin, G.L., Mullin, J.C. and Mullin, W.P. (1995) 'The competitive effects of mergers: stock market evidence from the U.S. Steel dissolution suit', *Rand Journal of Economics*, 26: 314–30.

Neufeld, J.L. (2008) 'Corruption, quasi-rents, and the regulation of electric utilities', *Journal of Economic History*, 68: 1059–97.

Nonnenmacher, T. (2001) 'State promotion and regulation of the telegraph industry, 1845–60', *Journal of Economic History*, 61: 19–30.

Novak, W.J. (1996) *The People's Welfare: Law and Regulation in Nineteenth-Century America*, Chapel Hill, NC: University of North Carolina Press.

Olson, M. (1982) *The Rise and Fall of Nations: Economic Growth, Stagflation, and Social Rigidities*, New Haven, CT: Yale University Press.

Pashigian, B.P. (1976) 'Consequences and causes of public ownership of urban transit facilities', *Journal of Political Economy*, 84: 1239–59.

Peltzman, S. (1971) 'Pricing at public and private enterprises: electric utilities in the United States', *Journal of Law and Economics*, 13: 109–47.

——(1989) 'The economic theory of regulation after a decade of deregulation', *Brookings Papers on Economic Activity: Microeconomics*, 1: 1–49.

Prager, R.A. (1989) 'Using stock price data to measure the effects of regulation: the Interstate Commerce Act and the railroad industry', *Rand Journal of Economics*, 20: 280–90.

Prager, R.A. (1992) 'The effects of horizontal mergers on competition: the case of the Northern Securities Company', *Rand Journal of Economics*, 23: 123–33.

Priest, G.L. (1993) 'The origins of utility regulation and the "theories of regulation debate"', *Journal of Law and Economics*, 36: 289–324.

Seager, H.R. and Gulick, C.A. (1929) *Trust and Corporation Problems*, New York: Harper.

Sklar, M.J. (1988) *The Corporate Reconstruction of American Capitalism, 1890–1916*, Cambridge: Cambridge University Press.

Stephenson, N.W. (1930) *Nelson W. Aldrich: A Leader in American Politics*, New York: Charles Scribner's Sons.

Stigler, G.J. (1985) 'The origin of the Sherman Act', *Journal of Legal Studies*, 14: 1–12.

Stigler, G.J. and Friedland, C. (1962) 'What can regulators regulate? The case of electricity', *Journal of Law and Economics*, 5: 1–16.

Stotz, L.P. and Jamison, A. (1938) *History of the Gas Industry*, New York: Stettiner Brothers.

Thompson, C.D. (1925) *A Survey of Public Enterprises, Municipal, State, and Federal, in the United States and Elsewhere*, New York: Thomas Y. Crowell Company.

Thorelli, H.B. (1955) *The Federal Antitrust Policy: Origination of an American Tradition*, Baltimore, Md: Johns Hopkins University Press.

Troesken, W. (1995) 'Antitrust enforcement before the Sherman Act: the break-up of the Chicago Gas Trust Company', *Explorations in Economic History*, 32: 109–36.

——(1996) *Why Regulate Utilities? The New Institutional Economics and the Chicago Gas Industry, 1849–1924*, Ann Arbor, MI: University of Michigan Press.

——(1997) 'The sources of public ownership: historical evidence from the gas industry', *Journal of Law, Economics, and Organization*, 13: 1–27.

——(1998) 'Exclusive dealing and the whiskey trust, 1890–95', *Journal of Economic History*, 58: 755–78.

——(1999) 'Typhoid rates and the public acquisition of private waterworks, 1880–1920', *Journal of Economic History*, 59: 927–48.

——(2000) 'Did the trusts want a federal antitrust law: an event study of state antitrust enforcement and passage of the Sherman Act', in J. Heckelman and R. Whaples (eds) *Public Choice Interpretations of American Economic History*, New York: Kluwer Academic Press.

——(2001) 'Race, disease, and the provision of water in American cities, 1889–1921', *Journal of Economic History*, 61: 750–76.

——(2002) 'The letters of John Sherman and the origins of antitrust', *Review of Austrian Economics*, 15: 275–97.

——(2006) 'Regime change and corruption: a history of public utility regulation', in E. Glaeser and C. Goldin (eds) *Corruption and Reform: Lessons from America's Economic History*, Chicago, IL: University of Chicago Press.

Troesken, W. and Geddes, R. (2003) 'Municipalizing American waterworks, 1897–1914', *Journal of Law, Economics, and Organization*, 19: 546–67.

Vitale, R. (2001) 'Privatizing water systems: a primer', *Fordham International Law Journal*, 24: 1382–404.

Wallis, J.J. (2005) 'Constitutions, corporations, and corruption: American states and constitutional change, 1842–52', *Journal of Economic History*, 65: 211–56.

——(2006) 'The concept of systematic corruption in American history', in E. Glaeser and C. Goldin (eds) *Corruption and Reform: Lessons from America's Economic History*, Chicago, IL: University of Chicago Press.

Wilcox, D.F. (1910) *Municipal Franchises: A Description of the Terms and Conditions upon which Private Corporations enjoy Special Privileges in the Streets of American Cities*, vol. I, New York: McGraw Hill.

Williamson, O. (1985) *The Economic Institutions of Capitalism*, New York: Free Press.

Winston, C. (1981) 'The welfare effects of ICC rate regulation revisited', *Bell Journal of Economics*, 12: 232–44.

Zerbe, R.O. (1980) 'The costs and benefits of early regulation of the railroads', *Bell Journal of Economics*, 11: 343–50.

Zueblin, C. (1918) *American Municipal Progress*, New York: MacMillan Company.

9

THE EVOLUTIONARY ROOTS OF ECONOMIC HISTORY

Philip R.P. Coelho

The Mecca of the economist lies in economic biology rather than in economic dynamics.

Alfred Marshall (1890: 19)

Evolutionary biology

Evolution is the fundamental paradigm of modern biology; it lays the scientific foundations of biology beyond the visually descriptive. Evolution postulates a demand for resources by living things (organisms) that exceed the environment's capacity to provide them. The paradigm of economics – scarcity – limits an organism's ability to survive and reproduce. How well species (different organisms) adapt to the environment depends upon their genes – the building blocks of all living things. Scarcity reduces or precludes the reproduction of organisms that are relatively less effective in acquiring resources. Differential rates of reproduction ensure that the innate (genetic) traits that made organisms more effective in acquiring resources are more frequent in the next generation's gene pool. Conversely, the lack of reproduction reduces the presence in the gene pool of traits that hindered an organism's successful reproduction. There is some circularity here that is revealed in the definition of evolutionary success: survival through succeeding generations. Genes make the organism and affect all its characteristics; so, ultimately the survival (ability to successfully reproduce) of species is determined by their genes, and how well suited the genes are within the environment in which they exist.[1] Over time, the physical and biological worlds interact, producing changes in the environment to which species must adapt or cease to exist. Gene pools (the relative frequency of various genes in a breeding population) change because of natural selection, and these changes in the gene pool affect the species. Adding complexity, species can change the environment, and environmental changes may have repercussions (favorable or unfavorable) upon the species that created them.

Organisms that share enough common genes to continually reproduce are classified as belonging to the same species.[2] Another way of saying this is that a group of organisms that successfully reproduce with one another constitute a species. Still, within a given gene pool there is a sufficient variation among the genes of individual organisms (of the same species) to ensure substantial differences among organisms. For example, the domestic dog varies in size from smallest to largest by close to 100-fold (small Chihuahuas have an average minimum weight of approximately 3 pounds, while large St. Bernards have a maximum average of about 240 pounds), yet they all belong to the same species. It is necessary to point out that variation among dog breeds is not the result of natural selection; it is the result of numerous human interventions in the breeding of dogs. Regardless, within each species there are enough variations in the common gene pool to vary the characteristics of the species tremendously over generations. The results are startling; from pygmies to giants within the same species. This is also the basis for Darwinian evolution: variation through natural selection.

Natural selection leads to evolution. In successful (surviving) species, succeeding generations will be the descendants of ancestors who were able to survive the culling process of the environment, and to gather enough resources to reproduce. As noted, the genetic (innate) characteristics that facilitated the process of relative reproductive success will become more widely represented in each succeeding generation. Each generation will tend to be more genetically homogeneous as long as there are no isolated breeding populations. Countering this homogenization is the occurrence of random mutations of genes within each generation. If the net effects of the mutations assist the organism in reproducing, the mutations are pro-adaptive; if instead they reduce reproductive success, they are deemed maladaptive. Pro-adaptive genes will become more common in the gene pool as time passes, while maladaptive genes will become less frequent. But there are, as always, complications.

In sexual reproduction (many organisms are not sexual) one copy of each gene is inherited from male and female parents.[3] Human beings have two copies of each gene, but in many cases only one expresses itself in individuals. The gene that expresses itself in the individual is termed dominant; the gene that is not expressed is termed recessive. For example, in a union of a person with brown eyes with another person who has blue eyes, the resulting child has brown eyes.[4] However, the brown-eyed child will carry the blue-eye gene in its genome, and when it grows up it may have a blue-eyed child if its partner also carries that gene. Blue-eyed humans are homozygous (inherit genes for blue eyes from both parents). A brown-eyed child who is the offspring of one parent who is blue-eyed and the other who is brown-eyed is heterozygous in genes for eye color because the parent with blue eyes can only contribute the gene for blue eyes. The reason that this knowledge is relevant is because some genes that are expressed heterozygously can have beneficial effects, while if the genes are expressed homozygously they are very maladaptive. Two examples are the sickle cell gene and the Tay-Sachs gene. In a highly malarious environment, being heterozygous for the sickle cell gene is highly beneficial because it provides resistance to malaria; however, a child who is homozygous in the sickle cell gene will, in the absence of modern medicine, typically die before early adulthood.[5] A child who is homozygous in the Tay-Sachs gene dies in infancy, while people who are heterozygous in the Tay-Sachs gene are disproportionately endowed with exceptional mental powers ("geniuses"). Consequently, the specification of the *net* effects of genes is important; in certain environments even genes that are fatal homozygously expressed can have positive net effects upon a population when expressed heterozygously.

Interactions

Evolution is the story of change; but change is neither unidirectional nor simple. Change begets further change, in biology and the physical environment. For example, when the earth was newly formed the atmosphere was oxygen poor. Over billions of years living organisms (cyanobacteria are frequently implicated) through photosynthesis expired oxygen. Prior to about 2.4 billion years ago, the oxygen was sequestered in iron oxides and organic matter; when these recipients of oxygen became saturated, the expired oxygen was expelled into the atmosphere.

As the atmosphere became oxygen rich, radical changes occurred in the ecological and biological environments. Free-ranging anaerobic bacteria vanished from the earth's surface because the oxygen–rich environment that they had created over eons was inimical to their existence. An ecological niche was created and filled by oxygen-tolerant/using life-forms; these came to dominate the planet's surface. The lessons here are: 1) evolution is random and unpredictable; 2) pollution to one life-form may be paradise to another; 3) feedback effects are ubiquitous; 4) evolutionary processes are path dependent; 5) life-forms and the environment are engaged in an eternal duet, with each responding to the other; and 6) evolutionary processes work over time spans that are so long that they escape human intuition.

Evolution has no direction; it is just the unthinking process of natural selection (reproductive success) of species in environments over time. The usage of the plural, "environments," is to emphasize that environments are dependent upon evolutionary processes. Just as in history and life, there are no biological equilibria and no endings. This makes telling an evolutionary story somewhat less compelling than a narrative with heroes, villains, and a denouement. When we talk about the history of various groups, "races," peoples, and nations, it is more than a little misleading because there is just one human race. The frequencies of various genes, however, can differ among ethnic groups and the differing frequencies (caused by natural selection) can manifest themselves in visual differences that are sometimes identified with "race." The history of African slavery in the New World, racism, and regional concentration of slavery are all linked by the evolutionary heritage of the ethnic groups that came from the Old World to the New.

African slavery

Economic history places history into an economic context. The material world and humanity's ability to understand and manipulate it constrain all economic activities. The biological environment is an integral and major part of the material world. All this is common knowledge; what is less widely recognized are the profound changes that biological processes can have upon the economic and physical environments. In order to make sense of the history of African slave labor in America (the 13 colonies and, later, the United States), knowledge of the evolutionary impact of disease environments and how different populations, given their ancestral heritage, were affected by different disease ecologies is essential.

African slave labor lasted about two and a half centuries in America. Slavery and the issues surrounding it are the subject of intense debates. One important question is why American slavery was regionally specific. The South and slavery are inextricably linked, and absent the regional concentration of slavery in the South there would have been no war between North and South. Why wasn't African slavery spread uniformly about the American landscape? African slavery was tried throughout colonial North America, yet it only survived, grew, and prospered in the American South. Apparently, slavery failed the evolutionary test in the North. McGuire and Coelho (2011) argue that it failed because it was insufficiently profitable to guarantee its survival where and when it was tried in the North. Why was slavery profitable in the South and uneconomical in the North? Until recently, the commonly accepted answer to this question was climatic.[6] Because African slaves came from the tropics, they were supposedly inured to the heat, and were consequently assumed to be more productive than Europeans in hot weather. This explanation runs afoul of both physics and history. Physics because darker colors absorb more heat from sunshine, and people with darker skin pigmentation (*ceteris paribus*) are at greater risk from sunstroke. The climatic explanation runs afoul of history because in the tropics there are examples of labor of European ancestry being employed as agricultural workers; in Queensland, Australia, labor of predominately European ancestry was profitably employed in sugar cane cultivation, while in the Western Hemisphere sugar was primarily cultivated by peoples of African ancestry.

McGuire and Coelho (2011) argue that slavery was confined to the American South because those with African ancestry were more productive in the *disease* environment that eventually prevailed there. The ecology of tropical West Africa is home to a host of warm-weather diseases that parasitize human populations. Descendants of tropical West Africans are relatively resistant to these diseases because their ancestors were healthy enough to reproduce and raise their children in that disease environment. The genome of the typical European colonist was the product of a disease ecology that was deficient in warm-weather diseases, and instead the product of an environment that was replete with cold-weather diseases (influenza, pleurisy, other lung infections, tuberculosis, plague, etc.). Europeans did not have the innate defenses that tropical West Africans had to warm-weather disease because of the deleterious effects that these genes had upon populations that were not afflicted by the diseases to which the genes provided some protection.[7] The lack of any net benefits prevented these genes from becoming established in the European gene pool. When Europeans were infested with parasitic diseases, helminthic and protozoan infections that were imported from Africa with the enslaved Africans, the productivity of the European peoples declined, relative to that of people of tropical West African ancestry. Conversely, in cold-weather disease ecologies, tropical West Africans were sick more frequently and had lower productivities than peoples of European ancestries. In the tropical West African disease ecology, the side-effects of genes that endowed a resistance to cold-weather diseases were greater than any benefits these genes conferred to humans; the genes were maladaptive in tropical West Africa and could not establish themselves in that gene pool. It was not climatic conditions, but disease ecologies and ethnic differences in the susceptibility to diseases that determined the regional viability and profitability of African slavery.[8] Ironically, the American disease ecology, in turn, was heavily modified by the African slave trade. Evolution endowed tropical West Africans with genes that allowed them to survive and reproduce in the disease ecology that eventually prevailed in the South. In contrast, people of Northwestern European ancestry were relatively resistant to cold-weather diseases but had few genetic immunities to warm-weather diseases.

The differences in productivity between peoples of African and European ancestries were mirrored in the differences in infection and mortality rates for different diseases. Malaria, yellow fever, and hookworm were and are much milder when contracted by people of tropical West African ancestry; when contracted by peoples of European ancestry (in the absence of modern medicines), malaria and yellow fever are very serious diseases and frequently fatal. Helminthic diseases that are abundant in tropical West Africa have similar ethnic disparities; in early twentieth-century South Carolina, hookworm was more than twice as frequent in the white (Euro-American) population relative to South Carolina's black (African-American) population. This is even more astounding when one considers that in this era in South Carolina blacks were systematically discriminated against and routinely denied public services. Death rates (again, before modern medicine) in tropical West Africa for Europeans were typically estimated to be from the low two hundreds per thousand per year to low six hundreds per thousand per year; life expectancies for Europeans living (dying seems a more appropriate term) were around two years.[9] We do not have data for the life expectancies of Africans living there, but we know they were much higher otherwise there would have been no Africans. The data that Susan Klepp (1994) derived show that, in the cold-weather climate of Boston, Massachusetts, the life expectancies of newly imported African slaves were 12 years, while European immigrants could expect to live an additional 29+ years. These data are real and substantial; differential susceptibilities to diseases were a cause of the unprofitability of African slavery in the North, and the regional specificity of slavery.[10]

Entrepreneurship

An explicitly evolutionary approach to the history of entrepreneurship challenges the accepted canon. The conventional approach to entrepreneurship focuses on individuals or firms striving towards success. The approach explains how efforts to achieve success fared, and why they failed, succeeded, or were sidetracked. But when the future is unknown and there is no road map to follow, entrepreneurs cannot know the avenue to success.

Armen Alchian (1950) suggests an analogy: suppose people driving cars wish to leave a city but the routes they take are entirely random. Some will end up running into obstacles, some will drive into areas where there are no roads, others will be on roads where there is no fuel, and others will be lucky enough to have taken routes that are passable and are replete with fueling stations. Over historical time, we would observe that the people who had gone the furthest had acted *as if* they had a road map, when it was done entirely without conscious choice. Milton Friedman (1953) suggested another metaphor; plants act as if they want to maximize the amount of sunlight they receive. We know that the reason trees grow so high is that their genetic heritage was chosen by evolutionary processes for their relative ability to acquire sunlight. Volition had nothing to do with it. This overstates the role of chance in entrepreneurial history because humans do have memory and intelligence: copying success is a strategy that sentient beings can select. Mimicking behavior may result in success; still it does not imply understanding of why the behavior results in success. This is akin to the old story of champion pool-players acting as if they had a complete understanding of geometry, Newtonian physics, and mechanics, when they are completely innocent of such knowledge; but they do play pool superbly.

In understanding actual human behavior as distinct from the actual causes of business success, the evolutionary approach may serve better than profit maximization because profit maximization is non-operational given random processes. Even if one abstracts from uncertainty (where outcomes and distributions are unknown – what has been termed "unknown unknowns"), profit maximization is not sensible. Suppose there are two possible choices that involve different distributions of outcomes: one possible choice results in a higher mean value but it has a wide distribution of possible outcomes. The other choice has a lower mean value but a narrower set of possible outcomes. Further, suppose the distributions overlap. Which distribution is a maximum? This question does not have a meaningful answer because the choice is between *distributions*. One can reasonably ask: what is the optimal distribution? But if uncertainty exists, then profit maximization is impossible. Uncertainty (a necessary condition for the existence of profits) requires that both the distributions of outcomes and means are unknown. With uncertainty there are no criteria that can lead to profit maximization. So how can one characterize business decision making?

One solution is the evolutionary approach: to observe outcomes. Firms surviving in the competition for returns greater than costs will behave *as if* they were attempting to garner profits. To survive over time, firms must have access to resources; in a market system this means that for surviving firms expenditures have to be less than revenues. The fundamental scarcity of resources guarantees this. Each generation of surviving firms has to survive, and, assuming no change (an assumption that is demonstrably false) in the economic ecology, generation after generation of surviving firms will more closely resemble the textbook models of profit maximization.

Observing the history of firms typically means observing the *survivors* of competitions for resources; this is very like the evolutionary processes. Referring to a previous analogy, genes that impart height to trees in a jungle are pro-adaptive; we can say that the trees "want" to maximize the sunlight that they capture, but this is engagingly false. Trees have no minds; the competition for scarce sunlight selects trees for height. The genes that enable height will survive and spread through the species. This is the evolutionary process. Returning to entrepreneurs, they cannot maximize any objective function because uncertainty ensures that the knowledge necessary to maximize is nonexistent. In their ignorance, all entrepreneurs grope to find ways to survive; typically this means having revenues exceed costs. Those firms whose entrepreneurs succeed at this task may continue to populate the economic ecology; those that do not are culled from the economic landscape. Entrepreneurs do not have a text to follow; what behaviors they adopt may or may not be suitable for their environment. Surviving firms will have to acquire more resources than they expend; in market exchange the positive difference between revenues and expenditure is called profit. So passing the evolutionary test (survival) does mimic profit maximization, but is it because of knowledge, innate genius, random chance, or something else? The study of entrepreneurs is often predicated upon the genius inherent in the successful; on the other hand, a close examination of individual entrepreneurs (see Thomas [1969] on Henry Ford and the automobile) suggests that the economic ecology, luck, and slightly more talent and/or foresight are what determine success in entrepreneurship. Genius is nice, but it assures neither success nor wealth. Persistence, attention to detail, and monomania appear to be more prescriptive of success than pure genius. Nevertheless, innumerable studies (granted these are typically not in the literature of economic history) appear extolling the genius of various moguls of industry and finance.[11]

The point is that the survival of firms may be characterized by the marketplace culling unsuitable products and high-cost providers; indeed, this is the competitive marketplace. The profit maximization postulate is useful as an explanation of *why* firms survive and an *as if* prescription for the behavior of firms and entrepreneurs. The assumption that entrepreneurs want their firms to survive explains why there is a non-*ad hoc* explanation of why firms mimic other firms. In the recent past, IBM, General Electric, and Japanese industry in general have all served as models to be emulated by businesses. Why was there so much copying? Because these firms were, at the time, perceived to be highly successful and it was thought that, if firms emulated them, the imitators were more likely to prosper. Management wanted their firms to survive, and what better way to survive in an unknown environment than to imitate the successful? After all, there are multitudes of ways to fail, ways to succeed are scarce; this is why we have books and speakers extolling particular paths to success, and children of all species depend upon family instinctively copying older generations. Imitation and tried-and-true paths may not be exciting, but not being exciting is a survival strategy.

Again, many of the results of employing the survival hypothesis resemble the results of conscious profit maximization, but the stories are very different; it is not the genius of the particular individuals (like Ayn Rand's John Galt) but the environment that allows multitudes of would-be entrepreneurs to strive and succeed in the marketplace. The survival hypothesis is more dynamic than profit maximization (which is by definition part of static economic analysis) because it involves continual feedback effects, and the survival hypothesis does not depend on any single being or event (the historical equivalent of the dramatist's *deus ex machina*). Economic growth, industrial and other "revolutions" depend not on individual genius but on the economic ecology. The study of entrepreneurs focuses upon the individual; this would be analogous to studying an individual tree, like the General Sherman in the Giant Forest of Sequoia National Park. We can learn from the study of individual trees, but we learn a great deal more from studying the forest ecology that allowed giant trees to come into existence and endure. In economic history, what type of story provides more knowledge? Stories that focus on individual entrepreneurs have more drama because readers can identify with the individuals and their struggles; they do pass a market test because they are popular. Less popular are stories that emphasize market conditions, constraints, and an evolving economic ecology, but they more accurately explain the ultimate causes of the development and history of economies. There are substantive differences between the two approaches; histories that focus upon rational explanations may never be popular literature, but they attempt to explain and educate, tasks that an emphasis on the individual has yet to achieve.

Industrial revolutions

Economic history has devoted considerable attention to issues surrounding industrialization and, in particular, why England does or does not deserve to be credited as the first and prime mover in what is termed the "Industrial Revolution." Biological processes and metaphors cast these debates into somewhat different perspectives. First, *was* there an industrial revolution? If there were one, then some very perceptive observers (Adam Smith, David Hume, Samuel Johnson, and Edmund Burke, to name a few) did not recognize that they were living through a "revolution." Second, if we ask, "When did you become old?", what would the answer be? This is not a sensible question because both age and its perception are relative. A child of 3 years old thinks of a child of 12 as grown; the aging process is continual and, indeed, it never stops until death. Aging is an ongoing process that continues as long as life; dating a fixed point as old is neither accurate nor does it provide insights. We talk about the development of artists, writers, and scholars as ongoing processes; dating it as we do wars obscures the maturational process. Similarly, the transition from a primarily agricultural and mercantile society to one that had a large, if not dominant, manufacturing sector was a process that was arguably less rapid than the process of human aging. Consequently, if there were an industrial revolution, like the aging process, it was only noticed retrospectively. The impertinent, yet revealing question that the child asks – "When did you grow old?" – is in this same vein.

Whether England deserves primacy in any industrial revolution is an issue that does not concern this chapter; its concern is what the answer to this question reveals. Assuming that England was first to industrialize, does this mean that, if it had been unable (e.g. if some natural or man-made catastrophe occurred) to fulfill this role, humanity would still be confined to speed limits dependent upon animal power, or, a little bit more realistically, that industrialization would have been postponed by decades or longer? Most serious scholars do not entertain these extreme alternatives, and leave them to the authors of fantasy. If England were somehow not able, there were other candidates to lead the process, perhaps not as soon and less rapidly, but still over historic time, absent England's primacy, the economic landscape of the early twentieth century would not have been much changed.

Consider the "new economic history" and the hypothetical alternative; the importance of any single innovation, individual, or resource is of relatively small importance because there are always substitutes. Relative to gross domestic product, the assessments of the magnitude of any beneficial development are relatively small because economy-wide there are relatively good substitutes. In the case of England, there were textile industries throughout Europe where innovations were being pursued because they were perceived as potentially lucrative; in the absence of English innovations, there would most probably have been Dutch, French, Irish, Scottish, Welsh, or German innovations. This is a probabilistic statement; but consider the biological analogies – eyesight and flight have arisen numerous times through mindless evolution; so what is the likelihood that substitutes for John Kay, Richard Arkwright, and James Hargreaves (to name some of the more prominent in the historiography of the textile "revolution") would have come forth from non-English textile producers consciously seeking cheaper production techniques? Observing the history of technology, there has been no new successful technology that was the creation of one individual who had no close rivals.

Alternatively, what is so important about being first? In a competitive landscape (both biological and economic) natural selection chooses winners and losers from among the competitors. Going back to the trees seeking sunlight analogy, the genetic characteristics of the tree determine its height and its ability to garner sunlight, and these determine the growth of trees; but discovering which individual tree germinated first is a question that is relatively uninteresting. So why should economic historians be concerned with primacy? Sony was first with the Betamax, yet it was replaced by the VHS system, which was supplanted by DVDs, that are/were supplanted by other developments. The video-recording industry is illustrative; the times are changing, and this is not a new development. Still one very good reason for examining primacy is the ability to discern the background conditions conducive to economic growth; yet within the same economic ecology one would expect similar economic institutions to emerge, and, if they do not, then why they did not is an interesting question.

How did the economic ecology differ between England and its continental competitors? One difference that has been commented upon (but still deserves more attention) is that until 1844 most firms in England were unincorporated (they had no corporate charter, thus no legal identity separate from owners). Legislation adopted in 1844 changed that, but it was still 10 years later before limited liability was adopted. On the continent, corporations were more common than in England until at least the mid-nineteenth century; how was the growth of England and its firms affected by the absence of corporate charters and limited liability? Obviously it was possible to have large firms without these institutions, but what were the differential costs entailed in finding substitutes, and then working with them? Because of the rapid adoption of the corporate form and limited liability when they became available, we know that their substitutes did not function as well as the corporate form. But we do not know what the actual costs were that British firms had to bear because of the difficulties in adopting the corporate form.

Biology helps get a handle on these costs. The evolution of flight, eyesight, echolocation, and communal living all developed in entirely different species many times. This suggests that, if there is an ecological (read economic) niche, random processes and evolution will eventually fill that niche. If in the prevailing environment there is a feasible (one that can reasonably arise through random processes from the resources at hand) mechanism that provides a competitive advantage, then some variant of the mechanism will evolve. Yet there remain unanswered questions: how soon did substitutes arise and how adequate were they? Extrapolating from biology and applying it to the economic ecology, the extra costs to the British economy because of the absence of incorporation seem to have been small. Issues remain. If institutions are crucial to the development process, what is the contribution of a single institutional innovation, and, if there are many substitutes for a particular innovation, are there causes more fundamental that create the conditions for the growth of institutions?

These questions are easy to ask but hard to answer; still it appears that institutions reflect the economic ecology in which they evolved. Economic institutions, like biological species, transplanted to a foreign environment frequently have difficulties in establishing themselves.

Final comments

The epigraph of Marshall's *Principles of Economics* (1890) has inscribed on it the Latin phrase: *Natura non facit saltuum.* Roughly translated, it means: Discontinuities do not appear in nature. This means that economics is about observable reality, and there is a long lineage directly linking past to the present: history does matter. We cannot escape the past. Who we are is determined by our genes and history. Our genes are the results of a long line of evolutionary selection, going back to the beginnings of life on this planet; they were selected for combinations of traits that enhance the probabilities of survival and reproduction. The ancestral environment in which our forebears lived manifests itself in who we are; the results range from the inconsequential to those that alter history. We ignore biology at our peril because it is part and parcel of material reality. The stories of natural selection and evolution help us understand our history: past, present, and future. The biological leash that constrains humanity is a long one, but it is still a leash.

Notes

1 The "selfish gene" metaphor popularized by Richard Dawkins (1976) suggests that individual organisms are "survival machines" for genes. The implication is that genes have evolved animal bodies to carry genes forward through time. More than a few have objected to this terminology; still, the fact remains that the vast majority of genes that make people have been around for millions of years. Humans have finite life expectancies, but the genes that comprise and make individuals are potentially immortal; this gives meaning to the "survival machine" terminology.

2 "Continually" is an important condition; hybrids (a cross between two separate species – for example, a mule, which is a cross between a donkey and a horse) are usually sterile; one of the definitions of a (sexual) species is that the offspring of males and females can reproduce. A horse and donkey can mate but their offspring are usually sterile; thus, horses and donkeys are different species.

3 Sexual reproduction is important because it provides a way of disseminating genes relatively rapidly through a population and it is an additional avenue for creating genetic variations. In human history this is important because different people (ethnic groups) have different frequencies of genes within their chromosomes (chromosomes are groupings of genes; each human has 23 chromosomal pairs for a total of 46 chromosomes: 23 from each parent). Over generations, people (the individual organisms that concern us most) who are most able to survive and reproduce in a given environment will have a chromosomal heritage that is the result of natural selection in their ancestral environment. There is only one human race (*H. sapiens*); nevertheless, since the Earth's environment is not homogeneous, we neither expect nor observe genetic homogeneity among the peoples of the world.

4 This assumes the brown-eyed parent was not carrying a recessive gene for blue eyes. Even here there are exceptions; people are (infrequently) born with one eye blue, the other brown. While exceptions are fascinating to specialists, they are of lesser interest to people who just want a familiarity with the subject.

5 A child born to parents heterozygous for the sickle cell trait has a 1 chance in 4 of receiving the sickle cell trait from both parents; a child with two copies of the sickle cell trait has the genetic abnormality termed "sickle cell anemia" and, in the absence of modern medicine, will usually die before reproducing. For more about both sickle cell anemia and Tay-Sachs disease, see Wailoo and Pemberton (2006).

6 Racism (or, more broadly, xenophobia) is sometimes utilized as an ancillary, or even primary, explanation for the existence of African slavery. However, racism is neither a sufficient nor necessary condition for slavery, nor does it explain why the use of African slaves in agriculture was regionally specific during the colonial era. Many New England colonialists experimented with using slave labor in agriculture; various forms of slave labor were used throughout the New England colonies during the colonial period, although, because of fears of uprisings and high death rates, American Indian slavery diminished and was finally eliminated in the early eighteenth century. (See Mann [2011] for a general depiction of Northern slavery, and Manegold [2011] for a case history of slavery on farms in New England.) New England merchants, sailors, and speculators were heavily involved in slave trading. The evidence indicates that the regional distaste for slavery was not embedded in the colonial New England soil. There was racism in both the North and South throughout the colonial period; consequently, if racism were the cause of slavery, why did it not survive in the North? Both racism and slavery existed in the North, yet a widespread, slave-based agricultural economy did not persist because it was less profitable than agriculture based on free (non-African) labor. The attempts to establish slave-based agriculture in the North and racism's existence in the North during the colonial era illustrate the difficulties of using non-economic reasoning (racism) as an explanation for widespread African slavery persisting only in the South.

7 Recall that, on average, every fourth baby born to parents who are heterozygous in the sickle cell trait will be homozygous in the trait and, thus, doomed to an early and painful death. It should be recognized that the North American New World was sufficiently less malarious than tropical West Africa; the protection the sickle cell gene (and other genes) provided against malaria was more than offset by their negative effects. The result was that these genes were maladaptive in America. Evidence for this statement is provided by genomic research; the anti-malarial genes are expressed substantially less frequently in the contemporaneous African-American gene pool than in the present-day West African gene pool – the ancestral gene pool of most African-Americans. Conversely, genes that provide some protection against influenza are disproportionately expressed in the African-American gene pool relative to the West African gene pool, reflecting disparate evolutionary pressures of the influenza virus (see Wenfei et al. (2012).

8 In the Australian sugar plantations, there were much fewer warm-weather pathogens *because* there never was any consequential trade in Australia of African slaves; consequently, most pathogens that were abundant in tropical West Africa did not become established there.

9 On life expectancies for Europeans in tropical West Africa, see Mann (2011), McGuire and Coelho (2011), and Thornton (1992).

10 McGuire and Coelho (2011) provide details on the various disease environments in colonial North America.

11 See Jonathan Hughes (1986) for an explanation of why economists/historians should focus on the individual entrepreneur. The literature on the great man in business is abundant; two relatively recent examples are Chernow (1998) and Isaacson (2011).

References and additional sources

Alchian, A.A. (1950) 'Uncertainty, evolution, and economic theory', *Journal of Political Economy*, 58: 211–21.

Chernow, R. (1998) *Titan: The Life of John D. Rockefeller, Sr.*, New York: Random House.

Coelho, P.R.P. (1985) 'An examination into the causes of economic growth', *Research in Law and Economics*, 7: 89–116.

Crosby, A.W. (1986) *Ecological Imperialism*, New York: Cambridge University Press.

Curtin, P.D. (1968) 'Epidemiology and the slave trade', *Political Science Quarterly*, 83: 190–216.

Dawkins, R. (1976) *The Selfish Gene*, New York: Oxford University Press.

Dennett, D.C. (1995) *Darwin's Dangerous Idea: Evolution and the Meaning of Life*, New York: Simon & Schuster.

Diamond, J. (1997) *Guns, Germs, and Steel: The Fates of Human Societies*, New York: Norton.

Friedman, M. (1953) *Essays in Positive Economics*, Chicago, IL: University of Chicago Press.

Hirshleifer, J. (1977) 'Economics from a biological viewpoint', *Journal of Law and Economics*, 20: 1–52.

Hughes, J. (1986) *The Vital Few: The Entrepreneur and American Economic Progress*, New York: Oxford University Press.

Isaacson, W. (2011) *Steve Jobs*, New York: Simon & Schuster.

Klepp, S.E. (1994) 'Seasoning and society: racial differences in mortality in eighteenth-century Philadelphia', *William and Mary Quarterly*, 51: 473–507.

Manegold, C.S. (2011) *Ten Hills Farm: The Forgotten History of Slavery in the North*, Princeton, NJ: Princeton University Press.

Mann, C.C. (2011) *1493 Uncovering the New World Columbus Created*, New York: Alfred A. Knopf.

Marshall, A. (1890) *Principles of Economics*, London: Macmillan and Company.

McGuire, R.A. and Coelho, P.R.P. (2011) *Parasites, Pathogens, and Progress: Diseases and Economic Development*, Cambridge, MA: MIT Press.

McNeill, W.H. (1977) *Plagues and People*, New York: Anchor Books.

Ridley, M. (2010) *The Rational Optimist: How Prosperity Evolves*, New York: HarperCollins.

Thomas, R.P. (1969) 'The automobile and its tycoon', *Explorations in Entrepreneurial History*, 6: 139–57.

Thornton, J. (1992) *Africa and Africans in the Making of the Atlantic World 1400–1800*, New York: Cambridge University Press.

Wailoo, K. and Pemberton, S. (2006) *The Troubled Dream of Genetic Medicine: Ethnicity and Innovation in Tay-Sachs, Cystic Fibrosis, and Sickle Cell Disease*, Baltimore, Md: Johns Hopkins University Press.

Wenfei, J., Xu, S., Wang, H., Yu, Y., Shen, Y., Wu, B. and Jin, L. (2012) 'Genome-wide detection of natural selection in African Americans pre- and post-admixture,' *Genome Research*, 22: 1–9.

10

THE ECONOMIC HISTORY
OF WAR AND DEFENSE

Jari Eloranta

The modern period, beginning more or less with the French Revolution in 1789,[1] was marked by pivotal changes in the power relations among nations, the financing of wars, and the actual practices of warfare. European nations had already amassed great empires prior to that, but the real culmination of their ascendancy occurred in the nineteenth century, particularly for Great Britain. The nineteenth century also featured the rapid advance of industrialization, mostly in the West, which enabled Western European powers to create military machines of unparalleled proportions. The naval supremacy of the West was proven beyond doubt during the opening of China's and Japan's markets in the mid-nineteenth century. The age of total war that began in the modern sense with the French Revolution and Napoleon pushed European states to adopt increasingly efficient fiscal systems in the nineteenth and twentieth centuries and enabled some of them to dedicate more than half of their gross domestic product (GDP) to the war effort during the world wars. Whereas, in the pre-modern world, military spending was typically the dominant item for state budgets, thrusting the most eager rulers and nations toward default, industrialized nations developed more efficient budgeting systems to cope with the threat and execution of wars.

The most successful model to follow was the so-called "British Model," which entailed developing an elaborate fiscal and financial system to support military expansion, including the use of public debt. Subsequently, with the emergence of welfare state priorities by the early twentieth century, the representative share of military spending both in terms of budgets and the economy as a whole started to decline. The exceptions to these patterns were the periods of world wars and the Cold War period (or at least most of it). The fierce economic and military rivalry between the West and the Communist Bloc escalated tensions and military spending until the 1970s (and briefly in the 1980s), resulting in spending levels that represented substantially higher shares of GDP than in the nineteenth century. Finally, the collapse of the Soviet Union alleviated some of these tensions and lowered aggregate military spending. Newer security challenges such as terrorism and various interstate rivalries have again pushed the world towards growing overall military spending.

In a way, the historical evolution of the twentieth century represents a culmination of many of these processes: industrial expansion, total war, globalization, rapid development of lethal technologies, and profound structural changes in most economies. Was the twentieth century a period of mass killings and misery or a century of economic progress, despite all the warfare?

105

A pessimistic tradition represented by scholars like Eric Hobsbawm (1996) views the extreme political and military outcomes of the period of world wars as indicative of the decadence and economic failures of the twentieth century. In this view, the twentieth century was an era of total warfare in its perverse perfection, with state-sanctioned genocides, ethnic cleansing, and totalitarianism; a world brought to the brink of extinction during the Cold War arms race. Charles Tilly (1990) identified the twentieth century as the most bellicose in human history, featuring hundreds of bloody conflicts and over a hundred million battle deaths (Tilly 1990). Niall Ferguson agrees with Tilly, saying that the hundred years after 1900 "were without question the bloodiest century in modern history, far more violent in relative as well as absolute terms than any previous era." Yet the incidence of great power wars, measured as the number of years such a war was underway, was highest in the fifteenth century (95 per cent) and lowest in the nineteenth (40 per cent) (Tilly 1990: 72). During the nineteenth and twentieth centuries, industrialized nation states found new ways to mobilize their manpower and resources for warfare, and the technological advances of the age, in particular railroads, often served both the civilian as well as military production and planning (Ferguson 2001).

It is undeniable that the twentieth century featured two of the deadliest conflicts in human history. The world wars were unparalleled in their severity and concentration, and pioneered the widespread use of genocide (Ferguson 2006). The First World War (1914–18) thrust more than 30 countries into conflict with each other and led to 20 million premature deaths, only to be outdone by the Second World War (1939–45). In that conflict, more than 60 countries engaged in a global death match and prematurely ended the lives of more than 55 million people (Broadberry and Harrison 2005). The European region and many other battlefields around the globe were devastated in many ways by these conflicts. Yet, as Bradford DeLong and Alexander Field have emphasized, the underlying continuities of technological change through the first half of the century eventually made possible the massive increases in living standards in the second half (DeLong 2000; Field 2003). Others have noted this paradox of massive conflicts alongside tremendous economic progress, which manifested itself especially in terms of incomes, improved nutrition, life expectancy, and political voice (Ferguson 2006; Lindert 2003, 2004). This economic expansion was linked to the technological advances of the period, some of which were spurred on by the conflicts.

Trends in the study of economics of war and military spending

The study of war and its economic dimensions is a very interdisciplinary endeavor. Research can be found in the pages of books and journals in economics, history, political science, anthropology, psychology, demographics, and so on. In the past, many military historians attempted to understand periods of war almost in isolation from peacetime developments. However, over the last 50 years or so, this has no longer been the case due to the emergence of the so-called "New Military History." Now scholars are much more likely to study the social and economic contexts of conflicts, by combining interdisciplinary ideas about the causes and consequences of conflicts (see, for example, Brauer and Tuyll 2008). The study of a particular conflict would indeed be quite futile if one did not study the period that preceded it in order to gauge the short- and long-term processes that led to it. Moreover, many scholars have been interested in the economic and social aftermath of conflicts. Economic historians have also made significant contributions to the study of both peacetime impacts and causes of wars, as well as the processes that determine the outcome of these conflicts. (See, for example, Harrison 1998; Eloranta 2007; Harrison and Wolf 2012.)

Military spending is crucial for understanding many aspects of economic and political history: the cost, funding, and burden of conflicts, the creation of nation states, and in general the increased role of the state. Economic historians have tended to focus on the economics of global conflicts as well as the immediate short-term economic impacts of wartime mobilization (Milward 1965, 1977). Defense economists have been preoccupied mostly with the immense expansion of military budgets and military-industrial complexes in the Cold War era, and have, by and large, ignored other historical periods in their studies (e.g. Sandler and Hartley 1995). Conflict and peace scientists, a sub-field of political science, have focused on the causes of conflicts and, for example, the impact of democracies as a possible pacifying influence (so-called democratic peace debate) among states. Moreover, even though some cycle theorists and conflict scientists have been interested in the formation of modern nation states and the respective system of states since 1648, most conflict scientists have had less interest in the long-run analysis of the causes of warfare (see, especially, Geller and Singer 1998).

Many of the explanations of states' military-fiscal behavior focus on the short-run dimensions of the effects of wars and defense spending, and neglect to discuss the long-run economic outcomes. Carolyn Webber and Aaron Wildavsky maintain that each political culture generates its characteristic budgetary objectives – namely, productivity in market regimes, redistribution in groups dissenting from an established authority, and more complex procedures in hierarchical regimes (Webber and Wildavsky 1986). They, in turn, have implications for the respective regimes' revenue and spending needs. For example, despotic regimes would have a higher propensity to spend money for military purposes, to project power both internally and externally, and social democracies (e.g. Sweden from the 1930s onward) would be less likely to maintain massive military establishments in the long run.

Richard Bonney (1999) focuses on the evolution of fiscal regimes mainly for the early modern states. He emphasizes that the states' revenue and tax collection systems, the backbone of any militarily successful nation state, have evolved over time. During the Middle Ages, European fiscal systems were relatively backward and autarchic, whereas the modern fiscal state (embodying more complex fiscal and political structures) is able to maximize resources for possible conflicts. A superpower like Great Britain in the nineteenth century in fact had to be a fiscal state to be able to dominate the world, due to all the burdens that went with an empire. Niall Ferguson (2001, 2003) maintains that wars have shaped all the most relevant institutions of modern economic life. The invention of public debt instruments has gone hand-in-hand with more democratic forms of government and military supremacy, which is sometimes referred to as the British model. Such regimes have also been the most efficient economically, and military expenditures may have been the principal cause of fiscal innovation for most of history. A successful ascendancy to a leadership position requires higher expenditures, a substantial navy, fiscal and political structures conducive to increasing the availability of credit, and reoccurring participation in international conflicts. Most great powers had acquired such structures by the twentieth century, which also meant more intense military competition and more destructive conflicts.

Towards the British Model and industrialization of war

In the eighteenth century, with rapid population growth in Europe, armies grew in size, and most states had more resources at their disposal to fight longer wars. Or, they were forced to adopt British-style institutions to be able to do so in the long run. Those that did not follow this model seemed doomed to fail or face serious domestic challenges to authoritarian monarchic rule. In Western Europe, the scale and scope of warfare increased from the Seven Years War (1756–63) to the French Revolution and Napoleon's conquests (1792–1815). The new style of warfare brought on by the French Revolutionary and Napoleonic Wars – with conscription, blockades, civilian casualties, and war of attrition as new elements – meant that the great powers required larger and larger military capacity to survive. For example, the French army grew over 3.5 times in size from 1789 to 1793, up to 650,000 men. Respectively, the British army grew from 57,000 in 1783 to 255,000 men in 1816. The Russian army acquired the massive size of 800,000 men in 1816, and it exceeded 1 million men in the nineteenth century (Eloranta 2003).

The industrialized, more centralized governments with large, conscripted armies required new ways of financing. The fiscal reforms they implemented included centralized public administration, reliance on specific, balanced budgets, innovations in public banking and public debt management, and reliance on direct taxation of income for revenue. In particular, the most successful nations borrowed mostly from their own citizens, in exchange for more access to the political process, and this made the governments less likely to renege on their loan commitments. The industrialization and rapid economic development, which tended to favor the Western nations, brought more revenue for the governments in the nineteenth century. The nineteenth century was also the century of the industrialization of war, starting in the mid-century and gathering breakneck speed quickly. By the 1880s, military engineering was leap-frogging civil engineering, and more and more armaments firms were established; first to serve the domestic markets, and then to enter into growing international markets for arms. Furthermore, a revolution in transportation with steamships and railroads made massive, long-distance mobilizations possible, as seen in the Prussian victory over the French in 1870–1. The destructive bang for the buck increased rapidly, which was in fact the pattern for the nineteenth and twentieth centuries as a whole (McNeill 1982; Ferguson 2001).

The military spending patterns depicted in Table 10.1 indicate some broader patterns too. First, the British Empire was not as expensive as many assume; a pattern that applied to some other empires as well. But the British Model certainly produced the most stable financial basis for the maintenance and expansion of an empire. Second, there were relatively few great power conflicts in the nineteenth century (some of the exceptions included the Crimean War, 1853–6, and the Franco-Prussian War, 1870–1), and most of the conflicts during the period consisted of civil wars and colonial conflicts. Subsequently, some of the non-European powers like the

Table 10.1 Military spending patterns for France, Germany, Russia, Sweden, the United Kingdom, and the United States, 1815–1913

Year	France DF	France ML	Germany DF	Germany ML	Russia DF	Russia ML	Sweden DF	Sweden ML	UK DF	UK ML	U.S. DF	U.S. ML
1815	40.2	4.7	..	..	59.0	..	..	4.7	73.1	..	71.7	2.9
1825	34.8	2.8	..	..	43.4	..	..	3.1	28.1	..	42.3	0.8
1835	36.0	2.5	..	..	..	..	..	3.6	25.2	2.6	54.8	0.6
1845	33.3	2.6	..	..	..	..	..	3.1	25.0	2.5	52.5	0.7
1855	50.9	8.5	..	..	..	..	..	2.7	29.6	3.6	47.0	0.7
1865	34.2	3.0	..	..	25.4	..	49.9	2.3	39.2	2.5	88.9	17.6
1875	33.9	4.4	68.5	2.2	33.3	2.7	39.7	2.0	32.7	1.9	22.8	0.7
1885	31.5	4.4	69.3	2.2	26.9	3.6	37.4	2.0	32.6	2.3	22.6	0.6
1895	30.7	4.3	54.3	2.6	22.5	4.1	35.7	2.2	33.7	2.3	22.6	0.6
1905	33.0	2.9	48.2	2.5	50.9	12.0	34.0	2.2	44.9	3.2	42.9	1.0
1913	37.0	4.0	54.2	3.4	28.4	4.4	31.3	2.2	37.8	2.9	46.9	0.8

DF = defense share = military spending, per cent of central or federal government expenditures. ML = military burden = military spending per cent of GDP.
Source: See Eloranta (2005) for details.

United States were not interested in dominating international politics, which can be seen in its meager defense spending in the period. Third, the military spending of most nations increased in the pre-First World War period with the accelerating arms race. Yet, in comparison with the pre-Second World War military spending, this arms race was quite tame.

The European powers increased the absolute amount they spent on defense in the nineteenth century without actually increasing military expenditures as a relative share of fiscal or economic resources. In the French case, the average defense share (military spending as a per cent of central/ federal government expenditures) remained at similar levels in the nineteenth and early twentieth centuries, at little over 30 per cent, whereas the military burden (military spending as a per cent of GDP) increased from less than 3 per cent to 4 per cent, with 1905 being the exception. The British defense share increased slightly from the early nineteenth century to 1870–1913. However, the strength of the British economy made it possible that the military burden actually declined a little to 2.6 per cent, which is similar to what Germany was spending in the same period (1870–1913). For most countries the period leading to the First World War meant higher military burdens than the early nineteenth century, such as Japan's 6.1 per cent (see Eloranta 2007). The aggregate, systemic (based on a 16-country total) real military spending in this period increased consistently. Moreover, the impact of the Russo-Japanese War (1904–5) was immense for the great powers' military spending behavior: the unexpected defeat of the Russians, along with the arrival of dreadnoughts, launched an arms race, which increased military spending as a whole among great powers, even if some like the U.S. actually decreased their military burden (Eloranta 2007).

Age of total war

The new military might of European powers was unleashed in August 1914 with horrible consequences, leading to a war that many of the participants expected to win quickly. Yet they ended up fighting a protracted war in the Western front trenches and other parts of Europe, as well as in far-away colonies. The age of total war, or "war of the world" as Niall Ferguson coined this era, had become a reality (Ferguson 2006). It has been estimated that about 9 million combatants and 12 million civilians died during the so-called "Great War," with property damage especially acute in France, Belgium, and Poland. According to the most recent estimates, the economic losses arising from the war may be as high as over 11 trillion 2011 US dollars (Broadberry and Harrison 2005).

In the First World War, the French military burden was fairly high in addition to the size of its military forces and the number of battle deaths. France mobilized the most resources, relatively, for the war and, subsequently, suffered the greatest losses. The mobilization by Germany was also quite extensive, because most of the state budget was used to support the war effort. On the other hand, the United States barely mobilized economically for the war, and its personnel losses in the conflict were relatively small. In comparison, the massive population of Russia allowed them to incur fairly high personnel losses, quite similar to the Soviet experience in the Second World War, without collapsing. The First World War also disrupted international trade and left the gold standard in shambles (Eloranta and Harrison 2010).

The concept and practice of total war had, of course, been around for a long time, although the First World War brought it to a new level by combining industrialized empires with new types of weapons capable of mass killing. The participants in the war had to harness the entire society and economic resources to fight this war, as well as attempt to disrupt their enemies' trade and ability to mobilize by imposing blockades. European colonies and neutral countries were equally affected by this conflict. The war also brought the first era of globalization to an end and initiated an era of instability and protectionism. Conversely, it was also the beginning of the end for European empires and initiated a wave of democratization, at least in the long run.

In the interwar period, military spending levels of participants of the First World War plummeted, at least in the 1920s. New strains on spending included pension and healthcare concerns arising from the war, as well as reconstruction expenses. Many countries had financed the war by resorting to debt, particularly borrowing from the United States, and they tried to impose the cost on Germany in the form of reparations. Germany's inability to pay ultimately led to negotiations and *de facto* default in the early 1930s, and the United States was not paid back in full the war debts incurred by the Allies. In many countries, except the authoritarian regimes, the defense shares dropped noticeably, yet their respective military burdens stayed either at similar levels as before the war or even increased – for example, the French military burden rose to a mean level of 7.2 per cent in this period. In Great Britain also, the defense share mean dropped to 18.0 per cent, although the military burden mean actually increased compared with the pre-war period, despite military expenditure cuts. The mid-1930s marked the beginning of intense rearmament for the reluctant democracies, whereas many of the authoritarian regimes had begun earlier in the decade. Nazi Germany increased its military burden from 1.6 per cent in 1933 to 18.9 per cent in 1938, a rearmament program combining creative financing and promising both guns and butter for the Germans. Mussolini was not quite as successful in his efforts to recreate the Roman Empire, with a military burden fluctuating between 4 and 5 per cent in the 1930s. The Japanese rearmament drive, driven by a militaristic elite, was perhaps the most impressive, with a military burden as high as 22.7 per cent and a defense share of over 50 per cent in 1938. For many countries, such as France and Russia, the rapid pace of technological change in the 1930s rendered many of the earlier armaments obsolete only two or three years later (Eloranta 2005, and see Eloranta 2002 for the data sources).

Some smaller countries behaved similarly to the UK and France, which belonged to a higher spending group among European democracies. This was also similar to most of the East European states. Belgium and the Netherlands were among the low-spending group, perhaps due to the futility of trying to defend their borders amid a probable conflict involving their giant neighbors, France and Germany. Overall, the democracies maintained fairly steady military burdens throughout the period. Their rearmament was, however, much slower than the effort amassed by most autocracies, as seen in Figure 10.1, such as Germany and Japan. The Soviet Union was a bit slower than its authoritarian rivals. However, the military burdens of most great powers were substantially higher before the Second World War compared with 1914.

As seen in Figure 10.2, the 1930s featured a modest naval arms race, reminiscent of the pre-First World War arms race, especially after 1933. The naval arms limitation agreements of the 1920s became less and less effective as the League of Nations proved unable to mediate international disputes. While the British rearmament programs, often in connection with Depression-related employment efforts, produced a strong increase in tonnage in the 1930s, the French naval stock declined, both due to lack of funding and the aging of the ships. The German fleet, practically nonexistent before the 1930s, was built up quite fast, at least to provide a significant threat to the French, yet the naval lead of the United Kingdom and the United States remained clear. The great powers tended to expand and modernize their fleets in the 1930s, along with other rearmament efforts, leading to an arms race (Eloranta 2011).

The Second World War began in stages, first with Japanese aggression in Manchuria in the early 1930s, then with Italian aggression in North Africa in the middle of the decade, followed by Japanese invasion of China in 1937 as well as Hitler's annexation of territory in Central Europe. The final straw was Germany's invasion of Poland on September 1, 1939, following a pact with the Soviet Union. The ensuing conflict was truly a global war encompassing the

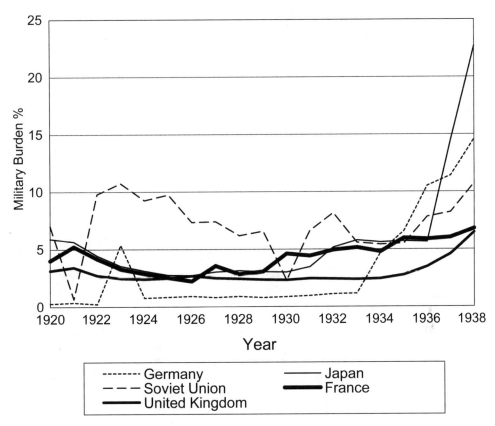

Figure 10.1 Military burdens for France, Germany, Japan, Soviet Union, and the UK, 1920–1938
Source: See Eloranta (2002) for details.

world. The initial phase from 1939 to early 1942 favored the Axis powers as far as strategic and economic resources and performance were concerned. After that, the war of attrition, with the United States and the USSR joining the Allies, turned the tide in favor of the Allies. For example, in 1943 the Allied total GDP was 3.84 trillion in 2011 dollars, whereas the Axis accounted for only 1.53 trillion 2011 dollars. It seems plausible that the "rich" countries, which often were democracies, ultimately won this conflict due to their superior resources and ability to mobilize even further than their typically more agricultural and authoritarian enemies.

The impact of the Second World War was profound for the participants' economies. For example, Great Britain at the height of the First World War incurred a military burden of about 27 per cent, whereas the military burden level consistently held throughout the Second World War was over 50 per cent (Eloranta 2005). The greatest military burden was likely incurred by Germany, even though the other great powers experienced similar levels (over 50 per cent). Only the massive economic resources of the United States made possible its lower military burden. Also the United Kingdom and the United States mobilized their central/federal government expenditures more effectively for the military effort, albeit slowly. The Soviet Union was the least effective in mobilizing its resources, although they did manage to squeeze enough out of their industrial base to help turn back the German invasion in 1942–3, and additionally the share of military personnel out of the population was relatively small compared with the

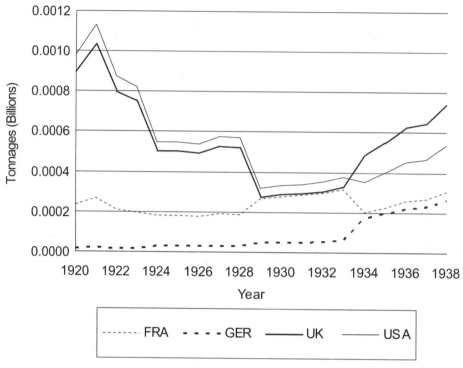

Figure 10.2 Total depreciated tonnages of France, Germany, the United Kingdom, and the United States, 1920–1938
Source: See Eloranta (2011) for details.

other great powers. As a whole, the largest personnel losses were incurred by Germany and the Soviet Union – many times those of the other great powers. Moreover, it should be noted that 70 per cent of German casualties occurred on the Eastern front. In comparison with the First World War, the Second World War was even more destructive and lethal, and the aggregate economic losses from the war were over 64 trillion in 2011 dollars. After the war, European industrial and agricultural production amounted to only one-half of the 1938 total (Eloranta and Harrison 2010).

The Cold War and its aftermath

The United States assumed a new military–political leadership role after the war, a role that would have been warranted by its dominant economic status established over 50 years earlier. With the establishment of NATO in 1949, a formidable defense alliance was formed by the major Western countries. The Soviet Union, rising to a new prominence after being on the winning side in the war, established the Warsaw Pact in 1955 to counter these efforts by capitalist economies. The Second World War also brought about a change in the public spending and taxation levels of most Western nations. The introduction of welfare states brought the OECD government expenditure average from just under 30 per cent of the GDP in the 1950s to over 40 per cent in the 1970s. Social and military spending levels followed suit and peaked during the early Cold War. The American military burden climbed over 10 per cent in 1952–4, and the

United States retained a high mean value for the Cold War period (1946–91) of 7.5 per cent. Great Britain and France followed the American example after the Korean War (Eloranta 2005).

The Cold War turned into a relentless arms race, with nuclear weapons and other modern technologies increasing both the destructive capacity of the weapons as well as the bang for the buck for the two superpowers. The USSR spent about 60 to 70 per cent of the American level in the 1950s, and possibly even more than the United States in the 1970s in terms of actual dollars spent. Nonetheless, the United States initially maintained a massive advantage over the Soviets in terms of nuclear warheads, as seen in Figure 10.3. The United States eventually lost this lead in the 1970s. However, the United States could count on a 2-to-1 lead in aggregate military spending in favor of the NATO countries over the Warsaw Pact members in the 1970s and early 1980s. The cost per soldier also increased – it has been estimated that technological advances produced a mean annual increase in real costs of about 5.5 per cent in the post-war period. Nonetheless, spending on personnel and their maintenance remained the biggest spending item for most countries (Eloranta 2005).

World military spending levels started to decline in the 1970s, although the early Reagan years were an exception for the U.S. In 1986, the U.S. military burden was up slightly to 6.5 per cent, whereas in 1999 it was down to 3.0 per cent. During the period 1977–99, in

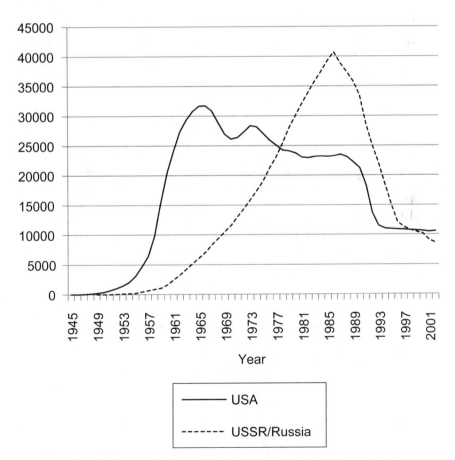

Figure 10.3 Number of nuclear warheads owned by the U.S. and the Soviet Union (or Russia), 1945–2001
Source: see http://www.rense.com/general47/global.htm for further details.

comparison, the French military burden declined from the high levels in the 1950s to a mean level of 3.6 per cent at the turn of the millennium. This was mostly the outcome of the reduction in tensions in the post-Cold War climate as well as the downfall of the USSR and the communist regimes in Eastern Europe. The USSR was spending almost as much on its armed forces as the United States up until the mid-1980s, and the official Soviet military burden was still 12.3 per cent in 1990 (Eloranta 2005). However, there is a lot of debate about how much the USSR actually spent on defense. Figures adjusted by Mark Harrison point toward a larger military burden for 1980 than previously assumed – in fact, it seems that the Soviets were spending about a quarter of their national income on defense fairly consistently (Harrison 2003).

Under the Russian Federation, with a declining GDP, this level dropped rapidly to 3.2 per cent by the end of the twentieth century. Similarly, other nations downscaled their military spending in the late 1980s and the 1990s. For example, German military spending in constant 1990 U.S. dollars was over 52 billion in 1991, whereas in 1999 it had declined to less than 40 billion. Overall there was a reduction of about one-third in real terms in world military spending in 1989–96. In the global scheme, world military expenditure was still highly concentrated in the hands of a few countries at the end of the twentieth century, with the 15 major spenders accounting for 80 per cent of the world total in 1999. The newest military spending estimates display a growth trend in the world military expenditures once again, due to new threats such as international terrorism and international rivalries in the twenty-first century. In terms of absolute figures, the United States still dominates the world military spending with almost 50 per cent of the rest of the world's military spending total, although the U.S. spending total becomes slightly less impressive when purchasing power parities (PPPs) are utilized (more details can be found at http://www.sipri.org, especially in the military spending database).

The cost of warfare has increased in the last centuries. The adoption of new technologies and massive standing armies has ensured that military expenditures have retained a central role for modern fiscal regimes. Although the growth of welfare states in the twentieth century has forced some trade-offs between "guns and butter," usually the spending choices have not been mutually exclusive. Thus, the size and spending of governments have increased. It is not likely that military spending will be displaced as a major spending item in national budgets despite new fiscal challenges brought on by welfare expansions, government debt crises, and the weight of entitlement programs for aging Western populations, although declines in the percentage of defense spending in federal budgets seems to be the order of the day. Having said that, however, various international threats and the lack of international cooperation will ensure that military spending will remain the main contender to social expenditures in the twenty-first century.

Notes

1 Some of the earlier wars of the eighteenth century already featured some of the characteristics of modern warfare, such as far-reaching practices of economic warfare and global conflict – for example, the Seven Years' War and the American Revolution. Nonetheless, the French Revolution and the Napoleonic conflicts brought about such widespread political, economic, and social changes that they are typically mentioned as a watershed moment in bringing about modernity.

References

Bonney, R. (ed.) (1999) *The Rise of the Fiscal State in Europe c. 1200–1815*, Oxford: Oxford University Press.

Brauer, J. and Tuyll, H.V. (2008) *Castles, Battles and Bombs: How Economics Explains Military History*, Chicago, IL: Chicago University Press.

Broadberry, S. and Harrison, M. (2005) 'The economics of World War I: an overview', in S. Broadberry and M. Harrison (eds) *The Economics of World War I*, Cambridge: Cambridge University Press.

DeLong, J.B. (2000) 'Cornucopia: the pace of economic growth in the twentieth century', NBER Working Paper No. 7602.

Eloranta, J. (2002) 'External security by domestic choices: military spending as an impure public good among eleven European states, 1920–38', European University Institute, Department of History and Civilisation, Florence, Italy.

——(2003) 'National defense', in J. Mokyr (ed.) *The Oxford Encyclopedia of Economic History*, Oxford: Oxford University Press.

——(2005) 'Military spending patterns in history', in R. Whaples (ed.) *EH.Net Encyclopedia of Economic and Business History*, http://eh.net/encyclopedia/article/eloranta.military

——(2007) 'From the great illusion to the Great War: military spending behaviour of the great powers, 1870–1913', *European Review of Economic History*, 11: 255–83.

——(2011) 'Why did the League of Nations fail?' *Cliometrica*, 5: 27–52.

Eloranta, J. and Harrison, M. (2010) 'War and disintegration, 1914–50', in S. Broadberry and K. O'Rourke (eds) *The Cambridge Economic History of Modern Europe: Volume 2, 1870 to the Present*, New York: Cambridge University Press.

Ferguson, N. (2001) *The Cash Nexus: Money and Power in the Modern World, 1700–2000*, New York: Basic Books.

——(2003) *Empire: The Rise and Demise of the British World Order and the Lessons for Global Power*, New York: Basic Books.

——(2006) *The War of the World: Twentieth-century Conflict and the Descent of the West*, New York: Penguin Press.

Field, A.J. (2003) 'The most technologically progressive decade of the century', *American Economic Review*, 93: 1399–414.

Geller, D.S. and Singer, J.D. (1998) *Nations at War: A Scientific Study of International Conflict*, New York: Cambridge University Press.

Harrison, M. (ed.) (1998) *The Economics of World War II: Six Great Powers in International Comparison*, Cambridge: Cambridge University Press.

Harrison, M. (2003) 'How much did the Soviets really spend on defence? New evidence from the close of the Brezhnev era', Warwick Economic Research Papers, 1–39.

Harrison, M. and Wolf, N. (2012) 'The frequency of wars', *Economic History Review*, 65: 1055–76.

Hobsbawm, E.J. (1996) *The Age of Extremes: A History of the World, 1914–1991*, New York: Vintage Books.

Lindert, P.H. (2003) 'Voice and growth: was Churchill right?' NBER Working Paper No. 9749.

——(2004) *Growing Public. Social Spending and Economic Growth since the Eighteenth Century*, Cambridge: Cambridge University Press.

McNeill, W.H. (1982) *The Pursuit of Power: Technology, Armed Force, and Society since A.D. 1000*, Chicago, IL: University of Chicago Press.

Milward, A.S. (1965) *The German Economy at War*, London: Athlone Press.

——(1977) *War, Economy and Society 1939–1945*, London: Allen Lane.

Sandler, T. and Hartley, K. (1995) *The Economics of Defense*, Cambridge: Cambridge University Press.

Tilly, C. (1990) *Coercion, Capital, and European States, AD 990–1990*, Cambridge, MA: Basil Blackwell.

Webber, C. and Wildavsky, A. (1986) *A History of Taxation and Expenditure in the Western World*, New York: Simon and Schuster.

11

BUSINESS CYCLES

Christopher Hanes

This chapter examines characteristics and causes of American business cycles in the era before the First World War – the "prewar" era – especially the years from 1879 on, which represent a distinct monetary regime. In January 1879, the U.S. Treasury began to redeem legal-tender currency in gold at a fixed rate, placing the U.S. within the international gold-standard system that had developed in the 1870s (Meissner 2005). Unlike most large gold-standard countries, the U.S. had no central bank. In 1914, the American monetary regime changed in two ways: the international gold standard broke down as other countries suspended gold convertibility, and the U.S. gained a central bank in the Federal Reserve system.

To describe the characteristics of prewar business cycles, I compare them with those of the "postwar" era since the Second World War. Thus, in the first section of the chapter, I review some established facts about postwar business cycles. The second section examines evidence about prewar cycles, emphasizing the limits on our knowledge due to lack of historical data. Finally, the third section discusses causes of prewar business cycles – that is, the events exogenous to the American economy (political, natural, or foreign developments) that explain why downturns and upturns occurred when they did. Recent research has identified the exogenous causes of most prewar business cycles.

Facts about post–Second World War business cycles

Many macroeconomic concepts such as unemployment and national income were developed or refined over the 1930s. By the late 1940s, the U.S. had put into place bureaucratic structures to collect the information needed to construct most of the statistics commonly used in macroeconomic research today, such as monthly unemployment rates and quarterly national income and product accounts (NIPAs). Because standard time-series data begin after the Second World War, so do the samples for most macroeconomic empirical work.

A business cycle is often defined as a short-term fluctuation in aggregate employment or aggregate output (real gross domestic product [GDP]) as indicated by variations in annual growth rates or deviations from longer-term trends. The business-cycle dating committee of the National Bureau of Economic Research (NBER) uses a more restrictive definition: a cyclical downturn is an absolute decline in real output across most sectors of the economy, not just a growth slowdown or dip below trend in real GDP. An NBER business-cycle "peak" (trough) is the point in time that output began to fall (rise again). Using the general definition, a variable can be classed as "acyclical," "procyclical," or "countercyclical" as its fluctuations are uncorrelated, positively or negatively correlated with those in real GDP. Using the NBER definition, it can be characterized on the basis of its behavior in recessions (peak to trough) and recoveries (trough to peak). The following characterizations hold either way.

Real GDP is the sum of various types of real spending: consumption, investment, government expenditure on goods and services, and net exports. Real GDP is also the sum of output (value added) of individual sectors: manufacturing, mining, agriculture, and services. Estimates of real GDP and its components for the postwar era, constructed by the Bureau of Economic Analysis (BEA), are based on an astounding mass of information. Some is about quantities of goods produced or shipped (e.g. number of automobiles sold), but most is about dollar values: of output and shipments, retail sales, receipts of service providers, payrolls, tax collections, exports and imports, and so on. To estimate quantities from dollar values (and vice versa), the BEA applies specialized price indices that match the dollar values in question (U.S. Bureau of Economic Analysis 2005).

In postwar NIPA data, across types of spending, consumption is procyclical; investment is more strongly procyclical; net exports are countercyclical. Across sectors, output is generally procyclical (highly correlated with other sectors' output) with one exception: agriculture. As early business-cycle researchers observed, outputs of crops and livestock "undergo cyclical movements, but they have little or no relation to business cycles" (Burns 1951: 7–8); "the basic industry of growing crops does not expand and contract in unison with mining, manufacturing, trading, transportation and finance" because "farmers cannot control the short-term fluctuations in their output … the factor that dominates year-to-year changes in the harvests is that intricate complex called weather. Plant diseases and insect pests also exert an appreciable influence" (Mitchell 1951: 56–7).

Postwar employment statistics are based on two types of surveys, carried out every month by the Bureau of Labor Statistics (BLS). Surveying firms, the BLS records total numbers and hours of employees. Surveying households, the BLS classifies adults as employed, unemployed, or neither. A person is classified as unemployed if he or she is not employed or self-employed but is actively looking for work or on temporary layoff. The number of unemployed plus the number employed, excluding those employed in the military, make up the "civilian labor force." The civilian unemployment rate is the fraction of unemployed in the civilian labor force.

Outside agriculture, total employment hours fluctuate with real value-added but with smaller amplitude, so nonagricultural output per hour is procyclical. Hours per employee is procyclical, but most variation in total hours is due to changes in the number employed or self-employed. The civilian unemployment rate is highly countercyclical. The civilian labor force is procyclical, which is to say that the number of people *out* of the labor force (not employed, not actively looking for work, not on temporary layoff) is countercyclical.

Postwar price indices include the Consumer Price Index (CPI), which measures prices paid by households for consumer goods and services and housing costs; and producer price indices (PPIs), which measure prices received by the firms that originally produce goods and services, as distinct from prices received by retailers, middlemen, and wholesalers. The price-index counterpart of real GDP is the GDP price index, a Fisher–ideal index for prices of all final goods and services produced in the U.S.

All these price indices show a cyclical pattern known as the "accelerationist Phillips curve" in postwar samples that stretch past the mid-1960s: the change in inflation is positively correlated with the level of real activity (e.g. real GDP deviations from trend), negatively correlated with the civilian unemployment rate. Across different price indices, the degree of sensitivity to real activity depends on the relative weight given to more-finished goods and services versus less-finished commodities such as farm products, minerals, and raw materials. Prices of less-finished commodities are more procyclical in inflation rates and levels. Thus, inflation in PPIs for crude or intermediate commodities shows more sensitivity to real activity than inflation in finished-good PPIs, CPIs or GDP price indices (Hanes 1999).

Postwar wage series include average hourly earnings (AHEs) and employment cost indices (ECIs). ECIs are derived from surveys of establishments that record wages and benefits for narrowly defined occupations within the establishment. For ECIs, changes in wages for individual jobs are aggregated up with fixed weights from one period to the next. Thus, ECIs are unaffected by changes in the mix of employees across jobs, firms, and industries: changes in ECIs reflect only changes in wage rates or salaries paid by given firms for given jobs. AHEs are derived from data on firms' total payrolls and hours. They reflect changes in wage rates but are also affected by the distribution of a given firm's employees between high-wage and low-wage jobs, and the distribution of employees between high- versus low-wage employers. Depending on the level of aggregation, AHEs can be affected by changes in the mix of workers across high- versus low-wage industries. For most purposes, ECIs are the more appropriate wage series, but they were not developed until the 1970s, so many older studies relied on AHEs. Rates of inflation in both ECIs and AHEs show the same accelerationist Phillips curve pattern apparent in price indices.

Disaggregated data on wage rates paid for individual jobs show a pattern known as "downward nominal wage rigidity." In any year, some jobs' wage rates rise much more than average while some rise less. Many wage rates are held absolutely fixed from year to year. But absolute *cuts* in wage rates are *extremely* rare even in recessions (Lebow *et al.* 2003).

Ratios of wages to prices are "real wages." "Real consumption wages" are wages relative to prices households pay for consumption goods, services, and housing. "Real product wages" are wages relative to prices received by employers for their workers' output. The obvious measure of real consumption wages is the ratio of ECIs to CPIs. This measure is procyclical. The proper measure of real product wages is not so obvious, because PPIs come in many categories. Using PPIs for more-finished goods, real wages are procyclical or acyclical. Using PPIs for less-finished goods, real wages are countercyclical. This is, of course, another side of the procyclical pattern in less-finished goods' relative prices (Hanes 1996). The goods in postwar CPIs, which is to say the goods postwar households buy, are mainly more-finished goods.

Facts about pre-First World War business cycles

There is a lot that we do not and *cannot* know about prewar business cycles. As Carter and Sutch (1990: 15) observe, research on the topic is like "inferring the shape of some long-extinct animal from bones collected in an ancient tar pit." Many of today's most useful macroeconomic statistics, such as unemployment rates and NIPAs, simply cannot be constructed for the prewar era at frequencies useful for business-cycle research, because no one collected the necessary information. Of course, it is fun to try to answer questions like "What would the civilian unemployment rate have been in 1893?" One can find annual, even quarterly frequency estimates of many standard macroeconomic variables for the prewar era, which were created by combining the scanty historical evidence with reasonable assumptions. But it is important to keep in mind that these estimates are largely distillations of their creators' assumptions. They are not *data* like postwar statistics. To avoid mistaking assumptions for data, it is usually best to work with time series that can be constructed from historical evidence without more assumptions than are required for their postwar counterparts. Often, that means relying on statistics that have a subsidiary role nowadays, such as indices of industrial production (IP) and wholesale prices.

Fortunately, the most reliable prewar statistics are enough to establish key facts. Prewar cycles were like postwar cycles in that both consumption and investment were procyclical; net exports were not procyclical; farm output was volatile but acyclical.

Prewar cycles were *different* in the behavior of wages and prices. In prewar data, the level of real activity is correlated with inflation, not the change in inflation. Real consumption wages, measured as wage rates over CPIs, were countercyclical or acyclical, not procyclical. The prewar era was also different in that many cyclical downturns were accompanied by national financial crises, with mass withdrawals of funding from key financial intermediaries, choked-off credit supply, and payment-system breakdowns. Such crises have been rare in subsequent eras, occurring only in the 1929–33 downturn of the Great Depression and in 2007–8.

Prewar employment and unemployment

Recall that postwar employment data are based on monthly BLS surveys of firms and households. In the prewar era, the decennial census surveyed households, determining whether people had jobs or were self-employed. It also surveyed businesses, determining the number of employees. Thus, for census years it is possible to estimate the number of people employed using definitions close to those applied by the postwar BLS. Years between censuses are another matter. There is very little annual-frequency, much less monthly, information of any kind about the number of people with jobs. Starting in 1890, the Interstate Commerce Commission (ICC) recorded annual employment in intercity railways (U.S. Census 1975: 726). About the same time, statistical bureaus in a few states began annual surveys of large manufacturing plants, inquiring about employment among other things. Building on the work of Lebergott (1964), Weir (1992) constructed annual estimates of total U.S. nonfarm employment starting with 1890. Weir and Lebergott had to guess at annual employment outside manufacturing and railroads, and employment in manufacturing outside the small number of states with surveys. To do this, they made assumptions about the relation between employment and variables for which they had annual, national data, mainly variables indicating the quantity of manufacturing output and railway traffic.

A variety of evidence from the prewar era shows that there must have been widespread unemployment, on the postwar definition, during depressions (Keyssar 1986). But no prewar survey asked questions like those the postwar BLS has used to categorize a person as unemployed, so it is not possible to estimate the unemployment rate in any prewar year on the postwar definition. Again building on Lebergott (1964), Weir (1992) used his annual estimates of total employment to construct annual figures for an essentially different notion of the unemployment rate, in terms of the "usual labor force." The usual labor force is the number of employed in a "normal" year, estimated from decennial census data and intercensal population growth in relevant demographic categories. The usual labor force is acyclical by construction, while the labor force in postwar BLS statistics is procyclical as noted earlier.

National income and product accounts

Prewar censuses (decennial censuses and additional censuses of manufacturing in 1905 and 1914) surveyed businesses and recorded dollar values of output or sales and most costs (such as wages and salaries and costs of materials) over the year preceding the census. Thus, for census years it is possible to construct estimates of many NIPA variables along the lines of postwar estimates. Using census data and price indices described later, Shaw (1947) constructed census-year estimates for an important component of GDP – nominal and real values of manufactured goods and other commodities produced for final use by households and firms. Building on Shaw's work, Kuznets (1946) constructed census-year estimates of nominal and real gross national product (GNP) and sectoral value-added, which were improved by Kendrick (1961) and Gallman (1966).

Years between censuses are, again, another matter. Annual-frequency information about dollar values of output or sales is quite limited. It includes merchandise exports and imports, values of shipments of some items in internal trade (for example, flour shipments received at New York City), and estimated value of planned construction in some large cities from construction permits. Starting in the late 1880s, the state surveys mentioned earlier give values of output in large manufacturing establishments in a few states. For manufacturing, mining, agriculture, and transportation services, there is more information about output quantities: measures of traffic on railways and waterways (in weight, volume, or mileage), quantities of manufactured goods produced (e.g. tons of steel) or raw materials consumed in manufacturing (e.g. raw cotton for textiles), output of coal (both anthracite and bituminous), petroleum and many other minerals, annual harvests of most crops (in pounds, bales, or bushels). For services other than transportation, such as wholesale and retail trade, there is practically no useful information on values *or* quantities.

Using the state surveys of manufacturing establishments and quantity data, Shaw (1947) constructed estimates for commodity output value in years between censuses, starting with 1889. Because the state surveys give values of products in specific categories, Shaw could estimate values for consumption versus investment goods. Using data on export and import values, Shaw could also estimate the flow of goods for domestic use – that is, production *less* exports plus imports. Kuznets (1946: 90–9) constructed annual estimates of commodity output value for 1880–8 and 1870–8 based on export and import value data (such as coffee imports) and quantity data for a remarkably small set of items.[1]

Kuznets, Kendrick, and Gallman did not believe it was possible to construct estimates of NIPA variables for years between censuses that would be good enough to indicate the magnitude of year-to-year fluctuations. Their only goal was to estimate longer-term trends. But, even for this limited purpose, census-year estimates were not enough. Trends calculated from census-year values would be distorted if a census happened to occur during a recession or boom. To deal with this problem, they created pseudo-annual estimates for real GNP by scaling up annual estimates of the value of commodity output – Shaw's series beginning with 1889, Kuznets's series for earlier years – with fixed coefficients based on the *long-term* relation between commodity output and total output. They produced series for "consumption" and "investment" in the same way, scaling up estimates of values of consumption or investment commodities for domestic use. They then estimated long-term trends in NIPA variables from five- or ten-year averages of the annual series. This was a good way to remove cyclical effects from long-term trends, but Kuznets, Kendrick, and Gallman never claimed it was a good way to estimate annual values. For serious annual estimates, one would want to use the *short-term*, year-to-year relation between commodity output and total output, and available information about annual output in transportation services and construction.

Gallman never published the pseudo-annual estimates, but he did make them available to other researchers on request. (With a few corrections by Paul Rhode, they are available in Carter *et al.* 2006: 23–5.) Gallman often warned that the figures were not suitable for use on an annual frequency. But this was like telling children not to put beans up their noses. Many researchers used the series to make inferences about year-to-year fluctuations – for example, comparing them with year-to-year fluctuations in postwar series.

Christina Romer (1989) pointed out the foolishness of such exercises. To construct a better annual series for prewar real GNP, she estimated the actual short-term, annual-frequency relation between commodity output value and real GNP in reliable data from later eras. She used this estimated relation to project annual figures for prewar real GNP off of the Shaw–Kuznets commodity value series. Balke and Gordon (1989) argued that estimates could be further improved by making use of annual series on transportation and construction, in addition to the Shaw–Kuznets commodity value series. The additional information they used was an annual index of real transportation and communication services that had been constructed by Edwin Frickey (1947), mainly from data on railroad traffic; a series on the dollar value of nonfarm construction by Manuel Gottlieb (1965) based mainly on building permits; and a dubious index of building costs to deflate the Gottlieb series.[2] Neither Romer nor Balke and Gordon constructed series for NIPA components such as sectoral value-added, consumption, or investment.

All three series for prewar real GNP – Kuznets–Kendrick–Gallman, Romer, and Balke–Gordon – are similar with respect to the direction and timing of deviations from trend. Thus, it may be safe to use any of them to observe the sign of correlations between fluctuations in aggregate output and other variables. Using the Kuznets-Kendrick-Gallman series, Backus and Kehoe (1992) observe that consumption and investment were both procyclical, and net exports were not, in the prewar U.S.

But there are substantial differences between the Gallman, Romer, and Balke–Gordon real GNP series with respect to the overall magnitude of fluctuations, and the relative magnitude of different fluctuations within the prewar era. There is no general agreement that one of the series is best. None of the series contains much actual information about cyclical-frequency fluctuations other than production of commodities, transportation services, and construction. Thus, anyone using annual estimates of prewar real GNP or other NIPA variables must think hard about the relative strengths and weaknesses of the various series and their potential biases with respect to the purpose at hand.

Output indices

Fortunately, for most purposes there is an easy out. The relatively abundant quantity of information from the prewar era can be used in the form of *production indices*. Annual indices of IP that cover all of the gold-standard era can be constructed from data on industrial outputs and inputs weighted by census-year estimates of value-added by industry. Many studies have used the indices for manufacturing and industrial production constructed by Frickey (1947). Recently, Davis (2004) constructed annual IP series that are better than Frickey's, incorporating information about more products and industries. Starting with January 1884, Miron and Romer (1990) constructed a *monthly* IP index from the smaller set of data available at that frequency.

Many facts about prewar business cycles can be established using production indices and their components. The uniquely acyclical nature of farm output can be observed in indices of crop production, IP, and transportation: in terms of first differences or deviation from trend, IP and transportation indices are strongly correlated with each other but not with crop production in the same year (Frickey 1942: 229; Calomiris and Hanes 1994). It can also be observed in disaggregated data. Romer (1991) examines fluctuations in output of individual crops (e.g. cotton, wheat), manufactured goods (e.g. steel, cotton textiles) and minerals (e.g. anthracite coal). She finds that mining and industrial products, but not farm products, were subject to strong common shocks in the prewar era.

Since business cycles are essentially fluctuations in nonagricultural output, the magnitude of prewar business cycles can be compared with postwar cycles by comparing prewar IP indices with the most similar postwar IP indices. In terms of per cent changes or deviations from trend, annual fluctuations in IP were somewhat larger in the prewar era but not a different order of magnitude (Romer 1986). The cyclical behavior of other variables can be observed in their correlations with IP. Hanes (1996) examines the cyclical behavior of consumption using Frickey's IP index and Shaw's series on output of consumption goods. Making comparisons with matching postwar data, he finds that consumption was about as procyclical in the prewar era as in the postwar era.

Wages and prices

Prewar business publications and government reports recorded long series of "wholesale" prices of commodities and standardized manufactured products (such as steel rails) from business publications ("prices current") and government reports. From this type of data, the federal agency that became the BLS constructed monthly-frequency "wholesale price indices" (WPIs) beginning with 1890. Warren and Pearson (1932) constructed monthly series for years prior to 1890 using data and techniques similar to those used by the BLS for the 1890s and 1900s. The Warren and Pearson aggregate or "all groups" WPI for years up through 1890, linked to the BLS aggregate WPI from 1890 on, is a commonly used price index for the prewar era and sometimes compared with postwar PPIs.

It is important to keep in mind, however, that WPIs are not the same as PPIs. Wholesale prices were not always the prices received by producers. In many cases they were prices received (or quoted) by middlemen. Also, the aggregate Warren and Pearson and prewar BLS WPIs put very heavy weight on prices of raw agricultural commodities, such as cotton and wheat. Prices received by manufacturers can be better indicated by constructing a WPI that excludes farm products and raw foodstuffs. Even with those components removed, prewar WPIs remain heavily weighted toward less-finished goods, to a degree that greatly exaggerates the actual composition of output in the era. They do not include prices of the more-finished or specialized goods that were produced at the time. Because less-finished goods' prices are relatively procyclical, that makes it hard to compare cyclical price behavior across eras. To facilitate such comparisons, Hanes (1998) constructed an annual WPI that covers the same set of goods (or very similar goods) in all eras, prewar, interwar, and postwar.

Prewar CPIs are tricky, too. A special report for the 1880 Census, known as the "Weeks Report," contains annual records of retail prices and rents from the 1850s through 1880. Hoover (1960) constructed a CPI from these data. Starting in 1890, the future BLS began to collect data on retail food prices. Rees (1961) constructed annual CPIs for 1890–1914 from these data, along with prices of clothing and other goods taken from mail-order catalogs, and rents from newspaper advertisements. That leaves a gap across 1880–90. Published CPIs for that decade (such as Long 1960) are constructed from very spotty data and cannot be relied on to show year-to-year changes.

Reliable GDP price indices or deflators cannot be constructed for any of the prewar era because there is no suitable information about prices of most services, more-processed or specialized manufactured goods, or construction. The deflators used by Shaw, Kuznets, Kendrick, and Gallman to create census-year and pseudo-annual NIPAs were based on WPIs for raw materials and intermediate products, and a lot of assumptions that are reasonable with respect to long-term trends but not annual fluctuations. The alternative GNP deflator constructed by Balke and Gordon (1989) is just an average of the Kuznets-Kendrick-Gallman deflator, the dubious construction cost index and prewar CPIs (including the WPI-based 1880s series).

Prewar wage information is surprisingly good for manufacturing. The Aldrich Report (a special report prepared in the early 1890s for a Congressional committee) gives wage rates paid for jobs in a fairly large set of manufacturing establishments from the 1850s through 1890. The federal agency that became the BLS collected the same type of data from 1890 through 1907. Douglas (1930), Long (1960) and Hanes (1992) present wage indices constructed from these data, which are quite comparable to postwar ECIs for manufacturing. Starting about 1890, there are annual series on weekly or daily earnings in manufacturing, railroads, and mining, based mainly on state surveys of manufacturing establishments and mines, and the ICC (Douglas 1930; Rees 1961). Unfortunately, there is no information on annual fluctuations in hours per day, so it is not possible to construct reliable postwar-style AHE series (Allen 1992). There is almost no annual information about wages outside manufacturing, railroads, and mining.

Many studies have examined the cyclical behavior of inflation of wages and prices in the prewar era. They find a different pattern from that in postwar series: inflation (not the change in inflation) is positively correlated with the level of real activity as indicated by deviation from trend in IP or one of the real GNP series. This is the original (not the accelerationist) Phillips curve that A.W. Phillips (1958) found in pre-1960s British wage series. The difference across eras can be observed by regressing inflation on lagged inflation and output deviation (as in Allen 1992; Gordon 1990: 1130; Hanes 1993, 1999). Postwar data give positive, statistically significant coefficients on output and on lagged inflation. Prewar data give positive and significant coefficients on output, of similar magnitude to postwar coefficients if the data are carefully matched across the eras.[3] But prewar coefficients on lagged inflation are not significantly different from zero and are usually close to zero in size.

Another difference from the postwar era appears in disaggregated data on wages paid for individual jobs. Prewar data show no sign of downward nominal wage rigidity. Nominal wage cuts were fairly common (Hanes and James 2003).

The cyclical behavior of real wages appears similar to the postwar era, or different, depending on the price series in the denominator (Hanes 1996). The cyclical behavior of real consumption wages looks different. As noted earlier, postwar ECIs in ratio to CPIs are procyclical. The prewar ECI-style wage index in ratio to prewar CPIs (available for years before and after the 1880s) is acyclical or countercyclical. Relative to Hanes's annual WPI that covers the same goods in both the prewar and postwar eras, the prewar ECI-style wage index and the postwar ECI are about equally countercyclical.

Business-cycle chronologies

The dates of business-cycle peaks and troughs chosen by the NBER in the postwar era, making up the business-cycle "chronology," are based on its definition of a downturn as an absolute decline in real output. Early NBER researchers developed a business-cycle chronology for the prewar era, but they did not apply the same standard. Romer (1994) shows that the NBER's prewar chronology dates some peaks too early, when output growth had begun to slow but prior to the absolute decline in output. It also incorrectly counts as downturns some occasions when nominal variables fell but real variables continued to grow. Romer developed another chronology for the era to better match the postwar NBER definition, based on fluctuations in the Miron–Romer monthly IP index. Romer's chronology suggests that business cycles were more frequent in the prewar era than in the postwar era she examined. Recessions (peak to trough) were perhaps a bit shorter prewar, expansions a bit longer postwar, with little change in the total peak-to-peak duration of a whole cycle. Watson (1994) came to similar conclusions based on individual production series.

As the monthly IP index begins in 1884, Romer's chronology misses much of the prewar era. Davis (2006) constructs a chronology that is rougher but covers all of the era, by marking turning points in his annual IP index. This may miss some short-lived fluctuations but reliably indicates the biggest fluctuations.

Table 11.1, column 1, gives per cent changes in the Davis (2004) index of industrial production from the previous year. Absolute declines occurred over 1883–5, 1892–3, 1895–6, 1903–4, 1907–8, 1910–11, and 1913–14. Columns 2–5 list months of cyclical peaks and troughs according to the old NBER chronology and the Romer chronology. All downturns in annual IP are associated with recessions in both chronologies, except 1883–4. The NBER chronology places a peak in 1882: this appears to be too early, a case of the inconsistencies noted by Romer. The Romer chronology cannot cover 1883–4 because the monthly IP index begins in January 1884. The Romer chronology includes two downturns, in 1887 and 1900, which were too brief to appear in annual IP; these also appear in the NBER chronology though with slightly different timing. The NBER chronology includes a downturn in 1890 that appears in neither Romer's chronology nor annual IP. IP growth slows down sharply from 1890 to 1891, but there is no absolute decline.

If one defines recessions specifically as absolute declines in IP, it still appears that consumption and inflation were procyclical, and net exports were not. Table 11.1, column 6, shows the per cent change in Shaw's (1947) annual series for the flow of real commodities available for domestic consumption (the sum of nondurable, semidurable, and durable commodities for household use); recall this series begins at 1889. Column 7 shows acceleration in consumption – the change in the growth rate. All downturns in IP were accompanied by slowdowns in consumption growth in the same year or the prior year. Column 8 shows acceleration in the ECI-style manufacturing wage index of Hanes (1992). The wage rates constituting the index are from pay periods in the middle of the summer, so it is not surprising that the slowdown in inflation often appears in the year following the IP downturn. Column 9 shows acceleration in a WPI constructed from the standard Warren and Pearson and BLS series but excluding prices of agricultural products. To match the timing of the wage index, inflation is calculated as the change in the average of monthly values for June, July, and August. The WPI shows the same pattern as the wage index. Column 10 shows the change in net exports, measured in dollars. This particular series (Lipsey 1963), begins with 1879 and gives figures on a calendar-year basis. (Other series go further back, but are for 12-month spans ending in June.) Columns 11 and 12 show per cent changes in Lipsey's calendar-year indices for real quantities of imports and exports. There is no clear cyclical pattern in net exports, but imports are clearly procyclical.

Financial crises

In the pre-1914 gold-standard era, America suffered financial crises more frequently than other countries (Bordo 1985). Most studies of prewar American financial crises (e.g. Sprague 1910; Wilson *et al.* 1990; Calomiris and Gorton 1991; Wicker 2000) define them in the same way, as a general run on banks in New York City, and identify these events objectively by the actions of the New York Clearing House (NYCH). The NYCH responded to a general run by issuing clearing house loan certificates (Wicker 2000: 116). Using this standard, nearly all studies say that crises occurred in May 1884, November 1890, May or June 1893, and October 1907 (e.g. Wicker 2000; Calomiris and Gorton 1991). These are the times the NYCH issued clearing house loan certificates. Calomiris and Gorton (1991) identify an additional crisis in October 1896, when the NYCH authorized certificates but did not issue any. Comparing these dates with the business-cycle chronologies in Table 11.1, one can see that nearly all of the crises occurred during recessions. The crisis of 1890 occurred during a recession according to the old NBER chronology, but not according to Romer's or the annual IP series.

A panic in New York City was a *national* crisis because of New York banks' central role in the financial system. Loans from New York banks were a key source of funds to nonbank financial intermediaries (private banks, brokerage houses, and commercial-paper houses). New York banks arranged most loans to firms and individuals who borrowed short term to finance purchases of long-term securities (Myers 1931: 265–87, 335) – a particularly obvious form of nonbank intermediation. On the liability side, New York banks drew interbank deposits – "bankers' balances" – from all regions of the country. Nearly all banks held deposits in a New York "correspondent" bank, or in a regional money-center bank that held New York balances (James 1978). An increase in banks' demand for cash reserves or the nonbank public's demand for cash anywhere in the country was ultimately covered by withdrawals of bankers' balances and shipments of cash out of New York. Thus, widespread bank runs in the hinterland were quickly transmitted to New York, while a general run in New York triggered suspensions by other cities' banks and clearing houses.

A New York financial crisis must have had real macroeconomic effects that tended to reduce aggregate output. Because New York bankers' balances were the chief medium of intercity payments, a New York run raised real transactions costs of employment and trade as payers resorted to long-distance cash shipments (James *et al.* 2009). As a run on New York hindered many types of financial intermediation, it raised the cost of credit and tightened credit rationing to potential borrowers (Mishkin 1991).

But the timing of financial crises suggests they were not *causes* of business cycles. Rather, they amplified cyclical downturns that were already underway. Crises occurred a few months after cyclical peaks. Calomiris and Gorton (1991) argue that cyclical downturns caused financial crises: depositors withdrew *en masse* when they observed or forecast a recession, because a recession meant defaults on business loans, and this would endanger banks' solvency. As evidence, Calomiris and Gorton point out that all crises, without exception, were preceded by stock-market crashes, which were another symptom indicating the public expected a recession (a recession would depress corporate earnings). Hanes and Rhode (2011) show that a stock-market crash could actually cause a crisis, because it threatened New York banks' solvency, or at least their liquidity. Some New York banks made large unsecured loans to brokerages and other stock "speculators," who could not repay in the event of a general decline in stock prices. Depositors ran on banks rumored to be exposed to stock prices in this way.

A political factor that contributed to the 1884, 1893, and 1896 crises was "silver risk": the perceived danger that the U.S. would link the dollar to silver and float against gold. Silver risk contributed to crises mainly because it reduced international demand for American securities (not by spurring Americans to withdraw bank deposits for conversion into gold [Sprague 1910: 165, 169; Friedman and Schwartz 1963: 108–9]). But silver risk did not trigger the crises. The more-or-less exogenous political events that created silver risk – the 1878 Bland-Allison Act, the 1890 Sherman Silver Purchase Act – occurred years before the crises in question. Existing research does not claim that exogenous hikes in silver risk set off crises but rather that potential silver risk was crystallized by, and amplified, cyclical downturns and financial crises already underway (Sprague 1910: 109–10, 162, 165, 168, 179; Fels 1959: 130–1, 184–7; Friedman and Schwartz 1963: 100–1).

Causes of business cycles

The cause of a business cycle may be generally defined as an event or combination of events exogenous to the economic system that is the reason a cyclical downturn occurred in a particular

Table 11.1a   Business-cycle data, 1879–1914

	Industrial Production	Business-cycle chronologies				"Consumption"	
	Per cent Change	NBER		Romer		Per cent Change	Acceleration
		Peak	Trough	Peak	Trough		
Year	1	2	3	4	5	6	7
1879	13.5			NA	NA		
1880	12.5			NA	NA		
1881	19.3			NA	NA		
1882	6.6	March		NA	NA		
1883	2.8			NA	NA		
1884	−3.5			NA	NA		
1885	−2.9		May				
1886	12.2						
1887	9.8	March		Feb.	July		
1888	8.6		April				
1889	2.8						
1890	15.6	July				−0.5	
1891	1.5		May			8.1	8.6
1892	7.4					4.9	−3.2
1893	−8.7	Jan.		Jan.		1.5	−3.4
1894	−7.2		June		Feb.	−3.4	−4.9
1895	17.3	Dec.				12.8	16.2
1896	−3.1			Jan.		−0.6	−13.4
1897	6.5		June		Jan.	8	8.5
1898	17.8					1.1	−6.8
1899	9.7	June				11.4	10.3
1900	4.6		Dec.	April	Dec.	−0.2	−11.6
1901	8					12.2	12.4
1902	7.2	Sept.				−0.1	−12.3
1903	3.7			July		5.3	5.4
1904	−4.7		Aug.		March	0.3	−5
1905	15.7					4.4	4.1
1906	5.1					11.2	6.8
1907	4.2	May		July		1.2	−10
1908	−15.6		June		June	−8.1	−9.3
1909	17.9					11.9	20.1
1910	4.6	Jan.		Jan.		2.4	−9.5
1911	−3.7				May	5.5	3.1
1912	10.5		Jan.			3.8	−1.7
1913	4	Jan.				4.3	0.5
1914	−10.2		Dec.	July	Dec.	−1.2	−5.5

Sources: Davis (2004), Romer (1994), Shaw (1947), Hanes (1992), and Lipsey (1963).

Table 11.1b Business–cycle data, 1879–1914

	Acceleration in inflation		Change in Net Exports ($millions)	Quantity index	
	Wages	Prices		Imports	Exports
				Per cent change	
Year	8	9	10	11	12
1879	−1.5	1.1	−50	NA	NA
1880	5.2	18.7	−62	22.8	5.7
1881	−2.6	−18.5	−35	0.9	−9.1
1882	3.9	4.8	−147	11.8	−10.7
1883	−2.5	−5.7	94	−3	9.5
1884	−2.8	−3.7	14	−2.2	−1.9
1885	0.3	0.7	−19	1.4	−1.6
1886	4.8	4.8	−49	13.2	10.3
1887	−1.7	2.7	−43	2.7	0.9
1888	−1.6	−1.6	−39	4.8	−8.1
1889	0.8	−0.6	88	0.5	25.1
1890	0.2	6.5	−20	7.6	5.2
1891	−0.4	−11.6	106	1.7	9.4
1892	−0.3	1.7	−47	5.7	3.6
1893	1.2	2.2	−3	−11.3	−5.5
1894	−4.6	−6.1	55	−0.7	7.4
1895	2.8	15.5	−128	25.5	−1.7
1896	3.3	−10.6	299	−16.3	23.4
1897	−3.4	−2.3	32	15.9	12.4
1898	−0.4	11.6	262	−14.3	15.5
1899	1.2	14.8	−145	16.8	−4
1900	4.7	−18	170	−1.7	3.6
1901	−3.5	−6.1	−66	11.7	1.6
1902	0.5	7.6	−194	12.8	−9.6
1903	0.3	2.1	99	−1.3	2.8
1904	−2.8	−12.4	−73	1.8	−2.6
1905	1.7	10.6	30	7.9	16.4
1906	2.1	5.4	32	7.2	3.2
1907	2.6	−1.4	20	2.8	1
1908		−21.5	141	−11.6	−3.6
1909		15.6	−388	32.2	−6
1910		−2.2	41	−1.4	−0.8
1911		−3.1	259	−3.5	23.1
1912		8.9	20	12.8	12.3
1913		−1.6	110	−0.4	−1.1
1914		−9.9	−373	6.5	−13.4

Sources: Davis (2004), Romer (1994), Shaw (1947), Hanes (1992), and Lipsey (1963).

year. Natural events such as weather and earthquakes are obviously exogenous. For purposes of understanding American economic history, it can also be useful to treat foreign economic developments as exogenous.

To establish that a particular event caused a particular business cycle, one must show that the event occurred with the right timing relative to that business cycle, that events of that type were generally correlated with fluctuations in aggregate output, and that the correlation reflects causation from the events to the economy, not the other way around. The last point is often hard to prove because potential causes of business cycles are rarely as exogenous as earthquakes. Usually, they *might* occur for exogenous reasons but also might be responses to economic developments. The best one can do is show that real activity was affected by a proposed causal event when one can be *fairly* sure that the event occurred for exogenous reasons; that the event *could* be a cause of business cycles in an economic model that depicts a plausible theory; and that the event was accompanied by other outcomes implied by the model. Thus, as Temin (1998) points out, claims about causes of business cycles depend on a theoretical framework. Different theories have different implications as to the type of event that could be responsible for a downturn and the other outcomes that would, if observed, pin the blame on the suspect. In macroeconomic theory there is unfortunately little agreement on frameworks. The monumental study of Friedman and Schwartz (1963) was built on the framework of monetarism. Currently, most macroeconomic research is in the framework of either Keynesian ("old" and "new") or real business cycle (RBC) theory.

In RBC models, wages and prices are perfectly flexible, markets clear continuously, and all decision makers are perfectly rational. In standard RBC models, the only shock that can generate the co-movements in output across nonagricultural sectors, consumption, and international trade that occurred in prewar business cycles is an exogenous, absolute, simultaneous decline in total factor productivity (TFP) across most sectors of the economy (King and Rebelo 1999). According to RBC theorists, real events corresponding to a negative TFP shock in an RBC model include not only deteriorations in production technology *per se*, but also "changes in the legal and regulatory system" that impair microeconomic efficiency (Hansen and Prescott 1993: 281). Ebell and Ritschl (2008) and Ohanian (2009) explain the 1929–33 downturn of the Great Depression this way, as the result of a sudden increase in union bargaining power and Hoover administration policies that forced employers to pay higher real wages. As far as I know, there have been no attempts to account for prewar business cycles in terms of RBC models, but I expect it would be hard to do so. There is no evidence for a general decline in technological *or* regulatory efficiency in 1883–4, 1892–3, 1895–6, 1903–4, 1907–8, 1910–11, or 1913–14. The gold-standard era was notable for a relative absence of government interference in the economy (Hughes 1991).

In both Keynesian and monetarist models, wages and/or prices are *not* perfectly flexible. They are "sticky," subject to nominal rigidity, so that an event affecting aggregate demand can disturb real activity from the level that would prevail under perfectly flexible wages and prices – the "natural rate" of output. (Using this definition, output fluctuations in RBC models are fluctuations in the natural rate.) In most models, wage and price stickiness takes the form of the "expectations-augmented" Phillips curve. In old-fashioned models, this is a structural equation that says inflation is equal to expected inflation *plus* a positive coefficient times the output gap – the difference between actual output and the natural rate. In New Keynesian models, an equation of similar form is derived from "fundamental" assumptions about microeconomic constraints on price adjustment (e.g. Roberts 1995) or information imperfections (e.g. Mankiw and Reis 2010).[4]

The apparent change in inflation behavior from the prewar original Phillips curve to the postwar accelerationist Phillips curve is consistent with an expectations-augmented Phillips curve of either the old or new-Keynesian variety (Alogoskoufis and Smith 1991; Ball and Mankiw 2002; Hanes and James 2010). An expectations-augmented Phillips curve generates the prewar pattern if expected inflation is uncorrelated with past inflation. It generates the postwar pattern if expected inflation is positively correlated with past inflation. Barsky (1987) shows that, in postwar samples including the 1970s and 1980s, serial correlation in inflation is so strong that inflation is statistically indistinguishable from a random walk – that is, current inflation is a good forecast of future inflation. In pre-1914 data, monthly or annual inflation shows little or no serial correlation – using standard tests, one cannot reject the hypothesis that the price *level* was a random walk. Thus, any roughly rational expectation of inflation would be strongly correlated with past inflation in the postwar era, and uncorrelated with past inflation in the prewar era. The lack of inflation persistence in the prewar U.S. was an outcome of the monetary regime: under the gold standard, a country's aggregate demand growth was subject to a long-term constraint that did not accommodate persistent inflation (Klein 1975).

The apparent change in the behavior of real consumption wages, from acyclical or counter-cyclical prewar to procyclical postwar, is also consistent with nominal rigidity. Hanes (1996) and Huang *et al.* (2004) show that real consumption wages become more procyclical over time if nominal wages are sticky and consumption goods become more finished, passing through more stages of production and sale prior to purchase by households. Historical evidence on the nature of consumption bundles shows that consumption goods indeed became more finished in this sense. In Hanes's model, more stages make real wages procyclical because firms' desired price markups over marginal cost are countercyclical. In the model of Huang *et al.*, it is because wages and prices are both subject to adjustment costs and more stages make production more roundabout in the sense of Basu (1995).

In the framework of a model with an expectations-augmented Phillips curve, one would say that the cause of a business-cycle downturn is the exogenous event(s) that causes a large decline in aggregate demand to occur in a given year. The distinctive monetarist view was that nearly all fluctuations in aggregate demand were immediately due to changes in the "money stock" – an aggregate of cash and assets that are relatively close substitutes for cash, such as demand deposits. Friedman and Schwartz (1963) analyzed the prewar era in this framework, accounting for money-stock fluctuations in terms of the supply of high-powered money, the fraction of the money stock the public wants to hold in cash versus deposits, and the fraction of deposits banks want to hold in cash reserves – the reserve ratio. It is not always clear whether Friedman and Schwartz view changes in money-stock determinants such as the reserve ratio to be exogenous, but they do propose a clear, causal explanation of the Depression of 1893. They argue that a downturn took place in that year because of fluctuations in wheat harvests.

Wheat and wheat flour were important American exports. The size of the wheat harvest had a big effect on American export revenue. Shocks to export revenue could affect the high-powered money supply because of the gold standard and America's lack of a central bank.

Under the gold standard, an international flow of monetary gold covered a country's balance of payments – the sum of net exports, international capital inflow, and net income from foreign assets – unless the country's authorities managed stocks of foreign assets. An international flow of monetary gold affected the high-powered money supply, unless a monetary authority such as a central bank "sterilized" it with an adjustment to the supply of non-gold currency or central-bank balances. Because the U.S. had no central bank, there was an unusually direct link between the money supply and the balance of payments. The high-powered money supply consisted of monetary gold *plus* non-gold currency issued by the Treasury *minus* cash held in Treasury vaults (removed from banks and the public) (Friedman and Schwartz 1963: 124–34). The net inflow of monetary gold was equal to the balance of payments, as U.S. authorities did not hold stocks of foreign assets. Non-gold currency growth was unresponsive to economic conditions and mostly out of the Treasury's control.[5] On occasion, Treasury officials deliberately managed vault cash to affect the money supply (Myers 1931: 370–86; Timberlake 1978) but they did not generally sterilize international gold flows.

According to Friedman and Schwartz (1963: 107), the Sherman Silver Purchase Act of 1890 raised fears that the U.S. would leave the gold standard, which tended to reduce the flow of international investment in the U.S., the balance of payments, and hence growth in the high-powered money supply. But this effect was staved off by a bumper wheat harvest in autumn 1891, an "accident of weather," coincident with poor harvests abroad. The positive shock to net exports "fostered a spurt in the stock of money from 1891 to 1892 … This surcease, however, was bound to be temporary," so a downturn occurred in 1893. Wheat export revenues remained relatively low until a "fortuitous" increase in 1897, which contributed to the 1897 upturn.

A recent study in the monetarist spirit of Friedman and Schwartz is Moen and Tallman (1998), who examine the relation between the American monetary gold stock and the Miron-Romer monthly IP index over 1890–1909. They claim that exogenous shocks to gold flow can be distinguished from endogenous variations (e.g. shocks to American demand for gold) by regressing the gold stock on IP, short-term interest rates and a few other variables: the residuals from this regression are the exogenous shocks (that is, they perform a vector autoregression [VAR] with the gold stock as one of the variables). They show that these residual fluctuations in gold flow were positively related to subsequent growth in IP, and that there were large negative shocks prior to the downturns of 1893, 1896, and 1907.

In the Keynesian view, the money stock is not the key intermediate factor for aggregate demand; what matters is the difference between prevailing real interest rates and the "natural rate of interest" – that is, the real interest rate level consistent with the natural rate of output in the IS curve. In many Keynesian models (e.g. Bernanke *et al.* 1999) real effects of interest-rate changes are amplified by their effects on the supply of credit from financial intermediaries.

Within a Keynesian framework, Davis *et al.* (2009) claim that the downturns of 1884, 1893, 1896, and 1910 were caused by fluctuations in cotton harvests. They show that there was a strong, general positive relation between the size of the cotton harvest and the following year's IP, within the 1879–1913 gold-standard era specifically, and cotton harvests were *extremely* poor in the harvest seasons prior to these downturns (autumn 1883, 1892, 1895, and 1909). To establish the direction of causality, they show that there was an effect from cotton harvest fluctuations specifically due to weather, an obviously exogenous factor. (That is, they use weather data to form instruments for harvest fluctuations in two-stage least squares.) Davis *et al.* argue that the apparent effect of cotton harvest fluctuations on IP makes sense within a Keynesian model, and they show that cotton harvest fluctuations were associated with other outcomes implied by such a model.

Cotton, like wheat, was an important export. Cotton harvest fluctuations were positively related to export revenue. Davis *et al.* argue that export-revenue shocks affected the non-agricultural economy because of interactions with the monetary regime, but not through the money supply. The key intermediate factor was interest rates. American interest rates were determined by the interaction between the gold standard, net exports, and international capital flows. International demand for American assets was sensitive (but not infinitely sensitive) to the spread between expected returns on American versus European assets (as in models of imperfect international capital mobility). Under the international gold standard, absent a central bank, the balance of payments was equal to the change in the high-powered money supply, so the sum of net exports and capital inflow was constrained by the change in high-powered money *demand*.

Putting these conditions together, a negative shock to American net exports was balanced either by an increase in American interest rates, or by an exogenous negative shock to high-powered money demand. Davis *et al.* hypothesize that a poor cotton harvest tended to reduce American export revenue but had little immediate effect on money demand, while wheat harvest fluctuations had strong effects on high-powered money demand as well as export revenue. This implies that, during the gold-standard regime specifically, poor cotton harvests would be associated with higher interest rates, gold outflows and slow high-powered money growth, as well as a decline in IP. Poor wheat harvests would be associated with gold outflows and slow money growth but not higher interest rates or lower IP. Davis *et al.* show that these patterns are clear in the data.

In a related paper, Hanes and Rhode (2011) argue that cotton harvests were responsible for the financial crises of 1884, 1893, and 1896 in the same way, not only by causing business-cycle downturns but also by reducing international demand for American assets, which had a further effect on stock prices. Their hypothesis implies that poor cotton harvests, but not poor wheat harvests, tended to drain deposits from New York banks, and depress stock prices and bond prices *prior* to IP. These patterns are also clear in the data.

On the same Keynesian argument, monetary tightening by European central banks or other factors reducing Europeans' demand for American assets should have affected American financial markets and real activity like a poor cotton harvest. The financial crisis of 1890, the financial crisis and cyclical downturn of 1907, and the downturn of 1914 can all be accounted for in this way.

1890 was the year of the famous Barings Crisis. Events in Argentina depressed prices of Argentine bonds held by financial intermediaries in London. To raise funds, Barings and other European financial houses began fire sales of assets including American stocks.[6] Meanwhile, a monetary tightening by the Bank of England raised London bill rates, discouraging American finance-bill borrowing (Sprague 1910: 133). These conditions caused the 1890 stock-market crash and financial crisis in New York, according to many contemporaries and modern economists (e.g. Sprague 1910: 132; Fels 1959: 167; Friedman and Schwartz 1963: 104; Bordo 2006; Reinhart and Rogoff 2009: 243). Hanes and Rhode (2011) argue that they did not cause a cyclical downturn only because they were largely counteracted by the financial effects of a large cotton harvest and export revenues in autumn 1890.

The Panic of 1907 followed sharp hikes in European interest rates due to tightening actions by the Bank of England and other European central banks. In addition to raising its discount rate, the Bank blocked American borrowing in London with informal threats (Sprague 1910: 241; Sayers 1976: 54–6). Friedman and Schwartz (1963: 156) and Eichengreen (1992: 51) identify these actions as the cause of the 1907 crisis in the U.S. According to Odell and Weidenmier (2004), European central banks took these actions to counter a persistent international gold drain caused by payments by European insurance companies associated with the San Francisco earthquake of April 1906 – an event that took place within the U.S., but may be viewed as essentially exogenous.

At the end of July 1914, the effects of the First World War's outbreak were initially similar to 1890 and 1907. An increase in European demand for monetary gold and fire sales of American assets by European investors caused hikes in American interest rates and declines in American stock and bond prices. But there soon followed unprecedented disruptions to the mechanisms of international payments and trade finance, demand for American exports, and the closing of the New York Stock Exchange for more than four months (Sprague 1915; Silber 2006). Because these disruptions were unprecedented, it is hard to quantify their real effects, but it is no surprise that they were accompanied by a business-cycle downturn: July 1914 was a cyclical peak (according to Romer).

Conclusion

Deficiencies in historical data may mean the characteristics of prewar business cycles are seen only as through a glass, darkly, but their causes are surprisingly clear. Within the prewar era from 1879 to 1914, there were seven recessions big enough to show up as a decline in annual IP: in 1884, 1893, 1896, 1904, 1907, 1910, and 1914. At least six can be attributed to clearly exogenous events. 1884, 1893, 1896, and 1910 were caused by poor American cotton crops in the prior harvest seasons. 1907 was caused by the San Francisco earthquake of 1906. 1914 was caused by a politically motivated shooting in Sarajevo. All of these events created disturbances in American financial markets equivalent to exogenous hikes in interest rates, through mechanisms created by the American gold-standard monetary regime.

Notes

1 Romer (1989: 5) judged that the data used by Kuznets to estimate annual commodity output prior to 1889 were "similar to those used by Shaw" to estimate output after 1889. I do not agree.
2 The construction-cost index they used, from Blank (1954), is the building materials component of the Warren and Pearson WPI, discussed later, weighted together with a wage series.
3 Some studies found larger coefficients on real activity in prewar eras, concluding that there had been a decrease over time in cyclical "flexibility" (e.g. Cagan 1975; Sachs 1980), but this result was a relic of bad data.
4 Depending on the particular assumptions, the "expected inflation" in the augmented Phillips curve that affects current inflation may be past expectations of current inflation (as in Mankiw and Reis 2010) or current expectations of future inflation (Roberts 1995).
5 Non-gold money consisted of greenbacks, silver notes, national banknotes, and silver coins. The quantity of greenbacks was simply fixed; the rate at which the Treasury created new silver notes was governed by long-standing political factors (Myers 1931: 396–8, 402); and the rate at which banks created national banknotes was remarkably insensitive to variations in interest rates and business activity (Myers 1931: 403; Cagan 1965: 91).
6 Noyes (1898: 157) and Lauck (1907: 64) describe relevant Argentine events. The *Economist* (supplement, February 21, 1891) describes the embarrassments of London financial houses holding Argentine securities; Wilkins (1989: 194, 222, 471) describes the effects of foreign sales of American securities on American financial markets.

References

Allen, S.G. (1992) 'Changes in the cyclical sensitivity of wages in the United States, 1891–1987', *American Economic Review*, 82: 122–40.

Alogoskoufis, G.S. and Smith, R. (1991) 'The Phillips curve, the persistence of inflation and the Lucas critique: evidence from exchange-rate regimes', *American Economic Review*, 81: 1254–75.

Backus, D.K. and Kehoe, P.J. (1992) 'International evidence on the historical properties of business cycles', *American Economic Review*, 82: 864–88.

Balke, N.S. and Gordon, R.J. (1989) 'The estimation of prewar gross national product: methodology and new evidence', *Journal of Political Economy*, 97: 38–92.

Ball, L. and Mankiw, N.G. (2002) 'The NAIRU in theory and practice', *Journal of Economic Perspectives*, 16: 115–36.

Barsky, R.B. (1987) 'The Fisher effect and the forecastability and persistence of inflation', *Journal of Monetary Economics*, 19: 3–24.

Basu, S. (1995) 'Intermediate goods and business cycles: implications for productivity and welfare', *American Economic Review*, 85: 512–31.

Bernanke, B.S., Gertler, M. and Gilchrist, S. (1999) 'The financial accelerator in a quantitative business cycle framework', in J.B. Taylor and M. Woodford (eds) *Handbook of Macroeconomics*, Amsterdam: Elsevier Science Publications.

Blank, D.M. (1954) *The Volume of Residential Construction, 1889–1950*, NBER Technical Paper No. 9.

Bordo, M. (1985) 'The impact and international transmission of financial crises: some historical evidence, 1870–1933', *Revista di Storia Economica*, 2: 41–78.

——(2006) 'Sudden stops, financial crises and original sin in emerging countries: deja vu?' NBER Working Paper No. 12393.

Burns, A.F. (1951) 'Mitchell on what happens during business cycles', in *Conference on Business Cycles*, New York: NBER.

Cagan, P. (1965) *Determinants and Effects of Changes in the Stock of Money, 1875–1960*, New York: Columbia University Press.

——(1975) 'Changes in the recession behavior of wholesale prices in the 1920s and post-World War II', *Explorations in Economic Research*, 2: 54–104.

Calomiris, C.W. and Gorton, G. (1991) 'The origins of banking panics: models, facts and bank regulation', in R.G. Hubbard (ed.) *Financial Markets and Financial Crises*, Chicago, IL: University of Chicago Press.

Calomiris, C.W. and Hanes, C. (1994) 'Consistent output series for the antebellum and postbellum periods: issues and preliminary results', *Journal of Economic History*, 54: 409–22.

Carter, S.B. and Sutch, R. (1990) 'The labour market in the 1890s: evidence from Connecticut manufacturing', in E. Aerts and B. Eichengreen (eds) *Unemployment and Underemployment in Historical Perspective*, Studies in Social and Economic History 12. Leuven: Leuven University Press.

Carter, S.B., Gartner, S.S., Haines, M.R., Olmstead, A.L., Sutch, R. and Wright, G. (2006) *Historical Statistics of the United States Millennial Edition*, Vol. 3, New York: Cambridge University Press.

Davis, J.H. (2004) 'An annual index of U.S. industrial production, 1790–1915', *Quarterly Journal of Economics*, 119: 1177–215.

——(2006) 'An improved annual chronology of U.S. business cycles', *Journal of Economic History*, 66: 103–21.

Davis, J.H., Hanes, C. and Rhode, P.W. (2009) 'Harvests and business cycles in nineteenth-century America', *Quarterly Journal of Economics*, 124: 1675–727.

Douglas, P.H. (1930) *Real Wages in the United States, 1890–1926*, Boston: Houghton Mifflin.

Ebell, M. and Ritschl, A. (2008) 'Real origins of the Great Depression: monopoly power, unions and the American business cycle in the 1920s', Centre for Economic Performance Discussion Paper No. 0876.

Eichengreen, B. (1992) *Golden Fetters: The Gold Standard and the Great Depression, 1919–39*, Oxford: Oxford University Press.

Fels, R. (1959) *American Business Cycles 1865–1897*, Chapel Hill, NC: University of North Carolina Press.

Frickey, E. (1942) *Economic Fluctuations in the United States*, Cambridge, MA: Harvard University Press.

——(1947) *Production in the United States 1860–1914*, Cambridge, MA: Harvard University Press.

Friedman, M. and Schwartz, A.J. (1963) *A Monetary History of the United States, 1867–1960*, Princeton, NJ: Princeton University Press.

Gallman, R.E. (1966) 'Gross national product in the United States, 1834–1909', in D.S. Brady (ed.) *Output, Employment and Productivity in the United States after 1800*, Studies in Income and Wealth 30, New York: Columbia University Press.

Gordon, R.J. (1990) 'What is New-Keynesian economics?' *Journal of Economic Literature*, 28: 1115–71.

Gottlieb, M. (1965) 'New measures of value of nonfarm building for the United States, annually 1850–1939', *Review of Economics and Statistics*, 47: 412–19.

Hanes, C. (1992) 'Comparable indices of wholesale prices and manufacturing wage rates in the United States, 1865–1914', *Research in Economic History*, 14: 269–92.

——(1993) 'The development of nominal wage rigidity in the late 19th century', *American Economic Review*, 83: 732–56.

——(1996) 'Changes in the cyclical behavior of real wage rates, 1870–1990', *Journal of Economic History*, 56: 837–61.

——(1998) 'Consistent wholesale price series for the United States, 1860–1990', in T. Dick (ed.) *Business Cycles Since 1820: New International Perspectives from Historical Evidence*, Cheltenham: Elgar.

——(1999) 'Degrees of processing and changes in the cyclical behavior of prices in the United States, 1869–1990', *Journal of Money, Credit and Banking*, 31: 35–53.

Hanes, C. and James, J. (2003) 'Wage adjustment under low inflation: evidence from U.S. History', *American Economic Review*, 93: 1414–24.

——(2010) 'Wage rigidity in the Great Depression', working paper.

Hanes, C. and Rhode, P.W. (2011) 'Harvests and financial crises in gold-standard America', working paper.

Hansen, G.D. and Prescott, E.G. (1993) 'Did technology shocks cause the 1990–91 recession?' *American Economic Review*, 83: 280–6.

Hoover, E.D. (1960) 'Retail prices after 1850', in NBER, *Trends in the American Economy in the Nineteenth Century*, Studies in Income and Wealth 24, Princeton, NJ: Princeton University Press.

Huang, K.X.D., Liu, Z. and Phaneuf, L. (2004) 'Why does the cyclical behavior of real wages change over time?' *American Economic Review*, 94: 836–56.

Hughes, J. (1991) *The Government Habit Redux: Economic Controls from Colonial Times to the Present*, Princeton: Princeton University Press.

James, J. (1978) *Money and Capital Markets in Postbellum America*, Princeton, NJ: Princeton University Press.

James, J., McAndrews, J. and Weiman, D.F. (2009) 'Wall Street and main street: the macroeconomic consequences of bank suspensions in New York on the national payments system, 1866 to 1914', working paper.

Kendrick, J.W. (1961) *Productivity Trends in the United States*, Princeton, NJ: Princeton University Press.

Keyssar, A. (1986) *Out of Work: The First Century of Unemployment in Massachusetts*, New York: Cambridge University Press.

King, R.G. and Rebelo, S.T. (1999) 'Resuscitating real business cycles', in J.B. Taylor and M. Woodford (eds) *Handbook of Macroeconomics*, Amsterdam: Elsevier Science Publications.

Klein, B. (1975) 'Our new monetary standard: the measurement and effects of price uncertainty, 1880–1973', *Economic Inquiry*, 13: 461–84.

Kuznets, S.S. (1946) *National Product since 1869*, New York: NBER.

Lauck, W.J. (1907) *The Causes of the Panic of 1893*, Boston, MA: Houghton-Mifflin.

Lebergott, S. (1964) *Manpower in Economic Growth: The American Record Since 1800*, New York: McGraw-Hill.

Lebow, D.E., Saks, R.E. and Wilson, B.A. (2003) 'Downward nominal wage rigidity: evidence from the employment cost index', *Advances in Macroeconomics*, 3.

Lipsey, R.E. (1963) *Price and Quantity Trends in the Foreign Trade of the United States*, Princeton, NJ: Princeton University Press.

Long, C.D. (1960) *Wages and Earnings in the United States, 1860–1890*, Princeton, NJ: Princeton University Press for NBER.

Mankiw, N.G. and Reis, R. (2010) 'Imperfect information and aggregate supply', NBER Working Paper No. 15773.

Meissner, C. (2005) 'A new world order: explaining the international diffusion of the gold standard', *Journal of International Economics*, 66: 385–406.

Miron, J.A. and Romer, C.D. (1990) 'A new monthly index of industrial production, 1884–1940', *Journal of Economic History*, 50: 321–32.

Mishkin, F.S. (1991) 'Asymmetric information and financial crises: a historical perspective', in R.G. Hubbard (ed.) *Financial Markets and Financial Crises*, Chicago, IL: University of Chicago Press.

Mitchell, W.C. (1951) *What Happens During Business Cycles: A Progress Report*, New York: NBER.

Moen, J. and Tallman, E. (1998) 'Gold shocks, liquidity, and the United States economy during the national banking era', *Explorations in Economic History*, 35: 381–404.

Myers, M.G. (1931) *The New York Money Market, Volume I: Origins and Development*, New York: Columbia University Press.

Noyes, A.D. (1898) *Thirty Years of American Finance*, New York: G.P. Putnam.

Odell, K.A. and Weidenmier, M.D. (2004) 'Real shock, monetary aftershock: the 1906 San Francisco earthquake and the panic of 1907', *Journal of Economic History*, 64: 1002–27.

Ohanian, L. (2009) 'What – or who – started the Great Depression?' *Journal of Economic Theory*, 144: 2310–35.

Phillips, A.W. (1958) 'The relationship between unemployment and the rate of changes of money wages in the United Kingdom, 1861–1957', *Economica*, 25: 283–99.

Rees, A. (1961) *Real Wages in Manufacturing, 1890–1914*, Princeton, NJ: Princeton University Press.

Reinhart, C. and Rogoff, K.S. (2009) *This Time is Different: Eight Centuries of Financial Folly*, Princeton, NJ: Princeton University Press.

Roberts, J.M. (1995) 'New Keynesian economics and the Phillips curve', *Journal of Money, Credit and Banking*, 27: 975–84.

Romer, C.D. (1986) 'Is the stabilization of the postwar economy a figment of the data?' *American Economic Review*, 76: 314–34.

——(1989) 'The prewar business cycle reconsidered: new estimates of gross national product, 1869–1908', *Journal of Political Economy*, 97: 1–37.

——(1991) 'The cyclical behavior of individual production series, 1889–1984', *Quarterly Journal of Economics*, 106: 1–31.

——(1994) 'Remeasuring business cycles', *Journal of Economic History*, 54: 573–609.

Sachs, J. (1980) 'The changing cyclical behavior of wages and prices: 1890–1976', *American Economic Review*, 70: 78–90.

Sayers, R.S. (1976) *The Bank of England, 1891–1944*, Cambridge: Cambridge University Press.

Shaw, W.H. (1947) *Value of Commodity Output since 1869*, New York: NBER.

Silber, W.L. (2006) 'Birth of the Federal Reserve: crisis in the womb', *Journal of Monetary Economics*, 53: 351–68.

Sprague, O.M.W. (1910) *History of Crises under the National Banking System*, Washington: Government Printing Office.

——(1915) 'The crisis of 1914 in the United States', *American Economic Review*, 5: 499–533.

Temin, P. (1998) 'The causes of American business cycles: an essay in economic historiography', in J.C. Fuhrer and S. Schuh (eds) *Beyond Shocks: What Causes Business Cycles*, Boston, MA: Federal Reserve Bank of Boston.

Timberlake, R. (1978) *The Origins of Central Banking in the United States*, Cambridge, MA: Harvard University Press.

U.S. Bureau of Economic Analysis (2005) 'Updated summary NIPA methodologies', *Survey of Current Business*, 85: 11–28.

U.S. Census Bureau (1975) *Historical Statistics of the United States Bicentennial Edition*, Washington: Government Printing Office.

Warren, G.F. and Pearson, F.A. (1932) *Wholesale Prices for 213 Years, 1720 to 1932*, Ithaca, NY: Cornell University Agricultural Experiment Station Memoir 142.

Watson, M.W. (1994) 'Business-cycle durations and postwar stabilization of the U.S. economy', *American Economic Review*, 84: 24–46.

Weir, D.R. (1992) 'A century of U.S. unemployment, 1890–1990: revised estimates', *Research in Economic History*, 14: 301–46.

Wicker, E. (2000) *Banking Panics of the Gilded Age*, Cambridge: Cambridge University Press.

Wilkins, M. (1989) *The History of Foreign Investment in the United States to 1914*, Cambridge, MA: Harvard University Press.

Wilson, J.W., Sylla, R.E. and Jones, C.P. (1990) 'Financial market panics and volatility in the long run, 1830–1988', in E. White (ed.) *Crashes and Panics: The Lessons from History*, Homewood, IL: Dow Jones-Irwin.

12

THE ECONOMIC HISTORY OF FINANCIAL PANICS

Andrew Jalil

Banks are wonderful things, when they work. And they usually do. But when they don't, all hell can break loose.

(Krugman 2008: 152)

The financial crisis of 2008 has brought renewed interest to the study of the history of financial panics. When did panics occur? What were their effects? What caused them? What should be the goals of policy? What lessons can history provide for today?

Prior to the onset of the crisis of 2008, to most people, banking panics were relics of the past – stories told to them by parents or grandparents who had lived through the Great Depression. All of that changed in 2008 as a banking crisis – originating in the United States – spread across the globe. On the surface, it might have appeared different – with few exceptions, mobs of distressed depositors were not racing to withdraw money from banks. But it was, in fact, a twenty-first century version of an old-fashioned banking panic.

What is a financial panic?

There are many different types of financial panics: banking panics, stock market crashes, currency crises, the collapse of speculative bubbles. Most economists would probably agree, however, that a financial panic occurs when agents panic in financial markets – that is, when agents rush to dispose of assets out of fears that an asset will suddenly decline in value or be rendered illiquid. This chapter focuses primarily on the history of banking panics, partly because the events of the past few years have focused attention on banking instability, but also because banking panics have proven to be particularly severe types of financial panics.[1] Nevertheless, it is important to note that there are many different types of financial panics.

What are banks?

It is often said that the origins of modern banking date to medieval-era goldsmiths (Krugman 2008). According to this story, holders of gold coins realized that goldsmiths' vaults were safe places to store their wealth. For a small fee, goldsmiths agreed to store gold deposits for individuals. However, goldsmiths quickly realized that they could earn additional profits by lending a fraction of these deposits at interest, and, in the process, modern banking was born.

This simple story describes the key function of banks: banks provide liquidity transformation services. By accepting short-term liquid deposits and making long-term illiquid loans, banks bridge gaps between savers and investors and channel the supply of loanable funds to the demand for loanable funds, providing essential financial intermediation services to an economy.

What is a banking panic? The Diamond–Dybvig framework

Diamond and Dybvig (1983) provide the classic formulation of a banking panic. They develop a model in which an unregulated banking system without deposit insurance is vulnerable to a panic. In their view, the main function of banks is their ability to allow investors to maintain liquid, short-term assets, while simultaneously channeling those funds to finance illiquid, long-term projects. For the most part, such an arrangement operates smoothly – on any given day, only a fraction of depositors are expected to withdraw their deposits, permitting banks to lend out most of their reserves on a long-term basis. However, as Diamond and Dybvig note, such a system is susceptible to a panic. For instance, suppose an event or trigger causes depositors to fear that their bank might fail, inducing depositors to run to convert their deposits into currency. In such a setting, the run could break the bank. A fundamentally solvent bank could fail simply because it did not have enough cash on hand to meet depositor demands.

Kindleberger's anatomy of a crisis

In a famous historical study of financial crises, Kindleberger (1978) provides an anatomy of a typical crisis. According to Kindleberger's historical analysis, financial crises follow certain stages: manias, panics, and crashes.

Manias – also known as "bubbles" – occur when a shock to the economic system changes profit opportunities, inducing investors to enter the market to take advantage of these new opportunities. The developing bubble – which is generally fueled even further by an expansion of credit – leads to speculative pressures that bid prices up over time.

At some point, however, prices stop rising and investors begin to leave the market, sparking a full-scale panic. The trigger can include a variety of forces: the failure of an overstretched bank, revelation of fraud, or a sudden realization that an object is overvalued. However, as soon as a few investors leave the market, the bubble bursts, precipitating a rush for liquidity.

The panic quickly degenerates into a crash. The run for liquidity causes large declines in the prices of goods and securities, increased bankruptcies, and bank failures. Ultimately, the crisis ends when price declines make investment profitable again, trading is closed, or a lender of last resort successfully calms markets.

Bagehot and the lender of last resort

How should central banks respond to financial panics? In his classic work *Lombard Street*, Walter Bagehot (1873) argues that, in the midst of a panic, the central bank can fulfil its responsibility to act as the lender of last resort by lending at a penalty rate against good collateral, which can include securities that may have no market value during the panic, even though they are easily tradable in normal times. As evidence, Bagehot describes how the Bank of England's swift intervention during the Panic of 1825 contained a growing crisis:

> In wild periods of alarm, one failure makes many, and the best way to prevent the derivative failures is to arrest the primary failure which causes them. The way in which

the Panic of 1825 was stopped by advancing money has been described in so broad and graphic a way that the passage has become classical. "We lent it" said Mr. Harman, on behalf of the Bank of England, "by every possible means and in modes we had never adopted before; we took in stock on security, we purchased Exchequer bills, we made advances on Exchequer bills, we not only discounted outright, but we made advances on the deposit of bills of exchange to an immense amount in short, by every means possible consistent with the safety of the Bank, and we were not on some occasions over-nice. Seeing the dreadful state in which the public were, we rendered every assistance in our power." After a day or two of this treatment, the entire panic subsided, and the "City" was quite calm. (Bagehot 1873: 51–2)

Financial panics throughout history

Financial panics are not a recent feature of modern economies. For example, Temin (2001) describes a financial crisis that occurred in Ancient Rome. In 33 AD, a liquidity crisis – characterized by a collapse in land prices, increases in interest rates, and a curtailment of loans – broke out, inducing the Roman Emperor Tiberius to rush large sums of money to landowners in the form of interest-free loans.

The seventeenth-century Netherlands also experienced a famous financial panic: tulip mania. Between November 1636 and February 1637, frenzied, speculative purchases of tulips led to dramatic price increases, with some estimates indicating that prices rose at one point to more than ten times the annual income of a skilled craftsman. However, the bubble eventually burst and tulip prices collapsed (Garber 1989).

Moreover, in a recent study, *This Time is Different: Eight Centuries of Financial Folly*, Reinhart and Rogoff (2009a) chronicle eight centuries of financial crises across the world. Specifically, they identify hundreds of banking crises across 66 countries. The title of their book, *This Time is Different*, mocks the recurring tendency to believe that each crisis – when one unexpectedly hits – is truly different from past crises. Reinhart and Rogoff argue that eight centuries of financial crises demonstrate the folly of those beliefs. According to their work and the known historical record, financial crises are recurring features of nearly all economies.

The United States is also no stranger to financial panics. In a classic account, Sprague (1910) describes five episodes of financial instability during the National Banking Era. In a recent study, Jalil (2011) constructs a listing of banking panics for the pre-Great Depression era by searching through 100 years of contemporary newspapers. He identifies seven major banking panics between 1825 and 1929 – 1833, 1837, 1839, 1857, 1873, 1893, and 1907 – as well as twenty minor banking panics.

The Panic of 1907 and the founding of the Federal Reserve

One of the most significant economic and political developments of the twentieth century – the founding of the Federal Reserve – was a consequence of a financial panic. It was the Panic of 1907 that led to the formation of the Federal Reserve System. The Panic of 1907 began when news broke that banking officials from a few trust companies in New York City had misappropriated funds for speculative purposes (Tallman and Moen 1992). A depositor run on the trusts implicated in the scandal quickly spread to virtually every bank in New York City. Within a few days, the Panic spread throughout the entire nation. The real economic consequences of the Panic were dramatic: industrial production plummeted by roughly 25 per cent in the six months following the crisis (Miron and Romer 1990).

The desire to avoid a repeat of the financial upheaval of 1907 motivated the U.S. Congress to pass the Aldrich-Vreeland Act. The Act established the National Monetary Commission, a study group assigned the task of assessing the strengths and weaknesses of the country's financial system. Its report, published in 1910, argued for the creation of a central bank. The report drew attention to the key issue contemporary scholars – academics, government officials, and bankers – considered the primary weakness of the U.S. monetary system: the perverse elasticity of the money supply. According to the report, seasonal agricultural monetary shocks weakened the financial system at recurring periods throughout the year, increasing the likelihood of a financial panic. Specifically, increased demands for currency and credit during the fall crop-moving season and the spring planting season caused higher seasonal interest rates, lower bank reserve–deposit ratios, and recurring periods of seasonal monetary stringencies. According to the Commission's findings, a central bank designed to furnish an elastic currency – one that could contract and expand as needed – was the necessary cure for the financial instability. Their arguments and recommendations became enshrined into law with the passage of the Federal Reserve Act of 1913, establishing the Federal Reserve System.

The banking panics of the Great Depression

The unfortunate irony in the history of the Federal Reserve – an institution designed to eliminate financial panics – is that, within 15 years following the founding of the Fed, the United States experienced the worst economic downturn in its history – a downturn that was accompanied by waves of banking panics. Moreover, there is widespread agreement among economic historians that the collapse of the nation's banking system from 1929 to 1933 contributed enormously to the severity of the Great Depression.

Wicker (1996) provides the most detailed narrative of the banking panics of the Great Depression. In his masterful work, Wicker analyzes newspaper records from cities throughout the country to reconstruct a history of the banking panics of the Depression. His work examines the geographical incidence, origins, magnitude, and effects of the banking panics of the Depression. He describes the four major banking panics of the Depression – November 1930 to January 1931, April to August 1931, September to October 1931, and February to March 1933 – and calls attention to the fact that 9,000 banks failed in the United States between 1930 and 1933.

A classic debate exists in the literature between Friedman and Schwartz (1963) and Temin (1976) over the nature of the banking panics of the Great Depression. Friedman and Schwartz argue that a wave of banking panics turned a relatively normal downturn into a much more severe depression. They place special emphasis on the Panic of October 1930, the first major banking panic of the Great Depression, arguing in their famous words that there was "a change in the character of the contraction" following the first panic. However, Temin challenges the Friedman and Schwartz view, noting that the banking panics of the Great Depression might have been consequences – rather than causes – of the downturn. In his study, Temin examines the Panic of 1930 and concludes that agricultural distress – which was, he argues, a component of the Depression – caused the banking Panic of 1930. Thus, in Temin's view, the banking panics of the Great Depression were consequences of the Depression. These arguments are representative of some of the much larger debates over the causes of the Great Depression.

The Federal Reserve System failed to intervene to successfully contain the banking panics of the Great Depression. One of the key questions from history is: As bank after bank failed, why did the Federal Reserve fail to act? Why would an institution – explicitly formed as a response to an earlier financial panic – fail to intervene to halt a collapse of the banking system?

Friedman and Schwartz (1963) argue that a misguided view of how the economy operates, coupled with a power vacuum and infighting among Federal Reserve officials, constrained policy makers. Temin (1989) and Eichengreen (1992) argue that the gold standard, an international system of fixed exchange rates, prevented the Federal Reserve from adopting expansionary measures. In a recent study, Romer (2006) finds evidence that corroborates the view of Friedman and Schwartz. According to Romer's analysis of the minutes of Federal Open Market Committee meetings, the Federal Reserve failed to intervene due to a flawed ideological understanding of how the economy operated and a diffuse power structure.

Regardless of the forces behind inaction, a key question remains: Would a different policy course have been effective? Could the Federal Reserve have stopped the banking panics of the Depression had it injected liquidity into the banking system and acted as a lender of last resort earlier on – that is, had it adopted the policies advocated by Bagehot a half-century before? Two recent studies have attempted to empirically test these questions. Calomiris and Mason (2003) argue that the banking panics of the Great Depression were primarily solvency crises, rather than liquidity crises. They assemble bank-level data and model the determinants of bank failure risk. Because bank fundamentals explain bank failure risk well in their model, they conclude that most of the banks that failed during the Depression were insolvent (that their liabilities exceeded their assets) rather than simply illiquid. Accordingly, liquidity intervention to prop up ailing banks would not have been sufficient to contain the panics since the banks that failed were fundamentally unhealthy, rather than simply illiquid.[2]

Richardson and Troost (2009) look at this same question in a very novel way. They use Mississippi – a state that was divided into two distinct Federal Reserve Districts – as a natural experiment for identifying the effects of liquidity intervention. The northern half of Mississippi was under the jurisdiction of the St. Louis Federal Reserve District, whereas the southern half was under the jurisdiction of the Atlanta Federal Reserve District. Policies differed across these districts during the Depression. Whereas the St. Louis Fed did little to contain the banking panics, the Atlanta Fed aggressively intervened to support its banking system. The Atlanta Fed rushed cash to banks undergoing runs and acted as a lender of last resort. Richardson and Troost note that banks suspended at far lower rates in the portion of Mississippi under the jurisdiction of the Atlanta Fed. Hence, they conclude that liquidity intervention mitigated banking panics during the early stages of the Depression. Moreover, they conjecture that the course of the Depression might have been different had the Federal Reserve System as a whole acted as a lender of last resort.[3]

The end of the Quiet Period and the banking Panic of 2008

The period in the United States from the end of the Great Depression to the onset of the crisis of 2008 has frequently been referred to as the "Quiet Period" in U.S. financial history. The financial reforms designed in the wake of the Great Depression – increased regulation of the banking sector and the introduction of deposit insurance – proved successful: the U.S. economy did not experience a major, systemic banking panic for more than 70 years.

The financial crisis of 2008 ended the Quiet Period. Gorton (2009) describes how the crisis resembled an old-style banking panic – one that was concentrated in the largely unregulated shadow banking sector. Specifically, Gorton places particular importance on the repo market, which he describes as a form of depository banking for firms and financial institutions. Similar to individual depositors, firms and financial institutions also have a need to deposit their money somewhere. The repo market satisfies this need. On one side of a repo transaction, a firm or financial institution wants to deposit (lend) its money, whereas, on the other side, a firm or financial institution wants to borrow the money. The borrowers and lenders in the repo market include banks, hedge funds, institutional investors, pension funds, insurance companies, and other financial institutions. Thus, the repo market resembles traditional depository banking with one notable exception: a lack of deposit insurance.

However, as the Diamond–Dybvig framework implies, such a system is vulnerable to a panic. And we know from 2008 that a panic did indeed break out. The bursting of the housing bubble and the corresponding decline in the value of mortgage-backed securities impaired the balance sheets of financial institutions, creating fears that some institutions might fail and sparking a system-wide run in the repo market. Thus, in a classic Diamond–Dybvig sense, the shadow banking sector experienced a panic.

Indeed, for most economists, the panic in the shadow banking system is the primary cause of the crisis of 2008. Moreover, the economic effects of the crisis were similar to those of the banking panics of the Great Depression. Eichengreen and O'Rourke (2009) note that during the initial stages of the crisis, according to a variety of economic indicators including world industrial output, the value of world equity markets, and the volume of world trade, the world economy was deteriorating in as rapid a manner as the initial descent into the Great Depression. However, largely because the policy response differed so dramatically – countries across the world implemented bank-stabilization programs and undertook expansionary monetary and fiscal policies – the recent worldwide downturn, while severe, pales in comparison to the economic collapse of the 1930s.

The effects of banking crises

The experience of Japan following its banking crisis in the early 1990s – a crisis that was brought on by a real estate bubble and crash – has served as a warning to the United States in the wake of its crisis. Following its banking crisis, Japan experienced a lost decade of growth. While the United States did indeed emerge from recession in 2009, output growth has been so sluggish that unemployment has remained high. Moreover, current forecasts do not indicate that a rapid recovery is on the way. Given this gloomy outlook, researchers are asking a host of questions: Why has unemployment remained high for so long? Will output return to its pre-crisis trend path? Is the United States already one-third of the way through a lost decade of prosperity?

Much of the recent empirical work on financial panics has rightly focused on the key question: What are the effects of financial panics? In a recent study of the banking panics of the pre-Great Depression era, Jalil (2011) derives four main empirical findings regarding the macroeconomic effects of banking panics of that period: (1) banking panics had large and strongly negative effects on both output and prices, (2) banking panics were a primary source of economic instability throughout much of U.S. history – either causing or amplifying roughly half of all business-cycle downturns between 1825 and 1914, (3) in the post-Civil War era, downturns with major banking panics were, on average, substantially more severe than downturns without them, and output recoveries for downturns with major banking panics were two to three times the length of downturns without them, and (4) output did not always rapidly return to its pre-crisis trend path following major banking panics.

Reinhart and Rogoff (2009b) conducted an international study of the aftermath of financial crises. Among their sample of major banking crises, they found that, during a typical crisis, real housing prices fall by 36 per cent over 6 years, real equity prices decline by 56 per cent over 3 years, the unemployment rate increases by 7 percentage points over 5 years, and real gross domestic product (GDP) per capita declines by 9.3 per cent over 1.9 years. In addition, among their sample of postwar crises, it takes, on average, 4.4 years for real GDP per capita to return to its pre-crisis level. Moreover, in the three years following the crisis, public debt levels increase by 86 per cent on average.

Given the serious macroeconomic consequences of banking panics, researchers have also focused on another key question: Through what channels do banking panics affect the economy? In a classic early study, Friedman and Schwartz (1963) argue that banking panics have large effects on output through their effects on the money supply. According to the Friedman and Schwartz view, for much of its history, the United States experienced periodic financial panics for exogenous reasons: people in the economy panicked and there was a run on liquidity, leading to large declines in the stock of money. Friedman and Schwartz cite financial panics as crucial natural experiments that show that changes in the money supply have effects on output.

However, in a study of the banking panics of the Great Depression, Bernanke (1983) identifies an additional channel through which banking panics have effects on output other than their impact on the money supply. Bernanke argues that banking panics increase the costs of credit intermediation services. According to Bernanke, banks do not merely create money: they engage in a host of other activities that affect economic activity. They examine the credit of potential borrowers. They bridge gaps between savers and investors. They invest in long-term relationships with clients and accumulate relationship capital. They provide financial intermediation services that relax credit constraints. Bernanke argues that the banking panics of the Great Depression disrupted these efficiency-enhancing services and raised the costs of credit intermediation, reducing output through a nonmonetary channel. To show this, Bernanke estimates a regression with the growth rate of industrial production as the dependent variable and unanticipated changes in the money supply and measures of financial crisis as independent variables. Because the coefficients on the crisis variables are negative and statistically significant, Bernanke argues that the banking panics of the Great Depression reduced output through a channel other than their effects on the money supply. Bernanke's paper has deservedly remained one of the most influential studies on the causes of the Great Depression. It also led to the emergence of a new literature on the nonmonetary effects of financial crises and the impact of credit disruptions.

More recent studies have examined the persistence of the effects of banking crises. Using a panel data set covering a large number of countries in the post-1960 era, Cerra and Saxena (2008) conclude that after financial crises output does not, on average, return to its pre-crisis trend. In a study of 88 banking crises since 1970, the IMF's 2009 *World Economic Outlook* finds that output typically does not return to its pre-crisis trend over the medium term – within the first seven years following the crisis. In a study of 40 banking crises since 1980, Cecchetti *et al.* (2009) find that, while the behavior of output varies widely following financial crises, many banking crises have long-lasting effects on output, and trend reversion (that is, the reversion of output to its pre-crisis trend path) tends to be a sluggish process, if it even occurs.

Several papers have recently attempted to explain why banking crises might have persistent effects on output. Cecchetti *et al.* (2009) speculate that increased risk aversion in the aftermath of banking crises could lower capital accumulation in the long run and that sharp increases in the size of government debt could lead to crowding-out effects that dampen economic growth for years.[4] Ramirez (2009) presents evidence that, before the advent of deposit insurance, banking panics reduced trust in the banking system and induced depositors to keep their money out of the banking system, thereby impairing an economy's ability to conduct effective financial intermediation services over time. The IMF's 2009 *World Economic Outlook* speculates that banking panics are associated with declines in potential output – the level of output consistent with stable inflation and full employment. However, while the findings from these empirical studies are suggestive, there remain several candidate explanations for the sluggish performance of output in the aftermath of financial crises. Indeed, whether the poor performance of output in the aftermath of financial crises reflects long-lasting effects on potential output, long-lasting effects on aggregate demand, or the return of an overheating economy to a more normal level of production, remain competing explanations.

The next financial panic

When will the next financial panic hit? In July 2010, Congress passed and President Obama signed into law the Dodd-Frank Wall Street Reform and Consumer Protection Act, a financial reform bill designed to prevent future crises. Will the reform bill be successful? Will it prevent financial crises for decades to come? Have we entered a new Quiet Era? Or have we returned to the days in which major banking panics reoccur every 10 to 20 years? The answers to these questions are anyone's guess. The financial reforms in the wake of the Great Depression created a 70-year Quiet Period. Yet, recreating it might not be so simple. As Gorton (2009) notes, prior to the Great Depression, when financial reforms were enacted, contemporaries praised the reforms, even though they ultimately proved to be unsuccessful and were followed by subsequent panics. Moreover, one of the lessons from history is that financial panics tend to reappear, and seldom if ever manifest themselves in the same way. Regulators are always fighting the last war and financial innovation is usually three steps ahead of the regulators. History tells us quite plainly that there surely will be a future financial panic. It is only a question of when.

Notes

1 For example, Schwartz (1986: 12) distinguishes between real and pseudo financial crises. According to Schwartz, real financial crises occur when the banking system experiences a crisis. By contrast, Schwartz describes all other financial disturbances – those that do not threaten the stability of the banking sector – as pseudo crises. Schwartz asserts, "All the phenomena of recent years that have been characterized as financial crises – a decline in asset prices of equity stocks, real estate, commodities; depreciation of the exchange value of a national currency; financial distress of a large non-financial firm, a large municipality, a financial industry, or sovereign debtors – are pseudo financial crises." Regardless of the merits of this claim, it speaks to the view that banking panics are particularly severe types of financial crises and worthy of discussion in their own right.
2 Calomiris and Mason (2003) argue, however, that earlier macroeconomic intervention – perhaps in the form of expansionary open market operations – could have prevented a general deflation and averted the worst of the downturn, thereby alleviating bank distress. Moreover, their findings indicate that bank recapitalization policies, similar to those enacted by the Reconstruction Finance Corporation after 1933, could have helped prevent bank failures in 1930–32.
3 This debate is particularly relevant in light of the financial crisis of 2008. In a recent article, Anna J. Schwartz argues that whereas the banking panics of the Great Depression were liquidity crises, the banking crisis of 2008 was primarily a solvency crisis (Carney 2008). Regardless of the merits of this view, it is clear that a better understanding of the nature of the banking panics of the Depression can help inform policymakers about the appropriate policy response to combat financial crises.
4 In a recent study, Rinehart and Rogoff (2010) find a correlation between high debt levels and lower growth, though Irons and Bivens (2010) provide a critical appraisal of their study.

References

Bagehot, W. (1873) *Lombard Street: A Description of the Money Market*, London: Henry S. King & Co.
Bernanke, B. (1983) 'Nonmonetary effects of the financial crisis in the propagation of the Great Depression', *American Economic Review*, 73: 257–76.
Calomiris, C.W. and Mason, J.R. (2003) 'Fundamentals, panics, and bank distress during the depression', *American Economic Review*, 93: 1615–47.

Carney, B.M. (2008) 'Bernanke is fighting the last war', *Wall Street Journal*, October 18.

Cecchetti, S., Kohler, M. and Upper, C. (2009) 'Financial crises and economic activity', NBER Working Paper No. 15379.

Cerra, V. and Saxena, S. (2008) 'Growth dynamics: the myth of economic recovery', IMF Working Paper, WP/05/147.

Diamond, D. and Dybvig, P. (1983) 'Bank runs, deposit insurance, and liquidity', *Journal of Political Economy*, 91: 401–19.

Eichengreen, B. (1992) *Golden Fetters: The Gold Standard and the Great Depression, 1919–1939*, New York: Oxford University Press.

Eichengreen, B. and O'Rourke, K. (2009) 'A tale of two depressions', VoxEU.

Friedman, M. and Schwartz, A.J. (1963) *A Monetary History of the United States, 1867–1960*, Princeton, NJ: Princeton University Press.

Garber, P. (1989) 'Tulipmania', *Journal of Political Economy*, 97: 535–60.

Gorton, G. (2009) 'Slapped in the face by the invisible hand: banking and the panic of 2007', paper prepared for the Federal Reserve Bank of Atlanta's 2009 Financial Markets Conference: Financial Innovation and Crisis, May 11–13, 2009.

International Monetary Fund (2009) *World Economic Outlook*, Washington: International Monetary Fund.

Irons, J. and Bivens, J. (2010) 'Government debt and economic growth: overreaching claims of debt "threshold" suffer from theoretical and empirical flaws', Economic Policy Institute Briefing Paper No. 271.

Jalil, A. (2011) 'A new history of banking panics in the United States, 1825–1929: construction and implications', unpublished paper, Reed College.

Kindleberger, C. (1978) *Manias, Panics, and Crashes: A History of Financial Crises*, London: Macmillan.

Krugman, P. (2008) *The Return of Depression Economics and the Crisis of 2008*, New York: Norton.

Miron, J. and Romer, C. (1990) 'A new monthly index of industrial production', *Journal of Economic History*, 50: 321–37.

Ramirez, C.D. (2009) 'Bank fragility, "money under the mattress," and long-run growth: U.S. evidence from the "perfect" panic of 1893', *Journal of Banking and Finance*, 33: 2185–98.

Reinhart, C. and Rogoff, K. (2009a) *This Time is Different: Eight Centuries of Financial Folly*, Princeton, NJ: Princeton University Press.

——(2009b) 'The aftermath of financial crises', *American Economic Review*, 99: 466–72.

——(2010) 'Growth in a time of debt', *American Economic Review*, 100: 573–8.

Richardson, G and Troost, W. (2009) 'Monetary intervention mitigated banking panics during the Great Depression: quasi-experimental evidence from a Federal Reserve district border, 1929–33', *Journal of Political Economy*, 117: 1031–73.

Romer, C. (2006) 'Was the Federal Reserve constrained by the gold standard during the Great Depression? Evidence from the 1932 open market purchase program', *Journal of Economic History*, 66: 140–76.

Schwartz, A.J. (1986) 'Real and pseudo-financial crises', in F. Capie and G.E. Wood (eds) *Financial Crises and the World Banking System*, London: Macmillan.

Sprague, O.M.W. (1910) *History of Crises under the National Banking System*, Washington: U.S. Government Printing Office.

Tallman, E. and Moen, J. (1992) 'The bank panic of 1907: the role of trust companies', *Journal of Economic History*, 42: 611–30.

Temin, P. (1976) *Did Monetary Forces Cause the Great Depression?* New York: Norton.

Temin, P. (1989) *Lessons from the Great Depression*, Cambridge, MA: MIT Press.

Temin (2001) 'A market economy in the early Roman Empire', *Journal of Roman Studies*, 91: 169–81.

Wicker, E. (1996) *The Banking Panics of the Great Depression*, Cambridge: Cambridge University Press.

PART III

Individual economic sectors

13

ECONOMIC HISTORY
AND RELIGION

John E. Murray

The historical study of economics and religion has been approached in two directions. The first uses economic reasoning to understand religious behavior in the past, and the second seeks to understand how religious beliefs influence the performance of economies over time. This chapter incorporates both approaches in order to make sense of both economic and religious history. It first addresses the audacious notion that economic reasoning might inform the study of religion.

The economic approach to the study of religion

The most fundamental assumption in economics is that of rationality. It is axiomatic that people understand the choices before them and the costs and benefits of each particular option. This is not to say that people hold perfect information about all possible options; obtaining and assessing information is costly, and so people collect as much of it as will yield benefits greater than costs. And then they act on that cost-benefit assessment. The validity of such an approach to religious behavior may not be immediately apparent in the wake of nineteenth-century writers such as Marx, Freud, and Comte, who emphasized the utter irrationality of religion. But that is simply to say that before reaching any conclusions earlier analyses had committed themselves to, in the words of one sociologist, "the positivist view that religion in the modern world is merely a survival from man's primitive past, and doomed to disappear in an era of science and general enlightenment" (Gerhard Lenski, quoted in Iannaccone 1998: 1468).

In a post-Enlightenment era, assuming human rationality in religious behavior would seem anomalous. But of course, independent of the existence of God, the study of theology itself embodies a standard of rationality that dates back to Augustine's engagement with neoplatonism and Aquinas's Aristotelianism. Economists do not employ logic to study the characteristics or activities of God, but rather the characteristics and activities of persons in their search for and response to God. This approach makes no judgments about the likelihood of actual contact with God in religious acts. In that sense, imputing rationality to religious humans is no more unreasonable than imputing rationality to consumers who exchange their time or wealth for goods or services in ordinary markets. Whether the exchange is a "success" by some standard is not of immediate interest, but whether the exchange occurs in the first place, and whether the market participants and others persist in such exchanges, is of great interest. And even in the absence of explicit prices these exchanges are costly. In the case of religion, to participate one must sacrifice time to the religious activity. The process of determining whether the time lost to religious activity repays the participant provides an initial point of entry into the economics of religion.

If participation in religious activities is costly certainly in time terms and in most cases in money terms as well, what exactly are the benefits that participants derive? Different strands of research have posited a variety of possible objective functions: religious activity might lead to a higher probability of passing the final judgment and thus avoiding hell, or it might lead to a deeper relationship with God in the present (Stolz 2006). In a more mundane sense, it might be pursued for its own sake as an element in fellowship with other worshippers or for its aesthetic consequences: an appreciation of beautiful music, ritual, or architecture. These are not mutually exclusive alternatives, but they serve to illustrate the open-ended nature of the ends of religious activity. Once one has accepted the open-ended nature of both the benefits and costs of religious activity, it is natural to examine such activity from an economic perspective. In this view the choices made by religious actors are as rational as those made by a consumer in a store, and the insights that economic analysis makes available are just as acute.

Debates about the impact of religious beliefs on economic performance

Probably the best-known writer on the interaction of religion and economics, particularly as a way to explain historical processes, was Max Weber. Weber's essay *The Protestant Ethic and the Spirit of Capitalism* (1905 [1958]) was a landmark in the analysis of economic history through religious motives. From Luther's foundations into John Calvin's writings, proposed Weber, an indirect line could be drawn thence to modern economic growth. The Lutheran notion of the priesthood of believers had a leveling effect on individual salvation: no longer was one occupation seen as preferable in the eyes of God. In addition, justification by faith alone introduced a further element of uncertainty regarding ultimate salvation. Calvin emphasized that the power of the final judgment was so completely in God's hands that none of man's actions could even slightly influence his final fate; this was the doctrine of total depravity. Mere man, then, had not the slightest inkling of his status in the eyes of God. This lack of knowledge of the most urgent kind then led Reformed Christians to live, not so as to convince God of their righteousness, for that was pointless, but as if they were in fact among the elect. The appearance of election was best presented by, in Weber's words, a worldly asceticism: "the clean and solid comfort of the middle class home as an ideal." The hard work, savings habits, and lack of ostentation among these worldly ascetics identified them as among the elect, or so they hoped. This too was a calling as much as any other particular occupation, but its righteousness required the person – be he a humble manual worker, a skilled tradesman, or a business owner or manager – to execute his daily toil for the greater glory of God. It just so happened that the qualities that led to this ascetic Protestantism happened also to be activities that rising markets for labor, capital, and products rewarded generously as well. And so, it appeared, one reason for economic growth in Northwestern Europe was that much of the land had already been prepared for capitalism by Reformed Christianity.

From the time of its publication, the Weber thesis elicited admiration and criticism. R.H. Tawney, in *Religion and the Rise of Capitalism* (1926 [1948]), criticized Weber's use of English Puritanism to stand for all of Protestantism, but otherwise expanded on the Weber thesis with approval. Tawney noted that capitalism in a broad sense predated the Reformation, and that the two phenomena developed in parallel. Weber defined capitalism in a relatively narrow sense as the rational organization of formally free labor. Kurt Samuelsson, in *Religion and Economic Action* (1961 [1993]), treated the Weber thesis as explaining economic growth more generally, and this was the version of Weber that he criticized thoroughly. In the Low Countries themselves, he noted, the Netherlands was oriented towards market-based trade long before the Reformation, and predominantly Catholic Belgium industrialized much more rapidly than the Netherlands, or indeed anywhere else on the Continent. The Weber thesis might best be seen as plausible and provocative. In the best scholarly tradition, it has inspired responses that have led to a deeper understanding of religious activity in economic history, despite – or because of – its shortcomings.

A debate closely related to the development of the Weber thesis associated economic growth in Protestant parts of Europe with higher literacy levels. To be sure, from an early date the Lutheran countries, and Sweden in particular, had emphasized near-universal literacy acquisition so that the individual believer could read Scripture on his or her own. Conveniently for the historian, Swedish custom and law required pastors to examine members of their flock on their reading ability and report the results to their bishop. Results of these examinations show that Swedish literacy rates were extraordinarily high not long after the Reformation. Among birth cohorts of the mid-seventeenth century, according to parish registers, some two-thirds were able to read in their adult years (Johansson 1977). While the effect of religion on human capital acquisition is clear in this case, both the consequences for Sweden and the generalizability to the rest of Europe are much less clear. The meaning of literacy acquisition and the uses to which it was put were not always in accord with modern notions of economic growth. Luther, in particular, was as fond of catechism-type primers, recitation, and rote memorization as the Catholic schools against which he rebelled. In the early modern period, confessionally mixed areas of France and Germany often displayed higher literacy rates among Catholics than among Protestants. And while in both Germany and Sweden higher literacy rates were associated with economic growth, the lag time between literacy acquisition and growth dependent on such human capital could be as long as a century (Murray 2000b).

The relationship between a particular kind of Protestantism and the consequences, rather than the causes, of economic growth was the subject of Élie Halévy's *History of the English People in the Nineteenth Century* (1912–32 [1949]). Here Halévy considered the dire conditions of the working class in England during the Industrial Revolution of the late eighteenth and early nineteenth centuries. Why was Britain so politically calm when France, which had experienced much less economic dislocation, convulsed with political revolution and made war on its neighbors? Halévy proposed his famous thesis that the difference between the two countries was the rise of evangelical Christianity in England. Methodism grew out of economic distress in the early eighteenth century, but in a conservative direction that led to respect for existing institutions. Although relatively few of the working classes became Methodists, the revivalists such as Wesley and Whitefield carried an importance out of proportion to their numbers, and well beyond Wesley's death in 1791 (Itzkin 1975).

Economic analysis of religious history

Weber, Halévy, and their interlocutors provide ample evidence that religious activity can influence the course of economic history. We now turn this argument around and consider how economic theory might help explain religious history. In the Judeo-Christian tradition, certain Scriptural stories contain tantalizing details of economic life. The exchange by Esau of his birthright for a mess of pottage is an example of a binding contract for sale (Miller 1993). The development of monotheistic cult activity of Yahweh may be explained by theories of monopoly formation (Raskovich 1996). The parable of the workers in the vineyard (Matthew 20:1–16) may describe characteristics of spot market labor contracts at the time, and it certainly describes an economy that had been at least partially monetized, because all the workers are paid in coin and not in scrip or promises of future compensation. The economic studies of these narratives tend to be richly theorized but somewhat lacking in empirical support. The a posteriori nature of examining given religious texts through social scientific lenses is inherently *ad hoc*, and perhaps less enlightening than more formally quantitative studies.

The spread of Christianity

These begin – at least, the study of *estimated* quantities – with the onset of the Christian era and the rise of organized Christianity. The sociologist Rodney Stark (1996) provided an excellent example using contemporary records, simple models, and present-day comparisons to address the question: how did Christianity grow from such unprepossessing beginnings? From *Acts* to Eusebius to prominent present-day historians, the standard version attributes rapid growth to mass conversions. Stark proposes that within a decade of Jesus's death (and resurrection, according to tradition) there were about 1,000 believers. Then, just before the conversion of Constantine, this had grown to 5 to 7.5 million Christians, according to a variety of scholarly estimates. Combining the two figures with an exponential growth formula yields an annual growth rate of 3.4 per cent, or about 40 per cent per decade. This rate is not unique in the annals of religious sects; in fact it is very close to the growth rate of the Mormon church over the last century. Of particular interest is the correlation of estimated Christian population levels from both this model and from historians' independent estimates at various times along the way: between 40,000 (model) and 50,000 (Robert Wilken 1984) in the mid-second century; about 1.9 per cent of the population (model) and 2 per cent (Robin Lane Fox 1987) in the mid-third century. The model, as in many historians' accounts, also indicates a sharp increase in the Christian share of the population in the late third century, just before the Constantinian legal changes of the new religion's status.

While adherence to a model implies a certain predictability in behavior, joining a particular new religion need not be interpreted as a rational choice. But in this case there were sound reasons for choosing Christianity that went well beyond a taste for a particular kind of religious activity. Practical arguments also favored Christianity. Stark emphasizes the novelty in antiquity of the command to love your neighbor. Indeed in the first ecclesial communities (i.e. "chur-ches"), charity towards the less fortunate was institutionalized in the position of the deacon, who ensured that the sick, poor, infirm, and disabled were aided and cared for. Such care for those struck down by epidemic disease led to higher survival rates among Christians than pagans. Christian women were respected in their community, not married off to strangers before they had reached menarche, and Christians treated infants with kindness as well, forbidding abortion and infanticide from an early date. Thus, internal relations within Christian communities offered strong incentives for outsiders to join. But those who joined simply to take advantage of Christian welfare benefits would have dragged down the intensity of communal worship, a phenomenon well known to social scientists as free riding. Christian practices of sacrifice and stigma mitigated this free riding, which made the group all the stronger (Iannaccone 1992). Once baptized, or initiated, the Christian was expected to care for the sick, infirm, and dependent, and to forgo convenient but barbarous pagan practices towards infants, children, and women. The willingness of martyrs (Greek for "witnesses") to give their lives on behalf of the church solved two difficult problems of credibility. The earliest martyrs were those who had seen the risen Christ, or at least claimed to have seen him. But if they were misrepresenting their interactions with Jesus then their willingness to die for his sake was strange indeed. Deaths of later martyrs gave credibility to a different but related claim, that they believed in the truth of Christian doctrine and, more precisely, its truth claims that conflicted with those of the state.

Supporting doctrinal and historical claims with the lives of believers made the church more attractive to prospective converts, and membership grew as a result.

Religious monopoly and competition in the United States

The notion that relations within a church could create powerful incentives to join and maintain membership through donations of time and money powered Roger Finke and Rodney Stark's revisionist work in American religious history (1992). Careful quantitative work directed by some basic social scientific theorizing led them to refute a bushelful of chestnuts. Already well known to early American historians if not the general reading public, at the time of the Revolution only about a sixth of Americans belonged to any particular congregation. What was new was Finke and Stark's explanation for this small share: this was a typical result in a monopolized market. Schoolchildren might remember of the Thirteen Colonies that most of New England was Congregationalist, Rhode Island Baptist, New York Dutch Reformed, Maryland Catholic, and the rest Anglican. However, other than Rhode Island and Maryland, these identifications reflected establishment of particular churches as much as chain migration of new Americans who brought their religious loyalties with them. Establishment in early America meant simply that the state (or colony in earlier times) collected taxes through its coercive powers, which it then handed over to the established church. Consequences were, at least retrospectively, predictable: churches that were unresponsive to their congregation's needs for contact with God, and a less than optimal provision of religious services. Indeed, the first amendment to the federal Constitution only prohibited the *federal* government from establishing a church, so that the states of Massachusetts and Connecticut continued to support the Congregational church into the nineteenth century. When that support ended, competing churches flourished, and the overall demand for ministers rose sharply (Olds 1994).

What drove the exceptional level of American religiosity in the nineteenth century was this privatization of religious markets. New denominations grew with great speed into spaces vacated by old-line churches. Over the antebellum period, the share of Americans who belonged to a church more than doubled, from a sixth to over a third, at a time when the overall population level increased elevenfold. It was not the most prominent colonial churches that grew. The share of the population that was Congregationalist dropped from 20 per cent to 4 per cent between 1776 and 1860, and the Episcopal and Presbyterian churches met similar fates. It was new, "upstart" – perhaps better described as start-up – churches that led the way. The share of the population that was Methodist grew from 2.5 per cent to 34 per cent at mid-century, and the share Catholic from less than 2 to nearly 14 per cent. None of this simply happened. The newer churches reached out to members of long standing, and evangelized vigorously. The great Methodist preacher Francis Asbury was only the best known of his brother clergy who travelled many thousands of miles on their circuits to bring the Word to the people. As for the Catholics, the German priest Franz Xavier Weninger travelled almost as many hundreds of thousands of miles as did Asbury, planting churches and conducting parish missions. Meanwhile, the old mainline churches failed to adapt to new market conditions, and settled back into their seminaries, more content with reading and writing than with preaching and teaching.

The idea that a monopolized, established, state church would not minister to its members as energetically as a hustling minority church that lived by donations did not originate with Finke and Stark (1992). Adam Smith discussed this idea in Book V, Chapter 1, of *Wealth of Nations* in 1776. Smith proposed, "The clergy of an established and well-endowed religion frequently become men of learning and elegance." In response to a challenge by outsiders, they were likely to call for the state to crush the newcomers, much as Anglican clergy had done to dissenters. As a result, wrote Smith, "all the arts of gaining proselytes are constantly on the side of ... the dissenters and ... the methodists (sic)." As for the Catholics, "the voluntary oblations of the people" ensured that priests maintained their "industry and zeal" (Smith 1776 [1937]). The reasonableness of this claim was tested by Iannaccone (1991). Excluding countries that were predominantly Catholic, he showed that the more concentrated that attendance was among just a few churches, the lower the share of overall population that attended. Thus, in the United States and Canada with a variety of churches, over a third of people participated in services weekly, while in Scandinavia, with its established Lutheran churches, attendance rates hovered around 5 per cent. Indeed, even within those Scandinavian countries attendance was much higher in non-established Catholic, Baptist, and other churches than in Lutheran churches. The low attendance rates, high costs associated with unionized, civil service clergy, and excess capacity in Scandinavian Lutheran churches are textbook symptoms of monopoly (Iannaccone *et al.* 1997).

The phenomenon of stabilization of once vibrant churches and their subsequent decline, combined with the simultaneous start-up of new, stricter churches that grew rapidly, marked American church history well into the twentieth century. Over the middle third of the century, the share of the church-going population who were United Methodists declined from 12 per cent to 6 per cent; the Episcopalians declined from 3 to 2 per cent. Meanwhile, Evangelicals gained in relative and absolute terms, with membership in Southern Baptist churches rising from 7.7 to over 10 per cent. Finke and Stark (1992) emphasize that the decline of more familiar churches does not imply a decline in American religiosity altogether; it is part of a cyclic shift in religious activity from staid to lively churches that has been in motion since 1776. Over the course of this cycle, a single church, such as the Methodists, might experience growth in its strict and active phase, to a peak characterized by the establishment of seminaries and a highly educated clergy, and then begin a decline in which it becomes much like other shrinking churches. But then another young and vibrant church – in the Methodist case, those growing out of the Holiness movement – comes along to take its place. Christianity is not in decline in America, but its components are perpetually rising and falling in popularity.

Monasticism

Given the power of incentives and market structure to influence the growth and well-being of churches, it is reasonable to wonder just how strong these incentives are over a very long-term period. For example, throughout Christian history some followers have wanted to observe Jesus's instruction to sell all one's worldly goods, give the proceeds to the poor, and then follow Him. Forswearing wealth would seem to be the least rational choice economically possible, and yet examples of such action abound, even if the share of Christians who attempt it are few. The history of monastic life resembles the model laid out by Finke and Stark (1992) for the American case. As monastic foundations age and become more set in their ways – indeed, more worldly in their ways – reform movements set out, not to create new forms of monastic life, but to return to the charisms of the founders. In response to decline in observance of the Rule of St. Benedict (early sixth century), the monks of Cluny early in the tenth century reformed their daily lives with an emphasis on more reverent liturgy. This did not last, and another reform movement began in Cîteaux in the late eleventh century, the Cistercians, who aimed for a stricter observance to the rule. But this too, after many centuries, inspired another reform movement from the abbey at La Trappe, which became the Order of Cistercians of the Strict Observance, or the Trappists. Thus, monastic history exhibits a certain cycling much like Christianity as a whole. From growth during a time of strict simplicity, monastic orders have moved to stagnation during a time of laxity, thus spawning a reform that re-emphasizes strictness.

The Cistercians, because of their role in building up late medieval Europe, and in particular the pioneer movements of German speakers into the wastes of Northeast Europe, have attracted the attention of economic historians (Roehl 1972). Consistent with Finke and Stark's stress on the fruits of strictness, the immediate consequence of Cistercian efforts was growth throughout Western Europe. The Cistercians practiced an austere Christianity much in line with Jesus's teachings on poverty and prayer. In the eyes of relatively wealthy landholders, Cistercian holiness and industry made the order an attractive candidate for charity, since donations – of land, the primary form of wealth holding at that time – might not only advance the Cistercian project but also provide for posthumous prayers for the donors' souls. While at first the accumulating landholdings seemed to signal Cistercian success, eventually they led to a less intense exercise of their monastic gifts. As their land holdings grew beyond the ability of the monks themselves to work them, the Cistercians sought help from *conversi*, lay brothers who worked the farms but were not full members of the order. Typically within three monastic generations, those monasteries that had received substantial land gifts had retreated to a less strict life. Eventually this opened up the monastic field for the new order of the Trappists.

A similar case that showed the difficulty of maintaining religious strictness over time appeared among the American communal group the Shakers. Begun in the Revolutionary era as an essentially monastic group in the Northeast United States, they followed news of revivals in the West to plant new communes in Ohio and Kentucky. At some point not long before the Civil War – in other words, about the three monastic generations that the Cistercians experienced – the Shakers began to slip away from their unique customs of active dance during prayer (hence their name) and towards practices resembling other Protestant churches of the day. The societies attracted less committed members during economic hard times, and tended to lose educated Shakers to apostasy. As with the Cistercians, they became more dependent on the labor of non-members. By the later nineteenth century, they were sharply declining in numbers and participating in ecumenical exercises with other shrinking churches (Murray 1995a, 1995b, 2000b; Cosgel and Murray 1998).

Judaism and Islam

Although the examples provided so far pertain primarily to varieties of Christianity, it need not be assumed that only Christians behave rationally in making religious decisions. Carmel Chiswick (2008) has documented the changing practices of American Jews and the correlation with the rising value of their time. That is, as Jews assimilated and became more successful materially, the opportunity cost of participation in religious ritual rose. To economize on time that could be spent in other activities, Reform synagogues in particular abbreviated their services and conducted more of them in English rather than Hebrew. Further, interactions of timing of assimilation and educational choices early in the twentieth century influenced such later phenomena as intermarriage rates. Rational choice in Jewish practice and custom appears not only in the United States but Israel as well. Population patterns in kibbutzim suggest an exodus of the more productive members reminiscent of the Shaker situation (Abramitzky 2008).

Nor need we limit our view to the Judeo-Christian tradition. Timur Kuran (2010) has written extensively on the role of Islam in the economic underdevelopment of the Middle East. He finds in particular that nothing inherent in Islamic doctrine held the region back. Rather the fundamental problem stemmed from later institutions developed to be consistent with Islamic teaching, which then took on a life of their own. While they could be replaced or reformed with more modern institutions that would also be in conformity with Koranic and Hadithic doctrine, their longevity implies a necessity that simply is not there in the foundation documents. Among these institutions Kuran emphasizes group inheritance laws that impeded capital accumulation, an emphasis on individualism in Islamic law that discouraged such collective institutions as corporations, and the *waqf* or trust, which tied up resources into organizations that eventually became inefficient (Kuran 2004). These might not have mattered much, except that the West embraced corporations, a variety of ways to accumulate capital, and reasonably efficient and integrated capital markets. As a result, from rough equality in economic development terms at the opening of the second millennium, Western Europe began to outpace the Middle East. Strangely, Kuran (2004: 88) notes, Islamic extremists who want to return the *Dar al Islam* to a golden age of parity with the West hope to restore only parts of the old economy. They seem to accept joint stock corporations, equity markets, and modern accounting techniques, but cannot abide interest and insurance, advertising and consumerism. Kuran concludes on an optimistic note. He distinguishes between (1) what is "inherent" in Islam, which comes from the Koran and Hadithic addenda, and (2) later institutions that developed such as the *waqf*. He sees nothing in the former that would impede economic growth, but plenty of problems in the latter. Should predominantly Islamic countries return to the oldest sources of their religion for economic policy guidance, they might reasonably expect economic development to follow. Such is a recommendation the possible consequences of which Max Weber would recognize.

References

Abramitzky, R. (2008) 'The limits of equality: insights from the Israeli kibbutz', *Quarterly Journal of Economics*, 123: 1111–59.

Chiswick, C.U. (2008) *Economics of American Judaism*, New York: Routledge.

Cosgel, M. and Murray, J. (1998) 'Productivity of a commune: the Shakers, 1850–1880', *Journal of Economic History*, 58: 494–510.

Finke, R. and Stark, R. (1992) *The Churching of America 1776–1990: Winners and Losers in Our Religious Economy*, New Brunswick, NJ: Rutgers University Press.

Fox, R.L. (1987) *Pagans and Christians*, New York: Knopf.

Halévy, E. (1912–32 [1949]) *History of the English People in the Nineteenth Century*, 6 vols, London: Ernest Benn.

Iannaccone, L.R. (1991) 'The consequences of religious market structure: Adam Smith and the economics of religion', *Rationality and Society*, 3: 156–77.

——(1992) 'Sacrifice and stigma: reducing free-riding in cults, communes, and collectives', *Journal of Political Economy*, 100: 271–91.

——(1998) 'Introduction to the economics of religion', *Journal of Economic Literature*, 36: 1465–96.

Iannaccone, L.R., Finke, R. and Stark, R. (1997) 'Deregulating religion: the economics of church and state', *Economic Inquiry*, 35: 350–64.

Itzkin, E.S. (1975) 'The Halévy thesis: a working hypothesis? English revivalism: antidote for revolution and radicalism, 1789–1815', *Church History*, 44: 47–56.

Johansson, E. (1977) 'The history of literacy in Sweden', *Educational Reports, Umeå* 12: 2–42; reprinted in H.J. Graff (ed.) (2007) *Literacy and Historical Development*, Carbondale, CO: Southern Illinois University Press.

Kuran, T. (2004) 'Why the Middle East is economically underdeveloped: historical mechanisms of institutional stagnation', *Journal of Economic Perspectives*, 18: 71–90.

——(2010) *The Long Divergence: How Islamic Law Held Back the Middle East*, Princeton, NJ: Princeton University Press.

Miller, G.P. (1993) 'Contracts of Genesis', *Journal of Legal Studies*, 22: 15–45.

Murray, J.E. (1995a) 'Determinants of membership levels and duration in a Shaker commune', *Journal for the Scientific Study of Religion*, 34: 35–48.

——(1995b) 'Human capital in religious communes: literacy and selection among nineteenth century Shakers', *Explorations in Economic History*, 32: 217–35.

——(2000a) 'Communal viability and employment of non-member labor: testing hypotheses with historical data', *Review of Social Economy*, 58: 1–16.

——(2000b) 'Literacy and industrialization in modern Germany', in C. Rider and M. Thompson (eds) *The Industrial Revolution in Comparative Perspective*, Malabar, FL: Krieger.

Olds, K.J. (1994) 'Privatizing the church: disestablishment in Connecticut and Massachusetts', *Journal of Political Economy*, 102: 277–97.

Raskovich, A. (1996) 'You shall have no other gods besides me', *Journal of Institutional and Theoretical Economics*, 152: 449–71.

Roehl, R. (1972) 'Plan and reality in a medieval monastic economy: the Cistercians', in H.L. Adelson (ed.) *Studies in Medieval and Renaissance History 9*, Lincoln, NE: University of Nebraska Press.

Samuelsson, K. (1961 [1993]) *Religion and Economic Action: The Protestant Ethic, the Rise of Capitalism, and the Abuses of Scholarship*, Toronto: University of Toronto Press.

Smith, A. (1776 [1937]) *An Inquiry into the Nature and Causes of the Wealth of Nations*, New York: Random House.

Stark, R. (1996) *The Rise of Christianity: A Sociologist Reconsiders History*, Princeton, NJ: Princeton University Press.

Stolz, J. (2006) 'Salvation goods and religious markets: integrating rational choice and Weberian perspectives', *Social Compass*, 53: 13–32.

Tawney, R.H. (1926 [1948]) *Religion and the Rise of Capitalism: A Historical Study*, London: John Murray.

Weber, M. (1905 [1958]) *The Protestant Ethic and the Spirit of Capitalism*, New York: Charles Scribner's Sons.

Wilken, R. (1984) *The Christians as the Romans Saw Them*, New Haven, CT: Yale University Press.

14

THE ECONOMIC HISTORY OF AGRICULTURE

Giovanni Federico[1]

Introduction: two centuries of successes

In the last two centuries, world agriculture has succeeded in feeding a growing population (from about 1 billion in 1800 to more than 6 billion two centuries later) and in producing enough raw materials for industry, while using proportionally less land, capital, and labor. This chapter sketches out and tries to explain this outstanding performance.

Mapping the growth of world gross agricultural output for the first 70 years of the period is difficult, because estimates refer almost exclusively to a few countries in Europe and North America. Output increased in all these countries but Portugal, and in the majority of cases it increased faster than population. We cannot rule out that these gains were offset by a decline in output per capita elsewhere in the world, but this hypothesis is not terribly plausible. The growing population was mostly employed in agriculture and new farmers could find new land to till in almost all countries. After 1870, it is possible to estimate an index of "world" output from national production series for 25 countries, accounting for about 50 to 55 per cent of world population (see Figure 14.1). Production per capita increased by about a quarter from 1870 to the First World War and stagnated from 1913 to 1938. If, as it is reasonable to hypothesize, output per capita in the remaining countries remained constant, world production almost doubled over the whole period, increasing by 10 per cent in per capita terms. Figure 14.1 links this index to the official series by the Food and Agricultural Organization (FAO) of the United Nations), which covers all countries (except the Soviet Union to 1948). The acceleration in the second half of the twentieth century is dramatic: in 50 years, total output trebled and per capita production increased by a third. Current production would be sufficient for comfortably feeding the world population. One billion people are still undernourished, however, because of shortcomings in its distribution.

Production can be augmented by using more inputs – capital, labor, and land – and/or by using them more efficiently. The next section outlines the growth in inputs, and shows it to have accounted for only a part of the increase in output. The rest reflects an increase in efficiency, so the other sections deal with the causes of increasing productivity. The third section focuses on technical progress, describing the main innovations and their adoption. However, efficiency depends also on how factors are allocated and techniques are used – and thus

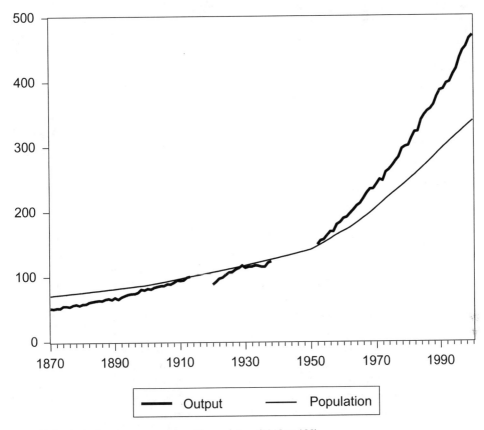

Figure 14.1 Agricultural output and world population (1913 = 100)
Source: Federico (2005).

ultimately also on institutions (the fourth section) and policies (the fifth section). The last section speculates about the prospects for the future.

How success was achieved: the growth of inputs

The evidence on the growth of inputs is fairly abundant, but incomplete. Before 1913 it refers mostly to Europe and North America, and during the interwar years the coverage, although greater, is still partial. All-world data are available from the FAO database since 1960. In order to minimize the impact of these differences in coverage, the tables report chained indexes, adding absolute figures for the reference year 2000.

Table 14.1 proxies the amount of labor with the number of workers, of both genders. In traditional rural societies, including all less developed countries (LDCs) before the 1960s, employment in agriculture grew as much as population. By definition, modern economic growth caused its share of total workers to decrease. However, the total number of workers, and thus the labor input, declined only in a handful of advanced countries and only long after the start of their modern economic growth. The agricultural work force did peak in the UK around 1850, but in other advanced countries of Europe and North America it peaked sometime in the first half of the twentieth century, and it collapsed only after the Second World

Giovanni Federico

Table 14.1 Number of agricultural workers (Year 2000 = 100)

Continent	Circa 1880	Circa 1910	Circa 1938	1960	2000	2000 (millions)
Africa			31	51	100	197.1
Europe	240	358	359	309	100	17.6
North America	43	84	112	90	100	20.7
South America	2	36	69	88	100	26.9
Asia	12	43	68	64	100	1031.8
Oceania	24	35	42	59	100	2.8
Former USSR			203	178	100	21.7
World				64	100	1318.6

Sources: Van Zanden (1961), Federico (2005, Statistical Appendix Table IV), and Lains and Pinilla (2009).

War. The number of workers may differ from labor inputs for a number of reasons, but these biases tend to compensate – so as a whole the headcount is a fairly accurate measure of total work.

Table 14.2 reports comparable indexes for the extension of cropland and tree-crops, the best available proxy for land input. Europe seems to have been an outlier. Before 1880, total acreage increased somewhat in "peripheral" countries such as the Iberian Peninsula, but afterwards it remained stable, and it even declined in some countries in the two last decades of the nineteenth century. In contrast, in other continents, cropland grew, albeit at a reduced rate, until the end of the twentieth century. The story of the settlement of the American West is well known thanks to many Hollywood movies, but the pattern has been repeated, with some delay, in all other regions of European immigration, such as Canada, South America, and Oceania. Cropland increased also in Asia and Africa, with little or no contribution from Europeans. Even in a supposedly overpopulated country such as China, there was a considerable amount of land to exploit. The figures do not include pastures nor take into account the quality of land. However, the scarce available evidence does not suggest any systematic bias from these omissions.

There is no good proxy for the total capital stock, which consists of a number of widely different items. An item-by-item analysis suggests that the stock has increased in all areas, according to four different paths:

Table 14.2 Acreage, cropland and tree crops (Year 2000 = 100)

Continent	Circa 1880	Circa 1910	Circa 1938	1960	2000	2000 (millions of hectares)
Africa		34	86	77	100	201.8
Europe	110	112	112	114	100	133.2
North America	41	77	90	97	100	268.1
South America		44	71	59	100	116.1
Asia	29	58	64	85	100	511.7
Oceania	7	22	34	66	100	53.0
Former USSR	48	52	55	110	100	217.5
World			81	90	100	1501.5

Sources: Van Zanden (1961), Federico (2005, Statistical Appendix Table IV), and Lains and Pinilla (2009).

1) By 1800, the capital stock in the Western Settlement countries was small, but colonization entailed massive investments. Following a lull, investments boomed after the 1930s with the start of massive mechanization.

2) The advanced, long-settled countries of Western Europe traditionally had a very substantial capital stock. Thus, it grew decidedly slower than in the Western Settlement countries until the Second World War and then boomed after the war.

3) In "backward," long-settled countries, most notably China, the capital stock around 1800 was quite large, possibly even greater than in Europe because rice growing needed extensive irrigation. Rice grew very slowly or did not grow at all until quite recently and then boomed, with the intensive use of fertilizers and also mechanization.

4) In "backward" unsettled countries (i.e. those in Africa), the capital stock was initially minimal, and it grew as much as population, probably until the Second World War. Since 1950, the per capita stock of capital has increased, but much less than in Asia.

Summing up, all inputs have been growing throughout the whole period, but there is evidence of a slowdown after 1950, at least for labor and land. This slowdown was to some extent balanced by the acceleration in the rate of growth of the capital stock. It seems highly unlikely that this was large enough to cause the total amount of inputs to increase faster after the Second World War than before it.

The conclusion implies that the acceleration in the growth of output after 1950 reflects an increase in efficiency – or total factor productivity (TFP). TFP is routinely measured as the difference between the rate of growth for output and a weighted average of growth rates for inputs. Table 14.3 reports the available estimates (in average yearly growth rates) for the period before the Second World War, by continent. Two stylized facts stand out. First and foremost, TFP grew almost everywhere, and this by itself is a major change from the (alleged) stagnation of traditional agriculture. A 0.5 per cent yearly growth rate may seem slow, but, when compounded over 40 years, corresponds to a 25 per cent increase, and this is far from trivial. Second, with very few exceptions, such as the Philippines, productivity growth has accelerated over time. A simple unweighted mean of all country estimates is "only" 0.6 per cent but this figure is lowered by the very poor performance of some African and former socialist countries. Indeed, the rate of growth of "world" TFP growth (i.e. the difference between growth of total output and total inputs) is decidedly higher. From 1960 to 2000, the estimates vary, according to the method of computation, between 1 per cent and 1.25 per cent per annum. The growth was decidedly faster in OECD countries than in the rest of the world. Indeed, for these developed countries, TFP growth was on average three times faster after the war than before,

Table 14.3 Growth in total factor productivity to the Second World War

	Before 1870		1870–1910		1910–1940	
	Number	Average	Number	Average	Number	Average
Europe	5	0.3	13	0.65	8	1
Europe (Van Zanden)			15	0.78		
Western Settlement	1	0.4	2	0.74	2	0.56
Asia			3	1.24	6	0.08
Africa	1	3.41	1	0.83	1	−0.21
South America			1	−1.9	2	1.57

Sources: Van Zanden (1961), Federico (2005, Statistical Appendix Table IV), and Lains and Pinilla (2009).

confirming the acceleration already detected in previous periods. Contrary to a widespread fear, the estimates for the 1990s and 2000s do not show evidence of slowdown in TFP growth (Headey *et al.* 2010).

Innovations and their adoption

The thousands of innovations adopted in agriculture over the last two centuries can be grouped into four main categories: new practices of cultivation, new plants and animals, chemicals, and machines.

Most new practices aimed at reducing the length of periods of rest, which was the traditional way to restore the soil fertility depleted by cultivation. Thus, in traditional agriculture, the number of crops per year (or cropping ratio) was usually below one, down to 0.05 in the so-called slash-and-burn systems (i.e. two or three crops followed by long periods of rest, up to 40–60 years). In most of Europe, the ratio was around 0.6 – that is, land was left idle (fallow) 1 year out of 3. The ratio was increased by substituting rest with fertility-restoring plants, such as grass or roots. In the late eighteenth and early nineteenth centuries, the practice spread in the UK and all over Europe. Fallow disappeared and later in the century the succession of crops (rotation) become increasingly sophisticated. On the eve of the Second World War, cropping ratios were slightly below 1 in Europe and the United States, and over 1.3 in Asia. Since then, the ratio has increased further, approaching 1 worldwide at the end of the 1990s.

New plants (or animals) can come from three different sources – the casual discovery of a new species or variety, the transfer from other areas, and the production of a new variety of a known species via the hybridization of existing ones. Casual discoveries have always been rare and they played a minor role in the last two centuries, with the sole exception of the sugarbeet, discovered around 1750 and cultivated since the early nineteenth century. Long-range transfers were still important in the nineteenth century. European migrants to the New World brought with them the seeds and plants of native countries and many governments tried to foster the economic potential of agriculture with systematic collection and testing of varieties all over the world. Their attempts often failed, but there were some notable successes. Early experiments of hybridization had started in the mid-nineteenth century, but with poor results. The first great success was the production of hybrid corn in the 1930s. In the 1940s, researchers started to work on varieties suitable for poor countries. The effort paid off handsomely: the new varieties, aptly named high-yield varieties (HYV), in the right conditions, produced up to eight times the traditional ones. The results were stunning enough that they have been called the Green Revolution. Since the 1980s, the potential for improvement has been boosted by genetic engineering.

The major contribution of the chemical industry to agricultural progress was the solution, apparently for good, of the problem of restoring soil fertility. The production of phosphates started in the 1840s and of potash fertilizers in the mid-1850s, while production of nitrogen took off only after the discovery of the Haber-Bosch method of producing ammonium sulfate in 1909. Chemical products were used since the late nineteenth century to fight diseases and parasites, but results were rather poor until the 1940s and the discovery of DDT.

The first modern animal-powered machine for fieldwork was the wheat harvester, or reaper, which Hussey and McCormick patented independently in 1833–4. In the next decades, investors focused on increasing labor productivity in harvesting, with some notable success, but mechanization was delayed by the lack of a suitable source of inanimate power. Neither water nor steam was, for different reasons, really suitable. The mechanization of agriculture really took off only after the introduction of tractors powered by internal combustion engines in the early

1900s, and of the power–take–off shaft (or PTO), which transformed the pulling power of the engine into a rotatory movement.

All innovations cut production costs by reducing the amount of factors per unit of product, but in different ways. Some innovations save all factors in the same proportion (neutral), others save prevalently one factor (say land), and some others need more of a factor to save others. With the possible exception of crop rotation, agricultural innovations needed additional investments (i.e. were capital intensive). Machinery saved labor, by definition, while chemical products and new varieties augmented yields and thus reduced the need of land per unit of product. Thus, one would expect the transfer of technologies from advanced to LDC countries to have been hampered by LDC's scarcity of capital and by the poor development of their financial institutions. One would also expect that the countries of land-scarce Europe were on the forefront of the adoption of fertilizers and new varieties, while labor-scarce Western Settlement countries pioneered mechanization.

The evidence confirms these hypotheses. The difference in patterns of adoption of new technologies between Europe and the United States were huge before the Second World War and, although reduced, are still sizeable today. In a controversial book, Hayami and Ruttan (1985) go a step further along this line of reasoning. They argue that factor endowment affects not only the adoption of innovations but also their production. Land-scarce countries invest more in research on land-saving innovations, and vice versa. However, Olmstead and Rhode (2008) disagree, stressing the relevance of research in land-saving innovations in the United States.

Most innovations are the outcome of expensive investments in research. Chemical and engineering firms can recover the costs while they sell fertilizers or machinery to farmers, but this is often not the case for new varieties or new practices of cultivation. They can be imitated fairly easily and thus inventors risk the loss of part of the potential returns from their investments. Expenditures on research and development (R&d) may not be socially optimal. This problem has been mitigated by granting patenting rights for plants – first in the European Union in 1960, then in the United States in 1970–1, and afterwards in most countries. As of 2011, 69 countries have joined the international association for the mutual recognition of plant patents (UPOV). Under this new regime, private expenditure in agricultural R&D grew steadily, to become the main source of funding in advanced countries – in the United States as early as the late 1980s.

Before the 1970s, much research was financed by non–profit organizations or by the state. A few enlightened landlords funded research in their own estates, while many others gathered in learned societies, such as the Royal Agricultural Society of England. The research in high-yielding varieties started in Mexico with funds from the Ford and Rockefeller Foundations of the United States. Governments funded agricultural R&D research indirectly via universities and directly by setting up specialized agencies, called agricultural stations. The first station was established in Mockern (Saxony) in 1851 and in the second half of the century the United States and most European countries imitated this example. At the turn of the century, colonial powers funded R&D in tropical cash crops for exports (cocoa, rubber), while research in food crops took off after the Second World War. The total investment was substantial. In the United States, expenditures increased from the equivalent of 0.03 per cent of gross agricultural output in 1883 to over 2 per cent in the late 1990s. According to the best estimates, worldwide public expenditure in agricultural R&D increased by 150 per cent in the 1960s, by 50 per cent in the 1970s and by a further half from 1980 to 1995. Expenditure on agricultural extension (i. e. the diffusion of best practices among farmers) doubled from 1959 to 1971 and increased by 25 per cent in the next decade. Since the late 1990s, public expenditure in R&D has stagnated or declined.

Institutions and agricultural performance in the long run

Institutions can be defined as the set of formal or informal rules that determine the ownership of goods and factors (property rights) and regulate the interactions among individual agents or households (contracts, markets, and other forms of distribution). There is a wide consensus among historians, economists, agricultural experts and policy makers on the relevance of institutions as a whole for agricultural growth, but also wide differences of opinion about the importance of each type of institution and their effects.

1) Economists believe that modern property rights are necessary to exploit the full potential of an economy (De Soto 2000). They argue that modern property rights on land – including the right to sell and bequeath it – prevent an excessive exploitation of land for short-term gains (the so-called "tragedy of the commons"), stimulate location-specific investments (e.g. buildings, tree-crops) and allow the use of land as collateral for borrowing. By 1800, these individual rights extended to only a minor part of agricultural land – in Western Europe, in the countries of the Western Settlement, and in some areas in Asia, including most of China (Pomeranz 2008). Elsewhere, the rights to land were jointly held by several individuals. In some areas, feudal lords or other powerful people had the right to claim a part of the product and/or of the time of workers. In others, the rights to land were owned collectively by tribes of hunter-gatherers or by communities of farmers. In this latter case, each household was allocated a plot of land for its sole use for a pre-determined period.

   In the last two centuries, these traditional property rights have been disappearing. The process has been slow, featuring massive reversals, such as the collectivization of previously private land in the Soviet Union in the 1930s and in China in the late 1950s, and is not yet fully over. In the first half of the nineteenth century, the feudal estates of Eastern Europe were divided between the former serfs and the former lords. In other areas, temporary allocation of land to members of farming villages was slowly turned into permanent ownership. In contrast, the rights of hunter-gatherers or slash-and-burn (swidden) agriculturalists in Africa and Asia were ignored by European colonizers. The areas of the New World with temperate climate attracted large numbers of European settlers and thus the natives lost almost all their rights. In tropical countries, the demand for land by Europeans was smaller and thus the native tribes managed to keep most of the land. Colonial administrations started to register the ownership of individual native farmers ("titling") in the 1940s and the process has continued since then, with strong support by international organizations such as the World Bank. The benefits, although substantial, may have been smaller than hoped for. In some cases, titling was unfair or blatantly rigged and peasants lost their rights. Furthermore, anecdotal evidence suggests that traditional property rights were not as inefficient as assumed, because farmers found ways to circumvent their shortcomings.

2) Historians and agricultural experts tend to pay a lot of attention to the patterns of size and ownership of farms. They generally deem the concentration of land in the hands of absentee landlords (latifundia) as a major hindrance to technical progress. However, the evidence for this conclusion is very weak to non-existent. Presumably absentee landlords will introduce innovations whenever profitable. On the other hand, large farms rarely enjoy any advantage in cultivation (processing is altogether different, but it has become an industrial activity). The economies of scale are small, if any, and large farms manned by hired workers are less efficient than family farms. Family farmers have strong incentives to work hard, while preventing wage workers from shirking is much more difficult in agriculture than in

manufacturing. It is possible to effectively monitor agriculture workers only while they perform simple tasks, most notably harvesting.

The superiority of family-owned farms is revealed by their growing share of agricultural land. In the nineteenth century, they prevailed in Western Settlement countries, in many countries of Europe, especially in the North, and possibly in China. In the late 1930s, according to the agricultural censuses by the FAO, "farms managed by owners" accounted for about 55 per cent of acreage in the 1930s, and this figure rose to almost 80 per cent at the end of the twentieth century. In a number of countries, the diffusion of family farms was helped by the intervention of government, by titling and land reform – that is, the forcible division of large estates. The first reforms were enacted in the early 1920s by new countries of Eastern Europe and they multiplied rapidly after the Second World War. However, the share of owner-operated farms rose also in countries or areas where states did not intervene in land ownership.

3) When landowners are not willing (or forced) to sell, the advantage of small-scale self-monitoring cultivation may be captured by hiring a tenant and his family, for a pre-determined sum (fixed rent tenancy) or for a share of the product (sharecropping). Sharecropping is a very contentious institution. Many historians argue that it hinders technical progress, while economists, following Marshall, suspect it to be inefficient. Marshall's argument spawned a huge but ultimately inconclusive theoretical literature. Hard data are scarce, but show that sharecropping was less diffused than fixed rents in the nineteenth century and that its share of total tenanted land, and thus *a fortiori* on total acreage, has been declining in the twentieth century (Federico 2006). The few available tests have uncovered no evidence that sharecropping is less efficient or less innovation-fostering than fixed rent contracts.

4) Agriculture is plagued by serious problems of asymmetric information. Farmers have much more information than buyers about the quality of their products, and more information than providers of credit about their own creditworthiness. Thus, buyers and investors may refrain from purchasing or lending, or may ask farmers, who cannot pledge real assets, very high interest rates. This behavior can be economically rational, but it reduces output and investments below their potential. A quite frequent institutional solution to the asymmetric information problem is cross-monitoring among farmers via cooperation in production and banking. The members of a production cooperative can monitor each other to avoid cheating, which could endanger the quality of the product; those of a cooperative bank can assess the credit risk of another farmer in the same village much better than a bank clerk from the city. Thus, cooperatives have been a great success story. The first were set up in the early nineteenth century, and, in spite of some setbacks, they have been growing since then. In the mid-1990s, when world agriculture employed about 1.3 billion people, agricultural cooperatives had 180 million members. About 80 per cent of these people were in LDCs – over 140 million in India alone. However, advanced countries, including Japan, accounted for 80 per cent of the total value of output by cooperatives. In these countries, cooperatives now have very high market shares in perishable or not homogenous products, such as fruit and vegetables, wine, and, above all, dairy products. Some of them have built highly successful consumer brands, becoming, in some extreme cases, a threat to competition.

5) Last but not least, both technical progress and specialization need the development of markets. The evidence on the development of markets for capital and labor is too sketchy to be of much use, and overall trends, such as the increase in family farming, have affected factor markets in a complex way. In contrast, there is no doubt that the markets for agricultural products have experienced extensive development. In fact, the gross output per worker has increased well beyond the consumption needs of farming households, while urban

population, which has to be fed via markets, has been rising throughout the whole period. Worldwide, its share of total world population has increased from about 30 per cent in 1950 to above a half in 2000. This argument is supported by evidence on the share of marketed production in total output, which shows a steady increase in all countries. In the 1960s, it exceeded 95 per cent of output in the United States and 80 per cent in all advanced countries, and it hovered around 40 per cent in the least developed African countries. It is likely that the share has increased since then.

Agriculture and the state

The list of policies that may affect agriculture is very long. Some of them, such as support for R&d, have been discussed previously. Thus, this section concentrates on policies that directly affect farmers' income.

At the beginning of the nineteenth century, state intervention was very limited. Production and domestic commerce in agricultural products were almost everywhere uninhibited by the state, and this was true also for international trade, with the notable exception of protection against imports of wheat in the UK and some other European countries. These duties were abolished in the 1840s and 1850s and were re-imposed in most countries, excluding the UK, after the 1880s. As a rule, other products were affected much less than cereals. A compact measure of the effects of product-specific policies is the nominal rate of assistance (NRA) – that is, the difference between the domestic price and the world price as percentage of the latter. The ratio remained very low or even negative in European countries until the First World War (Swinnen 2009) and, after a short spell of war-time regulations, also in the 1920s.

The outbreak of the Great Depression caused a fall in relative prices of agricultural goods, triggering an epoch-making change. The European countries protected farmers by increasing duties and by adding quantitative restrictions and regulations of the markets, pushing their NRAs well above 50 per cent. Overseas exporters such as the United States tried to help farmers by setting up marketing boards to prop up exports or by subsidizing their incomes. State intervention was not phased out after the war, for different reasons – the fear of shortages in Europe and the successful lobbying of farmers in the New World. In Europe, the level of protection declined relative to the peaks of the 1930s, but it increased again in the 1960s under the Common Agricultural Policy. Some newly developed countries, such as South Korea, imitated the European countries, while other developed countries continued to subsidize producers. In contrast, poor countries in Latin America and former colonies in Africa and Asia used agriculture, especially the production of cash crops for exports, as a cash cow to finance their dreams of industrialization. In the 1960s, the NRAs for developing countries were heavily negative – that is, domestic prices were lower than world ones (Anderson et al. 2009). Since the 1990s, state intervention has been slowly phased out, although not entirely. Poor countries liberalized their domestic markets and dismantled state-owned marketing boards, while advanced OECD countries switched from price setting and market intervention to directly subsidizing farmers. Thus, in advanced countries, the NRAs, which had peaked at around 80 per cent in the 1980s, declined to about 40 per cent, while in developing countries they became moderately positive.

Economists generally take the view that state intervention is justified only when it can foster competition or redress some market failure. Neither criterion applies to these policies. In the 1980s, consumers in OECD countries lost on average 1.35 per cent of their income because of artificially high prices for agricultural products. According to other estimates, about three-quarters of these sums accrued to farmers, while the rest was a net loss for the whole economy

(Federico 2009). The liberalization of the 1990s reduced consumer losses by about two-thirds. The effects of policies in LDCs were the opposite: producers lost and urban consumers gained. In all likelihood, the welfare losses were greater than in advanced countries, although there are not really representative estimates. Cline (2004) estimates that, in 1997, simply liberalizing agricultural trade, without modifying other domestic subsidies, would have increased world income by 0.5 per cent.

Conclusions: the challenges ahead

In spite of its past achievements, the prospects for world agriculture are not bright and there are myriad problems that need to be addressed. World agriculture must increase production at least as rapidly as world population, which according to United Nations forecasts by 2050 will be 20 to 65 per cent larger than in 2000. On top of this, the increase in income is bound to shift demand towards fruits, vegetables, and, above all, dairy and meat, which use land more intensively than cereals per unit of calories produced. Unfortunately, however, available land is scarce, and it is constantly reduced by urbanization, even neglecting the possible losses from climate change. A massive extension of cropland is possible only at the expense of forests, but massive deforestation would cause huge environmental and social problems. Scarcity of land is not the only problem. Agricultural manpower is bound to decrease in the future as workers migrate to cities. Thus, the only solution to the problem of production increase seems to be a further increase in capital intensity and technical progress. Unfortunately, modern techniques, although extremely efficient, often damage the environment. Irrigation may cause losses of land, chemical products are harmful for farmers and for the whole population, and the massive adoption of selected seeds and improved breeds threatens biodiversity and thus the stock of potentially useful varieties. The impact of genetically modified organisms is controversial. Thus, the needs of increasing production and of preserving the environment are in conflict. This conflict cannot be solved with a return to traditional agriculture, which, although environmentally more sustainable, would be unable to feed the current and projected world population. Developing efficient and environmentally sustainable techniques is the great challenge for the future of agriculture and of humankind.

Notes

1 The chapter relies heavily on Federico (2005) and quotes only additional material and references.

References

Anderson, K., Croser, J., Sandri, D. and Valenzuela, E. (2009) 'Agricultural distortion patterns since the 1950s: what needs explaining?' Agricultural Distortion Working Paper No. 90.

Cline, W.R. (2004) *Trade Policy and Global Poverty*, Washington: Institute for International Economics.

De Soto, H. (2000) *The Mystery of Capital: Why Capitalism Triumphs in the West and Fails Everywhere Else*, New York: Basic Books.

Federico, G (2005) *Feeding the World: An Economic History of Agriculture, 1800–2000*, Princeton, NJ: Princeton University Press.

——(2006) 'The "real" puzzle of share-cropping: why is it disappearing?' *Continuity and Change*, 21: 261–85.

——(2009) 'Was the CAP the worst agricultural policy of the 20th century?' in K. Patel (ed.) *Fertile Ground for Europe? The History of European Integration and the Common Agricultural Policy since 1945*, Baden-Baden: Nomos.

Hayami, Y. and Ruttan, V. (1985) *Agricultural Development*, 2nd edition, Baltimore, Md: Johns Hopkins University Press.

Headey, D., Alauddin, M. and Prasada Rao, D.S. (2010) 'Explaining agricultural productivity growth: an international perspective', *Agricultural Economics*, 41: 1–14.

Lains, P. and Pinilla, V. (2009) *Agriculture and Economic Development in Europe since 1870*, London: Routledge.

Olmstead A. and Rhode, P.W. (2008) *Creating Abundance: Biological Innovation and American Agricultural Development*, New York: Cambridge University Press.

Pomeranz, K. (2008) 'Land markets in late imperial and republican China', *Continuity and Change*, 23: 101–50.

Swinnen, J.F.M. (2009) *Agricultural Protection Growth in Europe, 1870–1969*, World Bank, Agricultural Distortion Working Paper No. 80.

Van Zanden, J.L. (1991) 'The first green revolution: the growth of production and productivity in European agriculture, 1870–1914', *Economic History Review*, 44: 215–39.

15

THE ECONOMIC HISTORY OF TRANSPORTATION

Dan Bogart

Introduction

Around the year 1700, much of humanity was stuck in the mud. Unimproved roads made it extremely costly to move goods and people overland. Many rivers had navigation problems and ocean vessels were slow and risky. Of course there were exceptions. Some roads leading into major cities were well maintained and constructed using techniques dating to the Romans. Navigable rivers like the Thames in Britain or the Yangtze in China served as major thoroughfares for their respective economies. But these were areas privileged by geography. Most of the pre-industrial world languished under poor transport systems.

This state of affairs changed dramatically from 1700 to 2000. Much like the rest of the global economy, transportation experienced a "revolution" in technology, investment, and management. The speed of the revolution varied dramatically across time and space. In general, Western European nations led the way in improving their transport systems during the eighteenth and early nineteenth centuries. From 1850 onwards, European technologies and practices diffused throughout most of the world. For instance, almost every country in the world had a railway or steamship arriving at its major port by 1913. Although there were many advances by the early twentieth century, the speed and freedom of travel was still quite limited. Two innovations changed the nature of transport once again. The airplane and the automobile were initially adopted in the world's leading economies, most notably the United States. Subsequently, automobiles and airplanes became commonplace. Today one can travel by car or by plane even in the poorest countries of the world.

Technological change is only part of the story of the modern transport sector. Improvements required substantial infrastructure investments. The building of highways, railways, airports and the like involved substantial risks. Their irreversible nature meant that costs could not be easily recovered if revenue expectations were not realized. Partly for this reason, governments stepped in and either built the network or designed a framework in which private companies built, owned, and operated infrastructure. Governments also developed a large body of regulations determining where infrastructure could be developed and how it was used and priced.

This chapter reviews the major technological and infrastructural developments in overland, water, and air transport. Next, it reviews the major trends in prices and quantities. Like any other sector, outcomes in the transportation sector were the result of "equilibrium" forces. As

167

technology, income, and market structures evolved, so did fares and the quantities of services purchased. The general trend was towards cheaper transport and higher traffic volume because of a combination of income and productivity growth. However, there remained substantial differences in outcomes across space, even after holding technology and income levels constant. Some of these differences in fares and traffic volumes were due to broader economic and political forces. For example, regulatory authorities sometimes acted to protect favored firms by imposing minimum fares or restricting entry. In other instances, authorities limited the monopoly power of transport providers or they imposed safety standards. Several cases are given later to illustrate some of the factors influencing outcomes in transport markets.

This chapter also examines the contribution of transport improvements to economic development. The classic approach is to measure the social savings, or the gain in consumer surplus that occurred due to a transport innovation. Another approach uses regional or state variation to measure the effect of transport improvements on income or population. The general conclusion is that transport improvements contributed to development, but there are sizeable differences across time and space. The effect of any single transport innovation depends on the quality of alternative transport modes in addition to managerial and regulatory decisions. Excessive market power, poor network design, and inefficiency in operations have all worked to limit the social benefits from transport innovations.

Finally, some have argued that transport improvements have introduced a number of social costs, particularly greater pollution. However, the evidence suggests that transport improvements and innovations have done more good than harm and thus this chapter takes a decidedly positive tone when discussing innovations like the automobile and airplane. Because the literature has yet to satisfactorily measure the social costs of transport over the last 300 years, it is hoped that in the future more can be said about this important issue.

Technological and infrastructural developments

The history of transport can be told through a series of technological breakthroughs and infrastructural developments. With this in mind, it is useful to start with the eighteenth-century context where road and river transport were dominant in much of the world. Advances in civil engineering knowledge marked one of the major breakthroughs of this period. Perhaps the most famous are the British engineers John Macadam and Thomas Telford, who developed new techniques for building roads and bridges. Dutch and French engineers also made advances in navigation that led to "canalizing" rivers and eventually canals.

New systems of public finance were developed concurrently with advances in engineering know-how. Governments in several Western European countries entered into contractual arrangements with the private sector to build and operate roads, canals, and bridges in exchange for levying tolls. These public–private partnerships of the pre-industrial era were predicated on the existence of relatively stable political systems in which investments were secure from expropriation (both public and private). Just as important, these societies could draw on a range of informal institutions to govern infrastructure providers, making their exactions more palatable to the society. Governments also began to heed the call by providing public funds for large projects. One example is the royal highways of France, which were coordinated and financed by the monarchy. Another example is the British Navy, which played a key role in policing the seas, principally for British ships. More broadly, however, governments rarely spent large sums on transport infrastructure before 1800. It was only when military and economic interests coincided that public spending levels exceeded a few percentage points of central government budgets.

Transport progress was modest outside of Western Europe until the mid-nineteenth century. The available statistics on transport infrastructure provide one indicator that Europe was ahead. By the 1880s, Europe had 925,000 highway miles and 62,000 miles of navigable waterways. By comparison, the U.S. and Canada had 266,000 highway miles and 25,000 waterway miles. India was further behind: it had 58,000 and 5,000 miles of highways and waterways respectively (Mulhall 1884: 395).

The nineteenth century witnessed more dramatic changes in technology and infrastructure with the coming of the railway and the steamship. Steam locomotives were first shown to be economically superior to wagon transport in the densely populated regions of Britain in the 1820s. Relatively quickly railways spread to the rest of Britain, Europe, and the United States. By 1910, emerging railway networks could be found in most parts of the world, including India, China, Latin America, and Africa.

Railway penetration was more extensive in the advanced countries. Table 15.1 shows European railway networks were most developed in terms of railway miles per square mile. North and South American railway networks were not as dense geographically but they were well developed in terms of population. Asian networks were the least developed. China stands out in that it had the smallest railway network among all major countries. Even so, the penetration of railways in poor countries was greater than in other technologies, such as mechanization of textiles (Clark 1987).

Several factors account for the success of railways as a global technology. One was the substantial improvements in the design of locomotives, wagons, and rails. By the early 1900s, the

Table 15.1 Railway diffusion for selected countries in 1910

	Rail Miles per 1000 people	Rail Miles per Square Mile
Europe		
Austria	0.50	0.12
France	0.74	0.15
Germany	0.58	0.18
Italy	0.29	0.09
Russia	0.27	0.02
Spain	0.46	0.05
Sweden	1.58	0.05
U.K.	0.56	0.19
North America		
Canada	3.44	0.002
Mexico	1.03	0.02
U.S.	2.69	0.07
South America		
Argentina	2.64	0.02
Brazil	0.60	0.004
Asia		
China	0.01	0.001
India	0.11	0.02
Japan	0.11	0.04

Source: Bogart (2009).

cost of adopting railway technologies had decreased dramatically compared to the initial designs. Developments in global financing and corporate governance also proved crucial. For the first time in world history it was possible for foreign capitalists to invest and own transportation facilities in other countries. Colonialism helped to grease the wheels of investment, but other factors like social networks and the adoption of commercial codes also facilitated diffusion (Roth and Dinhobl 2008). Last but not least, rising global incomes fostered railways. Vast amounts of railway track were laid in Latin America, India, Russia, and the United States because these regions had abundant land and Europeans had great demand for their products.

The introduction of the steamship was arguably just as important as the railway in bringing the nineteenth-century world closer together. Steamships came on line in the mid- to late 1800s. They first replaced sail ships along routes where coal was plentiful. They eventually achieved dominance in the early 1900s. Like railways, steamships offered capacity and speed. They were the main vehicle for immigration from Europe to America (Keeling 2008). Probably the most famous example of a steamship is the *Titanic*. Its sinking in 1912 was notable in part because it marked the latest design, combining speed, size, and luxury.

The automobile and the airplane are the two most important transport technologies of the twentieth century. Prior to 1900, there were experiments with steam-powered automobiles but none was economically successful. The major breakthrough occurred in the late nineteenth century when the German Karl Benz developed the internal combustion engine for vehicles. Automobiles became increasingly common in the 1910s. The development of the assembly line was one factor. Henry Ford perfected the use of the assembly line at his plants in Michigan and is credited with a number of organizational innovations. The automobile industry grew enormously over the ensuing decades. Near its peak in the 1970s, production of motor vehicles, bodies and trailers, and parts accounted for 15 per cent of durable goods production in the U. S.[1] The significance of auto production was underlined in 1953 by the assertion of General Motors' chairman, Charles Wilson, that "what's good for the country is good for General Motors, and vice-versa."

Highway expansion was also crucial to the diffusion of automobiles. The auto industry needed public authorities to provide paved roads. Otherwise their new cars would have been stuck in the mud. As in the eighteenth century, new systems of public finance were developed to meet this need. For example, the gasoline tax was increased in the United States in order to help build the Interstate Highway System. Gasoline taxes increased from 1.2 per cent of the U. S. federal government internal tax revenues in the late 1940s to 2.5 per cent in the 1960s when the interstate highway network was being built. After the network was built, gasoline taxes declined as a per cent of total federal revenues. In the 1990s, they represented 1.7 per cent of all federal internal tax revenues (Carter *et al.* 2006: Table Ea609–35).

The airline industry began with the innovations of numerous entrepreneurs and engineers. The Wright brothers were the first to achieve flight with an airplane. Their design was improved in the 1920s and 1930s, including the introduction of the jet engine. Initially, most commercial aviation firms were small, but by the 1930s the industry became more concentrated. Following a series of regulations, the U.S. airline industry came to be dominated by Eastern, American, United, Trans-continental, Western, and Pan American airlines. Each firm was given a regional monopoly. In some cases their market power has persisted even to the present day.

Like most transport sectors, government involvement in the airline industry is extensive. Cities or regional governments often own airports. Allocation of scarce airport "slots" has proved to be a key regulatory tool and has sometimes led to restrictions on entry by rival airlines. Governments are also largely responsible for safety in air travel. Major accidents and threats to security have led to greater government involvement, much like the attacks on the World Trade Center in 2001 led to the creation of Transportation Safety Administration in the United States.

The evolution of the transport market

Purchases of transportation services have exploded over the past three centuries. Declines in fares and freight charges have been equally dramatic, as have been quality improvements. This section provides a brief overview of the market for domestic flights in the U.S. since 1930 to illustrate these trends for one sector. Comparisons with other sectors are discussed as well.

Table 15.2 reports selected statistics for the domestic airline sector using data from the *Historical Statistics of the United States* (Carter *et al.* 2006). Passenger miles flown (the main measure of output) increased from just 85 million in 1930 to more than 340,000 million in 1990. The average annual growth rate in services was 15 per cent and was especially rapid between 1930 and 1970 when air travel was an emerging industry.

Trends in real average passenger fares can be gleaned from revenues per passenger mile divided by a consumer price index. Airfares differ by time of purchase, thus there is no single market price even for the same flight. According to this metric, passenger fares have fallen substantially. In 1950, a typical 500-mile flight in the U.S. would have been purchased for approximately $260 in 2010 constant prices. By 1990, a 500-mile flight could be purchased for approximately $115 dollars. There was an even greater decline in average passenger fares between 1930 and 1950 at the same time that services were becoming more widespread.

Speed and safety are two of the most important aspects of quality in air travel. Domestic air travel has become dramatically safer based on the number of fatalities per passenger mile travelled. The chances of dying in a plane crash in 1990 were a small fraction of what they were in 1940. The speed of air travel has also increased. Average speeds went from 180 to 350 miles per hour between 1950 and 1970.

Sectors exhibiting radical decreases in prices and quality improvements usually see a greater growth relative to other sectors. Air travel was no exception. U.S. domestic airline revenues as a percentage of gross domestic product (GDP) increased from less than 0.1 per cent in 1940 to 1 per cent by 1990. A similar story could be told for other transport sectors as they progressed from novelty to a mature industry. For example, rail freight services in the U.S. grew by an average of 9.4 per cent per year between 1850 and 1910. The most rapid growth occurred in

Table 15.2 Selected statistics for domestic air travel sector in the U.S.

Year	Millions of passenger miles	Revenue per passenger mile in constant 2010 dollars	Fatalities per 100 million passenger miles	Average speed in mph	Revenues as a per cent of U.S. GDP
1930	85	1.123			
1940	1052	0.818	3		0.076
1950	8007	0.520	1.1	180	0.19
1960	30567	0.466	0.9	235	0.404
1970	104156	0.341	0	350	0.691
1980	200829	0.314	0.005	404	0.93
1990	340231	0.233	0.0085	408	0.999

Source: Carter *et al.* (2006): Tables Df1112-1125, Df1229-1245, Df1177-1189, Df1203-1215, Cc1-2, and Ca9-19.

the 1850s, 1860s, and 1870s. Railroad freight rates and travel times also declined to a fraction of their initial level (Fishlow 1966).

What accounts for the rapid growth in output in the transport sector? Higher incomes are certainly one factor. Travel is a normal good: an individual wants to travel more as his or her income increases. The same holds in the aggregate as well. Britain was the richest economy in the early nineteenth century. It also had the largest transport sector (Ville 1990). In the late nineteenth century, the U.S. became the richest economy in the world. It soon became the largest consumer of transport services as well.

Greater investment and productivity growth were also driving the growth in transport output. As mentioned earlier, infrastructure investments like the construction of roads, seaports, canals, railway tracks, and airports played a crucial role. The role of productivity is perhaps less obvious. Productivity growth implies that the same amount of goods or services can be supplied with fewer inputs, like labor and capital. Productivity growth is significant in any industry because it allows firms to charge lower prices and still cover their fixed costs of investment. In the U.S. domestic airline sector, labor productivity (or passenger miles flown per worker) increased by a factor of 18 between 1930 and 1990.[2] Although not as spectacular, labor productivity has increased in other transport sectors as well. In U.S. railroads, for example, labor productivity is estimated to have increased by a factor of 3 between 1840 and 1910 (Fishlow 1966).

Technological change is one of the key drivers of productivity growth. In the air and rail sectors, improvements in jet engines and locomotive power increased average haul sizes and fuel efficiency. "Organizational" change is another contributing factor. One example was the reduction in risks associated with the British Navy routing out piracy in the Caribbean Sea (North 1958). There is debate in the literature as to the significance of the British Navy's contribution to productivity growth when compared with steam power and steel hulls (Harley 1988); nevertheless, it is clear that investments in safety were a public good, and, without the assistance of the British Navy, ocean shipping would have been more expensive. Another example of organizational change involved the turnpike roads of eighteenth-century Britain. In this case, tolls were used to finance road improvements because the existing system for financing highways was inadequate. Following the introduction of turnpikes, carriers adopted larger wagons and faster carriages, eventually contributing to lower transport costs. Private investments in vehicles and public investments in roads were complementary (Bogart 2005).

Increases in economic "density" have been another important factor in determining productivity growth. As urban populations increase, planes, trains, and automobiles can run more frequently and at a higher percentage of capacity. An excellent example comes from the shipping of grain and cattle in the nineteenth century. Beef was a desired American import in Europe but a problem arose because ships could not be filled with beef cattle alone. As it turns out, grain was used to fill the empty cargo space, and, when combined in the same ship, cattle and grain freight rates were reduced to very low levels. However, the opportunity to combine complementary freight was only available on certain routes, such as New York to London, where there was a high volume of services (Harley 2008).

Cost decreases translate into the greatest price reductions when competition is most vigorous. But obviously competition does not always prevail in transportation. Entry is costly because of the large fixed costs in setting up transport services. The small number of firms is significant because it aids efforts in collusion. The Joint Executive Committee is one telling case where collusion seems to have been partially successful. The Committee fixed the market share among several railroads shipping grain from the Midwest to the Eastern seaboard of the U.S. in the 1880s. According to some accounts, individual railroads were deterred from cheating on the cartel because they expected to be sanctioned by the other railroads belonging to the Joint Executive Committee (Porter 1983).

The fear of collusion has led transport users to lobby for government regulation of fares and freight charges. However, the implementation of regulation has been difficult in practice. Perhaps the most famous example is the Interstate Commerce Commission (ICC), which was made responsible for regulating railroads in the U.S. during the late 1800s. Its early success was limited by a Supreme Court decision that weakened its powers to set railroad rates (Kolko 1965). In another case, the colonial government of India introduced maximum freight charges for railways in the nineteenth century. But it also introduced minimum freight charges to limit ruinous competition. There is some evidence that the colonial government kept minimum rates high because it wanted to maintain high profits on the railway lines that it owned (Bell 1894: 205–15). In both of these cases, government regulation was compromised to some degree by the conflicting interests of governing authorities.

The extent of government ownership has been another important factor in transport markets. Governments were always involved in building and operating transport infrastructure, but prior to railways they rarely owned the wagons and ships that provided the transport services. In the nineteenth century, governments began to take over these functions. As one indication, the fraction of world railway miles owned and operated by private companies declined from over 90 per cent in 1860 to just above 70 per cent in 1912. Government ownership increased because of both new construction and nationalizations of privately owned railways. Many of the nationalizations occurred on a line-by-line basis, as national authorities targeted particular railway companies. In other cases, like Switzerland and Japan, laws were passed transferring ownership over much of the network to the central government. The reasons for greater government ownership varied. Military interests were certainly a factor since railways were an input into the state's war machine. Political and economic factors mattered as well. For example, democratic countries tended to have less nationalization than more autocratic countries (Bogart 2009).

The effect of government ownership on transport performance is a topic of major interest among scholars and policy makers. In a number of cases it appears that nationalizations of railways in the nineteenth century reduced operating efficiency (Bogart 2010). One explanation is that governments tend to care more about rewarding constituencies with extra railway stations and employment. Matters are more complicated, however, when privately owned railways receive substantial government subsidies or when railways represent an important source of tax revenue. India provides one case in point. Here greater government ownership in the nineteenth century seems to have reduced operating costs (Bogart and Chaudhary 2012).

The impact of transport on economic development

It has long been argued that transport improvements generate development. But the size of these developmental effects is still in debate. This final section reviews the literature studying the impact of transport improvements. It also discusses the channels by which transport influences development.

Nineteenth-century boosters often argued that railroads were crucial to economic development, but they did not have a clear method to test their argument. Economic historians of the 1960s approached this issue using a novel approach known as the "social savings" methodology. The goal is to measure how much consumer surplus was gained from railways at some benchmark date, say 1860 or 1890. The reasoning is that railway customers would have relied on alternative transport modes, like wagons and boats, in the absence of railways. A simple approximation for the gain in consumer surplus is the difference between freight rates for wagons and railroads multiplied by quantity of rail traffic in 1860 or 1890. Prices are meant to capture the marginal costs of each technology under perfect competition and the quantity of traffic proxies for consumer demand.

Early research showed that the social savings of railways were surprisingly small in the U.S. According to two prominent studies, U.S. GDP would have been lowered by only a few percentage points in 1860 or 1890 had railways never existed (Fishlow 1965; Fogel 1970). Similar conclusions were reached for railways in European countries (O'Brien 1983). The view that railways were indispensible for nineteenth-century development was largely debunked for more developed economies. For less developed countries, like Mexico and Brazil, railways had much larger social savings and could be considered "crucial" if not indispensable (Summerhill 2005; Coatsworth 1979).

The social savings methodology is controversial, however. Critics point to a number of problems. First, it is not clear what the price of road or water transport would have been in the absence of railways. Congestion would have increased on roads and rivers with the increased traffic volume. The cost of using alternative transport modes is arguably underestimated as a result (McClelland, 1968: 114). Second, the social savings calculation omits spillovers. Railways increased demand for iron and steel and increased competition in manufacturing. The size of these backward and forward linkages is unclear. There are also changes in economic geography to consider. In theory, lower transport costs can lead to agglomeration of economic activity, like the emergence of cities. The standard social savings methodology has no way of measuring the effects on urbanization.

Yet, the social savings methodology has yielded a number of insights that are worth mentioning. First, railways offered time savings as well as monetary savings. One study quantifies the value of time saved on British railways and shows it was equal to approximately 10 per cent of GDP in 1913. Railways were important in this regard because walking was the alternative for many low-income passengers (Leunig 2006). Second, the social savings methodology shows how different transport modes can serve as substitutes. Countries without effective road and water transport often had higher social savings from railways. A case in point is Brazil, where mule trains represented the alternative to railways (Summerhill 2005). A third insight concerns technology diffusion and access. Necessarily there must be a large number of customers if any transport improvement is going to have a large social savings. In some countries, like Spain, the railway had a smaller impact than it might have had because its total revenues represented a small share of GDP (Herranz-Loncán 2006). One potential culprit is poor regulation or network design.

A second general method seeks to measure the effects of transport on economic outcomes more directly. It uses regression analysis to compare income or population density in economies with and without transport innovations, or to measure economic changes before and after transport innovations are introduced. Most studies in this second vein find that transport improvements have effects on income and population density. Often the key questions revolve around the size of the effect. One study estimates the effect of highways on suburbanization in the U.S. between 1950 and 1990. During this period, central city population declined by 17 per cent. The analysis compares the differences in population across cities depending on the number of new highway miles. The estimates imply that one new highway passing through a central city reduced its population by about 18 per cent (Baum-Snow 2007).

Estimates of the effects of transport improvements are useful in informing policy discussions. Transportation improvements are often expensive. If the developmental effects are small relative to the costs, then transport funding should be reduced. More generally, if transport innovations change the way we live, as in the case of suburbanization, then it is useful to know how much.

The literature also speaks to the importance of transport improvements in the development of economies over the long run. As transport costs are crucially linked with trade costs and the extension of markets, transport improvements have been shown to be one of the most important developments in any economy.

As a final remark, transport innovations have been difficult to implement historically because they involve vexing issues like eminent domain and taxation. In addition, some economies have made inefficient use of their transport infrastructure due to excessive monopoly power and regulatory failures. History tells us that attention needs to be paid to transport effectiveness if the social gains of transport are to be realized.

Notes

1 Figures obtained from U.S. Department of Commerce, Bureau of Economic Analysis, http://www.bea.gov/industry/gdpbyind_data.htm
2 Author's calculation based on Carter *et al.* (2006): Df1112–25.

References

Baum-Snow, N. (2007) 'Did highways cause suburbanization?' *Quarterly Journal of Economics*, 122: 775–805.

Bell, H. (1894) *Railway Policy of India: With Map of Indian Railway System*, Rivington: Percival.

Bogart, D. (2005) 'Turnpike trusts and the transportation revolution in eighteenth century England', *Explorations in Economic History*, 42: 479–508.

——(2009) 'Nationalizations and the development of transport systems: cross-country evidence from railroad networks, 1860–1912', *Journal of Economic History*, 69: 202–37.

——(2010) 'A global perspective on railway inefficiency and the rise of state ownership, 1880–1912', *Explorations in Economic History*, 47: 158–78.

Bogart, D. and Chaudhary, L. (2012) 'Regulation, Ownership, and Costs: A Historical Perspective from Railways in Colonial India', *American Economic Journal: Economic Policy*, 4: 28–57.

Carter, S.B., Gartner, S.S., Haines, M.R., Olmstead, A.L., Sutch, R. and Wright, G. (eds) (2006) *Historical Statistics of the United States Millennial Edition*, New York: Cambridge University Press.

Clark, G. (1987) 'Why isn't the whole world developed? Lessons from the cotton mills', *Journal of Economic History*, 47: 141–73.

Coatsworth, J. (1979) 'Indispensable railroads in a backward economy: the case of Mexico', *Journal of Economic History*, 39: 939–60.

Fishlow, A. (1965) *American Railroads and the Transformation of the Ante-bellum Economy*, Cambridge: Harvard University Press.

——(1966) 'Productivity and technological change in the railroad sector, 1840–1910', in D.S. Brady (ed.) *Output, Employment, and Productivity in the United States after 1800*, New York: NBER.

Fogel, R. (1970) *Railroads and American Economic Growth: Essays in Econometric History*, Baltimore, Bd: Johns Hopkins Press.

Roth, R. and Dinhobl, G. (eds) (2008) *Across the Borders: Financing the World's Railways in the Nineteenth and Twentieth Centuries*, Aldershot: Ashgate.

Harley, C.K. (1988) 'Ocean freight rates and productivity, 1740–1913: the primacy of mechanical invention reaffirmed', *Journal of Economic History*, 4: 851–76.

——(2008) '"Steers afloat": the North Atlantic meat trade, liner predominance, and freight rates, 1870–1913', *Journal of Economic History*, 68: 1028–58.

Herranz-Loncán, A. (2006) 'Railroad impact in backward economies: Spain, 1850 1913', *Journal of Economic History*, 66: 853–81.

Keeling, D. (2008) 'Transport capacity management and transatlantic migration, 1900–1914', *Research in Economic History*, 25: 225–83.

Kolko, G. (1965) *Railroads and Regulation: 1877–1916*, Princeton, NJ: Princeton University Press.

Leunig, T. (2006) 'Time is money: a re-assessment of the passenger social savings from Victorian British railways', *Journal of Economic History*, 66: 635–73.

175

McClelland, P.D. (1968) 'Railroads, American growth, and the new economic history: a critique', *Journal of Economic History*, 28: 102–23.

Mulhall, M. (1884) *Mulhall's Dictionary of Statistics*, London: George Routledge and Sons.

North, D.C. (1958) 'Ocean freight rates and economic development, 1750–1913', *Journal of Economic History*, 18: 537–55.

O'Brien, P.K. (1983) *Railways and the Economic Development of Western Europe: 1830–1914*, New York: St. Martin's.

Porter, R. (1983) 'A study of cartel stability: a study of the Joint Executive Committee, 1880–86', *Bell Journal of Economics*, 14: 301–14.

Summerhill, W.R. (2005) 'Big social savings in a small laggard economy: railroad-led growth in Brazil', *Journal of Economic History*, 65: 72–102.

Ville, S. (1990) *Transport and the Development of the European Economy, 1750–1918*, London: Macmillan.

16

ECONOMIC HISTORY AND THE HEALTHCARE INDUSTRY

Melissa Thomasson

Over the past 100 years, the healthcare industry in the United States has radically transformed. In 1900, hospitals were places where only people without family to care for them would go. There were no effective pharmaceuticals, and the average person spent only $134 (in 2011 dollars) per year on medical care (Craig 2006: 3–232). Physicians could not effectively treat disease, and physician training was rudimentary. Over the course of the twentieth century, significant changes occurred in physician education, technological development, hospital care, health insurance, and in the level of government involvement in the provision of healthcare. Together, these changes reshaped the industry. By 2009, healthcare expenditures reached $8,086 per capita, and healthcare spending accounted for 17.6 per cent of gross domestic product (GDP) (Centers for Medicare and Medicaid Services 2011).

Figure 16.1 shows the trend in healthcare expenditure in the United States as a share of GDP. To ensure consistency over time, it aggregates consumer spending on hospitals, physicians' services, dental and other professional services, drugs, and ophthalmology. Figure 16.1 demonstrates that the healthcare industry grew slowly until the 1930s, grew at a somewhat faster pace between 1930 and 1950, with growth spiking after 1960. In many ways, the trends depicted in Figure 16.1 mirror the underlying developments in the industry. Until the 1930s, the state of medical technology was low and health insurance was virtually non-existent. As technology began to advance and the number of people with health insurance coverage increased, medical expenditures started to rise. The passage of Medicare in 1965 and continued growth in medical technology accelerated the trend. This chapter discusses the evolution of the healthcare industry and the forces that shaped it, including health insurance, providers, and technology.

1900–30

At the turn of the twentieth century, the healthcare industry in the United States bore little resemblance to its modern form. The state of medical technology was in its infancy such that even the best doctors could do no more than educate patients on hygiene and perhaps diagnose their afflictions. There were no effective pharmaceuticals, and surgery was high risk because of the danger of infection. Hospitals only cared for people who lacked family or friends who could care for them at home, and medical education was for the most part substandard and did not even

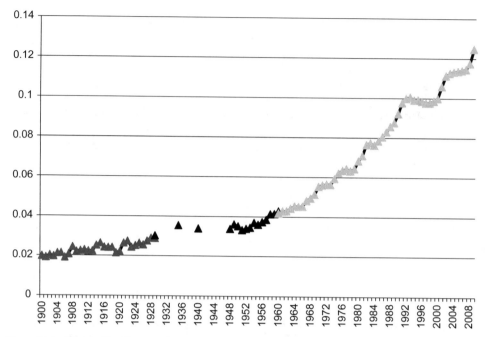

Figure 16.1 National health expenditures as a per cent of GDP, 1900–2008

Sources: To create a consistent series over time, data were pulled from three sources. From 1900 to 1929, data are from Table Cd1-77, column Cd39 (total consumer expenditures on medical care) less Cd44 (expenditures on health insurance) in Craig (2006: 3–232). An annual series does not exist from 1930 to 1960; these data are from Table Bd1-16, column Bd2 (total expenditures on health services and supplies) less columns Bd9 (nursing home care), Bd10 (home healthcare), Bd11 (expenses for prepayment and administration), Bd12 (government public health activities), and Bd13 (other health services) in Steckel (2006: 2–509). For the post-1960 period, data are from National Health Expenditures (2009) and include expenditures on hospitals, physicians, dentists, other professionals, pharmaceuticals, and medical durables and non-durables (see http://www.cms.gov/Research-Statistics-Data-and-Systems/Statistics-Trends-and-Reports/NationalHealth
ExpendData/index.html).

require a baccalaureate degree (Starr 1982: 112–16). In 1900, the life expectancy for white males was 48.2 years (and between 33.5 and 41.8 years for black males). Much of the mortality occurred at younger ages; especially in urban areas where crowding and poor water quality put infants particularly at risk from contagious diseases and gastroenteritis (Haines 2001: 3–7).

Over the early part of the twentieth century, the transformation of the healthcare industry occurred as science progressed, medical education improved, and more medical training took place in hospitals. Among these factors, reforms in medical education were the first to occur. Driving these educational reforms was a significant increase in the number of newly (and usually poorly) trained physicians in the late nineteenth century. In 1870, there were 75 medical schools. By 1900, there were 160 (Starr 1982: 112). Physicians complained that they could not earn a decent income due to physician oversupply. The problem of "overcrowding" in the profession was referred to in several articles at the turn of the century. A *Journal of the American Medical Association* editorial written in October 1901 stated, "It is evident from the census statistics that we must be rapidly approaching the limit of additions to the medical profession if the individual members are to find the practice of medicine a lucrative occupation" (*Journal of the American Medical Association*, October 26, 1901: 1119).

Johns Hopkins was the first university to substantially reform medical education. In 1893, it became the first school to treat medicine as a graduate degree. At the time, even the best medical schools (such as Harvard and the University of Pennsylvania) did not require a high school diploma. Johns Hopkins required students to attend medical school for four years, two of which were spent on hospital wards. Other schools offered two- or (among better schools) three-year programs where students attended only six months out of the year. Schools churned out poorly trained physicians who spent little time studying science or in laboratories, and virtually no time in hospitals. Medical students learned in their professors' offices and the homes of patients (Starr 1982: 112–16). After Johns Hopkins increased their admissions standards and requirements, other good schools followed suit.

In 1904, the American Medical Association (AMA) founded its Council on Medical Education (CME). The CME specified minimum requirements for "approved" medical schools, and began to inspect and rate medical schools. The number of medical schools fell from 162 in 1906 to 131 in 1910, the year that Abraham Flexner published his report indicting the quality of education that most medical schools offered (Starr 1982: 118). Flexner argued for higher entrance standards and more rigorous curricula, stating that the current system of medical education had resulted in an oversupply of poorly trained physicians and that present needs would be better "met by a reduced output of well trained men than by further inflation with an inferior product" (Flexner 1910: 16). After Flexner's report was issued, the number of medical schools (and the number of graduates) continued to decline, and fell to 81 by 1922 (*Journal of the American Medical Association*, August 12, 1922: 633). While Flexner's report hastened the closure of many schools, rising requirements by state licensing boards (such as increasing the required length of training) led to the closure of many subpar institutions (Starr 1982: 118).

Reforms in medical education had two primary impacts. First, the reforms served to shift the focus of practice from physicians' offices and patients' homes into hospitals. As physicians trained more routinely in hospitals, they came to view hospitals as their workshops. Doctors could see more patients in a hospital than if they spent time traveling to patients' houses, and hospitals became centers for medical care and science as some technological advances necessitated centralization. Discovered in 1895, the X-ray machine soon became a much used, but non-portable technology. With a greater understanding of bacteria, pathology laboratories were also developed and located in hospitals. Advances in the understanding of bacteriology also led to the development of aseptic techniques that could be more easily implemented in a hospital than in a patient's living room or kitchen. As Starr notes:

> [P]erforming surgery in the home became steadily more inconvenient for both the surgeon and the family, as the procedures became more demanding and more people moved into apartments. And the more busy surgeons became, the more costly was the lost time in traveling to the patient's home. (Starr 1982: 157)

In addition to shifting the focus of practice to hospitals, reforms in medical education also turned out qualified doctors who could better diagnose illnesses, educate patients on hygiene, and aid in public health efforts to identify sources of infection. Science played an ever-greater role in medicine, and technological developments occurred that made the public view doctors as effective and hospitals as a consumer good. Major technological developments included the development of diphtheria antitoxin and a vaccine for typhoid in the 1890s, a test for syphilis in 1906, the development in 1910 of salvarsan, a drug that was partially effective in the treatment of syphilis, and the development of "twilight sleep" anesthesia for childbirth (Starr 1982: 137–8; Thomasson and Treber 2008).

By the early 1910s, hospitals were learning to cater to the increasing demand for medical and hospital care. Hospitals focused on relatively simple procedures such as obstetrical deliveries, tonsillectomies, and appendectomies (Stevens 1989: 105). Despite the increase in demand for medical care at this point, the effectiveness of medical care was still fairly low. While life expectancy at birth had increased from 47.8 years in 1900 to 59.7 years in 1930, much of the decline in mortality was due to public health initiatives such as sanitation, sewer systems, and hygiene education efforts that better-educated physicians could indirectly aid (Haines 2001: 13). Physicians were still fairly limited in their ability to cure (rather than simply diagnose) illness, and increased medical attention did not necessarily improve outcomes. One such example is in childbirth. In 1900, only about 5 per cent of infants were born in hospitals. By 1935, 75 per cent of births in urban areas and half of all births occurred in hospitals (Wertz and Wertz 1977: 133). However, as births shifted to hospitals, maternal mortality rates did not decline. In hospital deliveries, physicians were more likely to engage in operative interventions that raised the risk of secondary infection. Thomasson and Treber (2008) examine the pre- and post-sulfa period and find that while medical care in the post-sulfa period lowered maternal deaths, medical care in the pre-sulfa period was of limited effectiveness.

As the demand for medical care increased, costs rose. Nevertheless, even by 1920, the primary costs associated with sickness were due to lost wages and not medical expenditures. A 1918 Bureau of Labor Statistics survey of 211 families in Ohio found their average annual medical bill to be $701 (2011 dollars), with expenditures on physicians' and surgeons' services accounting for 51.6 per cent of all spending, and hospital expenses accounting for only 7.6 per cent (Ohio Health and Old Age Insurance Commission 1919: 116). Similarly, a 1919 State of Illinois Commission that examined the total cost of sickness estimated that, for each dollar of wages lost by individuals, only an additional 24 cents had to be added to cover medical expenses (State of Illinois 1919: 15–17). Each year, the average cost of lost wages and medical expenses that were incurred by a typical wage-earning family totaled only $945 (2011 dollars). In comparison, the average cost of a funeral was nearly twice that at $1,670 (State of Illinois 1919: 17).

As a result of the relatively low expenses associated with medical care, there was not a real need for health insurance. Instead, wage-earning families typically purchased sickness insurance, which generally provided benefits similar to modern-day disability benefits. Most workers participated in sickness funds either through their firms or unions, or through fraternal societies (Murray 2007; Emery 1996; Emery and Emery 1999). Murray (2007) estimates that, by 1915, sickness funds covered about one-third of the non-agricultural labor force. This number is similar to that found by the State of Illinois Commission, which estimated 30 per cent of the working class had sickness insurance (State of Illinois 1919: 146).

The fact that health insurance – as opposed to sickness insurance – was not in high demand is also reflected in the failure of a Progressive Era effort to implement state-level compulsory health insurance. Following compulsory health insurance initiatives in Germany and Great Britain, the American Association for Labor Legislation (AALL) proposed a plan calling for comprehensive sickness and medical benefits for low-income workers. Under the plan, local mutual insurance companies would manage premium contributions shared by employers, workers, and the state. Employers and workers would each contribute 40 per cent of the plan's premium, while the state would contribute the remaining 20 per cent (Chasse 1994: 1067). The AALL's plan also included a $50 death benefit. Several groups were opposed to the legislation, including insurance companies, pharmacists, unions, and physicians. Insurance companies had a large stake in the burial insurance market that was threatened by the AALL's death benefit. Pharmacists worried that they would be replaced with government dispensaries. Unions feared that the state-run plans would diminish workers' need for unions, and physicians felt that state-run plans may limit their fees. In the face of serious opposition, the AALL's model bill may have passed in some states with enough popular support, but even this was lacking. A 1918 referendum in California on health insurance was defeated 358,324 to 133,858 (Murray 2007: 19).

While the failure of the AALL's efforts was indicative of a definite lack of demand for health insurance, there was also a lack of supply. Commercial insurance companies were very reluctant to offer health insurance because they doubted that health was an insurable commodity. *Insurance Monitor*, a trade journal, strongly stated its fears about the viability of health insurance, writing that:

> [T]he opportunities for fraud upset all statistical calculations ... Health and sickness are vague terms open to endless construction. Death is clearly defined, but to say what shall constitute such loss of health as will justify insurance compensation is no easy task. (*Insurance Monitor* 1919)

Insurance companies were worried about two problems associated with the provision of health insurance: adverse selection and moral hazard. Adverse selection occurs if people who are more likely to make a claim are more likely to try to buy insurance than other people. Some factors associated with the risk of making a claim (such as age) are observable, but many (such as lifestyle behaviors) may not be. If insurance companies are unable to discern the likelihood of an individual making a claim, it is difficult for them to offer insurance without losing money. Moral hazard is a problem that occurs when having insurance changes the behavior of the insured – for example, if a worker with sickness insurance malingers and takes longer to recover than a worker without insurance. Clearly, as the earlier quote reflects, insurance companies were quite worried about moral hazard and about how to measure "loss" due to sickness. As one author commenting on the development of sickness insurance noted, "to collect on life insurance, the insured must be dead, to collect on accident insurance, he must have had an accident, while to collect on sickness insurance he must have a policy" (McCahan 1954: 187).

While low medical expenses precluded a demand for health insurance before 1920, this began to change as the demand for medical care increased in the 1920s, driving up medical expenses. By 1929, the average American family had medical expenses totaling $108, with hospital expenditures contributing to about 14 per cent of medical expenses. Total medical expenses had become more variable as the costs of hospitalization increased. In 1929, urban families with incomes between $2,000 and $3,000 per year had medical expenses of $67 if no one had been admitted to the hospital, but medical expenses of $261 if someone in the family had been hospitalized (Falk *et al.* 1933: 89). As the costs associated with hospitalization increased, some people had trouble paying the large bills. In response, hospitals developed pre-paid hospital care plans. The first of these plans, which later organized under the name "Blue Cross," was founded in the late 1920s when Baylor University Hospital contracted with a group of Dallas teachers to provide 21 days of hospital care for a $6 annual payment. One official connected with the Baylor plan compared hospital bills with cosmetics, noting that the nation's cosmetic bill was actually more than the nation's hospital bill, but that:

> We spend a dollar or so at a time for cosmetics and do not notice the high cost. The ribbon counter clerk can pay 50¢, 75¢, or $1 a month, yet ... it would take about twenty years to set aside a large hospital bill. (American Foundation 1937: 1023)

The plans gained momentum during the Great Depression, as hospital beds sat empty because people could no longer afford care. Between 1929 and 1930, hospital occupancy rates fell from

71.28 per cent to 64.12 per cent, and hospital receipts per bed fell from $236.12 in 1929 to $59.26 (*Bulletin of the American Hospital Association* 1930). The American Hospital Association (AHA) encouraged the growth of the plans to prevent those with limited incomes from "financial embarrassment and even from disaster in the emergency of sickness" (Reed 1947: 14). The AHA also recognized that single-hospital plans generated competition between hospitals, and created Blue Cross to organize the plans and reduce interhospital price competition. Prepayment plans seeking the Blue Cross designation had to provide subscribers with free choice of physician and hospital, requirements that eliminated single-hospital plans from membership (see Eilers 1963 for more discussion). Blue Cross plans also benefited from state-level legislation that enabled them to act as nonprofit corporations and enjoy tax-exempt status, and that freed them from adhering to insurance regulations such as reserve requirements and assessment liability.[1]

Physicians were much slower than hospitals to provide pre-paid care plans. They had long mistrusted third-party insurance because they feared that insurance companies would restrict their income and limit their ability to price discriminate. In the 1930s, physicians were faced with two situations that spurred them to develop pre-paid plans that covered physicians' services. First, Blue Cross plans were becoming popular and physicians feared that hospitals would move into the realm of providing insurance for physicians' services. In addition, the emerging social security legislation had reinvigorated the debate about national healthcare. Compulsory health insurance was even more anathema to physicians than voluntary health insurance. It became clear to physicians that, in order to protect their interests, they would be better off preempting both hospitals and the government by creating their own plans (Hedinger 1966: 82). The AMA adopted a set of 10 principles to guide plan development. The principles included that the plans would remain under physician supervision, and that physicians could retain their ability to price discriminate by charging subscribers the difference between their fee and the level of reimbursement provided by the plan (Hedinger 1966: 82). The AMA encouraged state and local medical societies to form their own prepayment plans, which eventually became affiliated and "Blue Shield" in 1946.

The Blue Cross and Blue Shield prepayment plans were the first actual modern health insurance plans to be offered on a widespread scale, and they set the stage for the employment-based system of health insurance through which 70 per cent of Americans still receive insurance today. These plans succeeded by successfully reducing adverse selection and moral hazard. Offering insurance to groups of employees (i.e. people who are healthy enough to work) enabled the plans to overcome adverse selection. By providing benefits in the form of hospital services instead of a cash indemnity, the prepayment plans limited the problem of moral hazard. Once it was apparent that Blue Cross and Blue Shield had successfully overcome the problems of adverse selection and moral hazard, commercial, for-profit companies began to move rapidly into the market. The Superintendent of Insurance in New York, Louis H. Pink, noted in 1939 that 20 for-profit insurance companies were issuing health insurance in New York, and speculated that "it is no doubt the interest aroused by the non-profit associations that has induced the regular insurance companies to extend their activities in this way" (Pink 1939).

1940–60

The 1940s and 1950s witnessed large increases in the number of people with health insurance. In 1940, only about 9 per cent of the population had health insurance (Health Insurance Institute 1978: 22). By 1952, on the eve of a significant change in the tax treatment of employer-provided health insurance, roughly 63 per cent of people had coverage (Thomasson 2003: 1375). Several factors contributed to the rapid growth in health insurance over this period. First, significant technological developments in medicine occurred that increased both the demand for medical care and the demand for insurance. In 1937, sulfa drugs became available on a widespread basis. For the first time, physicians were able to effectively treat a range of previously fatal bacterial infections, including streptococcal infections, pneumonia, and meningitis. Jayachandran *et al.* (2010) estimate that overall mortality declined 2 to 3 per cent after sulfa drugs became available, and that life expectancy rose by 0.4 to 0.7 years. Diseases related to streptococcal infection were particularly susceptible to sulfa, and deaths due to these causes dropped dramatically. For example, deaths due to scarlet fever – a feared killer – dropped by 52 to 65 per cent, while maternal mortality declined between 24 per cent and 36 per cent (Jayachandran *et al.* 2010: 118).

This dramatic reduction in deaths due to bacterial infection ushered in a new confidence in medicine.[2] Significant medical advances continued with the advent of penicillin in the 1940s and the polio vaccine in 1955. With effective new technologies, demand for medical care increased and expenditures rose as well. Medical expenditures per capita in real 1935 dollars more than doubled between 1935 and 1955, rising from $22.65 to $54.06 (Steckel 2006: 511). Thomasson (2002) examines the various factors explaining the rise in health insurance from 1932 to 1955 and finds that factors such as changes in technology explain up to 43 per cent of the growth in the demand for health insurance over this period. Other important factors include rising income (35 per cent) and increases in the number of large firms (15 per cent) (Thomasson 2002: 249).

In addition to an increase in demand for health insurance due to more effective medical technologies, there were changes in government policy in the 1940s and 1950s that further spurred the growth of health insurance, particularly its growth as an employment-based benefit. Under the 1942 Stabilization Act, employers were allowed to offer health benefit packages to lure workers during a period of wage and price controls (Scofea 1994). The ability of unions to negotiate health benefits on behalf of workers was cemented in 1949, when the National Labor Relations Board ruled that, for the sake of negotiations, the term "wages" included health benefits (*Inland Steel Co. v. NLRB*, 170 F. 2d 247 [7th Cir. 1948]).

While these rulings certainly increased the growth of employment-based insurance, government tax policy in the 1940s and 1950s also proved very important. In 1943, an administrative tax ruling stated that employers' payments to commercial insurance companies for group medical and hospitalization premiums on behalf of their employees were not taxable as employee income (3 CCH 1943 Fed. Tax Rep. 6587 [1943]). While the lack of statutory provisions made the ruling uncertain and may have prevented some firms from deciding to offer health insurance, the uncertainty was eliminated in 1954, when changes to the Internal Revenue Code firmly established the tax exemption (Thomasson 2003: 1375). This tax change generated a significant shift in the provision of health insurance in the United States; Thomasson (2003) finds that the tax change increased the likelihood that a household would have coverage by 9 per cent, and increased the amount of coverage purchased by 9.5 per cent (Thomasson 2003: 1380–1). By 1957, about 76 per cent of the population held some form of private health insurance coverage (Thomasson 2003: 1373).

As the market for private health insurance was growing in the 1940s and 1950s, it did so against a backdrop of continued efforts to implement a government-based health insurance system. Previous attempts to implement compulsory health insurance in the 1910s and 1930s had failed. In the 1930s, although some members of the Committee on Economic Security (originally formed to study the issue of social security) were in favor of national health insurance as part of the Social Security Act, the Roosevelt Administration feared that including health insurance in the social security bill would cause it to be defeated, so it was never included (Starr 1982: 268–9).

In the 1940s, renewed efforts for universal health insurance coverage continued when President Harry Truman proposed a universal health insurance system. Just as in earlier attempts to implement national health insurance, the AMA strongly opposed the plan and spent $1.5 million (one of the most expensive lobbying efforts in history at that time) to convince the public to oppose the plan (Shi and Singh 2008: 103). The AMA printed pamphlets filled with allegations of socialism. An AMA pamphlet circulating in 1949 said that, under the plan, the government intended to control doctors and hospitals, and "direct both the citizen's and the doctor's participation in the program" (American Medical Association 1949: 8). Moreover, the pamphlet suggested that "socialized" medicine would lead to the socialization of other phases of American life. According to the pamphlet, "If the medical profession should be socialized because people need doctors, *why not the milk industry? ... Why not nationalize lawyers, miners, businessmen, farmers?* Germany did, Russia did. England is in the process" (American Medical Association 1949: 8). The AMA's campaign was successful. While 52 per cent of people polled in 1945 said they preferred a compulsory public health insurance plan over a voluntary one set up by the medical profession, this number had fallen to one-third by 1949 (Erskine 1975: 139–40).

While Truman did not succeed in implementing national health insurance, another of his ideas did come to fruition. Truman's proposed health reform measures included expanding hospitals. In 1946, he signed the Hospital Survey and Construction Act (more commonly referred to as the Hill-Burton Act) into law. The bill was proposed in response to the general belief that hospitals were poorly distributed in the U.S. and adequate hospital facilities were particularly lacking in rural areas – 40 per cent of U.S. counties did not have a hospital in 1945 – thus, contributing to the "national-health problem" (1945 Hearings on S. 191 1945: 7). Through the Hill-Burton program, the federal government became the single largest investor in hospitals. Nationwide over the period 1947–71, 10,748 projects at a total cost of $12.8 billion had been approved under the Hill-Burton program. Federal funds accounted for 29 per cent of expenditures, with state and local funds comprising the remainder. Overall, 344,453 new beds were added in general hospitals, accounting for 73.2 per cent of all new beds added under the program (Hill-Burton Project Register 1971) and approximately half of the existing beds in the U.S. (United States Department of Health, Education and Welfare 1966).

The expansion of the nation's supply of hospital beds occurred at the same time that money was being aggressively funneled into science. The rapid pace of technological discovery in medicine that occurred during the war was accommodated afterwards by increased federal funding for scientific research. Between 1941 and 1951, total expenditures by all sources on medical research increased by tenfold, from $18 million to $181 million (Endicott and Allen 1953: 337).

1960 and beyond: Medicare and Medicaid

By 1960, the healthcare industry looked much like its modern form. Most people received health insurance through their place of employment. People without health insurance either did not work, or did not work at a job that offered benefits. Under the 1950 amendments to the Social Security Act, the federal government provided matching funds to states to pay doctors and hospitals for providing medical care to welfare recipients (Starr 1982: 286). These "vendor payments" were expanded to include the elderly who were not welfare recipients but who needed help paying their medical bills under the Kerr–Mills bill, enacted into law in 1960 (United States Social Security Administration 2011).

The passage of Kerr–Mills was an intermediate step between the proposals under Truman and the creation of Medicare – the national health insurance program for the elderly – in 1965.

During his presidential campaign, Senator John F. Kennedy repeatedly argued that Kerr-Mills was inadequate. A Special Committee on Aging in the U.S. Senate investigated the health insurance coverage of the elderly and concluded that only one in four elderly Americans had adequate hospital insurance coverage. It also found that Blue Cross plans had been cutting benefits and increasing premiums to the point where older members were "virtually being priced out of the market," and were caught between higher premiums and lower benefit levels even as medical costs were rising. The report concluded that "increasing numbers of our older people are confronted with financial catastrophe brought on by illness" (United States Senate Special Committee on Aging 1964: 4–5). By 1964, political support for Medicare had gradually increased, and about two-thirds of Americans supported it. By mid-1965, Medicare was enacted into law as a federal program with two parts. Part A represented the compulsory hospital insurance program that the elderly were automatically enrolled in upon reaching age 65. Part B provided supplemental medical insurance for physicians' services. Funding for Medicare comes from payroll taxes, income taxes, and trust fund interest (United States Social Security Administration 2011).

Under the Medicare legislation, Medicaid was also created to cover other populations in need of assistance with medical bills. Unlike Medicare, which was funded by the federal government and provided uniform benefits to all enrollees, Medicaid was enacted as a means-tested, federal-state program to provide medical benefits originally to recipients of public assistance, although legislative changes over the years have expanded eligibility. The federal government specified minimum standards for eligibility and benefits; states could be more generous with either eligibility or benefit levels. Thus, eligibility and benefits in the Medicaid program vary widely across states (Gruber 2000).

Conclusion

Since 1965, medical technology has continued to advance and medical expenditures have continued to climb. Yet the structure of the healthcare industry in the U.S. has remained remarkably unchanged. A massive attempt at healthcare reform under President Bill Clinton failed in the early 1990s, and, with the exception of the State Children's Health Insurance Program (that went into effect in 1998), only relatively minor changes to Medicare and Medicaid have been enacted. The majority of Americans (55.8 per cent) still receive health insurance through their place of work. Medicaid covers about 15.7 per cent of Americans, Medicare covers 14.3 per cent, and 15.3 per cent have no insurance (DeNavas-Walt *et al.* 2010: 24).

After a decade of failed attempts, healthcare reform succeeded in March 2010 when President Barack Obama signed the Patient Protection and Affordable Care Act (ACA) into law. In addition to expanding Medicaid eligibility and instituting a host of insurance reforms, the law requires most U.S. citizens and legal residents to have health insurance or pay a penalty, and creates health insurance exchanges through which individuals and small businesses can purchase coverage. Families with incomes below 400 per cent of the federal poverty level are eligible for premium subsidies. With the exception of small firms, employers who do not provide coverage pay penalties if their employees receive subsidized coverage through the health insurance exchange (Henry J. Kaiser Family Foundation 2011: 1).

Why was the ACA enacted when so many previous attempts failed? Looking at history, successful attempts to change healthcare have only done so incrementally. For example, Medicare did not change the way the majority of Americans received insurance and services – it simply added coverage for the elderly, many of whom did not have coverage. The ACA in many ways does the same thing. Most Americans, at least initially, will see little or no change in how they receive health insurance coverage. The Act extends coverage to many of the uninsured, most of whom have trouble paying their medical bills. With coverage, the formerly uninsured will find it easier to see doctors, go to hospitals, and pay their medical bills. Perhaps this explains why the AMA – in a break from its longstanding tradition of opposing healthcare reform – supported the ACA.

The long-term impact of the ACA is difficult to determine. While previously uninsured people will find it easier to pay their medical bills and receive care, critics contend that the bill will cause healthcare expenditures to rise significantly. By lowering the price of care, the ACA will increase the quantity demanded. How much of an impact this will have is difficult to determine, but this is an area where history can provide guidance. Finkelstein (2007: 31) suggests that up to half of the six-fold increase in real per capita health expenditures between 1950 and 1990 may be explained by the implementation of Medicare in 1966, which provided health insurance coverage for 15 million elderly persons. While a direct comparison is difficult given that Medicare is a single-payer system (versus one in which private insurance companies compete), and that the elderly have higher medical expenditures than the non-elderly, Finkelstein's findings nevertheless suggest that the ACA will likely increase medical expenditures.

Notes

1 For a greater discussion of this "enabling legislation" and its impact, see Eilers (1963), *Michigan State Bar Journal* (1940), and *Yale Law Journal* (1943).
2 See Jayachandran *et al.* (2010), Lesch (2007), and Thomasson and Treber (2008) for a discussion of the development and health benefits of sulfa.

References

American Foundation (1937) *American Medicine, Volume II*, New York: American Foundation.
American Medical Association (1949) *The Voluntary Way is the American Way: 40 Questions – 40 Answers on Health Insurance*, Chicago, IL: National Education Campaign, American Medical Association.
Bulletin of the American Hospital Association (1930) Volume IV, July, 68.
Centers for Medicare and Medicaid Services (2011) Research, Statistics, Data and Systems, National Health Expenditure Data, Historical, Highlights, 20 January, http://www.cms.gov/Research-Statistics-Data-and-Systems/Statistics-Trends-and-Reports/NationalHealthExpendData/Downloads/highlights.pdf
Chasse, D.J. (1994) 'The American Association for Labor Legislation and the institutionalist tradition in national health insurance', *Journal of Economic Issues*, 28: 1063–90.
Craig, L.A. (2006) 'Consumer expenditures', in S.B. Carter, S.S. Gartner, M.R. Haines, A.L. Olmstead, R. Sutch and G. Wright (eds) *Historical Statistics of the United States, Earliest Times to the Present: Millennial Edition*, New York: Cambridge University Press.
DeNavas-Walt. C., Proctor, B.D. and Smith, J.C. (2010) U.S. Census Bureau, Current Population Reports, P60–238, *Income, Poverty, and Health Insurance Coverage in the United States: 2009*, Washington: U.S. Government Printing Office.
Eilers, R.D. (1963) *Regulation of Blue Cross and Blue Shield Plans*, Homewood, IL: Richard D. Irwin.
Emery, J.C.H. (1996) 'Risky business? Nonactuarial pricing practices and the financial viability of fraternal sickness insurers', *Explorations in Economic History*, 33: 195–226.
Emery, G. and Emery, J.C.H. (1999) *A Young Man's Benefit: The Independent Order of Odd Fellows and Sickness Insurance in the United States and Canada*, Montreal and Kingston: McGill-Queen's University Press.
Endicott, K.M. and Allen, E.M. (1953) 'The growth of medical research 1941–53 and the role of Public Health Service research grants', *Science*, 118(3065): 337–43.
Erskine, H. (1975) 'The polls: health insurance', *Public Opinion Quarterly*, 39: 128–43.
Falk, I.S., Rorem, C.R. and Ring, M.D. (1933) *The Cost of Medical Care*, Chicago, IL: University of Chicago Press.
Faulkner, E.J. (1960) *Health Insurance*, New York: McGraw-Hill.

Finkelstein, A. (2007) 'The aggregate effects of health insurance: evidence from the introduction of Medicare', *Quarterly Journal of Economics*, 122: 1–37.

Flexner, A. (1910) *Medical Education in the United States and Canada: A Report to the Carnegie Foundation for the Advancement of Teaching*, New York: Carnegie Foundation for the Advancement of Teaching.

Gruber, J.B. (2000) 'Medicaid', NBER Working Paper No. 7829.

Haines, M.R. (2001) 'The urban mortality transition in the United States, 1800–1940', NBER Historical Paper No. 134.

Health Insurance Institute (1978) *Source Book of Health Insurance Data, 1976–1977*, New York: Health Insurance Institute.

Hedinger, F.R. (1966) *The Social Role of Blue Cross as a Device for Financing the Costs of Hospital Care: An Evaluation*, Iowa City, IA: University of Iowa.

Henry J. Kaiser Family Foundation (2011) 'Summary of new health reform law', April 19, http://www.kff.org/healthreform/upload/8061.pdf

Insurance Monitor (1919), July, 67, 7: 38.

Jayachandran, S., Lleras-Muney, A. and Smith, K.V. (2010) 'Modern medicine and the twentieth century decline in mortality: evidence on the impact of sulfa drugs', *American Economic Journal: Applied Economics*, 2: 118–46.

Journal of the American Medical Association, various issues.

Lesch, J.E. (2007) *The First Miracle Drugs: How the Sulfa Drugs Transformed Medicine*, Oxford: Oxford University Press.

McCahan, D. (ed.) (1954) *Accident and Sickness Insurance*, Philadelphia, PA: University of Pennsylvania Press.

Michigan State Bar Journal (1940) Volume 19, December.

Murray, J.E. (2007) *Origins of American Health Insurance: A History of Industrial Sickness Funds*, New Haven, CT: Yale University Press.

Ohio Health and Old Age Insurance Commission (1919) *Health, Health Insurance, Old Age Pensions*, Columbus, OH: F.J. Heer Printing Co.

Pink, L.H. (1939) 'Voluntary hospital and medical associations and the state', address to the Meeting of the Medical Society of the County of Queens, Forest Hills, New York, February 28, *Journal of American Insurance*, 16.

Reed, L.S. (1947) *Blue Cross and Medical Service Plans*, Washington: U.S. Public Health Service.

Scofea, L.A. (1994) 'The development and growth of employer-provided health insurance', *Monthly Labor Review*, 117: 3–10.

Shi, L. and Singh, D.A. (2008) *Delivering Health Care in America: A Systems Approach*, 4th edition, Sudbury, MA: Jones and Bartlett Publishers.

Starr, P. (1982) *The Social Transformation of American Medicine*, New York: Basic Books.

State of Illinois (1919) *Report of the Health Insurance Commission of the State of Illinois, 1919*, Springfield.

Steckel, R.H. (2006) 'Health', in S.B. Carter, S.S. Gartner, M.R. Haines, A.L. Olmstead, R. Sutch and G. Wright (eds) *Historical Statistics of the United States, Earliest Times to the Present: Millennial Edition*, vol. 2, New York: Cambridge University Press.

Stevens, R. (1989) *In Sickness and in Wealth: American Hospitals in the Twentieth Century*, New York: Basic Books.

Thomasson, M.A. (2002) 'From sickness to health: the twentieth century development of U.S. health insurance', *Explorations in Economic History*, 39: 233–53.

——(2003) 'The importance of group coverage: how tax policy shaped U.S. health insurance', *American Economic Review*, 93: 1373–84.

Thomasson, M.A. and Treber, J. (2008) 'From home to hospital: the evolution of childbirth in the United States, 1928–40', *Explorations in Economic History*, 45: 76–99.

United States Department of Health, Education and Welfare (1966) *Hill-Burton Program, 1946–1966*, Washington: U.S. Government Printing Office.

United States Department of Health, Education and Welfare (1971) *Hill-Burton Project Register, July 1, 1947–June 30, 1971*, Rockville, MD: Public Health Service.

United States Senate (1945) Committee on Education and Labor, *S. 191, Hospital Construction Act*. Hearings, Feb. 26, 27, 28, Mar. 12, 13, 14, 79th Congress, 1st sess., Washington, Government Printing Office.

United States Senate Special Committee on Aging (1964) 'Blue cross and private health insurance coverage of older Americans', July, 88th Congress, 2nd. sess., Washington, Government Printing Office.

United States Social Security Administration (2011) *Social Security History*, Chapter 4: 'The Fourth Round – 1957 to 1965', June 8, http://www.ssa.gov/history/corningchap4.html

Wertz, R.W. and Wertz, D.C. (1977) *Lying-in: A History of Childbirth in America*, New Haven, CT: Yale University Press.

Yale Law Journal (1943) 'Group health plans: some legal and economic aspects', 53: 162–82.

17

THE ECONOMIC HISTORY OF BANKING

Richard S. Grossman

Introduction

Among the most important functions of a financial system is intermediation: channeling the aggregate savings of an economy toward productive use.[1] In the absence of intermediators, individuals, firms, and governments in need of finance and savers with surplus funds seeking investment opportunities would have to find each other and negotiate detailed contracts. These contracts would have to specify whether the funds are be loaned or to purchase a share of the enterprise. If loaned, the contract must stipulate the term and interest rate of the loan, as well as the amount and quality of collateral to be pledged as security. If the funds purchase an ownership share, the contract must stipulate the fraction of the profits and seats on the board of directors the new investor will be entitled to and, if the enterprise fails, how much liability the shareholder will bear. Without financial intermediators, negotiating such arrangements would be so costly and time consuming that many worthwhile projects would go unfunded. The consequences for economic development would be severe.

The importance of finance for long-term economic growth has been debated for years. Bagehot (1873), Schumpeter (1934), Gurley and Shaw (1955), Goldsmith (1969), Hicks (1969), McKinnon (1973), and Miller (1998) assert that finance plays a crucial role in fostering industrialization and long-term economic growth; Robinson (1952), Lucas (1988), and many development economists view it as being less essential. The weight of modern empirical analysis supports a finance–growth nexus, although the precise nature of the relationship and how financial systems and economies "co-evolve" is still not well understood (Levine 2005).

Of the two major components of the financial system, securities markets and financial institutions, economic theory suggests that securities markets are more efficient as intermediators. Those who need funds can offer their wares (i.e. securities) for sale in the financial marketplace, while savers can shop for the financial product with the attributes (e.g. maturity, risk, return, and collateral) that suit their preferences, and buy and sell those products as their personal circumstances change. If securities markets are active, transactions costs are low, and all parties have good information, both buyers and sellers will get the best price possible. Market prices will continuously adjust to reflect changes in supply and demand for securities which, in turn, reflect new information about underlying investments. If circumstances warrant, adjustments can take place through the market: firms and other demanders of funds can purchase their own debt or equity if the funds are no longer needed; savers can sell securities at any time in order to gain access to their funds.

Despite the many theoretical advantages of securities markets, highlighted in particular by Rajan and Zingales (2003), the conditions necessary to secure those advantages – an active market with many buyers and sellers, low transactions costs, and ample information – have been rare historically. Even with today's active and sophisticated securities markets, the transactions and information costs for small firms (e.g. securing a bond rating, complying with regulations imposed by regulators and exchanges) and firms in less developed countries may render access to securities markets impractical. Historically, the obstacles were much higher: active securities markets were scarce, information flows were poor by modern standards, and high transactions costs limited market access to only the largest and most credit-worthy borrowers, typically governments. By contrast, far less infrastructure is required for a bank – or an individual banker – to intermediate between depositors and borrowers.

Banking prerequisites

Although incorporated commercial banking is only about 225 years old, it represents the culmination of centuries, even millennia, of financial and legal developments (Grossman 2010: 28ff.). Among the oldest of these was the evolution of money, both as a medium of exchange and as a unit of account, and of money changing. Other important ancient innovations include bookkeeping and mechanisms for making transfers among customers without the need for the exchange of cash, as well as oral and written contracts. A medieval development that combined elements of written contracts and cashless transfers was the negotiable bill of exchange. The demand for the bills of exchange was bolstered by the advent of medieval trade fairs, where the need for relatively complex credit transactions that spanned both time and geography was great.

An outgrowth of these developments was the ability to create credit, an essential function of commercial banks. Credit creation consists of issuing notes or creating deposits (or other forms of credit) beyond what the issuer has on deposit. Money changing (i.e. exchanging one currency for another), a common activity of early bankers, does not create credit. Similarly, if banks merely provide depositors with safekeeping services, they do not create credit. Finally, if banks take in a quantity of money on deposit which they lend out, they do not create credit, since credit outstanding equals the total amount of deposits held. Put succinctly by Schumpeter (1934: 73), "It is always a question, not of transforming purchasing power which already exists in someone's possession, but of the creation of purchasing power out of nothing …"

London's goldsmith banks, which were active in the mid-seventeenth century, provide a good example of credit-creating banking. Suppose that gold is the only widely accepted money. Although the very wealthy might be able to afford sufficiently thick walls or armed guards to protect their treasure, those of more modest means might be prepared to pay a reputable third party with good security to keep their savings for them. Goldsmiths, since they dealt in large quantities of precious metals, would have had a safe or other means to secure their own gold and would have made ideal depositories. Thus, individuals could store their gold with a goldsmith for safekeeping, and in exchange receive a receipt indicating exactly how much gold was on deposit. Initially, depositors would have had to return to the goldsmith every time they wanted to make a transaction: the goldsmith paid out as much of the depositor's gold as requested and altered the receipt accordingly. With the passage of time, instead of making frequent trips to the goldsmith in order to make withdrawals, receipts were passed from hand to hand and functioned as currency. The receipts retained value since they represented a quantity of gold that could be withdrawn at any time.

Because a substantial portion of receipts remained in circulation, goldsmiths eventually came to realize that they could issue more receipts than they had gold on deposit, and could lend these excess receipts at interest. These loans constituted the beginning of credit creation or, in the words of Schumpeter, created "purchasing power out of nothing." Credit-creating loans (i.e. loans over and beyond the amount of gold reserves held) need not be receipts, but could take the form of deposits, as long as those deposits are somehow spendable, either via written order to a third party or via a transfer on the books of a banker.

Exchange banks, state banks, and private banks

The ability to transfer money without the use of cash was further developed by exchange banks, such as Venice's Banco della Piazza di Rialto and Amsterdam's Wisselbank. These banks, which were established in the sixteenth and seventeenth centuries, were municipally owned and provided a mechanism for local merchants to make and receive payments from each other and from outside sources. Prior to the introduction of exchange banks, many different types of currencies (including clipped or otherwise debased coins) circulated; an important consequence of the exchange banks was to standardize all transactions on a single currency unit.

The exchange banks provided inspiration – and sometimes a model – for the subsequent establishment of state banks.[2] In addition to their roles as the government's banker, state banks were often established in order to bring order to a chaotic monetary situation. The state banks of Austria-Hungary (established 1816), Belgium (1850), Denmark (1818), and Norway (1816) were granted monopolies on the right to issue bank notes upon their establishment or soon thereafter, frequently because a predecessor institution had collapsed because it had over-issued currency. Although originally these institutions had very little in the way of public responsibility beyond stabilizing the monetary situation and lending to the government, during the course of the nineteenth century they evolved into the central banks that we know today, operating as bankers' banks, lenders of last resort, and, sometimes, banking supervisors.

Another important predecessor institution was the private bank. Unlike state banks, which came into existence with a birth certificate in the form of a charter granted by a legislature or sovereign, the establishment of private banks required no special legislation. Instead, these institutions were set up and governed by the terms of their partnership agreements and were bound by no specific laws beyond those that applied to individuals. Because they operated without specific government sanction, they were not usually required to keep especially detailed records or submit reports to government authorities. Thus, our knowledge of specific private banking firms is limited to those firms with surviving records.[3]

Because private banks were unchartered, they were not restricted to specific types of business and hence could engage in a variety of banking and non-banking activities. These included money changing, pawn broking, and, most importantly, providing domestic and international trade credit. Frequently, private banks started out as purely commercial firms and, because of the need to extend credit for trade finance, evolved into institutions where banking functions soon overshadowed non-financial business. In discussing private banking in the Rhineland during the first half of the nineteenth century, Tilly (1966: 47) writes:

> [T]here is great uncertainty as to when a man was a banker and when he was not. Many persons provided banking services – either as a sideline or on a small scale – long before they called themselves bankers ... At the same time, the title "banker" was sometimes given to a businessman whose resources were employed mainly in non-banking lines.

Commercial banking

The first incorporated commercial banks emerged in the late eighteenth and early nineteenth centuries. Early examples include Australia's Bank of New South Wales (established 1817), Belgium's Société Générale (1822), Canada's Bank of Montreal (1820), Denmark's Fyens Discontokasse (1846), Germany's A. Schaaffhausen'scher Bankverein (1848), Norway's Christiana Bank og Kreditkasse (1848), and the U.S.'s Bank of North America (1782). Although commercial banks conducted many of the same operations as private banks, there were important differences.

Private banks were frequently family-run concerns, with resources limited to those of the extended family. Although some of these financial enterprises grew quite large (e.g. the Rothschilds), for the most part they were small by comparison with the commercial banks that would follow. Another constraint on the size of private banks was that they were not able to organize as corporations. Corporations are, in theory, immortal: when shareholders die, their ownership in the ongoing concern can be passed to others or sold; however, the firm itself should be unaffected. The lifespan of a partnership is less certain: the death of a partner may necessitate the liquidation of the firm. The uncertainty over the lifespan of private banks may have presented an obstacle to their growth. Additionally, corporations are likely to grow larger than partnerships because their shares can be more easily bought and sold, allowing them to achieve a more diffuse – and larger – ownership base. The effect on firm size was magnified by the fact that during the course of the nineteenth century limited liability became an option for incorporated banks. Limited-liability shares, which would not subject the shareholder to unlimited calls in case of failure, would have been more marketable to a wider audience than those of an unlimited liability partnership.

From its inception during the late eighteenth and early nineteenth centuries through the Great Depression, commercial banking in the industrialized countries followed a characteristic life-cycle pattern.[4] Although the specifics differ considerably from country to country, the pattern is robust, and consists of an early phase of rapid growth, followed by slower growth and an eventual peak, followed by a more or less rapid decline. Throughout this life cycle, the structure of the banking system is shaped by four key types of events: crises, bailouts, merger movements, and regulatory reforms (Grossman 2010).

The earliest stages of the banking life cycle are characterized by rapid expansion, during which both the number of banks and aggregate banking assets increase. The speed and strength of the initial growth depend positively upon the demand for banking services, derived from the current and expected future financing needs of commerce and industry, and negatively upon the severity of the regulatory constraints placed upon banks and competition from other intermediators. Commercial banking growth may accelerate by taking over the functions of private banks and other pre-existing intermediators (Lindgren 2002). This early growth will be subject to a variety of economic and regulatory shocks, and will not in any sense be smooth or constant.

The upward trend continues until a turning point is reached. The turning points in the number and assets of banks may not occur at the same time in any given country, nor need they take place at the same time in any particular country's economic development. The turning point in numbers usually occurs in close proximity to a banking crisis or a merger movement. Both of these events reduce the numbers of banks; however, crises typically lead to a reduction in aggregate banking assets, while mergers may be accompanied by a continued increase in banking assets.

Crises generate two reactions, both of which can have profound effects on banking structure. In the short run, government or private actors may attempt to rescue some or all of the failed banks. In the slightly longer run, governments may impose more stringent regulations in an attempt to bolster banking stability. Mergers, if they result in a substantial increase in banking concentration, may also encourage regulators to intervene in order to reduce the likelihood of a monopolized banking sector. Government efforts to rein in banks via regulation – whether due to crises or heightened merger activity – will be met with increasingly inventive attempts to circumvent such regulation. These may lead to additional regulations and, in turn, even more ingenious efforts at avoiding such regulation. Kane (1977) aptly refers to these cycles of moves and countermoves as the "regulatory dialectic."

This life-cycle pattern was repeated over and over in the industrialized world from the beginning of the nineteenth century through the Great Depression (Grossman 2010). The first commercial banks in Australia and Canada, for example, were established in 1817. By 1837, the banking populations of Australia and Canada were 11 and 20, respectively. In Australia, the number of banks peaked at 31 in 1890; in Canada, the number peaked at 45 in 1875. By the onset of the Great Depression, Australia had about a dozen banks; Canada had less than half a dozen. The banking populations of Denmark, Finland, Norway, and the United States all exhibited similar patterns, reaching peaks during the period between the end of the First World War and the onset of the Great Depression.

As previously noted, this life cycle is neither regular nor consistent. Although the early phase of banking growth usually accompanied rapid industrialization, in Britain, the first country to experience an industrial revolution, commercial banking growth lagged due to the influence of the Bank of England. The bank had been granted a charter by Parliament in 1694 in return for a substantial loan to the government; subsequent chartering acts prevented the establishment of banks with more than six partners. Thus, for the next century, English banking was the sole preserve of the Bank of England and a large number of small banking partnerships. By 1826, the instability of a banking system composed primarily of small banks, complaints from industry about the inadequate resources of those banks, and the diminishing importance of the Bank of England as a source of government revenue led to a repeal of the monopoly (Broz and Grossman 2004). The Netherlands, an early commercial, if not industrial power, was also slow to develop commercial banking. In the Dutch case, the slowness was due to the existence of a variety of alternative intermediators: *kassiers* (cashkeepers, a sort of financial agent), an active money market, and private merchant houses that provided ample intermediation.

As noted earlier, the life-cycle pattern was by no means smooth or regular and was frequently interrupted. Among the most important – and frequent – interruptions, were banking crises. Banking crises were ubiquitous during the nineteenth and early twentieth centuries: Grossman (2010: 297–313) catalogues more than 60 banking crises among the nations of Western Europe, the United States, Canada, Japan, and Australia during the century following 1825.[5] The majority of these resulted from "boom–bust" economic cycles. Irving Fisher (1932, 1933), one of the first modern economists to take an analytical approach to financial crises, argues that crises result from the cyclical nature of real economic activity.[6] Economic expansion leads to a growth in the number and size of bank loans, as well as to an increase in the relative indebtedness of non-bank firms. As economic expansion proceeds and bankers seek more profitable investments, less worthwhile projects receive funding. Fisher (1932: 43) laments the excessive buildup of debt during cyclical upswings: "If only the (upward) movement would stop at equilibrium!" When the expansion ends, these marginal firms are the first to be unable to meet their debt service obligations. This leads to loan defaults and declines in the prices of outputs and securities. The debt-deflation spiral generates a negative feedback loop: loan defaults lead to bank failures, exacerbating the macroeconomic downturn already underway.

The Great Depression and its aftermath

No matter where banking systems were within their evolutionary life cycle, the Great Depression and the Second World War stopped the process dead in its tracks. The 1930s saw banking crises in Austria, Belgium, France, Germany, Italy, Norway, Switzerland, and the United States, as well as a number of other countries; in many countries, the crisis was of unprecedented severity. Given that banking crises also afflicted many other countries during the early 1920s, it is safe to say that few industrialized countries emerged from the interwar period with their banking systems completely intact. In response to financial devastation and wartime needs, governments enacted strict, often anti-competitive rules and regulations aimed at stabilizing the banking system and directing credit towards favored sectors. These constraints – a sort of financial "lockdown" – combined with low, stable interest rates and robust economic growth, led to the longest period of banking stability the industrialized world has ever known.

In the United States, where state and federal law already prescribed detailed banking regulations, including branching restrictions, capital requirements, and reserve requirements, the Banking (Glass–Steagall) Act of 1933 further curtailed the scope of permitted bank activities by prohibiting commercial and investment banking functions from being carried out by the same institution. The Banking Act also established the Federal Deposit Insurance Corporation (FDIC), which insured commercial bank deposits up to $2,500 (soon doubled to $5,000; today $250,000). This marked the first time that an explicit deposit insurance program had been enacted on a national level anywhere. The American deposit insurance legislation was anti-competitive in that it both limited entry into banking and made entry more discretionary, since federal banking authorities were required to consider capital adequacy, earnings prospects, managerial character, and community need before allowing prospective banks to commence operations with deposit insurance (Spong 2000). The moral hazard consequences of deposit insurance subsequently played a role in generating the savings and loan crisis that emerged during the 1980s.

In countries that had no specific banking law prior to the First World War and enacted banking codes during the interwar period, the change in the regulatory environment was especially dramatic. In Belgium, Depression-era laws not only separated commercial banking from investment banking, but also forbade bankers from taking part in the operation of a non-financial company (Allen et al. 1938). The Belgian law also established capital and reporting requirements and established a banking commission with wide-ranging powers over all deposit-taking institutions, including private banks. The commission was empowered to limit entry into banking, to set interest rates and liquidity ratios, and to establish reporting and auditing requirements. Switzerland also enacted its first-ever banking code during this period, which established detailed capital and liquidity regulations, specified certain rules of corporate governance, and held managers liable for intentional damage to creditors and shareholders. The law also established a banking commission, which was empowered to regulate entry, approve articles of association, certify auditing associations, and set required financial ratios, as well as giving the Swiss National Bank the authority to veto the conditions of certain bank undertakings.

The crisis also led to greater government ownership in – and direct control of – the banking sector. In Germany, virtually all important commercial banks received an infusion of capital from the state in the aftermath of the 1931 banking crisis. It was estimated that in 1932 the state held 50 per cent of the capital of the large commercial banks (Allen et al. 1938). The 1931 crisis in Italy led to substantial government participation in the banking industry through the creation of the Istituto Mobiliari Italiano (IMI) in 1931 and the Istituto Ricostruzione Industriale (IRI) in 1933, which took over the industrial participations, loan portfolios, and, in some cases, the lending operations of distressed Italian banks (Gerbi 1956).

Even in countries where banking systems remained essentially intact, important Depression-era changes in the regulatory environment were enacted. In Canada, the Bank of Canada was established, not because there existed any pressing economic need for a central bank, but because of the government's desire to be *seen* to be doing something in response to the Great Depression (Bordo and Redish 1987). Sweden's banking system also weathered the 1930s without a serious crisis, despite the collapse of the Kreuger industrial empire in 1932, although it enacted legislation in 1933 making it more difficult for banks to own industrial shares. Sweden also established A/B Industrikredit, which, like IMI and IRI in Italy, was to take industrial shares off the hands of banks.

The Second World War led to the introduction of additional legislative and administrative measures to control the uses and cost of bank credit, as governments harnessed the banking industry to finance the war effort. Many of these reforms persisted long after the conflict ended, as did the Depression-era reforms. In February 1942, the Commonwealth Bank of Australia was given powers to set maximum interest rates as a wartime measure. At the war's end, these powers were continued by the Banking Act 1945 and lasted until the 1980s (Parliament of the Commonwealth of Australia 1991). In Germany, interest rates on deposits had been set during the war by the government and the bankers' association; following the war, the job was taken over by West German state governments, which maintained control until interest rate deregulation in 1967 (Irmler 1956). Sweden introduced credit controls at the beginning of the Second World War and interest rate controls at the war's end, both of which remained in force for nearly a half-century (Jonung 1993).

The era of deregulation – and instability – begins

The close of the 1960s marked the beginning of the end of tightly controlled domestic banking and financial markets. Financial liberalization can be traced, at least in part, to the exigencies of inflation-induced high and volatile market interest rates. Inflation contributed to, and was exacerbated by, the demise of the Bretton Woods regime in 1971–3 (Bordo and Eichengreen 1993). Important components of liberalization included the gradual elimination of interest rate controls on bank lending and deposit rates, the growth of market-oriented mechanisms for the allocation of capital, such as the development of money markets and auction techniques for the issue of government debt securities, and the elimination of direct controls on bank lending. Many countries made substantial strides towards liberalizing other aspects of bank regulation as well, including blurring the lines between securities firms, savings banks, commercial banks, and insurance companies, and relaxing rules that restricted branching and foreign entry into domestic banking markets.

Deregulation has been a double-edged sword for commercial banking. On the one hand, it has introduced dynamism into the financial industry that had been lacking since the Great Depression. Depositors are no longer at the mercy of government-imposed interest rate ceilings and banks have been mostly freed of the constraints that forced them to channel the accumulated savings of the economy toward government-favored objectives. Banks and other financial institutions are freer to develop new financial products that better suit the needs of their customers.

This freedom has come at a cost, however. Starting with the 1974 failures of Germany's Bankhaus I.D. Herstatt and the U.S.'s Franklin National Bank, the world banking system, which had been crisis-free since the Second World War, began to experience crises at a rate similar to the pre-First World War era (Bordo *et al.* 2001). Notable episodes have included the U.S. savings and loan crisis during the late 1980s, the Nordic banking crisis during the late 1980s and early 1990s, and Japan's "lost decade" of the 1990s. In each of these cases, the classic boom–bust cycle was aggravated by ill-timed deregulation and/or perverse government incentives, often combined with lax supervision.

The most severe post-Second World War crisis to date has been the sub-prime meltdown, which originated in the United States in 2008, but soon spread worldwide. Many of the same macroeconomic and regulatory forces that contributed to the other modern crises were at work in the run-up to this crisis. Expansionary fiscal and monetary policy, combined with unhelpful government intervention in the mortgage market, and weak regulatory oversight led to excessive leverage that fuelled a speculative boom in U.S. real estate. The boom was exacerbated by the growth – and misuse – of new and complex financial instruments which, thanks to increasing globalization and improvements in communications, facilitated worldwide participation in the boom – and the subsequent bust.

Notes

1 Financial systems provide other services as well: facilitating trade, monitoring managers and exerting corporate control, assisting in the trading, hedging, diversification, and pooling of risk, and allocating resources. See Levine (1997).
2 Johan Palmstruch's original plan for the Swedish Riksbank envisioned it containing two departments, one of which was to be called the *Wexelbank*, a direct translation from the Dutch *Wisselbank*.
3 See, for example, Joslin (1954), Pressnell (1956), and Temin and Voth (2008).
4 A literature on product life cycles posits a similar pattern in competitive industries. See Gort and Klepper (1982).
5 For other catalogues of banking and financial crises, both historical and modern, see Kindleberger (1978), Bordo *et al.* (2001), Lindgren *et al.* (1996), and Caprio and Klingebiel (2003).
6 He was not the first to notice this phenomenon. Writing 150 years ago, Evans (1859 [1969]) argued that the pattern had already been well established during the previous 60 years.

References

Allen, A.M., Cope, S.R., L.J.H. Dark and H.J. Witheridge (1938) *Commercial Banking Legislation and Control*, London: Macmillan and Co.

Bagehot, W. (1873) *Lombard Street*, London: H.S. King.

Bordo, M.D. and Eichengreen, B. (eds) (1993) *A Retrospective on the Bretton Woods System*, Chicago, IL: University of Chicago Press.

Bordo, M., Eichengreen, B., Klingebiel, D. and Martinez-Peria, M.S. (2001) 'Is the crisis problem growing more severe?' *Economic Policy*, 32: 53–82.

Bordo, M.D. and Redish, A. (1987) 'Why did the Bank of Canada emerge in 1935?' *Journal of Economic History*, 47, 2: 405–17.

Broz, J.L. and Grossman, R.S. (2004) 'Paying for privilege: the political economy of Bank of England charters, 1694–1844', *Explorations in Economic History*, 41: 48–72.

Caprio, G. and Klingebiel, D. (2003) 'Episodes of systematic and borderline financial crises', World Bank Working Paper.

Evans, D.M. (1859 [1969]) *The History of the Commercial Crisis, 1857–58, and the Stock Exchange Panic of 1859*, New York: Augustus M. Kelly.

Fisher, I. (1932) *Booms and Depressions: Some First Principles*, New York: Adelphi.

——(1933) 'The debt-deflation theory of great depressions', *Econometrica*, 1: 337–57.

Gerbi, A. (1956) 'Italy', in B.H. Beckhart (ed.) *Banking Systems*, New York: Columbia University Press.

Goldsmith, R.W. (1969) *Financial Structure and Development*, New Haven, CT: Yale University Press.

Gort, M. and Klepper, S. (1982) 'Time paths in the diffusion of product innovations', *Economic Journal*, 92: 630–53.

Grossman, R.S. (2010) *Unsettled Account: The Evolution of Banking in the Industrialized World since 1800*, Princeton, NJ: Princeton University Press.

Gurley, J.G. and Shaw, E.S. (1955) 'Financial aspects of economic development', *American Economic Review*, 45: 515–38.

Hicks, J.R. (1969) *A Theory of Economic History*, Oxford: Clarendon Press.

Irmler, H. (1956) 'Western Germany', in B.H. Beckhart (ed.) *Banking Systems*, New York: Columbia University Press.

Jonung, L. (1993) 'The rise and fall of credit controls: the case of Sweden, 1939–89', in M. Bordo and F. Capie (eds) *Monetary Regimes in Transition*, Cambridge: Cambridge University Press.

Joslin, D.M. (1954) 'London private bankers, 1720–1785', *Economic History Review*, 7: 167–86.

Kane, E.J. (1977) 'Good intentions and unintended evil: the case against selective credit allocation', *Journal of Money, Credit and Banking*, 9: 55–69.

Kindleberger, C.P. (1978) *Manias, Panics, and Crashes: A History of Financial Crises*, New York: Basic Books.

Levine, R. (1997) 'Financial development and economic growth: views and agenda', *Journal of Economic Literature*, 35: 688–726.

——(2005). 'Finance and growth: theory and evidence', in P. Aghion and S.D. Durlauf (eds) *Handbook of Economic Growth, Volume 1, Part 1*, Amsterdam: Elsevier.

Lindgren, C., Garcia, G.G. and Saal, M.I. (1996) *Bank Soundness and Macroeconomic Policy*, Washington: International Monetary Fund.

Lindgren, H. (2002). 'The modernization of Swedish credit markets, 1840–1905: evidence from probate records', *Journal of Economic History*, 62: 810–32.

Lucas, R.E. (1988) 'On the mechanics of economic development', *Journal of Monetary Economics*, 22: 3–42.

McKinnon, R.I. (1973) *Money and Capital in Economic Development*, Washington: Brookings Institution.

Miller, M.H. (1998) 'Financial markets and economic growth', *Journal of Applied Corporate Finance*, 11: 8–15.

Parliament of the Commonwealth of Australia (1991) *A Pocket Full of Change: Banking and Deregulation*, Canberra: Australian Government Publishing Service.

Pressnell, L.S. (1956) *Country Banking in the Industrial Revolution*, Oxford: Clarendon Press.

Rajan, R.G. and Zingales, L. (2003) *Saving Capitalism from the Capitalists: Unleashing the Power of Financial Markets to Create Wealth and Spread Opportunity*, New York: Crown Business.

Robinson, J. (1952) *The Rate of Interest and Other Essays*, London: Macmillan.

Schumpeter, J.A. (1934) *The Theory of Economic Development: An Inquiry into Profits, Capital, Credit, Interest, and the Business Cycle*, Cambridge: Harvard University Press.

Spong, K. (2000) *Banking Regulation*, Kansas City, MO: Federal Reserve Bank of Kansas City.

Temin, P. and Voth, H. (2008) 'Private borrowing during the financial revolution: Hoare's Bank and its customers, 1702–24', *Economic History Review*, 61: 541–64.

Tilly, R.H. (1966) *Financial Institutions and Industrialization in the Rhineland, 1815–1870*, Madison, WI: University of Wisconsin Press.

18

THE ECONOMIC HISTORY OF ENTERTAINMENT AND SPORTS

Michael Haupert

The entertainment industry evokes images of movie stars, exotic performances, regal theaters, and grand stadiums. However, from an economic standpoint, it is not much different from the market for most other goods and services. Entertainment is a normal good subject to the law of demand.

There are some properties of the entertainment industry that don't necessarily apply to other markets. These include uncertain product characteristics, producers who have an unusually high personal attachment to their product (think *art* as opposed to *commerce*), and goods that cannot readily be inventoried.

The quality of entertainment goods is seldom known in advance. What is more, no two are alike, so it is hard to predict exactly what the quality will be the next time they are produced. As a result, consumers rely on signals for quality indicators in entertainment more often than in other industries. In the movie industry, for example, the quality of a movie cannot be determined until it has been seen. In order to try to avoid buying tickets to bad movies, consumers rely on the opinion of critics and word-of-mouth reviews to give them an indication of quality. Bakker (2003a) looks at this unique market for films and finds evidence that product differentiation was important to the success of film companies. He also (2003b) finds that film companies became increasingly sophisticated in their methods of trying to obtain knowledge about consumer preferences over time. These changes were caused by the rise in fixed costs as well as technological and contractual changes. The increasing need for quick information led to the use of new market research techniques such as Gallup audience research.

Knowing what made one movie or recording popular usually adds nothing to the predictive ability of what makes the next one popular. No entertainer is a guaranteed hit every time, and no genre of film has proven to be eternally popular. Without really knowing what factors influence the quality of the final product, producers are at an extreme disadvantage, and the final result is the volatile entertainment industry we have today.

Live performances, such as plays, concerts, vaudeville, and sports, all share certain characteristics. In particular, they cannot be inventoried. The consumption of their product takes place at the same time as its final production, and customers must come to it, because it cannot be shipped to them or an intermediary for resale. Over time, technology has blurred these lines of distinction, since a live performance can be recorded and sold like any other commodity. However, while a taped version of a concert or play is a substitute for the live performance, the degree of substitution is highly variable. Listening to a high-quality digital recording of a concert may, for example, be a closer substitute for the concert than would be a similarly high-quality video recording of last night's championship football game. The high prices commanded for some live concerts and sporting events suggest the demand for them is highly inelastic.

Economic studies of the leisure industry in general are not common, but do exist. Cole and Lubin (1964) were among the first to consider the industry. Maoz (2010) attributes differences in the valuation of leisure in the U.S. and Europe during the twentieth century to differences in labor hours. He notes that U.S. annual hours per worker declined in general over the time period, but not always at the same rate as in Europe. Holler and Klose-Ullmann (2010) examine the effects of conspicuous consumption on the growth of the American art market between 1870 and the Second World War. Hunnicutt (1980) examines the political, economic, and intellectual events surrounding the increase in leisure time during the first four decades of the twentieth century, how its use changed and how it was viewed by society.

The demand for entertainment

Americans saw a fourfold increase in their real income over the twentieth century. The average manufacturing worker saw his real wage rise by a factor of five. And the percentage of personal consumption expenditures by Americans devoted to recreation and entertainment tripled from 3 per cent at the end of the nineteenth century to 9 per cent by the beginning of the twenty-first century. These patterns were common across developed countries, contributing to a worldwide increase in the demand for entertainment.

The decrease in the length of the workweek also contributed to an increase in the consumption of entertainment. The average workweek decreased by one-third over the century from 59 hours to 39 hours. Additional time for leisure has also been made available by technology, which had an impact on wages through its increase in labor productivity, and led to the reduction of the amount of time needed for household chores such as laundry, cleaning, and cooking. Numerous scholars have studied the evolution of wages and labor hours in the American economy, including Costa (2000), Garrett (2009), Higgs (2009), Whaples (1990), and Vandenbroucke (2009), who looked specifically at the impact of the length of the workweek on the consumption of recreation. He attributes the decrease in the length of the U.S. workweek in the first half of the twentieth century to technological progress, which increased wages and decreased the cost of recreation, making it possible for the average worker to afford more leisure time.

In addition to the higher incomes and lower work hours brought about by urbanization, the cost of pursuing entertainment is also lower for city dwellers because of the closer proximity of venues such as theaters and stadiums. There is also a greater supply of entertainment opportunities in the city. Population density leads to economies of scale in entertainment; thus, urban dwellers have access to more entertainment options, and it doesn't cost them as much to purchase them.

One specific technology that has had an impact on the entertainment industry has been the automobile. It created a more mobile society, increasing the scope of possible entertainment venues and lowering the cost of reaching them. Shaw (1986) looks at the complementary goods of transportation and entertainment by examining the ownership of amusement parks by street railways during the latter part of the nineteenth century. Economies of scale in the generation of electricity as street railways converted from horse power to electric power required efficient use of the capital plant, which involved running as many loaded cars as possible over the tracks. Railway interest in amusement parks arose from a desire to encourage use during non-peak hours. Clevinger and Vozikis (2007) look at the role of transportation on the spread of entertainment, finding the railroad to be a significant determinant of the growth of the American theater.

Technology also created more and newer ways to enjoy this newfound leisure time. The first big innovation of the century was recorded sound, followed closely by the motion picture industry and radio. These latter two industries ruled until the 1950s, when television exploded upon a postwar America ready to spend money and anxious to escape the drudgery of the Great Depression and the war years. Not until the personal computer became a household fixture at the end of the century would anything come along to rival television for the leisure time of Americans.

It is not merely technology that explains the emergence of new media, however. Stoeber (2004) combines Schumpeter's distinction between invention and innovation with evolution theory to argue that the emergence of new forms of media are not merely the consequence of new technology, but also "social institutionalizing," whereby the new technology takes on new possibilities and is adapted in new ways by society. The technology that provided text messaging, for example, begat a whole new way of communicating and social-networking possibilities.

Bowden and Offer (1994) provide an interesting view on technology and the use of time in the household. They look at the falling cost of electronic entertainment media and their role in the household budget, and conclude that electric appliances didn't shorten housework hours until television viewing expanded in the allocation of household time to the point where its marginal utility fell to that of housework. Chandler (2006) uses the example of the rise and fall of RCA in a broad, sweeping look at how high-technology industries transformed work and life.

The supply of entertainment

Technology also changed the supply of entertainment, progressing from live theater to the movies for public consumption and adding home entertainment in the form of recorded music, radio, television, and ultimately the Internet. The American entertainment industry responded to the demands of the public and adapted the latest technologies in an effort to capitalize on the growing demand for entertainment services.

The fact that the costs of producing entertainment are almost all borne before the product can be marketed means that the entire investment must be made before the producers know if it will be a success. These sunk costs cannot be recovered if the show is a bomb.

The skills of those producing entertainment goods are highly variable, and in many cases are not identifiable before hiring. For example, not all athletes are the same quality. In fact, there is a huge discrepancy in talent (defined here only as ability to generate revenue, usually through ticket sales). This leads to a market with high salaries for the few who are most easily identifiable as high-quality workers (i.e. superstars). This leads to a division of the marketplace into "superstar" and "secondary" employees. The difference is not in the known outcome of the quality of their product, but rather the likelihood of the quality being high. A superstar actor is more likely to produce a high-quality acting job (and high box-office revenues) than is a "secondary" actor. This "superstar effect" is explored by Berri *et al.* (2004, 2006) in the sports industry and by Frey (1988) who applies the theory to museums.

Vaudeville

Before technology made entertainment a packaged and stored commodity, live entertainment ruled the industry. This took the form of staged shows, such as symphony, theater, and vaudeville, and spectator sports. The former were attended primarily by the well educated and upper class. The latter were attended primarily by men. Only vaudeville appealed to the mass audience.

Vaudeville flourished in America for the first two decades of the twentieth century and spawned many of the actors who went on to propel the movie and television industries to their current dominant positions in the entertainment industry. Like theater and opera, vaudeville was performed live. Unlike theater and opera, however, it was neither as formal nor as exclusive. Vaudeville also contained elements of the circus and appealed to a much broader customer base than did the theater, opera, or symphony.

A typical vaudeville show lasted about two hours and featured as many as ten different acts, ranging from singers and comedians to acrobats and animal acts with the occasional appearance of the famous and bizarre. Prices were low compared with more formal stage shows, and the acts traveled from city to city, usually on a weekly basis. Thus, the local theater provided great variety, and the vaudeville acts performed before a wide range of audiences.

Vaudeville reached its peak in the early 1920s, about a decade before the entire industry collapsed under the weight of the Great Depression and competition from talking pictures. At the time, there were over 15,000 theaters in towns of every size, making it the most popular form of mass entertainment in America. It was easily accessible, affordable, and appropriate for the whole family. The bill changed on a weekly basis and the most famous names eventually landed in even the smallest of theaters, adding a sense of commonality to it all.

Vaudeville was a victim of the radio and movies on both the demand and the supply side of the equation. The demand for vaudeville shows fell off as demand for the movies increased and radios came down in price. In addition, talent was drained. Performers preferred the higher paychecks and reduced travel schedule offered by national radio networks and Hollywood. Finally, venues disappeared as theaters were converted from vaudeville shows to the more profitable motion pictures.

Vestiges of vaudeville live on in Las Vegas, though only in spirit. The Vegas entertainment scene offers the variety that vaudeville once did, but each act is a separate ticket purchase. Gragg (2010) addresses the evolution of the Las Vegas entertainment scene in his research on the growing use of nudity during the 1950s as a means of attracting customers during a period of overexpansion of hotels.

Variety shows still exist, but in a different format – the Internet. While vaudeville is dead and television thrives on reality shows, sitcoms, and dramas, the Internet is perhaps the ultimate example of the variety show. With the click of a mouse one can move from sports to music to whatever else is desired. The improvements in computer technology over the past decade have made video and audio streaming commonplace, making the computer a sophisticated and powerful entertainment medium.

Little attention has been paid to the economics of vaudeville. General histories of the industry have been written by Gilbert (1940), DiMeglio (1973), and Erdman (2004). A more general look at theater, especially in its earliest years, is covered by Milford (1999), who looks at the puritanical influence on early American theater. Sullivan and Pry (1991) use the eighteenth-century London theater market to study the capture theory of regulation. They find that the Licensing Act of 1737 restricted competition and successfully maintained the interest of three London theater companies.

Recorded sound

The basic scientific principle of converting sound into an electrical current has evolved into a massive entertainment industry that has advanced on two major fronts since 1900: art and technology. On the artistic front, the styles of popular music have changed and diversified from classical to jazz to rock and its many variations. The technological innovations in the recorded sound industry have been no less dramatic.

Despite changes in the types of music preferred by the listening public and the different means of delivering music, the industry looks remarkably like it did a century ago. The main issues are still the same. Manufacturers seek to push the envelope and deliver the highest-quality sound possible. Performers still strive to express themselves through their art. Producers compete for the opportunity to promote and distribute the best-selling stars, and consumers clamor for the best equipment to listen to the best music. Despite all the advances in technology, or perhaps because of them, the same problem besets all the players in the industry: how to control the rights to the final product. The dawning of the computer age in the recorded sound industry has only complicated this problem. Property rights issues in the recorded sound industry were first discussed by Coase (1966). Kruse (2002) takes a narrower view in her study of the evolution of property rights in the radio broadcasting spectrum.

Radio changed America in the twentieth century the way the computer has revolutionized it today. It brought immediacy to the news that had heretofore not existed. The telegraph wire reduced the time it took for news to travel from point to point, but it still had to be gathered by newspapers and converted to print before being distributed to the general public. Radio brought the news directly into the homes of listeners, who could sit by their radios and hear it happen live.

Fones-Wolf (1999) looks at the use of radio by corporate America during the period 1930 to 1950. Beginning in the 1930s, corporate America increased its use of radio for public relations campaigns aimed at improving their image. She concludes that radio was the most influential medium by which they could reach the public, which succeeded in helping business improve its status in American society. On the other hand, Lewis (1992) focuses on the social impact of radio during this same period of time. He describes the early radio broadcasting as a mix of culture, education, information, and entertainment and looks at the role of radio on American culture in the decades between the wars.

The advantage of wireless communication was the ability to bypass wires. The drawback was that it was not completely private, because anyone with a receiver tuned in to the specific frequency of the transmission could receive it, thus resulting in a classic public good problem. The inventions of Lee de Forest, Howard Armstrong, and others exploited this drawback and created the concept of "broadcasting" a signal to as wide an audience as possible. Walter Gifford, President of AT&T, solved the free-rider problem.

Under the leadership of Gifford, AT&T, in an effort to establish a foothold in the broadcasting business, established a high-watt radio station, WEAF in New York, and then used their telephone model to finance it. Telephone users paid for the time they used the wire, and AT&T applied the same model for use of the radio waves. AT&T set up their station and invited any and all to come and rent airtime, to say what they wanted during a broadcast that would reach hundreds of thousands of potential listeners. Customers flocked to the idea called "toll broadcasting." In order to fill the empty time between paid broadcasts (i.e. commercials), Gifford hired people to sing, play piano, lecture, and otherwise entertain. The model for radio, and eventually television broadcasting, was set: scheduled interruptions of paid advertisements.

The movie industry

The movie industry has been a popular subject of research for economists. Only the sports sector of the entertainment industry has received more attention. One of the earliest overviews of the economics of the movie industry was provided by Strick (1978). He noted at the time that little economic analysis was actually applied to the movie industry. This is no longer true. There have been numerous studies of the industry ranging from silent film-era labor markets (Kraft

1994; Ross 1991) to attempts to model the demand for movies (Hand 2002; De Vany and Wallis 1999).

At the dawn of the twentieth century, the movie industry was dominated not by movie stars, directors, and producers, but by inventors and business moguls. The kinetoscope, the fore-runner of the movie projector, debuted in the late nineteenth century and by the beginning of the twentieth century its commercialization was rapidly spreading. Businessmen, particularly the inventors themselves, moved to monopolize the potential profits of the kinetoscope by tying up the technology necessary for making and displaying the pictures. DeGraaf (1995) looks at the difference between innovation and marketing. He focuses on the failure of Thomas Edison to successfully market his phonograph, concluding that his strategies were ill-suited to the emerging mass consumer market.

The legal battles involving patents came to a head in 1908 with the organization of the Motion Picture Patents Corporation (MPPC). It was formed through a horizontal merger of 10 major companies that held most of the important industry patents. In 1910, a vertical merger combined the production and distribution levels of the industry. The MPPC purchased 68 distribution companies and merged them into one company, called the General Film Company (GFC). This created a virtual monopoly in the production and distribution sectors of the industry. The exhibition level of the industry was still competitive, with more than 10,000 theaters in operation. The exhibitors competed against each other, and this situation was exploited by the GFC. The theaters were forced into exclusive dealings with the GFC out of fear of being blackballed if they were caught showing films from one of the few remaining independent distributors. The exhibitors were kept in line by paying license fees to the GFC for the right to exhibit their films. This was a valuable right, since the GFC controlled so much of the traffic in new films, which were the lifeblood of a theater in the major markets. Without access to the newest films, an exhibitor would be unable to compete. Cassady (1959) analyzes the distribution monopoly in the early twentieth century.

The film trust composed of the MPPC and GFC, however, did not last long. Ultimately, the independent producers and distributors were able to make a large enough crack in the armor of the trust to bring it down entirely. Their failure to anticipate market changes ultimately led to their demise. Allen (1971) provides a nice overview of the history of the MPPC.

Independent producers were historically kept in line by the difficulty they had in finding distributors for their films, and ultimately exhibitors, given the threat of blackballing by the trust. Their rise coincided with important changes in the industry. Primary among those changes was the evolution of the movie-star system, the use of famous actors to market a film, and the metamorphosis of the industry from a novelty, showing generic motion pictures, to one telling stories. In addition to their market failure, the trust was attacked in the courts. The MPPC was found to be in violation of the Sherman and Clayton antitrust acts in 1915.

Until the end of the first decade of the twentieth century, actors in films were primarily anonymous characters. This anonymity served to keep actor salaries down, because it dampened the audience demand for any particular actor, making actors nearly perfect substitutes for one another. As moving pictures morphed into stories with plots and characters, individual actors began to emerge as public favorites. As film companies began publicizing their stars for marketing gains, they increased their own profits and the bargaining power of their stars. This star-driven market survived until the late 1920s, when it gave way to what is known as the "studio system."

Bakker (2001) shows that the high fixed costs and relatively short market window for films led producers to invest in name brand value, much as other consumer goods industries did. They built audience loyalty around stars and stories in order to lower the cost of delivering information about film quality to potential consumers.

By 1930, vertical integration had returned to the industry, which was dominated by eight studios. They owned theaters, distribution networks, and studios that employed the talent for making the movies. The movie industry oligopoly was made possible by a number of factors, among them the economies of scale resulting from technological changes in the industry, the shift in the balance of power from actors back to studio executives as a result of sound, and the economic hardships of the Great Depression.

The five largest studios each produced 40 to 60 movies per year, about half the industry total, but accounting for 75 per cent of the first-run product. Even though they owned less than 15 per cent of the theaters, their films accounted for 70 per cent of the total box office. The theaters they did own were concentrated in major urban areas, constituting the bulk of the first-run market.

Most of these pictures were what was known in the industry as B films. They were low-cost films, typically rented for flat fees, and serving as second features or fillers between releases of major pictures. Part of their low cost was due to the way in which actors were employed. During the studio system, actors were under contract to a studio for a fixed time period (often extended by the studio due to a system of renewing options, much the same way the professional sports industry tied up talent). The actors were essentially fixed costs to the studios.

The role of the B picture for the studios was to fill their theaters between first-run films, provide a second feature to enhance demand, and basically cover the fixed costs of the theater. They didn't make much money, but, because they sold for flat fees instead of a share of the box office, as the first-run films did, their revenues were predictable. There was a guaranteed market for B films on two fronts. First, studios owned theaters; thus, they could show any of their films, and they did so, keeping the theaters filled in between major hits. Second, studios that did not own theaters sold these low-budget pictures in a package deal with their blockbusters. This made for a guaranteed audience. Independent theaters were subject to these negotiating tactics and had little choice, since they did not have a guaranteed source of films. In order to keep movies in their theaters, they had to book what the studios offered. Kenney and Klein (1983, 2000) and Hanssen (2000) focus on the impact of this "block booking" practice.

The pricing scheme in the movie industry has long been based on revenue sharing. The distributor provides films to the exhibitor in return for a percentage of the box office. Hanssen (2002) finds this change was concomitant with the arrival of sound. The new technology altered the incentive structure of movie-theater owners, significantly reducing the scope for shirking on their part, thus lowering the cost of dividing attendance revenue. The distributor, being in the stronger oligopoly position, was able to pass risk on to the theaters. They got a percentage of the box office, good if the movie was a hit, but negotiated a floor fee payment, protecting them in case it was a bomb. In other work, Hanssen (2010) finds that the vertical integration of studios promoted efficiency in the industry because they were more likely to alter the run lengths of new releases after the initial run contract was written. This promoted efficiency since the demand for a given film is not known until after it begins to play in the cinema.

Gomery (1980, 1996) provides a historical overview of the studio system. Pokorny and Sedgwick have conducted numerous studies of the film industry during the studio-system era, taking a close look at profitability and the star system at Warner Brothers (2001); product differentiation (Sedgwick 2002); risk management, consumer behavior (Sedgwick and Pokorny 1998, 2010); and a comparative look at the U.S. and UK (Sedgwick and Pokorny 2005).

Bakker (2005) and Miksell (2006, 2009) also look toward the UK for clues to the American domination of the industry during the silent-film era. Bakker determines that the escalation of fixed costs during the rapid phase of U.S. movie industry growth resulted in American domination of international film production and distribution. Miksell attributes Hollywood's domination to its ability to tailor its films to the UK market, something the UK studios were ineffective at doing for the U.S. market.

The rise of television spelled the end for the double feature and the B movie – and along with it a host of production companies that survived on the B movie. The mid-1950s also saw the return of antitrust activity, forcing diversification of the major studios and dissolving the near-perpetual contract arrangements they had with the stars. As the era of "free agency" in talent returned, the B picture was priced out of the market. Finally, with so many entertainment options opening up in the postwar boom, consumers began to demand quality instead of mere quantity for their dollar. The cost of supplying B pictures increased, their demand waned, and a chapter of American movie history drew to a close. Gil (2010) looks at the change in production patterns by studios after the forced vertical disintegration of the industry.

By the 1970s, the industry had evolved into its present-day form, with the major studios operating essentially as bankers and distributors. They provide the financing to independent producers in return for the rights to distribute their pictures. Some own production stages that they lease or use primarily for television production. While they don't control the industry from top to bottom as they once did, the distributors are still the least competitive sector of the industry.

Television

The arrival of television was at first thought to be the death knell for the movie industry. Television was considered a cheaper and more convenient substitute. Ultimately, it evolved into a complement to the movie industry. Network and cable television have become havens for recycled older movies, and pay-per-view and movie rentals have become alternate outlets for movies just off the theater circuit. While there is a segment of the market for which television and the theater are close substitutes, there are many people who are not willing to wait for a movie to appear on the rental market or cable television.

Because of its fear of being replaced, the movie industry withheld its films from television until 1955. That year, RKO got out of the movie production business and sold its assets to General Teleradio. This marked the first time a major studio's film library was owned by a broadcaster. Studios that retained their film libraries, such as MGM and Columbia, set up separate departments to handle the leasing of their old films to television.

The licensing of films to television was the first step in an increasingly cooperative relationship between Hollywood and TV. The next step was the production of original programming for TV. As technology made the taping of shows for rebroadcast economically feasible, live television gave way to the taped broadcast. Hollywood studios began to produce filmed product for broadcast on television. Much of this market was filled by independent producers who leased studio space from the major film companies for the purpose of creating television programs.

The rise of the video and pay cable industry and the changing attitude of the major networks have altered the role of networks toward films. They no longer spend as much money buying theatrical releases for broadcast on network TV. In fact, that segment of the market has been in decline since the 1970s. By 1974, the networks began to spend more money to produce original, made-for-television movies than they did for rights to theatrical films. Now the four major networks finance the production of more original movies each year than all the studios combined. Despite this large number of films, the impact on the movie industry is negligible. The only sources of release for these films are domestic and foreign television, the least profitable of the venues for feature films. So, while they dominate the industry in sheer quantity, their quality does not rival that of feature films and their financial impact is minimal.

Spectator sports

Big-time sports leagues have all evolved in a monopoly framework, seeking to control the competition, the consumer base, and the labor pool, to varying degrees of success. In team sports, the owners formed cartels. Organizers of individual sports, like tennis and golf, attempted to control the tournaments, while boxing was dominated in the 1940s by promoters (some affiliated with the mob), who controlled the television rights and the heavyweight championship fights. Without fail, the most financially successful sports leagues have been cartels that grew and thrived on the back of exploited labor and monopolized geographic areas for teams. Competing leagues arose to cash in on the monopoly profits of the National Football League (NFL), National Hockey League (NHL), National Basketball Association (NBA), and Major League Baseball (MLB), but in every case they were either bankrupted or merged into the established league. As a result, despite a century of monopoly profits, each of these leagues still enjoys monopoly status. Professional sports leagues in the UK developed differently from those in America. Cain and Haddock (2005) compare and contrast the evolution of American baseball and British football leagues.

Baker *et al.* (2004) argue that stock ownership of clubs won out over player cooperative forms of ownership of baseball teams in the late nineteenth century because the team production problem resulted in players of unknown ability migrating to teams in co-op leagues. Based on this argument, the authors suggest that co-ops functioned as an early minor league system in which untried players could seek to prove themselves and eventually move up to wage teams. Empirical analysis of data on player performance and experience in early professional baseball provides support for this theory.

Off the field, teams have cooperated for many years in their efforts to control the market for their sport in order to maximize profits. These efforts have taken place in two primary ways: monopolization of the franchises and monopsonization of the labor markets. The franchises have established local monopolies to minimize competition among themselves. At the same time, professional sports leagues originally used a form of labor contract that restricted the ability of players to move to other teams and thus held down their wages. This combination of restrictions allowed teams to maximize their profits by increasing ticket revenue and lowering player salaries (the largest source of expenses for a professional sports team). The owners justified monopsony control on the basis of competitive balance. Rottenberg (1956) cast doubt on this claim, presaging Coase with his argument that the best ballplayers would end up on the teams in the biggest markets regardless of contract status. Hylan *et al.* (1996) and Surdam (2006) each use the Coase Theorem in case studies of professional baseball labor markets. Subsequent studies of sports labor markets have focused on measuring the degree of exploitation due to monopsony markets (Scully 1974a; Zimbalist 1992; Haupert 2009b), discrimination (Lanning 2010; Haupert 2009a; Kahn 1991, 1992, 2006; Kahn and Sherer 1988; Scully 1974b; Lavoie 2000; Krashinsky and Krashinsky 1997), labor relations (Lowenfish 1980; Zimbalist 2003; Abrams 2003), the determinants of salaries (Jones and Walsh 1988; Scully 2002; Haupert and Murray 2012), the Superstar effect (Rosen 1981; Hausman and Leonard 1997; Berri *et al.* 2004, 2006) and general sports labor markets (Fort 2005; Daly and Moore 1981; Kahn 2000; Rosen and Sanderson 2001).

Monopoly control of franchises is the backbone of any sports league. Sports leagues serve to control schedules and maintain the quality of play on the field. But even more importantly, they serve to maximize profits for the teams. This is done in a number of ways, beginning with attempts to corner the market on playing talent, desirable markets, and television income. Leagues do this by signing the best available players, and then tying up the next tier of talent at minor-league levels. This prepares them for the major leagues as well as keeping them away from potential competitor leagues.

Leagues also attempt to control the best markets. They locate teams in the largest markets in an effort to make it more difficult for a competitor league to start up. At the same time, leagues limit the number of franchises to fewer than the market will bear. This insures that they can exploit monopoly profits by limiting the output of their product. This is most obvious in the use of relocation of franchises as a threat to get government benefits such as tax breaks and new stadiums. Hardy (1997) provides an overview of the organization of the sports market and Gendzel (1995) provides a specific example of this sort of behavior in his look at the relocation of the MLB Braves from Milwaukee to Atlanta.

The organizational structure of professional sports was fortified by the U.S. Supreme Court when the shunned owner of the Baltimore club of the Federal League, a failed competitor to MLB in 1914 and 1915, sued MLB for violation of antitrust law. *Federal Baseball Club of Baltimore v. the National League* eventually reached the Supreme Court, where in 1922 the famous decision that baseball was not interstate commerce, and therefore was exempt from antitrust laws, was rendered. Baseball alone enjoys this exemption, but the basic league structure is the same for all team sports. Johnson (1979) and Abrams (1998, 2010) provide overviews of the relationship between Congress and professional sports.

The popularity of sports, the quality of competition at the highest level, the vast amounts of television and sponsorship dollars, and the monopoly status of leagues have generated revenues sufficient to guarantee large paychecks for athletes and profits for owners. The last few decades in American sports, however, have been marred by labor unrest between athletes and owners. This fighting has centered around the method of splitting the revenues, and has led to work stoppages in all four major team sports.

Surdam (2007) looks at the NFL revenue sharing in the 1950s and compares it with MLB. He finds that owners were willing to enact regressive aspects in their revenue-sharing plans, possibly to forestall moral hazard possibilities arising from automatically helping teams that remain poor draws or fail to improve.

Labor markets for players have evolved similarly across leagues and national boundaries. In team sports, the original labor pool was exploited because the league, as a monopoly, was the only employer. The standard player contract in professional sports leagues had a form of reserve clause, which the leagues instituted under the guise that it was required to keep teams balanced, games competitive, and the league viable. In the name of preservation, the team owners exercised tight control over athletes, exploiting their labor for monopoly profits. Players were signed to contracts that bound them to the signing team indefinitely. The team had the right to renew the player's contract each year, restricting the player's ability to bargain, thus depressing wages. This right was known as the "reserve clause."

Players began to level the playing field in the 1970s through legal victories and the growing strength of their unions. In all leagues, players eventually won the right to bargain freely with other teams, commonly referred to as "free agency," thus dramatically increasing their wages. While still controlled by the team early in their career, player wages (even for rookies) have climbed, in large part due to collective bargaining and the influx of television revenues.

The right to bargain with other teams for their services changed the landscape of the industry dramatically. No longer are players shackled to one team forever, subject to the whims of the owner for their salary and status. Now they are free to bargain with any team. The average salary of a professional athlete in the four major team sports skyrocketed from $45,000 in 1975 ($182,000 in 2010 dollars) to more than $3 million by 2010. The dramatic increase in television revenue caused by America's insatiable appetite for sports has contributed to this salary increase. The result is a much larger revenue pie to divide, with the players getting a larger piece of that pie.

The financial success of sports is due to its exposure on television. The most successful professional team sports in the world, soccer, American football, and baseball, generate more money from television rights fees than they do from live attendance. Golf and tennis owe their large purses to the growth of television fees in the last two decades. The less successful professional sports, such as hockey and basketball, have improved their status greatly with television packages, but are still not on the same par as the aforementioned sports.

Municipalities have come to view sports teams as an important and desired element in their economy, so they have used their powers of eminent domain, bond-issuing capacity, and taxation to secure sufficient land for stadiums and parking in the inner city, and to construct grand new cathedrals dedicated to sports in an effort to lure expansion franchises and teams looking to relocate. This is usually done in the name of urban renewal and economic development. Several economic studies of the value of sports facilities and teams to local economies have been conducted, including Baade and Sanderson (1997); Coates and Humphreys (1999); Johnson *et al.* (2001); Long (2005); Noll and Zimbalist (1997); and Siegfried and Zimbalist (2000).

Fans like to see their teams succeed, though evidence also suggests that, if they succeed too much for too long, interest may be lost (Knowles *et al.* 1992). The bottom line is that fans like to be entertained. When they are no longer entertained they will take their money elsewhere. In this regard, sports are no different from any other type of entertainment. Numerous economists have looked at the demand for baseball including Whitney (1988) who focuses on championships as a factor in demand; Schofield (1983) who looks at performance; and Schmidt and Berri (2006) and Ahn and Lee (2003) who develop a life-cycle demand model for MLB. Surdam (2009a, 2009b) looks at the financial records of the New York Yankees and Philadelphia Phillies during the 1930s in order to form his hypothesis about what determines the demand for baseball.

Conclusion

Increasing wealth and innovations in technology led Americans to pursue a variety of different means of entertainment. Still, there are only 24 hours in a day, so inevitably one new means of leisure-time pursuit comes at the expense of another. Radio and phonographs substituted for live music performances, talking films replaced silent films, and television encroached on the movies. Vaudeville could not compete with the movies and Broadway suffered with the rise of movie musicals in the 1930s. The automobile led to an increase in "going out" for entertainment, which in itself did not help the radio and phonograph industry. It was, however, a boon for ballparks and drive-in theaters. Americans have increased their demand for entertainment, but their tastes for specific types of entertainment are constantly evolving. The result is an industry that is monopolistically competitive.

Technology has blurred the distinction between entertainment media and caused upheavals in the industry along the way. Movie and television are good examples. The latter is an extension of the technology that created the former. When television first debuted, it was viewed as the eventual successor to the movie theater. Although it came after the movie industry, it is now difficult to tell the difference between the two industries. They share studio space and producers. Actors and directors frequently cross from one medium to the other in an industry that is composed of a shrinking number of companies that produce both television shows and movies. With the growing availability of cable movie channels, on-demand viewing capabilities, and the improvements in technology, the difference between watching a movie in a theater and at home is rapidly diminishing.

The same story can be told about the symbiotic relationships that have developed between radio, television, recorded music, and the movies. Indeed, at one time each of these industries saw one or more of the others as a potential threat to its existence, and instead they have grown to be close complements to one another.

Spectator sports, while initially wary of the growth of radio and television, learned to embrace them and evolve along with them. While technology is not necessary for the production of a sporting event, nor is it needed for it to be consumed, they are closely allied. Over time, spectator sports learned to see technology not as a substitute for ticket sales, but a complementary source of revenue.

Not only has technology revolutionized the quality of the entertainment industry, it has led to substantial price decreases as well. Television sets, radios, and music players are all cheaper today in real dollars than when they debuted. In addition, the quality has made quantum leaps. Nobody would argue that the first record players can compete with today's iPod, and certainly the radios of the 1920s and televisions of the 1950s are no match for today's sets.

The next chapter in the evolution of the entertainment industry is still being written. How the Internet, social media, and wireless reception impact the consumption and production of entertainment remains to be seen. And the property rights issues involved with the ability to share, transfer, and download video and audio files have yet to be clarified. While it is certain that the entertainment industry will survive, its exact nature is yet to be determined.

References

Abrams, R. (1998) *Legal Bases: Baseball and the Law*, Philadelphia, PA: Temple University Press.

——(2003) 'The public regulation of baseball labor relations and the public interest', *Journal of Sports Economics*, 4: 292–301.

——(2010) *Sports Justice: The Law and the Business of Sports*, Lebanon, NH: University Press of New England.

Ahn, C.C. and Lee, Y.H. (2003) 'Life-cycle demand for Major League Baseball', paper presented at the Western Economics Association International Conference, Denver, CO.

Allen, J.T. (1971) 'The decay of the Motion Picture Patents Company', *Cinema Journal*, 10: 34–40.

Baade, R. and Sanderson, A. (1997) 'The employment effect of teams and sports facilities,' in R.G. Noll and A. Zimbalist (eds) *Sports, Jobs and Taxes: The Economic Impact of Professional Sports Teams and Stadiums*, Washington: Brookings Institution.

Baker, M., Miceli, T.J. and Ryczek, W.J. (2004) 'The old ball game: organization of 19th-century professional baseball clubs', *Journal of Sports Economics*, 5: 277–91.

Bakker, G. (2001) 'Stars and stories: how films became branded products', *Enterprise and Society*, 2: 461–502.

——(2003a) 'Entertainment industrialized: the emergence of the international film industry, 1890–1940', *Enterprise and Society*, 4: 579–85.

——(2003b) 'Building knowledge about the consumer: the emergence of market research in the motion picture industry', *Business History*, 45: 101–27.

——(2005) 'The decline and fall of the European film industry: sunk costs, market size, and market structure, 1890–1927', *Economic History Review*, 58: 310–51.

Berri, D.J. and Schmidt, M.B. (2006) 'On the road with the National Basketball Association's superstar externality', *Journal of Sports Economics*, 7: 347–58.

Berri, D.J., Schmidt, M.B. and Brook, S.L. (2004) 'Stars at the gate: the impact of star power on NBA gate revenues', *Journal of Sports Economics*, 5: 33–50.

Bowden, S. and Offer, A. (1994) 'Household appliances and the use of time: the United States and Britain since the 1920's, *Economic History Review*, 47: 725–48.

Cain, L.P. and Haddock, D.D. (2005) 'Similar economic histories, different industrial structures: transat-lantic contrasts in the evolution of professional sports leagues', *Journal of Economic History*, 65: 1116–47.

Cassady, R. (1959) 'Monopoly in motion picture distribution, 1908–15', *Southern California Law Review*, 32: 325–90.

Chandler, A. (2006) 'How high technology industries transformed work and life worldwide from the 1880s to the 1990s', *Capitalism and Society*, 1: 1–55.

Clevinger, D.L. and Vozikis, G.S. (2007) 'A historical review of early entrepreneurial theatrical activity in a growing railroad center', *International Entrepreneurship and Management Journal*, 3: 159–69.

Coase, R. (1966) 'The economics of broadcasting and government policy', *American Economic Review*, 56: 440–7.

Coates, D. and Humphreys, B. (1999) 'The growth effects of sport franchises, stadia, and arenas', *Journal of Policy Analysis and Management*, 18: 601–24.

Cole, A.H. and Lubin, D. (1964) 'Perspectives on leisure-time business', *Explorations in Entrepreneurial History*, 1: 1–38.

Costa, D. (2000) 'The wage and the length of the work day: from the 1890s to 1991', *Journal of Labor Economics*, 18: 156–81.

Daly, G. and Moore, W.J. (1981) 'Externalities, property rights and the allocation of resources in Major League Baseball', *Economic Inquiry*, 19: 77–95.

DeGraaf, L. (1995) 'Confronting the mass market: Thomas Edison and the entertainment phonograph', *Business and Economic History*, 24: 88–96.

De Vany, A.S. and Wallis, W.D. (1999) 'Uncertainty in the movie industry: does star power reduce the terror of the box office?' *Journal of Cultural Economics*, 23: 285–318.

DiMeglio, J.E. (1973) *Vaudeville U.S.A.*, Bowling Green, OH: Bowling Green University Popular Press.

Erdman, A.L. (2004) *Blue Vaudeville: Sex, Morals and the Mass Marketing of Amusement, 1895–1915*, Jeffer-son, NC: McFarland.

Fones-Wolf, E. (1999) 'Creating a favorable business climate: corporations and radio broadcasting, 1934–54', *Business History Review*, 73: 221–55.

Fort, R. (2005) 'The golden anniversary of "The Baseball Players' Labor Market"', *Journal of Sports Economics*, 6: 347–58.

Frey, B.S. (1988) 'Superstar museums: an economic analysis', *Journal of Cultural Economics*, 22: 113–25.

Garrett, T.A. (2009) 'War and pestilence as labor market shocks: U.S. manufacturing wage growth, 1914–19', *Economic Inquiry*, 47: 711–25.

Gendzel, G. (1995) 'Competitive boosterism: how Milwaukee lost the Braves', *Business History Review*, 69: 530–66.

Gil, R. (2010) 'An empirical investigation of the Paramount antitrust case', *Applied Economics*, 42: 171–83.

Gilbert, D. (1940) *American Vaudeville: Its Life and Times*, New York: McGraw-Hill.

Gomery, D. (1980) 'Rethinking U.S. film history: the depression decade and monopoly control', *Film and History*, 10: 32–8.

——(1996) 'The Hollywood studio system', in G.N. Smith (ed.) *The Oxford History of World Cinema*, Oxford: Oxford University Press.

Gragg, L. (2010) 'A big step to oblivion for Las Vegas? The "battle of the bare bosoms," 1957–59', *Journal of Popular Culture*, 43: 1004–22.

Hand, C. (2002) 'The distribution and predictability of cinema admissions', *Journal of Cultural Economics*, 26: 53–64.

Hanssen, F.A. (2000) 'The block booking of films reexamined', *Journal of Law and Economics*, 43: 395–426.

——(2002) 'Revenue-sharing in movie exhibition and the arrival of sound', *Economic Inquiry*, 40: 380–402.

——(2010) 'Vertical integration during the Hollywood studio era', *Journal of Law and Economics*, 53: 519–43.

Hardy, S. (1997) 'Entrepreneurs, organization and the sports marketplace', in S.W. Pope (ed.) *The New American Sport History: Recent Approaches and Perspectives*, Urbana, IL: University of Illinois Press.

Haupert, M.J. (2009a) 'Pay, performance, and race during the integration era', *Black Ball*, 2: 37–51.

——(2009b) 'Player pay and productivity in the reserve clause and collusion eras', *Nine: A Journal of Baseball History and Social Policy Perspectives*, 18: 63–85.

Haupert, M. and Murray, J. (2012) 'Regime switching and wages in Major League Baseball under the reserve clause', *Cliometrica*, 6: 143–62.

Hausman, J.A. and Leonard, G.K. (1997) 'Superstars in the National Basketball Association: economic value and policy', *Journal of Labor Economics*, 15: 586–624.

Higgs, R. (2009) 'A revealing window on the U.S. economy in depression and war: hours worked, 1929–50', *Independent Review*, 14: 151–60.

Holler, M.J. and Klose-Ullmann, B. (2010) 'Art goes America', *Journal of Economic Issues*, 44: 89–112.

Hunnicutt, B. (1980) 'Historical attitudes toward the increase of free time in the twentieth century: time for work, for leisure, or as unemployment', *Society and Leisure*, 3: 195–218.

Hylan, T.R., Lage, M.J. and Treglia, M. (1996) 'The Coase theorem, free agency, and Major League Baseball: a panel study of pitcher mobility from 1961 to 1992', *Southern Economic Journal*, 62: 1029–42.

Johnson, A.T. (1979) 'Congress and professional sports, 1951–78', *Annals of the American Academy of Political and Social Science*, 445: 102–15.

Johnson, B.K., Groothuis, P.A. and Whitehead, J.C. (2001) 'The value of public goods generated by a major league sports team: CVM', *Journal of Sports Economics*, 2: 6–21.

Jones, J.C.H. and Walsh, W.D. (1988) 'Salary determination in the National Hockey League: the effects of skills, franchise characteristics, and discrimination', *Industrial and Labor Relations Review*, 41: 592–604.

Kahn, L. (1991) 'Discrimination in professional sports: a survey of the literature', *Industrial and Labor Relations Review*, 44: 395–418.

——(1992) 'The effects of race on professional football players' compensation', *Industrial and Labor Relations Review*, 45: 295–310.

——(2000) 'The sports business as a labor market laboratory', *Journal of Economic Perspectives*, 14: 75–94.

——(2006) 'Race, performance, pay, and retention among National Basketball Association head coaches', *Journal of Sports Economics*, 7: 119–49.

Kahn, L. and Sherer, P. (1988) 'Racial differences in professional basketball players' compensation', *Journal of Labor Economics*, 6: 40–61.

Kenney, R.W. and Klein, B. (1983) 'The economics of block booking', *Journal of Law and Economics*, 26: 497–540.

——(2000) 'How block booking facilitated self-enforcing film contracts', *Journal of Law and Economics*, 43: 427–36.

Knowles, G., Sherony, K. and Haupert, M. (1992) 'The demand for Major League Baseball: a test of the uncertainty of outcome hypothesis', *American Economist*, 36: 72–80.

Kraft, J.P. (1994) 'The "pit" musicians: mechanization in the movie theaters, 1926–34', *Labor History*, 35: 66–92.

Krashinsky, M. and Krashinsky, H.A. (1997) 'Do English Canadian hockey teams discriminate against French Canadian players?' *Canadian Public Policy-Analyse de Politiques*, 23: 212–16.

Kruse, E. (2002) 'From free privilege to regulation: wireless firms and the competition for spectrum rights before World War I', *Business History Review*, 76: 659–703.

Lanning, J.A. (2010) 'Productivity, discrimination, and lost profits during baseball's integration', *Journal of Economic History*, 70: 964–88.

Lavoie, M. (2000) 'The location of pay discrimination in the National Hockey League', *Journal of Sports Economics*, 1: 401–11.

Lewis, T. (1992) 'A godlike presence: the Impact of radio on the 1920s and 1930s', *OAH Magazine of History*, 6: 26–33.

Long, J.G. (2005) 'Full count: the real cost of public funding for major league sports facilities', *Journal of Sports Economics*, 6: 119–43.

Lowenfish, L. (1980) *The Imperfect Diamond: A History of Baseball's Labor Wars*, New York: Da Capo Press.

Maoz, Y.D. (2010) 'Labor hours in the United States and Europe: the role of different leisure preferences', *Macroeconomic Dynamics*, 14: 231–41.

Miksell, P. (2006) '"Selling America to the world?" The rise and fall of an international film distributor in its largest foreign market: United Artists in Britain, 1927–47', *Enterprise and Society*, 7: 740–76.

——(2009) 'Resolving the global efficiency versus local adaptability dilemma: U.S. film multinationals in their largest foreign market in the 1930s and 1940s', *Business History*, 51: 426–44.

Milford, T.A. (1999) 'Boston's theater controversy and liberal notions of advantage', *New England Quarterly*, 72: 61–88.

Noll, R. and Zimbalist, A. (eds) (1997) *Sports, Jobs and Taxes*, Washington, DC: Brookings Institution Press.

Pokorny, M. and Sedgwick, J. (2001) 'Stardom and the profitability of film making: Warner Bros. in the 1930s', *Journal of Cultural Economics*, 25: 157–84.

Rosen, S. (1981) 'The economics of superstars', *American Economic Review*, 71: 845–58.

Rosen, S. and Sanderson, A. (2001) 'Labour markets in professional sports', *Economic Journal*, 111: F47–F68.

Ross, S.J. (1991) 'Struggles for the screen: workers, radicals, and the political uses of silent film', *American Historical Review*, 96: 333–67.

Rottenberg, S. (1956) 'The baseball players' labor market', *Journal of Political Economy*, 64: 242–58.

Schmidt, M.B. and Berri, D.J. (2006) 'Research note: what takes them out to the ball game?' *Journal of Sports Economics*, 7: 222–33.

Schofield, J.A. (1983) 'Performance and attendance at professional team sports', *Journal of Sport Behavior*, 6: 196–206.

Scully, G. (1974a) 'Pay and performance in Major League Baseball', *American Economic Review*, 64: 915–30.

——(1974b) 'Discrimination: the case of baseball', in R. Noll (ed.) *Government and the Sports Business*, Washington: Brookings Institution Press.

——(2002) 'The distribution of performance and earnings in a prize economy', *Journal of Sports Economics*, 3: 235–45.

Sedgwick, J. (2002) 'Product differentiation at the movies: Hollywood, 1946 to 1965', *Journal of Economic History*, 62: 676–705.

Sedgwick, J. and Pokorny, M. (1998) 'The risk environment of film making: Warner Bros in the inter-war years', *Explorations in Economic History*, 35: 196–220.

——(2005) 'The film business in the United States and Britain during the 1930s', *Economic History Review*, 58: 79–112.

——(2010) 'Consumers as risk takers: evidence from the film industry during the 1930s', *Business History*, 52: 74–99.

Shaw, D.V. (1986) 'Making leisure pay: street railway owned amusement parks in the United States, 1900–925', *Journal of Cultural Economics*, 10: 67–79.

Siegfried, J. and Zimbalist, A. (2000) 'The economics of sports facilities and their communities', *Journal of Economic Perspectives*, 14: 95–114.

Stoeber, R. (2004) 'What media evolution is: a theoretical approach to the history of new media', *European Journal of Communication*, 19: 483–505.

Strick, J.C. (1978) 'The economics of the motion picture industry: a survey', *Philosophy of the Social Sciences*, 8: 406–17.

Sullivan, E.J. and Pry, K.B. (1991) 'Eighteenth century London theater and the capture theory of regulation', *Journal of Cultural Economics*, 15: 41–52.

Surdam, D.G. (2006) 'The Coase theorem and player movement in Major League Baseball', *Journal of Sports Economics*, 7: 201–21.

——(2007) 'A tale of two gate-sharing plans: the National Football League and the National League, 1952–56', *Southern Economic Journal*, 73: 931–46.

——(2009a) 'The New York Yankees cope with the Great Depression', *Enterprise and Society*, 9: 816–40.

——(2009b) 'What brings fans to the ball park? Evidence from New York Yankees' and Philadelphia Phillies' financial records', *Journal of Economics*, 35: 35–47.

Vandenbroucke, G. (2009) 'Trends in hours: the U.S. from 1900 to 1950', *Journal of Economic Dynamics and Control*, 33: 237–49.

Whaples, R. (1990) 'Winning the eight-hour day, 1909–19', *Journal of Economic History*, 50: 393–406.

Whitney, J.D. (1988) 'Winning games versus winning championships: the economics of fan interest and team performance', *Economic Inquiry*, 26: 703–24.

Zimbalist, A. (1992) *Baseball and Billions: A Probing Look Inside the Big Business of Our National Pastime*, New York: Basic Books.

——(2003) 'Labor relations in Major League Baseball', *Journal of Sports Economics*, 4: 332–55.

PART IV

The work force and human outcomes

19

INEQUALITY IN ECONOMIC HISTORY

Thomas N. Maloney and Nathaniel Cline

Income inequality is one of the most visible, and most controversial, characteristics of an economy. A short drive through any large city will reveal profound differences in the living conditions of the residents. The causes of this inequality and its broader effects are not so straightforward and indeed are the subject of a voluminous literature. This chapter examines the evolution of income inequality over the very long run and identifies its major determinants, focusing on the United States but placing patterns for the U.S. in an international context. It also examines related dimensions of inequality – in wealth, consumption, health, and broad measures of living standards. Finally, it examines the effects of economic inequality on other social phenomena, including economic growth, health, and happiness.

Inequality in the U.S. from the colonial era through the 1800s

Data on the distribution of income become scarce, as one might expect, the further one goes back in time. Indeed, the first relatively national series on wages paid for the U.S. begins only in 1820 (Margo 2000). Even this series is by no means complete. As all of the data from the nineteenth century suffer from various kinds of deficiencies, they should be viewed with some skepticism, even those for which several indicators agree. In general, the story of inequality in the nineteenth century seems to be driven largely by a long sectoral shift from agriculture to industry and slow regional integration. This suggests a pattern along the lines of Kuznets (1955), who emphasized the shift from agriculture to industry and regional differentials as drivers of inequality. Thus, in the early stages of growth, the transition from agriculture to industry may cause inequality to increase, while in later stages urban–industrial areas dominate trends and inequality falls. This generates a long-run inverse U-shaped curve relating inequality to growth. Though Kuznets's hypothesis has been met with some criticism, his overriding point that sectoral shifts may be at the heart of inequality trends has persisted (Conceição and Galbraith 2001).

The degree of inequality within and between the English colonies in North America has been the subject of much debate. For some, the colonial and early national period was a time of increasing inequality (for instance, Henretta [1965] and Kulikoff [1971]). Others have argued that colonial society was relatively equal and remained so without large changes up until the eve of the Revolutionary War (Williamson and Lindert 1980). Due to the greater availability of data on wealth as opposed to income, the focus of the debate has centered around the interpretation of various indicators of wealth.

Alice Hansen Jones (1978, 1980) produced the first broad picture of wealth inequality in the colonial period. Jones compiled estimates of wealth inequality from a set of 919 probate inventories randomly selected from all inventories of estates probated in 1774. She uses the estate multiplier method to reconstruct the distribution of wealth of the living from the distribution of wealth of the deceased. (This involves re-weighting the age distributions in accordance with the age distributions of the living, see Jones (1982).) Jones's probate data suggest a relatively egalitarian economy on the eve of the American Revolution. In addition, a comprehensive review of regional wealth studies by Williamson and Lindert (1980) suggests that, although wealth inequality may be rising in the New England and Middle Colonies along the Eastern seaboard, the ever-growing inland populations were more egalitarian, and thus Jones's picture may be roughly appropriate for the entire eighteenth century. In addition, it could be argued that the large number of immigrants to the colonies who came under indenture contracts were attracted by a degree of mobility not present in Europe (Galenson 1984; Lindert 2005). However, royal officials (and other British residents) are left out of the probate data. Making use of the first national tax in 1789, Soltow (1989) found a higher degree of inequality than Jones, which he largely attributes to the inability of the earlier probate data to fully capture wealthy residents.

Williamson and Lindert's (1980) view of a relatively equal aggregate distribution has to some extent become the dominant view of this era. However, disaggregated patterns have an important story to tell as well. Henretta (1965) examines tax lists in Boston and finds that wealth grew increasingly concentrated between 1687 and 1771, a fact that he attributes to the rapid expansion of industry and the development of a modern, urban social structure. Williamson and Lindert (1980) have suggested, however, that the wealth inequality in urban areas may be due to the high population of young men in the city. Smith (1984), using tax lists from Philadelphia between 1756 and 1774, finds that age structure cannot account for the full increase in inequality and argues that the source must be found in increasing mercantile activities.

In addition to possible rural–urban differences, the differences between Northern and Southern colonies seem pronounced. During the colonial period, Jones (1980) finds significant differences between the wealth and income of New England, the middle colonies, and the Southern colonies. Her estimates suggest higher wealth per free person in the South even when the value of slaves as wealth is excluded. If slaves are included, wealth per free person in the South is roughly twice the amount in the middle colonies and close to two and a half times that of New England. Of course, if slaves are counted as a part of the Southern population, the distribution of wealth appears even more unequal. Williamson and Lindert (1980) argue that the rising share of slaves in the Southern population between 1690 and 1770 likely increased inequality in the South because slaves can be considered as part of the wealth of free Southerners and as persons with no property.

There is some degree of consensus that overall inequality rose between the Revolutionary War and the Civil War. Much of this inequality is described using wage ratios (whether between occupation, skill level, or region), again due to the limitations of data. However, there is some evidence that occupational wage ratios are a good indicator of broader income inequality (Williamson and Lindert 1980). The seminal work here is Margo (2000). Margo's data are drawn from army reports of wages paid, stored at the National Archives. As he notes, the United States Army employed civilian workers at forts across the country, for a wide variety of jobs. These forts often acted as a tool to encourage frontier settlement and were, in some cases, small production centers. In addition, Margo makes use of the Censuses of Social Statistics in 1850 and 1860.

Margo finds that between 1820 and 1860 there was a moderate increase in skill differentials. Real wages for white-collar occupations rose much more rapidly than for artisans or common laborers. Artisans in particular saw very little wage growth over the period and actually witnessed declines in the Midwest. This contrasts with Williamson and Lindert's (1980) earlier suggestion that artisans benefited from antebellum industrialization, but it confirms their general conclusion that inequality increased over the period. In addition, it suggests a substitution of capital for certain artisanal labor. This is more in line with traditional notions about the de-skilling nature of the factory system than the Williamson and Lindert hypothesis (see, for instance, Brown and Philips 1986; Goldin and Sokoloff 1982). Rising managerial wages could also be attributed to the role of "bosses" in the factory system as suggested by Marglin (1974).

In addition, wages grew faster in the Northeast than in the South, which had the highest skill differentials. Easterlin (1960) also finds large differences in per capita income between the regions. Interestingly, Margo (2000) finds that wages for common labor and artisans in the Midwest were high compared with the Northeast (contrary to Easterlin). This in part explains the movement of labor westward. Though reallocation of labor between the regions served to limit the geographical wage gap, this process appears to have been insufficiently rapid to drive out these gaps entirely (Rosenbloom 1990). As we shall see, the North–South gap in particular persisted throughout the nineteenth century.

Finally, Margo finds the interesting result that, while wage differences between regions were arguably large, within regions, the sectoral wage differences between farm and non-farm labor were small (after cost of living adjustments). Thus, Margo prefers to explain the rise in inequality with regional differentials and the rise of a factory system that demanded white-collar workers, whose supply was inelastic. This result is somewhat surprising in light of research by Goldin and Sokoloff (1984), who suggest that women and children moved into factory work and off the farm due to higher potential wages that were the result of a productivity gap. In addition, a small wage gap between farm and factory seems out of line with the rapid growth in productivity in industry during the antebellum period.

The overall increase in wage inequality in the early 1800s is corroborated by data on wealth holding compiled by Steckel and Moehling (2001). They link manuscript schedules of the Census with Massachusetts property tax records to develop a series on wealth inequality from 1820 to 1910. Between 1820 and 1850 the proportion of wealth held by top fractiles increased significantly. Steckel and Moehling argue that population movements between rural and urban areas accounted for a large proportion of the rise in inequality. Thus it is likely that movements between regions, as suggested by Margo, and movements into the city both account for a portion of the rise in inequality in the antebellum period.

In general, it has been suggested that wage ratios may have drifted upwards after the Civil War (Williamson and Lindert 1980). An increase in inequality is confirmed by Atack *et al.* (2004), who examine manufacturing wages from the 1850 and 1880 manuscript Censuses of Manufacturing. Interestingly, they find evidence that this increase in inequality may be due to the de-skilling nature of factory work in this period. That is, average wages were declining in establishment size, which, following Goldin and Katz (1998), is interpreted as evidence of de-skilling. Anderson (2001) finds that immigration of the less skilled from Europe to America may also have contributed to the growth in wage inequality in the U.S. (and also in Canada and Australia) at the end of the nineteenth century.

Regional income differentials also persisted after the Civil War. Engerman (1971) has demonstrated a sharp drop in per capita incomes in the South. This has been attributed to a variety of factors, including a decline in labor productivity in Southern agriculture and a declining world demand for cotton (Fogel and Engerman 1974; Wright 1974). In addition, increased industrialization in other regions caused the South–non-South gap to persist.

It seems then that the period from the Revolution until the close of the nineteenth century was marked by increasing inequality in the distribution of income and wealth. Steckel and Moehling's (2001) wealth data suggest a relatively equal increase in inequality before and after the Civil War. Relative wage data, however, suggest that the latter half of the nineteenth century saw slower increases in inequality (Williamson and Lindert 1980). Several authors have pointed to the role of industrialization in promoting inequality. This is due both to its reward for managerial labor in the antebellum period (Margo 2000) and its deskilling nature in the postbellum period (Atack *et al.* 2004). Regional differences also contributed to inequality at this time. Wage differences between the Northeast, Mid-Atlantic, and Midwest tended to close over time as the U.S. began to develop an integrated labor market (Easterlin 1968). Despite this tendency, Rosenbloom (1990) found significant between-region wage differentials as late as 1898, suggesting a less than fully integrated market. Indeed, throughout the nineteenth century, the South's divergence was persistent, and this region likely did not begin to catch up until the twentieth century. Wright (1986) discusses the transition from the "Old" South, which had internally integrated, but nationally distinct, labor markets to the "New" South whose labor markets are national. This trend of rising inequality was not reversed until sometime around the turn of the twentieth century (Goldin and Katz 2001).

Inequality in the twentieth century

While broadly reported data on incomes remain scarce through 1940, other kinds of quantitative evidence become more readily available in the early 1900s, allowing longer-term measurement of inequality using consistent sources of data. In one of the most influential studies of this type, Thomas Piketty and Emmanuel Saez use income tax data to examine changes in income inequality from 1913 through 1998 (Piketty and Saez 2003). Because only top earners paid income taxes in the United States before the Second World War, this study is confined to examining inequality among the well-to-do, specifically the top 10 per cent of households (in terms of income). They find that the share of all income going to these top households fell sharply in the 1930s and did not recover much, as a percentage of the total, until after the Second World War. The incomes of the top 1 per cent did not recover in relative terms until the 1980s, but at that point this group experienced very rapid increases in their share of total income. Piketty and Saez also find that high-income households increasingly drew their incomes from payment for their labor rather than from returns to capital.

Changes in tax policy may affect how people report income on their tax returns, which may affect the inequality measures constructed by Piketty and Saez. In particular, the substantial reduction in top marginal tax rates in the mid-1980s may have prompted more complete reporting of income by high earners. The potential impact of these changes in reporting has generated a debate about the extent of the increase in inequality at the top after 1987 (Reynolds 2007; Burtless 2007). Even so, the general finding of a pronounced U-shaped pattern in income concentration in the twentieth century is corroborated in other, broader measures. Claudia Goldin and Lawrence Katz use average wages in various occupations (mainly production jobs) to construct three types of inequality measures: one describing inequality "below the middle" (the ratio of the median wage to the wage at the tenth percentile), one describing inequality "above the middle" (the ratio of the wage at the ninetieth percentile to the median), and one describing the full distribution (the ratio of the wage at the ninetieth percentile to the wage at the tenth percentile). They document substantial reductions in inequality from 1890 to 1950, especially in the bottom half of the income distribution. From 1960 on, the wage distribution began to widen again (Goldin and Katz 2001).

Goldin and Katz emphasize the relative supply of, and demand for, educated labor as a primary driving force in these patterns. The rapid expansion of high-school education from 1910 to 1950 drove down the value of a high-school diploma as workers with this credential composed a larger share of the overall work force. In the 1940s, a sharp increase in the demand for less educated workers (for use in heavy industry and war production) reinforced the process of "wage compression" (Goldin and Margo 1992). After 1960 or so, the supply of educated workers continued to expand, but technological changes greatly increased the demand for educated workers, so much so that wage inequality eventually began to rise again (Goldin and Katz 2001: 60–4).

Other views of these longer-run changes in the U.S. emphasize institutional forces. In the middle of the twentieth century, higher top-level tax rates and greater protection of collective bargaining rights (due to the passage of the Wagner Act) promoted greater equality in earnings. The early post-Second World War period cemented the place of the government in the economy as a stabilizing and equalizing force, and broad collective bargaining agreements in industry produced rising compensation levels for high-school-educated production workers in exchange for great employer discretion on the shop floor. Ongoing income growth into the early 1970s kept this system in place without dramatic change in inequality (from about 1950 to 1970 or so). However, macroeconomic crises in the mid-1970s – beginning with energy- and food-price shocks – generated new concerns about rapid wage inflation (tied to inflation more generally though collective bargaining and cost-of-living adjustments) and inefficiencies arising from government regulation. These forces resulted in defeats for labor unions and deregulation in a number of sectors. In the 1980s, a monetary policy regime switch to disinflation led to rising interest rates that increased the value of the dollar, thereby reducing the demand for exports and weakening the market for production workers in the U.S. At the same time, top marginal tax rates and tax rates on non-labor income were reduced. The resulting increases in inequality had self-reinforcing effects on social norms related to pay at the top (Levy and Temin 2007).

While these very long-term accounts have generated considerable attention, much of the recent debate about income inequality has focused on the post-Second World War period and more specifically the post-1970 period. Since the mid-1970s, the dispersion of income in the U.S. has grown substantially. Peter Gottschalk (1997) documents a very strong positive relationship between wage level and wage growth from 1973 to 1994. That is, wages near the top grew much more rapidly than wages at the middle or near the bottom. 90/10 wage ratios rose for both men and women over this period, though they rose more for men (Gottschalk 1997: 26–8).

While declining inequality between the middle and the bottom at mid-century helped drive patterns in those years, the recent rise in inequality has mainly reflected growing distance between the middle of the income distribution and the top. Outsourcing and technological change may play a role in these specific patterns. There are jobs in the middle of the income distribution – repetitive, non-interactive jobs in production work but also in accounting and bookkeeping, for instance – that can be substituted out to a degree by technology or by out-sourcing. Jobs at the top (CEO, lawyer, investment banker, doctor) are more interactive and cannot be automated away or moved offshore as easily. The demand for workers in these top jobs has remained strong while workers near the middle have faced weaker demand. As a result, income inequality has increased in the top half of the distribution (Gordon and Dew-Becker 2007: 175–6).

Not surprisingly, changes in the returns to education have tracked these changes in broader measures of inequality. The college wage premium (the difference in earnings between those with a college degree and those with a high school diploma) rose substantially in the 1980s and 1990s. On the other hand, about half of the increase in inequality among men was "within group" – growing inequality between people with similar levels of education and experience. About one-quarter of the increase in inequality among women was "within group" (Gottschalk 1997: 31–3). New technology may play a role here as well. In periods marked by significant new innovations (such as the development of information technology in recent decades), those who are best at learning and adapting to new methods quickly will have more rapid income growth. These forces can create growing inequality even among workers with similar levels of observable education and experience (Juhn *et al.* 1993). More work remains to be done before we have a thorough understanding of this growth in "within group" inequality (Acemoglu 2002).

The U.S. is not alone in its experience of growing income inequality since the 1970s. However, the U.S. experienced more rapid increases in inequality than did most other Western, industrialized nations, with only the UK being very close to the U.S. pattern (Gottschalk 1997: 34–5; Smeeding 2005: 956–7). While recent growth in inequality in the U.S. has been primarily in the top half of the distribution, the distinctive characteristic of inequality in the U.S. in comparison to other countries is the extent of inequality in the bottom half (Smeeding 2005: 959–61).

What explains the unusual amount of inequality in the bottom half of the income distribution in the U.S.? It is to a substantial degree a result of differences in redistributive policy between the U.S. and other nations. The overall inequality of market income – income before taxes and transfers – in the U.S. is actually lower than in France or Belgium and is similar to the level in the UK, Australia, and Sweden. However, taxes and transfers in the U.S. result in much less reduction in inequality than occurs elsewhere. Adjustments for differences in educational distribution and other demographic characteristics do not have much effect on these cross-country comparisons (Smeeding 2005: 972–8).

For the most part, these measures of inequality are based on cross-sectional "snapshots." They describe the pattern of wages and income at a point in time, but they do not give a complete representation of inequality across individuals because each person's income changes over the long run, either due to changes across the individual life course or due to cyclical changes in the economy. Measuring long-term income in this way is expensive to do, and as a result we have limited data of this type. One such study, a comparison of the U.S. and Germany in the 1980s, found that inequality in "permanent" (long-term) income was greater in the U.S. than in Germany, matching the patterns found in shorter-term measurements (Burkhauser and Poupore 1997).

Inequality on other dimensions

Wealth

As with income, efforts to measure the distribution of wealth over the very long term often rely on tax records. Using estate tax records, Wolff (1992) finds that the top 1 per cent of wealth holders accounted for 38 per cent of all wealth in 1922. Comparing this figure with calculations based on the 1870 Census indicates that the concentration of wealth increased over these 50 years (Rosenbloom and Stutes 2005). The share held by the top 1 per cent then fell sharply at the beginning of the Great Depression, reaching 28 per cent in 1933. Wealth concentration increased during the 1930s but then fell again by 1945 and remained at a persistently lower level into the mid-1970s. Wolff finds that these fluctuations track the change in the ratio of stock prices to housing prices rather closely, reflecting the fact that stock ownership and other forms of "financial" wealth are more concentrated than wealth embodied in housing. They also roughly follow the patterns of income inequality discussed earlier.

Wealth, unlike wages, can be directly transferred across generations, which would lead us to expect more persistence in the distribution of wealth in the long run. Using estate tax data for Wisconsin, linked across generations for the years 1916 to 1981, Wahl (2003) finds, not surprisingly, that the children of the very wealthy are themselves very wealthy. What may be surprising is just how slowly differences in wealth holding across families change over time. For instance, a 100 per cent wealth difference between two sets of parents corresponds to a predicted 84 to 86 per cent wealth difference between their children. At this rate, for a family with wealth 100 per cent above the average, 13 generations would have to pass before we would predict that the family had fallen to just 10 per cent above the average in its wealth holding.

For recent decades, Wolff (1994) and Kopczuk and Saez (2004) document rising wealth inequality after 1980. This increase is probably driven by the increasing concentration of income discussed earlier, though, notably, there is considerable variation in wealth holding among people who have similar incomes. Despite this rising concentration, wealth remained substantially less concentrated in 2000 than it had been around the First World War. This finding corroborates Piketty and Saez's evidence that, over the course of the twentieth century, high-income households increasingly drew their income from returns to labor rather than from interest on wealth.

Consumption

Measures of consumption arguably provide a better indication of persistent living standards than do measures of income. Consumption corresponds more directly to a household's estimate of its long-term income stream (which is hard to directly measure), while cross-sectional, short-term income measures may have large transitory components. Most analyses of consumption in the U.S. rely on data from the Consumer Expenditure Survey, produced by the Bureau of Labor Statistics. These data indicate that consumption inequality was less pronounced than income inequality in the 1980s and 1990s. While consumption inequality grew in these years, it increased less sharply than did income inequality. Based on the Gini coefficient, a commonly used index of inequality, consumption inequality was on average about 70 per cent as large as income inequality during these years, and it grew by about half as much as did income inequality (Johnson *et al.* 2005).

Health, schooling, leisure, and multidimensional measures

In a paper examining a wide variety of dimensions of inequality since the late 1800s, Clayne Pope argues that for some elements of living standards – health, leisure, and education – general improvement will almost inevitably lead to diminishing inequality, because these measures have rough maximum values that cannot be exceeded, unlike income. So, as health improves and mortality at young ages diminishes even for the relatively poor, the distribution of years lived will grow less unequally distributed. By this kind of measure, Pope finds dramatic reductions in inequality in health in the early twentieth century: total "years lived" became much less concentrated among just the most long-lived individuals. Similarly, as primary, secondary, and even some higher education has become much more widely diffused through the population, the concentration of years of schooling has diminished greatly. The concentration of high-quality education has probably diminished even more. Finally, Pope argues that earlier retirement and the decline of agriculture, which was marked by very long work hours, has reduced inequality in the distribution of lifetime leisure (Pope 2009).

While Pope considers each of these dimensions individually, Edward Wolff and colleagues have developed a composite index, the Levy Institute Measure of Economic Well-being (LIMEW), which is designed to combine a wide set of variables into a single "well-being" index. The index includes a broad measure of income – combining wages and salaries, health benefits, income from wealth, and government transfers (net of taxes) – along with measures of the consumption of public goods (like defense and transportation infrastructure) and the value of services that individuals produce for themselves through cooking, cleaning, and similar activities ("home production"). Well-being, by this calculation, was more equally distributed than was income throughout the period from 1959 to 2004. The incorporation of public consumption and home production had substantial equalizing effects on the LIMEW. Inequality in this measure increased between 1959 and 2004, rising most sharply in the 1990s due to growing wealth inequality and a decline in the value of net government transfers to the poor. There was a slight decline in inequality as measured by the LIMEW after 2000 as financial assets declined in value, reducing the income that the wealthiest received from these assets (Wolff and Zacharias 2007; Zacharias *et al.* 2009).

Effects of inequality: growth, health, and happiness

A central question of inequality research has been the relationship between inequality and general economic growth. The question has been answered from both directions, with growth and development driving different levels of inequality (as described by Kuznets), and with inequality having an impact on the timing and pace of economic growth. Sokoloff and Engerman (2000) have argued that initial levels of inequality among colonies in the New World created institutions that reinforced these inequality patterns and that also affected long-run growth. They suggest that highly unequal colonies (including those of the Spanish in South America) generated political structures that encouraged the dominance of a small elite and a large low-income population to enable the extraction of raw materials. On the other hand, regions with smaller (surviving) native populations and with agricultural environments not suited to scale economies and cash crops, such as the English colonies in North America, generated more democratic structures that caused their relative equality to persist. These more democratic institutions are associated with higher levels of growth as they encourage broader access to education, broader land ownership, and wider participation in financial markets.

The argument that greater equality may promote growth seems at odds with conventional economic theory. That is, inequality should be good for incentives in a market economy. In addition, to the extent inequality can increase aggregate savings, it should lead to further capital accumulation. More recent research in endogenous growth theory has, however, challenged this proposition, arguing that, in the face of imperfect capital markets, redistribution that encourages human capital acquisition may be growth enhancing (Aghion and Howitt 1998). Moreover, Keynesian models have emphasized the relationship between inequality and growth through effects on the level of effective demand. Keynes (1936) argues that income redistribution that increases the propensity to consume will increase growth as expenditures drive savings. Taylor (2004) provides a survey of modern Keynesian approaches along these lines.

As income inequality has become more pronounced in recent decades, especially in the United States, a large literature has emerged that examines the effect of this inequality on health. The argument is not just that poverty harms the health of the poor but rather that widening social inequalities create stress and reduce social cohesion and investment in the common good, harming the health of even relatively well-off individuals in highly unequal societies. Wilkinson and Pickett (2006) review 168 distinct analyses of these issues and find that 87 of these studies are strongly supportive of a relationship between income inequality and health, 44 more are partially supportive, and 37 are not supportive. (Notably, of those strongly supportive of a relationship between inequality and health, nine find a positive relationship.) Waitzman and Smith (1998) argue that the connection between inequality and health is mediated, at least in part, through residential segregation and the spatial distribution of poverty. Using data from 33 Metropolitan Statistical Areas in the United States, they find that, in cities where the poor reside in very highly concentrated neighborhoods, the health of residents in general (not just the poor) is harmed.

Deaton (2003) agrees that social context has implications for individual health but is not persuaded that there is a strong relationship between income inequality specifically and health. His examination of the evidence in cross-city and cross-state studies finds that, while there is a negative correlation between inequality and health, this correlation disappears once the racial composition of the local population (specifically the per cent black) is controlled. To be clear, Deaton finds that the health of both white and black residents is poorer in cities with a high percentage of blacks. This relationship may be reflective of some of the same underlying mechanisms – increased social tension, reduced cohesion – that are hypothesized by others to be the source of a relationship between income inequality and health. It may also reflect poorer provision of healthcare, due to more poorly funded hospitals, in predominantly black cities.

Finally, Alesina *et al.* (2004) go straight to the heart of the matter by examining the relationship between income inequality and happiness. They find that people in more unequal societies are less likely to report themselves as being happy. However, these patterns vary between the U.S. and Europe. Inequality is more strongly correlated with unhappiness in Europe (in cross-country data) than in the U.S. (in cross-state data). In particular, the poor are more unhappy in more unequal countries in Europe, while there is no strong correlation between unhappiness among the poor and overall inequality in the U.S. The authors hypothesize that these differences may reflect a greater expectation of socioeconomic mobility in the U.S. than in Europe.

References

Acemoglu, D. (2002) 'Technical change, inequality, and the labor market', *Journal of Economic Literature*, 40: 7–72.

Aghion, P. and Howitt, P. (1998) *Endogenous Growth Theory*, Cambridge, MA: MIT Press.

Alesina, A., Di Tella, R. and MacCulloch, R. (2004) 'Inequality and happiness: are Europeans and Americans different?' *Journal of Public Economics*, 88: 2009–42.

Anderson, E. (2001) 'Globalisation and wage inequalities, 1870–1970', *European Review of Economic History*, 5: 91–118.

Atack, J., Bateman, F. and Margo, R. (2004) 'Skill intensity and rising wage dispersion in nineteenth-century American manufacturing', *Journal of Economic History*, 64: 172–92.

Brown, M. and Philips, P. (1986) 'Craft labor and mechanization in nineteenth-century American canning', *Journal of Economic History*, 46: 743–56.

Burkhauser, R.N. and Poupore, J.G. (1997) 'A cross-national comparison of permanent inequality in the United States and Germany', *Review of Economics and Statistics*, 79: 10–17.

Burtless, G. (2007) 'Comments on "Has U.S. income inequality really increased?"', Brookings Institution. www.brookings.edu/~/media/Files/rc/papers/2007/0111useconomics_burtless/20070111.pdf (accessed June 16, 2011).

Conceição, P. and Galbraith, J.K. (2001) 'Toward a new Kuznets hypothesis', in J.K. Galbraith and M. Berner (eds) *Inequality and Industrial Change: A Global View*, Cambridge: Cambridge University Press.

Deaton, A. (2003) 'Health, inequality, and economic development', *Journal of Economic Literature*, 41: 113–58.

Easterlin, R. (1960) 'Interregional differences in per capita income, population, and total income, 1840–1950', in Committee on Research in Income and Wealth, *Trends in the American Economy in the Nineteenth Century*, Princeton, NJ: Princeton University Press.

——(1968) *Population, Labor Force, and Long Swings in Economic Growth: The American Experience*, New York: Columbia University Press.

Engerman, S. (1971) 'The economic impact of the Civil War', in R. Fogel and S. Engerman (eds) *The Reinterpretation of American Economic History*, New York: Harper & Row.

Fisher, J.D. and Johnson, D.S. (2006) 'Consumption mobility in the United States: evidence from two panel data sets', *Berkeley Electronic Journal of Economic Analysis and Policy: Topics in Economic Analysis and Policy*, 6: Issue 1, Article 16.

Fogel, R. and Engerman S. (1974) *Time on the Cross*, Boston, MA: Little, Brown.

Galenson, D.W. (1984) 'The rise and fall of indentured servitude in the Americas: An economic analysis', *Journal of Economic History*, 44: 1–26.

Goldin, C. and Katz, L.F. (1998) 'The origins of technology-skill complementarity', *Quarterly Journal of Economics*, 113: 693–732.

——(2001) 'Decreasing (and then increasing) inequality in America: a tale of two half-centuries', in F. Welch (ed.) *The Causes and Consequences of Increasing Inequality*, Chicago, IL: University of Chicago Press.

Goldin, C. and Margo, R. (1992) 'The great compression: the wage structure in the United States at mid-century', *Quarterly Journal of Economics*, 107: 1–34.

Goldin, C. and Sokoloff, K. (1982) 'Women, children, and industrialization in the early republic: evidence from the manufacturing censuses', *Journal of Economic History*, 42: 741–74.

——(1984) 'The relative productivity hypothesis of industrialization: the American case, 1820 to 1850', *Quarterly Journal of Economics*, 99: 461–87.

Gordon, R.J. and Dew-Becker, I. (2007) 'Selected issues in the rise of income inequality', *Brookings Papers on Economic Activity*, 2: 169–90.

Gottschalk, P. (1997) 'Inequality, income, growth, and mobility: the basic facts', *Journal of Economic Perspectives*, 11: 21–40.

Hatton, T.J. and Williamson, J.G. (1991) 'Wage gaps between farm and city: Michigan in the 1890s', *Explorations in Economic History*, 28: 381–408.

Henretta, J.A. (1965) 'Economic development and social structure in colonial Boston', *William and Mary Quarterly*, 22: 75–92.

Johnson, D.S., Smeeding, T.M. and Torrey, B. (2005) 'Economic inequality through the prisms of income and consumption', *Monthly Labor Review*, 128: 11–24.

Jones, A.H. (1978) *American Colonial Wealth: Documents and Methods*, New York: Arno Press.

——(1980) *Wealth of a Nation to Be: The American Colonies on the Eve of the Revolution*, New York: Columbia University Press.

——(1982) 'Estimating wealth of the living from a probate sample', *Journal of Interdisciplinary History*, 13: 273–300.

——(1984) 'Wealth and growth of the thirteen colonies: some implications', *Journal of Economic History*, 44: 239–54.

Juhn, C., Murphy, K.M. and Pierce, B. (1993) 'Wage inequality and the rise in returns to skill', *Journal of Political Economy*, 101: 410–42.

Keynes, J.M. (1936) *The General Theory of Employment, Interest, and Money*, London: McMillan.

Kopczuk, W. and Saez, E. (2004) 'Top wealth shares in the United States: evidence from Social Security data since 1937', *National Tax Journal*, 52: 445–87.

Kulikoff, A. (1971) 'The progress of inequality in revolutionary Boston', *William and Mary Quarterly*, 28: 375–412.

Kuznets, S. (1955) 'Economic growth and income inequality', *American Economic Review*, 45: 1–28.

Levy, F. and Temin, P. (2007) 'Inequality and institutions in 20th century America', NBER Working Paper No. 13106.

Lindert, P.H. (2005) 'Three centuries of inequality in Britain and America,' in A.B. Atkinson and F. Bourguignon (eds) *Handbook of Income Distribution*, Amsterdam: Elsevier.

Marglin, S. (1974) 'What do bosses do?', *Review of Radical Political Economics*, 6: 60–112.

Margo, R.A. (2000) *Wages and Labor Markets in the United States, 1820–1860*, Chicago, IL: University of Chicago Press.

Piketty, T. and Saez, E. (2003) 'Income inequality in the United States, 1913–98', *Quarterly Journal of Economics*, 118: 1–39.

Pope, C. (2009) 'Measuring the distribution of material well-being: U.S. trends', *Journal of Monetary Economics*, 56: 66–78.

Reynolds, A. (2007) 'Has U.S. income inequality really increased?' *Policy Analysis*, 586.

Rosenbloom, J.L. (1990) 'One market or many? Labor market integration in the late nineteenth-century United States', *Journal of Economic History*, 50: 85–107.

Rosenbloom, J.L. and Stutes, G.W. (2005) 'Reexamining the distribution of wealth in 1870', NBER Working Paper No. 11482.

Smeeding, T.M. (2005) 'Public policy, economic inequality, and poverty: the United States in comparative perspective', *Social Science Quarterly*, 86, supplement: 956–83.

Smith, B.G. (1984) 'Inequality in late colonial Philadelphia: a note on its nature and growth', *William and Mary Quarterly*, 41: 629–45.

Sokoloff, K.L. and Engerman, S.L. (2000) 'Institutions, factor endowments, and paths of development in the new world', *Journal of Economic Perspectives*, 14: 217–32.

Soltow, L. (1989) *Distribution of Wealth and Income in the United States in 1798*, Pittsburgh, PA: University of Pittsburgh Press.

Steckel, R.H. and Moehling, C.M. (2001) 'Rising inequality: trends in the distribution of wealth in industrializing New England', *Journal of Economic History*, 61: 160–83.

Taylor, L. (2004) *Reconstructing Macroeconomics*, Cambridge, MA: Harvard University Press.

Wahl, J.B. (2003) 'From riches to riches: intergenerational transfers and the evidence from estate tax returns', *Social Science Quarterly*, 84: 276–96.

Waitzman, N.J. and Smith, K.R. (1998) 'Separate but lethal: the effects of economic segregation on mortality in metropolitan America', *Milbank Quarterly*, 76: 341–73.

Wilkinson, R.G. and Pickett, K.E. (2006) 'Income inequality and population health: a review and explanation of the evidence', *Social Science and Medicine*, 62: 1768–84.

Williamson, J.G. and Lindert, P.H. (1980) *American Inequality: A Macroeconomic History*, New York: Academic Press.

Wolff, E.N. (1992) 'Changing inequality of wealth', *American Economic Review (Papers and Proceedings)*, 82: 552–8.

——(1994) 'Trends in household wealth in the United States, 1962–83 and 1983–89', *Review of Income and Wealth*, 40: 143–74.

Wolff, E.N. and Zacharias, A. (2007) 'The Levy Institute measure of economic well-being, United States, 1989–2001', *Eastern Economic Journal*, 33: 443–70.

Wright, G. (1974) 'Cotton competition and the post-bellum recovery of the American South', *Journal of Economic History*, 34: 610–35.

——(1986) *Old South, New South: Revolutions in the Southern Economy since the Civil War*, Baton Rouge: Louisiana State University Press.

Zacharias, A., Wolff, E.N. and Masterson, T. (2009) 'New estimates of economic inequality in America, 1959–2004', LIMEW reports, Levy Economics Institute.

20

THE EVOLUTION OF LABOR MARKETS

Michael Huberman

Informed by labor economics and labor history, the economic history of labor markets is an alternative and unified approach to study the wage and employment relation. This broad field encompasses the nature, organization, and conditions of work, as well as the non-wage compensation labor earned. It is an alternative approach because, unlike the economics' textbook model, the economic historian does not perceive the labor market as static. Rather, economic history provides a framework to examine the feedback mechanisms – the dynamic relation – between labor markets and technological change, business organization, government regulation, product markets, and the preferences of participants themselves. Put differently, history provides rich examples of the many margins of adjustment in labor markets across space and time, in addition to wage and employment dimensions.

In parallel fashion, the economic history of labor markets diverges from the historian's narrative of the sequential development of labor markets, according to which the epoch of fettered, mainly rural markets bound by custom was ultimately replaced by the epoch of unregulated and most often urban, competitive labor markets of the modern period. Economic historians generally reject teleology – that is, the philosophical proposition that final causes exist in nature. They do not hold to a linear or deterministic history of labor market development. In the eye of economic historians, the distinction between regulated and unregulated labor markets is blurred, because labor markets by themselves are institutions (Solow 1990). Even the most seemingly unregulated labor market had its own implicit and often explicit rules, while the most custom-based employment relation had market-like features. To be clear, the economic historian sees the exchange of work for pay as basic to all epochs, but recognizes that the labor market was and is malleable: its geographic scope and institutions adjusting to meet the challenges of the larger social and economic environments. At the same time, the labor market and its institutions can leave an indelible mark on this same environment. This chapter takes a historical glance at some of the major turning points in labor market history, without imposing any prescribed purpose, direction, or design on this development.

Pre-industrial labor markets

A functioning labor market exists when workers are free to change employment and location and are paid a wage or its equivalent corresponding with their productivity levels in order to signal which type of employment to choose. If these conditions are not met, the labor market cannot be said to exist because workers would be unrewarded for their toil.

The labor market in the Roman Empire serves as a useful starting point to examine these conditions in practice. It has been customary to take the widespread use of slave labor as an indication that the ancient economy was not a market economy. But this view is mistaken. The Roman labor market shared many features of pre-industrial and agricultural labor markets that were common into the nineteenth century (Temin 2004). While the number of slaves was sizeable, comprising about one-half of Rome's population and one-third of Italy's, their labor was integrated into the wider market, unlike slave labor in nineteenth-century United States and to a lesser extent Brazil whose activities were restricted. In Rome, slaves were inter-changeable with free labor in many activities. To be sure, even free labor until the twentieth century was not entirely voluntary, having to submit to arbitrary exactions, but the Roman system combined a mix of positive and negative rewards, and the rate of manumission was relatively high compared with that in the United States and Brazil. Like any functioning market, demand and supply adjusted to meet changes in product markets, and the larger economic and social environment, although this was much truer for the urban than rural sectors. Slaves and freemen were rewarded for investments in education, workers with various skills being compensated differently. Hereditary barriers were weak and guilds unrestrictive. Across the Empire, labor markets were integrated. Earnings of miners in Egypt and Dacia in Eastern Europe were comparable if not converging, differentials being the same order of magnitude found in Europe as late as the eighteenth century (Allen 2001). More fundamentally, wages moved in response to substantial shocks in the supply of labor, rising after environmental catastrophes, epidemics, and wars, and falling as population levels rebounded. This was a common trait of pre-industrial labor markets everywhere.

The Roman labor market adjusted to local needs and geopolitical concerns of the Empire. Compared with subsequent developments, it was mainly urban and its geographic scope was remarkably vast, but this does not imply that the regional, if not local, agricultural labor markets that dominated the next two millennia in Europe, and for that matter Asia, were not well functioning either. In Western Europe, serfdom had aspects of a contractual relation, peasants exchanging labor services for protection from their lords. Since peasants maintained, to a certain degree, the possibility of moving between manorial estates, competition assured that all lords provided the public good of protection, thereby putting limits on the surpluses lords could potentially extract from peasants. Because of limits on lords' extra-economic power, wages had some flexibility in adjusting to changes in the demand for and supply of labor.

By the thirteenth century, at least in Western Europe, the value of the protection side of the contract had diminished. The early agricultural labor force exhibited limited mobility, peasants being tied to the land in a patchwork of complex lease-holding arrangements. While peasants may not have always been landowners, they were deeply attached to land they occupied. Over the next centuries, as land markets evolved, a rural labor force emerged alongside the development of the property market. Overall wage levels were tied to demographic swings, declining in the population buildup before the plague of 1348, and then rising after.

As population pressures ebbed in the mid-fourteenth century, feudal relations in the West slowly disappeared, a good example of labor market changes having had large political implications. But the dynamic was not everywhere the same. In Eastern Europe, population scarcity had the opposite outcome, a clear illustration that labor markets were also embedded in larger social and political environments. From the late fifteenth to seventeenth centuries, the nobility exercised its power to restrict labor mobility by dictating harsh national systems of personal or tenurial serfdom. Labor in the East was at the service of their lords' extra economic powers.

To some observers, the labor market for agricultural workers in late medieval England can be considered to have been as competitive as that of industrial labor in the twenty-first century (Clark 2007). Wage contours, like that of the wage gap between men and women, mapped onto productivity differences. Another sign of well-functioning labor markets is that unemployment was negligible, the work year in England amounting to between 260 and 290 days. The evidence on mobility is mixed. As early as 1300, manors in western England attracted seasonal harvest workers from Wales, a distance of 250 kilometers, but in 1600, in the same region, workers in search of permanent jobs moved on average 5 or 6 kilometers (Grantham 1994: 16). Into the early modern period, the attachment to land deepened – the possibility of owning an individual plot was held to be an alternative to wage labor – and this would prove to be a major obstacle in the recruiting of the first industrial work forces, a subject discussed in greater detail later.

Urban and agricultural labor markets coexisted but did not necessarily overlap in early modern Europe. Adam Smith held that craft guilds were archaic institutions that regulated entry into occupations and the organization of work, and limited the type of items produced, thereby handcuffing the operations of labor markets. Long considered the archetype of customary or pre-capitalist labor markets, guilds had to be swept away before proceeding to subsequent stages of development. But closer examination suggests that, even in this classic case, labor markets functioned since they seem to have adjusted to imperfections in capital and product markets (Epstein 2008). The guild supplied members with financial support in a time when banking facilities were not well developed, negotiated on behalf of members with more powerful merchants, and enforced product controls and fixed prices, overcoming the problem of the lack of market information on the quality of items produced. As such, craft guilds were a stepping stone, not an obstacle, to later developments precisely because of their investments in human capital formation.

As production in urban centers expanded, and with improved credit facilities and product information, the authority of craft guilds weakened. Still, many guild requirements for apprenticeships persisted into the industrial era, and beyond. An outcome of this period is the melding of urban and agricultural labor markets. While merchants and certain stages of production remained urban based, other parts were outsourced to the countryside, where agricultural households supplemented incomes in handicraft production, mainly textiles, during the off seasons. The family household was the decision-making unit. Participation in the labor market reflected the balancing or allocation of family labor across activities having different combinations of earnings and risk. Women and children conducted much of this work. Induced by the availability of new products from home and afar, workers in the countryside and, towns were prepared to give more effort. The labor market thereby expanded to meet the growing national and international supply of and demand for manufactured items. Dutch labor markets were perhaps the most flexible, at least during the Golden Age of the late sixteenth and seventeenth centuries (De Vries 2008). Casual laborers moved between agricultural and non-agricultural activities seamlessly, and wage contours reflected skill levels.

For some of its history, China had a variant of this type of functioning labor market, although the attachment to the land was probably even stronger in the region than in Europe (Pomeranz 2000). In the Ming period, peasant freeholds in the Yangzi Valley began to supplant state and managerial farms using either wage or servile labor. Since urban guilds had no monopoly on textile production, state officials actively encouraged domestic production. They distributed cotton seeds, printed instructional pamphlets, sponsored the acquisition of skills, and officially promoted the gender division of labor, in which "man plows, woman weaves", as the basis of strong families. According to one authority (Pomeranz 2000: 87), almost every rural household in the lower Yangzi did some textile work for the market.

Labor markets in the age of industrialization

Labor recruitment was an overarching concern of the first generation of business owners in the industrial epoch. Of course, a solution was to bring factories to workers themselves and this meant locating in the countryside. To avoid costs of hiring, turnover, and discipline, some businesses located in regions where rural workers had accumulated skills. But this had its limits because unreliable sources of hydraulic energy constrained the application of new technologies, and perhaps, more importantly, there were agglomeration economies from locating in urban centers that were not available to the scattered mills in the countryside. The labor market and its institutions adjusted to meet these conditions, as much as factory organization and technology adapted to the labor supply. Faced by labor that was highly seasonal or undisciplined, certain employers opted for spot hiring – that is, short-term employment durations on demand. Others hoarded labor, offering workers long contracts and high wages, supplemented by housing and schooling for children. Another option was to substitute capital equipment for labor. If workers were not mobile, this would have the effect of putting downward pressure on wages themselves.

Business owners in Lancashire, the heartland of British industrialization, experimented with all these strategies. The early labor market in Manchester, the hub of the cotton textile trade, was a chaotic affair. There was high turnover of refractory male workers. Some firms sought to replace them with women and children, combined with investments in automatic equipment. In the heyday of British industrialization, say 1810, child labor was as prominent as in India 200 years later (Humphries 2010). Following Karl Polanyi (1944), the first industrial labor market has been cast as the paragon of the competitive model. Within one generation, however, a more coherent picture emerged. Male workers took on increased responsibility in the factories, tending the machines as well as supervising a team of assistant workers. The method of remuneration itself had been transformed into an incentive mechanism. Male workers were paid according to a piece wage list that assured them a share of their increased effort. Employment durations were extended (Huberman 1996). Even before the appearance of union contracts, layoffs were based on inverse seniority. This episode highlights how labor markets can become institutions themselves, meeting the requirements of both workers and employers.

Labor market institutions have a long legacy. All labor markets have rules of thumb because both workers and employers benefit from reduced costs of negotiation, including those associated with hiring, firing, and remuneration. On occasion, but not always, these informal rules, which may have had the appearance of custom, were codified. By the end of the nineteenth century, contemporaries often cited archaic workplace practices as an obstacle to sustained economic growth. Old practices had become locked in, making the adoption of new technologies and new products often difficult. But even rigid rules had offsetting effects. Consider the case of the modern cotton textile industry, the iconic global industry, which spread from Lancashire to continental Europe and then to low-wage countries abroad. How did high-wage Britain compete with low-wage India? It did so for nearly a century. Rigid pay lists assured workers a share of the gains of increased investments in new equipment, thereby providing them an incentive to sustain high levels of effort. In this respect, high wages promoted productivity growth, an outcome at cross currents with the textbook model in which wages adjust to productivity.

The development of U.S. manufacturing offers another illustration of the adaptation of technology to the supply of labor. In the absence of guilds, the United States did not have a long tradition of craftsmanship, and, initially, much of the demand for high-quality manufactured goods was met by European imports. As internal demand rose in the nineteenth century, producers, confronting scarce and high-priced skilled labor, substituted machines in their place and hired unskilled labor to operate them. The supply of labor in this instance had implications for product markets. To be sure, there were flows of skilled immigrants from the UK and Germany, but these never seem to have been sufficient. The bias in the United States was toward mass production of standardized items using semi-skilled labor. As technology developed along these lines, the dependence on unskilled labor was reinforced.

The geographic scope of labor supply in the United States expanded to meet the demand. Most industrial workers on the eve of the First World War were either immigrants or children of recent immigrants. The supply was not haphazard, however. Information flows were critical to the informal networks of friends and family behind the choice of destinations (Rosenbloom 2002). Many immigrants arrived on tickets paid for by someone already in the United States and they tended to settle in states where previous immigrants of the same ethnicity had settled. French Canadians, for instance, had a strong preference for textile employment in New England and Scandinavians went to the Midwest to become farmers. Informal networks thus perpetuated long-standing historical forces behind the operation of local labor markets. Not all regions were integrated into continental and transatlantic networks, however. The flow of immigrants to the U.S. North appears to have delayed the integration of the postbellum South, and, because labor markets in the regions were closed, age-old social and cultural values persisted (Wright 1986).

The first global labor market

The large waves of international and continental immigration between 1870 and 1914 had ramifications for national and global labor markets. Previously, much of long-distance migration was coerced or contractual. The early settlements in the United States were dependent on indenture servants, amounting to about one-quarter of European migrants until 1820. Under this system, individuals who signed multi-year contracts were given free passage to the colonies, and, upon arrival, their contracts were sold to merchants or farmers who needed labor. This type of arrangement had little effect on global labor markets. Contract labor was replaced by African slaves who were concentrated in resource-export sectors, like sugar and cotton. Unlike Roman slavery, there was little overlap between free and slave labor in the New World, thereby enabling the cruelty of the system to persist.

The transportation revolution, itself a product of the industrial revolution, changed fundamentally the nature and scope of the labor market. As transport costs fell, free migration became accessible to the masses. Over 50 million Europeans migrated to the New World and about an equal number moved within Europe. Mobility was universal. Another 50 million emigrants left India and China for labor-scarce and resource-abundant locations in Asia and Africa (Hatton and Williamson 2008: 127). Some of the movement was seasonal. By the eve of the First World War, Italian peasants made regular round trips to Argentina to harvest wheat during the European winter.

The geographic breadth of the market had expanded markedly with implications for wages and employment. Migration from the Old to the New World pushed wages downward in destination countries, while having the opposite effect in source countries. The result was the leveling of wages, or convergence, around the world. Trade operated in a similar fashion. Consumers and producers were able to substitute items produced by domestic labor for the same good, or a close substitute, produced by low wage workers elsewhere. As a result of the fall in transport costs, the demand for labor became more sensitive to changes in wages, and shocks in labor demand generated much greater fluctuations in both earnings and hours worked than had prevailed in the closed economy of the first half of the century. The period's gold standard exacerbated the effects of trade shocks on wages. As prices fell, the burden of adjustment was on labor. For workers producing similar goods, labor markets had become global.

Trade reconfigured the distribution of income within countries. Wages rose relative to land rents in labor-abundant regions specializing in labor-intensive production; wages fell relative to land rents in land-abundant regions specializing in agriculture and resources. Everywhere globalization promoted the demand for better social protection, but international integration restrained national labor movements. Migration weakened labor's ability in destination countries to mobilize, because heterogeneous groups of workers had difficulty in agreeing on collective or public goods. The contrast between the Old and New Worlds was telling in this regard. Certain labor movements in Europe's industrial core were hostile to foreign workers, but, since inflows of unskilled labor mapped onto existing factor supplies, the region's comparative advantage in labor-intensive items was unaltered. In North America, skilled workers were better organized than the unskilled and managed to defend their employment conditions. A divided labor movement in the New World was the result. An example of skilled workers' organizational capabilities was the rise of international trade unions that assured wage harmonization across the U.S.–Canadian border.

The pre-1914 period of globalization saw the beginning of the divergence in the labor histories of Old and New World countries that has persisted into the twenty-first century. In Europe, unions and their elected representatives succeeded in improving working conditions, embodied in new labor laws, even as the trade content of gross domestic product (GDP) rose. Hours of work in Europe fell dramatically as a result. In the New World, labor and social reformers had less success in pushing forward the social agenda. Despite a larger franchise in the settler economies, the various federal structures of the New World – labor law was the responsibility of sub-national units, provinces, or states – divided the nascent reform movement. With the exception of Australia, labor parties were weak. Moreover, in the New World, states sided more often with employers and were more open to use force to suppress strikes than was the case in the Old World. Much of the labor legislation that was adopted in the United States simply codified existing practice (Fishback 1998), or was the outcome of the general rise in prosperity (Whaples 1990). The end result was a growing divide between social Europe and liberal America. In the former, labor had better social protection, reduced hours of work, and longer employment spells, while, in the latter, labor was better paid and employment durations shorter. By the early twentieth century, these outcomes would become engrained in the respective industrial relations environments.

Labor markets since the First World War

The macroeconomic upheavals of the interwar years caused a change in direction in labor markets. If the period before 1914 witnessed the integration of world labor markets, after the First World War, the rising tide of economic nationalism pulled labor markets apart. The Great Depression deepened the divide between national economies. For a good part of the twentieth century, certainly until the recent wave of globalization beginning in the 1970s, the spatial dimension of labor markets was limited by national boundaries. The implication was that different types of labor markets and related institutions, promoted by states, business, and workers, and impervious to international competition, endured. In many countries, the advantage was tilted to labor's favor and its share of national income rose.

Developments in the United States were typical of the reversal in fortunes for labor. The war and legislation in the early 1920s put an end to mass European migration. The restrictions on labor supply raised real wages, ushering in sweeping changes in the functioning of markets. Turnover fell, employment durations lengthened, and labor conditions improved. The introduction of human resource departments in leading businesses contributed to this sea change. Compared with the prewar period, the average American worker was older, better educated, and more committed to industrial work. New Deal legislation had comparable effects on wages. Restrictions on the use of child labor and increases in the compulsory schooling age complemented the National Industrial Recovery Act (NIRA) and its follow-up legislation, and the Wagner Act, which promoted union organization in semi-skilled and skilled sectors. Earnings increased across the board, and particularly at the bottom end of the distribution. Because of restrictions in the labor market and cartelization promoted by the NIRA, unemployment did not exercise downward pressure on wages as in principle should have been the case. Business adapted to the high-wage labor market, investing in productivity-enhancing improvements and organizational changes. This in turn drove up the demand for skilled labor, which resulted in a long-term skill bias in technological change – that is, one favoring educated workers. In this fashion, labor market adjustments and reforms in the 1920s and 1930s had enduring effects on the distribution of rewards in the American labor market.

The labor market adjustments originating with the New Deal laid the basis for the golden age of labor lasting into the early 1970s, and which has been described as a high-wage national regime (Wright 2006: 147). While the Taft-Harley Act of 1947 rolled back some of the Depression gains for labor, union representatives and business in the automobile sector negotiated the Treaty of Detroit, which, because of pattern bargaining, had spillover effects throughout industry. With the imposition of high minimum wages, a pay floor was firmly established and hours of work declined. While management preserved the right to determine the direction of production, unions dictated the impact of these decisions on the shop floor. To be clear, minority groups were excluded from some of these benefits, but overall the average worker shared in productivity gains (Levy and Temin 2011). It should be noted that in the golden age of labor the trade content of U.S. GDP was small.

The paradox of post-war labor market history is that unions in Europe appear to have been more accommodating in their demands than their North American counterparts. A salient difference was that European labor, after the debacle of the interwar years, recognized the importance of trade for sustained growth. Workers opted for wage restraint. The strategy was favored because the reallocation of agricultural labor to industry in many parts of Europe that had begun before 1914 was not completed until the 1950s. With business, workers exchanged wage restraint for reinvestment of profits in enhanced technologies; with the state, workers committed themselves to social peace because they did not want to jeopardize the extension of unemployment insurance, and health and retirement benefits, and promises of more vacation time. As part of the social pact, all parties agreed to greater international exposure that also operated as a disciplinary device. Workers did not demand excessive wages for fear of over-pricing themselves, firms upgraded their plant and equipment in the face of stiff import competition, and states guaranteed market access for trading partners to get the benefits of membership in political and commercial unions (Eichengreen 2007).

Labor markets and globalization: the sequel

The 1973 oil shock ushered in a new chapter in world labor market history. Even before the crisis, the rise in part-time employment and the renewed labor market participation of women in developed countries had begun to alter the supply and demand for labor. Over time, a dual labor market had emerged: a primary labor market comprising full-time skilled workers, sometimes unionized, and a secondary market of the unskilled, minority groups, and immigrants, most often non-unionized. In the former, wages, and to a lesser extent employment, were invariant to economic shocks; in the latter, wages were flexible and job loss recurrent in periods of economic decline. However, labor market boundaries were not as sharp as some have claimed since workers moved between primary and secondary markets depending on skill levels and other attributes.

In advance of globalization, technological and ideological changes in the last decades of the twentieth century undermined existing labor market institutions. The technology revolution spurred a strong demand for skilled and educated workers. Since the rate of growth of supply did not always keep pace with demand, the wage gap between skilled and unskilled widened. In the United States, an ideological shift promoting reductions in the real minimum wage and de-unionization since the 1980s extinguished definitively the golden age of labor. With the exception of the United Kingdom, European labor resisted comparable political pressures and, by and large, labor regulation remained intact. By the early 1990s, the average European toiled about 200 hours less per year than a North American and had 2 more weeks of vacation time. Was the preference for leisure a statement of long-standing European social values? It may have been simply the outcome of reduced labor effort because of higher taxes, a phenomenon common to individuals everywhere. The regulated labor market had offsetting features, however. Unemployment was higher in continental Europe than in North America and young workers and immigrants had difficulty in finding entering positions.

Labor markets did not respond everywhere in the same fashion and not only because of different degrees of regulation. Even as the West was undergoing tumultuous changes, observers (Temin 1997) remarked that culture had made Japanese labor markets flexible and adaptive because employers and workers were predisposed to make long-term commitments to each other. Still, it is difficult to separate culture from economics as over time they have become blurred. Large enterprises invested in workers' general training, while employees had an incentive to be rotated among different activities to maintain the chance of upward mobility. Consequently, job specifications were far looser in Japan than in the United States.

Globalization at the dawn of the twenty-first century has had an impact on labor markets everywhere. While the process of releasing labor from agriculture to industry and creating an industrial labor force in the West was a long-term process, labor market developments in China and India have been rapid. In China, 300 million people have moved off the farm and into the factory in the last 25 years. Unlike the period before 1914 when immigration flows were considerable, trade forces by themselves have had powerful effects on labor markets and the distribution of income in the more recent wave of globalization. Low wages in labor-intensive industries in Asia have been seen to set earnings of workers in comparable sectors in rich countries (Freeman 1995). For the same reason, trade forces have challenged the social entitlements and labor standards of workers in the West. Outsourcing of production to low-wage countries has only magnified these effects. Even service-sector workers in richer countries compete against workers in poorer regions. In the new industrializing regions, skilled workers are in short supply. The result in the short term has been a widening of income distribution everywhere.

The long-term effects of globalization on labor markets are ongoing. There are signs of labor shortage in China and India that will moderate effects on earnings of low-wage workers everywhere (Bardhan 2010), while in the West the displacement of workers to industries producing higher-value goods will have a similar outcome. While the actual course of events remains uncertain, history makes clear that labor markets, sooner or later, will adjust.

References

Allen, R.C. (2001) 'The great divergence in European wages and prices from the Middle Ages to the First World War', *Explorations in Economic History*, 38: 411–47.

Bardhan, P. (2010) *Awakening Giants, Feet of Clay: Assessing the Economic Rise of China and India*, Princeton, NJ: Princeton University Press.

Carter, S.B. and Cullenberg, S. (1996) 'Labor economics and the historian', in T.G. Rawski, S.B. Carter, J.S. Cohen, S. Cullenberg, P.H. Lindert, D.N. McCloskey, H. Rockoff and R. Sutch (eds) *Economics and the Historian*, Berkeley, CA: University of California Press.

Clark, G. (2007) *A Farewell to Alms: A Brief Economic History of the World*, Princeton, NJ: Princeton University Press.

De Vries, J. (2008) *The Industrious Revolution: Consumer Behavior and the Household Economy, 1650 to the Present*, New York: Cambridge University Press.

Eichengreen, B. (2007) *The European Economy since 1945: Coordinated Capitalism and Beyond*, Princeton, NJ: Princeton University Press.

Epstein, S.R. (2008) 'Craft guilds in the pre-modern economy: a discussion', *Economic History Review*, 61: 155–74.

Fishback, P. (1998) 'Operations of "unfettered" labor markets: exit and voice in American labor markets at the turn of the century', *Journal of Economic Literature*, 36: 722–65.

Freeman, R. (1995). 'Are your wages set in Beijing?' *Journal of Economic Perspective*, 9: 15–32.

Grantham, G. (1994) 'Economic history and the history of labour markets', in G. Grantham and M. MacKinnon (eds) *Labour Market Evolution: The Economic History of Market Integration: Wage Flexibility and the Employment Relation*, London: Routledge.

Hatton, T.J. and Williamson, J.G. (2008) *Global Migration and the World Economy: Two Centuries of Policy and Performance*, Cambridge, MA: MIT Press.

Huberman, M. (1996) *Escape from the Market: Negotiating Work in Lancashire*, Cambridge: Cambridge University Press.

——(2012). *Odd Couple: International Trade and Labor Standards in History*, New Haven, CT: Yale University Press.

Humphries, J. (2010) *Childhood and Child Labour in the British Industrial Revolution*, Cambridge: Cambridge University Press.

Levy, F. and Temin, P. (2011) 'Inequality of institutions in twentieth century America', in P. Rhode, J.L. Rosenbloom and D. Weiman (eds) *Economic Evolution and Revolution in Historical Time*, Palo Alto, CA: Stanford University.

Polanyi, K. (1944) *The Great Transformation: The Political and Economic Origins of Our Time*, Boston, MA: Beacon Press.

Pomeranz, K. (2000) *The Great Divergence: China, Europe, and the Making of the Modern World Economy*, Princeton, NJ: Princeton University Press.

Rosenbloom, J.L. (2002) *Looking for Work: Searching for Workers*, New York: Cambridge University Press.

Solow, R.M. (1990) *The Labor Market as a Social Institution*, Oxford: Basil Blackwell.

Temin, P. (1997) 'Is it kosher to talk about culture?' *Journal of Economic History*, 57: 267–87.

——(2004) 'The labor market of the early Roman Empire', *Journal of Interdisciplinary History*, 34: 513–38.

Whaples, R. (1990) 'Winning the eight-hour day, 1909–19', *Journal of Economic History*, 50: 393–406.

Wright, G. (1986) *Old South, New South: Revolutions in the Southern Economy since the Civil War*, New York: Basic Books.

——(1987) 'Labor history and labor economics', in A. Field (ed.) *The Future of Economic History*, Boston, MA: Kluwer-Nijhoff.

——(2006) 'Productivity growth and the American labor market: the 1990s in historical perspective', in P.W. Rhode and G. Toniolo (eds) *The Global Economy in the 1990s: A Long-run Perspective*, New York: Cambridge University Press.

21

LABOR UNIONS AND ECONOMIC HISTORY

Gerald Friedman

Labor, industrialization, capitalism

Labor unions and socialist political movements are as much children of the spread of democracy in the late nineteenth and twentieth centuries as of the industrial revolution of the eighteenth and nineteenth centuries. By changing production technologies and the social relations among consumers, producers, and employers, industrialization created a working class able to challenge the organization of production and society and with a direct interest in disputing the distribution of income between workers and their employers. First in England, then throughout the industrializing world, the creation of a wage-earning class was followed by the creation of labor unions. Sustained union growth, however, began only in the late nineteenth century. By the middle of the twentieth century, unions became powerful forces throughout the developed world enrolling a substantial part of the labor force; this growth was not an inevitable result of industrialization, however, because it depended both on the extension of civil liberties to the working class and on government support for working-class collective action, usually during wartime or other national crises. This chapter discusses the nature and development of labor unions, including the role of industrial change, labor disputes, and political action in union growth. It concludes with a discussion of the decline of union membership in the late twentieth century.

Discussions of the industrial revolution and the labor movement begin with the theories of Karl Marx and Friedrich Engels (Marx 1974). In the *Communist Manifesto*, first published in 1847, Marx and Engels predict that the new proletarians created by the industrial revolution would revolutionize society. Capitalism, Marx and Engels argue, involves the creation of a labor force that is doubly free: free of control over the means of production and free of any ties to those (the capitalists) who own those means other than the exchange of labor time for wages.

Driven by competitive pressures to minimize the cost of production by finding the cheapest labor possible, capitalists will seek out low-wage workers and technologies to replace workers with skills and training with narrowly specialized workers requiring little specialized skill. Indeed, to replace relatively expensive craft workers with all-around skills, capitalists have created a new class of specialized workers whose narrow training allows them to perform simple tasks in a system of divided labor. Concentrated in large production units in big cities, Marx and Engels predict that the new proletarians would seek to improve their condition *within* capitalism by agitating for higher wages. Beginning with wage demands, they would form labor unions to manage their strikes. These unions would eventually fail and, Marx and Engels predict, their failures would teach proletarians that they can progress only through ever-wider solidarity and by building a *political* movement to overcome capitalism as a whole, creating a socialist society without commodity markets with distribution according to need.

The power of their analysis and their incisive writing led scholars of all politics to grapple with Marx and Engels's writings. For over a century after the *Manifesto*, socialists looked forward with anticipation, and their opponents with dread, to the unfolding of its predictions. But even the strongest socialist movements have failed to bring about a successful socialist revolution, and, today, socialist and labor movements are in retreat throughout the world. Whether relieved or disappointed with these failures, social scientists have had to reevaluate their approach to the labor movement. Instead of the precision of the Marxist model, recent scholars have seen the evolution of the labor movement as a contingent process. Within the economic and technological structures created by capitalist industrialization, the labor movement has been shaped by political factors and the outcomes of social conflicts. The rise of the labor movement has not been an inevitable product of the growth of capitalist industry; the labor movement is not necessarily destined to transform society.

This chapter reviews the growth of the labor movement in the course of industrialization from the perspective of this recent research. It begins with a discussion of relations between workers and their employers before the rise of capitalism. Next it discusses the industrial revolution and the way it changed labor relations. The rise of the labor movement is discussed in the next section; from the perspective of this research, the decline of the labor movement is evaluated in the final section.

Labor and society before the capitalist factory

Before modern labor unions, guilds united industrial workers, craftsmen, and their employees, setting minimum prices and quality, and regulating wages, employment, and output. Controlled by independent "masters" who employed journeymen and trained apprentices, guilds regulated industrial conditions and production to protect the comfort and status of the masters even while preserving a path to master status for apprentices and journeymen below them.

There were disputes between apprentices, journeymen, and masters within the guild system, but these conflicts differed fundamentally from modern capital–labor strife because they involved community action in defense of established privileges rather than worker solidarity to achieve progressive changes in conditions. Disgruntled guildsmen acted as members of communities in defense of traditional prerogatives rather than as wage workers with progressive grievances and demands for a general transformation of society. French journeymen, for example, would join their neighbors in *charivaris* to defend a traditional moral economy linking all members of the community in webs of reciprocal obligations and responsibilities (Tilly 1986). Highly routinized, even scripted, these were protests against violations of established rights rooted in community membership rather than demands for new rights or changes in conditions. Angry, for example, that a marriage was held without the customary wedding ball open to the community, or that a local merchant sold products made by outsiders, journeymen would gather with neighbors in a *charivari* outside the home of the miscreant. The *charivariseurs* would serenade the house, accompanying themselves on make-shift and improvised musical instruments while singing mocking, even obscene songs describing and condemning their putative miscreant's misdeeds. For small offenses, a gift of money or drinks would suffice to end the protest. More serious offenses required larger gifts, sometimes even including the departure of the guilty from the community.

Charivaris and other forms of community-based protest in defense of established moral claims were not restricted to wage earners, apprentices, or journeymen. Nor were they used to advance new claims or to demand an extension of popular control over production. Protesting high bread prices, for example, British women would occupy food markets and bakeries and sell the bread for what they held to be an appropriate and fair price; at the end of the protest, they would return the facility to its owner and hand over the proceeds from their sales. Rather than seizing the market to transform their situation, these women sought only to restore what they saw to be the community's traditional distribution of income and its established moral economy. Far from challenging the distribution of power, their protests reinforced established community ties by providing a means for workers to express their support for traditional values and the structures of the existing community (Thompson 1964; Wilentz 1984; Tilly 1986). By treating workers as members of communities, these struggles linked them with their non-wage-earning neighbors in defense of existing rights and responsibilities.

Conducted outside of the production process and without institutional support, *charivaris* united workers with homemakers, students, and others in defense of established claims. Focused on the development of the working class, Marxists have often discounted these earlier forms of protest along with their modern successors. By emphasizing grievances associated with capital–labor relations, they have discounted forms of oppression not linked to this relationship, including gender and racial oppression and discrimination against those with particular sexual or other orientations. Still, this older protest repertoire survives. By uniting members of different economic classes and social groups, community protests around moral issues and in defense of traditional values have been central in modern protest movements, including the Civil Rights movement of the 1950s and 1960s, and anti-war, feminist, and environmental actions, and the anti-abortion campaigns since then. Nor has this traditional repertoire excluded economic actions. Community action in defense of traditional values has been central to "living-wage" and anti-sweatshop campaigns, as well as union-organized campaigns such as the Justice-for-Janitors ones run by the Service Employees International Union since the 1990s.

Before the first factories, guild power was undermined by merchants and guild masters employing semi-skilled workers in their own homes in rural areas and small towns outside of the guild-dominated cities. While they were not capitalists because they did not directly control the means of production or supervise labor, these merchants had taken a giant step towards capitalism by freeing themselves of traditional community regulation, and freeing their workers of claims on the commodities they produced. It was a relatively short step then to the creation of factories where these workers were gathered together to work under supervision under one roof.

By the early 1800s, few in Britain, the United States, or France could anticipate moving up to becoming a master artisan or owning their own establishment. Instead, craftsmen began to seek a collective regulation of their individual employment. There may have been a surge in *charivari* and other popular protest in response to the declining opportunities for advancement within the guild system. Soon, sometimes inspired by the writings of Marx and Engels, many abandoned the defense of past positions to seek a collective regulation of employment and the extension of democratic rights to the workplace. In late eighteenth-century Britain, journeymen joined the growing republican movement; in the United States, they were "patriots" and "Sons of Liberty;" in France, they were radical *sans culottes* and supporters of the revolutionary *montaigne*.

The first "strikes" and labor associations came in the late eighteenth century. Unlike earlier protest, the strike is particular to wage workers fighting to advance new interests because it involves the conscious withdrawal of labor power from a capitalist exchange; no more labor unless wages are raised or other changes are granted. It was through strikes that workers came to develop new institutions specific to the wage earners, notably trade unions to organize and sustain strikes, and working-class socialist and labor parties to defend unions and the right to strike. Following Marx, scholars have looked to the semi-skilled workers of the new factories for these early strikes and unions. But the Marxist proletarians rarely struck and were poor prospects to inaugurate any new social movement. Often the most desperate and vulnerable workers took factory jobs (Pollard 1968). Poverty-stricken and without social or political resources or specialized skills, they were generally in a poor bargaining position. Rather than factory workers, the first strikes were organized by craft workers with the resources to remain outside of factories and who sought to develop a democratic alternative to the capitalist transformation of their trade. Carpenters, shoe makers, printers, tailors, and metal crafts workers organized some of the first strikes and the first labor unions. Further contradicting the expectations of a simplistic Marxian model, few of these strikes and unions were designed to promote worker solidarity. On the contrary, they were often intended to protect remaining craft privilege. Against the threat posed to their jobs and wages by semi-skilled wage workers in capitalist factories, they sought to reinforce established craft workers' control over the production process. Only after failing to secure their position as labor monopolists did craft workers seek to form a broad labor movement by spreading organization and solidarity to the new groups of semi-skilled factory workers.

The rise of labor unions

Some early nineteenth-century labor unions were formed on a broad basis uniting all wage workers without regard for craft or skill. Robert Owen's General National Consolidated Trades Union and the Workingmen's Parties formed in Philadelphia and other American cities in the 1830s were examples of these broad alliances (Thompson 1964; Wilentz 1984). None lasted long, however, because the new wage workers were slow to organize. Certainly, this was not for lack of grievances. Conditions in the early factories were often dismal. The work day was long, pay was low, and discipline was often abusive, especially for the young women who comprised a large share of the work force in textile and some other factories. But the *interest* factory workers had in forming unions was not enough to overcome the *collective action problems* that they faced (Olson 1965).

The lack of effective organization among the early wage workers is an example of why one cannot assume any simple connection between grievances and collective action. Quitting a bad job, exit, is a straightforward, simple act for an individual. But supporting collective action, like a strike or joining a labor union, requires that individuals commit themselves to produce *public goods* enjoyed by all regardless of their contribution. *Free riders* who contribute nothing to the group effort will receive the same benefits as do activists if the union succeeds; but, if it fails, the activists suffer while those who remained outside lose little or nothing. This makes *free riding* rational under virtually all circumstances.

Free riding is a problem for all collective action, including groups where there is no other barrier to effective action, such as religious communities, the Red Cross, and the Audubon Society. The one-sided nature of the Marxist model becomes clear when we consider that Marxists casually assume that unions will be formed even among relatively poor and weak workers facing the opposition of powerful employers and their political allies. Forming a union requires not only that some workers commit to a collective project, an irrational act for individuals, but it requires that enough individuals join against their better interest to overcome powerful opposition. Not only are workers crucial for unionization but so are employers and other opponents, and state officials.

The weaker side in the class conflict, labor, relies on the support of outsiders, especially state officials, to overcome the collective action problem and capitalist opposition (Friedman 1998; Hanagan 1980). Some unions may succeed because the workers want a union, or because employers do not oppose unionization very strongly, or because state officials are sympathetic. Some may succeed where workers are well positioned to overcome the collective-action problem because there are so few of them, because they know each other well so that they can police each other's contribution to the collective project, or because they are in a particularly strong bargaining position because the employer depends on their scarce skill. But focusing on workers and their grievances, Marxists almost act as if employers and state officials are indifferent to worker organization.

The slow development of labor protest in early factories reflected the difficulty workers in these industries had in overcoming free riding and resistant employers. To some degree, they shared these problems with craft and other workers who, at the time of the Industrial Revolution, were unfamiliar with the new repertoire of labor protest, strikes, unions, and socialist political organization, and hesitated to commit individual resources to it. Rather than hiring workers committed to improving conditions that they expected to work under for their lives, factories usually employed transient workers trained in a particular work process without lasting commitment to the job or even to the occupation. Preferring to see their factory work as a temporary status, their response to trouble was to exit, to seek other work, rather than to commit themselves to collective action to improve conditions.

Work in the early factories was recognized as particularly undesirable and the factories were largely filled with workers who lacked other alternatives, such as immigrants and ex-slaves, or workers who lacked personal autonomy, such as prisoners, children (including orphans), and young women. These new factory workers were from subservient groups who were hired because they were expected to accept work discipline without complaint. Collective protests by them not only challenged their employers but threatened other social hierarchies as well; their protests threatened established ethnic, familial, gender, or racial roles. Their protests were also inhibited because they often lacked political citizenship, the civil rights and political leverage needed to support their collective action. Instead, their challenges provoked state and community repression to reinforce the opposition of their employers.

Rather than recruiting from among the poorest-paid workers in factories or mines, the first unions were formed from among the best-paid workers, including craft workers in trades little influenced by modern factory methods: printers, construction workers, and workers in the most skilled metal trades and leather working (Friedman 1998; Hanagan 1980; Shorter 1974; Tilly 1986). Hoping to mobilize the power of a united working class to bring about a social revolution, socialists sought to transform these into inclusive unions uniting all wage workers in industries and regions on the basis of their common lack of productive property. Class-wide solidarity would spread the resources and bargaining leverage enjoyed by craft workers. It would also give inclusive unions greater political leverage due to a larger membership. But, well into the twentieth century, narrower unions dominated the labor movement. It was easier for small groups of skilled craftsmen to overcome the collective action problems both because they had bargaining leverage against their employers, and because their actions were not seen as challenges to other forms of social hierarchy and distinction.

By using a monopoly of knowledge to restrict access to their trade, the narrow craft unions of the early labor movement inflated their own wages at the expense not only of their employers, but of consumers and other workers as well. This craft strategy of organizing small groups of workers with control over exclusive skills offered nothing to factory laborers. As a tactic, it is not viable for large groups of workers with commonly available and easily taught skills. And, as a union policy, it hurts the larger number of unskilled and semi-skilled workers who are excluded by craft unions from their skilled positions and suffer when the skilled withdraw from any broader collective action to preserve their bargaining power for their own group without sharing any concessions won.

Into the early twentieth century, most strikes were conducted by craft workers to advance the interests of their particular craft, and most unions were organized by craft workers along narrow lines that excluded ordinary factory workers (Friedman 1998; Montgomery 1979; Shorter 1974; Perrot 1974; Sirot 2002; Caire 1978; Moss 1976). Even most socialist activists were craft workers with little sympathy for the modern semi-skilled factory worker (Hanagan 1980; Thompson 1964; Weir 1996; Wilentz 1984). A century after the Industrial Revolution began, the labor movement reflected the industrial revolution only negatively: labor militancy was directed at *limiting* the impact of factory production on craft workers rather than at organizing the new factory workers to advance their interests within the new industries.

It was a century after the industrial revolution began before there were lasting unions of factory workers, and even these depended on the organizing work and support of craft workers. Both ideology and self-interest led these craftsmen to seek to broaden their solidarity to include factory workers. Some were motivated by a commitment to democracy and to socialism. Ideology led American craftsmen like the machinists Ira Steward and Terence Powderly to organize factory workers and common laborers into inclusive industrial and regional unions; similar feelings and a commitment to socialist solidarity drove the French cobbler Victor Griffuelhes, and British machinists John Burns and Tom Mann. Paradoxically, Marxism, a materialist doctrine, contributed to the rise of the labor movement when socialist values led skilled craftsmen to neglect their own narrow interests to form alliances with the unskilled.

Experience led other craftsmen to promote industrial organization. Some had personal experience of factory work. This was the case, for example, with the American activist George McNeill. At the center of American labor struggles from the 1860s almost to the First World War, McNeill is known as a printer but he began his working life in 1847 as a 10-year-old at the Salisbury Corporation's Woolen Company textile mill in Amesbury, Massachusetts. The work day at the mill was 14 hours long, from 5:00 in the morning to 7:00 at night with three breaks allowed: 30 minutes for breakfast, 15 minutes for "luncheon privileges," and 45 minutes for dinner. In 1852, when McNeill was 15, the new manager, John Derby, decided this was too generous and eliminated the morning and afternoon breaks. When 100 employees defied his order to take their customary morning break on June 1, Derby fired them all. The following day, spinners, weavers, and workers in the carding room went out on strike. The strike failed, despite the support of the Amesbury town meeting, but it led McNeill to seek a trade (printing), and it launched his career as a labor activist. In 1863, he founded the Grand Eight-Hour League, with Ira Steward. By 1874, their efforts led the Massachusetts legislature to pass a law limiting children and women working in factory jobs to 10-hour days. McNeill himself moved on to organize for the Knights of Labor in the 1880s and the American Federation of Labor until his death in 1906. Throughout his life he retained the commitment he assumed in Amesbury to "plead for the little ones."

Other craft workers joined in inclusive unions when they were swept up in the excitement of what the American political scientist Aristide Zolberg has called "moments of madness." These are times when people are caught up in the excitement of the moment to join together without regard for individual interest to support a new collective project. Most union growth comes in such time, usually through major strike upheavals, where direct involvement in capital–labor disputes highlights class conflict, the need for organization, and the possibilities for collective action. Union membership growth has been associated with strike activity, especially massive strike waves involving workers previously outside of the labor movement. Such moments are rare, but they have been crucial for the growth in unions and the labor movement; almost all union growth has come during these few years of massive upheaval when unions grow by enrolling many of the striking workers caught up in the excitement of the strike. Strikes discourage free riding with activities ranging from demonstrations and peaceful picket lines designed simply to demonstrate the strike's support to physical intimidation and violence. And, by establishing a realm of working-class control, strikes also facilitate direct action to punish free riding (Friedman 2007). Strikes foster class consciousness by highlighting the division between labor and capital. The use of police and of private force against strikers, including strikes by craft workers, can persuade even selfish skilled workers that they share common interests with other wage workers and that they need to join together politically to change government policy.

But even this focus on transformative popular action misses a larger effect of popular upheavals: by presenting employers and state officials with a direct popular threat to their authority, strikes and popular upheavals frighten employers and state managers into dealing with unions as an alternative to disorganized labor protest. Collective bargaining does not come naturally to employers used to managing their businesses autocratically. But, frightened by popular unrest, some turn to unions as a relatively benign alternative to unorganized popular upheaval. Strikes can lead state officials to favor collective bargaining. Lacking faith in their own repressive powers, or unready to abandon democratic values, employers and state officials sometimes try to contain upheaval by seeking out *interlocateur valables*, labor leaders as partners who can deliver labor peace in exchange for tolerable concessions. If mass strikes and protest are seen as an "impetuous" wild revolt, then unions with bureaucracies and powerful leaders can be a means to restrain unrest and to substitute structured labor relations for strife and rank-and-file protest.

Here was the great discovery of late nineteenth-century social liberals, a way to assuage labor unrest by building on a materialist interpretation of the labor movement. Rather than reject all forms of popular and labor militancy, the new liberalism would appease and redirect this militancy, channeling it away from democratic challenges towards materialist issues that can be negotiated routinely between management and labor unions committed to restraining labor unrest. "Peaceable relations," a British Royal Commission pronounced in 1894, "are, upon the whole, the result of strong and firmly established trade unionism" (Great Britain 1892: 44; Howell 2005). Unions achieve this pacific result by restraining labor unrest in exchange for persuading management to correct inequities, by negotiating concessions on wages, hours, and working conditions, and by channeling worker demands away from the most contentious issues involving control over the production process. Employers and state officials reveal their true feelings when they agree to negotiate and sign contracts with unions representing their workers only because they are convinced that unions can use contracts to restrain popular unrest. Liberal capitalists and state reformers wanted unions that would regulate worker protest and channel it away from "unreasonable" demands for worker control towards wages and other issues amenable to compromise within the structures of capitalist authority (Friedman 2007).

Here was organized labor's Faustian bargain. Usually the product of popular upheaval, formal organizations have been established and have become powers in the land because they promise to put the genie back into the bottle, to end the very strife that brought workers together into unions. Again and again, periods of upheaval, moments of madness, were resolved by the establishment of formal labor movement institutions committed to the restoration of social peace through reform and the channeling of social unrest into paths that do not threaten employers' authority. Hardly had the French, in 1936, for example, discovered the power and possibility in the sit-down strike than their political and union leadership sought to restore tranquility in alliance with French capitalists and state officials. Communist Party leaders proclaimed that it was not revolution or militancy but "order that will assure success." Communists and the socialists in the new government of Léon Blum (elected as head of the Popular Front uniting Radicals, Socialists, and Communists) sought to restore calm and to channel the new energies into "possible" demands compatible with capitalist property and authority. In the subsequent *Matignon* Accords (named for the home of the French prime minister), unions exchanged a return to work and an end to the occupation of workplaces for collective bargaining, wage increases, and reduced hours of work (Kergoat 1986; Prost 1964; Tartakowsky 1986).

Grievous as the concessions at *Matignon* were to French employers, they were the grounds for a class compromise that left unchallenged the capitalist right to command workers' labor. (Many French employers never accepted *Matignon* and would proclaim "better Hitler than Blum" well into the Vichy years.) *Matignon* was the proving ground for the new French labor movement whose membership exploded during the strikes of 1936–7 because, after *Matignon*, labor leaders had to resolve the popular upsurges that had brought them power. Ignoring any nuance, the French Communist paper *L'Humanité* declared simply: "Victory is Obtained!" The improvement of salaries and of working conditions was presented as the full satisfaction of the strikers' demands. The workers were still under the authority of capitalists who retained the power to exclude them from their workplaces; but the new, responsible labor movement leaders told workers to settle for higher wages, benefits, and a shorter workweek. "Everything isn't possible," Maurice Thorez, leader of the French Communist Party, told a meeting of Parisian Communists on June 11, 1936. Strikers, he insisted, must abandon utopian notions of seizing power. They must "know how to agree to compromises in order not ... to make the fear and panic campaigns of reaction any easier." Above all, Thorez proclaimed in words echoed by labor leaders before and since: "one must know how to end a strike."

By demonstrating the failure of narrower strike strategies and craft organization, strike experiences led some craft workers to broaden their sense of solidarity, to spread solidarity beyond craft unions to involve common laborers and factory workers. The spontaneous involvement of these workers in strikes can stir sympathy from other workers. More powerful, however, can be the self-interest that craft workers find in broader solidarity when they watch their employers replace them with laborers and others previously excluded from their unions. Experience taught some the value of solidarity when craft unionists learned that to win strikes they needed the support of fellow workers, including workers in other crafts and even common factory workers. Advocates of broad unions and working-class solidarity argued that technological changes had reduced the value of specialized skill so that small groups of craft workers could no longer stop production on their own. In this view, which goes back to Marx's predictions about capitalism's trend towards homogenized labor, skilled workers cannot conduct effective strikes without the support of others. "Craft autonomy," the American labor leader Eugene V. Debs said, "denies industrial evolution. A modern industrial plant has a hundred trades and parts of trades represented ... To have these workers parceled out to a hundred unions is to divide and not to organize them" (Debs and YA Pamphlet Collection 1915: 20). Victor Griffuelhes, leader of the French *Confédération générale du travail*, agreed. He told the *Confédération*'s 1900 convention that machinery has rendered craft unions archaic. "We must," he argued, "find new means of struggle that respond well to this transformation. I estimate that only the creation of industry federations can give us the means to struggle" (Confédération générale du travail 1900: 153).

By the 1880s, craft workers throughout the advanced capitalist world had begun to abandon exclusive organizations for broader unions that included common laborers and semi-skilled factory workers. Craft workers brought to these new alliances the experience, resources, and bargaining leverage that allowed unions to be formed among semi-skilled counterparts; and the involvement of these additional workers in union struggles enhanced the unions' political claims while reducing the employers' ability to operate during strikes and other labor disputes. Socialists and other political radicals were especially active in promoting industrial organization and union amalgamation. Accepting Griffuelhes's arguments, revolutionary syndicalists, socialists, and anarchists led the French *Confédération générale du travail* to vote in 1900 to no longer accept craft unions as new affiliates and to promote the amalgamation of existing craft locals into industrial unions; perhaps as a consequence, French unions were especially effective in enrolling the semi-skilled workers in large factories. The spread of industrial and general unions in Germany and Britain was also associated with the enrollment of these workers. Effective industrial organization came later in the United States, in the 1930s with the passage of the Wagner Act and the rise of the Congress of Industrial Organization (CIO), many of whose leaders were socialists and communists. Unions belonging to the CIO organized some of the large factories of America's industrial heartland, including the steel industry (with the United Steelworkers of America), the automobile industry (the United Auto Workers), electronics manufacturing (United Electrical Workers), and, for a little while, textiles (with the United Textile Workers of America).

Basing their arguments on Marxian precepts, Griffuelhes, Debs, and other advocates of industrial unions emphasized the role of technological change in requiring new forms of union organization. Exaggerating the role of technological change and economic circumstances, they missed the greater impact of politics and state support in promoting unionization. Even with the support of craft workers, it is extraordinarily difficult to overcome the collective action problem in large establishments and continued employer opposition would make union organization nearly impossible. Instead, union success has almost always depended on the support of sympathetic outsiders, especially state officials led by sympathy or by electoral interest to favor unions. American industrial unions succeeded when supported by state officials, first during the First World War with the National War Labor Board, and then again during the New Deal and the early days of the National Labor Relations Board and the Second World War War Labor Board. The United Auto Workers was accepted by General Motors in 1937, not because a small minority of workers at a factory in Flint sat in and occupied the facility, but because the state's Democratic governor, Frank Murphy, refused to send the national guard in to clear the factory. Socialists and revolutionary syndicalists organized industrial unions in large French factories because they were able to manipulate France's fractured political system to gain the support of the dominant left Republicans against employers often allied with the right-wing and the monarchist opposition. British workers depended on the support of the Board of Trade to organize industrial unions. Without such state support, industrial organization would have been no more successful than it was in the United States in the 1920s, or since 1970.

The decline of the labor movement

The turmoil of the Second World War and the subsequent Cold War era led governments in Europe, America, and Australia and New Zealand to support unions as a means to rally support for national goals, and to prevent the economic disruptions of strikes and unrest (Lichtenstein 2003; McCartin 1997). In the United States, for example, in exchange for a no-strike pledge from unions, the Roosevelt Administration's War Labor Board pressed employers to recognize unions and granted unions "maintenance of membership" where new workers were auto-matically enrolled in the union and dues were deducted from pay. The support of the War Labor Board helped American unions to grow by over 50 per cent during the war years and the share of workers belonging to unions peaked at the end of the war (Friedman 2007).

This was the pattern throughout the world where unions grew rapidly because state support helped them to overcome collective action problems and employer resistance. During the Second World War, union membership doubled in Canada, and grew by over 60 per cent in Australia, the United Kingdom, and elsewhere. These membership gains persisted long after the war, and in most countries were magnified by continued state support for non-communist unions during the Cold War and by the support of organized labor's socialist and other allies. Political support contributed to a new wave of organization in the 1960s and 1970s among public sector workers including public school teachers, the uniformed services (police and fire), and workers in state-owned enterprises (Galenson 1994; Troy 1994). Some scholars have argued that, in some countries, union strength contributed to an extraordinary period of prosperity in the postwar decades, a period characterized by French economists as the "glorious thirty," when rapid economic growth and low rates of unemployment came with rapidly rising wages (Boyer 1986, 1993).

Postwar prosperity rested on cooperation between labor and capital to raise productivity while distributing the gains relatively amicably between wages and profits (Gordon 1982; Kerr 1964; Lichtenstein 2002). Notwithstanding examples of labor-management cooperation, there were fierce labor-management conflicts through the 1950s and 1960s, especially in Anglophone and Latin countries (Cowie 1999). But it was only in the late 1960s and 1970s that cooperation collapsed. Productivity growth plummeted in the 1970s in industries where there was a surge in wild-cat strikes, including mining and some of the auto industry in the U.S. and UK. The problem was always that labor peace was based on workers accepting management authority in exchange for higher wages; and it was the rank-and-file who ended this period of labor cooperation by rejecting this arrangement and joining in a massive wave of unauthorized strikes. In places, this tide of popular militancy brought new militant leaders to power; elsewhere, it prevented established union leaders from trading labor peace for higher wages (Cowie 2010; Friedman 2007).

For a time, governments pressed employers to accommodate labor discontent in the old way by granting still higher wages. In France, for example, the conservative government of Charles de Gaulle ended the national general strike of May–June 1968 *Matignon*-style with large wage concessions in the so-called "Grenelle Accords." In Britain, the newly elected Labour government of Harold Wilson ended a national coal strike with even larger wage increases in 1974. Rising wages preserved capitalist authority but at the price of inflation and falling profits; and authority was preserved only temporarily because rank-and-file militants returned with more demands for higher wages and concessions on managerial authority.

The dilemma of growing rank-and-file militancy was resolved only after 1979 with a change in state policy towards labor. Employers and state officials abandoned the old strategy of cooperation and labor peace for market deregulation and restrictive macroeconomic policies that restrained unrest with threats of unemployment. Beginning in Britain in 1979 with the election of a conservative government led by Margaret Thatcher and the installation of Paul Volcker as head of the United States Federal Reserve, governments attacked labor unrest and wage inflation without relying on the support of unions. Instead of seeking labor peace and wage restraint through cooperation with union leaders, Thatcher and Volcker, and their successors including President Ronald Reagan in the United States, restrained inflation with a cold bath of high unemployment.

The state turn against organized labor has led to a dramatic fall in union membership throughout the advanced capitalist world. German union membership has fallen by over a fourth since 1991; in Britain, the share of workers belonging to unions has fallen by over half since 1979; Australian unions have lost over half their membership since 1975; and Dutch unions have lost a third of their membership since 1977. Union collapse has been greatest in manufacturing and other industries particularly vulnerable to international trade and product market competition. This has led to a gap among unions with isolated bastions of union membership surviving among public sector and other service workers.

Union decline has been associated with economic changes and an end to the era of the "glorious thirty." Inflation has fallen but unemployment rates have been higher in many countries and national income has shifted away from wage workers towards managers, their employers, and the owners of capital. Union decline has been associated with other social changes. The labor movement has pressed to redistribute power and respect in society, and unions have provided much of the political muscle for coalitions in support of civil liberties and extending democratic rights. One may wonder how well such campaigns will fare in a world with a much weaker labor movement.

References

Boyer, R. (1986) *La Théorie de la Régulation: Une Analyse Critique*, Paris: La Découverte.

——(1993) *L'après-Fordisme*, Paris: Syros.

Caire, G. (1978) *La Grève Ouvrière*, Paris: Éditions Économie et humanisme.

Confédération générale du travail (1900) *Compte rendu du congrès national, 1900*, Paris: Confédération générale du travail.

Cowie, J. (1999) *Capital Moves: RCA's Seventy-Year Quest for Cheap Labor*, Ithaca, NY: Cornell University Press.

——(2010) *Stayin' Alive: The 1970s and the Last Days of the Working Class*, New York: New Press.

Debs, E.V. and YA Pamphlet Collection (Library of Congress) (1915) *Unionism and Socialism; A Plea for Both*, New York: Union Publishing.

Friedman, G. (1998) *State-Making and Labor Movements: France and the United States, 1876–1914*, Ithaca, NY: Cornell University Press.

——(2007) *Reigniting the Labor Movement: Restoring Means to Ends in a Democratic Labor Movement*, Abingdon: Routledge.

Galenson, W. (1994) *Trade Union Growth and Decline: An International Study*, Westport, CT: Praeger.

Gordon, D.M. (1982) *Segmented Work, Divided Workers: The Historical Transformation of Labor in the United States*, Cambridge: Cambridge University Press.

Great Britain (1892) *Report[s], [minutes of Evidence, Indexes, Answers to Questions]*, London: Printed for H.M. Stationery Office by Eyre and Spottiswoode.

Hanagan, M.P. (1980) *The Logic of Solidarity: Artisans and Industrial Workers in Three French Towns, 1871–1914*, Urbana, IL: University of Illinois Press.

Howell, C. (2005) *Trade Unions and the State: The Construction of Industrial Relations Institutions in Britain, 1890–2000*, Princeton, NJ: Princeton University Press.

Kergoat, J. (1986) *La France du Front Populaire*, Paris: La Découverte.

Kerr, C. (1964) *Industrialism and Industrial Man: The Problems of Labor and Management in Economic Growth*, 2nd edition, New York: Oxford University Press.

Lichtenstein, N. (2002) *State of the Union: A Century of American Labor*, Princeton, NJ: Princeton University Press.

——(2003) *Labor's War at Home: The CIO in World War II*, Philadelphia, PA: Temple University Press.

Marx, K. (1974) *The Communist Manifesto*, Belmont, MA: American Opinion.

McCartin, J.A. (1997) *Labor's Great War: The Struggle for Industrial Democracy and the Origins of Modern American Labor Relations, 1912–1921*, Chapel Hill, NC: University of North Carolina Press.

Montgomery, D. (1979) *Workers' Control in America: Studies in the History of Work, Technology, and Labor Struggles*, Cambridge: Cambridge University Press.

Moss, B.H. (1976) *The Origins of the French Labor Movement, 1830–1914: The Socialism of Skilled Workers*, Berkeley, CA: University of California Press.

Olson, M. (1965) *The Logic of Collective Action; Public Goods and the Theory of Groups*, Cambridge, MA: Harvard University Press.

Perrot, M. (1974) *Les Ouvriers en Grève, France 1871–1890*, Paris: Mouton.

Pollard, S. (1968) *The Genesis of Modern Management: A Study of the Industrial Revolution in Great Britain*, Harmondsworth: Penguin.

Prost, A. (1964) *La C.G.T. à L'époque du Front Populaire, 1934–1939; Essai De Description Numérique*, Paris: A. Colin.

Shorter, E. (1974) *Strikes in France, 1830–1968*, London: Cambridge University Press.

Sirot, S. (2002) *La Grève en France: Une Histoire Sociale: XIXe–XXe Siècle*, Paris: O. Jacob.

Tartakowsky, D. (1986) *Des Lendemains Qui Chantent?: La France Des Années Folles et du Front Populaire*, Paris: Messidor/Editions Sociales.

Thompson, E.P. (1964) *The Making of the English Working Class*, New York: Pantheon Books.

Tilly, C. (1986) *The Contentious French*, Cambridge, MA: Belknap Press.

Troy, L. (1994) *The New Unionism in the New Society: Public Sector Unions in the Redistributive State*, Fairfax, VA: George Mason University Press.

Weir, R.E. (1996) *Beyond Labor's Veil: The Culture of the Knights of Labor*, University Park, PA: Pennsylvania State University Press.

Wilentz, S. (1984) *Chants Democratic: New York City and the Rise of the American Working Class, 1788–1850*, New York: Oxford University Press.

22

THE ECONOMIC HISTORY OF EDUCATION

David Mitch[1]

That humans would make provision for the development of their offspring is to be expected, given the length of time between birth and maturity we experience as a species. And there is evidence from early in recorded human history of provision for apprenticeship and markets in training and instruction. Nevertheless, it is only in the last few centuries that provision of formal instruction and schooling has become widespread and indeed has become a gauge of potential for economic development. Economists since Adam Smith, if not earlier, have argued that the performance of an economy has been influenced by the education of its work force (Johnson 1937). These developments call for consideration of both the causes and consequences of the rise of education in historical perspective.

Students and their parents have purchased instructional services from ancient times onwards and there is evidence that in some ancient Greek city states the society and state were involved as well (Cubberley 1920). One can distinguish two types of instructional markets. One is characterized by direct outlays in payment and by the transmission of knowledge and skills from teacher to student. In contrast, a second type of market, apprenticeship, which can be documented from the Code of Hammurabi circa 1700 BC (Westermann 1914: 304) onwards, can be characterized by access to experiential learning opportunities financed by making the labor services of the learner available to sponsors of apprenticeship. By the high Middle Ages, apprenticeship came to be associated with guilds. Some historians have argued that the time required for completing an apprenticeship considerably exceeded that required to master a given craft and that guild-sponsored apprenticeship largely constituted a barrier to entry into skilled occupations rather than a means of conveying skill (Ogilvie 2008). However, other scholars have argued that apprenticeship constituted an efficient means of facilitating and financing access to experiential training opportunities (Epstein 1998, 2008; Humphries 2003). Institutional procedures, such as the Statute of Artificers established in England in 1563, developed to foster and regulate apprenticeship (Minchinton 1972).

There is little indication of systematic, centralized provision of schools and instructional services prior to the Protestant Reformation. Botticini and Eckstein (2005, 2007) argue that Judaism as a "religion of the Book" cultivated far higher rates of adult literacy than other populations in ancient and medieval times. Instructional services in the medieval period were available through local and itinerant teachers and schools run by the clergy themselves, with affiliated religious sponsorship, by lay philanthropic foundations or for profit (Graff 1987; Moran Cruz 1985).

While the medieval university has been associated with arid, academic scholasticism, it was in fact often centered around the professional faculties of Law, Medicine, and Theology (Cubberley 1920). Joan Simon's summary description of education resources in the English county of Leicestershire in the early seventeenth century, admittedly from the early modern period, can be deemed to apply to the medieval period as well: "a nucleus of organized schools in the main centres, then parish schools interspersed with lesser foundations in the countryside and, on a more casual basis, curates and schoolmasters engaged in teaching whose qualifications gradually rose" (Simon 1966: 376).

Trends in educational participation and attainment

Although available estimates are quite fragmentary, the extent of schooling and corresponding literacy attainment in the later Middle Ages and early Renaissance appears to have varied considerably according to social class and gender and also according to locality and between town and country (Houston 2002). While major gaps remain, available evidence suggests considerable improvement in schooling and literacy activity following the onset of the Protestant Revolution in the early sixteenth century. Cressy's (1980: 176–7) rough estimates of literacy for England, based on signature ability, show an increase from only around 10 per cent for men and 2 or 3 per cent for women in 1500 to around 60 per cent for men and 40 per cent for women in 1750. Johansson's estimates for Swedish parishes show increases from under 50 per cent prior to 1620 to over 80 per cent by 1690 (Johansson 1987: 87). Allen (2003: 415) develops estimates of adult signature ability based on urbanization shares. He finds that in 1500 the proportion of adults who could sign their names across Europe varied from a low of 6 per cent for England, Germany, Austria-Hungary, and Poland to a high of 10 per cent in Belgium and the Netherlands; he puts the percentage for France at 7 per cent and for Italy and Spain at 9 per cent. He then reports based on firmer evidence that in 1800 the adult signature rate varied from low values of 20 per cent for Spain, 21 per cent for Austria-Hungary and Poland, and 22 per cent for Italy to intermediate levels of 35 per cent for Germany, 37 per cent for France, 49 per cent for Belgium, and 53 per cent for England to a high of 68 per cent for the Netherlands.

By the eighteenth century, a distinct minority of adult populations throughout most regions of the world possessed even minimal literacy and numeracy skills. In 1800, the only areas of the world in which a clear majority of adults had basic literacy skills were North America, Germany, and Scandinavia. In 1900, these areas had been joined by much of the rest of Western Europe, most notably Britain and France. Throughout the rest of the world, literacy and exposure to primary education were still relatively uncommon at this time (Graff 1987).

Benavot and Riddle's (1988) compilation of primary school enrollment rates indicates that in 1890 the majority of children in the world aged 5–14 were not enrolled in primary schooling at any particular point in time, though a substantial proportion probably saw the inside of a schoolroom at some point during childhood. For a collection of 66 countries for which there are consistent data, they report (see Figure 22.1) that the primary school enrollment rate for children aged 5–14 was 32.9 per cent in 1890 and had risen to 51.7 per cent by 1935–40. For a broad group of 120 countries for which data are available in the latter time period, primary school enrollment rate was 40.9 per cent. Across regions, this ranged from 79.1 per cent for North America and Oceania, 72.1 per cent for Northern Europe, 48.2 per cent for Eastern Europe, 30.6 per cent for Asia, and 19.6 per cent for sub-Saharan Africa.

Economic historians have recently used age-heaping as an alternative way to measure trends in human capital development. The logic behind this measure is that populations with little exposure to numeracy tend to report numerical ages disproportionately ending in either 0 or 5.

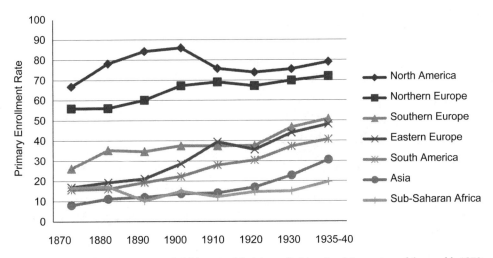

Figure 22.1   Trends in percentage of children aged 5–14 enrolled in school, by region of the world, 1870–1940

Source: Benavot and Riddle (1988).

As populations become more accustomed to working with numbers, the tendency for ages to heap at numbers ending in either 0 or 5 tends to decline. Employing indexes based on this measure, one recent study found that in Western Europe the percentage of adults correctly reporting their numerical age had already reached 70 per cent by 1600 and rose to 90 per cent by 1700. For Northern Italy, where longer-run estimates are available, this percentage rose from 31 per cent in 1350 to 89 per cent in 1750. The authors employ data from a study of grave inscriptions to infer that in Rome between 0 and 200 AD, the rate was 55 per cent (A'Hearn *et al.* 2009: 803). They suggest that, by this measure, numeracy became widely diffused in these populations prior to literacy as measured by signature ability. While they find that in the Eastern European areas of Bohemia, Hungary, and Russia numeracy rates in the mid-1600s were in the range of 30 to 45 per cent, considerably lower than what they report for Western Europe, by 1800 considerable convergence had occurred towards Western European levels. In a separate study of global age-heaping trends, Crayen and Baten (2010) find that in 1850 numeracy levels in South Asia, the Middle East, North Africa, and Southeast Asia were considerably lower than in industrialized areas of Western Europe, Japan, and North America, but that considerable convergence had occurred between these regions by 1940.

As Table 22.1 and Figure 22.2 indicate, by the end of the twentieth century, the rest of the world was clearly catching up with developed countries at the primary schooling level. For the world as a whole, male gross primary enrollment rates were 102 per cent in 1999 rising to 109 per cent in 2010. Since gross enrollment rates are measured relative to the primary school-aged population, countries enrolling students out of age range in primary schools can have gross enrollment rates exceeding 100 per cent.

World literacy rates have been estimated at 80 per cent in the year 2000 with literacy rates for countries classified as least developed at 50 per cent. By 2005–9, adult literacy had increased to 84 per cent and for Africa had reached 63 per cent, with female literacy rates at 79 per cent for the world and in Africa at 54.6 per cent. Enrollment rates of primary school-aged children indicate rapid catch-up across regions of the world over the last decade (1999–2010), with rates approaching 100 per cent even for sub-Saharan Africa. Differences by gender have

Table 22.1   Primary school enrollments around 2000

	Males 1999	*Males* 2010	*Females* 1999	*Females* 2010
World	102	109	94	105
South and West Asia	97	113 (2007)	81	107 (2007)
Arab States	93	102	81	94
Sub-Saharan Africa	86	105	73	97

Source: UNESCO Institute for Statistics (2001), Reports, Table 20D.

Note: Primary gross enrollment rate is defined as number of students enrolled in primary school as a percentage of the primary school-age population. This percentage can exceed 100 due to enrollment of students older than primary age.

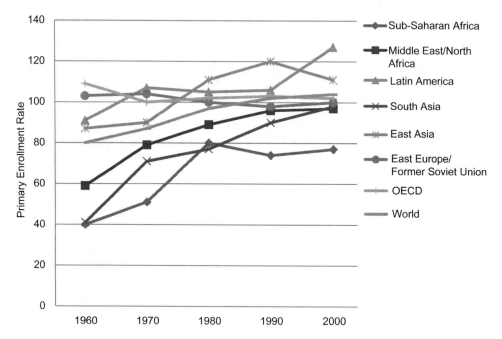

Figure 22.2   Primary gross enrollment rates by regions of the world, 1960–2000

Source: Glewwe and Kremer (2006).

Note: Primary gross enrollment rate is defined as number of students enrolled in primary school as a percentage of the primary school-age population. This percentage can exceed 100 due to enrollment of students older than primary age.

persisted. Nevertheless, for the world as a whole, the ratio of female to male literacy rates rose from 0.77 in 1970 to 0.86 in 2000 and for countries classified as least developed from 0.41 in 1970 to 0.67 in 2000 (UNESCO Institute for Statistics 2011).

Although enrollments in primary schooling have grown remarkably in the last half-century, especially in developing countries, the impact of these gains on educational attainment has been impeded by erratic patterns of school attendance and the frequently very low quality of schooling in developing countries (Glewwe and Kremer 2006).

The evidence of convergence for secondary and tertiary education over the last century is less pronounced (see Figure 22.3). Prior to 1900, only a small minority of adults completed

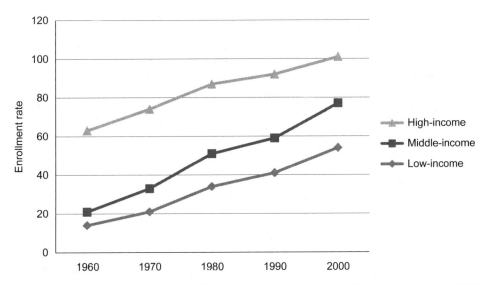

Figure 22.3   Trends in secondary gross enrollment rates for countries grouped by income per capita, 1960–2000

Source: Glewwe and Kremer (2006).

Note: Secondary gross enrollment rate is defined as the number of students enrolled in secondary schools as a percentage of the total population of secondary age. This percentage can exceed 100 if students of non-secondary age enroll in secondary school.

secondary or higher education even in the most developed countries of the world. Between 1970 and 2000, enrollments for those of secondary age in developed countries rose from 76 to 100 per cent and for least developed countries from 10 to 19.3 per cent. For higher education, the percentage rose from 26 to 52 per cent for developed countries and from 1 to 3.2 per cent for least developed countries. And similar trends have continued since 2000 (UNESCO Institute for Statistics 2011). In 1990, the mean years of schooling completed in the developed world was 10 years, but only 3.7 years for the developing world.

While the catch-up in enrollment rates in higher education has been modest for developing countries, their absolute population size has implied that they have started to overtake the United States as global suppliers of highly educated workers. From the 1970s onwards, enrollment rates have grown faster in developing countries, such as India and China, in higher education. In 1970, 29 per cent of the world's college students regardless of nationality were studying in the United States; by 2006, this share had fallen to 12 per cent while in the same year the share of developing countries was almost 75 per cent. By 2004, China produced 57 per cent as many PhDs in science and engineering as the United States and it is projected to soon overtake the U.S. (Freeman 2009). (It should be noted, however, that this makes no allowance for quality differences in higher and doctoral education between developed and developing countries.)

Also striking has been the overtaking of men by women in enrollment in higher education in most developed countries in recent decades. Beginning in the 1970s, enrollment of women in higher education grew at a faster rate than men and, by 2004, the majority of university students in 21 of 25 advanced countries were women (Freeman 2009; Goldin *et al.* 2006).

Expenditure shares of national income devoted to schooling appear to have risen during the first half of the twentieth century. Edding estimates for a group of five developed countries that expenditure on public education rose from about 1–2 per cent of national income around 1900 to 4–5 per cent by 1960 (Edding 1966: 26; Blaug 1970: 127–36). However, by 1999, the OECD average expenditure on non-tertiary schooling relative to gross domestic product (GDP) had leveled at 3.6 per cent (OECD 2002). Glewwe and Kremer (2006) note that, while expenditure on education relative to GDP in 2000 was larger in higher-income than lower income countries, the differences were not pronounced. And while expenditure per student relative to GDP per capita was higher in higher-income than lower-income countries, the gaps narrow considerably once allowance is made for price differences in non-traded goods and services across countries.

The rise of mass schooling: factors influencing public provision of schooling

Instruction of any sort can be privately supplied in the marketplace. Why, then, have societies increasingly turned toward the public provision of schooling?

The primary reason may be that people have increasingly come to see education as having significant benefits to society at large. Over time and cross-sectionally, the public share in total educational expenditure and enrollment in publicly managed schools relative to privately managed schools generally rises with the level of economic development (James 1993; Lott 1990; Fernandez and Rogerson 2001). Thus, in explaining the rise of schooling in recent centuries, a central focus has been the rise of public support for schooling.

Although there has not been a uniform path to the diffusion of mass schooling, scholars have distinguished some basic factors at work. Regarding motives, one useful distinction is between the public provision of education due to neighborhood effects – effects that fall beyond those obtaining the education – and the public provision of education as a means of redistribution from segments that pay a disproportionate share of the cost of education to those who realize a disproportionate share of the benefits. Both motives appear to have been present historically. Regarding the means of providing and funding public education, some accounts have emphasized the role of centralized institutions such as national governments or church hierarchies. This perspective argues that centralized governments and religious institutions can fund and set high standards for mass schooling as well as pursue universal involvement much more effectively than localized entities. However, other accounts have emphasized the importance of local commu-nity interests. And the counterargument for this position is that, without local support and enthusiasm for the spread of education, individual schools would have been unlikely to attract students or be effectively supervised. Beadie (2010a) provides a useful overview of the historical literature on these contrasting perspectives. John Stuart Mill (1861) set forth the classic argument for federalism in the provision of schooling with both centralized setting of standards and local monitoring suggesting the contrasting virtues of both centralized and decentralized provision. Beadie's (2010b) careful case study of a New York State antebellum community delineates the effective interaction between local community-level and regional-level actors in the rise of public schooling in the first half of the nineteenth century.

Even free-market advocates have noted that mass schooling has distinctive features from other commodities and services that can generate market failures. Both Adam Smith and Milton Friedman exhibited a clear preference for private provision and the role of profit incentives in instructional markets. Nevertheless, both also acknowledged a significant role for government in the market for schooling. Smith (1776) acknowledged the value in his native Scotland of the schools that localities had funded in each parish. As Friedman (1962) notes, the schooling of children raises both neighborhood effects – the schooling of other people's children affects me and my own children – and paternalism effects – poor or good decisions by parents can affect their children's schooling and life outcomes.

An important historical influence on the rise of mass education has come from religious groups. They have been important not only as sources of financial support for schooling but also for establishing doctrines and ideology either supportive of or impeding the spread of popular schooling. They have frequently been active in the establishment and funding of schools not only as a way of cultivating literacy and other cognitive skills but also as ways of propagating their own religious beliefs and related non-cognitive behaviors. For some religious groups such as the Jews and early modern Scandinavian Lutherans, the cultivation of religion seems to have been complementary with that of literacy and related cognitive skills (Botticini and Eckstein 2005, 2007; Johansson 1987). However, there is also evidence of opposition by religious elites (among others) to working-class schooling in early nineteenth-century England (Kaestle 1976) and evidence that Muslim emphasis on religious schooling displaced secular schooling in early twentieth-century India, even though the secular schooling was likely to have been more effective in propagating literacy (Chaudhary and Rubin 2011).

Historians of education often associate the Protestant Reformation with the perception of neighborhood and paternalism effects for popular schooling. The simplest and most commonly articulated version of this association is that Martin Luther and other Protestant leaders of his era emphasized the importance of the ability of the individual believer to read the Bible, and this in turn led church and lay leaders to paternalistically diffuse instruction in reading among the general populace. As a *post hoc propter hoc* explanation, this seems to work well in broad-brush cross-country terms. Scandinavia and Germany became early leaders in the spread of popular instruction following the Reformation in those countries (see Becker and Woessmann 2009 for detailed statistical and econometric analysis). However, deeper examination by historians has revealed considerable ambiguity in the causal mechanisms and channels of influence at work, and in the timing of the spread of reading ability and literacy following the Reformation in the sixteenth and seventeenth centuries (Craig 1981). Gawthrop and Strauss (1984) have challenged the direct connection between Lutheran or other Protestant doctrine and the promotion of popular Bible reading.

Another related line of analysis has emphasized the value to national religious and political leaders of using schooling to promote doctrinal and cultural uniformity whether in religious practice, patriotism, or loyalty to political ideology. Gawthrop and Strauss (1984), in their analysis of the relationship between Protestantism and the development of schooling networks, argue for the importance of local rulers, Catholic as well as Protestant, in using control over schooling to promote homogeneity of religious belief. Melton (1988) as well as Gawthrop and Strauss (1984) argue that an important follow-up impetus to Luther's Reformation was the late seventeenth- and eighteenth-century Pietist movement, which viewed popular education as a means of social control in eighteenth-century Austria and Prussia. Vaughan and Archer (1971) and Green (1990) consider the role of centralized control over schools as a way of promoting social uniformity in their comparative studies of Britain, France, and the U.S. Beadie (2010a) contrasts the decentralized provision in the U.S. with these European comparative studies.

For the twentieth century, Lott (1990) argues that totalitarian regimes have been disproportionately likely to promote schooling as a way of promoting ideology supportive of their regimes.

It should be noted that the motives for educational provision and funding in all these cases often focuses on the impact of schooling on the non-cognitive behaviors of students, what could loosely be labeled social control, because it aimed to instill order in populations and reduce tendencies to crime, disorder, and improvident behavior, rather than schooling as a way of enhancing labor market productivity.

Much recent work by economic historians has emphasized the importance of redistributive coalitions in motivating the development of public education. The general claim is that public schooling has emerged and developed when it has been feasible for political coalitions to arise that favor redistribution of resources via taxes to support schools. A number of analyses of the uneven development and access to schooling and literacy by race in the postbellum U.S. South reflect the distributional dimensions of schooling (see, for example, Margo 1990). In contrast, Goldin and Katz (2008), in their assessment of what they term the "virtues" of U.S. schooling, argue that homogeneity of local communities implied that agreement could be reached on acknowledging the neighborhood and paternalistic externalities of schooling and hence for support of schooling, thus avoiding gridlock over distributional conflicts. Consistent with this view, Alesina *et al.* (1999) argue that diversity and fragmentation among interest groups has impeded support for funding public goods such as schooling in the late twentieth-century U.S. Lindert's (2004) international comparative analysis of the rise of mass schooling gives prominent place to the timing of the franchise, which he argues reflects the use of popular voting power to support public schooling as a way of redistributing resources to the masses, as does Stasavage's (2005) study of Africa. Engerman *et al.* (2009) suggest that differences in inequality in access to political power explain the stark differences between North and South America in the timing and extent of support for mass education. In the United States and Canada, egalitarian ideology and increasing access to the franchise implied the use of public funding to redistribute resources to lower- and middle-income groups in the funding of schooling. However, in South America, the much greater inequality of wealth and political power implied much greater reluctance of elites to fund popular education or of lower classes to demand it. Recent studies of developing areas have also pointed to the presence of distributional coalitions hostile to support of mass education (see, for example, Chaudhary 2009 on India). However, research on India has also suggested that the colonial British establishment of secondary education contributed to higher levels of secondary enrollment in the early twentieth century than in France or Japan, and contributed to the development of India's service sector (Chaudhary 2009; Broadberry and Gupta 2010).

A number of scholars, including Engerman and Sokoloff (2000), Galor *et al.* (2009), Galor (2011), and Cinnirella and Hornung (2011), have argued that inequality in land ownership has been a key impediment to the development of mass schooling with its associated inequality of control over economic resources, and that ameliorating this inequality has been key to the spread of popular schooling.

Stoddard (2009) tests the relative importance of distributive versus external benefits in explaining the timing of support for public schooling for the United States in the mid-nineteenth century. She finds that an increase in wealth dispersion tended to lower the share of public spending in the U.S. at this time and interprets this as consistent with the perception of external benefits to public schooling as dominant over redistributive motives. Her argument is that, in a model with external benefits dominant, an increase in wealth dispersion will increase the percentage of the population with a tax price of schooling exceeding perceived external benefits, while in a model emphasizing redistributive motives an increase in dispersion should increase the benefit to the median voter of supporting public schooling. However, Gallego's (2010) analysis of variation in primary school enrollment for a global sample of countries in both 1900 and 1985–95 finds that the degree of democratization has tended to have a positive influence on primary school enrollments, which could be interpreted as supporting the presence of redistributive elements in the support for primary schooling. James's (1993) analysis of cross-country variation in public share in secondary enrollments finds that allowing for religious diversity weakens the impact of income level, which she interprets as showing the presence of redistributive motives. Stoddard (2011), based on analysis of increasing support for fee subsidization and ultimately free schooling in nineteenth-century New York State, finds that the relative importance of the distributive motive increased over time, as the distribution of wealth and voting power changed. She argues that initially successful political coalitions were dominated by middle-income groups over both elites and the poor, neither of which would patronize public schools. However, as the century progressed, lower-income groups dominated the coalition but also experienced rising demands for schooling for their children that shifted support towards completely free schooling. Thus, as suggested earlier, the relative importance of external benefit versus redistributive motives for the funding of public schooling would appear to have varied by time and place.

Centralization of the provision of education can be seen as having made a number of contributions to the rise of mass schooling. It insured the diffusion of school buildings and teachers and thus growing access throughout a given population to instructional services. It also set in place and presumably improved standards for curriculum and for teacher training. And it insured that even more backward areas, reluctant to support education, received compensating funding from centralized sources. Furthermore, compulsory schooling legislation and enforcement could insure that even reluctant parents ended up sending their children to school. Skeptics have argued that compulsory schooling legislation was effectively enforced only after widespread popular support for schooling was present. But recent estimates suggest a substantive impact on enrollments for the U.S. Clay *et al.* (2010) estimate that compulsory schooling laws in the late nineteenth-century U.S. raised enrollment rates (which for the relevant age groups were initially in the 60 to 80 per cent range) by a further 2 to 7 percentage points. Moreover, centralized mandates could override more localized discrimination against certain racial and ethnic groups as with the case of civil rights legislation in the twentieth-century U.S. (Donohue *et al.* 2002; Margo 1990).

One important stage in this increased public funding concerns the decision to eliminate school fees. In the U.S., this occurred relatively early with the elimination of rate bills in the mid-nineteenth century throughout the United States (Go and Lindert 2010; Stoddard 2011). In the case of England, it did not occur until the 1890s. In developing countries, fees are still often present for primary schooling (James 1993). Other scholars have emphasized the role of local support for schooling. The U.S. in particular is a case noteworthy for the very limited role of the national government in the provision of schooling but with very early and active provision of schooling at the local and state level. Some of the factors seen as contributing to the success of local initiative in the U.S. are the homogeneity of communities supporting education and the egalitarian ethic (Goldin and Katz 2008). Go and Lindert (2010) have argued that decentralization and local autonomy in school provision and funding in the antebellum Northern United States allowed public support for schooling to emerge in high-demand localities without being blocked by low-demand groups elsewhere. They argue that the more centralized arrangements in the U.S. South impeded the emergence of local coalitions supportive of public schooling. Similar arguments have been made about regional diversity in support of education in late nineteenth- and early twentieth-century Brazil (Martinez-Fritscher *et al.* 2010). But even in areas where education expansion has been characterized by top-down initiative, local community support has been identified as important, as in Prussia and Austria in the eighteenth century (Melton 1988). Going back to at least early modern times, some regions and communities in Europe had traditions of providing communal resources to support teachers, often providing additional sources of livelihood for those agreeing to engage in teaching duties (see Maynes 1979 and Melton 1988).

Gallego's (2010) international analysis for the later twentieth century finds decentralization of political power had a positive effect on secondary school enrollments. He suggests that decentralization implies more local autonomy in the provision and management of schools, which can lead to more responsiveness and tailoring of instruction more closely to local demands. He also notes that more decentralized systems may be able to more effectively mobilize local funding for schools. However, Glewwe and Kremer (2006) offer a more mixed assessment of the advantages of decentralized compared with centralized provision of schooling in current developing countries. On the one hand, they acknowledge that centralized funding arrangements can result in substantial wastage due to corruption of funds actually reaching local schools. On the other hand, they note studies of Kenya indicating that communities with substantial ethnic diversity had difficulty in coping with collective action problems and ruling elites established decentralized control of schools in ways that tended to allocate resources to regions most favored by these elites. In addition, Chaudhary (2009) finds that for late nineteenth- and early twentieth-century India caste and religious diversity reduced the level and effectiveness of local private provision of schooling.

In sum, this survey suggests the variety of historical experience with provision of mass schooling and the various roles in specific historical circumstances that can be played by addressing the neighborhood effects of schooling, the redistributive aspects of public funding for schools, and the contribution of both centralized and decentralized aspects to the provision of schooling.

The private demand for education

While historians have emphasized the role of public efforts in promoting the expansion of schooling, it has also been recognized that any such expansion will be greatly amplified insofar as it is reinforced by the eagerness of parents and their children to attend school. These private motives can vary ranging from perceived labor market advantages of education to a desire for self-improvement for its own sake. However, as already noted, economists such as Smith and Friedman have recognized that the markets for education may fail due to factors such as capital market imperfections, imperfect information by parents and children on the labor market advantages of schooling, and barriers to entering occupations making use of education, including societal attitudes toward gender roles. The discussion here will proceed by first considering labor market trends in the demand for education based on the arguable premise that labor markets have functioned reasonably efficiently. Then consideration will turn to one major influence that can shift demand for schooling even in the presence of market failures (i.e. rising income levels). Finally, very brief consideration will be given to non-labor market uses of schooling.

The pecuniary return to schooling provides the most obvious economic explanation for private investment in schooling and other forms of training such as apprenticeship.

It can be argued that in the long run, with constant supply costs of providing skill and schooling, the premiums to skill and education should be constrained to provide a normal rate of return to the investments involved. Any excess in returns above that should encourage additional entry, which lowers returns accordingly. While subject to considerable margins of error, some attempts at estimating skill premia over several centuries based on differences between skilled and unskilled building workers have found constant premia consistent with this perspective (Clark 2005; van Zanden 2009). However, there is abundant evidence of strong swings in skill premia over shorter time periods (Goldin and Margo 1992; Goldin and Katz 2008; Hornstein *et al.* 2005; Williamson 1985).

An increasing premium placed on education is often associated with rising demands for education due to the scientific and technological revolutions and industrialization from the seventeenth century onwards (Easterlin 1981; Kuznets 1966). Other longer-term developments may have generated demands for educated workers as well. Johnson (1964) suggested that the centrality of art and practice in contrast to science in pre-industrial societies pointed to on-the-job experiences as the most effective approach to learning. However, there were pre-industrial developments contributing to the rise of more formal instruction. The earliest systems of writing seem to have emerged in ancient Babylonia and Egypt as ways to monitor government tax collections (Goody 1986). And this would lead to some sort of provision for instruction in writing and deciphering these writing systems, albeit most likely for a quite small proportion (under 10 per cent) of the adult population. In the early Middle Ages, there was increased use of writing as a substitute for memory (Clanchy 1993; de Roover 1965: 59) and in particular the development of double entry bookkeeping that could be attributed to the rise of commercial activity at this time.

The expansion of education in the United States and elsewhere in the twentieth century has been depicted, as originally suggested by Tinbergen (1975), as a race between schooling and technology (see, for example, Berman *et al.* 1998; Machin and Van Reenen 1998). This suggests that technological advance is skill-biased, or, in other words, skill- or education-using. One way to explain the presence of skill- or education-using technological advance is to argue that technological advance has been increasingly knowledge-based and hence has increased the demand for educated workers who can use advances in knowledge (Easterlin 1981; Kuznets 1966; Abramovitz and David 1996) and can adapt to the disequilibria associated with changes in knowledge (Schultz 1975). However, this does not account for how widespread the use of knowledge or education is in the labor force. Thus, other accounts have argued that skill-biased technical change has arisen due to specific historical circumstances and to particular types of technological advance (Goldin and Katz 1998). Some have argued that any education-using bias of technology is itself endogenous, and in particular has been affected by the premia paid for education. Economies facing relatively low premia for education would have greater incentives to demand and hence to generate more education-using technologies (Acemoglu 2002).

Unified growth theorists, in attempting to explain the apparently changing role of education over the last few centuries, have argued that the economic system itself has longer-term triggers, which set off interactions between education and technology, and which have led to the onset of modern economic growth (Galor 2011). The nature of these triggers remains sketchy. However, one scenario by which they would work is that an initial surge in education levels – for example, fueled in early modern Europe by the Reformation – has in turn generated new technologies that in their turn lead employers to increasingly value education of their workers, setting in motion ongoing positive interactions between education and technology. In the case of manufacturing, Goldin and Katz (1998) have mapped out changing relationships in the case of the United States.

Given the complexity of possible interactions and limitations on evidence regarding educational attainment, especially in conjunction with earnings or measures of economic activity, much remains obscure about how the demand for education has changed in the course of economic change and growth. The three following sectoral examples illustrate the issues and possibilities.

Agriculture is often regarded as a tradition-bound economic activity, and as such one that would have relatively little call for education. However, Adam Smith among others noted the diversity and irregularity of activity in agriculture compared with factory work. And much of the early work on education as a factor of production in the 1960s and 1970s recognized the value of education in agriculture in enhancing decision-making ability in response to technological and economic change (Griliches 1964; Welch 1970; Schultz 1975; Huffman 2001).

In the case of manufacturing, Sanderson (1972) pointed to evidence that early English textile factories made extensive use of illiterate labor. It was also noted by investigators for the

Newcastle commission in mid-Victorian England that in relatively affluent industrial districts, where little labor market advantage was perceived to schooling, enrollment rates were relatively low, while in port cities, with a higher perceived advantage, enrollment rates tended to be higher (Mitch 1992). Goldin and Katz (1998) mapped out for the United States from the late nineteenth century onwards how complementarity between capital and skill evolved as manufacturing shifted from a more artisanal orientation towards factory and then to batch, assembly line, and other continuous process methods of production. They suggest that the shift from artisanal workshops to the factory may on net have lowered the relative demand for skilled labor, but that the subsequent shift to batch and continuous process methods of production increased it. The skilled labor was embodied in the machine-building and maintenance segment rather than in the machine-operation and product-assembly segment of manufacturing operations.

The service sector has become notorious for relatively slow productivity growth due to the difficulty of substituting capital for human judgment and skill in this sector, thus leading to Baumol's so-called "cost-disease problem" (Baumol and Bowen 1966; Baumol, 1993). Recent work on the impact of computers has suggested that computers can substitute for humans in tasks involving clear procedural logic, while leaving untouched tasks where procedures are much more problematic to specify in a formal or systematic manner. This can lead to declining demand for less skilled labor with increasing demand for educated labor more capable of exercising judgment (Baumol 1993; Autor *et al.* 2002).

This work points to the importance of considering skill and task content of jobs and how these can change over time in an endogenous manner as sketched by Autor *et al.* (2002, 2003) and Acemoglu and Autor (2011). This factor would seem especially critical for determining the extent of demand for educated labor throughout the work force as a whole.

Although females had achieved parity in college completion in the United States earlier in the twentieth century, changing social attitudes and labor market opportunities contributed to women overtaking men in college completion in the later twentieth century. Comparable recent trends in female advantage over males in college completion in other OECD countries would suggest similar influences at work (Goldin *et al.* 2006).

One obvious explanatory factor on the demand side that transcends pecuniary motives and market imperfections is rising living standards throughout the world over the last few centuries. Simple cross-section scatter plots of educational expenditure on income per capita as well as pooled time-series cross-country regressions support some role for rising income (Blaug 1970: 127–36; Edding 1966). However, the issue of direction of causation arises – whether rising educational attainment has also contributed substantially to rising income per capita. The issue of mutual causation between schooling and income has featured centrally in discussions of education and economic development going back as far as Bowman and Anderson's classic study (1963). The more general issue arises of why people value education regardless of their income levels. One can argue that with perfect capital markets and only a pecuniary return to education – that is, with schooling only as an investment – an optimizing model of schooling choice would not predict any impact of wealth changes on educational attainment (Behrman and Knowles [1997] and Glewwe and Jacoby [2004] following Becker [1967]). Findings of a positive effect of wealth on educational attainment can be interpreted as reflecting the presence of some combination of capital market imperfections and consumption value (i.e. non-pecuniary) to schooling. A number of studies of late twentieth-century developing countries do indicate causation from income to schooling but also point to the importance of care in measurement and to differences in how children's school careers can differ by level of poverty (Behrman and Knowles 1997; Filmer and Pritchett 1999; Glewwe and Jacoby 2004; Thomas *et al.* 2004).

Filmer and Pritchett (1999) also note distinctive patterns across the world in whether the very poor are unlikely to send their children to primary school at all or whether the wealth gaps in schooling occur because of higher attrition rates by age according to poverty. They identify a Latin American pattern in which there is universal enrollment in the first year of schooling or lower primary education that then drops off to zero for the poor for subsequent schooling, and they distinguish this pattern from an East African one where many poor do not send their children for any schooling.

Historical studies looking at variation over time and across countries have found a positive effect of per capita income on school enrollment rates; however, this evidence has been confined to examining macro-level country variation in income and enrollment measures. It doesn't provide direct estimates of income elasticities (Engerman *et al.* 2009: 134; Lindert 2004).

The development of the printing press and associated rise of book production enhanced the value of literacy (Dittmar 2011; Eisenstein 1979). One non-labor market factor increasing the private demand for basic education has been the falling price of print media and increased value to writing through the service sector (Altick 1957; Mitch 1992; St. Clair 2004; Vincent 1989, 2000).

Consequences of mass schooling

The expansion of schooling would seem to be an obvious factor contributing to modern economic growth. However, the actual impact of schooling expansion depends on the channels through which it influences output per capita and on historical circumstances that influence those channels. The most direct channel is through enhancing the productivity of individual workers. With this channel, the contribution to growth over some period would depend on both how much the productivity of the individual worker is enhanced by any given increment of education and the percentage of the labor force increasing its levels of educational attainment. Insofar as the return to education is high and the proportion of the labor force affected is large, then the contribution of education to economic growth is likely to be high. And in some situations such as for the United States in the twentieth century this appears to have happened. Denison (1962) estimated that, for the period 1929 to 1957, as much as 42 per cent of the growth in real GDP per capita in the United States could be attributed to improvements in work force educational attainment. However, more recently, Goldin and Katz (2008: 40) obtain a more modest estimate of 15 per cent for this contribution over the period 1915 to 2005. In other situations, either or both returns to education and expansion of schooling have been limited, while other factors such as capital accumulation or technological advance unrelated to rising educational attainment appear to have contributed more substantially to economic growth; England during the industrial revolution is one conspicuous example.

However, another channel that has been emphasized is that the level of education affects the generation and adoption of technological advance and adaptability more generally. Here causal effects are more difficult to pin down. Benhabib and Spiegel (1994) find evidence for this in the late twentieth century supporting the original conceptual foundation proposed by Nelson and Phelps (1966). That is, through cross-country analysis, they find that levels of educational attainment rather than changes in educational attainment affect growth rates. Their argument is that the overall level of schooling contributes to adaptability and the possibility of technological advance rather than changes in schooling changing the quality of individual workers. Becker *et al.* (2011) find support for this framework in their examination of cross-county differences in the rate of industrialization relative to schooling levels in nineteenth-century Prussia.

Empirical attempts to estimate the impact of education on economic growth from cross-country studies have varied considerably in their findings and much depends on model specification (Mitch 2005; Pritchett 2001; Bils and Klenow 2000). One conclusion would seem to be that the impact of education on growth varies with particular context and not in obvious ways. Thus education can have as large an impact in agriculture as in manufacturing because possibilities for technological advance and adaptation can be at least as large in that traditional sector.

Going beyond economic impacts to the impact on human welfare more generally and attempting to incorporate likely positive externalities of schooling, analysts and investigators are increasingly emphasizing the importance of women's education. Schultz's (2002: 211–21) assessment of a large interdisciplinary and international literature of micro-studies concludes that the external benefits of women's schooling are considerably larger than men's schooling. These studies indicate that enhancements in women's schooling are more likely to raise educational attainment of their children, lower their mortality rates, and improve their nutrition and health outcomes than equivalent enhancements in men's schooling. A presumption of greater female involvement with childrearing and household production in past times would suggest that these findings would generalize to previous periods in history as well, but this is a matter requiring further investigation.

Conclusion

The rise of mass education is one of the most striking developments of recent centuries. It clearly should be viewed as a historical phenomenon rather than some universal tendency of human nature. The protean nature of education implies that it can serve different purposes for different groups in different places and times. This chapter suggests diverse paths to the spread of education – and the consequences for economic development and economic well-being have also been diverse. Resource commitments to public education have been no more than a few percentage points of national income. Yet the consequences for economic performance and human welfare suggest that this sector warrants continued monitoring.

Notes

1 I would like to thank without implicating Latika Chaudhary and Robert Whaples for quite helpful comments on an earlier draft of this chapter.

References

Abramovitz, M. and David, P. (1996) 'Technological change and the rise of intangible investments: the U.S. economy's growth-path in the twentieth century', in OECD Documents, *Employment and Growth in the Knowledge-based Economy*, Paris: OECD.

Acemoglu, D. (2002) 'Technology and the labor market', *Journal of Economic Literature*, 40: 7–72.

Acemoglu, D. and Autor, D. (2011) 'Skills, tasks, and technologies: implications for employment and earnings', in O. Ashenfelter and D. Card (eds) *Handbook of Labor Economics*, vol. 4B, Amsterdam: Elsevier.

A'Hearn, B., Baten, J. and Crayen, D. (2009) 'Quantifying quantitative literacy: age heaping and the history of human capital', *Journal of Economic History*, 69: 783–808.

Alesina, A., Baqir, R. and Easterly, W. (1999) 'Public goods and ethnic divisions', *Quarterly Journal of Economics*, 114: 1243–84.

Allen, R. (2003) 'Poverty and progress in early modern Europe', *Economic History Review*, 56: 403–43.

Altick, R. (1957) *The English Common Reader*, Chicago, IL: University of Chicago Press.

Autor, D.H., Levy, F. and Murnane, R.J. (2002) 'Upstairs, downstairs: computers and skills on two floors of a large bank', *Industrial and Labor Relations Review*, 55: 432–47.

——(2003) 'The skill content of recent technological change: an empirical exploration', *Quarterly Journal of Economics*, 118: 1279–333.

Baumol, W.J. (1993) 'Health care, education, and the cost disease: a looming crisis for public choice', *Public Choice*, 77: 17–28.

Baumol, W.J. and Bowen, W.G. (1966) *Performing Arts: The Economic Dilemma*, New York: Twentieth Century Fund.

Beadie, N. (2010a) 'Education, social capital and state formation in comparative historical perspective: preliminary investigations', *Paedagogica Historica*, 46: 15–32.

——(2010b) *Education and the Creation of Capital in the Early American Republic*, New York: Cambridge University Press.

Becker, G.S. (1967) 'Human capital and the personal distribution of income: an analytical approach', Woytinsky Lecture No. 1, Ann Arbor, MI: Institute of Public Administration.

Becker, S. and Woessmann, L. (2009) 'Was Weber wrong? A human capital theory of Protestant economic history', *Quarterly Journal of Economics*, 124: 531–96.

Becker, S., Hornung, E. and Woessmann, L. (2011) 'Education and catchup in the industrial revolution', *American Economic Journal: Macroeconomics*, 3: 92–126.

Behrman, J. and Knowles, J.C. (1997) 'How strongly is child schooling associated with household income', University of Pennsylvania CARESS Working Paper No. 97–022.

Benavot, A. and Riddle, P. (1988) 'The expansion of primary education, 1870–1940: trends and issues', *Sociology of Education*, 61: 191–210.

Benhabib, J. and Spiegel, M. (1994) 'The role of human capital in economic development: evidence from aggregate cross-country data', *Journal of Monetary Economics*, 34: 143–73.

Berman, E., Bound, J. and Machin, S. (1998) 'Implications of skill-biased technological change: international evidence', *Quarterly Journal of Economics*, 113: 1245–69.

Bils, M. and Klenow, P.J. (2000) 'Does schooling cause growth?' *American Economic Review*, 90: 1160–83.

Blaug, M. (1970) *An Introduction to the Economics of Education*, Harmondsworth: Penguin.

——(1975) 'The economics of education in English classical political economy: a re-examination', in A.S. Skinner and T.Wilson (eds) *Essays on Adam Smith*, Oxford: Oxford University Press.

Botticini, M. and Eckstein, Z. (2005) 'Jewish occupational selection: education, restrictions, or minorities?' *Journal of Economic History*, 65: 922–48.

——(2007) 'From farmers to merchants, conversions and diaspora: human capital and Jewish history', *Journal of the European Economic Association*, 5: 885–926.

Bowman, M.J. and Anderson, C.A. (1963) 'On the role of education in economic development', in C. Geertz (ed.) *Old Societies and New States*, New York: Free Press.

Broadberry, S. and Gupta, B. (2010) 'The historical roots of India's service-led development: a sectoral analysis of Anglo-Indian productivity differences, 1870–2000', *Explorations in Economic History*, 47: 264–78.

Chaudhary, L. (2009) 'Determinants of primary schooling in British India', *Journal of Economic History*, 69: 269–302.

Chaudhary, L. and Rubin, J. (2011) 'Reading, writing, and religion: institutions and human capital formation,' *Journal of Comparative Economics*, 39: 17–33.

Chin, A., Juhn, C. and Thompson, P. (2006) 'Technical change and the demand for skills in the second industrial revolution: evidence from the merchant marine, 1891–1912', *Review of Economics and Statistics*, 88: 572–8.

Cinnirella, F. and Hornung, E. (2011) 'Landownership concentration and the expansion of education', University of Munich working paper.

Clanchy, M.T. (1993) *From Memory to Written Record: England, 1066–1307*, 2nd edition, Oxford: Blackwell.

Clark, G. (2005) 'The condition of the working class in England, 1209–2004', *Journal of Political Economy*, 113, 6: 1307–40.

Clay, K., Lingwall, J. and Stephens, M. (2010) 'Compulsory attendance laws and nineteenth-century schooling', SITE conference paper.

Craig, J. (1981) 'The expansion of education' in D.C. Berliner (ed.) *Review of Research in Education*, 9: 151–213.

Crayen, D. and Baten, J. (2010) 'Global trends in numeracy 1820–1949 and its implications for long-term growth', *Explorations in Economic History*, 47: 82–99.

Cressy, D. (1980) *Literacy and the Social Order: Reading and Writing in Tudor and Stuart England*, Cambridge: Cambridge University Press.

Cubberley, E. (1920) *The History of Education: Educational Practice and Progress Considered as a Phase of the Development and Spread of Western Civilization*, Boston, MA: Houghton Mifflin.

Denison, E. (1962) 'Education, economic growth, and gaps in information', *Journal of Political Economy*, 70: 124–8.

de Roover, R. (1965) 'The organization of trade' in M.M. Postan, E.E. Rich, and E. Miller (eds) *The Cambridge Economic History of Europe, Vol. III*, Cambridge: Cambridge University Press.

Dittmar, J. (2011) 'Information technology and economic change: the impact of the printing press', *Quarterly Journal of Economics*, 126: 1133–72.

Donohue, J.J., Heckman, J.J. and Todd, P.E. (2002) 'The schooling of southern blacks: the roles of legal activism and private philanthropy, 1910–60', *Quarterly Journal of Economics*, 117: 225–68.

Easterlin, R. (1981) 'Why isn't the whole world developed?' *Journal of Economic History*, 41: 1–19.

Edding, F. (1966) 'Expenditure on education: statistics and comments', in E.A.G. Robinson and J.E. Vaizey (eds) *The Economics of Education: Proceedings of a Conference Held by the International Economic Association*, London: Macmillan.

Eisenstein, E. (1979) *The Printing Press as an Agent of Change: Communications and Cultural Transformations in Early Modern Europe*, Cambridge: Cambridge University Press.

Engerman, S. and Sokoloff, K. (2000) 'Institutions, factor endowments, and paths of development in the new world', *Journal of Economic Perspectives*, 14: 217–32.

Engerman, S., Mariscal, E. and Sokoloff, K. (2009) 'The evolution of schooling in the Americas, 1800–1925', in D. Eltis, F.D. Lewis, and K.L. Sokoloff (eds) *Human Capital and Institutions: A Long-Run View*, New York: Cambridge University Press.

Epstein, S.R. (1998) 'Craft guilds, apprenticeship, and technological change in pre-industrial Europe', *Journal of Economic History*, 53: 684–713.

——(2008) 'Craft guilds in the pre-modern economy: a discussion', *Economic History Review*, 61: 155–74.

Fernandez, R. and Rogerson, R. (2001) 'The determinants of public education expenditure: longer-run evidence from the states', *Journal of Education Finance*, 27: 567–83.

Filmer, D. and Pritchett, L. (1999) 'The effect of household wealth on educational attainment: evidence from 35 countries', *Population and Development Review*, 25: 85–120.

Freeman, R.B. (2009) 'What does global expansion of higher education mean for the U.S.?' NBER Working Paper No. 14962, Cambridge: MA: NBER.

Friedman, M. (1962) 'The role of government in education', in *Capitalism and Freedom*, Chicago, IL: University of Chicago Press.

Gallego, F. (2010) 'Historical origins of schooling: the role of democracy and political decentralization', *Review of Economics and Statistics*, 92: 228–43.

Galor, O. (2011) *Unified Growth Theory*, Princeton, NJ: Princeton University Press.

Galor, O., Moav, O. and Vollrath, D. (2009) 'Inequality in landownership, the emergence of human-capital promoting institutions, and the great divergence', *Review of Economic Studies*, 76, 1: 143–79.

Gawthrop, R. and Strauss, G. (1984) 'Protestantism and literacy in early modern Germany', *Past & Present*, 104: 31–55.

Glewwe, P. and Jacoby, H. (2004) 'Economic growth and the demand for education: is there a wealth effect?' *Journal of Development Economics*, 74: 33–51.

Glewwe, P. and Kremer, M. (2006) 'Schools, teachers, and education outcomes in developing countries', in E. Hanushek and F. Welch (eds) *Handbook of the Economics of Education*, vol. 2, Amsterdam: Elsevier.

Go, S. and Lindert, P. (2010) 'The uneven rise of American public schools to 1850', *Journal of Economic History*, 70: 1–26.

Goldin, C. and Katz, L. (1998) 'The origins of technology-skill complementarity', *Quarterly Journal of Economics*, 113: 693–732.

——(2008) *The Race Between Education and Technology*, Cambridge, MA: Harvard University Press.

Goldin, C., Katz, L. and Kuziemko, I. (2006) 'The homecoming of American college women: the reversal of the college gender gap', NBER Working Paper No. 12139, Cambridge, MA: NBER.

Goldin, C. and Margo, R. (1992) 'The great compression: the wage structure in the United States at mid-century', *Quarterly Journal of Economics*, 107: 1–34.

Goody, J. (1986) *The Logic of Writing and the Organization of Society*, Cambridge: Cambridge University Press.

Graff, H. (1987) *The Legacies of Literacy: Continuities and Contradictions in Western Culture and Society*, Bloomington, IN: Indiana University Press.

Green, A. (1990) *Education and State Formation: The Rise of Education Systems in England, France, and the USA*, New York: St. Martin's.

Griliches, Z. (1964) 'Research expenditures, education, and the aggregate production function', *American Economic Review*, 54: 961–74.

Hornstein, A., Krusell, P. and Violante, G. (2005) 'The effects of technical change on labor market inequalities', in P. Aghion and S. Durlauf (eds) *Handbook of Economic Growth*, vol. 1B, Amsterdam: Elsevier.

Houston, R.A. (2002) *Literacy in Early Modern Europe: Its Growth, Uses, and Impact*, 2nd edition, London: Longman.

Huffman, W. (2001) 'Human capital: education and agriculture', in B. Gardner and G.C. Rausser (eds) *Handbook of Agricultural Economics*, vol. 1, Amsterdam: Elsevier.

Humphries, J. (2003) 'English apprenticeship: a neglected factor in the first industrial revolution', in P.A. David and M. Thomas (eds) *The Economic Future in Historical Perspective: Essays in Honour of Charles Feinstein*, Oxford: Oxford University Press.

James, E. (1993) 'Why do different countries choose a different public–private mix of educational services?' *Journal of Human Resources*, 28: 571–92.

Johansson, E. (1987) 'Literacy Campaigns in Sweden', in R.F. Arnove and H.J. Graff (eds) *National Literacy Campaigns: Historical and Comparative Perspectives*, New York: Plenum.

Johnson, E.A.J. (1937) *Predecessors of Adam Smith: The Growth of British Economic Thought*, New York: Prentice-Hall.

——(1964) 'The place of learning, science, vocational training and "art" in pre-Smithian economic thought', *Journal of Economic History*, 24: 129–44.

Kaestle, C.F. (1976) '"Between the Scylla of brutal ignorance and the Charybdis of a literary education": elite attitudes toward mass schooling in early industrial England and America', in L. Stone (ed.) *School and Society: Studies in the History of Education*, Baltimore, Md: Johns Hopkins University Press.

Kuznets, S. (1966) *Modern Economic Growth: Rate, Structure, and Spread*, New Haven, CT: Yale University Press.

Lindert, P. (2004) *Growing Public. Social Spending and Economic Growth since the Eighteenth Century*, Vols 1 and 2, Cambridge: Cambridge University Press.

Lott, J. (1990) 'An explanation for public provision of schooling: the importance of indoctrination', *Journal of Law and Economics*, 33: 199–232.

Machin, S. and Van Reenen, J. (1998) 'Technology and changes in skill structure: evidence from seven OECD countries', *Quarterly Journal of Economics*, 113: 1215–44.

Margo, R.A. (1990) *Race and Schooling in the South, 1880–1950: An Economic History*, Chicago, IL: University of Chicago Press.

Martinez-Fritscher, A., Musacchio, A. and Viarengo, M. (2010) 'The great leap forward: the political economy of education in Brazil, 1889–1930', Harvard Business School Working Paper No. 10–075.

Maynes, M.J. (1979) 'The virtues of archaism: the political economy of schooling in Europe, 1750–1850', *Comparative Studies in Society and History*, 21: 611–25.

Melton, J. (1988) *Absolutism and the Eighteenth-century Origins of Compulsory Schooling in Prussia and Austria*, Cambridge: Cambridge University Press.

Mill, J.S. (1861) 'Of local representative bodies', Chapter XV of *Considerations on Representative Government* in Vol. XIX of J.M. Robson (ed.) (1977) *The Collected Works of John Stuart Mill*, Toronto: University of Toronto Press.

Minchinton, W. (ed.) (1972) *Wage Regulation in Pre-Industrial England*, Newton Abbott: David & Charles.

Mitch, D. (1992) *The Rise of Popular Literacy in Victorian England: The Influence of Private Choice and Public Policy*, Philadelphia, PA: University of Pennsylvania Press.

——(2005) 'Education and economic growth in historical perspective', R. Whaples (ed.) *EH.Net Encyclopedia of Economic and Business History*, eh.net/encyclopedia/article/mitch.education

Moran Cruz, J. (1985) *The Growth of Schooling, 1340–1548: Learning, Literacy and Laicization in Pre-reformation York Diocese*, Princeton, NJ: Princeton University Press.

Nelson, R. and Phelps, E. (1966) 'Investment in humans, technological diffusion, and economic growth', *American Economic Review*, 56: 69–75.

OECD (2002) *Financing Education – Investments and Returns: Analysis of the World Education Indicators 2002 Edition*, Paris: OECD Publications.

Ogilvie, S. (2008) 'Rehabilitating the guilds: a reply', *Economic History Review*, 61: 175–82.

Pritchett, L. (2001) 'Where has all the education gone?' *World Bank Economic Review*, 15: 367–91.

St. Clair, W. (2004) *The Reading Nation in the Romantic Period*, Cambridge: Cambridge University Press.

Sanderson, M. (1972) 'Literacy and social mobility in the industrial revolution in England', *Past & Present*, 56: 75–104.

Schultz, T.P. (2002) 'Why governments should invest more to educate girls', *World Development*, 30: 207–25.

Schultz, T.W. (1975) 'The value of the ability to deal with disequilibria', *Journal of Economic Literature*, 13: 827–46.

Simon, J. (1966) *Education and Society in Tudor England*, Cambridge: Cambridge University Press.

Smith, A. (1776, reprinted 1976) *The Wealth of Nations*, Chicago, IL: University of Chicago Press.

Stasavage, D. (2005) 'Democracy and education spending in Africa', *American Journal of Political Science*, 49: 343–58.

Stoddard, C. (2009) 'Why did education become publicly funded? Evidence from the nineteenth-century growth of public primary schooling in the United States', *Journal of Economic History*, 69: 172–201.

——(2011) 'Voting for free public schools', Montana State University working paper, Department of Agricultural Economics and Economics.

Thomas, D., Beegle, K., Frankenberg, E., Sikoki, B., Strauss, J. and Teruel, G. (2004) 'Education in a crisis', *Journal of Development Economics*, 74: 53–85.

Tinbergen, J. (1975) *Income Distribution. Analysis and Policies*, Amsterdam: North-Holland.

UNESCO Institute for Statistics (2011), UNESCO Global Education Digest, www.uis.unesco.org

Van Zanden, J.L. (2009) 'The skill premium and the "great divergence"', *European Review of Economic History*, 13: 121–53.

Vaughan, M. and Archer, M. (1971) *Social Conflict and Educational Change in England and France, 1789–1848*, Cambridge: Cambridge University Press.

Vincent, D. (1989) *Literacy and Popular Culture: England, 1750–1914*, Cambridge: Cambridge University Press.

——(2000) *The Rise of Mass Literacy: Reading and Writing in Modern Europe*, Cambridge: Polity Press.

Welch, F. (1970) 'Education in production', *Journal of Political Economy*, 78: 35–59.

Westermann, W.L. (1914) 'Apprenticeship contracts and the apprenticeship system in Roman Egypt', *Classical Philology*, 9: 295–315.

Williamson, J.G. (1985) *Did British Capitalism Breed Inequality?* Boston, MA: Allen & Unwin.

23

THE ECONOMIC HISTORY OF IMMIGRATION

Raymond L. Cohn

This chapter discusses immigration historically. Most of the discussion centers on the United States, though the U.S. experience is placed in an international context. After an examination of the volume of immigration, the chapter analyzes where the immigrants came from, who they were, why they came, how many came, where they went to, what jobs they obtained, and the economic effects immigration had on the native born and the country.

The volume of immigration

Before 1914, international migration was dominated by the movement of individuals from Europe to the United States. Table 23.1 provides the relevant numbers. Some immigration occurred to all of the countries listed during all periods, but the years before 1820 saw few people freely choose to go anywhere other than the United States. Even between 1820 and 1870, the United States dominated as the receiving country since many of those who arrived in Canada continued on to the United States. Free immigration to Australia picked up in the 1850s after the discovery of gold. Before 1870, almost 82 per cent of the immigrants to the five countries shown

Table 23.1 Historical world immigration to Australia and the New World, 1630–1914 (thousands)

Receiving County	1630–1819	1820–1850	1851–1860	1861–1870	1871–1914
Australia	——	28	226	167	863
Argentina	——	——	20	28	4,511
Brazil	——	19	122	98	3,388
Canada[a]	——	668	277	176	4,649
United States	896	2,464	2,598	2,315	29,587

Note: [a] Figures through 1860 are for arrivals at Montreal and Quebec. Later figures are for all immigrant arrivals. In both cases, some of the individuals arriving in Canada travelled on to the United States.

Sources: Australia: Calculated from Mitchell (1995: 86). These figures ignore the forced migration of convicts to Australia before 1843. Argentina, Brazil, and Canada: figures before 1860 are calculated from Mitchell (1993: 90–1, 94); later figures are provided in Nugent (1992: 14). United States: Columns 1 and 2 are calculated from Table 23.2 in this chapter, the other columns are provided in Nugent (1992: 14).

in Table 23.1 went to the United States. It was only after 1870, because the development of the transatlantic steamship shortened voyage times, that large numbers of people went to South American countries. Even so, during the entire period before 1914, over 71 per cent of all immigrants to the five countries shown went to the U.S. From the perspective of Europe, some 52 million people left between 1815 and 1930, with 33 million going to the United States (Baines 1991: 1–2).

With the outbreak of the First World War, the volume of international migration declined substantially. After the war ended, the United States and many other countries adopted wide-spread restrictions on the number of immigrants. These laws, combined with the Great Depression and the Second World War, kept international migration volumes low into the 1960s. Since then, volumes have increased as countries modified their restrictions. The biggest change is that Europe in now a net receiver of immigrants. In 2009, the net migration rates (immigrants minus emigrants) per 1,000 inhabitants were: the United States = 3, Canada = 8, Europe = 3 (though the rate into Southern Europe was 6), and Australia = 12. Losing areas were Latin America and the Caribbean, where the net migration rate was −2 and Africa, where it was −1 (though there has been positive net migration into South Africa). Asia had a net migration rate of zero, though East and South Asia had a negative rate and West Asia a positive one (Population Reference Bureau 2009).

The volume and sources of immigration into the United States over the course of its history are presented in Table 23.2. The periods chosen show the large fluctuations that occurred in the average yearly volume and rate of immigration. In terms of absolute numbers, immigrant volume was highest between 1900 and 1914, and since 1989. The period with the largest immigration rate (the number of immigrants per 1,000 inhabitants) was 1847 through 1854, during and immediately after the potato famine. Immigration rates were high though quite variable over the entire period from 1832 through 1914, with an average yearly rate of 7.7 per 1,000 inhabitants. In line with the discussion in the preceding paragraph, immigration rates declined during and after the First World War and stayed low into the 1960s. Rates began to increase again in the 1970s and have continued to increase into the twenty-first century, though they remain lower than the rates before 1915 because of continued restrictions and the larger U.S. population. The rate between 1989 and 1991 is artificially high because it counts illegal immigrants, mostly from Mexico, who were given amnesty in those years but who arrived earlier. It is important to realize that the official estimates in Table 23.2 do not include illegal immigrants. An estimated 11 million individuals were illegally in the United States in 2009 with 62 per cent of these being Mexican (U.S. Department of Homeland Security 2010).

The source of immigrants to the United States has changed substantially over time. For the period before the 1880s, the major sending countries were Ireland, Great Britain, and Germany with sizeable components from other areas of Northwest Europe and Scandinavia. In the 1880s, Central and Southern Europe became more important sources and these areas comprised over 70 per cent of the immigrants between 1900 and 1914. Immigration from China was restricted in the 1880s and that from Japan in 1905. After the First World War, immigration from Europe was restricted while it was virtually prohibited from Asia. It was not restricted from Latin America, which began to account for 40 to 50 per cent of the total. With the loosening of immigration restrictions in the 1950s and 1960s, Asian countries became more important sources of immigrants and Latin America remained important. More recently, immigration has been increasing from African countries. Between 2001 and 2010, 85 per cent of legal immigrants into the United States came from Asia, Latin America, and Africa.

Table 23.2 United States immigration volume and rates

Years	Average Yearly Total – All Countries	Immigration Rates (per 1000 Population)	Per cent of Average Yearly Total										
			Great Brit.	Ireland	Scandinavia and Other NW Europe	Germany	Central and Eastern Europe	Southern Europe	Asia	Africa	Australia and Pacific Islands	Mexico	Other America
1630–1700	2,200	—	—	—	—	—	—	—	—	—	—	—	—
1700–1780	4,325	—	—	—	—	—	—	—	—	—	—	—	—
1780–1819	9,900	—	—	—	—	—	—	—	—	—	—	—	—
1820–1831	14,538	1.3	22	45	12	8	0	2	0	0	—	4	6
1832–1846	71,916	4.3	16	41	9	27	0	1	0	0	—	1	5
1847–1854	334,506	14.0	13	45	6	32	0	0	1	0	—	0	3
1855–1864	160,427	5.2	25	28	5	33	0	1	3	0	—	0	4
1865–1873	327,464	8.4	24	16	10	34	1	1	3	0	0	0	10
1874–1880	260,754	5.6	18	15	14	24	5	3	5	0	0	0	15
1881–1893	525,102	8.9	14	12	16	26	16	8	1	0	0	0	6
1894–1899	276,547	3.9	7	12	12	11	32	22	3	0	0	0	2
1900–1914	891,806	10.2	6	4	7	4	45	26	3	0	0	1	5
1915–1919	234,536	2.3	5	2	8	1	7	21	6	0	1	8	40
1920–1930	412,474	3.6	8	5	8	9	14	16	3	0	0	11	26
1931–1946	50,507	0.4	10	2	9	15	8	12	3	1	1	6	33
1947–1960	252,210	1.5	8	2	7	17	5	10	6	1	1	15	38
1961–1970	332,168	1.7	6	1	4	6	4	13	13	1	1	14	38
1971–1980	449,331	2.1	3	0	1	2	4	8	35	2	1	14	30
1981–1988	578,739	2.4	2	0	1	1	3	3	45	3	1	12	28
1989–1991	1,484,213	6.0	1	0	1	1	3	2	22	2	0	46	22
1992–2000	805,993	3.0	1	1	1	1	11	1	34	4	1	18	26
2001–2010	1,050,053	3.6	2	0	2	1	8	1	34	7	1	17	27

Notes: Row percentages may not sum to 100 per cent due to rounding. Cells where "0" is entered represent less than 0.5 per cent.
Sources: Years before 1820: Grabbe (1989); 1820–1970: Carter et al. (2006); years since 1970: U.S. Department of Homeland Security (various years).

Why does immigration occur?

In the absence of government restrictions, the answer is straightforward. Though at certain times religious and political reasons were important factors in immigration, for most individuals the motivation has been economic. Simply put, immigrants expect to earn more in the destination country than the source country, though the gain may not be immediate and it may also include an expected gain to one's descendants (Sjaastad 1962).

The most comprehensive attempt to explain the volume and source of immigration historically has been by Hatton and Williamson (1998), who focus on the United States for the period between 1860 and 1914. They view immigration from a country during these years as being caused by up to five different factors: (a) the difference in average real wages between the country and the United States; (b) the rate of population growth in the country 20 or 30 years before; (c) the degree of industrialization and urbanization in the home country; (d) the volume of previous immigrants from that country or region; and (e) economic and political conditions in the United States. To this list can be added factors not relevant between 1860 and 1914, such as (f) the potato famine; and (g) declines in transportation costs. Finally, (h) the imposition of restrictions obviously affected immigration. Thus, at least eight important factors affected the volume and source of immigration.

Factors (e) through (g) explain many of the fluctuations in immigrant volume. Declines in transatlantic transportation costs during the 1820s led to volume increasing around 1830 (Cohn 2009). The potato famine in the late 1840s led to a sudden and large increase in volume. The adoption of steamships around 1870 and the move to intercontinental airline travel in the 1950s each caused immigration to become easier. The former led to an increase in volume while the change to air travel would have increased volume in the absence of restrictions. Changes in economic and political conditions in the United States caused many of the year-to-year fluctuations in immigrant volume. In particular, volume declined during the nativist outbreak in the 1850s, the major depressions of the 1870s and 1890s, and the Great Depression of the 1930s. In fact, during economic downturns not only does immigration fall but emigration increases, a combination that keeps the unemployment rate smaller than otherwise.

In turn, the first four factors primarily explain changes in the source countries of immigration. A larger difference in real wages between the country and the United States increased immigration from the country because it meant immigrants had more to gain from the move. Because most immigrants were between 15 and 35 years old, a higher population growth 20 or 30 years earlier meant there were more individuals in the potential immigrant group. In addition, a larger volume of young workers in a country reduced job prospects at home and further encouraged immigration. A greater degree of industrialization and urbanization in the home country initially increased immigration because traditional ties with the land were broken during this period, making laborers in the country more mobile. Finally, the presence of a larger volume of previous immigrants from that country or region encouraged more immigration because potential immigrants now had friends or relatives to stay with who could smooth their transition to living and working in the United States.

Based on these four factors, Hatton and Williamson explain the rise and fall in the volume of immigration from a country to the United States. Immigrant volume initially increased as a consequence of more rapid population growth and industrialization in a country, and the existence of a large gap in real wages between the country and the United States. Within a number of years, volume increased further due to the previous immigration that had occurred. Volume remained high until changes caused immigration to decline. Population growth slowed. Most of the country underwent industrialization, which increased the number of jobs and real wages at home. Partly due to the previous immigration, the real wage rose at home and became closer to that in the United States. Thus, each source country went through stages where immigration increased, reached a peak, and then declined.

Differences in the timing of these effects led to changes in the source countries of the immigrants. The countries of Northwest Europe were the first to experience rapid population growth and industrialization. By the latter part of the nineteenth century, immigration from these countries was in the stage of decline. At about the same time, countries in Central, Eastern, and Southern Europe were experiencing the beginnings of industrialization and more rapid population growth. This model holds directly only through the 1920s, because U.S. government policy changed. At that point, quotas were established on the number of individuals allowed to immigrate from each country. Even so, many countries, especially those in Northwest Europe, had passed the point where a large number of individuals wanted to leave and thus did not fill their quotas. The quotas were binding for many other countries in Europe in which the pressure to emigrate was still strong. Even today, the countries providing the majority of immigrants to the United States and Europe – that is, those south of the United States and in Asia – are places where population growth is high, industrialization is breaking traditional ties with the land, and real wage differentials with the wealthier areas are large.

As noted, restrictions interfere with the workings of this model. The U.S. laws adopted in the 1920s originally limited the number of immigrants in total and from each country not in the Western Hemisphere. An important change was made in the Immigration and Nationality Act of 1965, which abolished the quotas based on national origins. Instead, a series of preferences was established to determine who would gain entry. The most important preference was given to relatives of U.S. citizens and permanent resident aliens. Preferences were also given to professionals, scientists, artists, and workers in short supply. Restrictions imposed by other countries tend to emphasize these types of economic preferences more than U.S. law. The 1965 U.S. law kept an overall quota on total immigration for Eastern Hemisphere countries, originally set at 170,000, and no more than 20,000 individuals were allowed to immigrate to the United States from any single country. This law was designed to treat all countries equally. Asian countries were treated the same as any other country, so the virtual prohibition on immigration from Asia disappeared. In addition, for the first time the law also limited the number of immigrants from Western Hemisphere countries, with the original overall quota set at 120,000. It is important to note that neither quota was binding because immediate relatives of U.S. citizens, such as spouses, parents, and minor children, were exempt from the quota. Moreover, at different times the United States has admitted large numbers of refugees from Cuba, Vietnam, Haiti, and other countries. Finally, many individuals enter the United States on student visas, enroll in colleges and universities, and eventually get companies to sponsor them for a work visa. Thus, the total number of legal immigrants to the United States since 1965 has always been larger than the combined quotas. This law has led to an increase in the volume of immigration and, by treating all countries the same, has led to Asia recently becoming a more important source of immigrants to the United States.

The characteristics of the immigrants

The gender breakdown and age structure remained fairly constant in the period before 1930. Generally, about 60 per cent of the immigrants were male. As to age structure, about 20 per cent were children, 70 per cent were aged 14–44, and 10 per cent were older than 44. In most of the period and for most countries, immigrants were typically young single males, young couples, or, especially in the era before the steamship, families. For particular countries, such as Ireland, a large number of the immigrants were single women (Cohn 2009: 98–120). The primary exception to this generalization was the 1899–1914 period, when 68 per cent of the immigrants were male and those aged 14–44 accounted for 82 per cent of the total. This period saw the immigration of a large number of single males who planned to work for a period of months or years and return to their homeland, a development made possible by the steamship shortening the voyage (Nugent 1992). The immigrant stream also included a large number of Jewish families from Eastern Europe who sought to escape repressive economic and political conditions.

The characteristics of the immigrant stream since 1930 have been somewhat different (Gabaccia 1996). Males have consistently comprised slightly less than one-half of all immigrants while the percentage of immigrants over the age of 44 has increased at the expense of those aged between 14 and 44. The only exception occurred between 1989 and 1991 when many of the newly legalized immigrants were Mexican males who had lived and worked in the United States for a period of years. During this period, two-thirds of the "immigrants" were male and over three-quarters were between 14 and 44 years of age.

Table 23.3 presents data on the percentage of immigrants who did not report an occupation (or whose occupation is unknown) and the percentage breakdown of those reporting an occupation (presumably the occupation held in the source country). The percentage not reporting an occupation declined through 1914, reflecting the increasing number of single males who arrived over time. Though a change in the classification scheme complicates the analysis, skilled workers usually comprised over one-fourth of the immigrant stream through 1970. The immigration of farmers and farm workers was important before the Civil War but declined steadily over time. The percentage of laborers has varied over time, though during some time periods they comprised one-half or more of the immigrants. Commercial workers, mainly merchants, were an important group of "immigrants" (the data actually record passengers at this time) very early when immigrant volume was low, but their percentage fell substantially until the 1930s. Professional workers were always a small part of U.S. immigration until the 1930s. Since 1930, professional and managerial workers have become a larger percentage of all immigrants. In fact, during the first decade of the twenty-first century they accounted for close to half of the legal U.S. immigrants.

The skill level of the immigrant stream is important because it potentially affects the U.S. labor force, an issue considered later. Before turning to this issue, a number of comments can be made concerning the occupational skill level of the U.S. immigration stream. First, skill levels fell substantially in the period before the Civil War. Between 1820 and 1831, only 39 per cent of the immigrants were farmers, servants, or laborers – the least skilled groups. By the 1847–54 period, however, the less-skilled percentage had increased to 76 per cent. Second, the less-skilled percentage had changed relatively little by the last decades of the nineteenth century. During the 1899–1914 period, farmers, servants, and laborers accounted for 78 per cent of the total. In fact, in both periods, these percentages were not much different from those for the native-born labor force, so the skill levels of the two groups were not radically different (Cohn 2009: 190–7). Third, restrictions on immigration imposed during the 1920s had a sizable effect on the skill level of the immigrant stream. Between 1930 and today, the percentage in the least-skilled group has fallen if the entry of illegal workers is ignored. Thus, one clear effect of the imposition of restrictions on the volume of immigration has been to increase the average skill level of the legal immigrant stream. The increasing skill level of the immigrant stream, however, has almost certainly been outdone by the increased skill level of the native-born labor force. Thus, the immigrant stream during more recent times has almost certainly become less skilled than the labor force they entered.

Table 23.3 United States Immigration by occupation

Year	Per cent with no occupation listed or unknown	Per cent of immigrants with an occupation in each category						
		Professional	Commercial	Skilled	Farmers	Servants	Laborers	Miscellaneous
1820–1831	61	3	28	30	23	2	14	—
1832–1846	56	1	12	27	33	2	24	—
1847–1854	54	0	6	18	33	2	41	—
1855–1864	53	1	12	23	23	4	37	0
1865–1873	54	1	6	24	18	7	44	1
1873–1880	47	2	4	24	18	8	40	5
1881–1893	49	1	3	20	14	9	51	3
1894–1898	38	1	4	25	12	18	37	3

		Managers and Professional	Sales and Office Workers	Construction, Maintenance, Production, and Transportation Workers	Service Workers and Non-Farm Laborers	Farming, Farm Workers Fishing, and Forestry
1899–1914	26	4	2	18	49	28
1915–1919	37	10	5	21	49	15
1920–1930	39	8	7	24	49	13
1931–1946	59	34	13	21	26	6
1947–1960	53	21	17	31	23	9
1961–1970	56	28	17	25	25	6
1971–1980	59	32	12	36	15	5
1981–1988	58	28	13	34	19	5
1989–1991	37	10	8	27	17	38
1992–2000	70	35	13	29	17	5
2001–2010	76	45	13	20	18	5

Note: Row percentages may not sum to 100% due to rounding.
Sources: 1820–1970: Carter et al. (2006). Years since 1970: U.S. Department of Homeland Security (various years).

The effects of immigration on the receiving country

Determining the effects of immigration on the receiving country is complex and virtually none of the conclusions presented here is without controversy. Yet most economic historians believe the effects of immigration are much less harmful than commonly supposed and, in many ways, are beneficial.

Immigration is popularly thought to lower the overall real wage rate in the United States by increasing the supply of individuals looking for jobs. This effect may occur in a particular area during a short period of time. Over longer time periods, however, average real wages will only fall if average labor productivity declines. Labor productivity can fall if the amounts of other resources do not change. Historically, however, immigration has often triggered increases in the amounts of other resources. For example, historically, the large-scale immigration from Europe contributed to rapid westward expansion of the United States during most of the nineteenth century. The westward expansion, however, increased the amounts of land and natural resources that were available, factors that could have kept immigration from lowering wage rates. In addition, immigration spurred an increase in the capital stock when it induced Europeans to invest in American railroads and other industrial projects. Many immigrants saved large amounts and increased the amount of capital in the economy through building their own businesses. In addition, the simple fact that there were more workers in the economy would increase the productivity of capital and its return, causing entrepreneurs to increase its size over time. These factors suggest that immigration increases labor demand as well as labor supply and thus does not necessarily cause a decline in the average level of real wages, at least over a period of years.

At least since the Civil War, average real wages for native-born workers have consistently increased. Whether they would have increased more with a lower level of immigration is the crux of the issue. Some researchers have concluded that immigration during the nineteenth century did keep wages down (Hatton and Williamson 1998; Goldin 1994). Carter and Sutch (1999), however, claim the models used in these studies assume, either explicitly or implicitly, that only labor supply increased, and thus do not adequately analyze the issue. They find little effect of immigration on the average real wage during the nineteenth century. Turning to the more recent time period, most studies have found little effect of immigration on the level of real wages, though a few have found an effect (Borjas 1999). Overall, it is possible that immigration may decrease the average wage, but this result is far from certain.

Even if immigration leads to a fall in average real wages, it does not follow that native workers are worse off. Workers typically receive income from sources other than their own labor. Although wages may fall, other resource prices in the economy may rise. For example, immigration increases the demand for land and housing and many existing owners benefit from an increase in the current value of their property. It is not easy to determine whether any individual worker is better off or worse off in this case. It depends on the amounts of other resources each individual possesses. During the nineteenth century, many workers likely did not possess many resources other than their own labor skills and thus could have been harmed by immigration, at least in the short run. Other natives, however, were not wage workers but farmers, whose incomes rose as immigration increased the population and the demand for their products. During recent times, more workers possess additional resources and thus are less likely to be severely harmed by immigration.

Immigration is often thought to have its greatest effect on the wages of unskilled workers. If the immigrants arriving in the country are primarily unskilled, then the larger number of unskilled workers could cause their wage to fall if the overall demand for these workers does not change. A requirement for this effect to occur is that the immigrants be less skilled than the U.S. labor force they enter. During the 1830s and 1840s, immigration increased substantially and the skill level of the immigrant stream fell to approximately match that of the native labor force. Instead of lowering the wages of unskilled workers relative to those of skilled workers, however, the large inflow apparently led to little change in the wages of unskilled workers, while some skilled workers lost and others gained. The explanation for these results is that the larger number of unskilled workers resulting from immigration was a factor in employers adopting new methods of production that used more unskilled labor. As a result of this technological change, the demand for unskilled workers increased so their wage did not necessarily decline. As employers adopted these new machines, however, skilled artisans who had previously done many of these jobs – for example iron casting – suffered losses. Other skilled workers gained, including many white-collar workers who were not in direct competition with the immigrants. Some evidence exists to support a differential effect on skilled workers during the antebellum period (Williamson and Lindert 1980; Margo 2000). After the Civil War through the 1920s, as the skill level of the immigrant stream remained close to that of the native labor force, immigration probably did not further affect the wage structure (Carter and Sutch 1999; Cohn 2009).

The lower volume of immigration in the period from 1930 through 1960 meant immigration had little effect on the relative wages of different workers during these years. With the resumption of higher volumes of immigration after 1965, however, and with the immigrants' skill levels being low, an effect on relative wages again became possible. In fact, the relative wages of high-school dropouts in the United States deteriorated, especially after the mid-1970s. Researchers who have studied the question conclude that immigration accounted for about one-fourth of the wage deterioration experienced by high-school dropouts during the 1980s, though some researchers find a lower effect and others a higher one (Friedberg and Hunt 1995; Borjas 1999). Wages are determined by a number of factors other than immigration. In this case, it is thought the changing nature of the economy, such as the growing use of computers increasing the benefits to education, explains more of the decline in the relative wages of high-school dropouts than immigration does.

Beyond any effect on wages, there are a number of ways in which immigration might improve the overall standard of living in an economy. First, immigrants may engage in inventive or scientific activity, with the result being a gain to everyone. Evidence exists for both the historical and more recent periods that the United States has attracted individuals with an inventive and scientific nature (Cohn 2009: 218–21). Since the United States has generally been a leader in these areas, individuals are more likely to be successful in such an environment than in one where these activities are not as highly valued. Second, immigrants expand the size of markets for various goods, which may lead to lower unit costs due to an increase in firm size. The result would be a decrease in the price of the goods in question. One historical example of these economies of scale is in the transportation sector, where rising population allows fixed costs to be spread over higher levels of output, thus reducing average costs. Third, most individuals immigrate between the ages of 15 and 35, so the expenses of their upbringing and basic schooling are paid abroad. In the past, being of working age, most immigrants immediately got a job. Thus, immigration increased the percentage of the population in the United States that worked, a factor that raises the average standard of living in a country. Even in more recent times, most immigrants work, though the increased proportion of older individuals in the immigrant stream means the positive effects from this factor may be lower than in the past. Fourth, while immigrants may place a strain on government services in an area, such as the school system and healthcare delivery, they also pay taxes. Even illegal immigrants directly pay sales taxes on their purchases of goods and indirectly pay property taxes through their rent. Finally, the fact that immigrants are less likely to immigrate to the United States during periods of high unemployment is also beneficial. By reducing the number of people looking for jobs during these periods, this factor increases the likelihood U.S. citizens will be able to find or keep a job.

The experience of immigrants in the United States

This section examines the experiences of immigrants in the United States. The issues of discrimination against immigrants in jobs and the success immigrants experienced over time are investigated, as is the question of where immigrants settled. Interested readers are directed to Borjas (1999); Ferrie (1999); Carter and Sutch (1999); Hatton and Williamson (1998); Buffum and Whaples (1995); and Friedberg and Hunt (1995) for more technical discussions.

Wage discrimination exists when a worker's compensation is less than the value of his or her marginal contribution to the firm. Empirical tests generally do not find this type of discrimination. At any point in time, immigrants have been paid the same wage for a specific job as otherwise similar native workers. When immigrants received lower wages than native workers, the differences reflected the lower skills of the immigrants. Historically, as discussed earlier, the skill level of the immigrant stream was similar to that of the native labor force, so wages did not differ much between the two groups. During more recent years, the immigrant stream has been less skilled than the native labor force, leading to the receipt of lower wages by immigrants. A second form of discrimination is in the jobs an immigrant is able to obtain. Immigrant and native occupations have often differed significantly. For example, in 1910, immigrants accounted for over one-half of the work force in mining, apparel, steel manufacturing, meat packing, and baking. If a reason for the employment concentration was that immigrants were kept out of alternative higher-paying jobs, then the immigrants would suffer. This type of discrimination may have occurred against Catholics during the 1840s and 1850s and against the immigrants from Central, Southern, and Eastern Europe after 1890. Yet the open nature of the U.S. schooling system and economy has been such that this effect usually did not have an impact on the fortunes of the immigrants' children or did so at a much smaller rate. Illegal immigrants, however, have found it more difficult to exploit the open nature of the U.S. economy and would thus be more subject to possible discrimination.

An associated issue is explaining where the immigrants settled in the United States. Since newer immigrants usually settled near older immigrants, initial settlement patterns set during the antebellum years had a large impact. These settlement patterns generally reflected the location of manufacturing (Cohn 2009: 167–73, 180–5). The main exceptions pertained to those immigrants sufficiently wealthy to start or buy their own farm, to young Irish girls who became domestic servants, and to poorer individuals who worked on transportation projects or as farmhands. Otherwise, immigrants tended to settle where the manufacturing firms were. Compared with the native born, immigrants were thus more likely to live in the Northeast and to settle in cities, areas where manufacturing first developed. In 1850, the 15 largest cities contained 9 per cent of the U.S. population but 30 per cent of the foreign born. In the same year, the European born accounted for 10 per cent of the entire U.S. population but 14 per cent of the Northeastern total. In the latter half of the nineteenth century, manufacturing activity spread into the Midwest and so did the immigrants. These settlement patterns persisted into the twentieth century, with cities and manufacturing areas containing large numbers of immigrants. In turn, the willingness of immigrants to take these jobs probably slowed the movement of the native born to urban areas. Even in more recent times, immigrants are more likely to be found in urban areas, though the lower importance of manufacturing activity in the U.S. economy has lessened the relationship of this factor to the location of immigrants.

Another aspect of how immigrants fared in the U.S. labor market is their experiences over time with respect to wage growth, job mobility, and wealth accumulation. A study done by Ferrie (1999) for a small sample of immigrants arriving between 1840 and 1850, a period when the inflow of immigrants relative to the U.S. population was high, found immigrants from Britain and Germany generally improved their job status over time. By 1860, over 75 per cent of the individuals reporting a low-skilled job on entry into the country had moved up into a higher-skilled job, while fewer than 25 per cent of those reporting a high-skilled job on entry had moved down into a lower-skilled job. Thus, the job mobility for these individuals was quite high. For immigrants from Ireland, the experience was quite different; the percentage of immigrants moving up was only 40 per cent and the percentage moving down was over 50 per cent. It is not clear if the Irish did worse because they had less education and fewer skills or whether the differences were due to discrimination in the labor market. As to wealth, all the immigrant groups succeeded in accumulating larger amounts of wealth the longer they were in the United States, though their wealth levels fell short of those enjoyed by natives.

A broader approach to the same period taken by Cohn (2009: 173–80) generally agrees with Ferrie. Cohn compares the occupational distributions of individuals born in Great Britain, Ireland, and Germany using samples from the 1850, 1860, and 1870 U.S. Censuses. He finds that all three groups achieved success over time in the U.S. labor market. This finding includes the Irish, though they were much less skilled as a group. Thus, the evidence indicates that most antebellum immigrants were successful over time in matching their skills to the available jobs in the U.S. economy.

The extent to which immigrants had labor market success in the period since the Civil War is not clear. Hanes (1996) found that immigrants, even those from Northwest Europe, had slower earnings growth over time than natives, a result he argues was due to poor assimilation. Hatton and Williamson (1998: 124–41) reexamined the data and concluded that Hanes' result disappeared if immigrants who arrived before age 16 and those who arrived after their sixteenth birthday were examined separately. In fact, the wages for both groups increased at rates at least as high as those of the native born. Hatton and Williamson's study thus suggests that late nineteenth-century immigrants assimilated relatively easily into the U.S. labor market.

For the period after the Second World War, Chiswick (1978) argues that immigrants' wages have increased relative to those of natives the longer the immigrants have been in the United States. Borjas (1999) has criticized Chiswick's finding by suggesting it is caused by a decline in the skills possessed by the arriving immigrants between the 1950s and the 1990s. Borjas finds that 25- to 34-year-old male immigrants who arrived in the late 1950s had wages 9 per cent lower than comparable native males, but by 1970 had wages 6 per cent higher. In contrast, those arriving in the late 1970s had wages 22 per cent lower at entry. By the late 1990s, their wages were still 12 per cent lower than those of comparable natives. A growing mismatch between the skills of recent immigrants and the native born may have also reduced the former's ability to assimilate. Overall, the degree of success experienced by immigrants in the U.S. labor market remains an area of controversy.

References

Baines, D. (1991) *Emigration from Europe, 1815–1930*, London: Macmillan.

Borjas, G.J. (1999) *Heaven's Door: Immigration Policy and the American Economy*, Princeton, NJ: Princeton University Press.

Briggs, V.M. (1984) *Immigration and the American Labor Force*, Baltimore, Md: Johns Hopkins University Press.

Buffum, D. and Whaples, R. (1995) 'Fear and lathing in the Michigan furniture industry: employee-based discrimination a century ago', *Economic Inquiry*, 33: 234–52.

Carter, S.B. and Sutch, R. (1999) 'Historical perspectives on the economic consequences of immigration into the United States', in C. Hirschman, P. Kasinitz, and J. DeWind (eds) *The Handbook of International Migration: The American Experience*, New York: Russell Sage Foundation.

Carter, S.B., Gartner, S.S., Haines, M.R., Olmstead, A.L., Sutch, R. and Wright, G. (eds) (2006) *Historical Statistics of the United States: Earliest Times to the Present – Millennial Edition, Volume 1: Population*, New York: Cambridge University Press.

Chiswick, B.R. (1978) 'The effect of Americanization on the earnings of foreign-born men', *Journal of Political Economy*, 86: 897–921.

Cohn, R.L. (2009) *Mass Migration under Sail: European Immigration to the Antebellum United States*, New York: Cambridge University Press.

Ferrie, J.P. (1999) *Yankeys Now: Immigrants in the Antebellum United States, 1840–1860*, New York: Oxford University Press.

Friedberg, R.M. and Hunt, J. (1995) 'The impact of immigrants on host country wages, employment and growth', *Journal of Economic Perspectives*, 9: 23–44.

Gabaccia, D. (1996) 'Women of the mass migrations: from minority to majority, 1820–1930', in D. Hoerder and L.P. Moch (eds) *European Migrants: Global and Local Perspectives*, Boston, MA: Northeastern University Press.

Goldin, C. (1994) 'The political economy of immigration restrictions in the United States, 1890 to 1921', in C. Goldin and G.D. Libecap (eds) *The Regulated Economy: A Historical Approach to Political Economy*, Chicago, IL: University of Chicago Press.

Grabbe, H-J. (1989) 'European immigration to the United States in the early national period, 1783–1820', *Proceedings of the American Philosophical Society*, 133: 190–214.

Hanes, C. (1996) 'Immigrants' relative rate of wage growth in the late 19th century', *Explorations in Economic History*, 33: 35–64.

Hatton, T.J. and Williamson, J.G. (1998) *The Age of Mass Migration: Causes and Economic Impact*, New York: Oxford University Press.

Margo, R.A. (2000) *Wages and Labor Markets in the United States, 1820–1860*, Chicago, IL: University of Chicago Press.

Mitchell, B.R. (1993) *International Historical Statistics: The Americas, 1750–1988*, 2nd edition, New York: Stockton Press.

——(1995) *International Historical Statistics: Africa, Asia & Oceania, 1750–1988*, 2nd edition, New York: Stockton Press.

Nugent, W. (1992) *Crossings: The Great Transatlantic Migrations, 1870–1914*, Bloomington, IN: Indiana University Press.

Population Reference Bureau (2009) *2009 World Population Data Sheet*, http://www.prb.org/Publications/Datasheets/2009/2009wpds.aspx (accessed April 6, 2011).

Sjaastad, L.A. (1962) 'The costs and returns of human migration', *Journal of Political Economy*, 70: 80–93.

U.S. Department of Homeland Security (2010) Office of Immigration Statistics, *Population Estimates*, http://www.dhs.gov/xlibrary/assets/statistics/publications/ois_ill_pe_2009.pdf (accessed April 8, 2011).

U.S. Department of Homeland Security (various years), Office of Immigration Statistics, *Yearbook of Immigration Statistics*, http://www.dhs.gov/files/statistics/immigration.shtm (accessed April 1–5, 2011).

Williamson, J.G. and Lindert, P.H. (1980) *American Inequality: A Macroeconomic History*, New York: Academic Press.

24

THE ECONOMIC HISTORY OF SLAVERY

Jenny Bourne

Throughout history, slavery has existed where it has been economically worthwhile to those in power. The most-studied example is the enslavement of those of African descent in the Americas. Millions of Africans were forcibly transported across the Atlantic Ocean, often stacked into sweltering cargo holds; they and their descendants generated returns to slaveowners comparable to those on other assets. Yet sea captains, cotton and sugar consumers, slave traders, banks and insurance companies, and industrial enterprises benefited handsomely from slavery as well.

Out of Africa

From 1500 to 1900, an estimated 12 million Africans went west to the New World, with about 10 million of them completing the journey. Nearly 3 million departed between 1811 and 1867. Africans were sold East as well as West, with some 6 million making the long trek across their own continent to Arab, Asian, and even some European countries. Another 8 million remained enslaved on their own soil (Lovejoy 1983).

African slaves came to the New World from the very beginning. Not long after Columbus set sail, Europeans brought slaves on various expeditions. Slaves accompanied Ponce de Leon to Florida in 1513, for example. The first African slaves in what became British North America arrived in Virginia in 1619 on a Dutch ship.

But institutionalized trading arrangements soon replaced casual theft. Although early Spanish settlers at first enslaved native Americans, the indigenous population perished in droves from smallpox and punishingly hard work. Via licensing agreements, Portugal and Spain started importing African slaves into their colonies in the early 1500s to replace the dying natives. In 1517, Charles I began to import Africans, first to the West Indies, then to the Spanish-controlled mainland. Brazil commenced legal importation of black slaves in 1549. Traders could acquire slaves in specific African zones, then sell them in America – up to 120 per year per Brazilian planter, for example. Because prices for Brazilian licenses were cheaper than other licenses, traders applied for these, then rerouted their vessels in search of extra profits.

The evils of the trade expanded when Britain replaced Spain and Portugal as the major trafficker in African slaves. Elizabethan-era captain Sir John Hawkins had transported slaves, but England did not figure large in the African trade until the seventeenth-century Royal African Company became the biggest slaver in the world.

Many parties participated in the infamous "trading triangle": European captains provided the chieftains of West and Central Africa with liquor, guns, cotton goods, and decorative ornaments. In exchange, Africans supplied slaves to suffer through the arduous middle passage across the Atlantic. Slaves worked on sugar plantations in the West Indies, grew coffee and sugar as well as mining precious metals in Brazil, and raised tobacco, sugar, rice, and eventually cotton in North America. These goods, along with molasses and rum, went back to Europe.

Few imported slaves actually ended up in what became the U.S. By 1808, when the trans-Atlantic slave trade to the U.S. officially ended, only about 6 per cent of African slaves landing in the New World had come to North America. The remainder went further south, with the majority landing in the Caribbean and the rest primarily in Brazil.

Commanders of slave vessels and their financial backers amassed considerable wealth from the Atlantic trade. Transporting slaves was a major industry in the seventeenth and eighteenth centuries, with the Royal African Company a principal player for five decades. David Galenson's study of the Company unveiled a picture of closely connected competitive economic markets in Africa and America that responded quickly to economic incentives (Galenson 1982).

Despite its size, the Company was hardly a monopoly – hordes of small ship captains found the trade worthwhile, with the principal costs being those associated with capturing and transporting Africans, and the prospective profits at least comparable to returns on other sorts of ventures. Many researchers have devoted themselves to ascertaining the exact rate of return that these captain–traders earned, with the most plausible estimates being about 9 to 10 per cent.

Other interests also made much from the Atlantic trade. European banks and merchant houses helped develop the New World plantation system through complicated credit and insurance mechanisms, enjoying substantial returns as part of the bargain. Well-placed African dealers benefited as well. In sickening cycles, Sudanic tribes of the fifteenth and sixteenth centuries sold slaves for horses, then used the horses to obtain more slaves. Tribes of the seventeenth and eighteenth centuries similarly traded slaves for guns, then used guns to hunt down more slaves.

But of all who reaped rewards from the Atlantic trade, British and U.S. citizens stand out. In the 1940s, West Indian scholar Eric Williams went so far as to suggest that British industrialization was intimately linked to slavery. Without the slave trade to fuel growth in her colonies, Williams claimed, Great Britain could not have become the industrial superpower of the eighteenth and nineteenth centuries that she was (Williams 1944). Although Williams's thesis has largely been discarded, other scholars nevertheless agree that the slave trade benefited England. Even Elizabeth I made money by investing in slaving ships and captains. David Eltis speculates, in fact, that Britain would have enjoyed higher living standards by continuing as a slave trader rather than becoming an abolitionist power. Early industry in New England such as cotton textiles and shipbuilding also had strong connections to the slave trade and slavery. Among those who benefited were the New England families of Browns, Cabots, and Faneuils.

The spread of profitable slavery in the United States

Colonial slavery had a slow start, particularly in the North. At the time of the American Revolution, fewer than 10 per cent of the half million slaves in the 13 colonies lived in the North, working primarily in agriculture. Most of the original Northern colonies implemented a process of gradual emancipation in the late eighteenth and early nineteenth centuries; other regions above the Mason-Dixon Line ended slavery upon statehood early in the nineteenth century. A substantial portion of Northern slaves were sold South rather than obtaining freedom, however.

Throughout colonial and antebellum history, U.S. slaves lived primarily in the South. Slaves comprised less than a tenth of the total Southern population in 1680 but grew to a third by 1790. After the American Revolution, the Southern slave population exploded, reaching about 1.1 million in 1810 and over 3.9 million in 1860.

An earlier explosion had occurred in the Caribbean, although a much higher percentage of slaves there were imported rather than native born. In Jamaica, for example, the black population did not become self-sustaining until after the mid-1830s. The total Caribbean slave population increased from 150,000 in 1700 to 1.2 million in 1790, with slaves comprising about 90 per cent of the population in the late eighteenth century.

The value of slaves arose in part from the value of labor generally in the New World. Scarce factors of production command economic rent, and labor was by far the scarcest available input in the Americas.

But using slaves was especially lucrative when production processes could be divided into a series of simple, easily monitored tasks and when the resulting products were sold in well-developed markets. A large proportion of the reward from owning and working slaves resulted from innovative labor practices among growers of cash crops. In the West Indies, for instance, sugar slaves worked in three separate gangs: one harvesting the crop, a second cleaning up after the first, and a third bringing water and food to the others. Planters in the U.S. South also used the gang system to their advantage, particularly on cotton plantations.

Integral to many gang-oriented operations across the Americas were plantation overseers, who served as agents for oft-absent plantation owners. Overseers certainly had some authority so they could elicit work from their charges. Yet law and custom alike circumscribed overseers' abilities to administer correction, because slaves represented such a large chunk of their masters' wealth. This balance between authority and accountability worked well enough to turn handsome profits for many planters, particularly those who entrusted reliable slave drivers as liaisons. By the mid-1820s, slave managers actually took over much of the day-to-day operations in the West Indies.

Antebellum slaveowners experimented with other methods to increase productivity. Masters developed an elaborate system of "hand ratings" in order to improve the match between the slave worker and the job. Slaves could sometimes earn bonuses in cash or in kind, or quit early if they finished tasks quickly. Perhaps surprisingly, slaves often had Sundays off. Some masters allowed slaves to keep part of the harvest or to work their own small plots. In places, slaves could even sell their own crops and produce. To prevent stealing, however, many masters limited the crops that slaves could raise and sell, confining them to corn or brown cotton, for example.

Most slaves in the U.S. South lived in small groups rather than on large plantations. Less than one-quarter of white Southerners held slaves, with half of these holding fewer than five and fewer than 1 per cent owning more than 100. Slavery was worth protecting as an institution in certain regions because of the large payoff to plantation owners, yet slaveholders of all sorts reaped rewards from the existence of the peculiar institution within their borders. The South grew half to three-quarters of the corn crop harvested in the U.S. between 1840 and 1860, for example, often with the help of family or hired slaves. And masters capitalized on the native intelligence of slaves by using them, for instance, as agents to receive goods and keep books. In antebellum Louisiana, slaves even had under their control a sum of money called a peculium. This served as a sort of working capital, enabling slaves to establish thriving businesses that often benefited their masters as well.

In the U.S., masters profited from reproduction as well as production. Southern planters encouraged slaves to have large families because U.S. slaves lived long enough (past about age 27) to generate more revenue than cost over their lifetimes. Low mortality plus high fertility meant an exceptional rate of natural increase among U.S. slaves. Researchers have found little evidence of slave breeding; instead, masters encouraged slaves to live in nuclear or extended families for stability. Lest one think sentimentality triumphed on the Southern plantation, one need only recall the willingness of most masters to break up families by sale if the bottom line was big enough.

In contrast to U.S. slaves, the average slave elsewhere in the Americas did not live past his or her mid-20s. Mortality rates were higher due to a harsher disease climate and more grueling work conditions. Masters in Brazil and the West Indies therefore behaved differently, establishing much longer periods of breastfeeding (which helped provide natural protection against subsequent pregnancy). The demographic ratio was also skewed heavily toward males. As a result, birth rates among West Indian and Brazilian slaves were relatively much lower.

During the three-and-a-half centuries of New World slavery, slave-produced goods – especially sugar – dominated world trade. The great sugar plantations in the eighteenth century and cotton plantations in the nineteenth were the largest privately owned enterprises of their time, and their owners among the richest men in the world. But others reaped rewards as well: French, Spanish, Portuguese, Dutch, and Danish citizens thrived on buying from or selling to slave colonies. So did cotton and sugar consumers who enjoyed low prices, ship owners and captains who transported goods, and Northern entrepreneurs who helped finance plantation operations.

Central to the economic success of slavery were political and legal institutions that validated the ownership of other persons. Masters enjoyed the usual rights of property ownership, including the right to buy, sell, hire, exchange, give, and bequeath slaves and their offspring, as well as seize them for debt and put them up as collateral. What few due-process protections slaves possessed stemmed from desires to grant rights to their owners. Still, when slaves stole, rioted, set fires, or killed free persons, the law subverted the property rights of masters so as to preserve slavery as a social institution.

Other restrictions existed as well, particularly on manumission. Allowing masters to free slaves at will would have created incentives to manumit unproductive slaves. Consequently, the community at large could have borne the costs of these former slaves, particularly rebellious ones. Antebellum U.S. Southern states worried considerably about this adverse selection problem and eventually enacted restrictions on the age at which slaves could go free, the number freed by any one master, and the number manumitted by last will.

Society as a whole shared in maintaining the machinery of slavery as well as protecting its existence and enjoying its yields. All Southern states except Delaware passed laws to establish citizen slave patrols that had the authority to round up suspicious-looking or escaped slaves, for example. Patrollers were a necessary enforcement mechanism in a time before standing police forces were customary. Essentially, Southern citizens agreed to take it upon themselves to protect their neighbors' interests as well as their own so as to safeguard slavery.

Northern citizens often worked hand-in-hand with their Southern counterparts, returning fugitive slaves to masters either with or without the prompting of national and state law. Yet not everyone was so civic-minded. As a result, the profession of "slave catching" evolved – often highly risky (enough so that insurance companies denied such men life insurance coverage) and just as often highly lucrative.

One element that contributed to the profitability of New World slavery was the African heritage of the slaves. Africans, more than native Americans, were accustomed to the discipline of agricultural practices and knew metalworking. Some scholars surmise that Africans, relative to Europeans, could better withstand tropical diseases and, unlike native Americans, also had some exposure to the European disease pool.

Perhaps the most distinctive feature of Africans, however, was their skin color. Because they looked different from their masters, their movements were easy to monitor. Denying slaves education, property ownership, contractual rights, and other things enjoyed by those in power was simple: one need only look at people to ascertain their likely status. Using color was a low-cost way of distinguishing slaves from free persons. For this reason, perhaps, early colonial practices that freed slaves who converted to Christianity quickly faded away. Deciphering true religious beliefs is far more difficult than establishing skin color.

Among those who profited from slavery were the slave catchers who received fees for returning escaped slaves to their masters. Because skin color was the principal identifying mark, however, free blacks also faced the horrifying possibility of capture and sale.

Internal markets and prices

Slaves benefited their owners via their productive labor and, in the U.S., by bearing children. But they also provided profit opportunities because they could be hired out or sold for cash. In his writings, for instance, Hernando Cortés described the large number of slaves brought to auction at the great marketplace near Tenochtìtlan (present-day Mexico City). Slave markets existed across the antebellum U.S. South as well. Even today, one can find stone markers like the one next to the Antietam battlefield, which reads: "From 1800 to 1865 This Stone Was Used as a Slave Auction Block. It has been a famous landmark at this original location for over 150 years."

Private auctions, estate sales, and professional traders facilitated easy exchange. Established dealers like Franklin and Armfield in Virginia, Woolfolk, Saunders, and Overly in Maryland, and Nathan Bedford Forrest in Tennessee prospered alongside itinerant traders who operated in a few counties, buying slaves for cash from their owners, then moving them overland in coffles to the lower South.

Over a million slaves were taken across state lines between 1790 and 1860 with many more moving within states. Some of these slaves went with their owners; some were sold to new owners. In his monumental study, Michael Tadman (1990) found that slaves who lived in the upper South in the 1850s faced at least a 14 per cent chance of being sold by their owners for speculative profits during that decade. Along with U.S. slave sale markets came farseeing methods for coping with risk, such as explicit – and even implicit – warranties of title, fitness, and merchantability.

A robust hiring market for slaves also existed. Slave hiring took root by the Revolutionary period and thrived throughout the antebellum period. Hiring was important both in industry and agriculture; it was frequently used to keep slaves occupied after an owner died but before the estate was settled.

Scholars, particularly Robert Fogel and Stanley Engerman, have gathered slave sale and hire prices from a variety of sources, including censuses, probate records, plantation and slave-trader accounts, and proceedings of slave auctions. The exchange prices for slaves – often substantial – reflected their economic value. Prime field hands went for four to six hundred dollars in the U.S. in 1800, close to a thousand dollars in 1850, and up to three thousand dollars on the eve of the Civil War. Hire rates for young adult males approached $150 a year during the 1850s.

Even controlling for inflation, slave prices rose significantly in the six decades before secession, as Figure 24.1 shows. Slavery remained a thriving business on the eve of the Civil War: by some estimates, average slave sale prices by 1890 would have increased more than 50 per cent over their 1860 levels. It is no wonder that the South rose in armed resistance to protect its enormous investment.

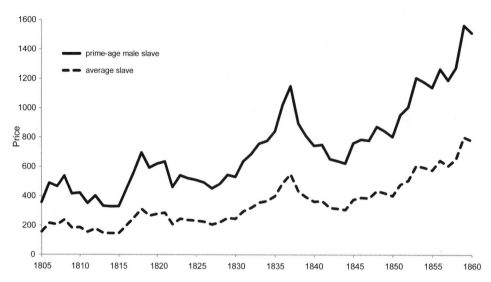

Figure 24.1 Real prices of average and prime-age male slaves in the U.S. South, 1805–1860 ($ 1860)
Sources: Series Cc2, Bb210, Bb212 in Carter *et al.* (2006)

Prices reflected the characteristics of particular slaves, including their sex, age, skill level, and physical condition. Important individual features also included temperament and, for females, childbearing capacity. In addition, the supply of slaves, demand for products produced by slaves, and seasonal factors helped determine market conditions and therefore prices.

Prices for both male and female slaves tended to follow similar life-cycle patterns, as Figure 24.2 indicates. Infant slaves sold for a positive price in the antebellum South because masters expected them to live long enough to make the initial costs of raising them worthwhile. Prices rose through puberty as productivity and experience increased. In nineteenth-century New Orleans, for example, prices peaked at about age 22 for females and age 25 for males. In the Old South, boys aged 14 sold for 71 per cent of the price of 27-year-old men, whereas girls aged 14 sold for 65 per cent of the price of 27-year-old men. After the peak age, prices declined slowly for a time, then fell off rapidly as slaves' ability to work disappeared. Girls cost more than boys at young ages; the genders then switched places in terms of value. Compared with men, women were worth 90 to 95 per cent as much in Cuba, 80 to 90 per cent as much in the U.S. and West Indies, and 70 to 80 per cent as much in Brazil.

One characteristic in particular set females apart: their ability to bear children. In the U.S., fertile females commanded a premium. The mother–child link also proved important in a different way: people sometimes paid extra to purchase intact families.

Besides age and sex, skills helped determine a slave's price. Premiums paid for skilled workers interacted with mortality rates and rates of depreciation for different characteristics. The U.S. had a relatively low slave mortality rate and skilled workers sold for premiums of 40 to 55 per cent. Slaveowners in areas with higher death rates could not reap as large a benefit from their skilled workers, due to shorter life spans. In Peru, the skill premium was about 35 per cent; in Cuba, about 10 to 20 per cent. Because the human capital associated with strength drops off more quickly as people age than the human capital associated with skills and training, prices for unskilled slaves in the Spanish colonies fell more rapidly with a slave's age than prices for skilled slaves.

Physical traits, mental capabilities, and other qualities contributed to price differentials as well. Crippled and chronically ill slaves sold for deep discounts. Slaves who proved

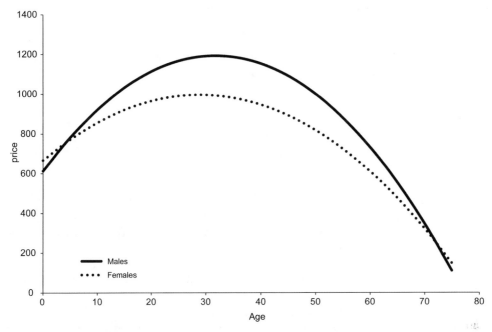

Figure 24.2 Estimated slave prices in the cotton South, by age and gender, 1860

Source: Robert W. Fogel and Stanley L. Engerman Slave Sales and Appraisals, 1775–1865 [Computer file]. ICPSR07421. Rochester, NY: University of Rochester [producer], 1976. Ann Arbor, MI: Inter-university Consortium for Political and Social Research [producer and distributor], 2006–10–11.

troublesome – runaways, thieves, layabouts, drunks, slow learners, and the like – also sold for lower prices. Taller slaves cost more, perhaps because height acted as a proxy for nutritional status. In New Orleans, light-skinned females (who enjoyed greater popularity as concubines) sold for a 5 per cent premium.

One pricing variant appeared in the West Indian "scramble." Here, owners and agents devised a fixed-price system, dividing slaves into four categories, penning them up accordingly, and assigning a single price per pen. Potential buyers then jumped into the pens, attempting to pick off the best prospects for the given price.

Slave prices fluctuated with market conditions as well as with individual characteristics. Supply factors mattered, for example. U.S. slave prices fell around 1800 as the Haitian revolution sparked the movement of slaves into the Southern states. Less than a decade later, slave prices climbed when the international slave trade was abolished, cutting off legal external supplies.

Many Southern slaveholders actually supported closing the Atlantic trade because the resulting reduction in supply drove up prices of slaves already living in the U.S. and, hence, their masters' wealth. U.S. slaves had high enough fertility rates and low enough mortality rates to reproduce themselves, so Southerners did not worry about having too few slaves to go around. Unlike elsewhere in the New World, the South did not require constant infusions of immigrants to keep its slave population intact. In fact, by 1825, 36 per cent of the slaves in the Western Hemisphere lived in the U.S.

Demand helped determine prices as well. The demand for slaves derived primarily from the demand for the commodities and services that slaves provided. Changes in slave occupations and variability in prices for slave-produced goods therefore created movements in slave prices. As slaves replaced increasingly expensive indentured servants in the New World, their prices went up. In the period 1748 to 1775, slave prices in British America rose nearly 30 per cent. As cotton prices fell in the 1840s, Southern slave prices also fell. But, as the demand for cotton and tobacco grew after about 1850, the prices of slaves increased as well. The connection between commodity and slave prices is not confined to the U.S. South. Some scholars have speculated that abolition in Cuba occurred because sugar prices had fallen too low to make slavery worthwhile.

Demand sometimes had to do with the time of year a sale took place. For example, slave prices in the New Orleans market were 10 to 20 per cent higher in January than in September. Why? One possible explanation is that the opportunity cost of spending time away from the plantation was high during harvest season, making the net willingness to pay for slaves relatively low in September.

Differences in demand across regions led to transient regional price differences, which in turn meant large movements of slaves. Yet, because planters experienced greater stability among their work force when entire plantations moved, 84 per cent of U.S. slaves were taken to the lower South in this way rather than being sold piecemeal.

One additional demand factor loomed large in determining slave prices: the expectation of continued legal slavery. As the American Civil War progressed, slave prices dropped dramatically because people could not be sure that the peculiar institution would survive. In New Orleans, prime-age male slaves sold on average for $1,381 in 1861 and for $1,116 in 1862. Burgeoning inflation meant that real prices fell considerably more. Not surprisingly, by the end of the Civil War, slaves sold for a small fraction of their 1860 price.

The debate over the profitability of slavery

Slavery was a profitable enterprise in the New World, although it never generated superprofits because people always had the option of putting their money elsewhere. Nevertheless, investment in slaves offered a rate of return – about 10 per cent – comparable to returns on other assets (Fogel 1989).

That slavery in the American South was profitable seems almost obvious. Yet scholars have argued furiously about this matter. On one side stand antebellum writers such as Hinton Rowan Helper and Frederick Law Olmstead, and contemporary scholars like Eugene Genovese (at least in his early writings), who speculated that American slavery was unprofitable, inefficient, and incompatible with urban life. On the other side are those who contend that slavery was profitable and efficient relative to free labor, and that slavery suited cities as well as farms, industry as well as agriculture. These researchers stress the similarity between slave markets and markets for other sorts of capital.

Perhaps the most controversial book ever written about American slavery is *Time on the Cross*. Authors Robert Fogel and Stanley Engerman (1974) were among the first to use modern statistical methods, computers, and large data sets to answer a series of empirical questions about the economics of slavery. Building on earlier work by Alfred Conrad and John Meyer (1958), Fogel and Engerman used data from probate and plantation records, invoices from the New Orleans slave-sale market, coastwise manifests for shipped slaves, and manuscript census schedules to find profit levels and rates of return. Fogel and Engerman pioneered the use of "total factor productivity," which measures output per average unit of all inputs.

Among Fogel and Engerman's findings are these: antebellum Southern farms were 35 per cent more efficient overall at turning inputs into output than Northern ones, and slave farms in the cotton South were 28.5 per cent more efficient than free farms. Moreover, slavery generated a rate of economic growth in the U.S. South comparable to that of many European countries.

Despite criticism (notably a collection of articles entitled *Reckoning with Slavery* edited by Paul David and others [1976]), *Time on the Cross* and Fogel's subsequent *Without Consent or Contract* (1989) have solidified the economic view of Southern slavery. Even Eugene Genovese, long an ardent proponent of the belief that Southern planters held slaves for prestige value, finally acknowledged that slavery was probably a profitable enterprise. Much like any businessmen, New World slaveowners responded to market signals – adjusting crop mixes, reallocating slaves to more profitable tasks, hiring out idle slaves, and sometimes selling slaves for profit. One instance well known to labor historians shows that contemporaneous free laborers thought that urban slavery may even have worked too well: workers at the Tredegar Iron Works in Richmond, Virginia, went out on their first strike in 1847 to protest the use of slave labor at the Works.

One potent piece of evidence supporting the notion that slavery provided pecuniary benefits is this: slavery often gave way to other forms of organizing the labor force when the costs and risks of maintaining slaves become too large. Within Africa in the nineteenth century, certain developments shifted some of the risk of poor crop yields away from masters: slaves began to pay masters for the right to work on their own as masters stopped paying for the slaves' upkeep. And the Spanish Crown for a time favored a system of forced labor called *encomienda*, whereby the indigenous population could not be bought, sold, rented, bequeathed, or removed from the area. Scholars have speculated that this form of coercion, relative to outright slavery, reduced threats to the security of the Crown's interest. Thus, other types of labor took the place of slaves when slavery cost too much.

In like fashion, slavery replaced other labor when it became relatively cheaper. In the early U.S. colonies, for example, indentured servitude was common. As the demand for skilled servants (and therefore their wages) rose in England, the cost of indentured servants went up in the colonies. At the same time, second-generation slaves became more productive than their forebears because they spoke English and did not have to adjust to life in a strange new world. Consequently, the balance of labor shifted away from indentured servitude and toward slavery. Georgia offers a compelling example. Its original 1732 charter prohibited ownership of black slaves. Yet by 1750 the trustees of the new colony had to relax the prohibition because Georgia growers simply could not compete with producers elsewhere who utilized lower-cost slave labor.

Was New World slavery efficient?

So New World slavery was profitable; was it an efficient way of organizing the work force? On this question, considerable controversy remains. Slavery might well have profited masters, but only because they exploited their chattel. What is more, slavery could have locked people into a method of production and way of life that might later have proven burdensome.

Fogel and Engerman claim that slaves kept about 90 per cent of what they produced. They also note that, because slaves constituted a considerable portion of individual wealth, masters fed and treated their slaves reasonably well. Although some evidence indicates that infant slaves suffered much worse conditions than their freeborn counterparts, juvenile and adult slaves lived in conditions similar to – sometimes better than – those enjoyed by many free laborers of the same period. Because Fogel and Engerman find as well that agricultural slavery was 35 per cent more efficient than family farming in the North, they argue that slaves actually may have shared in the overall benefits resulting from the gang system. Other scholars contend that slaves in fact kept less than half of what they produced and that slavery, while profitable, certainly was not efficient.

Gavin Wright (1978) critiques Fogel and Engerman by focusing on the exceptional nature of the crop year they used to calculate their statistics and by using alternative data to attack their estimates of total factor productivity. Wright calls attention as well to the difference between the short run and the long run. He notes that slaves accounted for a very large proportion of most masters' portfolios of assets. Although slavery might seem an efficient means of production at a point in time, it ties masters to a certain system of labor that may not adapt quickly to changed economic circumstances.

Wright's argument has some merit. Although the South's growth rate compared favorably with that of the North in the antebellum period, a considerable portion of wealth was held in the hands of planters – and much of that "wealth" depended upon the accounting convention of treating the human capital embodied by slaves as personal property owned by slaveholders. The consequence was a far different portfolio from that of the North, where immobile land was the largest investment. Consequently, commercial and service industries lagged in the South. The region also had far less rail transportation and internal improvements than the North.

Yet many plantations used the most advanced technologies of the day, and certain innovative commercial and insurance practices appeared first in transactions involving slaves. In Cuba, planters were behind the move to construct railroads. Slaveowners led in using new inventions, such as the circular saw. What is more, although the South fell behind the North and Great Britain in its level of manufacturing, it compared favorably with other advanced countries of the time. In sum, no clear consensus emerges as to whether the antebellum South created a standard of living comparable to that of the North or, if it did, whether it could have sustained it.

Slavery outside the New World and in more recent times

Rising British sentiment against slavery culminated in the Somerset case, which outlawed slavery in England in 1772 (*Somerset v. Stewart*, 98 English Reports 499–510 [King's Bench, 22 June 1772]). Britain and the U.S. abolished the international slave trade in 1807–8; Britain freed slaves in its colonies (except India) in 1833, with full emancipation in 1838. Slavery in the U.S. officially disappeared by the end of the American Civil War in 1865.

Abolition came later elsewhere, often accompanied by a rise in other forms of servitude. Eastern Europe and Russia kept slavery alive into the late nineteenth century. In 1890, all major European countries, the U.S., Turkey, Persia, and Zanzibar signed the General Act of Brussels in an attempt to suppress slavery. Forty years later, an international labor convention acted to outlaw forced labor in the former Ottoman and German colonies. In 1948, the United Nations General Assembly declared that all forms of slavery and servitude should be abolished.

Yet slavery in Southeast Asia, the Arabian peninsula, and parts of Africa continued well into the twentieth century. Perhaps the saddest legacy of American slavery is that the system established to supply the New World with slaves also shaped society at home. Some scholars believe that slavery was endemic to Africa, others date its origins to medieval Muslim society or the later European infiltration. Regardless of beginnings, slavery within Africa burgeoned along with the Atlantic trade – in 1600 Africa had a minority of the world's slaves, in 1800 the overwhelming majority. The Great Scramble for Africa spread slavery further. Although some scholars suggest that African slavery was more benign than the American version, recent research indicates that the two were not very different. Regrettably, the tragedy continues:

Angolan slaves fought bloodily for freedom in 1961; Mauritania kept slavery legal until 1980; Nigeria still had slave concubinage in the late 1980s; and numerous African regions actively practice slavery today.

Some of the harshest forms of slavery have arrived only recently. Modern weaponry, increased population density, and mass communication and transportation technology have made it that much easier to capture and move purported enemies as well as to incite one's allies to do the same. The classic mechanism of modern slavery, patterned after the practices of Nazi Germany and the Soviet Union, is this: officials in power arrest suspected opponents of the current political regime, or those considered racially or nationally unfit, and incarcerate them in forced-labor camps to work under terrible conditions.

Unlike slaves in earlier societies, the unfortunates who landed in Nazi and Soviet concentration camps were not privately owned and traded in open markets. Rather, they served as property of the state, sometimes to be rented out to private interests.

These sorts of modern slaves consequently represent something far different from their historic counterparts. From pre-classical times through the nineteenth century, masters – including public entities – typically viewed their slaves as productive investments, as bookkeeping entries in their wealth portfolios, as forms of valuable capital. Slaves in these circumstances could often count on minimal food, shelter, and clothing, and time for rest and sleep. This was true even for government-owned slaves, because these slaves were typically used in money-making enterprises that just happened to be government run, and they could potentially be sold to private owners. Not so for the "publicly owned" slaves of the twentieth century. Because these people were "acquired" at very low cost with public dollars and served primarily as political symbols, their masters had little incentive to care for them as assets.

To be sure, when Nazi Germany needed labor to fuel production of her war machinery, the country turned to the inmates of concentration camps. Likewise, the Soviets rounded up peasants to work on public projects and mineral extraction. Various regions across Africa, Asia, America, and Europe have done the same. Yet these sorts of "slaves" are often worth more dead than alive. Killing one's political adversaries makes the state that much easier to run. Exterminating those labeled as unfit "cleanses" society – in a truly twisted sense of the word – and binds together the "chosen." Accordingly, modern forms of mass slavery seem far different institutions from those of earlier times.

Revisiting the economics of slavery

Despite differences between twentieth-century slavery and its earlier counterparts, slavery in any time and place cannot be considered benign. In terms of material conditions, diet, and treatment, slaves in some societies may have fared as well as the poorest class of free citizens. Yet the root of slavery is coercion. By its very nature, slavery involves involuntary transactions. Slaves are property, whereas free laborers are persons who make choices (at times constrained, of course) about the sort of work they do and the number of hours they work.

The behavior of American ex-slaves after abolition clearly reveals that they cared strongly about the manner of their work and valued their non-work time more highly than masters did. Even the most benevolent former masters in the U.S. South found it impossible to entice their former chattels back into gang work, even with large wage premiums. Nor could they persuade women back into the labor force: many female ex-slaves simply chose to stay at home. In the end, slavery is an economic phenomenon because slave societies fail to account for the incalculable costs borne by the slaves themselves.

References

Aitken, H. (ed.) (1971) *Did Slavery Pay? Readings in the Economics of Black Slavery in the United States*, Boston, MA: Houghton-Mifflin.

Anstey, R. (1975) *The Atlantic Slave Trade and British Abolition, 1760–1810*, London: Macmillan.

Bailey, R. (1986) 'Africa, the slave trade, and the rise of industrial capitalism in Europe and the U.S.: A historiographic review', *American History: A Bibliographic Review*, 2: 1–91.

——(1990) 'The slave(ry) trade and the development of capitalism in the United States: the textile industry in New England', *Social Science History*, 14: 373–414.

Bancroft, F. (1931) *Slave Trading in the Old South*, New York: Ungar.

Barzel, Y. (1977) 'An economic analysis of slavery', *Journal of Law and Economics*, 20: 87–110.

Berlin, I. and Gutman, H. (1983) 'Natives and immigrants, free men and slaves: urban workingmen in the antebellum American south', *American Historical Review*, 88: 1175–200.

Berlin, I. and Morgan, P. (eds.) (1991) *The Slave's Economy: Independent Production by Slaves in the Americas*, London: Frank Cass.

——(1993) *Cultivation and Culture: Labor and the Shaping of Slave Life in the Americas*, Charlottesville, VA: University Press of Virginia.

Blackburn, R. (1997) *The Making of New World Slavery: From the Baroque to the Modern*, London: Verso.

Brydon, L. (2001) 'Slavery and labour in West Africa', *Review of African Political Economy*, 28: 137–40.

Bush, M. (ed.) (1996) *Serfdom and Slavery: Studies in Legal Bondage*, New York: Addison Wesley Longman.

Campbell, S. (1968) *The Slave Catchers*, Chapel Hill, NC: University of North Carolina Press.

Carter, S.B., Gartner, S.S., Haines, M.R., Olmstead, A.L., Sutch, R. and Gavin Wright (eds) (2006) *Historical Statistics of the United States, Earliest Times to the Present: Millennial Edition*, New York: Cambridge University Press.

Coelho, P. and McGuire, R. (1997) 'African and European bound labor in the British new world: the biological consequences of economic choices', *Journal of Economic History*, 57: 83–117.

Conrad, A. and Meyer, J. (1958) 'The economics of slavery in the antebellum south', *Journal of Political Economy*, 66: 95–130.

Conrad, A. and Meyer, J. (1964) *The Economics of Slavery and Other Studies*, Chicago, IL: Aldine.

Cooper, F. (1977) *Plantation Slavery on the East Coast of Africa*, New Haven, CT: Yale University Press.

Darity, W. (1985) 'The numbers game and the profitability of the British trade in slaves', *Journal of Economic History*, 45: 693–703.

——(1989) 'Comment: profitability of the British trade in slaves once again', *Explorations in Economic History*, 26: 380–4.

David, P., Gutman, H., Sutch, R., Temin, P. and Wright, G. (1976) *Reckoning with Slavery: A Critical Study in the Quantitative History of American Negro Slavery*, New York: Oxford University Press.

Dew, C. (1991) *Slavery in the Antebellum Southern Industries*, Bethesda, Md: University Publications of America.

——(1994) *Bond of Iron: Master and Slave at Buffalo Forge*, New York: Norton.

Domar, E. (1970) 'The causes of slavery or serfdom: a hypothesis', *Journal of Economic History*, 30: 18–32.

Drescher, S. (1999) *From Slavery to Freedom: Comparative Studies in the Rise and Fall of Atlantic Slavery*, London: Macmillan Press.

Drescher, S. and Engerman, S. (eds) (1998) *A Historical Guide to World Slavery*, New York: Oxford University Press.

Dunn, R. (1972) *Sugar and Slaves: The Rise of the Planter Class in the English West Indies, 1624–1713*, Chapel Hill, NC: University of North Carolina Press.

Elkins, S. (1976) *Slavery: A Problem in American Institutional and Intellectual Life*, Chicago, IL: University of Chicago Press.

Eltis, D. (1977) 'The export of slaves from Africa, 1821–43', *Journal of Economic History*, 37: 409–33.

——(1986) 'Slave departures from Africa, 1811–67: an annual time series', *African Economic History*, 15: 143–71.

——(1987) *Economic Growth and the Ending of the Transatlantic Slave Trade*, New York: Oxford University Press.

——(2000) *The Rise of African Slavery in the Americas*, New York: Cambridge University Press.

Eltis, D. and Engerman, S. (2000) 'The importance of slavery and the slave trade to industrializing Britain', *Journal of Economic History*, 60: 123–44.

Eltis, D. and Richardson, D. (1995) 'Productivity in the transatlantic slave trade', *Explorations in Economic History*, 32: 465–84.

Eltis, D., Behrendt, S. and Richardson, D. (1999) *The Atlantic Slave Trade: A Database on CD-Rom*, New York: Cambridge University Press.

Eltis, D., Lewis, F. and Richardson, D. (2005) 'Slave prices, the African slave trade, and productivity in the Caribbean, 1674–1807', *Economic History Review*, 58: 673–700.

Eltis, D., Lewis, F. and Sokoloff, K. (eds) (2004) *Slavery in the Development of the Americas*, New York: Cambridge University Press.

Engerman, S. (1972) 'The slave trade and British capital formation in the 18th century: a comment on the Williams thesis', *Business History Review*, 46: 430–43.

——(1992) 'Coerced and free labor: property rights and the development of the labor force', *Explorations in Economic History*, 29: 1–29.

Engerman, S. and Genovese, E. (1975) *Race and Slavery in the Western Hemisphere: Quantitative Studies*, Princeton, NJ: Princeton University Press.

Evans, E.W. and Richardson, D. (1995) 'Hunting for rents: the economics of slaving in pre-colonial Africa', *Economic History Review*, 48: 665–86.

Fehrenbacher, D. (1981) *Slavery, Law, and Politics*, New York: Oxford University Press.

Finkelman, P. (1988) *Slavery, Race, and the American Legal System, 1700–1872*, 16 vols, New York: Garland.

——(1989a) *State Slavery Statutes*, Frederick, MD: University Publications of America (microfiche).

——(1989b) *Articles on American Slavery*, 18 vols, New York: Garland.

Franklin, J. (1988) *From Slavery to Freedom*, New York: Knopf.

Friedman, G. and Manning, R. (1992) 'The rent and hire of slaves', in R. Fogel, R. Galantine and R. Manning (eds) *Without Consent or Contract: Evidence and Methods*, New York: Norton.

Fogel, R. (1989) *Without Consent or Contract*, New York: Norton.

Fogel, R. and Engerman, S. (1974) *Time on the Cross: The Economics of American Negro Slavery*, Boston, MA: Little, Brown.

Foner, L. and Genovese, E. (eds) (1969) *Slavery in the New World: A Reader in Comparative History*, Englewood Cliffs, NJ: Prentice-Hall.

Foner, P. (1941) *Business and Slavery*, Chapel Hill, NC: North Carolina Press.

Galenson, D. (1981) *White Servitude in Colonial America: An Economic Analysis*, New York: Cambridge University Press.

——(1982) 'The Atlantic slave trade and the Barbados market, 1673–1723', *Journal of Economic History*, 42: 491–511.

——(1984) 'Rise and fall of indentured servitude in the Americas: an economic analysis', *Journal of Economic History*, 44: 1–26.

——(1986) *Traders, Planters, and Slaves: Market Behavior in Early English America*, New York: Cambridge University Press.

Genovese, E. (1974) *Roll, Jordan, Roll*, New York: Pantheon.

——(1989) *The Political Economy of Slavery: Studies in the Economy and Society of the Slave South*, Middletown, CT: Wesleyan.

Goldin, C. (1976) *Urban Slavery in the American South, 1820–1860: A Quantitative History*, Chicago, IL: University of Chicago Press.

Goodell, W. (1853) *The American Slave Code*, New York: Antislavery Society.

Grindle, D. (1990) 'Manumission: the weak link in Georgia's law of slavery', *Mercer Law Review*, 41: 701–22.

Grubb, F. (1985) 'Immigrant servant labor: their occupational and geographic distribution in the late eighteenth century mid-Atlantic economy', *Social Science History*, 9: 249–75.

——(1994) 'The end of European immigrant servitude in the U.S.: an economic analysis of market collapse, 1772–1835', *Journal of Economic History*, 54: 794–824.

Helper, H.R. (1857) *The Impending Crisis of the South*, New York: Burdick Brothers.

Higman, B. (1976) *Slave Population and Economy in Jamaica, 1807–34*, New York: Cambridge University Press.

Hindus, M. (1980) *Prison and Plantation*, Chapel Hill, NC: University of North Carolina Press.

Hughes, S. (1978) 'Slaves for hire: the allocation of black labor in Elizabeth City County, Virginia, 1782 to 1810', *William and Mary Quarterly*, 35: 268–86.

Hurd, J. (1858) *Law of Freedom and Bondage in the United States*, Boston, MA: Little, Brown.

Inikori, J. (1981) 'Market structure and the profits of the British African trade in the late 18th century', *Journal of Economic History*, 41: 745–76.

Klein, M. (1990) 'The impact of the Atlantic slave trade on the societies of the western Sudan', *Social Science History*, 14: 231–54.

——(1993) *Breaking the Chains: Slavery, Bondage, and Emancipation in Modern Africa and Asia*, Madison, WI: University of Wisconsin Press.

Kolchin, P. (1987) *Unfree Labor: American Slavery and Russian Serfdom*, Cambridge, MA: Harvard University Press.

Kotlikoff, L. (1979) 'The structure of slave prices in New Orleans, 1804–62', *Economic Inquiry*, 17: 496–518.

Licht, W. (1983) *Working for the Railroad: The Organization of Work in the Nineteenth Century*, Princeton, NJ: Princeton University Press.

Lovejoy, P. (1983) *Transformations in Slavery: A History of Slavery in Africa*, New York: Cambridge University Press.

Mancall, P., Rosenbloom, J. and Weiss, T. (2001) 'Slave prices and the South Carolina economy, 1722–1809', *Journal of Economic History*, 61: 616–39.

Manning, P. (1990) 'The slave trade: formal demography of a global system', *Social Science History*, 14: 255–79.

——(2006) *Slavery and African Life: Occidental, Oriental, and African Slave Trades*, Cambridge: Cambridge University Press.

Manzo, K. (2005) 'Modern slavery, global capitalism and deproletarianization in West Africa', *Review of African Political Economy*, 32: 521–34.

Margo, R. and Steckel, R. (1982) 'The heights of American slaves: new evidence on slave nutrition and health', *Social Science History*, 6: 516–38.

Martin, J. (2004) *Divided Mastery: Slave Hiring in the American South*, Cambridge, MA: Harvard University Press.

Menard, R. (1977) 'From servants to slaves: the transformation of the Chesapeake labor system', *Southern Studies*, 16: 355–90.

——(2006) *Sweet Negotiations*, Charlottesville, VA: University of Virginia Press.

Metzer, J. (1975) 'Rational management, modern business practices and economies of scale in the antebellum southern plantations', *Explorations in Economic History*, 12: 123–50.

Mintz, S. (1974) *Caribbean Transformations*, New York: Columbia University Press.

Moreno Fraginals, M., Klein, H. and Engerman, S. (1993) 'The level and structure of slave prices on Cuban plantations in the mid nineteenth century: Some comparative perspectives', *American Historical Review*, 88: 1201–18.

Morris, T. (1996) *Southern Slavery and the Law: 1619–1860*, Chapel Hill, NC: University of North Carolina Press.

Newland, C. and San Segundo, M. (1996) 'Human capital and other determinants of the price life cycle of a slave', *Journal of Economic History*, 56: 694–701.

Oakes, J. (1982) *The Ruling Race: A History of American Slaveholders*, New York: Knopf.

Olmstead, F.L. (1861, reprinted 1953) *The Cotton Kingdom: A Traveler's Observation on Cotton and Slavery in the American Slave States*, ed. A.M. Schlesinger, New York: Knopf.

Parish, P. (1989) *Slavery: History and Historians*, New York: Westview Press.

Patterson, O. (1982) *Slavery and Social Death: A Comparative Study*, Cambridge, MA: Harvard University Press.

Phillips, U.B. (1918) *American Negro Slavery: A Survey of the Supply, Employment and Control of Negro Labor as Determined by the Plantation Regime*, New York: Appleton.

——(1927) *Life and Labor in the Old South*, Boston, MA: Little, Brown.

Pritchett, J. (1997) 'The interregional slave trade and the selection of slaves for the New Orleans market', *Journal of Interdisciplinary History*, 28: 57–85.

Ramsdell, C. (1929) 'The natural limits of slavery expansion', *Mississippi Valley Historical Review*, 16: 151–71.

Ransom, R. (1989) *Conflict and Compromise*, New York: Cambridge University Press.

Ransom, R. and Sutch, R. (1977) *One Kind of Freedom: The Economic Consequences of Emancipation*, New York: Cambridge University Press.

——(1988) 'Capitalists without capital: the burden of slavery and the impact of emancipation', *Agricultural History*, 62: 133–60.

Richardson, D. (1987) 'The costs of survival: the transport of slaves in the middle passage and the profitability of the 18th century British slave trade', *Explorations in Economic History*, 24: 178–96.

——(1989) 'Accounting for profits in the British trade in slaves: a reply to Darity', *Explorations in Economic History*, 26: 492–9.

Roark, J. (1977) *Masters Without Slaves*, New York: Norton.

Scarborough, W. (1966) *The Overseer: Plantation Management in the Old South*, Baton Rouge, LA: Louisiana State University Press.

Schafer, J. (1994) *Slavery, The Civil Law, and the Supreme Court of Louisiana*, Baton Rouge, LA: Louisiana State University Press.

Schmitz, M. and Schaefer, D. (1981) 'Paradox lost: westward expansion and slave prices before the Civil War', *Journal of Economic History*, 41: 402–7.

Sheridan, R. (1947) *Sugar and Slavery: An Economic History of the British West Indies, 1607–1776*, Barbados: Caribbean University Press.

Snyder, T. (2010) *Bloodlands: Europe between Hitler and Stalin*, New York: Basic Books.

Solow, B. and Engerman, S. (1987) *Capitalism and Caribbean Slavery: The Legacy of Eric Williams*, New York: Cambridge University Press.

Stampp, K. (1956) *The Peculiar Institution: Slavery in the Antebellum South*, New York: Knopf.

Starobin, R. (1970) *Industrial Slavery in the Old South*, New York: Oxford University Press.

Steckel, R. (1986a) 'Birth weights and infant mortality among American slaves', *Explorations in Economic History*, 23: 173–98.

——(1986b) 'A peculiar population: the nutrition, health, and mortality of American slaves from childhood to maturity', *Journal of Economic History*, 46: 721–41.

Steinfeld, R. (1991) *The Invention of Free Labor: The Employment Relation in English and American Law and Culture, 1350–1870*, Chapel Hill, NJ: University of North Carolina Press.

Stroud, G. (1856) *A Sketch of the Laws Relating to Slavery in the Several States of the USA*, New York: Negro University Press.

Tadman, M. (1990) *Speculators and Slaves*, Madison, WI: University of Wisconsin Press.

Tushnet, M. (1981) *The American Law of Slavery, 1810–60: Considerations of Humanity and Interest*, Princeton, NJ: Princeton University Press.

Vedder, R. (1975) 'The slave exploitation (expropriation) rate', *Explorations in Economic History*, 12: 453–7.

Wahl, J. (1998) *The Bondsman's Burden: An Economic Analysis of the Common Law of Southern Slavery*, New York: Cambridge University Press.

——(2007) 'Stay east, young man? Market repercussions of the *Dred Scott* decision', *Chicago-Kent Law Review*, 82: 361–91.

Walvin, J. (1992) *Black Ivory: A History of British Slavery*, Washington: Howard University Press.

Watson, A. (1989) *Slave Law in the Americas*, Athens, GA: University of Georgia Press.

Watson, J. (ed.) (1980) *Asian and African Systems of Slavery*, Berkeley, CA: University of California Press.

Westermann, W. (1943) 'Slavery and the elements of freedom in ancient Greece', *Quarterly Bulletin of the Polish Institute of Arts and Sciences in America*, 1: 1–16.

Wheeler, J. (1837) *A Practical Treatise on the Law of Slavery*, New York: Allan Pollack, Jr.

Wiecek, W. (1977) 'The statutory law of slavery and race in the thirteen mainland colonies of British America', *William and Mary Quarterly*, 34: 258–80.

Williams, E. (1944) *Capitalism and Slavery*, Chapel Hill, NC: University of North Carolina Press.

Wright, G. (1978) *The Political Economy of the Cotton South: Households, Markets, and Wealth in the Nineteenth Century*, New York: Norton.

——(2006) *Slavery and American Economic Development*, Baton Rouge, LA: Louisiana State University Press.

Yasuba, Y. (1961) 'The profitability and viability of slavery in the U.S.', *Economic Studies Quarterly*, 12: 60–67.

Yeager, T. (1995) 'Encomienda or slavery? The Spanish crown's choice of labor organization in sixteenth century Spanish America', *Journal of Economic History*, 55: 842–59.

25

THE ECONOMIC HISTORY OF URBANIZATION

Fred Smith

The city is the engine for human achievement. From engineering feats to solve the sanitation needs of ancient Rome, to the flood of art, literature, and music from the Italian city-states of the Renaissance, cities facilitate interactions that allow human beings to improve their quality of life. While social scientists clearly understand the importance of cities in promoting human well-being, the origins of the city remain shrouded in the darkness of ancient history. Jericho (located in the Jordan Valley) appears to be the strongest candidate for the title of "first city," for archaeologists have uncovered evidence of a city of some 2,000 inhabitants dating back to at least the ninth millennium BC (O'Sullivan 2006). Wherever and whenever they first appeared, however, cities took shape for one simple reason: the benefits to human beings from clustering and living in close contact with one another exceeded the costs of doing so (Glaeser 1998).

Although simple cost-benefit analysis tells us why cities form, it tells us nothing about key questions that are of interest to urban economists. What causes the benefits of human clustering to outweigh the costs? Why do cities form where they do? Why do cities form at a specific point in time, and why do some cities decline or even disappear? Does the city have a future?

In 2011, more than one half of the globe's inhabitants choose to live in urban areas (Glaeser 2011). This fact alone speaks to the importance of understanding the role of the city in shaping the human experience. In order to better understand the economic history of urbanization, this chapter will begin by examining the basic economic forces that cause cities to form. Then, after providing a brief snapshot of urbanization before 1800, the remainder of the chapter will focus on the history of urbanized areas in the United States.

Urbanization

What is an urban area? Economists define an urban area as a location with higher population density than the countryside that surrounds it. While this definition lacks precision, it captures the essence of what is important about urbanization to an economist. A city facilitates interactions among human beings by putting them in close contact with one another. More formal definitions of cities abound, and for social scientists conducting research on urban topics the U.S. Census Bureau's classification scheme is especially useful. For the Census Bureau, an Urban Area is a geographical area with at least 2,500 inhabitants and a population density of no fewer than 500 persons per square mile. A Metropolitan Area is a geographical area with a densely populated core area surrounded by communities that are "economically integrated" with the core area; a Metropolitan Area has no fewer than 50,000 inhabitants (O'Sullivan 2009).

If an urban area is a cluster of human beings living in close proximity to one another, then urban areas must be locations where the benefits of clustering exceed the costs. However, before examining these costs and benefits, it is necessary to recognize that cities cannot form without an agricultural surplus. Urban workers who are engaged in activities unrelated to the production of food draw resources away from the agricultural sector of the economy. Thus, the workers who remain employed in food production must produce enough to feed themselves as well as those working in the other sectors of the economy. While an agricultural surplus is a necessary condition for the formation of cities, it is not a sufficient condition.

In his seminal article, "Transportation and patterns of urban development," Edwin Mills identified the conditions that are needed for city formation by envisioning the circumstances in which we might live in a world without cities (Mills 1967). By working through this thought experiment, Mills demonstrates that an economy must possess one critical feature in order for cities to arise: economies of scale in production. Economies of scale in production can arise from a wide range of sources, but Mills identifies one key source – the transport of goods. Economies of scale in transportation come about when an individual (or firm) is able to move multiple units of a good on the same trip. Consider an individual moving boxes from her home to her office. Without any outside resources or tools, she would have to move the boxes by walking between her home and office, carrying one single box at a time. By loading all of her boxes on to a truck, and then driving the truck from her home to her office, she is able to reduce the average moving cost per box. Throughout history, cities have formed at locations where humans are able to exploit economies of scale in transportation. Until the nineteenth century, those locations almost invariably involved proximity to trading routes or access to water. (Boston, New Orleans, and New York are well-known examples.) Modern cities (like Atlanta, Chicago, and Denver) have exploited similar locational advantages formed by railroad junctures, airports, and intersections of major roadways.

Arthur O'Sullivan expands Mills's analysis to argue that cities may arise when a combination of four features of an economy cause the benefits of human clustering to outweigh the costs. O'Sullivan begins by reestablishing the core point made by Mills – namely, that an economy must possess scale economies in transportation or "trade services" (O'Sullivan 2006: 41). However, O'Sullivan argues that three additional features may lead to the benefits of human clustering exceeding the costs. First, if a firm possesses "internal" economies of scale in production, then the workers employed by that firm will cluster in an area that will become a city. Next, firms clustering in a single location may lead to what urban economists call "agglomeration economies" or "external economies of scale" due to factors such as labor pooling or information sharing and knowledge spillovers. Finally, the presence of a public good that must be consumed in a specific location – O'Sullivan cites religious facilities and defensive fortifications as two common examples – will lead to clustering that is beneficial (O'Sullivan 2006).

While the principal forces that cause urbanization are relatively straightforward and clear, complex economic forces shape the location, size, and viability of cities. The next section of this chapter seeks to better understand these forces by analyzing them in historical context.

Urbanized areas in history: the pre-industrial city

Cities formed across the globe many millennia ago. Paul Bairoch (1988) dates the origins of urbanization to the eighth millennia BC in the Middle East, the third millennia BC in the Indus Valley, the second millennia BC in China and the New World, and the first millennia BC in sub-Saharan Africa. Founded around 750 BC, by the second century AD Rome had, in all likelihood, become the first city to reach a population of 1 million inhabitants. Rome owes its location to a ford in the Tiber River; thus it serves as an excellent example of a city that formed due to locational advantages. Trading routes made use of the ford, and Rome's location also allowed easy access to the sea. Formed as a trading city, at the height of its economic power the citizens of Rome may well have enjoyed a material well-being comparable to that of seventeenth-century Europeans. While Roman citizens enjoyed material well-being that wouldn't be experienced again in Europe for over a thousand years, life expectancy in Rome was only 25 years. Nonetheless, Peter Temin (2006) points to technological innovation (concrete, aqueducts, baths, and theaters), advanced institutions (financial intermediaries), and literacy as evidence that life in Rome during the late-Republic and early Empire was relatively prosperous.

If the prosperity of Rome suggests that the benefits of urbanization outweighed the costs, then the fall of Rome signaled that was no longer the case. Indeed, cities in Europe were to remain in decline for over 500 years after the fall of Rome. The largest cities in the world during this period were found in China and the Middle East (Bairoch 1988). Regardless of the location or the time period, though, a clear theme emerges for the cities that existed during the period from the sixth to the eighteenth centuries. These cities functioned as trading centers, places for religious worship, places that allowed for the common defense, or places of centralized administration (capital cities). Thus, of the four factors identified by O'Sullivan as the principal causes of urbanization, cities from this time period typically existed only because of scale economies in transportation and the presence of location-specific public goods.

By 1600, Europe still lacked a city the size of ancient Rome, and only ten European cities had as many as 100,000 inhabitants. One hundred and fifty years later, on the eve of the Industrial Revolution, this number had only grown to sixteen. London and Paris – Europe's two largest cities – had populations of only slightly over 500,000 as late as 1750. Prior to the Industrial Revolution, the world's cities formed for similar reasons; similarly, the size of these cities remained constrained by the same technological limitations. The first, and most important, constraint on city size was the cost of transporting goods between a city and surrounding hinterlands (Mills and Hamilton 1994). Transporting agricultural goods to the city and manufacturing goods to the countryside was extraordinarily expensive without the use of waterways. George Rogers Taylor (1962) estimates that it cost 30 cents (or more) to move one ton of cargo one mile in 1815 using existing roadways. In comparison, shipping goods by inland waterways cost 6 cents or less per ton-mile; sending cargo on ocean-going vessels reduced the cost to 1 cent or less per ton-mile. Thus, a city's size was limited by the size of the region with which it could engage in trade.

Technological concerns also placed limits on urban infrastructure, which served as another constraint on a city's ability to grow. First, transportation technology limited the ability of urban residents to move themselves and their wares within and between urban areas. Carts, wagons, and coaches that could be pulled by a team of animals were the only alternatives to walking. These methods of transport failed to provide much in the way of economies of scale, for it was impossible to load many goods or many people into a single vehicle. Moreover, the animals needed to pull the carts and coaches required care while simultaneously generating waste that city residents were forced to contend with.

Building technology limited building height prior to the late nineteenth century, which created yet another constraint on city size. While it was technologically feasible to build tall structures before the 1800s, the cost of doing so was prohibitive. Major building projects – cathedrals, amphitheaters, and ceremonial structures – were some of the few examples of structures taller than a few stories. Building taller buildings forced firms to face two major challenges. First, as buildings increased in height, the walls for the lower stories needed to be thick enough to support the weight of the walls from the upper stories. (A late nineteenth-century example of this type of building still stands in Chicago – the Monadnock Building.) Second, prior to the invention of the elevator, stairs were the only means of accessing the upper floors of a structure (Glaeser 2011). For example, a person wishing to reach the top of the South tower of Notre Dame in Paris must climb 387 steps!

Finally, sanitation concerns also served as a major constraint on city size. Although urban dwellers understood the technology that would allow for the delivery of fresh drinking water and the disposal of sewage, the required investments in infrastructure necessary to obtain fresh water and safely dispose of sewage were prohibitively expensive.

The Industrial Revolution radically transformed the limits on urban growth. Whereas cities had once struggled to grow beyond a million residents, by the end of the nineteenth century more than 20 cities in Europe and three in the United States surpassed this population threshold.

Urbanization and the Industrial Revolution

By the late 1700s, urbanization had spread across the European continent and produced the world's first urban giants. Cities were not yet a major part of the North American landscape, though. The 1790 Census showed that only five cities in the United States had as many as 10,000 inhabitants. These cities were tied to coastal locations along the Atlantic, where residents could exploit the economies of scale in transportation that access to water provided them. As indicated in Table 25.1, the largest cities in the United States remained on or east of the Mississippi River until 1900.

Two transportation improvements dramatically changed the cost of shipping goods between the Midwest and the East Coast: the Erie Canal and the railroad. The Erie Canal, stretching from Lake Erie to the Hudson River, linked the agricultural heartland of the Midwest to New

Table 25.1 Population rank for selected U.S. cities, 1790–2000

City	1790	1850	1900	1950	2000
New York	1	1	1	1	1
Boston	3	3	5	10	20
Philadelphia	2	4	3	3	5
Baltimore	4	2	6	6	17
Washington, D.C.	–	18	15	9	21
Charleston, SC	5	15	68	–	–
New Orleans	–	5	12	16	31
Atlanta	–	–	43	33	39
Cleveland	–	41	7	7	33
Chicago	–	24	2	2	3
Detroit	–	30	13	5	10
St. Louis	–	8	4	8	49
Dallas	–	–	88	22	8
Houston	–	–	85	14	4
Phoenix	–	–	–	99	6
Los Angeles	–	–	36	4	2
San Francisco	–	–	9	11	13

Sources: Gibson (1998) and http://www.census.gov/statab/ccdb/cit1020r.txt

York City. By linking these markets, agricultural products could be moved to New York and trade goods could be moved to the hinterland cheaply and quickly. Similarly, the creation of the steam engine led to the construction of an extensive network of railroads across the United States. With a rail network in place, cities could develop in locations that were once impractical because of limited access to water transportation. Ultimately, water and rail transport radically reduced the travel time between the East Coast and the interior of the country. A trip from New York to Cleveland took two weeks in 1800, but by 1830 the trip time had been cut in half. Thirty years later, the same trip from New York took only one day. A trip from New York to Chicago was cut from six weeks (1800) to three weeks (1830) to two days (1860) (Atack and Passell 1994).

The development of improved transportation networks worked in tandem with changes in production technology to cause an explosion in urban population during the nineteenth century. Manufacturing technologies developed during the Industrial Revolution meant that firms producing goods were able to exploit substantial economies of scale. When these cost savings were coupled with lower transportation costs, factories enjoyed a dramatic increase in the size of their market area. ("Market area" is a term used by urban economists to describe the area in which a factory-produced good can be sold more cheaply than a comparable good produced at home.) Textile production serves as an excellent example that helps to illustrate this point. Prior to the Industrial Revolution, most households engaged in home production to satisfy their needs for garments. However, as production and transportation technology changed, and as factory-produced textiles became more affordable to a larger number of households, a larger number of households chose to purchase factory-produced textiles. Lowell, Massachusetts, is an excellent example of a city that grew as a result of this process. Lowell was America's first industrial city, for its location on the Merrimack River allowed textile mills to run power looms using water wheels. The city's population grew by more than 200 per cent between 1830 and 1840 as workers located near Lowell to take advantage of the jobs available in the thriving textile industry (Atack and Passell 1994).

Ultimately, Lowell provides insight into why the Industrial Revolution led to explosive population growth in major urban areas. Trade between a city and its hinterland ensured the economic prosperity of both. The residents of the rural areas benefited from the products manufactured in the city, while the urban dwellers required the food and raw materials from the countryside.

While industrialization fueled urban growth, cities would have been held in check without technological changes that allowed for improvements in intra-city transportation, building technology, and sanitation. Intra-city transportation changed dramatically during the nineteenth century. At the beginning of the century, animal-powered carts and coaches transported both people and goods. By the end of the century, transportation technology had allowed a city resident to move through the city on a streetcar or elevated train line. The streetcar or subway provided a great advantage for the urban resident: speed. Streetcars moved more rapidly than someone who was walking, which made it feasible for a city to expand its boundaries. The use of the streetcar was limited to those who could afford the fare, though. Zachary Schrag (2002) points out that it was principally a city's white-collar workers who were able to afford a roundtrip streetcar fare of 10 cents per day. Upper-class neighborhoods that could only be efficiently accessed by streetcar popped up in and near cities throughout the United States. One of the first, and most carefully planned, streetcar communities emerged on the east side of Cleveland, Ohio – the town of Shaker Heights.

While changes in intra-city transportation technology meant that cities could expand outward to occupy a larger footprint, changes in building technology meant that each square mile within a city's expanded borders could hold more residents. Iron, then steel, allowed for buildings to be built to heights that were once impractical. Tall buildings would have been unappealing, though, had it not been for the invention of the elevator and the Otis safety break (Glaeser 2011). One additional innovation allowed for urban dwellers to rapidly build houses: the mass-produced nail. Once nails became widely (and cheaply) available, frame houses could be built much more quickly than when construction methods had required beams to be fitted together using the mortise and tenon system (Mills and Hamilton 1994).

Poor sanitation had been another constraint on city size prior to the late nineteenth century, but Joseph Ferrie and Werner Troesken (2008) document the dramatic effect that improvements in Chicago's sanitation system had on mortality rates within the city. Chicago's experiences were certainly not unique, but the outcomes are no less startling as a result. Between 1860 and 1925, Chicago's crude death rate fell by 60 per cent, and Ferrie and Troesken attribute up to half of that decline to improvements in Chicago's sanitation system and the cleaner drinking water that resulted.

The technological changes from the Industrial Revolution had major effects on the size of urban areas, but they also had a profound impact on the shape of cities. A city's shape is often referred to as its "spatial structure," and throughout human history cities have typically been "monocentric." As the term suggests, monocentric cities have, literally, one center. The center of a monocentric city is commonly known as the "CBD" (central business district), and it functions as the core of the city, the place where economic activity is focused. CBDs typically formed around one of a handful of structures: a market or a port, or, later, in the nineteenth century, a rail terminal. Indeed, many CBDs contained a combination of a market and a transportation node. Because the residents of an urban area place great value on proximity to the transportation node and market in the center of a city, residents bid up the price for land that is located close to the center. The monocentric model formally develops this relationship, and William Alonso, Edwin Mills, and Richard Muth developed versions of the model independently in the 1960s. (The intellectual predecessor to Alonso, Mills, and Muth was J.H. von Thünen, an economist who worked in the late eighteenth and early nineteenth century.)

The monocentric model predicts that land values will be highest near the CBD, and that they will decline as one moves away from the center of the city. This relationship has clear implications for the city's spatial structure. Specifically, higher land values near the city center will lead firms and residents who wish to use this land to use it sparingly. Substituting capital for land leads to taller buildings in the center of the city. On the periphery of the urban area, where land is cheap, firms will choose to use more land and less capital. Thus, shorter buildings on the city's edges surround the tall buildings in the city's core.

The types of businesses (and individuals) that are best able to make use of the land in close proximity to the center of the city are the ones that will pay the higher prices associated with these parcels of land. The businesses that value proximity to the city center change depending on the period under consideration, but a common theme emerges. Businesses that face substantial transportation costs for moving inputs or outputs to the market (or transportation node) in the city center will place the highest value on proximity to the center. Historically, commercial firms occupied the space closest to the center of the city with manufacturing firms occupying the land immediately outside the CBD. Land used for housing a city's residents was typically located even farther away from the urban core, at locations beyond the manufacturing firms.

Before moving on to a discussion of urbanization in the twentieth century, it is worth exploring several additional urban economics concepts that can help to explain the pattern of firm location within (and between) cities. "Shopping externalities" is a term used to describe the benefit that a business receives by locating in close proximity to other businesses selling products that are either substitutes or complements for the products of the firm. More specifically, shopping externalities arise when a firm attracts more customers simply because it receives visits from customers who might not otherwise have visited the store. Consider an example. In the United States, there are shopping districts in New York (along Fifth Avenue) or in Chicago (along Michigan Avenue) that create and take advantage of shopping externalities. Chicago's Michigan Avenue offers the shopper nearly every conceivable type of clothing store. A person wishing to purchase a pair of pants from a department store might stop in at a specialty store selling jackets, not because he intended to buy a jacket but because he happened to see a jacket when he was on his trip to purchase the pair of pants.

The organization of retail firms within urban areas will frequently capture shopping externalities that may exist, but firms that aren't selling a retail product may also have their locational decisions affected by the presence of "externalities." Specifically, urban economists identify two types of forces – localization economies and urbanization economies – that can have a profound effect on where a firm locates.

Localization economies exist when firms in a related industry enjoy benefits from clustering together in a single location. Detroit's auto manufacturers provide an excellent historical example of localization economies affecting firm location. Automobile manufacturers opening in the early twentieth century chose Detroit to benefit from one or more of the three sources of localization economies – sharing input suppliers, sharing a labor pool, and knowledge spillovers. Auto manufacturers didn't produce all of the parts that went into their cars, so by locating in Detroit – where the auto parts manufacturers also ultimately chose to operate – allowed them to interact more easily with these firms. This promoted better communication between the firms, allowing the auto manufacturers to more precisely express their needs. Moreover, since so many of the auto manufacturing firms located in Detroit, and since these firms required many of the same parts, the firms manufacturing the car parts were able to exploit economies of scale in production. Auto manufacturers enjoyed the lower prices that parts suppliers could offer as a result. Similar efficiencies came about when auto manufacturing firms were able to benefit from sharing a common labor pool. By locating in the same city as Ford, General Motors could draw on a wide pool of workers who were interested in, or had experience in, working in the auto manufacturing industry. Finally, the day-to-day casual interactions that the employees from these auto manufacturing firms had with one another led to "knowledge spillovers." This is a term used by urban economists to describe the benefits that arise from the informal exchange of information that takes place when workers in a given industry live and work in close proximity to one another.

Localization economies occur when firms from a single industry locate in close proximity to one another; urbanization economies occur when firms enjoy these same benefits simply from locating in a large urban area. For example, not all of the top law firms in the nation locate in a single city in the United States. However, these firms typically choose to operate in large cities. By locating in a large city, a top law firm is able to take advantage of shared input suppliers (business services such as accounting, marketing, and consulting), a shared labor pool (other law firms will also locate in large cities, thereby creating a wide pool of legal talent that all firms may draw from), and knowledge spillovers. In the United States, firms are most likely to benefit from urbanization economies in cities such as Boston, Chicago, Los Angeles, New York, and San Francisco.

A final consideration about the location of firms and cities takes into account the way in which firms choosing to locate in a specific place can lead to the formation of a city around those firms. (Or, alternatively, cause an existing city to grow more rapidly.) Once again, economic history provides excellent examples to illustrate this point. In the United States, the oil refining industry was initially centered on Cleveland because of the city's proximity to the oil fields of Western Pennsylvania. As the refining industry thrived, Cleveland's population exploded. Checking in at under 100,000 residents in 1870, the city had nearly 400,000 residents 30 years later.

At the end of the nineteenth century, major U.S. cities such as New York, Chicago, and Philadelphia had grown to sizes that would have been unimaginable just 100 years earlier. The technological change brought about by the Industrial Revolution had allowed these cities to expand both out and up. These cities were densely populated, and the cities' infrastructure – especially intra-city transportation in the form of streetcars, elevated railways, or subways – meant that the CBD served as the focus of economic activity. Technological change would radically transform the urban spatial structure of the city once again, though. The railroad era was drawing to a close and the era of the automobile was about to begin.

Urbanization in the twentieth century

At the start of the twentieth century, 40 per cent of all Americans lived in an urban area. This represented a dramatic change from the nation's first Census (1790), when only 5.6 per cent of all Americans lived in cities. The process of urbanization continued throughout the twentieth century, and in 1990 nearly three out of every four Americans lived in an urban area. While the U.S. was evolving into an urbanized nation, the process didn't follow the same trajectory in all cities or regions.

As shown in Table 25.2, cities that were involved with the production or widespread use of the automobile expanded in dramatic fashion between 1900 and 1950. Most notably, the population of Detroit increased by a factor of more than six, Cleveland's population more than doubled, and Los Angeles expanded by a factor of nearly 20.

Cities that flourished because of the widespread use of the automobile continued to grow in the second half of the twentieth century; the cities that were linked to the production of the

Table 25.2 Population in select American cities in 1900, 1950, and 2000

City	1900	1950	2000
Atlanta	89,872	331,314	416,474
Baltimore	508,957	949,708	651,154
Boston	560,892	801,444	589,141
Chicago	1,698,575	3,620,962	2,896,016
Cleveland	381,768	914,808	478,403
Dallas	42,638	434,462	1,188,580
Detroit	285,704	1,849,568	951,270
Houston	44,633	596,163	1,953,631
Los Angeles	102,479	1,970,358	3,694,820
New Orleans	287,104	570,445	484,674
New York	3,437,202	7,891,957	8,008,278
Philadelphia	1,293,697	2,071,605	1,517,550
Phoenix	5,544	106,818	1,321,045
St. Louis	575,238	856,796	348,149
San Francisco	342,782	775,357	776,733
Washington, D.C.	278,718	802,178	572,059

Sources: Gibson (1998) and http://factfinder.census.gov

automobile didn't fare nearly as well. Once again, Detroit stands out. A city of nearly 2 million people in 1950, Detroit lost half of its population between 1950 and 2000. The decline continued in the first decade of the twenty-first century. Detroit lost another 25 per cent of its population, and the city is estimated to have had 713,777 residents in 2010 (Linebaugh 2011).

Los Angeles, Phoenix, Dallas, and Houston, cities whose residents rely heavily on the automobile for their transportation needs, have flourished in the past 60 years. Phoenix was a sleepy town of only 100,000 residents as recently as 1950. By 2000, it was the sixth largest city in the country. Although the automobile helped to facilitate the growth of Southern and Western cities, and it surely shaped the spatial structure of those cities, it is worth noting that without the widespread availability of air conditioning these cities would not have experienced their explosive rates of growth.

As the data in Table 25.2 show, the automobile had a profound impact on the growth (and decline) of American cities in the twentieth century. However, what the data fail to reveal is that the automobile not only affected the size of U.S. cities in the twentieth century, it also affected the shape of American cities. The car severed the economic connection between firms (and workers) and the central city. With the arrival of the car, and, more importantly, intra- and inter-city trucking, it was no longer necessary for firms to ship inputs or finished products through a port or a railhead. Instead, trucks made it possible to transport inputs from the field, forest, or mine directly to the factory or finished products directly to the store.

A factory that no longer needed to transport inputs or outputs to a centrally located port or railhead had the freedom to choose any location that had a plentiful supply of workers and cheap land. Land near the city center that had once been highly desirable rapidly became undesirable because it was so expensive. Manufacturing plants moved from within the city limits of cities like Cleveland, Detroit, and Pittsburgh into the suburbs of these cities or to states in the South or West. Cleveland's National Screw serves as an excellent example of this type of move. The firm moved from within Cleveland city limits to a distant suburb on the Southwest side of the city, a location with excellent freeway access.

Ultimately, the automobile led to two dramatic changes in urban spatial structure that urban economists have been able to successfully quantify. First, as firms moved to cheaper land in the suburbs, land in the city center became relatively less valuable. (This is especially true of cities that experienced urban decay.) This meant that the "bid-rent" function for decaying cities became flatter. A bid-rent function is a mathematical relationship that emerges from the economic theory presented in the monocentric city model. It posits a relationship between the price of a parcel of land and the distance of that parcel from the city center – namely that parcels near the city center will be worth more (in dollars per square foot) than parcels at the edge of the city. Figure 25.1 illustrates bid-rent functions that are representative of cities before and after the development of the automobile. Economists have used land value data from cities such as Cleveland and Chicago to determine the shape of bid-rent functions. For example, the value of a square foot of land in the city center of Cleveland, Ohio, fell from $85 in 1915 to just under $10 in 1980 (measured in 1980 dollars) (Smith 2003b). As economic theory predicts, the slope of the bid-rent functions for Cleveland and Chicago flattened dramatically between 1910 and 1930. Early in the twentieth century a 1-mile movement from the city center led to a reduction in land value of 64 per cent in Cleveland and 48 per cent in Chicago; by the middle of the century the same 1-mile movement from the city center led to a reduction in land value of only 29 per cent in Cleveland and 2 per cent in Chicago (Smith 2003a).

Taken to the extreme, the automobile allowed for a complete break from the monocentric city model. Figure 25.2 illustrates a bid-rent function for a modern, multicentric city. In this figure, land values reach peaks at distance zero as well as D_1 and D_2. This type of situation

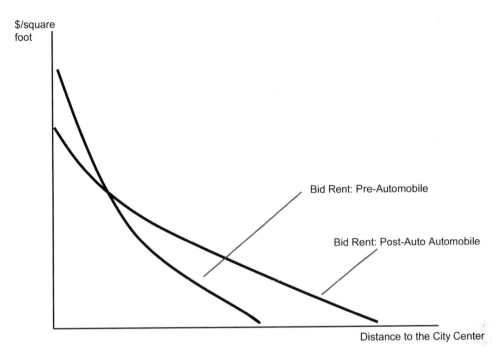

$/square foot

Bid Rent: Pre-Automobile

Bid Rent: Post-Auto Automobile

Distance to the City Center

Figure 25.1 Monocentric city bid–rent functions

could be found in modern Los Angeles (with a center in downtown Los Angeles and subcenters in places like Anaheim or Pasadena) or Chicago (with a center in downtown Chicago and subcenters in places like the O'Hare corridor and Naperville).

Urban economists have identified a second quantifiable trend caused by the spread of the automobile. As businesses moved from the city center, workers no longer had an incentive to pay the larger housing rents commanded by dwellings built near the center of the city. Thus, workers moved to locations distant from the old city center and the city's population density declined near the center. The relationship between population density and distance from a city's center is described with a "density gradient," and the ultimate effect of the widespread use of the automobile was to cause a flattening of cities' density gradients. Empirical work by Edmonston (reported in Kopecky and Suen [2010]) gives a clear indication of how dramatically density gradients flattened in a collection of 41 U.S. cities during the twentieth century. In 1900, a 1–mile movement away from the city center led to an 83 per cent reduction in population density (persons/square mile) for the average city. Seventy years later the same 1–mile movement led to only a 23 per cent reduction in population density. Figure 25.3 provides a different perspective on changing population density. The graphs in Figure 25.3 illustrate the change in population density within the city of Cleveland between 1960 and 1980. (The x axis measures distance East and West, the y axis measures distance North and South, and the z axis measures change in population density – measured as inhabitants per square mile. The city center – Public Square – is located at [x,y] coordinates [0,0].) The story in Figure 25.3 is clear: population density increased markedly at the edges of the city and remained stagnant in Cleveland's core. Thus, as the manufacturing firms that had once been located near Cleveland's downtown moved to the suburbs, residents moved to neighborhoods at the edges of the city.

Fred Smith

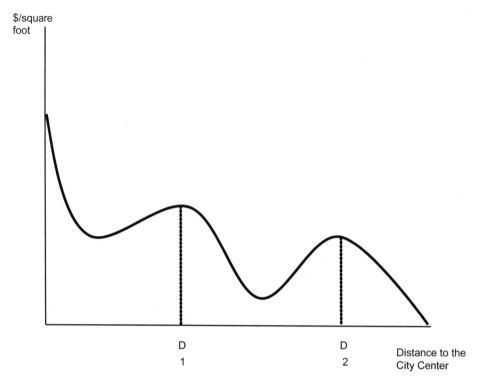

Figure 25.2 Multicentric city bid-rent function

As the automobile brought about dramatic changes in urban spatial structure, other features of urban life in U.S. cities changed too. While Americans were choosing to live in cities in ever-greater numbers, African-Americans moved to cities episodically. Only one out of every five African-Americans lived in a city in 1910; 90 years later, that number had increased to four out of every five. African-Americans moved to the city in especially large numbers during the second wave of the Great Migration. Only 41 per cent of blacks lived in metropolitan areas in 1940, yet 30 years later more than 75 per cent of all African-Americans lived in an urban area (Boustan and Margo 2011).

As Americans were choosing to live in cities, they were also choosing to live in owner-occupied housing with ever-increasing frequency. In 1900, only 46 per cent of all Americans lived in owner-occupied housing. This figure had climbed to 55 per cent by 1950, and at the beginning of the twenty-first century 66 per cent of Americans lived in an owner-occupied home. Not only were more Americans living in owner-occupied homes, they were living in higher-quality homes too. In 1940, 45 per cent of all homes lacked complete plumbing facilities (defined by the Census as a home with hot and cold running water, shower/bath, and a toilet). This figure had fallen to about 1 per cent by 1990. Not all Americans benefited equally from these changes though. William Collins and Robert Margo (2003) show that the value of owner-occupied housing differed by race throughout the twentieth century. Using observations from homeowners across the United States, they find that the black/white ratio of home values was 0.37 in 1940. The gap narrowed over time, and by 1990 the ratio was 0.65. While the black/white gap narrowed for the nation as a whole, it did not do so uniformly. The black/white ratio for owner-occupied homes in central cities barely changed: the ratio was 0.51 in 1940 and 0.52 in 1990.

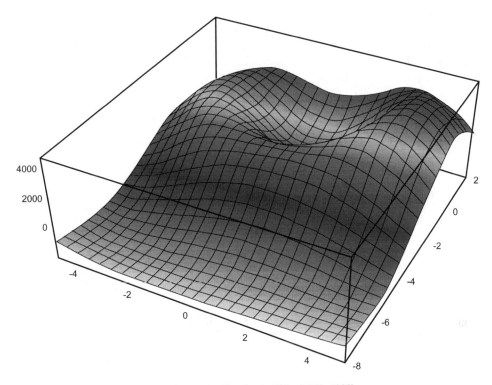

Figure 25.3 Change in population density in Cleveland, Ohio (1960–1980)
Source: Collins and Smith (2005).

Finally, the widespread use of the automobile not only changed where people lived within a metropolitan area. It also had the predictable effect of changing the way that workers commuted to their jobs. In 1960, 64 per cent of American workers relied on private automobiles to get to and from work. More than 22 per cent of Americans rode public transportation or walked to work. Just 40 years later, 87.9 per cent of Americans relied on private automobiles for their commute; only 7.6 per cent still opted to walk or ride public transportation.

Conclusion

Cities remain the engine for human achievement in the twenty-first century. Looking at measures of economic achievement, urban dwellers are doing better than Americans living in rural areas. By the year 2000, more than 50 per cent of all urban residents had attended at least some college and fewer than 20 per cent of urban dwellers failed to graduate from high school. These results compare very favorably with the nearly 24 per cent of rural residents who failed to graduate from high school and the 41 per cent who attended some college. Better educational outcomes for urban residents translate into better standards of living. Monica Fisher (2007) documents the lower poverty rates that have prevailed in metropolitan areas (when compared with non-metro areas), and she attributes the superior economic outcomes to two factors: better educational outcomes enjoyed by urban dwellers and the more prevalent economic opportunities that exist in urban areas due to the benefits of agglomeration. The metro/non-metro poverty rate gap remains substantial. Fisher shows that it was nearly 10 percentage points in the mid-1960s, and remained larger than 3 percentage points at the turn of the twenty-first century.

Although metropolitan areas are still the engine for economic growth in the United States in the twenty-first century, many American cities face serious challenges. More than one-third of the residents in Detroit and Cleveland now live below the poverty line, and in Buffalo, Miami, Milwaukee, and St. Louis one-fourth of the residents live below the poverty line. And the path out of poverty – a quality education – is blocked for all too many of the residents of these cities. Once again, Detroit serves as an unfortunate example of what can happen in an urban area on the decline. In 2011, Detroit was compelled to close half of its schools and to increase the maximum class size in public schools to sixty students (Linebaugh 2011).

The economic decline of Detroit, Cleveland, and other rust-belt cities is unfortunate, but exceptional. On the whole, U.S. cities continue to survive and grow for one simple reason: the benefits to clustering outweigh the costs. Technology and people's tastes and preferences for urban living may affect the costs and benefits associated with clustering, but it seems clear that the benefits of clustering will continue to outweigh the costs for the foreseeable future.

References

Alonso, W. (1964) *Location and Land Use: Towards a General Theory of Land Rent*, Cambridge, MA: Harvard University Press.

Atack, J. and Passell, P. (1994) *A New Economic View of American History*, 2nd edition, New York: W.W. Norton.

Bairoch, P. (1988) *Cities and Economic Development*, Chicago, IL: University of Chicago Press.

Boustan, L. and Margo, R. (2011) 'White suburbanization and African-American home ownership, 1940–80', NBER Working Paper No. 16702.

Collins, W. and Margo, R. (2003) 'Race and the value of owner-occupied housing, 1940–90', *Regional Science and Urban Economics*, 33: 255–86.

Collins, W.J. and Smith, F.H. (2005) 'A neighborhood-level view of riots, property values, and population loss: Cleveland 1950–1980', Working Paper 0528, Department of Economics, Vanderbilt University.

Dolan, M. (2011) 'Detroit's population crashes', *Wall Street Journal*, March 23.

Ferrie, J. and Troesken, W. (2008) 'Water and Chicago's Mortality Transition, 1850–1925', *Explorations in Economic History*, 45: 1–16.

Fisher, M. (2007) 'Why is U.S. poverty higher in nonmetropolitan than in metropolitan areas?' *Growth and Change*, 38: 56–76.

Gibson, C. (1998) 'Population of the 100 largest cities and other urban places in the United States: 1790 to 1990', U.S. Bureau of the Census, Population Division Working Paper No. 27.

Glaeser, E. (1998) 'Are cities dying?' *Journal of Economic Perspectives*, 12: 139–60.

——(2011) *Triumph of the City: How Our Greatest Invention Makes Us Richer, Smarter, Greener, Healthier, and Happier*, New York: Penguin Press.

Hohenberg, P. and Lees, L. (1985) *The Making of Urban Europe, 1000–1950*, Cambridge, MA: Harvard University Press.

Kopecky, K.A. and Suen, R.M.H. (2010) 'A quantitative analysis of suburbanization and the diffusion of the automobile', *International Economic Review*, 51: 1003–37.

Linebaugh, K. (2011) 'Detroit schools' cut plan approved', *Wall Street Journal*, February 22.

Mills, E. (1967) 'Transportation and patterns of urban development: an aggregative model of resource allocation in a metropolitan area', *American Economic Review*, 57: 197–210.

Mills, E. and Hamilton, B. (1994) *Urban Economics*, 5th edition, New York: HarperCollins.

Muth, R. (1969) *Cities and Housing*, Chicago, IL: University of Chicago Press.

O'Sullivan, A. (2006) 'The first cities', in R. Arnott and D. McMillen (eds) *A Companion to Urban Economics*, Malden, MA: Blackwell Publishing.

——(2009) *Urban Economics*, 7th edition, New York: McGraw-Hill.

Schrag, Z. (2002) 'Urban Mass Transit in the United States', in R. Whaples (ed.) *EH.Net Encyclopedia*, http://eh.net/encyclopedia/article/schrag.mass.transit.us

Smith, F. (2003a) 'Historical evidence on the monocentric urban model: a case study of Cleveland, 1915–80', *Applied Economics Letters*, 10: 729–31.

——(2003b) 'Decaying at the core: urban decline in Cleveland, Ohio', *Research in Economic History*, 21: 135–84.

Taylor, G.R. (1962) *The Transportation Revolution*, New York: Holt, Rinehart.

Temin, P. (2006) 'The economy of the early Roman Empire', *Journal of Economic Perspectives*, 20: 133–51.

Von Thünen, J. (1826 [1966]) *The Isolated State*, New York: Pergamon Press.

26

THE CHANGING ECONOMIC ROLES OF WOMEN

Joyce Burnette

Women have always been important economic producers, though the work they do, and the income they receive from that work, is often different from that of men. The wages women receive for their work are nearly always less than the wages men receive for their work, a fact which has contributed to women's lower social status.

The two main causes of gender differences in work and wages have been biological differences and institutions limiting women's opportunities. Women's lesser strength and their role in childbearing steered them towards occupations that required less strength and less travel. Men are stronger than women and, unlike many other gender differences, the male and female strength distributions overlap very little, so that it is rare for a woman to be stronger than a man. This strength difference gives men an advantage in many strength-intensive tasks. Some activities are so strength-intensive that women rarely do them (plowing, harvesting with a scythe, digging ditches, felling trees, hewing coal). In other tasks, strength is less important but still an advantage (hoeing, weaving); these activities often switch gender when circumstances change.

If men specialized in strength-intensive tasks, then tasks not requiring strength should have been female occupations. Often this was the case, as for lace-making and embroidery. Hand spinning was nearly always a female task, though there are instances in which men took up spinning. At times, though, women were prevented from entering occupations for which they were well suited because men found it profitable to exclude them. The practice of law does not require strength, but men long monopolized the profession. The professionalization of medicine even squeezed women out of the traditionally female occupation of assisting at childbirth. Men benefit from excluding women because a smaller labor supply means higher wages for the men. Access to education and guild, union, or professional regulations often prevented women from pursuing profitable occupations, forcing them to make do with lower-paying work. Gender differences in occupations, then, were partly due to biological differences between the sexes, and partly due to artificial restrictions privileging men.

This chapter examines women's work and wages, and will include not only waged work but also production for household use or sale in the market. Throughout much of history, independent production was more important than waged work for both men and women; therefore, limiting the discussion to waged work would create a seriously biased view of women's contributions to the economy.

Pre–industrial period

The earliest texts of the Western tradition depict women who were economically active, particularly in textile production. In *The Odyssey* (*c.* 700 BC), women are universally engaged in textile production (Calypso and Circe spend their time weaving; Helen and the Queen of Phaeacia spin; Penelope both spins and weaves). In *Proverbs* (*c.* 500 BC), the industrious wife is praised mainly for textile production, but also for some agricultural work:

> A capable wife who can find? ...
> She considers a field and buys it;
> with the fruit of her hands she plants a vineyard. ...
> She puts her hands to the distaff
> and her hands hold the spindle. ...
> She makes linen garments and sells them;
> she supplies the merchant with sashes.
> (*Proverbs* 31: 10, 16, 19, 24. New Revised Standard Version)

While women were certainly economically active, they usually did different work from men. The pattern of work that we see was strongly influenced by comparative advantage. Men specialized in tasks requiring the most strength, and in tasks that required travel.

Women's role in childbearing and childrearing made travel more difficult, so we generally see men engaged in activities that take them far from home such as hunting, fishing, and engaging in long-distance trade. In much of Africa, women specialized in crop production while men hunted. In Europe and Asia, men specialized in agricultural work while women produced textiles.

Most women did not have a job in the modern sense of the word: they did not work for an employer who paid them a wage, but produced goods or services that could be consumed or sold. Often women did not do the same type of work every day, but engaged in different activities on different days, pursuing what has been called "an economy of makeshifts." Women with access to common land might collect firewood and berries, make brooms from heath, and keep a cow. None of these activities was a full-time job, but all contributed to the family's income. Sometimes women's work consisted of selling household services: making food or clothing, doing laundry. In London *c.* 1700, two-thirds of working women were engaged in extensions of household labor. Sixty per cent of married women engaged in some form of paid employment, though often this work was not regular (Earle 1989).

Boserup (1970) notes that there are female farming systems, where women do most of the agricultural labor, and male farming systems, where men are the primary laborers. In much of Africa, land was cultivated by hand, few animals were kept, and the majority of agricultural work was done by women. Men specialized in felling trees, hunting, and waging war. Since women were an economic asset, there was a strong incentive for polygamy in these regions.

Where the plow is used, men do more agricultural work. This is consistent with men's greater strength. Women have been known to plow, but they are not as efficient as men, so it is not their comparative advantage. The plow seems to be an important determinant of the sexual division of labor, since areas that start to use the plow also shift towards using male labor in agriculture. Boserup notes that "the advent of the plow usually entails a radical shift in sex roles in agriculture; men take over plowing even in regions where the hoeing had formerly been women's work" (Boserup 1970: 21). Confirming the importance of the plow, Alesina *et al.* (2011) find that the suitability of the local geography for crops that need plowing has long-lasting negative effects on women's participation, not only in agriculture but also in business and politics.

European women worked in agriculture as wives and daughters of farmers, as wage laborers, and as farmers in their own right. Women in less prosperous families tended gardens, or used the commons to keep a cow. Women were hired both as casual day-laborers and as farm servants on annual contracts. While men did most of the plowing, women were commonly hired to weed, make hay, and help in the harvest. For women hired as servants, it was often difficult to distinguish farm work from housework, leading to confusion about how to count female servants in the British censuses. Higgs (1987) estimates that 10 per cent of women listed as domestic servants in the 1851 English census were really agricultural workers.

Textile production generally requires less strength than agriculture, and there have been many societies in which men specialize in agriculture while women specialize in textile production. As noted earlier, Homer depicts a world in which women are universally engaged in textile production, while men engaged in war or agriculture. Chinese society seems to have followed a similar pattern. Households were taxed in kind, and each household was expected to produce both grain and cloth. It was understood that men produced the grain and women produced the cloth.

Not every society followed this pattern. By the mid-seventeenth century, men wove most of the cloth in China. Men also did most of the weaving in early modern Europe. In Germany, women were prevented by guild restrictions from weaving cloth. Spinning, which required less strength than weaving, was almost always a female occupation, though there were occasions when men spun as well.

Agriculture and textiles engaged the majority of the pre-industrial work force, but women were also found in many other occupations, including mining, retail trade, and medicine. Women in Britain and the Netherlands were extensively employed in retail trade. Women brewed most of the ale until the use of hops allowed for larger-scale production and highly capitalized male-owned firms forced out small-scale female producers.

Not all occupations, though, were open to women. In China women's opportunities were limited by the expectation that they remain secluded indoors. In Europe, guilds limited women's occupational opportunities. While a guild member's wife was allowed to help her husband and a widow was usually allowed to carry on her husband's trade, few girls were apprenticed and guilds did not allow other women to work.

The effectiveness of guild regulations varied. Guilds were relatively effective in Germany, where they controlled all occupations except farming, laboring, and spinning. German guilds did not allow single women to work and did not allow girls to be apprenticed. These restrictions effectively kept women out of all remunerative crafts, crowding women into spinning and farm work. The range of occupations open to women was so restricted that German women plowed the fields, even though they were much less efficient at this task than men (Ogilvie 2003).

Elsewhere guilds were less effective. The Parisian tailors' guild tried to prevent women from making clothes, but without much success. Dutch guild restrictions were less strict than elsewhere in Europe; women were admitted to the tailors', surgeons', and shopkeepers' guilds, though not with the same rights as men. In Britain, girls could be apprenticed, though few actually were. More importantly, though, the power of the guilds declined, and by the end of the eighteenth century guilds had little power over who did what work in Britain (Burnette 2008: 239). In some cases, women established their own guilds. In Paris, the linen drapers' guild dated from medieval times, and the women of the guild did not allow their husbands to participate in the trade. The seamstresses' guild was established as a female guild in 1675 (Coffin 1994).

Governments were occasionally the source of occupational restrictions. The German government closed down unofficial schools. By limiting competition from private schools, the government protected the incomes of the official schoolmasters, but also prevented women from entering the profession. In Britain, where the government did not limit competition, there were many small private schools and no barriers to entry, and the majority of school teachers were female.

While women's legal status might seem restrictive, in practice the law did not prevent women from engaging in business. Married women were under *couverture*, meaning they had no legal status separate from their husbands and could not enter contracts in their own names. While we might expect this legal status to limit women's participation in business, in fact it did not because exceptions were made for women who operated their own businesses. In most European countries, it was possible for a married woman to operate as *femme sole* and enter contracts in her own name. Women could and did operate their own businesses. In eighteenth-century London, about 6 per cent of insurance policies on business assets were taken out by women (Kay 2009: 38).

Most economically active women of the pre-industrial era produced goods for use or sale rather than working for wages. When work is not waged, it is difficult to compare the earnings of men and women. On occasion, women could earn more than men. In China, the value of the cloth produced by the woman of the household may have been greater than what a man could earn as an agricultural laborer. The earnings of hand spinners fluctuated with the demand for yarn, and when demand was particularly high a good female spinner could earn as much as a male laborer. In seventeenth-century Devon, female lace makers could earn twice as much as male agricultural laborers (Sharpe 1991). However, the disadvantages women faced, their lesser strength, and guild restrictions preventing them from entering lucrative trades meant that women's earnings were more commonly lower than men's.

When working for time-rate wages, women were consistently paid less per day than men. In England, women's daily wages were one-half to two-thirds of male wages. In nineteenth-century France, women were paid about 60 per cent as much as men. Wage ratios were similar in India, where women working in agriculture earned two-thirds the male wage in 1800 and in the 1950s (Dutt 1956: 207; Agarwal 1975: 361). When working on piece-rates, men and women were paid the same rates per unit of output. When reaping, women were paid the same rate per acre, and, when weaving, women were paid the same rate per length of cloth. Women earned less than men, but this was due to their lower output rather than lower piece-rates.

Industrialization

The Industrial Revolution brought rapid changes in technology, particularly in textile production. The shift from human or animal power to machines driven by water or steam power encouraged the shift to production in factories. These technological changes altered the pattern of comparative advantage, and thus the gender division of labor. Early machines for spinning yarn, the spinning jenny and the water frame, were worked by females. However, as spinning machinery progressed, it became larger and more difficult for women to operate. Smaller mules could be operated by women, but larger mules required the strength of a man. Thus, spinning, which had for centuries been women's work, became a male activity.

Most of the new machinery, however, did not require strength or skill, and factory owners were eager to use cheap female labor to operate these machines. Goldin and Sokoloff (1984) argue that the U.S. cotton textile industry located in the North, rather than in the South where the cotton was grown, because the opportunity cost of female labor was lower in the North.

Women were relatively productive in the cultivation of cotton and tobacco, which were grown in the South, but were less productive in the grain-producing agriculture of the North, so factories in the North could hire women more cheaply.

While the earliest U.S. factories employed family groups, a new system employing exclusively female production workers, called the Waltham system, quickly became dominant. The new system used the throstle rather than the mule to spin, and thus did not need the strength and skill of adult men. Companies owned by the Boston Associates group attracted single women to Lowell, Massachusetts, by offering supervised accommodation in dormitories. In the early nineteenth century, the vast majority of production workers in U.S. textile factories were native women. Towards the middle of the century, however, more immigrants were hired and the labor force began to include more men.

British factories were also staffed mainly by women and children. In 1833, nearly half of the labor force was under 18 and 30 per cent were adult women. Only 23 per cent of workers were adult males, mainly overseers, mule spinners, and skilled craftsmen. Most of the women who worked in factories were relatively young. Two-thirds of female factory workers were under 21 and 90 per cent were under 31 (Mitchell 1834).

While the factory labor force was heavily female, the new factory jobs were not numerous enough to replace the hand-spinning work that had employed large portions of the female labor force. In some regions, hand spinning had been a universal female employment. When hand-spinning work suddenly disappeared, many women moved into handloom weaving, but in some regions, such as Southeast England, women found themselves unemployed.

Few women were employed in heavy industries such as iron and steel, railways, or the manufacture of steam engines. Women were employed in lighter manufacturing such as boots and shoes. Cigar making was well integrated, and cigarettes were made mainly by females. In Sweden in 1898, 70 per cent of cigar workers were female. In the Philippines in 1900, 72 per cent of cigar rollers and 96 per cent of cigarette makers were female (Murray and Keith 2004). In the U.S., where the cigar-makers' union was relatively strong, fewer women were employed.

The Industrial Revolution was an important watershed in women's work in that it shifted the location of work out of the home. Because of the importance of machines powered by water wheels or steam engines, textiles began to be produced in factories rather than in workers' homes. This change in the location of work made it more difficult for women to combine income-earning activities with childminding and other domestic duties. During the nineteenth century, higher household income, increased concern for cleanliness following the discovery of germs, and changes in social expectations combined to reduce women's participation in work outside the home. At the beginning of the twentieth century, married women's labor force participation reached a low point of about 10 per cent in Britain and 5 per cent in the U.S. (Hatton and Bailey 2001; Goldin 1990: 17).

During industrialization, guilds were no longer important sources of restrictions on women's work. Restrictions continued, but they were enforced by unions and professional organizations rather than guilds. In England, the mule-spinners' union was effective in keeping women out of mule spinning, even after the self-acting mule had reduced the need for strength. The book-binders', compositors', and hatters' unions also excluded women. While many unions tried to exclude women, only relatively high-skilled workers were successful. British handloom weavers tried to exclude women, but were not able to enforce their restrictions.

The rise of professional organizations also barred women from some occupations. Requiring a university education effectively debarred women from most professions because women were not admitted to universities until the late nineteenth century. By convincing the public that male physicians had more skill, the medical profession was able to force women out of the traditionally female occupation of midwifery. The term "man-midwife," in use during the eighteenth century, acknowledges that midwifery was typically a female occupation. By the middle of the nineteenth century, women had been marginalized and worked only in the low-paying parts of the field. Men dominated childbirth assistance for over a century.

In British factories, boys and girls earned approximately the same wages for factory work until age 18, when male wages jumped sharply upwards. Few adult males worked in textile factories, but those who did earned almost three times as much as adult women. Women in their 20s earned 38 per cent as much as men the same age, and women in their 30s earned only 35 per cent as much as men of the same age. These wage ratios were similar to wage ratios in agriculture, where women earned about 40 per cent as much as men in the 1830s (Mitchell 1834; Burnette 2008: 80).

As industrialization progressed, the gender wage gaps declined. By the 1930s, women in London earned 60 per cent as much as men (Johnson 2003). In the U.S., the female–male wage ratio was 30 per cent in 1820, rising to 40 per cent in 1832 and 50 per cent in 1850 (Goldin and Sokoloff 1982: 760). Relative female wages in manufacturing continued to rise, reaching 70 per cent of male wages in the 1930s (Goldin 1990: 60). In the late nineteenth century, female weavers were almost as productive as male weavers; females weaving on piece-rates produced 90 per cent as much cloth per day as males. However, because women tended to work in lower-paying jobs, the gender gap was greater for cotton factory workers as a whole (Burnette 2011).

Elsewhere in the world, women also earned less than men in factory work. In the mid-nineteenth century, women working in textile factories earned 60 per cent as much as male factory workers in France, and 65 per cent as much in Sweden (Cox and Nye 1989; Bagge *et al.* 1933). In the early twentieth century, women working in industry earned half as much as men in India, 68 per cent in the Soviet Union, and 78 per cent in China.

Post-industrialization

It was not until after industrialization that strength declined in importance. Today strength is not irrelevant in determining the division of labor, but occupations where it is important are few in number, so strength no longer drives the gender wage gap. Ironically, just as strength was becoming less important, wage discrimination became more important. During the nineteenth century, women earned less than men because they were less productive, or because they were prevented from entering the most rewarding occupations. Wage discrimination, which occurs when women earn less than their marginal product, was rare in the nineteenth century. In the early twentieth century, however, wage discrimination became an important component of the wage gap (Goldin 1990: Ch. 4).

The rise of wage discrimination seems to have been the result of changes in the employment relationship. Nineteenth-century labor markets were flexible. Turnover was high, and a woman who quit work to have a baby could easily return to the same job a year later. While experience in an occupation increased wages, firm tenure was rarely important, so there was no wage penalty for changing firms. In this context, childbearing did not reduce the wage a woman earned. In the twentieth century, as firms worked to reduce turnover, women found that if they quit it was difficult to return to the same job; Hareven (1982: 136) notes that, by the 1920s, textile factory workers "could no longer afford the luxury of leaving their jobs and being rehired." The new less flexible regime disadvantaged women because it was more difficult to combine childbearing and work.

311

These changes were likely driven by the rising importance of firm-specific skills. Employers responded by moving away from spot labor markets and introducing incentives to lower worker turnover.

Retirement and other benefits encouraged workers to stay at the same firm. Unfortunately, women did not benefit from the rise of internal labor markets as much as men did (Owen 2001). While firms designed increasing wage profiles and retirement packages to encourage men to stay with the firm, they expected and encouraged high turnover among women. Marriage bars, which required a woman to quit when she got married, were popular in the U.S. from the 1920s to the 1950s. While women gained as much from experience as men did in nineteenth-century manufacturing, when internal labor markets were instituted, women's wages did not rise as far as men's. A similar pattern can be seen in English banking, where male and female tellers started at the same wage. After 15 years, though, women hit a wage ceiling, while men's wages continued to rise (Seltzer 2011).

In the U.S. and Europe, female labor force participation reached a low point at the beginning of the twentieth century, and then rose throughout the century. At the beginning of the century, social expectations made middle-class women hesitant to work outside the home. A married woman working outside the home was seen as a sign that her husband could not support her. During the twentieth century, economic incentives encouraged women to work more, and as more women did so the social stigma associated with work outside the home declined. Declining fertility reduced the value of time spent at home, and rising female wages increased the cost of staying home. Rising education levels contributed to women's increasing wages, and education was itself encouraged by expectations of greater labor force participation. After controlling for women's education and fertility and the economic opportunities they faced, the Second World War had little long-term effect on female labor force participation (Goldin 1990: 152–3).

The 1960s and 1970s saw rapid change in the expectations of young women. In the 1960s, most teenage girls expected to be at home with their families at age 35. These expectations shifted in a relatively short time, and by 1980 most teenage girls expected to be in the labor force at age 35. The pill, which was introduced in 1960, changed the timing of births. Total fertility was already low by historical standards, but the ability to delay births and marriage made investment in education less risky, and the enrollment of women in postgraduate programs expanded rapidly (Goldin and Katz 2002; Bailey 2006). Male and female labor force participation rates converged over the twentieth century, but have not reached equality. In the U.S., men have a participation rate of 73 per cent, while women have a participation rate of 60 per cent (Bureau of Labor Statistics 2011).

Women's economic position improved greatly during the twentieth century, and many longstanding sources of inequality have been eroded. Until very recently, women's lower wages could be partially explained by lower levels of education. Currently, though, women in the U.S. are more likely to be enrolled in college than men, and women under 45 are more likely to have a college degree than men. Civil rights legislation made it illegal to exclude women from jobs simply because they are women. Women's opportunities remain severely limited in some areas of the world, however. Women do not have equal access to education or work in Islamic countries, and in some countries are not even allowed to drive. By contrast, communist countries encouraged female participation, and communist or formerly communist countries have relatively high levels of female labor force participation.

Even in countries with equal rights legislation, though, women still earn less than men. While the gender gap is declining, the family gap, the difference in the earnings of mothers and women without children, shows no sign of dissipation. Women in the U.S. and Britain incur substantial wage penalties for childbearing, particularly if they cannot return to the same job after giving birth. However, the child penalty is not universal, and in Scandinavia, where women are more likely to have job-protected maternity leave, having a child does not reduce women's wages.

Wage discrimination exists if the relative wage paid to women is less than their relative productivity. Women's relative productivity is best measured by estimating production functions with male and female labor as separate inputs. Studies that estimate relative female productivity this way find that women are less productive than men, and some of these studies find evidence of wage discrimination. In some cases, women earn less than men but this difference is explained by their lower productivity. In Norwegian and Israeli manufacturing, women earn 20 per cent less than men and are 20 per cent less productive (Haegeland and Klette 1999; Hellerstein and Neumark 1999). In these cases, the productivity differences may be due to inequality in training or domestic duties, but there is no wage discrimination. This contrasts with U.S. manufacturing, where there is evidence of discrimination. Wage discrimination exists when the wage gap is greater than the productivity gap. If wage discrimination exists, employers could earn higher profits by hiring more women, but give up some profits in order to indulge their tastes for discrimination. Hellerstein *et al.* (1999, 2002) find that in U.S. manufacturing in 1989 women were 84 per cent as productive as men, yet they only earned 55 per cent as much, and that manufacturing firms hiring more women were more profitable, both of which suggests wage discrimination against women.

Conclusion

Women have always participated in economic production, though not always on an equal footing with men. The gender division of labor has been driven by both biology and social institutions. Some societies have chosen to give their women more economic freedom. Interestingly, the societies that have given women the most economic freedom experienced the most economic growth. In the seventeenth century, the fastest-growing economy in Europe was the Netherlands. This was a society where women were active and accepted in the business world. In the nineteenth century, guilds were more effective in keeping women out of a large number of occupations in Germany than they were in Britain. Britain also grew faster than Germany, and experienced the first Industrial Revolution in the late eighteenth and early nineteenth centuries. Men have often tried to set aside the best occupations for themselves; while some men benefit from the male monopoly, the society as a whole seems to suffer.

By the early twenty-first century, women in the Western world have returned to full participation in the world of work. Labor markets, however, have not reached full equality. Women are acquiring more education than men, but still earn less. While gender differences in strength have become less important, women's role in childbearing still contributes to lower wages for women. Restrictions on women's employment are smaller than in the past, but wage discrimination has not yet been eliminated.

References

Agarwal, A.N. (1975) *Indian Economy*, Delhi: Vikas.

Alesina, A., Giuliano, P. and Nunn, N. (2011) 'On the origins of gender roles: women and the plough', Institute for the Study of Labor (IZA) Discussion Paper No. 5735.

Bagge, G., Lundberg, E. and Svennilson, I. (1933) *Wages, Cost of Living and National Income in Sweden, 1860–1930, Vol. II, Wages in Sweden*, Westminster: P.S. King & Son.

Bailey, M. (2006) 'More power to the pill: the impact of contraceptive freedom on women's lifecycle labor supply', *Quarterly Journal of Economics*, 121: 289–320.

Bennett, J. (1996) *Ale, Beer, and Brewsters in England: Women's Work in a Changing World, 1300–1600*, Oxford: Oxford University Press.

Boserup, E. (1970, reprinted 2007) *Women's Role in Economic Development*, London: Earthscan.

Bray, F. (1997) *Technology and Gender: Fabrics of Power in Late Imperial China*, Berkeley, CA: University of California Press.

Bureau of Labor Statistics (2011) 'The employment situation – September 2011', http://stats.bls.gov/news. release/empsit.nr0.htm

Burnette, J. (2006) 'How skilled were English agricultural labourers in the early nineteenth century?' *Economic History Review*, 59: 688–716.

——(2008) *Gender, Work and Wages in Industrial Revolution Britain*, Cambridge: Cambridge University Press.

——(2011) 'Decomposing the wage gap: within- and between-occupation gender wage gaps at a nineteenth-century textile firm', unpublished manuscript.

Coffin, J. (1994) 'Gender and the guild order: the garment trades in eighteenth-century France', *Journal of Economic History*, 54: 768–93.

Cox, D. and Nye, J.V. (1989) 'Male–female wage discrimination in nineteenth-century France', *Journal of Economic History*, 49: 903–20.

Dublin, T. (1979) *Women at Work: The Transformation of Work and Community in Lowell, Massachusetts, 1826–1860*, New York: Columbia University Press.

Dutt, R. (1956) *The Economic History of India under Early British Rule*, London: Routledge.

Earle, P. (1989) 'The female labour market in London in the late seventeenth and early eighteenth centuries', *Economic History Review*, 42: 328–53.

Freifeld, M. (1986) 'Technological change and the "self-acting" mule: a study of skill and the sexual division of labour', *Social History*, 2: 319–43.

Goldin, C. (1990) *Understanding the Gender Gap: An Economic History of American Women*, New York: Oxford University Press.

——(2006) 'The rising (and then declining) significance of gender', in F. Blau, M. Brinton and D. Brusky (eds) *The Declining Significance of Gender?* New York: Russell Sage Foundation.

Goldin, C. and Katz, L. (2002) 'The power of the pill: oral contraceptives and women's career and marriage decisions', *Journal of Political Economy*, 110: 730–70.

Goldin, C. and Sokoloff, K. (1982) 'Women, children, and industrialization in the early republic: evidence from the manufacturing censuses', *Journal of Economic History*, 42: 741–74.

Goldin, C., Katz, L. and Kuziemko, I. (1984) 'The relative productivity hypothesis of industrialization: the American case, 1820 to 1850', *Quarterly Journal of Economics*, 99: 461–87.

——(2006) 'The homecoming of American college women: the reversal of the college gender gap', *Journal of Economic Perspectives*, 20: 133–56.

Gullickson, G. (1986) *Spinners and Weavers of Auffay: Rural Industry and the Sexual Division of Labor in a French Village, 1750–1850*, Cambridge: Cambridge University Press.

Haegeland, T. and Klette, T.J. (1999) 'Do higher wages reflect higher productivity? Education, gender and experience premiums in a matched plant-worker data set', in J.C. Haltwanger, J.I. Lane, J.R. Spletzer, J. J.M. Theeuwes and K.R. Troske (eds) *The Creation and Analysis of Employer–Employee Matched Data*, Amsterdam: Elsevier.

Hareven, T. (1982) *Family Time and Industrial Time: The Relationship between the Family and Work in a New England Industrial Community*, Cambridge: Cambridge University Press.

Hatton, T. and Bailey, R. (2001) 'Women's work in census and survey, 1911–31', *Economic History Review*, 54: 87–107.

Hellerstein, J. and Neumark, D. (1999) 'Sex, wages, and productivity: an empirical analysis of Israeli firm-level data', *International Economic Review*, 40: 95–123.

Hellerstein, J., Neumark, D. and Troske, K. (1999) 'Wages, productivity, and worker characteristics: evidence from plant-level production functions and wage equations', *Journal of Labor Economics*, 17: 409–46.

——(2002) 'Market forces and sex discrimination', *Journal of Human Resources*, 37: 353–80.

Higgs, E. (1987) 'Women, occupations and work in the nineteenth century censuses', *History Workshop*, 23: 59–80.

Homer, *The Odyssey* (c. 700 BC) (trans. Robert Fagles 1996), Harmondsworth: Penguin.

Humphries, J. (1990) 'Enclosures, common rights and women: the proletarianization of families in the late eighteenth and early nineteenth centuries', *Journal of Economic History*, 50: 17–42.

Johnson, P. (2003) 'Age, gender and the wage in Britain, 1830–1930', in P. Scholliers and L. Schwarz (eds) *Experiencing Wages: Social and Cultural Aspects of Wage Forms in Europe since 1500*, New York: Berghahn Books.

Kay, A. (2009) *The Foundations of Female Entrepreneurship: Enterprise, Home and Household in London c. 1800–1870*, London: Routledge.

Mitchell, J. (1834) 'Report of Dr. James Mitchell to the central board of commissioners', *British Parliamentary Papers*, vol. XIX.

Murray, J. and Keith, K. (2004) 'Male–female earnings differentials in early 20th-century Manila', *Explorations in Economic History*, 41: 361–76.

Ogilvie, S. (2003) *A Bitter Living: Women, Markets, and Social Capital in Early Modern Germany*, Oxford: Oxford University Press.

Owen, L. (2001) 'Gender differences in labor turnover and the development of internal labor markets in the United States during the 1920s', *Enterprise & Society*, 2: 41–71.

Pomeranz, K. (2000) *The Great Divergence: China, Europe and the Making of the Modern World Economy*, Princeton, NJ: Princeton University Press.

Seltzer, A. (2011) 'Female salaries and careers in the British banking industry, 1915–41', *Explorations in Economic History*, 48: 461–77.

Sharpe, P. (1991) 'Literally spinsters: a new interpretation of local economy and demography in Colyton in the seventeenth and eighteenth centuries', *Economic History Review*, 44: 46–65.

Tomkins, A. and King, S. (2003) *The Poor in England, 1700–1850: An Economy of Makeshifts*, Manchester: Manchester University Press.

Van Den Heuvel, D. (2007) *Women and Entrepreneurship: Female Traders in the Northern Netherlands, c. 1580–1815*, Amsterdam: Aksant.

Van Nederveen Meerkerk, E. (2010) 'Market wage or discrimination? The remuneration of male and female wool spinners in the seventeenth-century Dutch Republic', *Economic History Review*, 63: 165–86.

Waldfogel, J. (1998) 'Understanding the family gap in pay for women with children', *Journal of Economic Perspectives*, 12: 137–56.

27

AFRICAN-AMERICANS IN THE U.S. ECONOMY SINCE EMANCIPATION

William A. Sundstrom[1]

Introduction

The Emancipation Proclamation and Union victory in the Civil War brought freedom to some 4 million African-American slaves, who at that time made up about 90 per cent of the nation's black population. African-Americans resided overwhelmingly in the country's Southern states, concentrated in the cotton plantation belt. The large majority of newly freed blacks would find their economic fates tied to the rural Southern economy, as would most of their descendants for the next half-century.

Under the best of circumstances, the freed people would have faced daunting economic challenges. The large majority were propertyless and illiterate; they lacked the financial or real wealth to enter farming as proprietors and lacked the human capital to advance beyond unskilled employments. These deficits assured that any convergence toward the economic status of white Americans would have taken several generations, even with a level playing field (DeCanio 1979; Sacerdote 2005; Miller 2011). But the playing field was anything but level. Especially after the close of the Reconstruction Era in 1877, race relations in the American South came to resemble what the economist Gunnar Myrdal (1944) characterized as a "color caste" system, with African-Americans occupying a position of legal, political, and social inferiority.

Despite these adverse conditions, the economic status of African-Americans improved over the ensuing century, if haltingly and unevenly. Progress was driven by three major forces. First, both inside and outside the South, black–white skill gaps gradually closed as the educational attainment of successive generations of African-Americans approached that of whites. Economic historians have referred to the twentieth century as the "human capital century," on account of the contributions of dramatic increases in educational attainment to increasing productivity and rising per capita real incomes.[2] African-Americans eventually shared in these gains, in spite of the legacy of separate and unequal schooling for blacks within what was already a low-education region.

Second, black workers successfully moved to opportunities in burgeoning urban labor markets, especially outside the South. The Great Migration of Southern-born blacks to the urban centers of the Northern, Midwestern, and Western parts of the country commenced in earnest during the First World War, and was especially dramatic during the 1940s and 1950s.[3] Although much of this migration could be attributed to the "pull" of urban labor demand, diminishing demand for tenant farmers in Southern agriculture, especially during and after the 1930s, reinforced the move, as did chain migration, whereby successive waves of migrants followed their acquaintances and kin.

Finally, racial discrimination in labor and other markets declined, especially under pressure from the civil rights movement of the 1950s and 1960s, equal opportunity law, changes in managerial practices, and diminishing racial prejudice on the part of whites. Economists continue to debate the relative importance of the gradual relative improvements in human capital versus the more episodic forces of legal, political, and social change, but the evidence points strongly to the significant impact of both (Smith and Welch 1989; Donohue and Heckman 1991).

The decades since the achievements of the 1960s present a decidedly more mixed picture of African-American progress. On the one hand, there is little doubt that overt racial discrimination plays a less substantial role in limiting the opportunities of African-Americans in the U.S. economy than it did half a century ago, with the evidence coming from both statistical analysis and the prominent role of blacks in all walks of American life, right up to the presidency. These changes had the greatest impact in the South. On the other hand, the overall income, wealth, and employment gaps between blacks and whites remain stubbornly large, and by some measures have widened since the 1970s. Particularly concerning has been the concentration of poverty and social dislocation in U.S. inner-city neighborhoods, associated with the dramatic rise in black single-parent households and exploding black male incarceration rates. To the extent that human capital remains a key ticket to economic success, the continuing racial gap in student achievement test scores is another troubling issue. These phenomena pose extraordinary challenges and suggest that the long struggle to correct the profound inequities created by the legacy of slavery and racial discrimination is far from complete.

The sections that follow begin with a description of the economic experience of African-Americans in the U.S. South during the decades immediately following emancipation, including institutional arrangements in the agricultural sector, the implications of segregation and Jim Crow, and labor markets outside farming. The chapter then turns to the Great Migration of blacks to cities outside the South and its economic consequences. The impact of the civil rights revolution and developments since the 1970s conclude the chapter.

A note on racial classifications: This chapter generally treats race as a well-defined and widely recognized characteristic of individuals that has social and economic importance. No position is taken on the extent to which race is biological versus socially constructed. The chapter uses the terms "black" and "African-American" interchangeably, and generally abstracts from issues relating to gradations of color or racial mix within the African-American population, although these may have been important in some contexts (Bodenhorn and Ruebeck 2007). Most of the statistics presented in the chapter are based on IPUMS samples of the U.S. Census (Ruggles *et al.* 2010) and employ the Census's standard self-reported racial categories (see Appendix).[4]

Emancipation and postbellum Southern labor markets

The end of slavery transferred property rights in labor from white planters to their former slaves, who thus took possession of the wealth embodied in their own human capital, but not the hoped-for 40 acres and a mule. The large majority had no formal schooling and limited skills: according to Census data, as of 1870, fully five-sixths of Southern-born blacks were illiterate, compared with only about a quarter of Southern-born whites (Collins and Margo 2006).

Land and other forms of productive capital remained in the hands of the white landowners, and the immediate postwar years saw experimentation in alternative labor contracts between them and the landless ex-slaves. Sharecropping emerged as the most prevalent arrangement for black farm workers, although it coexisted with other contractual forms, including wage labor, cash tenancy, and farm ownership. The typical sharecropping contract was an annual arrangement whereby the landlord provided a plot, lodging, and basic implements, in exchange for half the harvest. Variations on this theme existed as well, including share tenancy, whereby the worker provided more capital and received a larger share of the output than under sharecropping.

Sharecropping had certain clear advantages over wage labor for both parties to the transaction. By giving the cropper a stake in the output, sharecropping provided an effort incentive that reduced or eliminated the need for close supervision by the landlord; it also shared crop risk between the parties. Importantly, by deferring payment in full until the end of the growing season, sharecropping assured the landowner a stable supply of labor through the seasonal ups and downs of cotton production. It also allowed the cropper to deploy family members in the work.

Historians and economists have long debated the extent to which racial discrimination, legal restrictions, and market structure in Southern agriculture limited the mobility and opportunities of black workers. The picture is complex. On the one hand, there is ample evidence of an active and regionally integrated market in wage labor, with significant mobility between employers (Jaynes 1986; Wright 1986). The Jim Crow laws that enforced racial segregation in public accommodations and schools and effectively disenfranchised Southern blacks placed relatively few restrictions on the operation of wage labor markets (Wright 1986).

On the other hand, the recognized path to economic advancement for Southern agricultural workers – both black and white – was to escape the untethered life of the wage laborer. Casual day labor for a wage was largely a game for young, single men; settling in one place and becoming a sharecropper was the important first step in climbing an agricultural ladder that could lead to share tenancy, cash tenancy, and ultimately independent farm ownership. Climbing this ladder required access to working capital, which in turn required establishing creditworthiness and a reputation for reliability in a particular locale. Both blacks and whites moved up (and down) this ladder, although blacks undoubtedly tended to occupy a lower average rung. Among Southern farm operators in 1920, for example, some 60 per cent of whites were owners, compared with only 22 per cent of blacks; only 11 per cent of whites were croppers, compared with 37 per cent of blacks (Wright 1986: 121). Nevertheless, evidence from early in the twentieth century suggests that black and white sharecroppers earned roughly equal incomes, *ceteris paribus*, which may be taken as crude evidence that markets for tenancies were competitive enough to equalize returns, at least on the lower rungs of the ladder (Alston and Kauffman 2001). African-Americans in the South succeeded in accumulating property more rapidly than whites during decades leading up to the First World War, although of course starting from a much lower base (Higgs 1982; Margo 1984).

Although becoming established locally was the route to advancement for poor unskilled Southern workers of both races, it simultaneously created the potential for dependency and exploitation. Sharecropping has sometimes been portrayed as effectively reinstating a form of bound labor through so-called debt peonage – annual debt obligations to the landlord or local merchant that could be rolled over annually and used to tie the cropper to a particular farm and to dictate crop choice. High interest rates on loans to croppers probably reflected local monopsony power of planters and merchants as well as default risk (Ransom and Sutch 1977, 2001).

In addition to land, credit, and equipment, Southern landlords often provided a range of paternalistic in-kind benefits to secure the loyalty and effort of their tenants, including "old-age assistance, quasi-unemployment insurance (carrying the tenant through a poor season), emergency medical care, intercession with legal authorities, recreational amenities, among others" (Alston and Ferrie 1985: 101). Mobility of sharecroppers was further constrained by enticement laws – which provided for criminal penalties if an employer or landlord "enticed" a sharecropper to break an annual contract with a different employer – as well as contract-enforcement statutes and vagrancy laws (Roback 1984).

These impediments to mobility increased the cost of search for better pay and working conditions and reduced the bargaining power of tenants with their landlords, which could have reduced their incomes relative to what they would have earned in a more fluid market. Indeed, Naidu (2010) provides some evidence that enticement laws depressed the incomes of Southern agricultural workers. In principle, many of the factors that reduced labor mobility among Southern farm tenants affected both races, but the impact was likely to have been greater on African-Americans. Black workers were more vulnerable merely by virtue of their relative poverty, lower skills, and lower average starting position on the agricultural ladder. In addition, racism and legally enforced segregation made black workers particularly vulnerable to legal and extra-legal harassment and violence, increasing their dependence on the paternalistic protection of white elites.

The Southern sharecropping system came under increasing pressure during the Great Depression of the 1930s and beyond. As alternative employment opportunities dried up in the presence of high unemployment, landowners could shift a greater proportion of their land from sharecropping to wage labor without worrying so much about losing workers during the seasonal peaks in demand. Perhaps more importantly, New Deal agricultural policies created an incentive for landowners to displace croppers and employ wage labor instead in order to collect agricultural subsidy payments (Whatley 1983). With the coming of the Second World War boom in labor demand, black migration from the South resumed in earnest, and the ties of most African-Americans to the rural, agrarian economy were increasingly and permanently severed.

Non-farm employment: the color line

Even during the decades before the Great Migration, an increasing percentage of Southern black workers found work outside agriculture. Table 27.1 shows the evolution of the industrial distribution of male and female black workers over the period 1880–2000.[5] By 1920, more than half of black men were working outside of agriculture, particularly in such industrial pursuits as manufacturing, mining, construction, and transportation. Black working women were also shifting from agriculture, overwhelmingly into the personal and household services sector.

Non-agricultural labor markets in the South were racially segregated along both industrial and occupational lines. Although black farmers often grew the cotton, the workers who spun and wove it into cloth in Southern textile mills were overwhelmingly white; when blacks were employed in the cotton mills at all, they almost never operated textile machinery, but served as unskilled laborers, cleaning and moving materials. In contrast, some industries were disproportionately black, including sawmills, tobacco processing, and iron and steel production. These racial patterns were not simply a reflection of the geographical distribution of the races and industries, as all-white factories and industries could be found in areas with large numbers of black workers (Wright 1986). Nor were they strictly a consequence of racial gaps in formal

Table 27.1 Industrial distribution of African-American workers, ages 25–54 (per cent)

	1880	1900	1920	1940	1960	1980	2000
Males							
Agriculture, forestry, fisheries	75.5	66.8	42.8	31.0	10.2	2.4	1.5
Manufacturing, mining, transportation, utilities	11.1	18.9	33.4	26.7	39.1	41.5	30.8
Construction	3.3	3.7	5.7	13.6	11.1	9.0	8.3
Trade, finance	1.7	2.9	6.5	11.6	15.2	15.7	20.9
Services, excluding personal	3.0	3.1	3.4	6.0	10.1	17.1	26.1
Public administration	0.5	0.4	2.1	2.1	9.3	12.4	10.3
Personal services	4.9	4.3	6.0	9.1	5.0	1.9	2.1
Females							
Agriculture, forestry, fisheries	52.9	44.7	31.5	13.0	3.7	0.7	0.3
Manufacturing, mining, transportation, utilities	0.7	1.1	4.9	5.7	12.4	24.9	16.1
Construction	0.0	0.1	0.1	0.3	0.3	0.6	0.7
Trade, finance	0.4	0.7	3.4	5.6	12.4	16.3	21.3
Services, excluding personal	0.5	1.8	3.5	7.1	20.1	40.3	47.4
Public administration	0.0	0.0	0.5	0.9	4.2	9.2	9.8
Personal services	45.4	51.4	56.1	67.3	47.0	7.9	4.5

Notes: Sample consists of individuals in the labor force who reported an industry. Industries were identified using the 1950 Census classification scheme, which is consistent across IPUMS samples.
Source: IPUMS samples of the U.S. Censuses of 1870–2000 and the 2009 American Community Survey (Ruggles *et al.* 2010).

education: white cotton-mill operatives probably needed no more formal schooling to do their jobs than did black foundry workers.

Segregation of individual business firms or establishments (plants) is fully consistent with the predictions of standard economic models of labor-market discrimination by employers or co-workers (Becker 1971; Arrow 1973). If interracial contact is costly, it is profitable to minimize that contact by employing only blacks or only whites in any given workplace. But segregation by entire industries is more puzzling: why were not some cotton mills all-white and others all-black, rather than the entire industry predominantly white? Part of the explanation lies in external economies associated with racial homogeneity in industrial labor markets. In many industries and occupations, workers learned of job opportunities through referral networks of relatives and acquaintances, which typically would have been racially segregated. If search and hiring costs decreased with the size of the network, all the firms within a given industry might have found it more profitable to focus their search for experienced workers within one racial group. Industrial segregation was further reinforced by training patterns. Although operating a spinning machine or power loom may not have required much in the way of formal education, it did require a period of learning in the presence of other experienced workers and supervisors, who would presumably be of the same race. For a black worker to get started in an all-white industry would thus have required finding a segregated, all-black plant with a trained work force.

White employers' hiring behavior reflected not only their "distaste" for employing African-Americans, but also their prior beliefs about the ability and reliability of workers of different races. As Whatley (1990) has shown, employer learning could overturn inaccurate stereotypes about the suitability of black workers, but in highly segregated markets experiments would have been uncommon. Even with experience, racial stereotypes could be self-reinforcing if they resulted in feedback effects on the effort and skill acquisition of workers (Lundberg and Startz 1983; Coate and Loury 1993).

Labor markets were also highly segregated by occupation and stratified by skill level. Figures 27.1 and 27.2 show trends in the percentage of male workers of each race holding occupations in two broad categories of skilled labor: professional, technical, and managerial occupations (e.g. teachers, doctors, managers) and skilled craft occupations (e.g. carpenters, machinists), respectively. Until the 1960s, fewer than 5 per cent of black men held professional or managerial jobs; white men were five times as likely to have such an occupation.[6] Before the Second World War, white men were three to four times as likely as blacks to hold skilled craft positions.

The limited access of African-Americans to higher-paid skilled positions was a product of both the large racial gap in average human capital (education) and discrimination in advancement. The education gap is discussed in the following section. But even controlling for education, black workers were less likely to hold higher-paying skilled jobs (Margo 1990). For many skilled jobs, such as those represented in Figure 27.2, formal schooling was less important than on-the-job training and advancement up a job ladder. The racial prejudice of white employers, co-workers, and labor unions, coupled with social norms governing appropriate interaction between the races, created obstacles to occupational advancement for black workers. Blacks were commonly excluded from supervisory jobs – especially in cases that might involve supervision of whites, which would violate accepted norms of the racial hierarchy (Dewey 1952; Sundstrom 1994); jobs involving substantial interaction with white customers were also

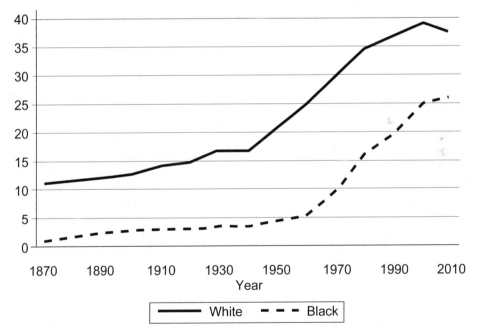

Figure 27.1 Per cent in professional occupation, 1870–2009 (males 25–54 in labor force reporting an occupation)

Source: IPUMS samples of the U.S. Censuses of 1870–2000 and the 2009 American Community Survey (Ruggles *et al.* 2010).

Notes: Professional, technical, and managerial workers as a percentage of all workers. Occupations were identified using the 1950 Census classification scheme, which is consistent across IPUMS samples.

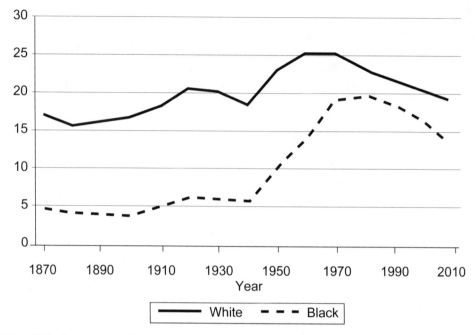

Figure 27.2 Per cent in craft occupation, 1870–2009 (males 25–54 in labor force reporting an occupation)

Source: IPUMS samples of the U.S. Censuses of 1870–2000 and the 2009 American Community Survey (Ruggles *et al*. 2010).

Notes: Skilled craft workers as a percentage of all workers. Occupations were identified using the 1950 Census classification scheme, which is consistent across IPUMS samples.

often taboo. In industries with job ladders, black workers were frequently blocked from advancing beyond a certain level or restricted to separate "dead-end" occupational clusters (e.g. Johnson 1943; Sundstrom 1990). White-dominated craft unions further limited black entry into organized skilled trades (Spero and Harris 1931; Higgs 1989; Moreno 2006).

These obstacles to advancement were manifested in a significant racial wage gap, even after controlling for the quantity and quality of schooling. Using 1940 Census data, Sundstrom (2007) shows that the pattern of the racial pay gap across Southern county groups was consistent with two main predictions of Becker's (1971) discrimination model: first, other things equal, the racial pay gap was larger in markets with a higher proportion of black workers, because the marginal worker had to seek employment from a more prejudiced employer; and second, that the pay gap was greater where whites exhibited stronger racial prejudice.

Schooling and human capital: separate and unequal

Historically, the South was the country's low-education region, and within it African-Americans received less and lower-quality schooling. In an advanced economy in which formal education was becoming essential for attaining high-wage employment, these educational deficits had deleterious long-run implications for black economic equality. Tables 27.2 and 27.3 summarize long-run trends in self-reported illiteracy and educational attainment, based on analysis of U.S. Census data (Collins and Margo 2006). Table 27.2 shows that, at the time of emancipation, 80

Table 27.2 Illiteracy rates, 1870–1930

Year	Blacks			Whites		
	All	Southern born	Non-southern born	All	Southern born	Non-southern born
1870	.808	.837	.408	.125	.255	.083
1880	.689	.717	.317	.100	.211	.066
1890	.557			.076		
1900	.482	.507	.157	.063	.126	.044
1910	.336	.355	.109	.053	.083	.044
1920	.242	.258	.064	.041	.054	.037
1930	.146			.024		

Note: Illiteracy defined as cannot write. Individuals aged 10–69.
Source: Collins and Margo (2006): Tables 1, 2.

per cent of African-Americans aged 10–69 were illiterate, but successive cohorts made rapid progress and by 1930 only 15 per cent were illiterate.

Table 27.3 summarizes completed years of education by five-year birth cohorts. Both races showed advances in average years of completed schooling, but the third column suggests that cohorts of blacks born in the late nineteenth century actually fell relatively further behind whites. As Collins and Margo (2006) point out, this apparent divergence may have been spurious, the product of a shift away from ungraded schools over this period in rural areas. After 1910, at any rate, the evidence of racial convergence in years of education is stronger, both nationwide and within the South.[7]

Not only did black children generally attain fewer total years of schooling than whites, but also the education they received was of lower quality. Because Southern schools were segregated by race, it is possible to compare indicators of school quality for black versus white students,

Table 27.3 Mean years of education, by race and year of birth (5-year cohorts)

Birth cohort [Census]	White	Black	Difference
1880–84 [1940]	7.79	4.66	3.13
1885–89 [1940]	7.99	4.95	3.04
1890–94 [1940]	8.35	5.37	2.98
1895–99 [1940]	8.83	5.58	3.25
1900–04 [1940]	9.27	5.92	3.35
1905–09 [1940]	9.81	6.36	3.45
1910–14 [1950]	10.23	7.23	3.00
1915–19 [1950]	10.62	7.83	2.79
1920–24 [1960]	11.09	8.73	2.36
1925–29 [1960]	11.25	9.22	2.03
1930–34 [1970]	11.70	10.15	1.55
1935–39 [1970]	11.93	10.54	1.39
1940–44 [1980]	12.67	11.67	1.00
1945–49 [1980]	13.04	12.11	0.93
1950–54 [1980]	12.99	12.21	0.78

Note: Educational attainment from Census samples. Date in brackets refers to the census from which the cohort's data were drawn. 1940 was the first year that the Census asked for years of schooling.
Source: Collins and Margo (2006): Table 7.

including per-pupil expenditure, class size, and length of the school year. The general findings suggest mixed progress from 1890 to 1910, with an overall decline in black-white ratio of per-pupil spending. Progress continued in absolute terms from 1910 to 1935, with relative black–white progress in some states and not others. More substantial relative improvements for black students are observed within the South for the period 1935–50:

> In absolute terms, there was more racial equality in the distribution of school resources within the South, and between the South and the rest of the nation, on the eve of the Supreme Court's historic decision in *Brown vs. Board of Education*, than in the previous half-century. (Collins and Margo 2006: 136)

The inequities of Southern schooling for black children were rooted in the disenfranchisement of African-Americans during the decades following Reconstruction and the *de facto* unequal implementation of "separate but equal" public schooling (Anderson 1988; Margo 1990). With white domination of the political process at the state and local levels, white school boards were able to funnel state educational funds disproportionately to white students. Laws that disenfranchised black voters had a large and significantly negative impact on school quality for black students, helping account for the deterioration in relative schooling from 1890 to 1910 (Collins and Margo 2006; Naidu 2009). The exclusion of black workers from skilled occupations reduced the return to education and with it the incentive to pursue schooling beyond a basic level (Anderson 1988). Racial differences in school attendance and literacy were also due to family background, including parents' occupational status, literacy, and single parenthood (Margo 1986; Moehling 2004).

While the distribution of school resources gradually became more equal during the period up to 1950, desegregation of Southern public schools occurred much more suddenly. Although the Supreme Court's 1954 *Brown* decision is often viewed as the landmark legal event, Southern white resistance delayed any significant reduction in school segregation for another decade. As of 1964, about 80 per cent of Southern blacks still attended an all-black high school, but by 1972 the figure had dropped to 10 per cent (Ashenfelter *et al.* 2006). The impact of desegregation on educational and economic outcomes for blacks is difficult to disentangle from other factors, but appears to have been significantly positive (Guryan 2004; Ashenfelter *et al.* 2006; Hanushek *et al.* 2009; Reber 2010).

The Great Migration

Trends in the regional distribution of the African-American population are summarized in Figure 27.3. Until the First World War, about 90 per cent of blacks lived in the Southern states, and there was little net out-migration. But beginning in the 1910s, black migration from the South to other parts of the country accelerated. Table 27.4 provides estimates of decadal net migration of African-Americans from the South for the period 1870–1980. Net out-migration picked up steam during the 1920s, slowed during the Great Depression decade, and reached its peak rates during the three decades from 1940 to 1970. In fact, Census data suggest that the Great Migration from the South had largely ended by the mid-1960s. By 1970, the net migration flow of blacks had reversed.

The Great Migration is one of the defining events in the history of African-Americans. From the perspective of economic history, there are two central questions: What caused the migration to occur when it did? And what were its impacts on the economic status of African-Americans? The first question might be better framed as: Why did it not occur sooner? The very lack of

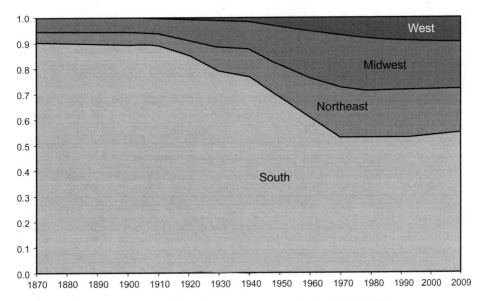

Figure 27.3   Regional distribution of the African-American population, 1870–2009

Source: IPUMS samples of the U.S. Censuses of 1870–2000 and the 2009 American Community Survey (Ruggles *et al.* 2010).

migration between the South and the rest of the country contributed to the isolation of Southern labor markets, with a resulting large and persistent regional wage deficit in the South (Wright 1986). This regional gap was particularly pronounced for black workers: as of 1940, Southern whites earned in the order of 10 per cent less than their non-Southern counterparts, whereas the regional wage gap for blacks was about 30 per cent (Smith and Welch 1989). Growing labor demand at higher wages outside the South should have created a strong economic "pull" factor for migration. At the same time, segregation, political disempowerment,

Table 27.4   Black out-migration from the South, 1870–1980 (thousands)

Period	Black population at start of period	Estimated net out-migration	Rate per thousand initial population
1870–1880	4421	71	16.1
1880–1890	5954	80	13.4
1890–1900	6761	174	25.7
1900–1910	7923	197	24.9
1910–1920	8749	525	60.0
1920–1930	8912	877	98.4
1930–1940	9362	398	42.5
1940–1950	9905	1468	148.2
1950–1960	10225	1473	144.1
1960–1965	11312	1164	102.9
1965–1970	11226	216	19.2
1970–1975	11970	−14	−1.2
1975–1980	12720	−195	−15.3

Source: Farley and Allen (1987): 113, 118.

violence, and other forms of racial oppression worsened in the South during the decades following Reconstruction (Woodward 1955), raising the costs of staying in the South and providing a "push" factor that complemented the economic pull of the North (Tolnay and Beck 1990).

Despite the apparent alignment of pull and push incentives, several factors delayed the large-scale out-migration by Southern blacks. The first was the poor education and mismatched agrarian skills of black workers. Although many unskilled non-farm jobs did not require extensive schooling, literacy at the very least was important in learning about and taking advantage of distant opportunities (Margo 1990). A second important factor was competition for Northern jobs from low-skilled European immigrants, who poured into American cities during the decades leading up to the First World War. Whether Northern employers exhibited a racial preference at the margin for white Europeans over black Southerners or simply viewed immigrants as a less risky "known entity" given limited experience dealing with black workers, blacks stood behind immigrants in the job queue. Higher Northern wages were thus offset by a lower Northern probability of employment. Collins (1997) shows that states and cities with larger European immigrant in-flows were significantly less likely to receive black migrants. In the absence of this immigrant-as-deterrent effect, the Great Migration would probably have started earlier.

Finally, migration tends to exhibit path dependence, operating through so-called chain migration. Once a migration flow is established between locations, the flow of information via kinship and acquaintance networks and a growing migrant community reduce the cost of moving for subsequent migrants: migration begets more migration. The flip side of this dynamic is that some kind of significant shock (push or pull) may be required to start the self-reinforcing flow. Inertia was probably a significant factor delaying African-American migration to the North (Carrington *et al.* 1996). A sequence of shocks to national labor markets and the Southern agrarian economy in the early 1900s helped jump-start mass black migration. The cutoff of mass European immigration during and after the First World War largely eliminated the immigrant deterrent effect (Collins 1997). Devastation to Southern agriculture caused by the cotton boll weevil may have been overrated in some historical narratives, but it undoubtedly weakened the local ties of many black Southerners, setting the stage for longer-distance moves (see Higgs 1976; Lange *et al.* 2009). New Deal agricultural policies further weakened those ties in the 1930s (Whatley 1983, 1987).

Turning to the impact of the Great Migration on the economic status of African-Americans, there seems little doubt that on average black migrants gained economically from their move. The fact that they willingly incurred the pecuniary and non-pecuniary costs of moving is one piece of qualitative evidence. In 1960, the gap between the wages of Southern-born blacks residing within the South and Southern-born blacks residing elsewhere was about 30 per cent (Smith and Welch 1989). Because the individuals who moved were positively self-selected (more skilled than the average black Southerner), the typical migrant presumably did not increase her or his wages by a full 30 per cent (see Vigdor 2006; also Margo 1990). But given the considerable evidence that wage discrimination was more severe in the South than elsewhere, at least before the 1960s, migrants of any skill level were likely to find more favorable opportunities outside the South.

However, African-Americans already residing and working in the North suffered increased competition from the new arrivals. As of 1940, about 3 million blacks already resided outside the South, and over the ensuing three decades an additional 4 million would migrate there from the South. Boustan (2009) estimates that, in the absence of that migration, black wages in the North would have been about 7 per cent higher in 1970. The size of the (presumably positive) impact of reduced competition on the wages of blacks who stayed behind in the South is not known.

Black economic progress in the North

African-Americans who moved to the urban centers of the North found new opportunities but faced considerable challenges. In the labor market, low skills and discrimination placed limits on the industries and occupations that were open to black workers. Many industrial firms simply refused to hire black workers at all (Gelber 1974; Higgs 1977; Whatley 1990; Sugrue 1996; Katz *et al.* 2005). Where they were hired, blacks were often restricted to low-level occupations and undesirable working conditions, with limited opportunities for advancement (Cayton and Mitchell 1939; Dewey 1952; Maloney 1995). Black women were excluded almost entirely from desirable clerical occupations. In 1940, about half of white working women with a high-school diploma held clerical jobs, whereas only 7 per cent of their black counterparts did (King 1993). The very fact that black workers' opportunities were severely limited permitted the firms that did hire them (such as the Ford Motor Company) to obtain a stable work force even in the kinds of dangerous and unpleasant jobs that would have led to high turnover among whites with better alternatives (Whatley and Wright 1994; Maloney and Whatley 1995; Foote *et al.* 2003).

Residential segregation and the black "ghetto" emerged as important features of African-American life in the cities. By 1940, Northern cities were highly segregated by race – as much so as Southern cities (Massey and Denton 1993; Cutler *et al.* 1999). By 1970, "segregation in America had reached staggering levels" (Cutler *et al.* 1999: 470). In the average Metropolitan Statistical Area, almost 80 per cent of the black population would have had to move to achieve full residential integration across Census tracts. Since 1970, segregation has diminished substantially in most U.S. cities. As of 2000, residential segregation was at its lowest level since roughly the 1920s, although achieving integration in the average Metropolitan Area would still have required that more than 60 per cent of blacks move, and segregation remained particularly high in the large, economically stagnant cities of the Northeast and Midwest (Glaeser and Vigdor 2001).

It is not uncommon for new migrants to choose to live in ethnic enclaves with others who share their language and culture, but racial segregation in U.S. cities was exacerbated by active white resistance that took both legal and extralegal forms. Restrictive racial covenants in deeds were used to prohibit the sale of homes in white neighborhoods to blacks until 1948, when the Supreme Court ruled them unenforceable; even thereafter covenants continued to be written and referenced by agents in the real estate markets and helped coordinate behavior that reinforced segregation (Brooks 2011). Racial composition of neighborhoods was explicitly taken into account in the mortgage underwriting standards promulgated by such federal housing programs as the Home Owners' Loan Corporation, the Federal Housing Administration, and the Veterans' Administration, reinforcing the widespread practice of redlining (Massey and Denton 1993). Collective action by white residents and steering by real estate agents further discouraged integration (Sugrue 1996). By the late 1960s, federal policy had changed course, at least on the books, banning discrimination in private housing and credit markets and encouraging integration in federally supported housing with the passage of such laws as the 1968 Fair Housing Act and the 1977 Community Reinvestment Act (Massey and Denton 1993).

In theory, residential segregation and the resulting isolation of the African-American community could have had both positive and negative effects on social and economic outcomes (Cutler and Glaeser 1997). Potential benefits of living in a concentrated ethnic population could include lower transaction costs because of a shared culture and dialect, and less exposure to discrimination by outsiders. But most scholars have emphasized the negative consequences of segregation, including the concentration of poverty with its associated social dislocations (Massey and Denton 1993) and the spatial mismatch between residence and jobs under a changing geography of labor demand (e.g. Kasarda 1989; Wilson 1996; Sugrue 1996; Boustan and Margo 2009). Cutler and Glaeser (1997) find that the net impact of segregation on black urban residents is decidedly negative for a variety of measured outcomes, although Collins and Margo (2000) show that these adverse impacts are not evident in the data before 1970.

Discrimination, human capital, and relative black economic progress since 1940

Rising educational attainment and migration to economic opportunities outside the South helped African-Americans share in the economic growth of the U.S. economy, especially after 1910. But the racial *gap* in outcomes remained large before the Second World War, and probably narrowed little if at all. In the absence of consistent data on wages and incomes before 1940, little definitive can be said about trends in the racial income gap. However, Figures 27.1 and 27.2 indicate that black representation in the higher-paying skilled and professional occupations hardly moved during the first decades of the twentieth century. Overall, employment segregation in the South was actually greater in 1940 than it had been at the turn of the century, even after controlling for schooling (Margo 1990).

Beginning in 1940, relative black–white incomes can be tracked using Census data. Figures 27.4 and 27.5 show the black–white ratio of annual wage and salary income for male prime-age wage and salary workers by region, with 100 representing earnings parity. The case of black women's labor market status warrants separate treatment and is also discussed. Figure 27.4 is age adjusted to control for potential racial differences in the age structure; Figure 27.5 adds controls for years of schooling. These figures must be interpreted cautiously for a number of reasons: the income measure does not take account of differences in work hours; only workers are included, so there is potential for selection bias; and the educational controls do not account for racial or regional differences in school quality and do not directly measure actual cognitive or other skills.[8]

Caveats aside, Figure 27.4 indicates that black men earned substantially less than white men throughout the 70-year period. As of 1960, black men in the South earned only half of what white men did. The racial gap was smaller outside the South, but still substantial. The period 1960–80 saw significant improvement in relative black earnings, with almost all of the progress taking place within the South. Outside the South, there were essentially no relative gains after 1970.

Comparison of Figures 27.4 and 27.5 shows that controlling for schooling narrows the racial gap somewhat, especially in the earlier decades. Relative gains in educational attainment (see Table 27.3) paid off in the labor market, an aspect of black progress that has been emphasized by Smith (1984) and Smith and Welch (1989). But human capital as measured by years of schooling is not the whole story: Figure 27.5 indicates that, in the South, the black–white earnings ratio increased by fully 10 percentage points between 1960 and 1980, even after controlling for schooling. Some – but not most – of these gains are attributable to relative improvements in educational quality, which are not captured by crude controls for years of schooling completed (Smith and Welch 1989; Card and Krueger 1992).

The use of decennial Census data obscures the speed with which relative black wages improved in the South after 1960. Using data from the annual March Current Population Survey, Donohue and Heckman (1991) show that essentially the entire convergence occurred

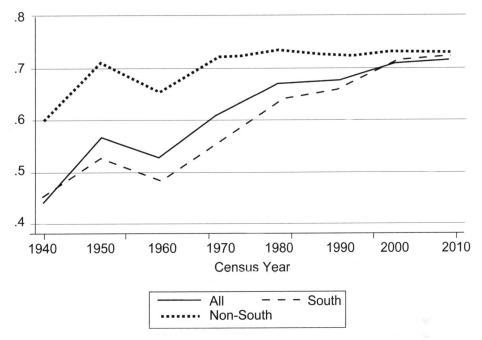

Figure 27.4 Black–white earnings ratios, 1940–2009 (males, ages 25–54, controlling for age)

Source: IPUMS samples of the U.S. Censuses of 1940–2000 and the 2009 American Community Survey (Ruggles *et al.* 2010).

Notes: The ratios are derived from least squares regressions of the natural log of wage and salary earnings on age, age squared, and a dummy variable for black race. The black–white ratio is calculated as the exponent of the coefficient on the race dummy. Samples are restricted to white and black wage and salary workers who reported positive wage and salary income during the preceding year, and use IPUMS person weights. For the regional series, separate South and non-South regressions were estimated.

between 1965 and 1975. The rapid, episodic nature of the change, its specific timing (coinciding with the civil rights movement and federal civil rights legislation), and its restriction to the Southern states all strongly suggest that declining discrimination played an important role (see also Freeman 1981).

An array of legal, social, and political forces during the 1960s undermined employment and wage discrimination against African-Americans, particularly in the South. The most prominent legal initiatives that directly affected employment practices included Title VII of the Civil Rights Act of 1964, which forbade racial discrimination in employment, and Executive Order 11246 in 1965, which prohibited discrimination by federal contractors.[9] Of course, having the policies on the books was one thing, actually enforcing them quite another; indeed, "enforcement budgets were low during the time black advance was so rapid" (Donohue and Heckman 1991: 1636). Yet the effect of the civil rights revolution on labor markets was felt almost immediately – most dramatically in the Southern cotton textile industry, where black employment jumped after 1965 (see Heckman and Payner 1989; Donohue and Heckman 1991; Wright 1999, 2010). Black workers and activists in the South immediately took advantage of the legal protections of the law to press for equal treatment in the labor market, and the threat of legal action may have spurred changes in employment practices even before many cases or complaints made their way into the system (Wright 1999). White employers who had refrained

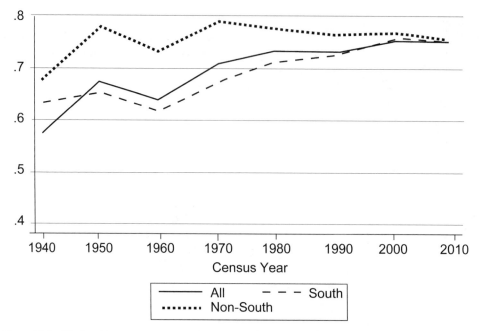

Figure 27.5 Black–white earnings ratios, 1940–2009 (males, ages 25–54, controlling for age and schooling)

Source: IPUMS samples of the U.S. Censuses of 1940–2000 and the 2009 American Community Survey (Ruggles *et al.* 2010).

Notes: The ratios are derived from least squares regressions of the natural log of wage and salary earnings on age, age squared, six categories of educational attainment, and a dummy variable for black race. The black–white ratio is calculated as the exponent of the coefficient on the race dummy. Samples are restricted to white and black wage and salary workers who reported positive wage and salary income during the pre-ceding year, and use IPUMS person weights. For the regional series, separate South and non-South regressions were estimated.

from employing blacks because of strong pressures to conform to community norms may have used the threat of action by federal authorities as a convenient excuse to hire black workers (Donohue and Heckman 1991; Wright 1999). Careful statistical analysis of the impact of the 1972 Equal Employment Opportunity Act, which expanded coverage of civil rights protections, shows that the law had a significant and positive impact on black employment and pay (Chay 1998). Studies of affirmative action policies also suggest modest positive impacts on black employment (Holzer and Neumark 2006).

To protect against actual or threatened legal actions, businesses adapted their existing per-sonnel and human resources procedures and bureaucracies to meet equal employment goals (Freeman 1981; Dobbin 2009). The intrinsic ambiguities in civil rights law and the absence of explicit regulatory directives from government meant that businesses and human resources professionals were forced to "invent" equal opportunity goals and affirmative action policies (Dobbin 2009). These innovations built on prior experience by racially progressive businesses as well as the model of modern personnel management that evolved in response to labor unions and New Deal labor law (Delton 2009). The impact of these management practices remains uncertain – as Dobbin (2009: 232) concludes, "We have little hard evidence that employer programs increase opportunity."

Since 1980, relative black–white economic progress has slowed substantially, and may actually have reversed. Figures 27.4 and 27.5 are misleading indicators of overall relative progress to the extent that lower-skilled black workers have dropped out of the paid work force at a disproportionate rate. Thus, the sample of black men with earnings is increasingly selected from the more skilled and higher-paid tail of the population distribution. Figure 27.6 shows the long-run trends in the employment–population ratio for white and black prime-age men. The racial gap in employment rates opened up during the Great Depression decade; after 1970, the trend in the employment–population ratio has been downward for both races, but especially so for blacks. Estimates of the bias in average black wages due to selective non-employment suggest that it is substantial, and imply a much less optimistic picture of relative gains (e.g. Brown 1984; Chandra 2003; Juhn 2003).

There are a number of explanations for the relatively high rates of black non-employment. At any point in time, the non-employed include the officially unemployed, who are not working but on temporary layoff or actively seeking reemployment, as well as labor force non-participants. The unemployment rate for black workers has fluctuated at around twice the rate for whites since 1960. The unemployment gap first appeared in national estimates after 1930 and widened thereafter, as regional and industrial shifts exposed more black workers to cyclical employment fluctuations. The size and persistence of the gap cannot be explained by standard measures of human capital (Fairlie and Sundstrom 1999).

The secular trend in non-participation (labor force "dropouts") reflects a number of factors. For both white and black men, changes in the eligibility requirements and generosity of government transfer and disability insurance programs since the 1960s increased the incentive for

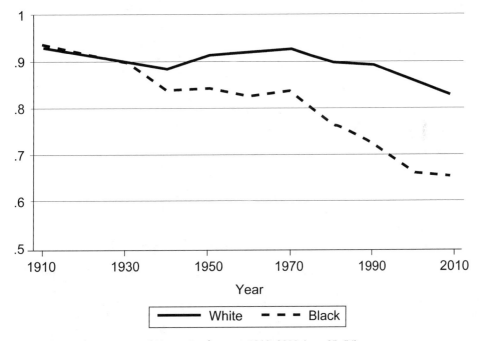

Figure 27.6 Employment–population ratios for men, 1910–2009 (ages 25–54)

Source: IPUMS samples of the U.S. Censuses of 1870–2000 and the 2009 American Community Survey (Ruggles *et al.* 2010).

Notes: Employed (including self-employed) workers as a proportion of the population.

more workers to drop out of the labor force (Butler and Heckman 1977; Autor and Duggan 2006). Especially significant for African-American men has been the dramatic increase in incarceration rates. Between 1970 and 2000, the incarceration rate for young black men (18–34) rose from about 3 per cent to over 8 per cent, compared with about 1 per cent for young white men. The prison boom of the 1980s and 1990s was fueled in part by social trends but in particular by changes in crime control policy. Using life table methods, Pettit and Western (2004: 162) estimate that the average black male born in the late 1960s had a cumulative risk of incarceration by age 30–34 of 20 per cent, a figure that rises to nearly 60 per cent for black high-school dropouts – comparable figures for non-Hispanic whites are 3 and 11 per cent, respectively (see also Western and Pettit 2005).

African-American women in the labor force

In the decades following emancipation, paid employment outside the home played a much more significant role in the lives of black women than white women. Figure 27.7 plots the long-run trend in labor-force participation rates for prime-age women, by race. As of 1900, black women were three times as likely as white women to be in the labor force; among married women, white

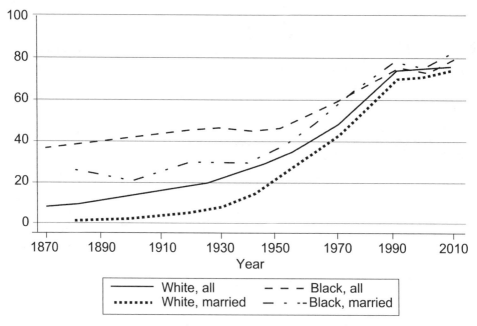

Figure 27.7   Women's labor force participation rate (%), 1870–2009 (ages 25–54, all, and married with spouse present)

Source: IPUMS samples of the U.S. Censuses of 1870–2000 and the 2009 American Community Survey (Ruggles *et al.* 2010).

Notes: Women in the labor force as a percentage of the relevant female population. For 1870–1930, labor force participation is defined as reporting a gainful occupation; for 1940–2009, the modern definition is used – namely, being employed for pay or profit, on temporary layoff, or actively seeking employment. Special instructions to census enumerators in 1910 led to an overcount of the gainfully employed relative to other years, which was particularly marked for black women (Sobek 2001: 80). Consequently, the 1910 census sample was not used for this figure; the observation for 1910 is simply the linear interpolation between 1900 and 1920.

women's participation was negligible, while fully a fifth of married black women were gainfully employed. After 1940, an increasing percentage of married women of both races entered the work force, but the pace of change was more rapid for whites, leading to a convergence in participation rates in the range of 70 to 75 per cent for both races by 2000.

The relative progress of black women's earnings during the postwar period was dramatic. Figure 27.8 presents the age-adjusted earnings ratio for women, analogous to Figure 27.4 for men.[10] Annual earnings of black working women converged toward the earnings of white women beginning in the 1940s and especially after 1960, with black earnings reaching 90 per cent of white within the South by 1980; outside the South, black women actually earned more than white women as early as 1970, although there was some retrenchment in the ratio after 1980. To some degree, these gains reflected shifting patterns in the demand for women's labor as early as the 1940s (e.g. Bailey and Collins 2006). But declining discrimination – especially in access to higher-paying clerical occupations – played a critical role after 1960. Employer survey evidence from 1940 indicates that black women were routinely barred from clerical positions on account of race (Goldin 1990: 147). Black women gained access to clerical work during the mid-1960s much more rapidly than would be predicted by advancing educational attainment alone (Cunningham and Zalokar 1992; King 1993, 1995).

Although the earnings convergence depicted in Figure 27.8 undoubtedly captures real relative progress for black women, earnings trends for women must be interpreted with caution. Given the large racial differences in labor-force participation rates and the dramatic increases in participation for women of both races over the period, there were substantial and shifting racial

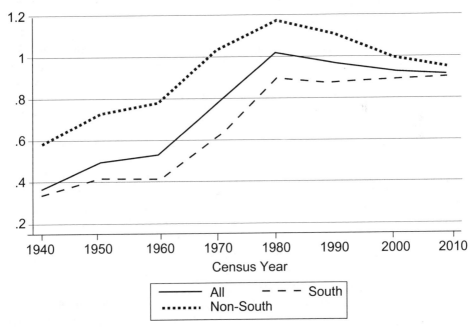

Figure 27.8 Black–white earnings ratios, 1940–2009 (females, ages 25–54, controlling for age)

Source: IPUMS samples of the U.S. Censuses of 1940–2000 and the 2009 American Community Survey (Ruggles *et al.* 2010).

Notes: See Figure 27.4 for explanation.

differences in the composition of the female work force. By 1990, the approximate wage parity between black and white working women largely reflected the fact that black working women were disproportionately selected from the upper tail of the black skill distribution, compared with whites (Neal 2004).

The persistent racial gap in economic status

Since roughly 1980, progress toward earnings equality between the races has slowed or stalled, and large gaps remain in many other measures of economic success, such as personal wealth, home ownership, and small business ownership (see Scholz and Levine 2004; Collins and Margo 2011; Fairlie 2004). By the early 1990s, economists were asking, "What went wrong?" (Bound and Freeman 1992). Recent research points to a number of factors. First, the broad trend toward increased income inequality disadvantaged workers with relatively low skills and less bargaining power, disproportionately affecting African-Americans, particularly during the 1980s (Juhn *et al.* 1991, Card and Lemieux 1996).[11]

Second, discrimination – although diminished – has not disappeared. Experimental and field studies in which carefully matched white and black applicants apply for jobs, housing, or other market transactions reveal evidence of ongoing disparate treatment by race (e.g. Ladd 1998; Bertrand and Mullainathan 2004; Pager *et al.* 2009). Although the implications of these findings for equilibrium labor-market gaps can be debated (e.g. Heckman 1998), the pattern of observed racial wage differentials is consistent with the predictions of the Becker model of discrimination (Charles and Guryan 2008).

Third, notwithstanding the evidence of ongoing discrimination in markets, there is good reason to believe that a large portion of the current racial gap in economic outcomes is due to continuing differences in "pre-market" skills. In an influential article, Neal and Johnson (1996) argued that the racial wage gap could be explained almost entirely by differences in individuals' cognitive test scores prior to entering the labor force, although the gap in employment still included a sizeable unexplained residual. More recent work largely confirms their findings, although, when educational attainment is also controlled for, there remains a sizable unexplained residual that is consistent with potential market discrimination (Urzúa 2008; Lang and Manove 2011).

As is the case for income convergence, progress in narrowing the racial skill gap has slowed (Neal 2006). The black–white test score gap opens up at an early age and tends to widen during the school years (Phillips *et al.* 1998; Fryer 2010). This pattern points to causal factors beginning during early childhood, which may include the family environment and parental resources (e.g. McLanahan 2004; Heckman 2011), deficiencies in the schools (Fryer 2010), and exposure to environmental pollutants (Currie 2011). Since the 1970s, the rate of single parenthood has risen substantially for all racial groups, but dramatically so for African-Americans, especially among less educated women. The correlation between skill deficits and economic disadvantage, on the one hand, and growing up with a single parent, on the other, is well established, although the direction of causation continues to be debated.

Disadvantages in childhood undoubtedly interact in complex ways with each other and with discrimination and racial stigma, creating adverse feedback dynamics, especially for African-Americans residing in neighborhoods with high concentrations of poverty and disrupted families (Wilson 1996; Loury 2002; National Research Council 2004: Ch. 11). Economic history suggests that forces of inertia may make it difficult to break these cycles, but also points to historical precedents for rapid and dramatic progress in the relative economic status of African-Americans.

Appendix: Census data

Table 27.1 and Figures 27.1–27.8 are based on analysis of individual-level samples of the decennial U.S. Census for the years 1870–2000, and the American Community Survey (ACS) for 2009. All samples were downloaded from the Integrated Public Use Microdata Series (IPUMS) (Ruggles *et al.* 2010). The following specific samples were used:

1870: 1 per cent sample with black oversample
1880: 10 per cent sample (50 per cent random subsample)
1900: 5 per cent sample
1910: 1.4 per cent sample with oversamples
1920–60: 1 per cent sample
1970: 1 per cent Form 1 state sample
1980: 5 per cent sample (20 per cent random subsample)
1990: 5 per cent sample (20 per cent random subsample)
2000: 1 per cent sample
2009: ACS (1 per cent national sample)

All analyses used person weights provided by IPUMS, with the exception of the earnings analysis for 1950, which used sample line weights. Racial identification was made using the IPUMS RACESING variable, which assigns a single race to individuals reporting multiple races (beginning in 2000). None of the findings reported here would be substantively different using alternative assignments of mixed-race individuals. Census samples do not exist for 1890, and in all charts the value for 1890 is simply the linear interpolation of the 1880 and 1900 data points. Details and Stata files are available from the author upon request.

Notes

1 I thank Leah Platt Boustan, William Collins, Robert Margo, and Gavin Wright for helpful suggestions.
2 See especially Goldin and Katz (2008).
3 For the sake of brevity in what follows, the non-Southern regions will often be referred to collectively as "the North."
4 Longitudinal surveys reveal that individuals sometimes change their reported race over time, and that these changes may be endogenous to the person's social or economic situation (e.g. Saperstein and Penner 2010; Charles and Guryan 2011). No attempt is made here to take account of the potential endogeneity of race.
5 This table and several other tables and figures in this chapter restrict the sample to prime-age adults (25–54) to avoid compositional changes associated with changing percentages of adults in school or retired.
6 These figures probably underestimate the racial disparity in skilled occupations, because within each occupational category African-Americans were more likely to be in the lower-paid occupations (e.g. among professionals, clergymen as opposed to doctors).
7 For cohorts born after 1954, comparisons with earlier generations are difficult because of major changes in the way the Census asked about educational attainment between 1980 and 1990.
8 The reader may note in Figures 27.4 and 27.5 that there are some years when the ratio for "All" falls below both the "South" and "Non-South" values. This can occur because the estimated racial gap for the country as a whole partly reflects the fact that blacks disproportionately resided in the South, where earnings tended to be somewhat lower for workers of either race. The general regional differential is implicitly controlled for in the separate regional series.
9 Anti-discrimination laws were already on the books in a number of states outside the South, and there is some evidence that these had at least modest effects on black employment and pay (Collins 2003).

10 For women, the education-adjusted chart is very similar to Figure 27.8 and is not included here.
11 Demand for the lowest-skilled workers recovered somewhat beginning in the 1990s (see Autor *et al.*
   2006).

References

Alston, L.J. and Ferrie, J.P. (1985) 'Labor costs, paternalism, and loyalty in southern agriculture: a
   constraint on the growth of the welfare state', *Journal of Economic History*, 45: 95–117.
Alston, L.J. and Kauffman, K.D. (2001) 'Competition and the compensation of sharecroppers by race: a
   view from plantations in the early twentieth century', *Explorations in Economic History*, 38: 181–94.
Anderson, J.D. (1988) *The Education of Blacks in the South, 1860–1935*, Chapel Hill, NC: University of
   North Carolina Press.
Arrow, K.J. (1973) 'The theory of discrimination', in O. Ashenfelter and A. Rees (eds) *Discrimination in
   Labor Markets*, Princeton, NJ: Princeton University Press.
Ashenfelter, O., Collins, W.J. and Yoon, A. (2006) 'Evaluating the role of Brown v. Board of Education
   in school equalization, desegregation, and the income of African-Americans', *American Law and
   Economics Review*, 8: 213–48.
Autor, D.H. and Duggan, M.G. (2006) 'The growth in the Social Security disability rolls: a fiscal crisis
   unfolding', *Journal of Economic Perspectives*, 20: 71–96.
Autor, D.H., Katz, L.F. and Kearney, M.S. (2006) 'The polarization of the U.S. labor market', *American
   Economic Review*, 96: 189–94.
Bailey, M.J. and Collins, W.J. (2006) 'The wage gains of African-American women in the 1940s', *Journal of
   Economic History*, 66: 737–77.
Becker, G.S. (1971) *The Economics of Discrimination*, 2nd edition, Chicago, IL: University of Chicago Press.
Bertrand, M. and Mullainathan, S. (2004) 'Are Emily and Greg more employable than Lakisha and Jamal?
   A field experiment on labor market discrimination', *American Economic Review*, 94: 991–1013.
Bodenhorn, H. and Ruebeck, C. (2007) 'Colourism and African-American wealth: evidence from the
   nineteenth-century south', *Journal of Population Economics*, 20: 599–620.
Bound, J. and Freeman, R.B. (1992) 'What went wrong? The erosion of relative earnings and
   employment among young black men in the 1980s', *Quarterly Journal of Economics*, 107: 201–32.
Boustan, L.P. (2009) 'Competition in the promised land: black migration and racial wage convergence in
   the North, 1940–70', *Journal of Economic History*, 69: 756–83.
Boustan, L.P. and Margo, R.A. (2009) 'Race, segregation, and postal employment: new evidence on
   spatial mismatch', *Journal of Urban Economics*, 65: 1–10.
Brooks, R.R.W. (2011) 'Covenants without courts: enforcing residential segregation with legally
   unenforceable agreements', *American Economic Review*, 101: 360–5.
Brown, C.C. (1984) 'Black–white earnings ratios since the Civil Rights Act of 1964: the importance of
   labor market dropouts', *Quarterly Journal of Economics*, 95: 31–44.
Butler, R. and Heckman, J.J. (1977) 'The government's impact on the labor market status of black
   Americans: a critical review', in F.E. Bloch and L.J. Hausman (eds) *Equal Rights and Industrial Relations*,
   Madison, WI: Industrial Relations Research Association.
Card, D. and Krueger, A. (1992) 'School quality and black–white relative earnings: a direct assessment',
   Quarterly Journal of Economics, 107: 151–200.
Card, D. and Lemieux, T. (1996) 'Wage dispersion, returns to skill, and black–white wage differentials',
   Journal of Econometrics, 74: 319–61.
Carrington, W.J., Detragiache, E. and Vishwanath, T. (1996) 'Migration with endogenous moving costs',
   American Economic Review, 86: 909–30.
Cayton, H.R. and Mitchell, G.S. (1939) *Black Workers and the New Unions*, Chapel Hill, NC: University of
   North Carolina Press.
Chandra, A. (2003) 'Is the convergence in the racial wage gap illusory?' NBER Working Paper No. 9476.
Charles, K.K. and Guryan, J. (2008) 'Prejudice and wages: an empirical assessment of Becker's *The
   Economics of Discrimination*', *Journal of Political Economy*, 116: 773–809.
Charles, K.K. and Guryan, J. (2011) 'Studying discrimination: fundamental challenges and recent progress',
   NBER Working Paper No. 17156.
Chay, K.Y. (1998) 'The impact of federal civil rights policy on black economic progress: evidence from
   the Equal Employment Opportunity Act of 1972', *Industrial and Labor Relations Review*, 51: 608–32.

Coate, S. and Loury, G.C. (1993) 'Will affirmative-action policies eliminate negative stereotypes?' *American Economic Review*, 83: 1220–40.

Collins, W.J. (1997) 'When the tide turned: immigration and the delay of the great migration', *Journal of Economic History*, 57: 607–32.

Collins, W.J. (2003) 'Labor market impact of state-level anti-discrimination laws, 1940–60', *Industrial and Labor Relations Review*, 56: 244–72.

Collins, W.J. and Margo, R.A. (2000) 'Residential segregation and socioeconomic outcomes: when did ghettoes go bad?' *Economics Letters*, 69: 239–43.

——(2006) 'Historical perspectives on racial differences in schooling in the United States', in E.A. Hanushek and F. Welch (eds) *Handbook of the Economics of Education*, Amsterdam: Elsevier.

——(2011) 'Race and home ownership from the Civil War to the present', NBER Working Paper No. 16665.

Cunningham, J.S. and Zalokar, N. (1992) 'The economic progress of black women, 1940–80: occupational distribution and relative wages', *Industrial and Labor Relations Review*, 45: 540–55.

Currie, J. (2011) 'Inequality at birth: some causes and consequences', *American Economic Review: Papers and Proceedings*, 101: 1–22.

Cutler, D.M. and Glaeser, E.L. (1997) 'Are ghettoes good or bad?' *Quarterly Journal of Economics*, 112: 827–72.

Cutler, D.M., Glaeser, E.L. and Vigdor, J.L. (1999) 'The rise and decline of the American ghetto', *Journal of Political Economy*, 107: 455–506.

DeCanio, S.J. (1979) 'Accumulation and discrimination in the postbellum South', *Explorations in Economic History*, 16: 182–206.

Delton, J. (2009) *Racial Integration in Corporate America, 1940–1990*, New York: Cambridge University Press.

Dewey, D. (1952) 'Negro employment in southern industry', *Journal of Political Economy*, 60: 279–93.

Dobbin, F. (2009) *Inventing Equal Opportunity*, Princeton, NJ: Princeton University Press.

Donohue, J.H. and Heckman, J. (1991) 'Continuous versus episodic change: the impact of civil rights policy on the economic status of blacks', *Journal of Economic Literature*, 29: 1603–43.

Fairlie, R.W. (2004) 'Recent trends in ethnic and racial business ownership', *Small Business Economics*, 23: 203–18.

Fairlie, R.W. and Sundstrom, W.A. (1999) 'The emergence, persistence, and recent widening of the racial unemployment gap', *Industrial and Labor Relations Review*, 52: 252–70.

Farley, R. and Allen, W.R. (1987) *The Color Line and the Quality of Life in America*, New York: Russell Sage Foundation.

Foote, C.L., Whatley, W.C. and Wright, G. (2003) 'Arbitraging a discriminatory labor market: black workers at the Ford Motor Company, 1918–47', *Journal of Labor Economics*, 21: 493–532.

Freeman, R.B. (1981) 'Black economic progress after 1964: who has gained and why?', in S. Rosen (ed.) *Studies in Labor Markets*, Chicago, IL: University of Chicago Press.

Fryer, R.G. Jr. (2010) 'Racial inequality in the 21st century: the declining significance of discrimination', NBER Working Paper No. 16256.

Gelber, S.M. (1974) *Black Men and Businessmen*, Port Washington, NY: Kennikat Press.

Glaeser, E.L. and Vigdor, J.L. (2001) 'Racial segregation in the 2000 census: promising news', Brookings Institution.

Goldin, C. (1990) *Understanding the Gender Gap: An Economic History of American Women*, New York: Oxford University Press.

Goldin, C. and Katz, L.F. (2008) *The Race Between Education and Technology*, Cambridge, MA: Harvard University Press.

Guryan, J. (2004) 'Desegregation and black dropout rates', *American Economic Review*, 94: 919–43.

Hanushek, E.A., Kain, J.F. and Rivkin, S.G. (2009) 'New evidence about *Brown v. Board of Education*: the complex effects of school racial composition on achievement', *Journal of Labor Economics*, 27: 349–83.

Heckman, J.J. (1998) 'Detecting discrimination', *Journal of Economic Perspectives*, 12: 101–16.

——(2011) 'The American family in black and white: a post-racial strategy for improving skills to promote equality', NBER Working Paper No. 16841.

Heckman, J.J. and Payner, B.S. (1989) 'Determining the impact of federal antidiscrimination policy on the economic status of blacks: a study of South Carolina', *American Economic Review*, 79: 138–77.

Higgs, R. (1976) 'The boll weevil, the cotton economy, and black migration 1910–30', *Agricultural History*, 50: 335–50.

——(1977) 'Firm-specific evidence on racial wage differentials and work force segregation', *American Economic Review*, 67: 236–45.

——(1982) 'Accumulation of property by southern blacks before World War I', *American Economic Review*, 72: 725–37.

——(1989) 'Black progress and the persistence of racial economic inequalities, 1865–1940', in S. Shulman and W. Darity (eds) *The Question of Discrimination: Racial Inequality in the U.S. Labor Market*, Middletown, CT: Wesleyan University Press.

Holzer, H.J. and Neumark, D. (2006) 'Affirmative action: what do we know?', *Journal of Policy Analysis and Management*, 25: 463–90.

Jaynes, G.D. (1986) *Branches Without Roots: Genesis of the Black Working Class in the American South, 1862–1882*, New York, Oxford University Press.

Johnson, C.S. (1943) *Patterns of Negro Segregation*, New York: Harper & Brothers.

Juhn, C. (2003) 'Labor market dropouts and trends in the wages of black and white men', *Industrial and Labor Relations Review*, 56: 643–62.

Juhn, C., Murphy, K.M. and Pierce, B. (1991) 'Accounting for the slowdown in black–white wage convergence', in M.H. Kosters (ed.) *Workers and Their Wages: Changing Patterns in the United States*, Washington: American Enterprise Institute Press.

Kasarda, J. (1989) 'Urban industrial transition and the underclass', *Annals of the American Academy of Political and Social Science*, 501: 26–47.

Katz, M.B., Stern, M.T. and Fader, J.T. (2005) 'The new African-American inequality', *Journal of American History*, 92: 75–108.

King, M.C. (1993) 'Black women's breakthrough into clerical work: an occupational tipping model', *Journal of Economic Issues*, 27: 1097–125.

——(1995) 'Human capital and black women's occupational mobility', *Industrial Relations*, 34: 282–98.

Ladd, H.F. (1998) 'Evidence on discrimination in mortgage lending', *Journal of Economic Perspectives*, 12: 41–62.

Lang, K. and Manove, M. (2011) 'Education and labor-market discrimination', *American Economic Review*, 101: 1467–96.

Lange, F., Olmstead, A.L. and Rhode, P.W. (2009) 'The impact of the boll weevil, 1892–1932', *Journal of Economic History*, 69: 685–718.

Loury, G.C. (2002) *The Anatomy of Racial Inequality*, Cambridge, MA: Harvard University Press.

Lundberg, S.J. and Startz, R. (1983) 'Private discrimination and social intervention in competitive labor markets', *American Economic Review*, 73: 340–7.

Maloney, T.N. (1995) 'Degrees of inequality: the advance of black male workers in the northern meat packing and steel industries before World War II', *Social Science History*, 19: 31–62.

Maloney, T.N. and Whatley, W.C. (1995) 'Making the effort: the contours of racial discrimination in Detroit's labor markets, 1920–40', *Journal of Economic History*, 55: 465–93.

Margo, R.A. (1984) 'Accumulation of property by southern blacks before World War I: comment and further evidence', *American Economic Review*, 74: 768–76.

——(1986) 'Educational achievement in segregated school systems: the effects of "separate-but-equal"', *American Economic Review*, 76: 794–801.

——(1990) *Race and Schooling in the South, 1880–1950: An Economic History*, Chicago, IL: University of Chicago.

Massey, D.S. and Denton, N.A. (1993) *American Apartheid: Segregation and the Making of the Underclass*, Cambridge, MA: Harvard University.

McLanahan, S. (2004) 'Diverging destinies: how children are faring under the second demographic transition', *Demography*, 41: 607–27.

Miller, M.C. (2011) 'Land and racial wealth inequality', *American Economic Review: Papers and Proceedings*, 101: 371–6.

Moehling, C.M. (2004) 'Family structure, school attendance, and child labor in the American South in 1900 and 1910', *Explorations in Economic History*, 41: 73–100.

Moreno, P.D. (2006) *Black Americans and Organized Labor: A New History*, Baton Rouge, LA: Louisiana State University Press.

Myrdal, G. (1944) *An American Dilemma: The Negro Problem and Modern Democracy*, New York: Harper and Row.

Naidu, S. (2009) 'Suffrage, schooling, and sorting in the post-bellum U.S. South', working paper, Harvard University.

——(2010) 'Recruitment restrictions and labor markets: evidence from the post-bellum U.S. South', working paper, Harvard University.

National Research Council (2004) *Measuring Racial Discrimination*, Washington: National Academies Press.

Neal, D. (2004) 'The measured black–white wage gap among women is too small', *Journal of Political Economy*, 112: S1–S28.

——(2006) 'Why has black–white skill convergence stopped?', in E.A. Hanushek and F. Welch (eds) *Handbook of the Economics of Education*, Amsterdam: Elsevier.

Neal, D.A. and Johnson, W.R. (1996) 'The role of premarket factors in black–white wage differences', *Journal of Political Economy*, 104: 869–95.

Pager, D., Western, B. and Bonikowski, B. (2009) 'Discrimination in a low-wage labor market: a field experiment', *American Sociological Review*, 74: 777–99.

Pettit, B. and Western, B. (2004) 'Mass imprisonment and the life course: race and class inequality in U.S. incarceration', *American Sociological Review*, 69: 151–69.

Phillips, M., Crouse, J. and Ralph, J. (1998) 'Does the black–white test score gap widen after children enter school?', in C. Jencks and M. Phillips (eds) *The Black–White Test Score Gap*, Washington: Brookings Institution Press.

Ransom, R.L. and Sutch, R. (1977) *One Kind of Freedom: The Economic Consequences of Emancipation*, Cambridge: Cambridge University Press.

——(2001) '*One Kind of Freedom:* reconsidered (and turbo charged)', *Explorations in Economic History*, 38: 6–39.

Reber, S.J. (2010) 'School desegregation and educational attainment for blacks', *Journal of Human Resources*, 45: 893–914.

Roback, J. (1984) 'Southern labor law in the Jim Crow era: exploitative or competitive?', *University of Chicago Law Review*, 51: 1161–92.

Ruggles, S., Alexander, J.T., Genadek, K., Goeken, R., Schroeder, M.B. and Sobek, M. (2010) Integrated Public Use Microdata Series: Version 5.0 [Machine-readable database], Minneapolis, MN: University of Minnesota.

Sacerdote, B. (2005) 'Slavery and the intergenerational transmission of human capital', *Review of Economics and Statistics*, 87: 217–34.

Saperstein, A. and Penner, A.M. (2010) 'The race of a criminal record: how incarceration colors racial perceptions', *Social Problems*, 57: 92–113.

Scholz, J.K. and Levine, K. (2004) 'U.S. black–white wealth inequality: a survey', in K. Neckerman (ed.) *Social Inequality*, New York: Russell Sage Foundation.

Smith, J.P. (1984) 'Race and Human Capital', *American Economic Review*, 74: 685–98.

Smith, J.P. and Welch, F.R. (1989) 'Black economic progress after Myrdal', *Journal of Economic Literature*, 27: 519–64.

Sobek, M. (2001) 'New statistics on the U.S. labor force, 1850–1990', *Historical Methods*, 34: 71–87.

Spero, S.D. and Harris, A.L. (1931) *The Black Worker: The Negro and the Labor Movement*, New York: Columbia University Press.

Sugrue, T.J. (1996) *The Origins of the Urban Crisis: Race and Inequality in Postwar Detroit*, Princeton, NJ: Princeton University Press.

Sundstrom, W.A. (1990) 'Half a career: discrimination and railroad internal labor markets', *Industrial Relations*, 29: 423–40.

——(1994) 'The color line: racial norms and discrimination in urban labor markets, 1910–50', *Journal of Economic History*, 54: 382–96.

——(2007) 'The geography of wage discrimination in the pre-civil rights South', *Journal of Economic History*, 67: 410–44.

Tolnay, S.E. and Beck, E.M. (1990) 'Black flight: lethal violence and the great migration, 1900–930', *Social Science History*, 14: 347–70.

Urzúa, S. (2008) 'Racial labor market gaps: the role of abilities and schooling choices', *Journal of Human Resources*, 43: 919–71.

Vigdor, J.L. (2006) 'The new promised land: black–white convergence in the American south, 1960–2000', NBER Working Paper No. 12143.

Western, B. and Pettit, B. (2005) 'Black–white wage inequality, employment rates, and incarceration', *American Journal of Sociology*, 111: 553–78.

Whatley, W. (1983) 'Labor for the picking: the New Deal in the South', *Journal of Economic History*, 43: 905–29.

——(1987) 'Southern agrarian labor contracts as impediments to cotton mechanization,' *Journal of Economic History*, 47: 45–70.

——(1990) 'Getting a foot in the door: "learning," state dependence, and the racial integration of firms', *Journal of Economic History*, 50: 43–66.

Whatley, W. and Wright, G. (1994) 'Race, human capital, and labour markets in American history', in G. Grantham and M. MacKinnon (eds) *Labour Market Evolution: The Economic History of Market Integration, Wage Flexibility and the Employment Relation*, London: Routledge.

Wilson, W.J. (1996) *When Work Disappears: The World of the New Urban Poor*, New York: Knopf.

Woodward, C.V. (1955) *The Strange Career of Jim Crow*, Oxford: Oxford University Press.

Wright, G. (1986) *Old South, New South: Revolutions in the Southern Economy since the Civil War*, New York: Basic Books.

——(1999) 'The civil rights revolution as economic history', *Journal of Economic History*, 59: 267–89.

——(2010) 'Desegregating southern labor markets', working paper, Stanford University.

INDEX